Vince
Bechtel

Exam 70-536: *Microsoft .NET Framework 2.0—Application Development Foundation*

Objective	Chapter	Lesson
1. Developing applications that use system types and collections		
1.1 Manage data in a .NET Framework application by using the .NET Framework 2.0 system types. (Refer System namespace)		
1.1.1 Value types	1	1, 2, 3
1.1.2 Reference types	1	2
1.1.3 Attributes	1	3
1.1.4 Generic types	1	3
1.1.5 Exception classes	1	2
1.1.6 Boxing and UnBoxing	1	4
1.1.7 TypeForwardTo Attribute Class	1	3
1.2 Manage a group of associated data in a .NET Framework application by using collections. (Refer System.Collections namespace)		
1.2.1 ArrayList class	4	1
1.2.2 Collection interfaces	4	3
1.2.3 Iterators	4	3
1.2.4 Hashtable class	4	3
1.2.5 CollectionBase class and ReadOnlyCollectionBase class	4	5
1.2.6 DictionaryBase class and DictionaryEntry class	4	3
1.2.7 Comparer class	4	1
1.2.8 Queue class	4	2
1.2.9 SortedList class	4	3
1.2.10 BitArray class	4	4
1.2.11 Stack class	2	2
1.3 Improve type safety and application performance in a .NET Framework application by using generic collections. (Refer System.Collections.Generic namespace)		
1.3.1 Collection.Generic interfaces	4	5
1.3.2 Generic Dictionary	4	5
1.3.3 Generic Comparer class and Generic EqualityComparer class	4	5
1.3.4 Generic KeyValuePair structure	4	5
1.3.5 Generic List class, Generic ListEnumerator structure, and Generic SortedList class	4	5
1.3.6 Generic Queue class and Generic Queue.Enumerator structure	4	5
1.3.7 Generic SortedDictionary class	4	5
1.3.8 Generic LinkedList	4	5
1.3.9 Generic Stack class and Generic Stack.Enumerator structure	4	5
1.4 Manage data in a .NET Framework application by using specialized collections. (Refer System.Collections.Specialized namespace)		
1.4.1 Specialized String classes	4	4
1.4.2 Specialized Dictionary	4	3, 4
1.4.3 NameValueCollection class	4	4
1.4.4 CollectionsUtil	4	4
1.4.5 BitVector32 structure and BitVector32.Section structure	4	4
1.5 Implement .NET Framework interfaces to cause components to comply with standard contracts. (Refer System namespace)		
1.5.1 IComparable interface	1	3
1.5.2 IDisposable interface	1	3
1.5.3 IConvertible interface	1	4
1.5.4 ICloneable interface	1	3
1.5.5 IEquatable interface	1	3
1.5.6 IFormattable interface	1	3
1.6 Control interactions between .NET Framework application components by using events and delegates. (Refer System namespace)		
1.6.1 Delegate class	1	3
1.6.2 EventArgs class	1	3
1.6.3 EventHandler delegates	1	3
2. Implementing service processes, threading, and application domains in a .NET Framework application		
2.1 Implement, install, and control a service. (Refer System.ServiceProcess namespace)		
2.1.1 Inherit from ServiceBase class	8	3
2.1.2 ServiceController class and ServiceControllerPermission class	8	3
2.1.3 ServiceInstaller and ServiceProcessInstaller class	8	3
2.1.4 SessionChangeDescription structure and SessionChangeReason enumeration	8	3
2.2 Develop multithreaded .NET Framework applications. (Refer System.Threading namespace)		
2.2.1 Thread class	7	1
2.2.2 Thread pool class	7	3
2.2.3 ThreadStart delegate and ParameterizedThreadStart delegate	7	1
2.2.4 Timeout class, Timer class, TimerCallback delegate, WaitCallback delegate, WaitHandle class, and WaitOrTimerCallback delegate	7	3
2.2.5 ThreadExceptionEventArgs class and ThreadExceptionEventHandler class	7	3
2.2.6 ThreadState enumeration and ThreadPriority enumeration	7	1
2.2.7 ReaderWriterLock class	7	2
2.2.8 AutoResetEvent class and ManualResetEvent class	7	2
2.2.9 IAsyncResult interface (Refer System namespace)	7	3
2.2.10 EventWaitHandle class, RegisteredWaitHandle class, SendOrPostCallback delegate, and IOCompletionCallback delegate	7	2
2.2.11 Interlocked class, NativeOverlapped class, and Overlapped class	7	2
2.2.12 ExecutionContext class, HostExecutionContext class, HostExecutionContext Manager class, and ContextCallback delegate	7	1
2.2.13 LockCookie structure, Monitor class, Mutex class, and Semaphore class	7	2
2.3 Create a unit of isolation for common language runtime in a .NET Framework application by using application domains. (Refer System namespace)		
2.3.1 Create an application domain.	8	1
2.3.2 Unload an application domain.	8	1
2.3.3 Configure an application domain.	8	2
2.3.4 Retrieve setup information from an application domain.	8	2
2.3.5 Load assemblies into an application domain.	8	1

Objective	Chapter	Lesson
3. Embedding configuration, diagnostic, management, and installation features into a .NET Framework application		
3.1 Embed configuration management functionality into a .NET Framework application. (Refer System.Configuration namespace)		
3.1.1 Configuration class and ConfigurationManager class	9	1
3.1.2 ConfigurationElement class, ConfigurationElementCollection class, and ConfigurationElementProperty class	9	4
3.1.3 ConfigurationSection class, ConfigurationSectionCollection class, ConfigurationSectionGroup class, and ConfigurationSectionGroupCollection class	9	1, 4
3.1.4 Implement ISettingsProviderService interface	9	4
3.1.5 Implement IApplicationSettingsProvider interface	9	4
3.1.6 ConfigurationValidatorBase class	9	1
3.2 Create a custom Microsoft Windows Installer for the .NET Framework components by using the System.Configuration.Install namespace, and configure the .NET Framework applications by using configuration files, environment variables, and the .NET Framework Configuration tool (Mscorcfg.msc).		
3.2.1 Installer class	9	2
3.2.2 Configure which runtime version a .NET Framework application should use.	9	3
3.2.3 Configure where the runtime should search for an assembly.	9	3
3.2.4 Configure the location of an assembly and which version of the assembly to use.	9	1
3.2.5 Direct the runtime to use the DEVPATH environment variable when you search for assemblies.	9	1
3.2.6 AssemblyInstaller class	9	2
3.2.7 ComponentInstaller class	9	2
3.2.8 Configure a .NET Framework application by using the .NET Framework Configuration tool (Mscorcfg.msc).	9	2
3.2.9 ManagedInstallerClass class	9	2
3.2.10 InstallContext class	9	2
3.2.11 InstallerCollection class	9	2
3.2.12 InstallEventHandler delegate	9	2
3.2.13 Configure concurrent garbage collection.	9	2
3.2.14 Register remote objects.by using configuration files.	9	1
3.3 Manage an event log by using the System.Diagnostics namespace.		
3.3.1 Write to an event log.	10	1
3.3.2 Read from an event log.	10	1
3.3.3 Create a new event log.	10	1
3.4 Manage system processes and monitor the performance of a .NET Framework application by using the diagnostics functionality of the .NET Framework 2.0. (Refer System.Diagnostics namespace)		
3.4.1 Get a list of all running processes.	10	3
3.4.2 Retrieve information about the current process.	10	3
3.4.3 Get a list of all modules that are loaded by a process.	10	3
3.4.4 PerformanceCounter class, PerformanceCounterCategory, and CounterCreationData class	10	3
3.4.5 Start a process both by using and by not using command-line arguments.	10	3
3.4.6 StackTrace class	10	3
3.4.7 StackFrame class	10	3
3.5 Debug and trace a .NET Framework application by using the System.Diagnostics namespace.		
3.5.1 Debug class and Debugger class	10	2
3.5.2 Trace class, CorrelationManager class, TraceListener class, TraceSource class, TraceSwitch class, XmlWriterTraceListener class, DelimitedListTraceListener class, and EventlogTraceListener class	10	2
3.5.3 Debugger attributes	10	2
3.6 Embed management information and events into a NET Framework application. (Refer System.Management namespace)		
3.6.1 Retrieve a collection of Management objects by using the ManagementObjectSearcher class and its derived classes.	10	4
3.6.2 ManagementQuery class	10	4
3.6.3 Subscribe to management events by using the ManagementEventWatcher class.	10	4
4. Implementing serialization and input/output functionality in a .NET Framework application		
4.1 Serialize or deserialize an object or an object graph by using runtime serialization techniques. (Refer System.Runtime.Serialization namespace)		
4.1.1 Serialization interfaces	5	1
4.1.2 Serialization attributes	5	1
4.1.3 SerializationEntry structure and SerializationInfo class	5	3
4.1.4 ObjectManager class	5	1
4.1.5 Formatter class, FormatterConverter class, and FormatterServices class	5	1
4.1.6 StreamingContext structure	5	3
4.2 Control the serialization of an object into XML format by using the System.Xml.Serialization namespace.		
4.2.1 Serialize and deserialize objects into XML format by using the XmlSerializer class.	5	2, 3
4.2.2 Control serialization by using serialization attributes.	5	2
4.2.3 Implement XML Serialization interfaces to provide custom formatting for XML serialization.	5	2
4.2.4 Delegates and event handlers are provided by the System.Xml.Serialization namespace	5	2
4.3 Implement custom serialization formatting by using the Serialization Formatter classes.		
4.3.1 SoapFormatter class (Refer System.Runtime.Serialization.Formatters.Soap namespace)	5	1
4.3.2 BinaryFormatter class (Refer System.Runtime.Serialization.Formatters.Binary namespace)	5	1
4.4 Access files and folders by using the File System classes. (Refer System.IO namespace)		
4.4.1 File class and FileInfo class	2	1
4.4.2 Directory class and DirectoryInfo class	2	1
4.4.3 DriveInfo class and DriveType enumeration	2	1
4.4.4 FileSystemInfo class and FileSystemWatcher class	2	1
4.4.5 Path class	2	1
4.4.6 ErrorEventArgs class and ErrorEventHandler delegate	2	1
4.4.7 RenamedEventArgs class and RenamedEventHandler delegate	2	1

Microsoft®

MCTS Self-Paced Training Kit (Exam 70-536): Microsoft® .NET Framework 2.0— Application Development Foundation

Tony Northrup and Shawn Wildermuth, with Bill Ryan of GrandMasters

PUBLISHED BY
Microsoft Press
A Division of Microsoft Corporation
One Microsoft Way
Redmond, Washington 98052-6399

ISBN-13: 978-0-7356-2277-7
ISBN-10: 0-7356-2277-9
Library of Congress Control Number 2006924468

Printed and bound in the United States of America.

6 7 8 9   QWT   1 0 9 8

Distributed in Canada by H.B. Fenn and Company Ltd.

A CIP catalogue record for this book is available from the British Library.

Microsoft Press books are available through booksellers and distributors worldwide. For further information about international editions, contact your local Microsoft Corporation office or contact Microsoft Press International directly at fax (425) 936-7329. Visit our Web site at www.microsoft.com/mspress. Send comments to tkinput@microsoft.com.

Acquisitions Editor: Ken Jones
Project Editor: Laura Sackerman
Technical Editors: Jim Fuchs and David Robinson
Indexers: Lee Ross and Tony Ross

Body Part No. X12-41817

For Sandi Edson

−Tony Northrup

To my mother, Pennie Wildermuth

−Shawn Wildermuth

To my parents, Walter and Carole Converse, for always being there for me.
To Kim and Sarah Finleyson for putting up with me always being busy and keeping me smiling.
Finally, to Walter Bellhaven and Herb Sewell, for helping me maintain my sanity for the past year.

−Bill Ryan

About the Authors

Tony Northrup

In the mid 1980s, Tony Northrup, CISSP, MCSE, and MVP, learned to program in BASIC on a ZX-81 personal computer built from a kit. Later, he mastered the 68000 assembly and ANSI C on the Motorola VERSAdos operating system before beginning to write code for MS-DOS. After a brief time with the NEXTSTEP operating system, Tony returned to a Microsoft platform because he was impressed by the beta version of Microsoft Windows NT 3.1. Although he has dabbled in other operating systems, Tony has since focused on Windows development in Microsoft Visual C++, Visual Basic, C#, and Perl (for automation projects). Tony now develops almost exclusively for the .NET Framework.

Tony started writing in 1997 and has since published more than a dozen technology books on the topics of development and networking. In addition, Tony has written dozens of articles at *http://www.microsoft.com*, covering topics ranging from securing ASP.NET applications, to designing firewalls to protect networks and computers. Tony spends his spare time hiking through the woods near his Phillipston, Massachusetts home. He's rarely without his camera, and in the past six years has created what might be the largest and most popular publicly accessible database of nature and wildlife photographs on the Internet. Tony lives with his wife Erica and his cat (also his favorite photographic subject) Sammy.

Shawn Wildermuth

Shawn Wildermuth is a Microsoft C# MVP and is the founder of Wildermuth Consulting Services, LLC, a company that is dedicated to delivering software and training solutions in the Atlanta, Georgia area. He is also a speaker on the INETA Speaker Bureau and has appeared at several national conferences to speak on a variety of subjects. Shawn is also the author of the book *Pragmatic ADO.NET* as well as the upcoming *Prescriptive Data Architectures*, both for Addison-Wesley. He has been writing articles for a number of years for a variety of magazines and Web sites, including MSDN, MSDN Online, DevSource, InformIT, Windows IT Pro, The ServerSide .NET, ONDotNet.com, and Intel's Rich Client Series. Shawn has enjoyed building data-driven software for more than 20 years.

Bill Ryan

Bill Ryan is a Senior Software Developer at InfoPro, Inc., a large medical records management company in Augusta, GA. Bill is a Microsoft MVP in the Windows Embedded category. Bill is also the co-author of *Professional ADO.NET 2* and *Professional WinFX Beta*, both by Wrox Press. He's currently authoring *Professional Microsoft Speech Server* by Apress. Bill is a frequent speaker at events such as Microsoft Code Camps, Speech Server Days, and .NET User's Groups. He also runs two .NET focused Web sites, *www.devbuzz.com* and *www.knowdotnet.com*.

Contents at a Glance

Table of Contents

8   Application Domains and Services 435

Acknowledgments

The authors' names appear on the cover of a book, but the authors are only part of a much larger team. First of all, thanks to Ken Jones at Microsoft for bringing us into this project. During the writing process, we worked most closely with Laura Sackerman and Maureen Zimmerman of Microsoft. Thanks for patiently and gently guiding us to better teach our readers. We didn't get to work with everyone at Microsoft directly, but we definitely appreciate the work of the rest of the Microsoft team:

- Rosemary Caperton and Sandi Resnick for coordinating the proofreading
- Carl Diltz for implementing the layout of this book
- Patty Masserman for coordinating the index
- Bill Teel for rendering the art and preparing the screen shots

From outside of Microsoft, Jim Fuchs and David Robinson were our technical editors. Thanks much, guys, for catching our mistakes so that our keen-eyed readers won't have to. Thanks also to our copy editor, Roger LeBlanc, for fixing all of our grammatical mistakes.

In addition, the authors would like to acknowledge the following people:

Tony Northrup: Many other people helped with this book, albeit a bit more indirectly. My friends—especially Tara, John, and Emilie Banks; Kristin Casciato; Kurt and Beatriz Dillard; Eric and Alyssa Faulkner; Chris and Diane Geggis; Bob Hogan; Sam Jackson; Tom Keegan; Eric and Alison Parucki; and Todd Wesche—helped me enjoy my time away from the keyboard. My in-laws distracted me with random drop-bys (which are only acceptable when bringing cookies): Mike, Michelle, Ray, and Sandi Edson. More than anyone, I have to thank my wife, Erica, for being so patient during many long days of writing.

Shawn Wildermuth: I'd like to thank Chris Sells for putting Ken Jones and I together on this project.

Introduction

This training kit is designed for developers who plan to take Microsoft Certified Technical Specialist (MCTS) exam 70-536, as well as for developers who need to know how to develop applications using the Microsoft .NET Framework 2.0. We assume that before you begin using this kit you have a working knowledge of Microsoft Windows and Microsoft Visual Basic or C#.

By using this training kit, you'll learn how to do the following:

- Develop applications that use system types and collections.
- Implement service processes, threading, and application domains to enable application isolation and multithreading.
- Create and deploy manageable applications.
- Create classes that can be serialized to enable them to be easily stored and transferred.
- Create hardened applications that are resistant to attacks and restrict access based on user and group roles.
- Use interoperability and reflection to leverage legacy code and communicate with other applications.
- Write applications that send e-mail messages.
- Create applications that can be used in different regions with different languages.
- Draw charts and create images, and either display them as part of your application or save them to files.

Hardware Requirements

The following hardware is required to complete the practice exercises:

- Computer with a 600-MHz or faster processor (1-GHz recommended)
- 192 MB of RAM or more (512 MB recommended)
- 2 GB of available hard disk space
- DVD-ROM drive

- 1,024 x 768 or higher resolution display with 256 colors
- Keyboard and Microsoft mouse, or compatible pointing device

Software Requirements

The following software is required to complete the practice exercises:

- One of the following operating systems:
  - ❑ Windows 2000 with Service Pack 4
  - ❑ Windows XP with Service Pack 2
  - ❑ Windows XP Professional x64 Edition (WOW)
  - ❑ Windows Server 2003 with Service Pack 1
  - ❑ Windows Server 2003, x64 Editions (WOW)
  - ❑ Windows Server 2003 R2
  - ❑ Windows Server 2003 R2, x64 Editions (WOW)
  - ❑ Microsoft Windows Vista
- Visual Studio 2005 (A 90-day evaluation edition of Visual Studio 2005 Professional Edition is included on DVD with this book.)

Using the CD and DVD

A companion CD and an evaluation software DVD are included with this training kit. The companion CD contains the following:

- **Practice tests** You can reinforce your understanding of how to create .NET Framework 2.0 applications by using electronic practice tests you customize to meet your needs from the pool of Lesson Review questions in this book. Or you can practice for the 70-536 certification exam by using tests created from a pool of 300 realistic exam questions, which is enough to give you many different practice exams to ensure that you're prepared.
- **Code** Most chapters in this book include sample files associated with the lab exercises at the end of every lesson. For some exercises, you will be instructed to open a project prior to starting the exercise. For other exercises, you will create a project on your own and be able to reference a completed project on the CD in the event you experience a problem following the exercise.

■ **An eBook** An electronic version (eBook) of this book is included for times when you don't want to carry the printed book with you. The eBook is in Portable Document Format (PDF), and you can view it by using Adobe Acrobat or Adobe Reader.

The evaluation software DVD contains a 90-day evaluation edition of Visual Studio 2005 Professional Edition, in case you want to use it with this book.

How to Install the Practice Tests

To install the practice test software from the companion CD to your hard disk, do the following:

1. Insert the companion CD into your CD drive, and accept the license agreement. A CD menu appears.

NOTE If the CD menu doesn't appear

If the CD menu or the license agreement doesn't appear, AutoRun might be disabled on your computer. Refer to the Readme.txt file on the CD-ROM for alternate installation instructions.

---

2. Click the Practice Tests item, and follow the instructions on the screen.

How to Use the Practice Tests

To start the practice test software, follow these steps:

1. Click Start/All Programs/Microsoft Press Training Kit Exam Prep. A window appears that shows all the Microsoft Press training kit exam prep suites installed on your computer.

2. Double-click the lesson review or practice test you want to use.

NOTE Lesson reviews vs. practice tests

Select the (70-536) Microsoft .NET Framework 2.0—Application Development Foundation *lesson review* to use the questions from the "Lesson Review" sections of this book. Select the (70-536) Microsoft .NET Framework 2.0—Application Development Foundation *practice test* to use a pool of 300 questions similar to those in the 70-536 certification exam.

Lesson Review Options

When you start a lesson review, the Custom Mode dialog box appears so that you can configure your test. You can click OK to accept the defaults, or you can customize the number of questions you want, how the practice test software works, which exam objectives you want the questions to relate to, and whether you want your lesson review to be timed. If you're retaking a test, you can select whether you want to see all the questions again or only those questions you missed or didn't answer.

After you click OK, your lesson review starts.

- To take the test, answer the questions and use the Next, Previous, and Go To buttons to move from question to question.

- After you answer an individual question, if you want to see which answers are correct—along with an explanation of each correct answer—click Explanation.

- If you'd rather wait until the end of the test to see how you did, answer all the questions and then click Score Test. You'll see a summary of the exam objectives you chose and the percentage of questions you got right overall and per objective. You can print a copy of your test, review your answers, or retake the test.

Practice Test Options

When you start a practice test, you choose whether to take the test in Certification Mode, Study Mode, or Custom Mode:

- **Certification Mode**   Closely resembles the experience of taking a certification exam. The test has a set number of questions, it's timed, and you can't pause and restart the timer.

- **Study Mode**   Creates an untimed test in which you can review the correct answers and the explanations after you answer each question.

- **Custom Mode**   Gives you full control over the test options so that you can customize them as you like.

In all modes, the user interface you see when taking the test is the basically the same, but with different options enabled or disabled depending on the mode. The main options are discussed in the previous section, "Lesson Review Options."

When you review your answer to an individual practice test question, a "References" section is provided that lists where in the training kit you can find the information that relates to that question and provides links to other sources of information. After you click Test Results to score your entire practice test, you can click the Learning Plan tab to see a list of references for every objective.

How to Uninstall the Practice Tests

To uninstall the practice test software for a training kit, use the Add Or Remove Programs option in Windows Control Panel.

Microsoft Certified Professional Program

The Microsoft certifications provide the best method to prove your command of current Microsoft products and technologies. The exams and corresponding certifications are developed to validate your mastery of critical competencies as you design and develop, or implement and support, solutions with Microsoft products and technologies. Computer professionals who become Microsoft-certified are recognized as experts and are sought after industry-wide. Certification brings a variety of benefits to the individual and to employers and organizations.

MORE INFO   **All the Microsoft certifications**

For a full list of Microsoft certifications, go to *www.microsoft.com/learning/mcp/default.asp*.

Technical Support

Every effort has been made to ensure the accuracy of this book and the contents of the companion CD. If you have comments, questions, or ideas regarding this book or the companion CD, please send them to Microsoft Press by using either of the following methods:

E-mail: tkinput@microsoft.com

Postal Mail:

Microsoft Press
Attn: MCTS Self-Paced Training Kit (Exam 70-536): Microsoft .NET Framework 2.0–
Application Development Foundation *Editor*
One Microsoft Way
Redmond, WA 98052–6399

For additional support information regarding this book and the CD-ROM (including answers to commonly asked questions about installation and use), visit the Microsoft Press Technical Support website at *www.microsoft.com/learning/support/books/*. To connect directly to the Microsoft Knowledge Base and enter a query, visit *http://support.microsoft.com/search/*. For support information regarding Microsoft software, please connect to *http://support.microsoft.com*.

Evaluation Edition Software Support

The 90-day evaluation edition provided with this training kit is not the full retail product and is provided only for the purposes of training and evaluation. Microsoft and Microsoft Technical Support do not support this evaluation edition.

Information about any issues relating to the use of this evaluation edition with this training kit is posted to the Support section of the Microsoft Press Web site (*www.microsoft.com/learning/support/books/*). For information about ordering the full version of any Microsoft software, please call Microsoft Sales at (800) 426-9400 or visit *www.microsoft.com*.

Chapter 1
Framework Fundamentals

The .NET Framework is an integral Microsoft Windows component designed to support next-generation applications and services. Many fundamentals of the .NET Framework will be familiar to developers who have worked in other object-oriented development environments; however, the .NET Framework also includes many unique elements that will be new to even the most experienced developers. This chapter provides an overview of .NET Framework programming, including knowledge required for every other chapter in this book.

NOTE .NET 2.0

If you have worked with versions of the .NET Framework released prior to version 2.0, much of this will be familiar. However, version 2.0 of the .NET Framework includes several new features: generics, partial classes, and type forwarding (all described in Lesson 3, "Constructing Classes").

Exam objectives in this chapter:

- Manage data in a .NET Framework application by using the .NET Framework 2.0 system types. (Refer *System* namespace)
    - Value types
    - Reference types
    - Attributes
    - Generic types
    - Exception classes
    - Boxing and UnBoxing
    - *TypeForwardedToAttribute* Class
- Implement .NET Framework interfaces to cause components to comply with standard contracts. (Refer *System* namespace)
    - *IComparable* interface
    - *IDisposable* interface
    - *IConvertible* interface

  ❑ *ICloneable* interface

  ❑ *IEquatable* interface

  ❑ *IFormattable* interface

- Control interactions between .NET Framework application components by using events and delegates. (Refer *System* namespace)

  ❑ *Delegate* class

  ❑ *EventArgs* class

  ❑ *EventHandler* delegates

Lessons in this chapter:

Before You Begin

This book assumes that you have at least two to three years of experience developing Web-based, Microsoft Windows-based, or distributed applications by using the .NET Framework 1.0, the .NET Framework 1.1, and the .NET Framework 2.0. Candidates should have a working knowledge of Microsoft Visual Studio 2005. Before you begin, you should be familiar with Microsoft Visual Basic or C# and be comfortable with the following tasks:

- Create a console or Windows Forms application in Visual Studio using Visual Basic or C#.

- Add namespaces and references to system class libraries to a project.

- Run a project in Visual Studio, set breakpoints, step through code, and watch the values of variables.

Lesson 1: Using Value Types

The simplest types in the .NET Framework, primarily numeric and Boolean types, are value types. Value types are variables that contain their data directly instead of containing a reference to the data stored elsewhere in memory. Instances of value types are stored in an area of memory called the *stack*, where the runtime can create, read, update, and remove them quickly with minimal overhead.

MORE INFO Reference types

For more information about reference types, refer to Lesson 2.

There are three general value types:

- Built-in types
- User-defined types
- Enumerations

Each of these types is derived from the *System.ValueType* base type. The following sections show how to use these different types.

After this lesson, you will be able to:
- Choose the most efficient built-in value type
- Declare value types
- Create your own types
- Use enumerations

Estimated lesson time: 30 minutes

Built-in Value Types

Built-in types are base types provided with the .NET Framework, with which other types are built. All built-in numeric types are value types. You choose a numeric type based on the size of the values you expect to work with and the level of precision you require. Table 1-1 lists the most common numeric types by size, from smallest to largest. The first six types are used for whole number values and the last three represent real numbers in order of increasing precision.

Table 1-1 Built-in Value Types

Type (Visual Basic/C# alias)	Bytes	Range	Use for
System.SByte (*SByte/sbyte*)	1	−128 to 127	Signed byte values
System.Byte (*Byte/byte*)	1	0 to 255	Unsigned bytes
System.Int16 (*Short/short*)	2	−32768 to 32767	Interoperation and other specialized uses
System.Int32 (*Integer/int*)	4	−2147483648 to 2147483647	Whole numbers and counters
System.UInt32 (*UInteger/uint*)	4	0 to 4294967295	Positive whole numbers and counters
System.Int64 (*Long/long*)	8	−9223372036854775808 to 9223372036854775807	Large whole numbers
System.Single (*Single/float*)	4	−3.402823E+38 to 3.402823E+38	Floating point numbers
System.Double (*Double/double*)	8	−1.79769313486232E+308 to 1.79769313486232E+308	Precise or large floating point numbers
System.Decimal (*Decimal/decimal*)	16	−79228162514264337593543950335 to 79228162514264337593543950335	Financial and scientific calculations requiring great precision

BEST PRACTICES **Optimizing performance with built-in types**

The runtime optimizes the performance of 32-bit integer types (*Int32* and *UInt32*), so use those types for counters and other frequently accessed integral variables. For floating-point operations, *Double* is the most efficient type because those operations are optimized by hardware.

These numeric types are used so frequently that Visual Basic and C# define aliases for them. Using the alias is equivalent to using the full type name, so most programmers use the shorter aliases. In addition to the numeric types, the non-numeric data types listed in Table 1-2 are also value types.

Table 1-2   Other Value Types

Type (Visual Basic/C# alias)	Bytes	Range	Use for
System.Char (*Char/char*)	2	N/A	Single Unicode characters
System.Boolean (*Boolean/bool*)	4	N/A	*True/False* values
System.IntPtr (none)	Platform-dependent	N/A	Pointer to a memory address
System.DateTime (*Date/date*)	8	1/1/0001 12:00:00 AM to 12/31/9999 11:59:59 PM	Moments in time

There are nearly 300 more value types in the Framework, but the types shown here cover most needs. When you assign between value-type variables, the data is copied from one variable to the other and stored in two different locations on the stack. This behavior is different from that of reference types, which are discussed in Lesson 2.

Even though value types often represent simple values, they still function as objects. In other words, you can call methods on them. In fact, it is common to use the *ToString* method when displaying values as text. *ToString* is overridden from the fundamental *System.Object* type.

NOTE   The *Object* base class

In the .NET Framework, all types are derived from *System.Object*. That relationship helps establish the common type system used throughout the Framework.

How to Declare Value Types

To use a type, you must first declare a symbol as an instance of that type. Value types have an implicit constructor, so declaring them instantiates the type automatically; you don't have to include the *New* keyword as you do with classes. The constructor assigns a default value (usually *null* or *0*) to the new instance, but you should always explicitly initialize the variable within the declaration, as shown in the following code block:

```
' VB
Dim b As Boolean = False
```

```
// C#
bool b = false;
```

NOTE   **Keyword differences in Visual Basic and C#**

One of the cosmetic differences between Visual Basic and C# is that Visual Basic capitalizes keywords, whereas C# uses lowercase keywords. In the text of this book, Visual Basic keywords will always be capitalized for readability. Code samples will always include separate examples for Visual Basic and C#.

NOTE   **Variable capitalizations in Visual Basic and C#**

C# is case-sensitive, but Visual Basic is not case-sensitive. Traditionally, variable names begin with a lowercase letter in C# and are capitalized in Visual Basic. For consistency between the languages, this book will use lowercase variable names for most Visual Basic examples. Feel free to capitalize Visual Basic variables in your own code—it will not affect how the runtime processes your code.

Declare the variable as *Nullable* if you want to be able to determine whether a value has not been assigned. For example, if you are storing data from a yes/no question on a form and the user did not answer the question, you should store a *null* value. The following code allows a Boolean variable to be *true*, *false*, or *null*:

```
' VB
Dim b As Nullable(Of Boolean) = Nothing
```

```
// C#
Nullable<bool> b = null;
```

```
// Shorthand notation, only for C#
bool? b = null;
```

NOTE   **.NET 2.0**

The *Nullable* type is new in .NET 2.0.

Declaring a variable as *nullable* enables the *HasValue* and *Value* members. Use *HasValue* to detect whether or not a value has been set:

```
' VB
If b.HasValue Then Console.WriteLine("b is {0}.", b.Value) _
  Else Console.WriteLine("b is not set.")
```

```
// C#
if (b.HasValue)Console.WriteLine("b is {0}.", b.Value);
  else Console.WriteLine("b is not set.");
```

How to Create User-Defined Types

User-defined types are also called *structures* or simply *structs*, after the language keyword used to create them. As with other value types, instances of user-defined types are stored on the stack and they contain their data directly. In most other ways, structures behave nearly identical to classes.

Structures are a composite of other types that make it easier to work with related data. The simplest example of this is *System.Drawing.Point*, which contains X and Y integer properties that define the horizontal and vertical coordinates of a point. The *Point* structure simplifies working with coordinates by providing the constructor and members demonstrated here:

```
' VB - Requires reference to System.Drawing
' Create point
Dim p As New System.Drawing.Point(20, 30)

' Move point diagonally
p.Offset(-1, -1)
Console.WriteLine("Point X {0}, Y {1}", p.X, p.Y)

// C# - Requires reference to System.Drawing
// Create point
System.Drawing.Point p = new System.Drawing.Point(20, 30);

// Move point diagonally
p.Offset(-1, -1);
Console.WriteLine("Point X {0}, Y {1}", p.X, p.Y);
```

You define your own structures by using the *Structure* keyword in Visual Basic or the *struct* keyword in C#. For example, the following code creates a type that cycles through a set of integers between minimum and maximum values set by the constructor:

```
' VB
Structure Cycle
    ' Private fields
    Dim _val, _min, _max As Integer
```

```vb
    ' Constructor
    Public Sub New(ByVal min As Integer, ByVal max As Integer)
        _val = min : _min = min : _max = max
    End Sub

    ' Public members
    Public Property Value() As Integer
        Get
            Return _val
        End Get
        Set(ByVal value As Integer)
            ' Ensure new setting is between _min and _max.
            If value > _max Then _val = _min _
              Else If value < _min Then _val = _max _
              Else _val = value
        End Set
    End Property

    Public Overrides Function ToString() As String
        Return Value.ToString
    End Function

    Public Function ToInteger() As Integer
        Return Value
    End Function

    ' Operators (new in 2.0)
    Public Shared Operator +(ByVal arg1 As Cycle, _
      ByVal arg2 As Integer) As Cycle
        arg1.Value += arg2
        Return arg1
    End Operator

    Public Shared Operator -(ByVal arg1 As Cycle, _
      ByVal arg2 As Integer) As Cycle
        arg1.Value -= arg2
        Return arg1
    End Operator
End Structure

// C#
struct Cycle
{
    // Private fields
    int _val, _min, _max;

    // Constructor
    public Cycle(int min, int max)
    {
        _val = min;
        _min = min;
        _max = max;
    }
```

```csharp
public int Value
{
    get { return _val; }
    set
    {
        if (value > _max)
            _val = _min;
        else
        {
            if (value < _min)
                _val = _max;
            else
                _val = value;
        }
    }
}

public override string ToString()
{
    return Value.ToString();
}

public int ToInteger()
{
    return Value;
}

// Operators (new in .NET 2.0)
public static Cycle operator +(Cycle arg1, int arg2)
{
    arg1.Value += arg2;
    return arg1;
}

public static Cycle operator -(Cycle arg1, int arg2)
{
    arg1.Value -= arg2;
    return arg1;
}
}
```

You can use this structure to represent items that repeat over a fixed range, such as degrees of rotation or quarters of a football game, as shown here:

```vb
' VB
Dim degrees As New Cycle(0, 359), quarters As New Cycle(1, 4)
For i As Integer = 0 To 8
```

```
    degrees += 90 : quarters += 1
    Console.WriteLine("degrees = {0}, quarters = {1}", degrees, quarters)
Next

// C#
Cycle degrees = new Cycle(0, 359);
Cycle quarters = new Cycle(1, 4);
for (int i = 0; i <= 8; i++)
{
    degrees += 90; quarters += 1;
    Console.WriteLine("degrees = {0}, quarters = {1}", degrees, quarters);
}
```

The *Cycle* sample can be easily converted to and from a value type to a reference type by changing the *Structure/struct* keywords to *Class*. If you make that change, instances of the *Cycle* class would be allocated on the managed heap rather than as 12 bytes on the stack (4 bytes for each private integer field) and assignment between two variables results in both variables pointing to the same instance.

While the functionality is similar, structures are usually more efficient than classes. You should define a structure, rather than a class, if the type will perform better as a value type than a reference type. Specifically, structure types should meet all of these criteria:

- Logically represents a single value
- Has an instance size less than 16 bytes
- Will not be changed after creation
- Will not be cast to a reference type

How to Create Enumerations

Enumerations are related symbols that have fixed values. Use enumerations to provide a list of choices for developers using your class. For example, the following enumeration contains a set of titles:

```
' VB
Enum Titles As Integer
    Mr
    Ms
    Mrs
    Dr
End Enum

// C#
enum Titles : int { Mr, Ms, Mrs, Dr };
```

If you create an instance of the *Titles* type, Visual Studio displays a list of the available values when you assign a value to the variable. Although the value of the variable is an integer, it is easy to output the name of the symbol rather than its value, as shown here:

```
' VB
Dim t As Titles = Titles.Dr
Console.WriteLine("{0}.", t) ' Displays "Dr."
```

```
// C#
Titles t = Titles.Dr;
Console.WriteLine("{0}.", t); // Displays "Dr."
```

The purpose of enumerations is to simplify coding and improve code readability by enabling you to use meaningful symbols instead of simple numeric values. Use enumerations when developers consuming your types must choose from a limited set of choices for a value.

Lab: Declaring and Using Value Types

The following exercises demonstrate how to create and use a structure and how to create an enumeration. If you encounter a problem completing an exercise, the completed projects are available on the companion CD in the Code folder.

▶ **Exercise 1: Create a Structure**

In this exercise, you will create a simple structure with several public members.

1. Using Visual Studio, create a new console application project. Name the project **CreateStruct**.

2. Create a new structure named *Person*, as the following code demonstrates:

```
' VB
Structure Person
End Structure
```

```
// C#
struct Person
{
}
```

3. Within the *Person* structure, define three public members:

   ❑ *firstName* (a *String*)

   ❑ *lastName* (a *String*)

   ❑ *age* (an *Integer*)

The following code demonstrates this:

```vb
' VB
Public firstName As String
Public lastName As String
Public age As Integer
```

```csharp
// C#
public string firstName;
public string lastName;
public int age;
```

4. Create a constructor that initializes all three member variables, as the following code demonstrates:

```vb
' VB
Public Sub New(ByVal _firstName As String, ByVal _lastName As String, ByVal _age As Integer)
    firstName = _firstName
    lastName = _lastName
    age = _age
End Sub
```

```csharp
// C#
public Person(string _firstName, string _lastName, int _age)
{
    firstName = _firstName;
    lastName = _lastName;
    age = _age;
}
```

5. Override the *ToString* method to display the person's first name, last name, and age. The following code demonstrates this:

```vb
' VB
Public Overloads Overrides Function ToString() As String
    Return firstName + " " + lastName + ", age " + age.ToString
End Function
```

```csharp
// C#
public override string ToString()
{
    return firstName + " " + lastName + ", age " + age;
}
```

6. Within the *Main* method of the console application, write code to create an instance of the structure and pass the instance to the *Console.WriteLine* method, as the following code demonstrates:

```vb
' VB
Dim p As Person = New Person("Tony", "Allen", 32)
Console.WriteLine(p)
```

```
// C#
Person p = new Person("Tony", "Allen", 32);
Console.WriteLine(p);
```

7. Run the console application to verify that it works correctly.

▶ **Exercise 2: Add an Enumeration to a Structure**

In this exercise, you will extend the structure you created in Exercise 1 by adding an enumeration.

1. Open the project you created in Exercise 1.

2. Declare a new enumeration in the *Person* structure. Name the enumeration *Genders*, and specify two possible values: *Male* and *Female*. The following code sample demonstrates this:

```
' VB
Enum Genders
    Male
    Female
End Enum

// C#
public enum Genders : int { Male, Female };
```

3. Add a public member of type *Genders*, and modify the *Person* constructor to accept an instance of *Gender*. The following code demonstrates this:

```
' VB
Public firstName As String
Public lastName As String
Public age As Integer
Public gender As Genders

Public Sub New(ByVal _firstName As String, ByVal _lastName As String, _
ByVal _age As Integer, ByVal _gender As Genders)
    firstName = _firstName
    lastName = _lastName
    age = _age
    gender = _gender
End Sub

// C#
public string firstName;
public string lastName;
public int age;
public Genders gender;

public Person(string _firstName, string _lastName, int _age, Genders _gender)
{
    firstName = _firstName;
    lastName = _lastName;
    age = _age;
    gender = _gender;
}
```

4. Modify the *Person.ToString* method to also display the gender, as the following code sample demonstrates:

```
' VB
Public Overloads Overrides Function ToString() As String
    Return firstName + " " + lastName + " (" + gender.ToString() + "), age " +
age.ToString
End Function

// C#
public override string ToString()
{
    return firstName + " " + lastName + " (" + gender + "), age " + age;
}
```

5. Modify your *Main* code to properly construct an instance of the *Person* structure, as the following code sample demonstrates:

```
' VB
Sub Main()
    Dim p As Person = New Person("Tony", "Allen", 32, Person.Genders.Male)
    Console.WriteLine(p)
End Sub

// C#
static void Main(string[] args)
{
    Person p = new Person("Tony", "Allen", 32, Person.Genders.Male);
    Console.WriteLine(p.ToString());
}
```

6. Run the console application to verify that it works correctly.

Lesson Summary

- The .NET Framework includes a large number of built-in types that you can use directly or use to build your own custom types.

- Value types directly contain their data, offering excellent performance. However, value types are limited to types that store very small pieces of data. In the .NET Framework, all value types are 16 bytes or shorter.

- You can create user-defined types that store multiple values and have methods. In object-oriented applications, a large portion of your application logic will be stored in user-defined types.

- Enumerations improve code readability by providing symbols for a set of values.

Lesson Review

You can use the following questions to test your knowledge of the information in Lesson 1, "Using Value Types." The questions are also available on the companion CD if you prefer to review them in electronic form.

NOTE Answers

Answers to these questions and explanations of why each answer choice is right or wrong are located in the "Answers" section at the end of the book.

---

1. Which of the following are value types? (Choose all that apply.)

    A. *Decimal*

    B. *String*

    C. *System.Drawing.Point*

    D. *Integer*

2. You pass a value-type variable into a procedure as an argument. The procedure changes the variable; however, when the procedure returns, the variable has not changed. What happened? (Choose one.)

    A. The variable was not initialized before it was passed in.

    B. Passing a value type into a procedure creates a copy of the data.

    C. The variable was redeclared within the procedure level.

    D. The procedure handled the variable as a reference.

3. Which is the correct declaration for a nullable integer?

    A.

    ```
    ' VB
    Dim i As Nullable<Of Integer> = Nothing

    // C#
    Nullable(int) i = null;
    ```

    B.

    ```
    ' VB
    Dim i As Nullable(Of Integer) = Nothing

    // C#
    Nullable<int> i = null;
    ```

C.

```
' VB
Dim i As Integer = Nothing

// C#
int i = null;
```

D.

```
' VB
Dim i As Integer(Nullable) = Nothing

// C#
int<Nullable> i = null;
```

4. You need to create a simple class or structure that contains only value types. You must create the class or structure so that it runs as efficiently as possible. You must be able to pass an instance of the class or structure to a procedure without concern that the procedure will modify it. Which of the following should you create?

   A. A reference class

   B. A reference structure

   C. A value class

   D. A value structure

Lesson 2: Using Common Reference Types

Most types in the .NET Framework are reference types. Reference types provide a great deal of flexibility, and they offer excellent performance when passing them to methods. The following sections introduce reference types by discussing common built-in classes. Lesson 4, "Converting Between Types," covers creating classes, interfaces, and delegates.

After this lesson, you will be able to:

- Explain the difference between value types and reference types.
- Describe how value types and reference types differ when assigning values.
- List the built-in reference types.
- Describe when you should use the *StringBuilder* type.
- Create and sort arrays.
- Open, read, write, and close files.
- Detect when exceptions occur and respond to the exception.

Estimated lesson time: 40 minutes

What Is a Reference Type?

Reference types store the address of their data, also known as a *pointer*, on the stack. The actual data that address refers to is stored in an area of memory called the *heap*. The runtime manages the memory used by the heap through a process called *garbage collection*. Garbage collection recovers memory periodically as needed by disposing of items that are no longer referenced.

BEST PRACTICES   Garbage collection

Garbage collection occurs only when needed or when triggered by a call to *GC.Collect*. Automatic garbage collection is optimized for applications where most instances are short-lived, except for those allocated at the beginning of the application. Following that design pattern will result in the best performance.

Comparing the Behavior of Reference and Value Types

Because reference types represent the address of data rather than the data itself, assigning one reference variable to another doesn't copy the data. Instead, assigning a reference variable to another instance merely creates a second copy of the reference, which refers to the same memory location on the heap as the original variable.

Consider the following simple structure declaration:

```vb
' VB
Structure Numbers
    Public val As Integer

    Public Sub New(ByVal _val As Integer)
        val = _val
    End Sub

    Public Overloads Overrides Function ToString() As String
        Return val.ToString
    End Function
End Structure
```

```csharp
// C#
struct Numbers
{
    public int val;

    public Numbers(int _val)
    { val = _val; }

    public override string ToString()
    { return val.ToString(); }
}
```

Now consider the following code, which creates an instance of the *Numbers* structure, copies that structure to a second instance, modifies both values, and displays the results:

```vb
' VB
Dim n1 As Numbers = New Numbers(0)
Dim n2 As Numbers = n1
n1.val += 1
n2.val += 2
Console.WriteLine("n1 = {0}, n2 = {1}", n1, n2)
```

```csharp
// C#
Numbers n1 = new Numbers(0);
Numbers n2 = n1;
n1.val += 1;
n2.val += 2;
Console.WriteLine("n1 = {0}, n2 = {1}", n1, n2);
```

This code would display "n1 = 1, n2 = 2" because a structure is a value type, and copying a value type results in two distinct values. However, if you change the *Numbers* type declaration from a structure to a class, the same application would display "n1 = 3, n2 = 3". Changing *Numbers* from a structure to a class causes it to be a reference type rather than a value type. When you modify a reference type variable, you modify all copies of that reference type variable.

Built-in Reference Types

There are about 2500 built-in reference types in the .NET Framework. Everything not derived from *System.ValueType* is a reference type, including these 2500 or so built-in reference types. Table 1-3 lists the most commonly used types, from which many other reference types are derived.

Table 1-3   Common Reference Types

Type	Use for
System.Object	The *Object* type is the most general type in the Framework. You can convert any type to *System.Object*, and you can rely on any type having *ToString*, *GetType*, and *Equals* members inherited from this type.
System.String	Text data.
System.Text.StringBuilder	Dynamic text data.
System.Array	Arrays of data. This is the base class for all arrays. Array declarations use language-specific array syntax.
System.IO.Stream	Buffer for file, device, and network I/O. This is an abstract base class; task-specific classes are derived from *Stream*.
System.Exception	Handling system and application-defined exceptions. Task-specific exceptions inherit from this type.

Strings and String Builders

Types are more than just containers for data, they also provide the means to manipulate that data through their members. *System.String* provides a set of members for working with text. For example, the following code does a quick search and replace:

```
' VB
Dim s As String = "this is some text to search"
s = s.Replace("search", "replace")
Console.WriteLine(s)
```

```
// C#
string s = "this is some text to search";
s = s.Replace("search", "replace");
Console.WriteLine(s);
```

Strings of type *System.String* are immutable in .NET. That means any change to a string causes the runtime to create a new string and abandon the old one. That happens invisibly, and many programmers might be surprised to learn that the following code allocates four new strings in memory:

```
' VB
Dim s As String

s = "wombat"            ' "wombat"
s += " kangaroo"        ' "wombat kangaroo"
s += " wallaby"         ' "wombat kangaroo wallaby"
s += " koala"           ' "wombat kangaroo wallaby koala"
Console.WriteLine(s)

// C#
string s;

s = "wombat";           // "wombat"
s += " kangaroo";       // "wombat kangaroo"
s += " wallaby";        // "wombat kangaroo wallaby"
s += " koala";          // "wombat kangaroo wallaby koala"
Console.WriteLine(s);
```

Only the last string has a reference; the other three will be disposed of during garbage collection. Avoiding these types of temporary strings helps avoid unnecessary garbage collection, which improves performance. There are several ways to avoid temporary strings:

- Use the *String* class's *Concat*, *Join*, or *Format* methods to join multiple items in a single statement.
- Use the *StringBuilder* class to create dynamic (mutable) strings.

The *StringBuilder* solution is the most flexible because it can span multiple statements. The default constructor creates a buffer 16 bytes long, which grows as needed. You can specify an initial size and a maximum size if you like. The following code demonstrates using *StringBuilder*:

```
' VB
Dim sb As New System.Text.StringBuilder(30)
sb.Append("wombat")     ' Build string.
sb.Append(" kangaroo")
sb.Append(" wallaby")
sb.Append(" koala")
Dim s as String = sb.ToString        ' Copy result to string.
Console.WriteLine(s)
```

```
// C#
System.Text.StringBuilder sb = new System.Text.StringBuilder(30);
sb.Append("wombat");       // Build string.
sb.Append(" kangaroo");
sb.Append(" wallaby");
sb.Append(" koala");
string s = sb.ToString();        // Copy result to string.
Console.WriteLine(s);
```

Another subtle but important feature of the *String* class is that it overrides operators from *System.Object*. Table 1-4 lists the operators the *String* class overrides.

Table 1-4   String Operators

Operator	Visual Basic	C#	Action on *System.String*
Addition	+ or &	+	Joins two strings to create a new string.
Equality	=	==	Returns *True* if two strings have the same contents; *False* if they are different.
Inequality	<>	!=	The inverse of the equality operator.
Assignment	=	=	Copies the contents of one string into a new one. This causes strings to behave like value types, even though they are implemented as reference types.

How to Create and Sort Arrays

Arrays are declared using parentheses (in Visual Basic) or square braces (in C#) as part of the declaration. As with the *String* type, *System.Array* provides members for working with its contained data. The following code declares an array with some initial data and then sorts the array:

```
' VB
' Declare and initialize an array.
Dim ar() As Integer = {3, 1, 2}

' Call a shared/static array method.
Array.Sort(ar)
```

```
' Display the result.
Console.WriteLine("{0}, {1}, {2}", ar(0), ar(1), ar(2))

// C#
// Declare and initialize an array.
int[] ar = { 3, 1, 2 };

// Call a shared/static array method.
Array.Sort(ar);

// Display the result.
Console.WriteLine("{0}, {1}, {2}", ar[0], ar[1], ar[2]);
```

How to Use Streams

Streams are another very common type because they are the means for reading from and writing to the disk and communicating across the network. The *System.IO.Stream* type is the base type for all task-specific stream types. Table 1-5 shows some of the most commonly used stream types. In addition, network streams are found in the *System.Network.Sockets* namespace, and encrypted streams are found in the *System.Security.Cryptography* namespace.

Table 1-5 Common Stream Types

System.IO Type	Use to
FileStream	Create a base stream used to write to or read from a file
MemoryStream	Create a base stream used to write to or read from memory
StreamReader	Read data from the stream
StreamWriter	Write data to the stream

The simplest stream classes are *StreamReader* and *StreamWriter*, which enable you to read and write text files. You can pass a filename as part of the constructor, enabling you to open a file with a single line of code. After you have processed a file, call the *Close* method so that the file does not remain locked. The following code, which requires the *System.IO* namespace, demonstrates how to write to and read from a text file:

```
' VB
' Create and write to a text file
Dim sw As StreamWriter = New StreamWriter("text.txt")
sw.WriteLine("Hello, World!")
sw.Close
```

```
' Read and display a text file
Dim sr As StreamReader = New StreamReader("text.txt")
Console.WriteLine(sr.ReadToEnd)
sr.Close

// C#
// Create and write to a text file
StreamWriter sw = new StreamWriter("text.txt");
sw.WriteLine("Hello, World!");
sw.Close();

// Read and display a text file
StreamReader sr = new StreamReader("text.txt");
Console.WriteLine(sr.ReadToEnd());
sr.Close();
```

MORE INFO   Streams

For more information about streams, refer to Chapter 2, "Input/Output (I/O)."

How to Throw and Catch Exceptions

Exceptions are unexpected events that interrupt normal execution of an assembly. For example, if your assembly is reading a large text file from a removable disk and the user removes the disk, the runtime will throw an exception. This makes sense because there is no way your assembly could continue running.

Exceptions should never cause your assembly to fail completely. Instead, you should plan for exceptions to occur, catch them, and respond to the event. In the preceding example, you could notify the user that the file was not available, and then await further instructions from the user. The following simplified code, which requires the *System.IO* namespace, demonstrates this:

```
' VB
Try
    Dim sr As StreamReader = New StreamReader("C:\boot.ini")
    Console.WriteLine(sr.ReadToEnd)
Catch ex As Exception
    ' If there are any problems reading the file, display an error message
    Console.WriteLine("Error reading file: " + ex.Message)
End Try

// C#
try
{
    StreamReader sr = new StreamReader(@"C:\boot.ini");
    Console.WriteLine(sr.ReadToEnd());
}
catch (Exception ex)
{
```

```
    // If there are any problems reading the file, display an error message
    Console.WriteLine("Error reading file: " + ex.Message);
}
```

In the preceding example, if any type of error occurs—including a file not found error, insufficient privileges error, or an error during the reading of the file—processing continues within the *Catch* block. If no problems occur, the runtime skips the *Catch* block.

The base *Exception* class is very useful and contains an error message and other application data. In addition to the base *Exception* class, the Framework defines hundreds of exception classes to describe different types of events, all derived from *System.SystemException*. Additionally, you can define your own exceptions when you need to describe an event in more detail than allowed by the standard exception classes by deriving from *System.ApplicationException*.

Having multiple exception classes allows you to respond differently to different types of errors. The runtime will execute only the first *Catch* block with a matching exception type, however, so order *Catch* blocks from the most-specific to the least-specific. The following code sample displays different error messages for a file not found error, an insufficient privileges error, and any other type of error that might occur:

```vb
' VB
Try
    Dim sr As StreamReader = New StreamReader("text.txt")
    Console.WriteLine(sr.ReadToEnd)
Catch ex As System.IO.FileNotFoundException
    Console.WriteLine("The file could not be found.")
Catch ex As System.UnauthorizedAccessException
    Console.WriteLine("You do not have sufficient permissions.")
Catch ex As Exception
    Console.WriteLine("Error reading file: " + ex.Message)
End Try
```

```csharp
// C#
try
{
    StreamReader sr = new StreamReader("text.txt");
    Console.WriteLine(sr.ReadToEnd);
}
catch (System.IO.FileNotFoundException ex)
{
    Console.WriteLine("The file could not be found.");
}
catch (System.UnauthorizedAccessException ex)
{
    Console.WriteLine("You do not have sufficient permissions.");
}
catch (Exception ex)
{
    Console.WriteLine("Error reading file: " + ex.Message);
}
```

This process is sometimes called *filtering exceptions*. Exception handling also supports a *Finally* block. The *Finally* block runs after the *Try* block and any *Catch* blocks have finished executing, whether or not an exception was thrown. Therefore, you should use a *Finally* block to close any streams or clean up any other objects that might be left open if an exception occurs. The following code sample closes the *StreamReader* object whether or not an exception occurs:

```vb
' VB
Dim sr As StreamReader
Try
    sr = New StreamReader("text.txt")
    Console.WriteLine(sr.ReadToEnd)
Catch ex As Exception
    ' If there are any problems reading the file, display an error message
    Console.WriteLine("Error reading file: " + ex.Message)
Finally
    ' Close the StreamReader, whether or not an exception occurred
    sr.Close
End Try
```

```csharp
// C#
StreamReader sr:
try
{
    sr = new StreamReader("text.txt");
    Console.WriteLine(sr.ReadToEnd());
}
catch (Exception ex)
{
    // If there are any problems reading the file, display an error message
    Console.WriteLine("Error reading file: " + ex.Message);
}
finally
{
    // Close the StreamReader, whether or not an exception occurred
    sr.Close();
}
```

Notice that the *StreamReader* declaration was moved outside the *Try* block in the preceding example. This is necessary because the *Finally* block cannot access variables that are declared within the *Try* block. This makes sense because depending on where an exception occurred, variable declarations within the *Try* block might not yet have been executed. To catch exceptions that occur both during and after the *StreamReader* declaration, use nested *Try/Catch/Finally* blocks.

Typically, all code except for simple variable declarations should occur within *Try* blocks. Robust error handling improves the user experience when problems occur and greatly simplifies debugging problems. However, exception handling does incur a slight performance penalty. To conserve space and focus on specific topics, sample code within this book will typically not include exception handling.

Lab: Working with Reference Types

The following exercises reinforce knowledge of reference types, strings, and exceptions. If you encounter a problem completing an exercise, the completed projects are available on the companion CD in the Code folder.

▶ **Exercise 1: Identify Types as Value or Reference**

In this exercise, you will write a console application that displays whether objects are value or reference types.

1. Using Visual Studio, create a new console application project. Name the project **List-Value-Types**.

2. Create instances of the following classes:

   ❑ *SByte*

   ❑ *Byte*

   ❑ *Int16*

   ❑ *Int32*

   ❑ *Int64*

   ❑ *String*

   ❑ *Exception*

   The following code demonstrates this:

```
' VB
Dim a As SByte = 0
Dim b As Byte = 0
Dim c As Int16 = 0
Dim d As Int32 = 0
Dim e As Int64 = 0
Dim s As String = ""
Dim ex As Exception = New Exception

// C#
SByte a = 0;
Byte b = 0;
Int16 c = 0;
Int32 d = 0;
Int64 e = 0;
string s = "";
Exception ex = new Exception();
```

3. Add each of the instances to a new object array, as the following code demonstrates:

```
' VB
Dim types As Object() = {a, b, c, d, e, s, ex}
```

```
// C#
object[] types = { a, b, c, d, e, s, ex };
```

4. Within a *foreach* loop, check the *object.GetType().IsValueType* property to determine whether the type is a value type. Display each type name and whether it is a value type or a reference type, as the following code demonstrates:

```
' VB
For Each o As Object In types
    Dim type As String
    If o.GetType.IsValueType Then
        type = "Value type"
    Else
        type = "Reference Type"
    End If
    Console.WriteLine("{0}: {1}", o.GetType, type)
Next
```

```
// C#
foreach ( object o in types )
{
    string type;
    if (o.GetType().IsValueType)
        type = "Value type";
    else
        type = "Reference Type";

    Console.WriteLine("{0}: {1}", o.GetType(), type );
}
```

5. Run the console application, and verify that each type matches your understanding.

▶ **Exercise 2: Work with Strings and Arrays**

In this exercise, you will write a function to sort a string.

1. Using Visual Studio, create a new console application project. Name the project **SortString**.

2. Define a string. Then use the *String.Split* method to separate the string into an array of words. The following code demonstrates this:

```
' VB
Dim s As String = "Microsoft .NET Framework 2.0 Application Development Foundation"
Dim sa As String() = s.Split(" ")
```

```
// C#
string s = "Microsoft .NET Framework 2.0 Application Development Foundation";
string[] sa = s.Split(' ');
```

3. Call the *Array.Sort* method to sort the array of words, as the following code demonstrates:

```
' VB
Array.Sort(sa)
```

```
// C#
Array.Sort(sa);
```

4. Call the *String.Join* method to convert the array of words back into a single string, and then write the string to the console. The following code sample demonstrates this:

```
' VB
s = String.Join(" ", sa)
Console.WriteLine(s)
```

```
// C#
s = string.Join(" ", sa);
Console.WriteLine(s);
```

5. Run the console application, and verify that it works correctly.

▶ **Exercise 3: Work with Streams and Exceptions**

Consider a scenario in which a coworker wrote a simple Windows Forms application to view text files. However, users complain that it is very temperamental. If the user mistypes the filename or if the file is not available for any reason, the application fails with an unhandled exception error. You must add exception handling to the application to display friendly error messages to users if a file is not available.

1. Copy the Chapter01\Lesson2-ViewFile folder from the companion CD to your hard disk, and open either the C# version or the Visual Basic .NET version of the ViewFile project.

2. Exceptions occur when users attempt to view a file. Therefore, edit the code that runs for the *showButton.Click* event. Add code to catch any type of exception that occurs, and display the error in a dialog box to the user. If an exception occurs after the *TextReader* object is initialized, you should close it whether or not an exception occurs. You will need two nested *Try* blocks: one to catch exceptions during the *TextReader* initialization, and a second one to catch exceptions when the file is read. The following code sample demonstrates this:

```
' VB
Try
    Dim tr As TextReader = New StreamReader(locationTextBox.Text)
    Try
        displayTextBox.Text = tr.ReadToEnd
```

```
        Catch ex As Exception
            MessageBox.Show(ex.Message)
        Finally
            tr.Close()
        End Try
    Catch ex As Exception
        MessageBox.Show(ex.Message)
    End Try

    // C#
    try
    {
        TextReader tr = new StreamReader(locationTextBox.Text);
        try
        { displayTextBox.Text = tr.ReadToEnd(); }
        catch (Exception ex)
        { MessageBox.Show(ex.Message); }
        finally
        { tr.Close(); }
    }
    catch (Exception ex)
    { MessageBox.Show(ex.Message); }
```

3. Run your application. First verify that it can successfully display a text file. Then provide an invalid filename, and verify that a message box appears when an invalid filename is provided.

4. Next add overloaded exception handling to catch *System.IO.FileNotFoundException* and *System.UnauthorizedAccessException*. The following code sample demonstrates this:

```
    ' VB
    Try
        Dim tr As TextReader = New StreamReader(locationTextBox.Text)
        Try
            displayTextBox.Text = tr.ReadToEnd
        Catch ex As Exception
            MessageBox.Show(ex.Message)
        Finally
            tr.Close()
        End Try
    Catch ex As System.IO.FileNotFoundException
        MessageBox.Show("Sorry, the file does not exist.")
    Catch ex As System.UnauthorizedAccessException
        MessageBox.Show("Sorry, you lack sufficient privileges.")
    Catch ex As Exception
        MessageBox.Show(ex.Message)
    End Try
```

```
// C#
try
{
    TextReader tr = new StreamReader(locationTextBox.Text);
    try
    { displayTextBox.Text = tr.ReadToEnd(); }
    catch (Exception ex)
    { MessageBox.Show(ex.Message); }
    finally
    { tr.Close(); }
}
catch (System.IO.FileNotFoundException ex)
{ MessageBox.Show("Sorry, the file does not exist."); }
catch (System.UnauthorizedAccessException ex)
{ MessageBox.Show("Sorry, you lack sufficient privileges."); }
catch (Exception ex)
{ MessageBox.Show(ex.Message); }
```

5. Run your application again, and verify that it provides your new error message if an invalid filename is provided.

Lesson Summary

- Reference types contain the address of data rather than the actual data.

- When you copy a value type, a second copy of the value is created. When you copy a reference type, only the pointer is copied. Therefore, if you copy a reference type and then modify the copy, both the copy and the original variables are changed.

- The .NET Framework includes a large number of built-in reference types that you can use directly or use to build your own custom types.

- Strings are immutable; use the *StringBuilder* class to create a string dynamically.

- Use streams to read from and write to files, memory, and the network.

- Use the *Catch* clause within *Try* blocks to filter exceptions by type. Close and dispose of nonmemory resources in the *Finally* clause of a *Try* block.

Lesson Review

You can use the following questions to test your knowledge of the information in Lesson 2, "Using Common Reference Types." The questions are also available on the companion CD if you prefer to review them in electronic form.

NOTE Answers

Answers to these questions and explanations of why each answer choice is right or wrong are located in the "Answers" section at the end of the book.

---

1. Which of the following are reference types? (Choose all that apply.)

   A. Types declared *Nullable*

   B. *String*

   C. *Exception*

   D. All types derived from *System.Object*

2. What is the correct order for *Catch* clauses when handling different exception types?

   A. Order from most general to most specific.

   B. Order from most likely to least likely to occur.

   C. Order from most specific to most general.

   D. Order from least likely to most likely to occur.

3. When should you use the *StringBuilder* class instead of the *String* class?

   A. When building a string from shorter strings.

   B. When working with text data longer than 256 bytes.

   C. When you want to search and replace the contents of a string.

   D. When a string is a value type.

4. Why should you close and dispose of resources in a *Finally* block instead of a *Catch* block?

   A. It keeps you from having to repeat the operation in each *Catch*.

   B. *Finally* blocks run whether or not an exception occurs.

   C. The compiler throws an error if resources are not disposed of in the *Finally* block.

   D. You cannot dispose of resources in a *Catch* block.

Lesson 3: Constructing Classes

In object-oriented languages, the bulk of the work should be performed within objects. All but the simplest applications require constructing one or more custom classes, each with multiple properties and methods used to perform tasks related to that object. This lesson discusses how to create custom classes.

> **After this lesson, you will be able to:**
> - Describe and use inheritance.
> - Describe and use interfaces.
> - Describe and use partial classes.
> - Create a generic type, and use the built-in generic types.
> - Respond to and raise events.
> - Add attributes to describe assemblies and methods.
> - Move a type from one class library to another using type forwarding.
>
> **Estimated lesson time: 40 minutes**

What Is Inheritance?

The .NET Framework has thousands of classes, and each class has many different methods and properties. Keeping track of all these classes and members would be impossible if the .NET Framework were not implemented extremely consistently. For example, every class has a *ToString* method that performs exactly the same task—converting an instance of the class into a string. Similarly, many classes support the same operators, such as comparing two instances of a class for equality.

This consistency is possible because of *inheritance* and *interfaces* (described in the next section). Use inheritance to create new classes from existing ones. For example, you will learn in Chapter 6, "Graphics," that the *Bitmap* class inherits from the *Image* class and extends it by adding functionality. Therefore, you can use an instance of the *Bitmap* class in the same ways that you would use an instance of the *Image* class. However, the *Bitmap* class provides additional methods that enable you to do more with pictures.

You can easily create a custom exception class by inheriting from *System.Application-Exception*, as shown here:

```vb
' VB
Class DerivedException
    Inherits System.ApplicationException
```

```
        Public Overrides ReadOnly Property Message() As String
            Get
                Return "An error occurred in the application."
            End Get
        End Property
End Class

// C#
class DerivedException : System.ApplicationException
{
    public override string Message
    {
        get { return "An error occurred in the application."; }
    }
}
```

You can throw and catch the new exception because the custom class inherits that behavior of its base class, as shown here:

```
' VB
Try
    Throw New DerivedException
Catch ex As DerivedException
Console.WriteLine("Source: {0}, Error: {1}", ex.Source, ex.Message)
End Try

// C#
try
{
    throw new DerivedException();
}
catch (DerivedException ex)
{
    Console.WriteLine("Source: {0}, Error: {1}", ex.Source, ex.Message);
}
```

Notice that the custom exception not only supports the throw/catch behavior, but it also includes a *Source* member (as well as others) inherited from *System.Application-Exception.*

Another benefit of inheritance is the ability to use derived classes interchangeably. For example, there are five classes that inherit from the *System.Drawing.Brush* base class: *HatchBrush, LinearGradientBrush, PathGradientBrush, SolidBrush,* and *TextureBrush.* The *Graphics.DrawRectangle* method requires a *Brush* object as one of its parameters; however, you will never pass an object of the base *Brush* class to *Graphics.DrawRectangle.* Instead, you will pass an object of one of the derived classes. Because they are each derived from the *Brush* class, the *Graphics.DrawRectangle* method can accept any of them. Similarly, if you were to create a custom class derived from the *Brush* class, you could also pass an object of that class to *Graphics.DrawRectangle*.

What Is an Interface?

Interfaces, also known as *contracts*, define a common set of members that all classes that implement the interface must provide. For example, the *IComparable* interface defines the *CompareTo* method, which enables two instances of a class to be compared for equality. All classes that implement the *IComparable* interface, whether custom-created or built in the .NET Framework, can be compared for equality.

IDisposable is an interface that provides a single method, *Dispose*, to enable assemblies that create an instance of your class to free up any resources the instance has consumed. To create a class that implements the *IDisposable* interface using Visual Studio 2005, follow these steps:

1. Create the class declaration. For example:

    ```
    ' VB
    Class BigClass
    End Class

    // C#
    class BigClass
    {
    }
    ```

2. Add the interface declaration. For example:

    ```
    ' VB
    Class BigClass
        Implements IDisposable
    End Class

    // C#
    class BigClass : IDisposable
    {
    }
    ```

3. If you are using Visual Basic, Visual Studio should automatically generate method declarations for each of the required methods. If it does not, delete the Implements command and try again; Visual Studio may still be starting up. If you are using C#, right-click the Interface declaration, click Implement Interface, and then click Implement Interface again, as shown in Figure 1-1.

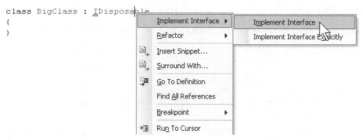

Figure 1-1 Visual Studio simplifies implementing an interface

4. Write code for each of the interface's methods. In this example, you would write code in the *Dispose* method to deallocate any resources you had allocated.

Table 1-6 lists the most commonly used interfaces in the .NET Framework.

Table 1-6 Commonly used interfaces

Class	Description
IComparable	Implemented by types whose values can be ordered; for example, the numeric and string classes. *IComparable* is required for sorting.
IDisposable	Defines methods for manually disposing of an object. This interface is important for large objects that consume resources, or objects that lock access to resources such as databases.
IConvertible	Enables a class to be converted to a base type such as *Boolean*, *Byte*, *Double*, or *String*.
ICloneable	Supports copying an object.
IEquatable	Allows you to compare to instances of a class for equality. For example, if you implement this interface, you could say "if (a == b)".
IFormattable	Enables you to convert the value of an object into a specially formatted string. This provides greater flexibility than the base *ToString* method.

You can create your own interfaces, too. This is useful if you need to create multiple custom classes that behave similarly and can be used interchangeably. For example, the following code defines an interface containing three members:

```vb
' VB
Interface IMessage
    ' Send the message. Returns True is success, False otherwise.
    Function Send() As Boolean
    ' The message to send.
    Property Message() As String
    ' The Address to send to.
    Property Address() As String
End Interface
```

```csharp
// C#
interface IMessage
{
    // Send the message. Returns True is success, False otherwise.
    bool Send();
    // The message to send.
    string Message { get; set; }
    // The Address to send to.
    string Address { get;  set; }
}
```

If you implement that interface in a new class, Visual Studio generates the following template for the interface members:

```vb
' VB
Class EmailMessage
    Implements IMessage

    Public Property Address() As String Implements IMessage.Address
        Get
        End Get
        Set(ByVal value As String)
        End Set
    End Property

    Public Property Message() As String Implements IMessage.Message
        Get
        End Get
        Set(ByVal value As String)
        End Set
    End Property

    Public Function Send() As Boolean Implements IMessage.Send
    End Function
End Class
```

```
// C#
class EmailMessage : IMessage
{
    public bool Send()
    {
    throw new Exception("The method or operation is not implemented.");
    }

    public string Message
    {
        get
        {
        throw new Exception("The method or operation is not implemented.");
        }
        set
        {
        throw new Exception("The method or operation is not implemented.");
        }
    }

    public string Address
    {
        get
        {
        throw new Exception("The method or operation is not implemented.");
        }
        set
        {
        throw new Exception("The method or operation is not implemented.");
        }
    }
}
```

If you create a custom class and later decide that it would be useful to have multiple classes with the same members, Visual Studio has a shortcut to extract an interface from a custom class. Simply follow these steps:

1. Right-click the class in Visual Studio 2005.

2. Click Refactor and then click Extract Interface.

3. Specify the interface name, select the public members that should form the interface, and then click OK.

Classes can implement multiple interfaces. Therefore, a class could implement both the *IComparable* and *IDisposable* interfaces.

What Are Partial Classes?

NOTE .NET 2.0

Partial classes are new in .NET 2.0.

Partial classes allow you to split a class definition across multiple source files. The benefit of this approach is that it hides details of the class definition so that derived classes can focus on more significant portions.

The Windows Form class is an example of a built-in partial class. In Visual Studio 2003 and earlier, forms classes included code generated by the form designer. Now that code is hidden in a partial class named *form*.Designer.vb or *form*.Designer.cs.

In Visual Basic, you must select Show All Files in the Solution Explorer to see the partial class files. In C#, that view is enabled by default. Partial classes aren't part of the exam objectives, but you need to know about them so that you can find the Form Designer code when you create a new Windows Form.

What Are Generics?

Generics are part of the .NET Framework's type system that allows you to define a type while leaving some details unspecified. Instead of specifying the types of parameters or member classes, you can allow code that uses your type to specify it. This allows consumer code to tailor your type to its own specific needs.

Exam Tip   Generic types are new in .NET 2.0, and you will probably see an unusually large number of questions about generics on the exam.

The .NET Framework version 2.0 includes several generic classes in the *System.Collections.Generic* namespace, including *Dictionary*, *Queue*, *SortedDictionary*, and *SortedList*. These classes work similarly to their nongeneric counterparts in *System.Collections*, but they offer improved performance and type safety.

MORE INFO   Generic collections

The .NET Framework version 2.0 includes the *System.Collections.Generic* namespace, which provides built-in collections that offer improved performance over standard collections. For more information, refer to Chapter 4, "Collections and Generics."

Why Use Generics?

Versions 1.0 and 1.1 of the .NET Framework did not support generics. Instead, developers used the *Object* class for parameters and members and would cast other classes to and from the *Object* class. Generics offer two significant advantages over using the *Object* class:

- **Reduced run-time errors**   The compiler cannot detect type errors when you cast to and from the *Object* class. For example, if you cast a string to an *Object* class and then attempt to cast that *Object* to an integer, the compiler will not catch the error. Instead, the runtime will throw an exception. Using generics allows the compiler to catch this type of bug before your program runs. Additionally, you can specify constraints to limit the classes used in a generic, enabling the compiler to detect an incompatible type.

- **Improved performance**   Casting requires boxing and unboxing (explained later in Lesson 4, "Converting Between Types"), which steals processor time and slows performance. Using generics doesn't require casting or boxing, which improves run-time performance.

Real World

Tony Northrup

I haven't been able to reproduce the performance benefits of generics; however, according to Microsoft, generics are faster than using casting. In practice, casting proved to be several times faster than using a generic. However, you probably won't notice performance differences in your applications. (My tests over 100,000 iterations took only a few seconds.) So you should still use generics because they are type-safe.

How to Create a Generic Type

First, examine the following classes. Classes *Obj* and *Gen* perform exactly the same tasks, but *Obj* uses the *Object* class to enable any type to be passed, while *Gen* uses generics:

```
' VB
Class Obj
    Public V1 As Object
    Public V2 As Object
```

```
    Public Sub New(ByVal _V1 As Object, ByVal _V2 As Object)
        V1 = _V1
        V2 = _V2
    End Sub
End Class

Class Gen(Of T, U)
    Public V1 As T
    Public V2 As U

    Public Sub New(ByVal _V1 As T, ByVal _V2 As U)
        V1 = _V1
        V2 = _V2
    End Sub
End Class

// C#
class Obj
{
    public Object t;
    public Object u;

    public Obj(Object _t, Object _u)
    {
        t = _t;
        u = _u;
    }
}

class Gen<T, U>
{
    public T t;
    public U u;

    public Gen(T _t, U _u)
    {
        t = _t;
        u = _u;
    }
}
```

As you can see, the *Obj* class has two members of type *Object*. The *Gen* class has two members of type *T* and *U*. The consuming code will determine the types for *T* and *U*. Depending on how the consuming code uses the *Gen* class, *T* and *U* could be a *string*, an *int*, a custom class, or any combination thereof.

There is a significant limitation to creating a generic class: generic code is valid only if it will compile for every possible constructed instance of the generic, whether an *Int*, a *string*, or any other class. Essentially, you are limited to the capabilities of the base *Object* class when writing generic code. Therefore, you could call the *ToString* or

GetHashCode method within your class, but you could not use the + or > operator. These same restrictions do not apply to the consuming code because the consuming code has declared a type for the generic.

How to Consume a Generic Type

When you consume a generic type, you must specify the types for any generics used. Consider the following console application code, which uses the *Gen* and *Obj* classes:

```
' VB
' Add two Strings using the Obj class
Dim oa As Obj = New Obj("Hello, ", "World!")
Console.WriteLine(CType(oa.V1, String) + CType(oa.V2, String))

' Add two Strings using the Gen class
Dim ga As New Gen(Of String, String)("Hello, ", "World!")
Console.WriteLine(ga.V1 + ga.V2)

' Add a Double and an Integer using the Obj class
Dim ob As Obj = New Obj(10.125, 2005)
Console.WriteLine(CType(ob.V1, Double) + CType(ob.V2, Integer))

' Add a Double and an Integer using the Gen class
Dim gb As New Gen(Of Double, Integer)(10.125, 2005)
Console.WriteLine(gb.V1 + gb.V2)

// C#
// Add two strings using the Obj class
Obj oa = new Obj("Hello, ", "World!");
Console.WriteLine((string)oa.t + (string)oa.u);

// Add two strings using the Gen class
Gen<string, string> ga = new Gen<string, string>("Hello, ", "World!");
Console.WriteLine(ga.t + ga.u);

// Add a double and an int using the Obj class
Obj ob = new Obj(10.125, 2005);
Console.WriteLine((double)ob.t + (int)ob.u);

// Add a double and an int using the Gen class
Gen<double, int> gb = new Gen<double, int>(10.125, 2005);
Console.WriteLine(gb.t + gb.u);
```

If you run that code in a console application, the *Obj* and *Gen* classes produce exactly the same results. However, the code that uses the *Gen* class actually works faster because it does not require boxing and unboxing to and from the *Object* class. Additionally, developers would have a much easier time using the *Gen* class. First, developers would not have to manually cast from the *Object* class to the appropriate types.

Second, type errors would be caught at compile time rather than at run time. To demonstrate that benefit, consider the following code, which contains an error:

```vb
' VB
' Add a Double and an Integer using the Gen class
Dim gb As New Gen(Of Double, Integer)(10.125, 2005)
Console.WriteLine(gb.V1 + gb.V2)

' Add a Double and an Integer using the Obj class
Dim ob As Obj = New Obj(10.125, 2005)
Console.WriteLine(CType(ob.V1, Integer) + CType(ob.V2, Integer))
```

```csharp
// C#
// Add a double and an int using the Gen class
Gen<double, int> gc = new Gen<double, int>(10.125, 2005);
Console.WriteLine(gc.t + gc.u);

// Add a double and an int using the Obj class
Obj oc = new Obj(10.125, 2005);
Console.WriteLine((int)oc.t + (int)oc.u);
```

The last line in that code sample contains an error—the *oc.t* value is cast to an *Int* instead of to a *double*. Unfortunately, the compiler won't catch the mistake. Instead, in C#, a run-time exception is thrown when the runtime attempts to cast a *double* to an *Int* value. In Visual Basic, which allows narrowing conversions by default, the result is even worse—a miscalculation occurs. It's much easier to fix a bug that the compiler catches and much harder to detect and fix a run-time error, so the generic class provides a clear benefit.

How to Use Constraints

Generics would be extremely limited if you could only write code that would compile for any class, because you would be limited to the capabilities of the base *Object* class. To overcome this limitation, use constraints to place requirements on the types that consuming code can substitute for your generic.

Generics support four types of constraints:

- **Interface**   Allow only types that implement specific interfaces to use your generic.
- **Base class**   Allow only types that match or inherit from a specific base class to use your generic.
- **Constructor**   Require types that use your generic to implement a parameterless constructor.
- **Reference or value type**   Require types that use your generic to be either a reference or value type.

Use the *As* clause in Visual Basic or the *where* clause in C# to apply a constraint to a generic. For example, the following generic class could be used only by types that implement the *IComparable* interface:

```
' VB
Class CompGen(Of T As IComparable)
    Public t1 As T
    Public t2 As T

    Public Sub New(ByVal _t1 As T, ByVal _t2 As T)
        t1 = _t1
        t2 = _t2
    End Sub

    Public Function Max() As T
        If t2.CompareTo(t1) < 0 Then
            Return t1
        Else
            Return t2
        End If
    End Function
End Class

// C#
class CompGen<T>
    where T : IComparable
{
    public T t1;
    public T t2;

    public CompGen(T _t1, T _t2)
    {
        t1 = _t1;
        t2 = _t2;
    }

    public T Max()
    {
        if (t2.CompareTo(t1) < 0)
            return t1;
        else
            return t2;
    }
}
```

The preceding class will compile correctly. However, if you remove the *where* clause, the compiler will return an error indicating that generic type *T* does not contain a definition for *CompareTo*. By constraining the generic to classes that implement *IComparable*, you guarantee that the *CompareTo* method will always be available.

Events

Most projects are nonlinear. In Windows Forms applications, you might have to wait for a user to click a button or press a key, and then respond to that event. In server applications, you might have to wait for an incoming network request. These capabilities are provided by events in the .NET Framework, as described in the following sections.

What Is an Event?

An *event* is a message sent by an object to signal the occurrence of an action. The action could be caused by user interaction, such as a mouse click, or it could be triggered by some other program logic. The object that raises the event is called the *event sender*. The object that captures the event and responds to it is called the *event receiver*.

In event communication, the event sender class does not know which object or method will receive (handle) the events it raises. What is needed is an intermediary (or pointer-like mechanism) between the source and the receiver. The .NET Framework defines a special type (*Delegate*) that provides the functionality of a function pointer.

What Is a Delegate?

A *delegate* is a class that can hold a reference to a method. Unlike other classes, a delegate class has a signature, and it can hold references only to methods that match its signature. A delegate is thus equivalent to a type-safe function pointer or a callback. While delegates have other uses, the discussion here focuses on the event-handling functionality of delegates. A delegate declaration is sufficient to define a delegate class. The declaration supplies the signature of the delegate, and the common language runtime provides the implementation. The following example shows an event delegate declaration:

```
' VB
Public Delegate Sub AlarmEventHandler(sender As Object, e As EventArgs)
```

```
// C#
public delegate void AlarmEventHandler(object sender, EventArgs e);
```

The standard signature of an event handler delegate defines a method that does not return a value, whose first parameter is of type *Object* and refers to the instance that raises the event, and whose second parameter is derived from type *EventArgs* and holds the event data. If the event does not generate event data, the second parameter is simply an instance of *EventArgs*. Otherwise, the second parameter is a custom type derived from *EventArgs* and supplies any fields or properties needed to hold the event data.

EventHandler is a predefined delegate that specifically represents an event handler method for an event that does not generate data. If your event does generate data, you must supply your own custom event data type and either create a delegate where the type of the second parameter is your custom type, or you must use the generic *EventHandler* delegate class and substitute your custom type for the generic type parameter.

To associate the event with the method that will handle the event, add an instance of the delegate to the event. The event handler is called whenever the event occurs, unless you remove the delegate.

How to Respond to an Event

You must do two things to respond to an event:

- Create a method to respond to the event. The method must match the *Delegate* signature. Typically, this means it must return void and accept two parameters: an *Object* and an *EventArgs* (or a derived class). The following code demonstrates this:

```
' VB
Public Sub Button1_Click(sender As Object, e As EventArgs)
    ' Method code
End Sub

// C#
private void button1_Click(object sender, EventArgs e)
{
    // Method code
}
```

- Add the event handler to indicate which method should receive events, as the following code demonstrates:

```
' VB
AddHandler Me.Button1.Click, AddressOf Me.Button1_Click

// C#
this.button1.Click += new System.EventHandler(this.button1_Click);
```

NOTE .NET 2.0

The .NET Framework 2.0 includes a new generic version of the *EventHandler* type.

When the event occurs, the method you specified will run.

How to Raise an Event

At a minimum, you must do three things to raise an event:

- Create a delegate:

```
' VB
Public Delegate Sub MyEventHandler(ByVal sender As Object, ByVal e As EventArgs)
```

```
// C#
public delegate void MyEventHandler(object sender, EventArgs e);
```

- Create an event member:

```
' VB
Public Event MyEvent As MyEventHandler
```

```
// C#
public event MyEventHandler MyEvent;
```

- Invoke the delegate within a method when you need to raise the event, as the following code demonstrates:

```
' VB
Dim e As EventArgs = New EventArgs
RaiseEvent MyEvent(Me, e)
```

```
// C#
EventArgs e = new EventArgs();

if (MyEvent != null)
{
    // Invokes the delegates.
    MyEvent(this, e);
}

// Note that C# checks to determine whether handler is null.
// This is not necessary in Visual Basic
```

Additionally, you can derive a custom class from *EventArgs* if you need to pass information to the event handler.

NOTE   **Differences in raising events in Visual Basic and C#**

Visual Basic and C# differ when raising events. In C#, you must check whether the event is null before calling it. In Visual Basic, you can omit that check.

What Are Attributes?

Attributes describe a type, method, or property in a way that can be programmatically queried using a technique called *Reflection*. Some common uses for attributes are to

- Specify which security privileges a class requires
- Specify security privileges to refuse to reduce security risk
- Declare capabilities, such as supporting serialization
- Describe the assembly by providing a title, description, and copyright notice

Attribute types derive from the *System.Attribute* base class and are specified using <> or [] notation. The following code sample demonstrates how to add assembly attributes:

```
' VB - AssemblyInfo.vb
<Assembly: AssemblyTitle("ch01vb")>
<Assembly: AssemblyDescription("Chapter 1 Samples")>
<Assembly: AssemblyCompany("Microsoft Learning")>
<Assembly: AssemblyProduct("ch01vb")>
<Assembly: AssemblyCopyright("Copyright ©  2006")>
<Assembly: AssemblyTrademark("")>

// C# - AssemblyInfo.cs
[assembly: AssemblyTitle("ch01cs")]
[assembly: AssemblyDescription("Chapter 1 Samples")]
[assembly: AssemblyConfiguration("")]
[assembly: AssemblyCompany("Microsoft Learning")]
[assembly: AssemblyProduct("ch01cs")]
[assembly: AssemblyCopyright("Copyright ©  2006")]
[assembly: AssemblyTrademark("")]
```

Visual Studio automatically creates some standard attributes for your assembly when you create a project, including a title, description, company, guide, and version. You should edit these attributes for every project you create because the defaults do not include important information such as the description.

Attributes do more than describe an assembly to other developers, they can also declare requirements or capabilities. For example, to enable a class to be serialized, you must add the *Serializable* attribute, as the following code demonstrates:

```
' VB
<Serializable()> Class ShoppingCartItem
End Class

// C#
[Serializable]
class ShoppingCartItem
{
}
```

Without the *Serializable* attribute, a class is not serializable. Similarly, the following code uses attributes to declare that it needs to read the C:\boot.ini file. Because of this attribute, the runtime will throw an exception prior to execution if it lacks the specified privilege:

```vb
' VB
Imports System.Security.Permissions

<Assembly: FileIOPermissionAttribute(SecurityAction.RequestMinimum, Read := "C:\boot.ini")>
Module Module1
    Sub Main()
        Console.WriteLine("Hello, World!")
    End Sub
End Module
```

```csharp
// C#
using System;
using System.Security.Permissions;

[assembly:FileIOPermissionAttribute(SecurityAction.RequestMinimum, Read=@"C:\boot.ini")]
namespace DeclarativeExample
{
    class Class1
    {
        [STAThread]
        static void Main(string[] args)
        {
            Console.WriteLine("Hello, World!");
        }
    }
}
```

What Is Type Forwarding?

Type forwarding is an attribute (implemented in *TypeForwardedTo*) that allows you to move a type from one assembly (assembly A) into another assembly (assembly B), and to do so in such a way that it is not necessary to recompile clients that consume assembly A. After a component (assembly) ships and is being used by client applications, you can use type forwarding to move a type from the component (assembly) into another assembly and ship the updated component (and any additional assemblies required), and the client applications will still work without being recompiled. Type forwarding works only for components referenced by existing applications. When you rebuild an application, there must be appropriate assembly references for any types used in the application.

To move a type from one class library to another, follow these steps:

NOTE .NET 2.0

Type forwarding is a new feature in .NET 2.0.

1. Add a *TypeForwardedTo* attribute to the source class library assembly.
2. Cut the type definition from the source class library.
3. Paste the type definition into the destination class library.
4. Rebuild both libraries.

The following code shows the attribute declaration used to move *TypeA* to the *DestLib* class library:

```
' VB
Imports System.Runtime.CompilerServices
<Assembly:TypeForwardedTo(GetType(DestLib.TypeA))]>
```

```
// C#
using System.Runtime.CompilerServices;
[assembly:TypeForwardedTo(typeof(DestLib.TypeA))]
```

Lab: Create a Derived Class with Delegates

The following exercises demonstrate inheritance and events. If you encounter a problem completing an exercise, the completed projects are available on the companion CD in the Code folder.

▶ **Exercise 1: Derive a New Class from an Existing Class**

In this exercise, you will derive a new class from the *Person* class you created in Lesson 1.

1. Copy the Chapter01\Lesson3-Person folder from the companion CD to your hard disk, and open either the C# version or the Visual Basic version of the CreateStruct project.
2. Change the *Person* structure to a class.
3. Create a new class definition named *Manager* that inherits from the base *Person* class.

    ```
    ' VB
    Class Manager
    End Class
    ```

```
// C#
class Manager : Person
{
}
```

4. Add two new public members as strings: *phoneNumber* and *officeLocation*.

5. Override the constructor to accept a phone number and office location to define the new members. You will need to call the base class's constructor, as shown in the following code sample:

```
' VB
Public Sub New(ByVal _firstName As String, ByVal _lastName As String, _
ByVal _age As Integer, ByVal _gender As Genders, ByVal _phoneNumber As String, _
ByVal _officeLocation As String)
    MyBase.New(_firstName, _lastName, _age, _gender)
    phoneNumber = _phoneNumber
    officeLocation = _officeLocation
End Sub

// C#
public Manager(string _firstName, string _lastName, int _age,
Genders _gender, string _phoneNumber, string _officeLocation)
    : base (_firstName, _lastName, _age, _gender)
{
    phoneNumber = _phoneNumber;
    officeLocation = _officeLocation;
}
```

6. Override the *ToString* method to add the phone number and office location, as shown in the following sample:

```
' VB
Public Overloads Overrides Function ToString() As String
    Return MyBase.ToString + ", " + phoneNumber + ", " + officeLocation
End Function

// C#
public override string ToString()
{
    return base.ToString() + ", " + phoneNumber + ", " + officeLocation;
}
```

7. Modify the *Main* method to create a *Manager* object instead of a person object. Then run your application to verify that it works correctly.

▶ **Exercise 2: Respond to an Event**

In this exercise, you will create a class that responds to a timer event.

1. Using Visual Studio, create a new Windows Forms application project. Name the project TimerEvents.

2. Add a *ProgressBar* control to the form, as shown in Figure 1-2.

Figure 1-2 You will control this progress bar by responding to timer events

3. Within the form class declaration, declare an instance of a *System.Windows .Forms.Timer* object. *Timer* objects can be used to throw events after a specified number of milliseconds. The following code sample shows how to declare a *Timer* object:

```
' VB
Dim t As Timer
```

```
// C#
System.Windows.Forms.Timer t;
```

4. In the designer, view the properties for the form. Then view the list of events. Double-click the *Load* event to automatically create an event handler that will run the first time the form is initialized. Within the method, initialize the *Timer* object, set the interval to one second, create an event handler for the *Tick* event, and start the timer. The following code sample demonstrates this:

```
' VB
Private Sub Form1_Load(ByVal sender As System.Object, ByVal e As System.EventArgs) _
Handles MyBase.Shown
    t = New System.Windows.Forms.Timer
    t.Interval = 1000
    AddHandler t.Tick, AddressOf Me.t_Tick
    t.Start()
End Sub
```

```
// C#
private void Form1_Load(object sender, EventArgs e)
{
    t = new System.Windows.Forms.Timer();
    t.Interval = 1000;
    t.Tick += new EventHandler(t_Tick);
    t.Start();
}
```

5. Implement the method that will respond to the *Timer.Tick* event. When the event occurs, add 10 to the *ProgressBar.Value* attribute. Then stop the timer if the *ProgressBar.Value* attribute has reached 100. The following code sample demonstrates this:

```
' VB
Private Sub t_Tick(ByVal sender As Object, ByVal e As EventArgs)
    ProgressBar1.Value += 10
```

```
      If ProgressBar1.Value = 100 Then
          t.Stop()
      End If
  End Sub

  // C#
  void t_Tick(object sender, EventArgs e)
  {
      progressBar1.Value += 10;

      if (progressBar1.Value >= 100)
          t.Stop();
  }
```

6. Run the application to verify that it responds to the timer event every second.

Lesson Summary

- Use inheritance to create new types based on existing ones.

- Use interfaces to define a common set of members that must be implemented by related types.

- Partial classes split a class definition across multiple source files.

- Events allow you to run a specified method when something occurs in a different section of code.

- Use attributes to describe assemblies, types, and members.

- Use the *TypeForwardedTo* attribute to move a type from one class library to another.

Lesson Review

You can use the following questions to test your knowledge of the information in Lesson 3, "Constructing Classes." The questions are also available on the companion CD if you prefer to review them in electronic form.

NOTE   Answers

Answers to these questions and explanations of why each answer choice is right or wrong are located in the "Answers" section at the end of the book.

---

1. Which of the following statements are true? (Choose all that apply.)

   A. Inheritance defines a contract between types.

   B. Interfaces define a contract between types.

    C. Inheritance derives a type from a base type.

    D. Interfaces derive a type from a base type.

2. Which of the following are examples of built-in generic types? (Choose all that apply.)

    A. *Nullable*

    B. *Boolean*

    C. *EventHandler*

    D. *System.Drawing.Point*

3. You are creating a generic class, and you need to dispose of the generic objects. How can you do this?

    A. Call the *Object.Dispose* method.

    B. Implement the *IDisposable* interface.

    C. Derive the generic class from the *IDisposable* class.

    D. Use constraints to require the generic type to implement the *IDisposable* interface.

4. You've implemented an event delegate from a class, but when you try to attach an event procedure you get a compiler error that there is no overload that matches the delegate. What happened?

    A. The signature of the event procedure doesn't match that defined by the delegate.

    B. The event procedure is declared *Shared/static*, but it should be an instance member instead.

    C. You mistyped the event procedure name when attaching it to the delegate.

    D. The class was created in a different language.

Lesson 4: Converting Between Types

Often, you need to convert between two different types. For example, you might need to determine whether an *Integer* is greater or less than a *Double*. You might need to pass a *Double* to a method that requires an *Integer* as a parameter. Or you might need to display a number as text.

This lesson describes how to convert between types in both Visual Basic and C#. Type conversion is one of the few areas where Visual Basic and C# differ considerably.

After this lesson, you will be able to:

- Convert between types.
- Explain boxing and why it should be avoided.
- Implement conversion operators.

Estimated lesson time: 20 minutes

Conversion in Visual Basic and C#

By default, Visual Basic allows implicit conversions between types, while C# prohibits implicit conversions that lose precision. To turn off implicit conversions in Visual Basic, add Option Strict On to the top of each code file, or (in Visual Studio) select Project, choose Properties, select Compile, and select Option Strict On for the entire project.

Both Visual Basic and C# allow implicit conversion if the destination type can accommodate all possible values from the source type. That is called a *widening conversion*, and it is illustrated by the following example:

```
' VB
Dim i As Integer = 1
Dim d As Double = 1.0001
d = i        ' Conversion allowed

// C#
int i = 1;
double d = 1.0001;
d = i;   // Conversion allowed.
```

If the range or precision of the source type exceeds that of the destination type, the operation is called a *narrowing conversion*, which usually requires explicit conversion. Table 1-7 lists the ways to perform explicit conversions.

Table 1-7 Methods for Explicit Conversion

System Type	Visual Basic	C#	Converts
System.Convert			Between types that implement the *System.IConvertible* interface.
	CType	(*type*) cast operator	Between types that define conversion operators.
type.*ToString*, type.*Parse*			Between string and base types; throws exception if the conversion is not possible.
type.*TryParse*, type.*TryParseExact*			From string to a base type; returns false if the conversion is not possible.
	CBool, CInt, CStr, etc.		Between base Visual Basic types; compiled inline for better performance. (Visual Basic only.)
	DirectCast, TryCast		Between types. *DirectCast* throws an exception if the types are not related through inheritance or if they do not share a common interface; *TryCast* returns *Nothing* in those situations. (Visual Basic only.)

NOTE .NET 2.0

TryParse, TryParseExact, and *TryCast* are new in .NET 2.0. Previously, you had to attempt a *parsing* or *conversion* and then catch the exception if it failed.

Narrowing conversions may return an incorrect result if the source value exceeds the destination type's range. If a conversion between the types is not defined, you will receive a compile-time error.

What Is Boxing and Unboxing?

Boxing converts a value type to a reference type, and unboxing converts a reference type to a value type. The following example demonstrates boxing by converting an *Integer* (a value type) to an *Object* (a reference type):

```
' VB
Dim i As Integer = 123
Dim o As Object = CType(i, Object)
```

```
// C#
int i = 123;
object o = (object) i;
```

Unboxing occurs if you assign a reference object to a value type. The following example demonstrates unboxing:

```
' VB
Dim o As Object = 123
Dim i As Integer = CType(o, Integer)
```

```
// C#
object o = 123;
int i = (int) o;
```

BEST PRACTICES   Boxing and unboxing

Boxing and unboxing incur overhead, so you should avoid them when programming intensely repetitive tasks. Boxing also occurs when you call virtual methods that a structure inherits from *System.Object*, such as *ToString*. Follow these tips to avoid unnecessary boxing:

- Implement type-specific versions (overloads) for procedures that accept various value types. It is better practice to create several overloaded procedures than one that accepts an *Object* argument.
- Use generics whenever possible instead of accepting *Object* arguments.
- Override the *ToString*, *Equals*, and *GetHash* virtual members when defining structures.

How to Implement Conversion in Custom Types

You can define conversions for your own types in several ways. Which technique you choose depends on the type of conversion you want to perform:

- Define conversion operators to simplify narrowing and widening conversions between numeric types.
- Override *ToString* to provide conversion to strings, and override *Parse* to provide conversion from strings.

- Implement *System.IConvertible* to enable conversion through *System.Convert*. Use this technique to enable culture-specific conversions.

- Implement a *TypeConverter* class to enable design-time conversion for use in the Visual Studio Properties window. Design-time conversion is outside the scope of the exam and the *TypeConverter* class is not covered in this book.

MORE INFO   Design-time conversion

For more information about design-time conversion, read "Extending Design-Time Support" at *http://msdn2.microsoft.com/en-us/library/37899azc(en-US,VS.80).aspx*.

NOTE   .NET 2.0

Conversion operators are new in .NET 2.0.

Defining conversion operators allows you to directly assign from a value type to your custom type. Use the *Widening/implicit* keyword for conversions that don't lose precision; use the *Narrowing/explicit* keyword for conversions that could lose precision. For example, the following structure defines operators that allow assignment to and from integer values:

```
' VB
Structure TypeA
    Public Value As Integer

    ' Allows implicit conversion from an integer.
    Public Shared Widening Operator CType(ByVal arg As Integer) As TypeA
        Dim res As New TypeA
        res.Value = arg
        Return res
    End Operator

    ' Allows explicit conversion to an integer.
    Public Shared Narrowing Operator CType(ByVal arg As TypeA) As Integer
        Return arg.Value
    End Operator

    ' Provides string conversion (avoids boxing).
    Public Overrides Function ToString() As String
        Return Me.Value.ToString
    End Function

End Structure

// C#
struct TypeA
```

```
{
    public int Value;

    // Allows implicit conversion from an integer.
    public static implicit operator TypeA(int arg)
    {
        TypeA res = new TypeA();
        res.Value = arg;
        return res;
    }

    // Allows explicit conversion to an integer
    public static explicit operator int(TypeA arg)
    {
        return arg.Value;
    }

    // Provides string conversion (avoids boxing).
    public override string ToString()
    {
        return this.Value.ToString();
    }
}
```

The preceding type also overrides *ToString* to perform the string conversion without boxing. Now you can assign integers to the type directly, as shown here:

```
' VB
Dim a As TypeA, i As Integer
' Widening conversion is OK implicit.
a = 42   ' Rather than a.Value = 42
' Narrowing conversion must be explicit.
i = CInt(a) ' Rather than i = a.Value
' This syntax is OK, too.
i = CType(a, Integer)
Console.WriteLine("a = {0}, i = {1}", a.ToString, i.ToString)

// C#
TypeA a; int i;
// Widening conversion is OK implicit.
a = 42;   // Rather than a.Value = 42
// Narrowing conversion must be explicit.
i = (int)a; // Rather than i = a.Value
Console.WriteLine("a = {0}, i = {1}", a.ToString(), i.ToString());
```

To implement the *System.IConvertible* interface, add the *IConvertible* interface to the type definition. Then use Visual Studio to automatically implement the interface. Visual Studio inserts member declarations for 17 methods, including *GetTypeCode*, *ChangeType*, and *To*Type methods for each base type. You don't have to implement every method, and some—such as *ToDateTime*—will probably be invalid. For invalid methods, simply throw an exception—Visual Studio automatically adds code to throw an exception for any conversion methods you don't implement.

After you implement *IConvertible*, the custom type can be converted using the standard *System.Convert* class as shown here:

```
' VB
Dim a As TypeA, b As Boolean
a = 42
' Convert using ToBoolean.
b = Convert.ToBoolean(a)
Console.WriteLine("a = {0}, b = {1}", a.ToString, b.ToString)

// C#
TypeA a; bool b;
a = 42;
// Convert using ToBoolean.
b = Convert.ToBoolean(a);
Console.WriteLine("a = {0}, b = {1}", a.ToString(), b.ToString());
```

Lab: Safely Performing Conversions

The following exercises show how to avoid problems with implicit conversions so that your programs function predictably. If you encounter a problem completing an exercise, the completed projects are available on the companion CD in the Code folder.

▶ **Exercise 1: Examine Implicit Conversion**

In this exercise, you will examine conversion to determine which number types allow implicit conversion.

1. Create a new console application in Visual Studio.

2. Declare instances of three value types: *Int16*, *Int32*, and *double*. The following code sample demonstrates this:

   ```
   ' VB
   Dim i16 As Int16 = 1
   Dim i32 As Int32 = 1
   Dim db As Double = 1

   // C#
   Int16 i16 = 1;
   Int32 i32 = 1;
   double db = 1;
   ```

3. Attempt to assign each variable to all the others, as the following code sample demonstrates.

```
' VB
i16 = i32
i16 = db

i32 = i16
i32 = db

db = i16
db = i32

// C#
i16 = i32;
i16 = db;

i32 = i16;
i32 = db;

db = i16;
db = i32;
```

4. Attempt to build your project. Which implicit conversions did the compiler allow, and why?

▶ **Exercise 2: Enable Option Strict (Visual Basic Only)**

In this exercise, which is only for developers using Visual Basic, you will modify the compiler's options and then rebuild the project you created in Exercise 1.

1. In Visual Studio, open the project you created in Exercise 1.

2. Click the Project menu, and then click *ProjectName* Properties.

3. Click the Compile tab. For Implicit Conversion, change the *Notification* type to *Error*.

4. Attempt to build your project. Which implicit conversions did the compiler allow, and why?

Lesson Summary

- The .NET Framework can automatically convert between built-in types. Widening conversions occur implicitly in both Visual Basic and C#. Narrowing conversions require explicit conversion in C#, while Visual Basic allows narrowing conversions by default.

- Boxing allows any type to be treated as a reference type.

- You must specifically implement conversion operators to enable conversion in custom types.

Lesson Review

You can use the following questions to test your knowledge of the information in Lesson 4, "Converting Between Types." The questions are also available on the companion CD if you prefer to review them in electronic form.

NOTE Answers

Answers to these questions and explanations of why each answer choice is right or wrong are located in the "Answers" section at the end of the book.

---

1. Why should boxing be avoided? (Choose one.)

   A. It adds overhead.

   B. Users must have administrative privileges to run the application.

   C. It makes code less readable.

2. Structures inherit *ToString* from *System.Object*. Why would someone override that method within a structure? (Choose as many correct answers as apply.)

   A. To avoid boxing.

   B. To return something other than the type name.

   C. The compiler requires structures to override the *ToString* method.

   D. To avoid run-time errors caused by invalid string conversions.

3. If there is no valid conversion between two types, what should you do when implementing the *IConvertible* interface?

   A. Delete the *ToType* member that performs the conversion.

   B. Throw an *InvalidCastException*.

   C. Throw a new custom exception reporting the error.

   D. Leave the member body empty.

4. With strict conversions enabled, which of the following would allow an implicit conversion? (Choose all that apply.)

   A. *Int16* to *Int32*

   B. *Int32* to *Int16*

   C. *Int16* to *Double*

   D. *Double* to *Int16*

Chapter Review

To further practice and reinforce the skills you learned in this chapter, you can perform the following tasks:

- Review the chapter summary.
- Review the list of key terms introduced in this chapter.
- Complete the case scenarios. These scenarios set up real-world situations involving the topics of this chapter and ask you to create a solution.
- Complete the suggested practices.
- Take a practice test.

Chapter Summary

- Value types are small variables that store data directly rather than storing a pointer to a second memory location that contains the data. Assignment between value types copies the data from one variable to the other, creating a separate instance of the data. You can make value types nullable using the *Nullable* generic type, and you can create structures that combine multiple value types.

- Reference types contain the address of data rather than the actual data. The .NET Framework includes thousands of reference types to perform almost any task you could require. The most commonly used reference type is the *String* class. Because the *String* class is immutable, it behaves differently from other reference types. When you copy most reference classes, only the pointer is copied, which means changes made to one instance are also reflected in the other instance. When an unexpected event occurs, the .NET Framework throws an exception. You can handle these exceptions by creating *Try/Catch* blocks in your code.

- Classes in .NET Framework languages are custom types that can include value types, reference types, methods, attributes, and properties. To enable consistency between classes, you can use inheritance (where you derive a new class from an existing class) or an interface (where you are required to implement specified interfaces). Generics enable you to create a class or method that works with a variety of types. To enable applications to respond to planned events, you can raise and respond to events.

■ Conversion enables you to compare and copy values between different types. Implicit conversion happens automatically and behaves differently in Visual Basic and C#. C# allows implicit conversion for only widening conversions, where no information could be lost. Visual Basic allows implicit conversion for both narrowing and widening conversions. When values are converted from a value type to a reference type, it is considered boxing. Unboxing occurs if you assign a reference object to a value type.

Key Terms

Do you know what these key terms mean? You can check your answers by looking up the terms in the glossary at the end of the book.

- boxing
- cast
- constraint
- contract
- exception
- filtering exceptions
- garbage collection
- generic type
- heap
- interface
- narrowing
- nullable type
- signature
- stack
- structure
- unboxing
- widening

Case Scenario

In the following case scenario, you will apply what you've learned about types. You can find answers to these questions in the "Answers" section at the end of this book.

Case Scenario: Designing an Application

You have recently accepted a job as an internal application developer in the information technology department of an enterprise healthcare company. Your first task is to design an internal application that employees will use to manage information about customers (whom everyone calls "subscribers"), their current plans, medications, and chosen doctors. Answer your manager's questions about your design choices.

1. We need to manage information about both subscribers and doctors. How will you do this? Will you have one class for both, two separate classes, or what?

2. Our employees need to search for groups of subscribers or doctors. For example, if a doctor retires, we need to contact all that doctor's subscribers and assist them in finding a new physician. Similarly, we contact doctors annually to renew their contracts. How can you store a group of subscribers or doctors in your application?

3. One of the tasks your application will perform is generating mailing labels for groups of subscribers or doctors. Is there any way that you can write a single method that will handle addresses for both subscribers and doctors? How will you implement this?

4. The privacy of our information is extremely important to us. Our database developer is going to restrict permissions on the database to prevent unauthorized users from gaining access. If a user's privileges are rejected, I'd like you to instruct the user to contact their manager to gain access. How will you handle it if a database query is rejected for insufficient privileges?

Suggested Practices

To help you successfully master the exam objectives presented in this chapter, complete the following tasks.

Manage Data in a .NET Framework Application by Using .NET Framework 2.0 System Types

For this task, you should complete at least Practices 1 and 2. If you want a better understanding of how generics perform in the real world, complete Practice 3 as well.

- **Practice 1** Open the last project you created, and add exception handling to your code. Unless performance is a higher priority than reliability, all code outside of value type declarations should be in a *Try* block.

- **Practice 2**   Create a linked-list generic class that enables you to create a chain of different object types.

- **Practice 3**   Create two classes with identical functionality. Use generics for the first class, and cast the second class to *Object* types. Create a *For* loop that uses the class over thousands of iterations. Time the performance of both the generic class and the *Object*-based class to determine which performs better. You can use *DateTime.Now.Ticks* to measure the time.

Implement .NET Framework Interfaces to Cause Components to Comply with Standard Contracts

For this task, you should complete all three practices to gain experience implementing common interfaces with real-world classes and schema.

- **Practice 1**   Create a custom class that implements the necessary interfaces to allow an array of the class to be sorted.

- **Practice 2**   Create a custom class that can be converted to common value types.

- **Practice 3**   Create a custom class that can be disposed of using the *IDisposable* .*Dispose* method.

Control Interactions Between .NET Framework Application Components by Using Events and Delegates

For this task, you should complete both Practices 1 and 2.

- **Practice 1**   Open the last Windows Forms application you created, and examine the code Visual Studio automatically generated to respond to user interface events.

- **Practice 2**   Create a class that throws an event and derives a custom class based on *EventArgs*. Then create an assembly that responds to the event.

Take a Practice Test

The practice tests on this book's companion CD offer many options. For example, you can test yourself on just one exam objective, or you can test yourself on all the 70-536 certification exam content. You can set up the test so that it closely simulates the experience of taking a certification exam, or you can set it up in study mode so that you can look at the correct answers and explanations after you answer each question.

Practice tests

For details about all the practice test options available, see the "How to Use the Practice Tests" section in this book's Introduction.

Chapter 2
Input/Output (I/O)

In this chapter, you will learn how to work with the input/output (I/O) system within the Microsoft .NET Framework. The basics of the I/O system include accessing files and folders in the file system, working with read and write streams, using compression streams, and using isolated storage.

Exam objectives in this chapter:
- Access files and folders by using the File System classes. (Refer *System.IO* namespace)
  - *File* class and *FileInfo* class
  - *Directory* class and *DirectoryInfo* class
  - *DriveInfo* class and *DriveType* enumeration
  - *FileSystemInfo* class and *FileSystemWatcher* class
  - *Path* class
  - *ErrorEventArgs* class and *ErrorEventHandler* delegate
  - *RenamedEventArgs* class and *RenamedEventHandler* delegate
- Manage byte streams by using *Stream* classes. (Refer *System.IO* namespace)
  - *FileStream* class
  - *Stream* class (not *Reader* and *Writer* classes because they are a separate objective)
  - *MemoryStream* class
  - *BufferedStream* class
- Manage the .NET Framework application data by using *Reader* and *Writer* classes. (Refer *System.IO* namespace)
  - *StringReader* class and *StringWriter* class
  - *TextReader* class and *TextWriter* class
  - *StreamReader* class and *StreamWriter* class
  - *BinaryReader* class and *BinaryWriter* class

■ Compress or decompress stream information in a .NET Framework application (refer *System.IO.Compression* namespace) and improve the security of application data by using isolated storage. (Refer *System.IO.IsolatedStorage* namespace)

  ❏ *IsolatedStorageFile* class

  ❏ *IsolatedStorageFileStream* class

  ❏ *DeflateStream* class

  ❏ *GZipStream* class

Lessons in this chapter:

Before You Begin

To complete the lessons in this chapter, you should be familiar with Microsoft Visual Basic or C# and be comfortable with the following tasks:

■ Create a console application in Microsoft Visual Studio using Visual Basic or C#.

■ Add references to system class libraries to a project.

■ Create text files.

Real World

Shawn Wildermuth

I've written hundreds, if not thousands, of lines of code and invariably I come back to the I/O system for lots of it. The I/O section of the .NET Framework provides help for doing a myriad of tasks. Much of what is in the I/O system is the basis for other parts of the Framework as well as for third-party products. Learning the basics of how streams and files work has made doing my job much easier.

Lesson 1: Navigating the File System

In the everyday work of developers, one of the most common tasks is to work with the file system. This task includes navigating and gathering information about drives, folders, and files as well as waiting for changes to happen in the file system.

After this lesson, you will be able to:

■ Write code that uses the *File* and *FileInfo* classes.

■ Write code that uses the *Directory* and *DirectoryInfo* classes.

■ Use the *DriveInfo* and *DriveType* classes.

■ Enumerate files, directories, and drives using the *FileSystemInfo* derived classes.

■ Use the *Path* class to manipulate file system paths.

■ Watch for changes in the file system using the *FileSystemWatcher* class.

Estimated lesson time: 20 minutes

What Are the File System Classes?

Inside the *System.IO* namespace are a set of classes used to navigate and manipulate files, directories, and drives. The file system classes are separated into two types of classes: informational and utility.

Most of the informational classes derive from the *FileSystemInfo* base class. These classes expose all the system information about file system objects—specifically, files, directories, and drives. These classes are named *FileInfo* and *DirectoryInfo*.

In addition, the *DriveInfo* class represents a drive in the file system, but although it is still an informational class, it does not derive from the *FileSystemInfo* class because it does not share the common sorts of behavior (for example, you can delete files and folders, but not drives).

The utility classes provide static methods (or shared ones for Visual Basic) to perform certain operations on file system objects such as files, directories, and file system paths. These utility classes include the *File*, *Directory*, and *Path* classes.

The *FileSystemInfo* Class

The *FileSystemInfo* class provides the basic functionality for all informational file system classes. Table 2-1 shows the most important *FileSystemInfo* properties.

Table 2-1 *FileSystemInfo* **Properties**

Name	Description
Attributes	Gets or sets *FileAttributes* of the current file or directory.
CreationTime	Gets or sets the time that the current file or directory was created.
Exists	Determines whether the file or directory exists.
Extension	Gets a string representation of the extension part of the file or directory.
FullName	Gets the full path to the file or directory.
LastAccessTime	Gets or sets the time the file or directory was accessed.
LastWriteTime	Gets or sets the time the file or directory was last written to.
Name	Gets the simple name for the file or directory. For a file, this is the name within the directory. For a directory, this is the last directory name in the directory hierarchy.

Table 2-2 shows the most important *FileSystemInfo* methods.

Table 2-2 *FileSystemInfo* **Methods**

Name	Description
Delete	Removes the file or directory from the file system
Refresh	Updates the data in the class with the most current information from the file system

The *FileInfo* Class

The *FileInfo* class provides the basic functionality to access and manipulate a single file in the file system.

Table 2-3 shows the most important *FileInfo* properties.

Table 2-3 *FileInfo* **Properties**

Name	Description
Directory	Gets the *DirectoryInfo* object that represents the directory that this file is stored within
DirectoryName	Gets the name of the directory that this file is stored within
IsReadOnly	Gets or sets the flag that dictates whether the file can be modified or deleted
Length	Gets the length of the file

Table 2-4 shows the most important *FileInfo* methods.

Table 2-4 *FileInfo* **Methods**

Name	Description
AppendText	Creates a new *StreamWriter* that will allow appending text to the file. See Lesson 2 for more information.
CopyTo	Makes a copy of the file in a new location.
Create	Creates a file based on the current file information.
CreateText	Creates a new *StreamWriter* and a new file for writing text. See Lesson 2 for more information.
Decrypt	Decrypts a file that was encrypted by the current user.
Encrypt	Encrypts a file so that only the current user can decrypt the information within the file.
MoveTo	Moves the file to a new location.
Open	Opens the file with specific privileges (read, read/write, and so on).
OpenRead	Opens the file with read-only access.
OpenText	Opens the file and returns a *StreamReader* to allow reading of text within the file.
OpenWrite	Opens the file with write-only access.
Replace	Replaces a file with the file that is described in the current *FileInfo* object.

How to Get Information about a File

To obtain information about a specific file, follow this procedure:

- Create a new *FileInfo* object by using the path to the file.
- Access the *FileInfo* object's properties.

For example, you can check whether a file exists by calling the *FileInfo* object's *Exists* property, as shown in the following code:

```vb
' VB
Dim ourFile As FileInfo = New FileInfo("c:\boot.ini")

If ourFile.Exists Then
    Console.WriteLine("Filename : {0}", ourFile.Name)
    Console.WriteLine("Path     : {0}", ourFile.FullName)
End If
```

```csharp
// C#
FileInfo ourFile = new FileInfo(@"c:\boot.ini ");

if (ourFile.Exists)
{
    Console.WriteLine("Filename : {0}", ourFile.Name);
    Console.WriteLine("Path     : {0}", ourFile.FullName);
}
```

Using the *FileInfo* object this way allows code to interrogate the information about a file in the file system.

How to Copy a File

In addition to accessing data about a file, the *FileInfo* object allows operations to be performed on the file. Again, once a valid *FileInfo* object is obtained, all you have to do is call the *CopyTo* method to make a copy of your file, as the following code example shows:

```vb
' VB
Dim ourFile As FileInfo = New FileInfo("c:\boot.ini")

ourFile.CopyTo("c:\boot.bak")
```

```csharp
// C#
FileInfo ourFile = new FileInfo(@"c:\boot.ini");

ourFile.CopyTo(@"c:\boot.bak");
```

The same procedure is used for moving and creating files. Once you have a valid *FileInfo* object, you can access all its properties and call any of its methods.

The *DirectoryInfo* Class

The *DirectoryInfo* class provides the basic functionality to access and manipulate a single directory in the file system. Table 2-5 shows the most important *DirectoryInfo* properties.

Table 2-5 *DirectoryInfo* **Properties**

Name	Description
Parent	Gets the *DirectoryInfo* object for the parent directory of the current directory in the directory hierarchy
Root	Gets the root part of the directory's path as a DirectoryInfo object

Table 2-6 shows the most important *DirectoryInfo* methods.

Table 2-6 *DirectoryInfo* **Methods**

Name	Description
Create	Creates the directory described in the current *DirectoryInfo* object
CreateSubdirectory	Creates a new directory as a child directory of the current directory in the directory hierarchy
GetDirectories	Retrieves an array of *DirectoryInfo* objects that represent subdirectories of the current directory
GetFiles	Retrieves an array of *FileInfo* objects that represent all the files in the current directory
GetFileSystemInfos	Retrieves an array of *FileSystemInfo* objects that represent both files and subdirectories in the current directory
MoveTo	Moves the current directory to a new location

How to Enumerate Files in a Directory

Accessing the files in a directory is much like accessing file information. The following steps show how to enumerate the files in a directory:

1. Create a valid *DirectoryInfo* object by using the path to the directory.

2. Call the *GetFiles* method to enumerate the files in the directory.

The following code example shows how to accomplish this task:

```
' VB
Dim ourDir As DirectoryInfo = New DirectoryInfo("c:\windows")

Console.WriteLine("Directory: {0}", ourDir.FullName)

Dim file As FileInfo
For Each file In ourDir.GetFiles()
    Console.WriteLine("File: {0}", file.Name)
Next

// C#
DirectoryInfo ourDir = new DirectoryInfo(@"c:\windows");

Console.WriteLine("Directory: {0}", ourDir.FullName);

foreach (FileInfo file in ourDir.GetFiles())
{
    Console.WriteLine("File: {0}", file.Name);
}
```

By using the *GetFiles* method of the *DirectoryInfo* object, you are able to enumerate through the files within a single directory.

The *DriveInfo* Class

The *DriveInfo* class models a drive and provides methods and properties to query for drive information. Use *DriveInfo* to determine what drives are available, and what type of drives they are. You can also query to determine the capacity and available free space on the drive. Table 2-7 shows the most important *DriveInfo* properties.

Table 2-7 *DriveInfo* Properties

Name	Description
AvailableFreeSpace	Gets the amount of available space on the drive. The amount might be different from the amount returned by *TotalFreeSpace* (described later in this table), depending on disk quotas.
DriveFormat	Gets the format of the drive, such as NTFS or FAT32.

Table 2-7 *DriveInfo* Properties

Name	Description
DriveType	Gets the type of drive in the form of the *DriveType* enumeration (which is described in the following section).
IsReady	Gets the status of the drive, indicating whether it is ready to be accessed.
Name	Gets the name of the drive.
RootDirectory	Gets a *DirectoryInfo* object that represents the root directory of the drive.
TotalFreeSpace	Gets the total amount of free space on the drive.
TotalSize	Gets the total size of the drive.
VolumeLabel	Gets or sets the label of the drive. It might be set only on drives that are not readonly.

Table 2-8 shows the most important *DriveInfo* method.

Table 2-8 *DriveInfo* Method

Name	Description
GetDrives	A static method (or a shared one in Visual Basic) that returns all the drives on the current system.

The *DriveType* Enumeration

The *DriveType* enumeration provides the possible types of drives that can be represented by a *DriveInfo* object. Table 2-9 shows the members of the *DriveType* enumeration.

Table 2-9 *DriveType* Members

Name	Description
CDRom	An optical drive. It can be CD-ROM, DVD, and so on.
Fixed	A fixed disk.
Network	A network mapped drive.

Table 2-9 *DriveType* Members

Name	Description
NoRootDirectory	A drive that does not have a root directory.
Ram	A RAM drive.
Removable	A drive that has removable media.
Unknown	The drive type could not be determined.

How to Enumerate Drives

You follow this procedure to enumerate all the drives in a system:

1. Call the static *GetDrives* method (or a shared one in Visual Basic) of the *DriveInfo* class.

2. Loop through the array of *DriveInfo* objects returned by *GetDrives*.

The following code example illustrates this process:

```
' VB
Dim drives() As DriveInfo = DriveInfo.GetDrives()

Dim drive As DriveInfo
For Each drive In drives
    Console.WriteLine("Drive: {0}", drive.Name)
    Console.WriteLine("Type:  {0}", drive.DriveType)
Next

// C#
DriveInfo[] drives = DriveInfo.GetDrives();

foreach (DriveInfo drive in drives)
{
    Console.WriteLine("Drive: {0}", drive.Name);
    Console.WriteLine("Type:  {0}", drive.DriveType);
}
```

As you can see, the *GetDrives* method of the *DriveInfo* object greatly simplifies the process of enumerating the drives in a system.

NOTE **Optical drives**

All types of optical drives (CD, CD/R, DVD, DVD/R, and so on) are marked as *DriveInfo.CDRom*.

The *Path* Class

The *Path* class provides methods for manipulating a file system path. Table 2-10 shows the most important *Path* methods.

Table 2-10   Static *Path* Methods

Name	Description
ChangeExtension	Takes a path and returns a new path with the file name's extension changed. (Note that only the path string changes, not the actual file name extension.)
Combine	Combines two compatible path strings.
GetDirectoryName	Returns the name of the directory in the specified path.
GetExtension	Returns the name of the file extension in the specified path.
GetFileName	Returns the name of the file in the specified path.
GetFileNameWithout-Extension	Returns the file name without the extension in the specified path.
GetFullPath	Returns a full path to the specified path. This method can be used to resolve relative paths.
GetPathRoot	Returns the root directory name in the specified path.
GetRandomFileName	Generates a random file name.
GetTempFileName	Generates a temporary file in the file system and returns the full path to the file.
GetTempPath	Returns the path to the temporary file directory for the current user or system.
HasExtension	Indicates whether a specified path's file name has an extension.
IsPathRooted	Indicates whether the specified path includes a root directory.

How to Change a File Extension in a Path

The *Path* class allows you interrogate and parse the individual parts of a file system path. Instead of writing your own string parsing code, the *Path* class allows you to answer most common questions you would have about a file system path. For example, if you want to get and change the extension of a file, you can do so with the *Path* class, as shown in the following code snippet:

```
' VB
Dim ourPath As String = "c:\boot.ini"
Console.WriteLine(ourPath)

Console.WriteLine("Ext: {0}", Path.GetExtension(ourPath))

Console.WriteLine("Change Path: {0}", _
    Path.ChangeExtension(ourPath, "bak"))

// C#
string ourPath = @"c:\boot.ini";
Console.WriteLine(ourPath);

Console.WriteLine("Ext: {0}", Path.GetExtension(ourPath));

Console.WriteLine("Change Path: {0}",
    Path.ChangeExtension(ourPath, "bak"));
```

By using the *GetExtension* method of the *Path* class, you can get the current extension of a file system path. However, because the original goal was to change the path, you use the *ChangeExtension* method of the *Path* class.

The *FileSystemWatcher* Class

The *FileSystemWatcher* class provides methods for monitoring file system directories for changes. Table 2-11 shows the most important *FileSystemWatcher* properties.

Table 2-11   *FileSystemWatcher* Properties

Name	Description
EnableRaisingEvents	Gets or sets whether the watcher object should raise events. Normally, it's used to turn on and off the watching of a directory and/or files.
Filter	Gets or sets the file filter to use to determine which file changes to monitor. A blank filter indicates "all files."

Table 2-11   *FileSystemWatcher* Properties

Name	Description
IncludeSubdirectories	Gets or sets an indicator of whether the watching of a directory is to include subdirectories or only the directory specified in the *Path* property.
NotifyFilter	Gets or sets the type of changes to watch for. By default, all changes (creation, deletion, renamed files, and modifications) are notified.
Path	Gets or sets the path to the directory to monitor.

Table 2-12 shows the most important *FileSystemWatcher* method.

Table 2-12   *FileSystemWatcher* Method

Name	Description
WaitForChanged	Synchronous method for watching a directory for changes and for returning a structure that contains all the changes

Table 2-13 shows the most important *FileSystemWatcher* events.

Table 2-13   *FileSystemWatcher* Events

Name	Description
Changed	Occurs when a file or directory has changed in the watched directory
Created	Occurs when a file or directory has been created in the watched directory
Deleted	Occurs when a file or directory has been deleted in the watched directory
Renamed	Occurs when a file or directory has been renamed in the watched directory

How to Monitor a Directory for Changes

To monitor a directory for changes, follow this procedure:

1. Create a new *FileSystemWatcher* object, specifying the directory in the *Path* property.

2. Register for the *Created* and *Deleted* events.

3. Turn on events by setting *EnableRaisingEvents* to *true*.

The following code snippet demonstrates this process:

```vb
' VB
Dim watcher As FileSystemWatcher = New FileSystemWatcher()
watcher.Path = "c:\"

' Register for events
AddHandler watcher.Created, _
    New FileSystemEventHandler(AddressOf watcher_Changed)
AddHandler watcher.Deleted, _
    New FileSystemEventHandler(AddressOf watcher_Changed)

' Start Watching
watcher.EnableRaisingEvents = True

' Event Handler
Sub watcher_Changed(ByVal sender As Object, _
    ByVal e As FileSystemEventArgs)

    Console.WriteLine("Directory changed({0}): {1}", _
        e.ChangeType, _
        e.FullPath)

End Sub
```

```csharp
// C#
FileSystemWatcher watcher = new FileSystemWatcher();
watcher.Path = @"c:\";

// Register for events
watcher.Created +=
    new FileSystemEventHandler(watcher_Changed);
watcher.Deleted +=
    new FileSystemEventHandler(watcher_Changed);

// Start Watching
watcher.EnableRaisingEvents = true;

// Event Handler
static void watcher_Changed(object sender,
    FileSystemEventArgs e)
```

```
{
    Console.WriteLine("Directory changed({0}): {1}",
        e.ChangeType,
        e.FullPath);
}
```

The event handler simply reports each change found in the *FileSystemEventArgs* object that is sent to the event handler.

In addition to using the *Created*, *Deleted*, and *Changed* events, you can monitor the system for renamed files. To monitor a directory for renamed files, you can follow this procedure:

1. Create a new *FileSystemWatcher* object, specifying the directory in the *Path* property.

2. Register for the *Renamed* event.

3. Turn on events by setting *EnableRaisingEvents* to *true*.

The following code snippet demonstrates this process:

```
' VB
Dim watcher As FileSystemWatcher = New FileSystemWatcher()
watcher.Path = "c:\"

' Register for events
AddHandler watcher.Renamed, _
    New RenameEventHandler(AddressOf watcher_Renamed)

' Start Watching
watcher.EnableRaisingEvents = True

' Event Handler
Sub watcher_Renamed(ByVal sender As Object, _
    ByVal e As RenamedEventArgs)

  Console.WriteLine("Renamed from {0} to {1}", _
    e.OldFullPath, _
    e.FullPath)

End Sub

// C#
FileSystemWatcher watcher = new FileSystemWatcher();
watcher.Path = @"c:\";

// Register for events
watcher.Renamed +=
    new RenamedEventHandler(watcher_Renamed);

// Start Watching
watcher.EnableRaisingEvents = true;
```

```
// Event Handler
static void watcher_Renamed(object sender,
    RenamedEventArgs e)
{
  Console.WriteLine("Renamed from {0} to {1}",
      e.OldFullPath,
      e.FullPath);
}
```

When watching the file system, you can get more changes than the *FileSystemWatcher* can handle. When too many events occur, the *FileSystemWatcher* throws the *Error* event. To capture the *Error* event, follow these steps:

1. Create a new *FileSystemWatcher* object, specifying the directory in the *Path* property.

2. Register for the *Error* event.

3. Turn on events by setting *EnableRaisingEvents* to *true*.

The following code snippet demonstrates this process:

```
' VB
Dim watcher As FileSystemWatcher = New FileSystemWatcher()
watcher.Path = "c:\"

' Register for events
AddHandler watcher.Error, _
    New ErrorEventHandler(AddressOf watcher_Error)

' Start Watching
watcher.EnableRaisingEvents = True

' Event Handler
Sub watcher_Error(ByVal sender As Object, _
    ByVal e As ErrorEventArgs)

  Console.WriteLine("Error: {0}", _
    e.GetException())

End Sub

// C#
FileSystemWatcher watcher = new FileSystemWatcher();
watcher.Path = @"c:\";

// Register for events
watcher.Error +=
    new ErrorEventHandler(watcher_Error);

// Start Watching
watcher.EnableRaisingEvents = true;
```

```
// Event Handler
static void watcher_Error(object sender,
    ErrorEventArgs e)
{
  Console.WriteLine("Error: {0}",
    e.GetException());
}
```

Lab: Enumerate Files and Watch for Changes

In this lab, you will enumerate through the files of a folder and then watch to see whether any files have changed. If you encounter a problem completing an exercise, the completed projects are available on the companion CD in the Code folder.

▶ **Exercise 1: Enumerating Through the Files in a Folder**

In this exercise, you will enumerate through all the files in a particular folder.

1. Create a new console application named ShowFilesDemo.

2. Add an *Imports* (or a *using* statement in C#) for the *System.IO* namespace into the new project.

3. Add a new method that takes a *DirectoryInfo* object named *ShowDirectory*.

4. Within your new method, iterate through each of the files in your directory and show them in the console one at a time. Your code might look something like this:

```
' VB
Sub ShowDirectory(ByVal dir As DirectoryInfo)

    ' Show Each File
    Dim file As FileInfo
    For Each file In dir.GetFiles()
        Console.WriteLine("File: {0}", file.FullName)
    Next

End Sub
// C#
static void ShowDirectory(DirectoryInfo dir)
{
    // Show Each File
    foreach (FileInfo file in dir.GetFiles())
    {
        Console.WriteLine("File: {0}", file.FullName);
    }
}
```

5. Within the *ShowDirectory* method, iterate through each subdirectory and call the *ShowDirectory* method. Doing this will call the *ShowDirectory* recursively to find all the files for every directory. This code might look something like this:

```
' VB
' Go through subdirectories
' recursively
Dim subDir As DirectoryInfo
For Each subDir In dir.GetDirectories()
    ShowDirectory(subDir)
Next
```

```
// C#
// Go through subdirectories
// recursively
foreach (DirectoryInfo subDir in dir.GetDirectories())
{
    ShowDirectory(subDir);
}
```

6. In the *Main* method, write code to create a new instance of a *DirectoryInfo* class for the System directory and use it to call the new *ShowDirectory* method. For example, the following code would work:

```
' VB
Dim dir As DirectoryInfo = New DirectoryInfo(Environment.SystemDirectory)
ShowDirectory(dir)
```

```
// C#
DirectoryInfo dir = new DirectoryInfo(Environment.SystemDirectory);
ShowDirectory(dir);
```

7. Build the project and resolve any errors. Verify that the console application successfully lists all the files in the system directory (*Environment.SystemDirectory*).

▶ **Exercise 2: Watch for Changes in the File System**

In this exercise, you will watch the file system for changes in all files that end with the *.ini* extension.

1. Create a new console application named FileWatchingDemo.

2. Import the *System.IO* namespace into the new file.

3. Create a new instance of the *FileSystemWatcher* class, specifying the system directory. For example, you could use the following code:

```
' VB
Dim watcher As New FileSystemWatcher(Environment.SystemDirectory)
```

```
// C#
FileSystemWatcher watcher =
    new FileSystemWatcher(Environment.SystemDirectory);
```

4. Modify properties of the file system watcher to look only for .ini files, search through all subdirectories, and accept changes only if the attributes of the file change or if the file size changes. Your code might look like this:

```vb
' VB
watcher.Filter = "*.ini"
watcher.IncludeSubdirectories = True
watcher.NotifyFilter = _
    NotifyFilters.Attributes Or NotifyFilters.Size
```

```csharp
// C#
watcher.Filter = "*.ini";
watcher.IncludeSubdirectories = true;
watcher.NotifyFilter =
  NotifyFilters.Attributes | NotifyFilters.Size;
```

5. To see the changes, add a handler for the *Changed* event of your watcher object. For example, you could use the following code:

```vb
' VB
AddHandler watcher.Changed, _
    New FileSystemEventHandler(AddressOf watcher_Changed)
```

```csharp
// C#
watcher.Changed +=
    new FileSystemEventHandler(watcher_Changed);
```

6. Next you need the method that the *Changed* event is going to call. Inside this method, write out to the console the name of the changed file. Your code might look something like this:

```vb
' VB
Sub watcher_Changed(ByVal sender As Object, _
                    ByVal e As FileSystemEventArgs)

    Console.WriteLine("Changed: {0}", e.FullPath)

End Sub
```

```csharp
// C#
static void watcher_Changed(object sender,
    FileSystemEventArgs e)
{
    Console.WriteLine("Changed: {0}", e.FullPath);
}
```

7. Set the *EnableRaisingEvents* property to *true* to tell the watcher object to start throwing events.

8. Build the project and resolve any errors. Verify that the console application successfully reports when the attributes of any .ini file in the System directory change or when the file size changes.

Lesson Summary

- The *FileInfo*, *DirectoryInfo*, and *DriveInfo* classes can be used to enumerate and inspect the properties of file system objects.

- The *Path* class can be used to interrogate a file system path and should be used instead of parsing the string manually.

- The *FileSystemWatcher* class can be used to monitor the file system for changes such as additions, deletions, and renamings.

Lesson Review

You can use the following questions to test your knowledge of the information in Lesson 1, "Navigating the File System." The questions are also available on the companion CD if you prefer to review them in electronic form.

NOTE Answers

Answers to these questions and explanations of why each answer choice is right or wrong are located in the "Answers" section at the end of the book.

---

1. Which are acceptable ways to open a file for writing? (Choose all that apply.)

    A.

    ```
    ' VB
    File.Open("somefile.txt", FileMode.Create)

    // C#
    File.Open("somefile.txt", FileMode.Create);
    ```

    B.

    ```
    ' VB
    File.Open("somefile.txt", FileMode.Create, FileAccess.Write)

    // C#
    File.Open("somefile.txt", FileMode.Create, FileAccess.Write);
    ```

    C.

    ```
    ' VB
    File.Open("somefile.txt", FileMode.Create, FileAccess.Read)

    // C#
    File.Open("somefile.txt", FileMode.Create, FileAccess.Read);
    ```

D.

```
' VB
Dim file As new FileInfo("somefile.txt")
file.Open(FileMode.Create)

// C#
FileInfo file = new FileInfo("somefile.txt");
file.Open(FileMode.Create);
```

2. Which of the following are types of changes that can be detected by the *File-SystemWatcher*? (Choose all that apply.)

   A. New files

   B. New directories

   C. Changed files

   D. Renamed files

   E. None

3. The following code changes the extension of a file. (True or False)

```
' VB
Dim ourPath As String = "c:\boot.ini"
Path.ChangeExtension(ourPath, "bak")

// C#
string ourPath = @"c:\boot.ini";
Path.ChangeExtension(ourPath, "bak");
```

   A. True

   B. False

Lesson 2: Reading and Writing Files

Reading and writing files are two of the most common tasks in the world of development. As a .NET developer, you need to know how to read and write files. The .NET Framework makes it easy to perform these tasks.

After this lesson, you will be able to:

- Open a file and read its contents.
- Create an in-memory stream.
- Write and close a file.

Estimated lesson time: 20 minutes

Understanding Streams

Streams are a common way to deal with both sequential and random access to data within the .NET Framework. Streams are used throughout different parts of the Framework. They begin with an abstract class (by means of the *MustInherit* keyword in Visual Basic) that provides the basic interface and implementation for all streams in the Framework. Some of the properties and methods of the *Stream* class are shown in Table 2-14 and Table 2-15, respectively.

Table 2-14   *Stream* Properties

Name	Description
CanRead	Determines whether the stream supports reading.
CanSeek	Determines whether the stream supports seeking.
CanTimeout	Determines whether the stream can time out.
CanWrite	Determines whether the stream can be written to.
Length	Gets the length (in bytes) of the stream.
Position	Gets or sets the virtual cursor for determining where in the stream the current position is. The value of *Position* cannot be greater than the value of the stream's *Length*.
ReadTimeout	Gets or sets the stream's timeout for read operations.
WriteTimeout	Gets or sets the stream's timeout for write operations.

Table 2-15   *Stream* Methods

Name	Description
Close	Closes the stream and releases any resources associated with it.
Flush	Clears any buffers within the stream and forces changes to be written to the underlying system or device.
Read	Performs a sequential read of a specified number of bytes from the current position and updates the position to the end of the read upon completion of the operation.
ReadByte	Performs the read of a single byte and updates the position by moving it by one. Identical to calling *Read* to read a single byte.
Seek	Sets the position within the stream.
SetLength	Specifies the length of the stream. Will truncate the stream if the new length is less than the old length and will expand the stream if the reverse is true.
Write	Writes information to the stream as a number of bytes and updates the current position to reflect the new write position.
WriteByte	Writes a single byte to the stream and updates the position. Identical to calling *Write* with a single byte.

All other stream classes in the .NET Framework derive from the *Stream* class. These derived classes include the following:

- *FileStream* (*System.IO*)
- *MemoryStream* (*System.IO*)
- *CryptoStream* (*System.Security.Cryptography*)
- *NetworkStream* (*System.Net.Sockets*)
- *GZipStream* (*System.IO.Compression*)

The reason that these streams have a common base class is that working with data as a flow is a common way to work with data. By learning how to work with a stream in general, you can apply that knowledge to any type of stream. For example, you could write a simple method to dump the contents of a stream to the console like so:

```
' VB
Shared Sub DumpStream(ByVal theStream As Stream)
    ' Move the stream's position to the beginning
    theStream.Position = 0
```

```
        ' Go through entire stream and show the contents
        While theStream.Position <> theStream.Length
            Console.WriteLine("{0:x2}", theStream.ReadByte())
        End While
    End Sub

    // C#
    static void DumpStream(Stream theStream)
    {
        // Move the stream's position to the beginning
        theStream.Position = 0;

        // Go through entire stream and show the contents
        while (theStream.Position != theStream.Length)
        {
            Console.WriteLine("{0:x2}", theStream.ReadByte());
        }
    }
```

This code doesn't care what kind of stream it is sent; it can deal with any stream in the same way. Similarly, appending some information to a stream can be done in a common way, as demonstrated in this example:

```
    ' VB
    Shared Sub AppendToStream(ByVal theStream As Stream, _
        ByVal data() As Byte)
        ' Move the Position to the end
        theStream.Position = theStream.Length

        ' Append some bytes
        theStream.Write(data, 0, data.Length)
    End Sub

    // C#
    static void AppendToStream(Stream theStream,
                               byte[] data)
    {
        // Move the Position to the end
        theStream.Position = theStream.Length;

        // Append some bytes
        theStream.Write(data, 0, data.Length);
    }
```

What Classes Facilitate Reading and Writing Data?

A number of classes take part in the process of reading and writing files. Most operations begin with the *File* class. This class exposes static methods (or shared methods in Visual Basic) that allow for opening and creating files. The *File* class can perform several types of operations:

- Atomic operations to read or write all the contents of a file

- Operations to open files for reading
- Operations to create or open files for writing
- Simple file operations (*File.Exists*, *File.Delete*, and so on)

When a file is opened or created, the *File* class can return several types of objects. The most rudimentary of these is the *FileStream* object. This is a simple stream class, but it represents a file in the file system.

In addition, the *File* class also has methods that return *StreamReaders* and *StreamWriters*. These classes wrap a *FileStream* to support sequential reading and writing to a stream.

The simple file operations that the *File* class supports are identical to those of the *FileInfo* class discussed in Lesson 1.

In addition to these classes, the *MemoryStream* class is a specialized stream for manipulating data in memory. This class is often used to create stream objects in memory for optimizations.

The *File* Class

The *File* class provides the basic functionality to open file streams for reading and writing. Table 2-16 shows the most important *File* static/shared methods.

Table 2-16   *File* **Static/Shared Methods**

Name	Description
AppendAllText	Appends a specified string into an existing file, alternatively creating the file if it does not exist.
AppendText	Opens a file (or creates a new file if one does not exist) and returns a *StreamWriter* that is prepared to allow text to be appended to the file.
Copy	Copies a file to a new file. The new file must not exist for *Copy* to be successful.
Create	Creates a new file and returns a *FileStream* object.
CreateText	Creates or opens a file and returns a *StreamWriter* object that is ready to have text written into it.
Move	Moves a file from one place to another.

Table 2-16   *File* Static/Shared Methods

Name	Description
Open	Opens an existing file and returns a *FileStream* object.
OpenRead	Opens an existing file and returns a read-only *FileStream* object.
OpenText	Opens an existing file and returns a *StreamReader* object.
OpenWrite	Opens an existing file for writing and returns a *StreamWriter* object.
ReadAllBytes	Opens a file, reads the contents of it into a byte array, and closes the file in one atomic operation.
ReadAllLines	Opens a file, reads the contents of it into an array of strings (one per line), and closes the file in one atomic operation.
ReadAllText	Opens a file, reads the contents of it into a string, and closes the file in one atomic operation.
WriteAllBytes	Opens a file, writes the contents of a byte array into it (overwriting any existing data), and closes the file in one atomic operation.
WriteAllLines	Opens a file, writes the contents of a string array into it (overwriting any existing data), and closes the file in one atomic operation.
WriteAllText	Opens a file, writes the contents of a string into it (overwriting any existing data), and closes the file in one atomic operation.

The *Directory* Class

As it does with the *File* class, the .NET Framework supports the *Directory* class, which presents a static/shared interface for manipulating and creating directories in the file system. The *Directory* class provides the basic functionality to create, manage, delete, and analyze directories. Table 2-17 shows the most important *Directory* static/shared methods.

Table 2-17 *Directory* **Static/Shared Methods**

Name	Description
CreateDirectory	Creates all the directories in a supplied path
Delete	Deletes a specified directory
Exists	Determines whether a directory exists in the file system
GetCreationTime	Returns the creation time and date of a directory
GetCurrentDirectory	Returns a *DirectoryInfo* object for the current working directory of the application
GetDirectories	Gets a list of names for subdirectories in a specified directory
GetDirectoryRoot	Returns the volume and/or root information for a specified directory
GetFiles	Returns the names of files in a directory
GetFileSystemEntries	Returns a list of subdirectories and files in the specified directory
GetLastAccessTime	Returns the time that a specified directory was last accessed
GetLastWriteTime	Returns the time that a specified directory was last written to
GetLogicalDrives	Gets a list of drives in the current system as strings with the pattern of "C:\"
GetParent	Gets the parent directory of the specified directory
Move	Moves a file or directory (and its contents) to a specified place
SetCreationTime	Sets the time a specific directory was created
SetCurrentDirectory	Sets the specified directory to be the current working directory for an application
SetLastAccessTime	Sets the last time a directory was accessed
SetLastWriteTime	Sets the last time a directory was written to

The *FileAccess* Enumeration

The *FileAccess* enumeration provides members that are used to determine the rights required when opening a file. Table 2-18 shows the *FileAccess* members.

Table 2-18   *FileAccess* **Enumeration Members**

Name	Description
Read	Specifies that the file should be opened with read-only access.
Write	Specifies that the file should be opened to be written to. The file cannot be read, only appended to.
ReadWrite	Specifies full access to the file for reading or writing. Equivalent to combining *Read* and *Write* values.

The *FileMode* Enumeration

The *FileMode* enumeration provides members that specify how a file is to be opened or created. Table 2-19 shows most of the *FileMode* members.

Table 2-19   *FileMode* **Enumeration Members**

Name	Description
Append	Opens a file and moves the pointer in the *FileStream* to the end of the file. Can be used only with *FileAccess.Write*.
Create	Creates a new file. If the file already exists, it is overwritten.
CreateNew	Creates a new file. If the file already exists, an exception is thrown.
Open	Opens an existing file. If the file does not exist, an exception is thrown.
OpenOrCreate	Opens an existing file. If the file does not exist, it creates a new file.
Truncate	Opens an existing file but empties the existing file so that it is zero bytes long.

The *FileStream* Class

The *FileStream* class provides the basic functionality to open file streams for reading and writing. Table 2-20 and Table 2-21 show the most important *FileStream* properties and methods, respectively.

Table 2-20 *FileStream* **Properties**

Name	Description
CanRead	Determines whether the stream supports reading. (Inherited from the *Stream* class.)
CanSeek	Determines whether the stream supports seeking. (Inherited from the *Stream* class.)
CanTimeout	Determines whether the stream can time out. (Inherited from the *Stream* class.)
CanWrite	Determines whether the stream can be written to. (Inherited from the *Stream* class.)
Handle	Gets the stream's underlying file handle.
Length	Gets the length (in bytes) of the stream. (Inherited from the *Stream* class.)
Name	Gets the name of the file.
Position	Gets or sets the virtual cursor for determining where in the stream the current position is. The value of *Position* cannot be greater than the stream's length. (Inherited from the *Stream* class.)
ReadTimeout	Gets or sets the stream's timeout for read operations. (Inherited from the *Stream* class.)
WriteTimeout	Gets or sets the stream's timeout for write operations. (Inherited from the *Stream* class.)

Table 2-21   *FileStream* **Methods**

Name	Description
Close	Closes the stream and releases any resources associated with it. (Inherited from the *Stream* class.)
Flush	Clears any buffers within the stream and forces changes to be written to the underlying system or device. (Inherited from the *Stream* class.)
Lock	Prevents other processes from changing all or part of the file.
Read	Performs a sequential read of a specified number of bytes from the current position and updates the position to the end of the read upon completion of the operation. (Inherited from the *Stream* class.)
ReadByte	Performs the read of a single byte and updates the position by moving it by one. Identical to calling *Read* to read a single byte. (Inherited from the *Stream* class.)
Seek	Sets the position within the stream. (Inherited from the *Stream* class.)
SetLength	Specifies the length of the stream. Will truncate the stream if the new length is less than the old length and will expand the stream if the reverse is true. (Inherited from the *Stream* class.)
Unlock	Allows other processes to change all or part of the underlying file.
Write	Writes information to the stream as a number of bytes and updates the current position to reflect the new write position. (Inherited from the *Stream* class.)
WriteByte	Writes a single byte to the stream and updates the position. Identical to calling *Write* with a single byte. (Inherited from the *Stream* class.)

The *StreamReader* Class

The *StreamReader* class provides the basic functionality to read data from a *Stream* derived class. Table 2-22 and Table 2-23 show the most important *StreamReader* properties and methods, respectively.

Table 2-22 *StreamReader* **Properties**

Name	Description
BaseStream	Gets the underlying stream that the reader is writing into
CurrentEncoding	Gets the current encoding used for the underlying stream
EndOfStream	Determines whether the reader has encountered the end of the stream

Table 2-23 *StreamReader* **Methods**

Name	Description
Close	Closes the reader and the underlying stream
Peek	Returns the next character in the stream without moving the stream's current position
Read	Reads the next set of characters in the stream
ReadBlock	Reads the next block of characters in the stream
ReadLine	Reads the next line of characters in the stream
ReadToEnd	Reads all the characters through to the end of the stream

How to Read from a File

Opening a file is quite a common occurrence. In its most simple form, opening a file involves asking the *File* class to open a stream by specifying the path to the file. When opening a file to read its contents, you use the *FileMode.Open* enumeration member to specify an existing file, as well as *FileAccess.Read* to get read-only access to the file, as seen in this code example:

```
' VB
Dim theFile As FileStream = _
    File.Open("C:\boot.ini", FileMode.Open, FileAccess.Read)

// C#
FileStream theFile =
    File.Open(@"C:\boot.ini", FileMode.Open, FileAccess.Read);
```

The *File.Open* method returns a *FileStream* object. A file stream is just a stream, so you can view the contents by calling the *Read* or *ReadByte* methods of the *Stream* class. But to better facilitate reading the file, the I/O system supports *StreamReader* and *Stream-Writer* classes, which make reading and writing easier. For reading the file, you can simply create a new *StreamReader* that wraps the *FileStream*, as shown here:

```
' VB
Dim rdr As StreamReader = New StreamReader(theFile)
Console.Write(rdr.ReadToEnd())
rdr.Close()
theFile.Close()
```

```
// C#
StreamReader rdr = new StreamReader(theFile);
Console.Write(rdr.ReadToEnd());
rdr.Close();
theFile.Close();
```

The *StreamReader* class is intended to read a stream as a string, not as a series of bytes. In this way, the *StreamReader*'s methods for returning data all return either strings or arrays of strings.

The *File* class supports some additional methods to make it simpler to open a file for reading. In the previous example, you created a *FileStream* and then created a new *StreamReader*. The *File* class supports creating a *StreamReader* directly with the *Open-Text* method, as seen in this code snippet:

```
' VB
Dim rdr As StreamReader = File.OpenText("C:\boot.ini")
Console.Write(rdr.ReadToEnd())
rdr.Close()
```

```
// C#
StreamReader rdr = File.OpenText(@"C:\boot.ini");
Console.Write(rdr.ReadToEnd());
rdr.Close();
```

If all you need to do is read out the entire file, the *File* class supports reading the file in a single method call, hiding all the details of the stream and reader implementation by calling its *ReadAllText* method:

```
' VB
Console.WriteLine(File.ReadAllText("C:\boot.ini"))
```

```
// C#
Console.WriteLine(File.ReadAllText(@"C:\boot.ini"));
```

So, if you can get everything you need with the *File* class's *ReadAllText* method, why would you use these other methods? The usual reason is that you do not need the entire text file. This approach is especially helpful if you are searching for a particular piece of text. For example, in this code snippet, you pull the data out line by line and test for a string that matches, and if you find it, you don't need to load the entire string into memory:

```vb
' VB
Dim rdr As StreamReader = File.OpenText("C:\boot.ini")

' Search through the stream until we reach the end
While Not rdr.EndOfStream
    Dim line As String = rdr.ReadLine()
        If line.Contains("boot") Then
            ' If we find the word boot, we notify
            ' the user and stop reading the file.
            Console.WriteLine("Found boot:")
            Console.WriteLine(line)
        Exit While
    End If

End While

' Clean Up
rdr.Close()
```

```csharp
// C#
StreamReader rdr = File.OpenText(@"C:\boot.ini");

// Search through the stream until we reach the end
while (!rdr.EndOfStream)
{
    string line = rdr.ReadLine();
    if (line.Contains("boot"))
    {
        // If we find the word boot, we notify
        // the user and stop reading the file.
        Console.WriteLine("Found boot:");
        Console.WriteLine(line);
        break;
    }

}

// Clean Up
rdr.Close();
```

Scanning files with this method is especially helpful when looking through very large files.

The *StreamWriter* Class

The *StreamWriter* class provides the basic functionality to write data from a *Stream* derived class. Table 2-24 and Table 2-25 show the most important *StreamWriter* properties and methods, respectively.

Table 2-24   *StreamWriter* **Properties**

Name	Description
AutoFlush	Gets or sets an indicator that shows whether every call to the *Write* method should flush changes to the underlying stream.
BaseStream	Gets the underlying stream that the reader is reading.
Encoding	Gets the current encoding used for the underlying stream.
NewLine	Gets or sets a string that contains the line terminator string. Normally used only if you need to change the string that terminates an individual line.

Table 2-25   *StreamWriter* **Methods**

Name	Description
Close	Closes the writer and the underlying stream
Write	Writes to the stream
WriteLine	Writes data to the stream followed by the string that terminates an individual line

How to Write to a File

Before you can write to a file, you have to open the file for writing. This process is similar to opening a file for reading. For example, you can open a file for writing as shown here:

```
' VB
FileStream theFile = File.Create("c:\somefile.txt")
```

```
// C#
FileStream theFile = File.Create(@"c:\somefile.txt");
```

Unlike the code for opening a file for reading, this code actually creates a new file with a *FileStream* object ready to be written to. With the *FileStream* object in hand, you can write to the stream directly, if you want. More often, however, you will want to use a *StreamWriter* object to write data to the new file, as shown in this code:

```
' VB
Dim writer As StreamWriter = New StreamWriter(theFile)
writer.WriteLine("Hello")
writer.Close()
theFile.Close()
```

```
// C#
StreamWriter writer = new StreamWriter(theFile);
writer.WriteLine("Hello");
writer.Close();
theFile.Close();
```

You can use the *StreamWriter* to write text directly into your new file. This pattern is much like the pattern for reading a file. Also, as demonstrated earlier for reading, the *File* class supports creating a *StreamWriter* object directly with the *CreateText* method:

```
' VB
Dim writer As StreamWriter = _
    File.CreateText("c:\somefile.txt")
writer.WriteLine("Hello")
writer.Close()
```

```
// C#
StreamWriter writer = File.CreateText(@"c:\somefile.txt");
writer.WriteLine("Hello");
writer.Close();
```

The *File* class also supports the *WriteAllText* method that writes a string to a new file, as shown here:

```
' VB
File.WriteAllText("c:\somefile.txt", "Hello")
```

```
// C#
File.WriteAllText(@"c:\somefile.txt", "Hello");
```

This process is straightforward, but there are times when you need to write to an existing file. Writing to an existing file is similar except for how you actually open the file. To open a file for writing, you use the *File* class's *Open* method but specify that you want to write to the stream that is returned, as shown in this example:

```
' VB
Dim theFile As FileStream
```

```
theFile = File.Open("c:\somefile.txt", _
                    FileMode.Open, _
                    FileAccess.Write)

// C#
FileStream theFile = null;
theFile = File.Open(@"c:\somefile.txt",
                    FileMode.Open,
                    FileAccess.Write);
```

The *File* class has the *OpenWrite* method, which is a shortcut for accomplishing this and simplifies opening existing files for writing. Instead of calling the *Open* method of the *File* class and specifying that you want to open it for writing, you can simply use code like this:

```
' VB
theFile = File.OpenWrite("c:\somefile.txt")

// C#
theFile = File.OpenWrite(@"c:\somefile.txt");
```

These code snippets work only if the file exists. On many occasions, you will want to either open an existing file or create a new one. Unfortunately, the *OpenWrite* method will open only an existing file. You could write code to test for the existence of the file and create the file if it doesn't exist, but luckily, you can use the *Open* method of the *File* class to specify that you want to open or create a file, as shown here:

```
' VB
theFile = File.Open("c:\somefile.txt", _
                    FileMode.OpenOrCreate, _
                    FileAccess.Write)

// C#
theFile = File.Open(@"c:\somefile.txt",
                    FileMode.OpenOrCreate,
                    FileAccess.Write);
```

The *FileMode.OpenOrCreate* enumeration value allows you to avoid writing procedural code to deal with the issue of whether you are dealing with a new or existing file.

Understanding Readers and Writers

As shown in the previous sections, *StreamReader* and *StreamWriter* are classes that make it simple to write to and read from text streams. That is the purpose of the reader and writer classes. The *StreamReader* class derives from the abstract *TextReader* class (by means of the *MustInherit* keyword in Visual Basic). The *StreamWriter*, not surprisingly, derives from the abstract *TextWriter* class. These abstract classes represent the basic interface for all text-based readers and writers.

For example, there is an additional text reader and writer pair called *StringReader* and *StringWriter*. The purpose of these classes is to write to and read from in-memory strings. For example, to read from a string using *StringReader,* you use code such as the following:

```vb
' VB
Dim s As String = "Hello all" & _
    Environment.NewLine & _
    "This is a multi-line" & _
    Environment.NewLine & _
    "string"

Dim rdr As New StringReader(s)

' See if there are more characters
While rdr.Peek() <> -1
    Dim line As String = rdr.ReadLine()
    Console.WriteLine(line)
End While
```

```csharp
// C#
string s = @"Hello all
This is a multi-line
text string";

StringReader rdr = new StringReader(s);

// See if there are more characters
while (rdr.Peek() != -1)
{
    string line = rdr.ReadLine();
    Console.WriteLine(line);
}
```

Conversely, you write a string in an efficient way by using *StringWriter*. *StringWriter* uses a *StringBuilder*, so it is very efficient at creating ever larger strings. You use it like so:

```vb
' VB
Dim writer As New StringWriter()
writer.WriteLine("Hello all")
writer.WriteLine("This is a multi-line")
writer.WriteLine("text string")

Console.WriteLine(writer.ToString())
```

```csharp
// C#
StringWriter writer = new StringWriter();
writer.WriteLine("Hello all");
writer.WriteLine("This is a multi-line");
writer.WriteLine("text string");

Console.WriteLine(writer.ToString());
```

But because you do not need to always read or write only textual data, the .NET Framework *BinaryReader* namespace also supports two classes for reading or writing binary data. The *BinaryReader* and *BinaryWriter* classes can be used to handle getting binary data to and from streams. For example, if you want to create a new file to store binary data, you can use the *BinaryWriter* class to write various types of data to a stream like so:

```
' VB
Dim NewFile As FileStream = File.Create("c:\somefile.bin")

Dim writer As BinaryWriter = New BinaryWriter(NewFile)

Dim number As Long = 100
Dim bytes() As Byte = New Byte() {10, 20, 50, 100}

Dim s As String = "hunger"

writer.Write(number)
writer.Write(bytes)
writer.Write(s)

writer.Close()
```

```
// C#
FileStream newFile = File.Create(@"c:\somefile.bin");

BinaryWriter writer = new BinaryWriter(newFile);

long number = 100;
byte[] bytes = new byte[] { 10, 20, 50, 100 };
string s = "hunger";

writer.Write(number);
writer.Write(bytes);
writer.Write(s);

writer.Close();
```

If you have written the data with the *BinaryWriter*, you can use the *BinaryReader* to get the data in the same order. For every *BinaryWriter.Write* or *WriteLine* call, you will need to call the appropriate *BinaryReader.Read* method. For example, the following code will read the data written by the code just shown:

```
' VB
Dim NewFile As FileStream = File.Open("c:\somefile.bin", FileMode.Open)

Dim reader As New BinaryReader(NewFile)

Dim number As Long = reader.ReadInt64()
Dim bytes() As Byte = reader.ReadBytes(4)
Dim s As String = reader.ReadString()

reader.Close()
```

```
Console.WriteLine(number)
Dim b As Byte
For Each b In bytes
    Console.Write("[{0}]", b)
Next
Console.WriteLine()
Console.WriteLine(s)

// C#
FileStream newFile = File.Open(@"c:\somefile.bin", FileMode.Open);

BinaryReader reader = new BinaryReader(newFile);

long number = reader.ReadInt64();
byte[] bytes = reader.ReadBytes(4);
string s = reader.ReadString();

reader.Close();

Console.WriteLine(number);
foreach (byte b in bytes)
{
    Console.Write("[{0}]", b);
}
Console.WriteLine();
Console.WriteLine(s);
```

The *MemoryStream* Class

The *MemoryStream* class provides the basic functionality to create in-memory streams. Table 2-26 and Table 2-27 show the most important *MemoryStream* properties and methods, respectively.

Table 2-26 *MemoryStream* **Properties**

Name	Description
CanRead	Determines whether the stream supports reading. (Inherited from the *Stream* class.)
CanSeek	Determines whether the stream supports seeking. (Inherited from the *Stream* class.)
CanTimeout	Determines whether the stream can time out. (Inherited from the *Stream* class.)
CanWrite	Determines whether the stream can be written to. (Inherited from the *Stream* class.)
Capacity	Gets or sets the number of bytes allocated for the stream.

Table 2-26 *MemoryStream* Properties

Name	Description
Length	Gets the length (in bytes) of the stream. (Inherited from the *Stream* class.)
Position	Gets or sets the virtual cursor for determining where in the stream the current position is. The value of *Position* cannot be greater than the stream's length. (Inherited from the *Stream* class.)
ReadTimeout	Gets or sets the stream's timeout for read operations. (Inherited from the *Stream* class.)
WriteTimeout	Gets or sets the stream's timeout for write operations. (Inherited from the *Stream* class.)

Table 2-27 *MemoryStream* Methods

Name	Description
Close	Closes the stream and releases any resources associated with it. (Inherited from the *Stream* class.)
Flush	Clears any buffers within the stream and forces changes to be written to the underlying system or device. (Inherited from the *Stream* class.)
GetBuffer	Retrieves the array of unsigned bytes that were used to create the stream.
Read	Performs a sequential read of a specified number of bytes from the current position and updates the position to the end of the read upon completion of the operation. (Inherited from the *Stream* class.)
ReadByte	Performs the read of a single byte and updates the position by moving it by one. Identical to calling *Read* to read a single byte. (Inherited from the *Stream* class.)
Seek	Sets the position within the stream. (Inherited from the *Stream* class.)
SetLength	Specifies the length of the stream. This method will truncate the stream if the new length is less than the old length and will expand the stream if the reverse is true. (Inherited from the *Stream* class.)

Table 2-27   *MemoryStream* Methods

Name	Description
ToArray	Writes the entire stream to an array of bytes.
Write	Writes information to the stream as a number of bytes and updates the current position to reflect the new write position. (Inherited from the *Stream* class.)
WriteByte	Writes a single byte to the stream and updates the position. This method is identical to calling *Write* with a single byte. (Inherited from the *Stream* class.)
WriteTo	Writes the *MemoryStream* to another stream.

How to Use a *MemoryStream*

As you have seen, working with streams of data is an important skill for any developer. Unfortunately, often you will need to create a stream before you really need to store it somewhere (like in a file). The *MemoryStream* class has the job of helping you create streams in memory. Creating a memory stream is as simple as creating a new instance of the *MemoryStream* class:

```
' VB
Dim memStrm As New MemoryStream()
```

```
// C#
MemoryStream memStrm = new MemoryStream();
```

You can use the *StreamWriter* exactly as you used the *FileStream* class earlier to write data to your new *MemoryStream*:

```
' VB
Dim writer As New StreamWriter(memStrm)
writer.WriteLine("Hello")
writer.WriteLine("Goodbye")
```

```
// C#
StreamWriter writer = new StreamWriter(memStrm);
writer.WriteLine("Hello");
writer.WriteLine("Goodbye");
```

Now that you have data in your *MemoryStream* object, what do you do with it? The designers of the *MemoryStream* class understand that storing the stream in memory is usually a temporary situation. So the class supports writing the stream directly to another stream or copying the data to other storage. One common use of a *Memory-Stream* is to limit the time a file is open for writing (because that locks the file). So to continue this running example, you can tell the *MemoryStream* to write to a *FileStream*, as shown here:

```vb
' VB
' Force the writer to push the data into the
' underlying stream
writer.Flush()

' Create a file stream
Dim theFile As FileStream = File.Create("c:\inmemory.txt")

' Write the entire Memory stream to the file
memStrm.WriteTo(theFile)

' Clean up
writer.Close()
theFile.Close()
memStrm.Close()
```

```csharp
// C#
// Force the writer to push the data into the
// underlying stream
writer.Flush();

// Create a file stream
FileStream theFile = File.Create(@"c:\inmemory.txt");

// Write the entire Memory stream to the file
memStrm.WriteTo(theFile);

// Clean up
writer.Close();
theFile.Close();
memStrm.Close();
```

As you can see, the code performs these tasks:

1. It tells the *StreamWriter* to flush its changes to the underlying stream (in this case, the *MemoryStream*).

2. It creates the new file.

3. It tells the *MemoryStream* object to write itself to the *FileStream* object.

This process allows you to do time-intensive work in the *MemoryStream* and then open the file, flush the data to it, and close the file quickly.

The *BufferedStream* Class

The *BufferedStream* class provides the basic functionality to wrap streams to improve performance by buffering reads and writes through the stream. Table 2-28 and Table 2-29 show the most important *BufferedStream* properties and methods, respectively.

Table 2-28 *BufferedStream* **Properties**

Name	Description
CanRead	Determines whether the stream supports reading. (Inherited from the *Stream* class.)
CanSeek	Determines whether the stream supports seeking. (Inherited from the *Stream* class.)
CanTimeout	Determines whether the stream can time out. (Inherited from the *Stream* class.)
CanWrite	Determines whether the stream can be written to. (Inherited from the *Stream* class.)
Length	Gets the length (in bytes) of the stream. (Inherited from the *Stream* class.)
Position	Gets or sets the virtual cursor for determining where in the stream the current position is. The value of *Position* cannot be greater than the stream's length. (Inherited from the *Stream* class.)
ReadTimeout	Gets or sets the stream's timeout for read operations. (Inherited from the *Stream* class.)
WriteTimeout	Gets or sets the stream's timeout for write operations. (Inherited from the *Stream* class.)

Table 2-29 *BufferedStream* **Methods**

Name	Description
Close	Closes the stream and releases any resources associated with it. (Inherited from the *Stream* class.)
Flush	Clears any buffers within the stream and forces changes to be written to the underlying system or device. (Inherited from the *Stream* class.)
Read	Performs a sequential read of a specified number of bytes from the current position and updates the position to the end of the read upon completion of the operation. (Inherited from the *Stream* class.)

Table 2-29 *BufferedStream* Methods

Name	Description
ReadByte	Performs the read of a single byte, and updates the position by moving it by one. Identical to calling *Read* to read a single byte. (Inherited from the *Stream* class.)
Seek	Sets the position within the stream. (Inherited from the *Stream* class.)
SetLength	Specifies the length of the stream. This method will truncate the stream if the new length is less than the old length and will expand the stream if the reverse is true. (Inherited from the *Stream* class.)
Write	Writes information to the stream as a number of bytes and updates the current position to reflect the new write position. (Inherited from the *Stream* class.)
WriteByte	Writes a single byte to the stream and updates the position. This method is identical to calling *Write* with a single byte. (Inherited from the *Stream* class.)

How to Use a *BufferedStream*

At times, you want the convenience of using a stream, but writing out data to a stream directly does not perform very well. This situation is where you can use a *BufferedStream* class. The *BufferedStream* wraps another stream object to allow for writes to happen to a buffer, and only when the buffer is flushed does the data actually get pushed into the underlying stream. To use a *BufferedStream*, follow these steps:

1. Create a new *FileStream* object, using the *File* class to specify a new file.
2. Create a new buffered stream, specifying the file stream as the underlying stream.
3. Use a *StreamWriter* to write data into the buffered stream.

The following code snippet demonstrates this process:

```
' VB
Dim NewFile As FileStream =  File.Create("c:\test.txt")

Dim buffered As New BufferedStream(NewFile)
```

```
Dim writer As New StreamWriter(buffered)

writer.WriteLine("Some data")

writer.Close()

// C#
FileStream newFile = File.Create(@"c:\test.txt");

BufferedStream buffered = new BufferedStream(newFile);

StreamWriter writer = new StreamWriter(buffered);

writer.WriteLine("Some data");

writer.Close();
```

Lab: Reading and Writing Files

In this lab, you will create a new file, write some data to it, and close the file. You'll then re-open the file, read the data, and show that data in the console. If you encounter a problem completing an exercise, the completed projects are available on the companion CD in the Code folder.

▶ **Exercise 1: Writing to a New File**

In this exercise, you will create a new file and insert some text into it.

1. Create a new console application named FileDemo.

2. Add an *Imports* (or a *using* statement in C#) for the *System.IO* namespace into the new project.

3. In the *Main* method, create a new *StreamWriter* by callling the *CreateText* method of the *File* class.

4. Write some lines to the stream writer using the *WriteLine* method.

5. Close the *StreamWriter*. The code might look something like this when you are done:

```
' VB
Shared Sub Main(ByVal args() As String)
    Dim writer As StreamWriter = _
        File.CreateText("c:\newfile.txt")
    writer.WriteLine("This is my new file")
    writer.WriteLine("Do you like its format?")
    writer.Close()
End Sub

// C#
static void Main(string[] args)
{
```

```
StreamWriter writer = File.CreateText(@"c:\newfile.txt");
writer.WriteLine("This is my new file");
writer.WriteLine("Do you like its format?");
writer.Close();
}
```

6. Build the project and resolve any errors. Verify that the console application creates the file by manually checking the file in the file system.

▶ **Exercise 2: Reading a File**

In this exercise, you will open the file you created in Exercise 1 and show the contents in the console.

1. Open the FileDemo project you created in Exercise 1.

2. In the *Main* method after the *StreamWriter* object is closed, open the file using the *OpenText* method of the *File* class to create a new *StreamReader* object.

3. Create a new string named *contents* and call the *ReadToEnd* method of the *StreamReader* class to get the entire contents of the file.

4. Close the *StreamReader* object.

5. Write the string to the console. Your code might look something like this:

```
' VB
Dim reader As StreamReader = _
    File.OpenText("c:\newfile.txt")
Dim contents As String = reader.ReadToEnd()
reader.Close()
Console.WriteLine(contents)

// C#
StreamReader reader = File.OpenText(@"c:\newfile.txt");
string contents = reader.ReadToEnd();
reader.Close();
Console.WriteLine(contents);
```

6. Build the project, and resolve any errors. Verify that the console application successfully shows the contents of the file in the console window.

Lesson Summary

- The *File* class can be used to open files, create new files, read whole files atomically, and even write files.

- The *FileStream* class represents a file in the file system and allows for reading and writing (depending on how it is created).

- The *StreamReader* and *StreamWriter* classes are used to simplify the writing of strings to streams.

■ The *MemoryStream* is a specialized stream for creating content in memory and supports saving the stream to other streams.

Lesson Review

You can use the following questions to test your knowledge of the information in Lesson 2, "Reading and Writing Files." The questions are also available on the companion CD if you prefer to review them in electronic form.

NOTE Answers

Answers to these questions and explanations of why each answer choice is right or wrong are located in the "Answers" section at the end of the book.

---

1. Which methods of the *FileStream* class affect the *Position* property? (Choose all that apply.)

    A. *Read*

    B. *Lock*

    C. *Write*

    D. *Seek*

2. How do you force changes in a *StreamWriter* to be sent to the stream it is writing to? (Choose all that apply.)

    A. Close the *StreamWriter*.

    B. Call the *Flush* method of the *StreamWriter*.

    C. Set the *AutoFlush* property of the *StreamWriter* to *true*.

    D. Close the stream.

3. Which of the following create a *FileStream* for writing when you want to open an existing file or create a new one if it doesn't exist? (Choose all that apply.)

    A. Create a new instance of the *FileStream* class, with the *FileMode* option of *OpenOrCreate*.

    B. Call *File.Create* to create the *FileStream*.

    C. Call *File.Open* with the *FileMode* option of *OpenOrCreate*.

    D. Call *File.Open* with the *FileMode* option of *Open*.

Lesson 3: Compressing Streams

Now that you know the basics of how to work with streams, you're ready to learn about a new type of stream that will be important in certain types of projects. Often in real-world projects, you will find it useful to save space or bandwidth by compressing data. The .NET Framework supports two new stream classes that can compress data.

> **After this lesson, you will be able to:**
>
> - Compress streams with the *GZipStream* and *DeflateStream* classes.
> - Decompress streams with the *GZipStream* and *DeflateStream* classes.
>
> **Estimated lesson time: 10 minutes**

Introducing the Compression Streams

In the I/O system inside the .NET Framework, there are two methods for compressing data: GZIP and DEFLATE. Both of these compression methods are industry-standard compression algorithms that are also free of patent protection. Therefore, you are free to use either of these compression methods in your own applications without any intellectual property concerns.

NOTE   **Compression size limitations**

Both compression methods are limited to compression of uncompressed data up to 4 GB.

These compression methods are exposed by the .NET Framework as two types of streams that support both compression and decompression. These streams are implemented in the *GZipStream* and *DeflateStream* classes.

NOTE   **Should I be using DEFLATE or GZIP?**

Both the *DeflateStream* and *GZipStream* classes use the same algorithm for compressing data. The only difference is that the GZIP specification[1] allows for headers that include extra information that might be helpful to decompress a file with the widely used *gzip* tool. If you are compressing data for use only within your own system, the file written by using *DeflateStream* is slightly smaller because of its lack of header information, but if you intend to distribute the files to be decompressed via GZIP, use *GZipStream* instead.

---

[1] *http://www.ietf.org/rfc/rfc1952.txt?number=1952*

The *GZipStream* Class

GZipStream is a class that allows the compression and decompression of data through to another stream using the GZIP compression method. Table 2-30 and Table 2-31 show the most important *GZipStream* properties and methods, respectively.

Table 2-30 *GZipStream* **Properties**

Name	Description
BaseStream	Gets the underlying stream.
CanRead	Determines whether the stream supports reading. (Inherited from the *Stream* class.)
CanSeek	Determines whether the stream supports seeking. (Inherited from the *Stream* class.)
CanTimeout	Determines whether the stream can time out. (Inherited from the *Stream* class.)
CanWrite	Determines whether the stream can be written to. (Inherited from the *Stream* class.)
Length	Do not use. Will throw *NotSupportedException*. (Inherited from the *Stream* class.)
Position	Do not use. Will throw *NotSupportedException*. (Inherited from the *Stream* class.)
ReadTimeout	Gets or sets the stream's timeout for read operations. (Inherited from the *Stream* class.)
WriteTimeout	Gets or sets the stream's timeout for write operations. (Inherited from the *Stream* class.)

Table 2-31 *GZipStream* **Methods**

Name	Description
Close	Closes the stream and releases any resources associated with it. (Inherited from the *Stream* class.)
Flush	Clears any buffers within the stream and forces changes to be written to the underlying system or device. (Inherited from the *Stream* class.)

Table 2-31   *GZipStream* Methods

Name	Description
Read	Performs a sequential read of a specified number of bytes from the current position and updates the position to the end of the read upon completion of the operation. (Inherited from the *Stream* class.)
ReadByte	Performs the read of a single byte and updates the position by moving it by one. This method is identical to calling *Read* to read a single byte. (Inherited from the *Stream* class.)
Seek	Do not use. Will throw *NotSupportedException*. (Inherited from the *Stream* class.)
SetLength	Do not use. Will throw *NotSupportedException*. (Inherited from the *Stream* class.)
Write	Writes information to the stream as a number of bytes and updates the current position to reflect the new write position. (Inherited from the *Stream* class.)
WriteByte	Writes a single byte to the stream and updates the position. This method is identical to calling *Write* with a single byte. (Inherited from the *Stream* class.)

The *DeflateStream* Class

DeflateStream is a class that allows the compression of data through to another stream using the DEFLATE compression method. Table 2-32 and Table 2-33 show the most important *DeflateStream* properties and methods, respectively.

Table 2-32   *DeflateStream* Properties

Name	Description
BaseStream	Gets the underlying stream.
CanRead	Determines whether the stream supports reading. (Inherited from the *Stream* class.)
CanSeek	Determines whether the stream supports seeking. (Inherited from the *Stream* class.)

Table 2-32   *DeflateStream* Properties

Name	Description
CanTimeout	Determines whether the stream can time out. (Inherited from the *Stream* class.)
CanWrite	Determines whether the stream can be written to. (Inherited from the *Stream* class.)
Length	Do not use. Will throw *NotSupportedException*. (Inherited from the *Stream* class.)
Position	Do not use. Will throw *NotSupportedException*. (Inherited from the *Stream* class.)
ReadTimeout	Gets or sets the stream's timeout for read operations. (Inherited from the *Stream* class.)
WriteTimeout	Gets or sets the stream's timeout for write operations. (Inherited from the *Stream* class.)

Table 2-33   *DeflateStream* Methods

Name	Description
Close	Closes the stream and releases any resources associated with it. (Inherited from the *Stream* class.)
Flush	Clears any buffers within the stream and forces changes to be written to the underlying system or device. (Inherited from the *Stream* class.)
Read	Performs a sequential read of a specified number of bytes from the current position and updates the position to the end of the read upon completion of the operation. (Inherited from the *Stream* class.)
ReadByte	Performs the read of a single byte and updates the position by moving it by one. This method is identical to calling *Read* to read a single byte. (Inherited from the *Stream* class.)
Seek	Do not use. Will throw *NotSupportedException*. (Inherited from the *Stream* class.)

Table 2-33   *DeflateStream* Methods

Name	Description
SetLength	Do not use. Will throw *NotSupportedException*. (Inherited from the *Stream* class.)
Write	Writes information to the stream as a number of bytes and updates the current position to reflect the new write position. (Inherited from the *Stream* class.)
WriteByte	Writes a single byte to the stream and updates the position. This method is identical to calling *Write* with a single byte. (Inherited from the *Stream* class.)

How to Compress Data with a Compression Stream

Compression streams are a little different than the streams shown in the previous lessons. Instead of the stream writing to a resource (for example, a file for a *FileStream* or memory for a *MemoryStream*), it writes to another stream. The compression stream is used to take in data like any stream, but when it writes data, it pushes it into another stream in the compressed (or decompressed) format.

The following paragraphs provide a typical example: reading an existing file in the file system and writing a new compressed version of the file. First you need to open the file to be compressed and the file you are going to write to:

```
' VB
Dim sourceFile As FileStream = File.OpenRead(inFilename)
Dim destFile As FileStream = File.Create(outFilename)
```

```
// C#
FileStream sourceFile = File.OpenRead(inFilename);
FileStream destFile = File.Create(outFilename);
```

Compressing a stream requires that the compression stream wrap the outgoing (or destination) stream. This task is performed in the constructor of the compression stream, as shown here:

```
' VB
Dim compStream As _
    New GZipStream(destFile, CompressionMode.Compress)
```

```
// C#
GZipStream compStream =
    new GZipStream(destFile, CompressionMode.Compress);
```

This statement tells the compression stream to compress data and push it to the destination stream. The constructor takes a *CompressionMode* value that specifies whether the stream is going to be used to compress or decompress. In this case, you want to compress the stream, so you use *CompressionMode.Compress*. Once you have created the compression stream, it is simply a matter of reading data from the source stream and feeding it into the compression stream, as shown here:

```vb
' VB
Dim theByte As Integer = sourceFile.ReadByte()
While theByte <> -1
    compStream.WriteByte(CType(theByte, Byte))
    theByte = sourceFile.ReadByte()
End While
```

```csharp
// C#
int theByte = sourceFile.ReadByte();
while (theByte != -1)
{
    compStream.WriteByte((byte)theByte);
    theByte = sourceFile.ReadByte();
}
```

This code streams data one byte at a time from the source file (*sourceFile*) into the compression stream (*compStream*). Notice that you do not write directly into the destination file at all (*destFile*). Because you are writing into the compression stream, the destination stream is being filled with the compressed version of the data from the source file.

The streaming code just shown is not specific to the GZIP compression method. If we change the construction of the stream to use the *DeflateStream* instead, the rest of the code does not change at all. All that is required is that you create a *DeflateStream* instead, as shown here (notice the signature of the constructor is the same as that of the *GZipStream*):

```vb
' VB
Dim compStream As _
    New DeflateStream(destFile, CompressionMode.Compress)
```

```csharp
// C#
DeflateStream compStream =
    new DeflateStream(destFile, CompressionMode.Compress);
```

How to Decompress Data with a Compression Stream

Decompression uses the same program design as compression, except that the streams are dealt with slightly differently. For example, you still create your source and destination files like you did before:

```vb
' VB
Dim sourceFile As FileStream = File.OpenRead(inFilename)
Dim destFile As FileStream = File.Create(outFilename)
```

```
// C#
FileStream sourceFile = File.OpenRead(inFilename);
FileStream destFile = File.Create(outFilename);
```

In this case, the source file is a compressed file and the destination file is going to be written as a decompressed file. When you create the compression stream, you change it in two ways: you wrap the source file because that is where the compressed data exists, and you specify the *CompressionMode.Decompress* to specify that you are decompressing the wrapped stream:

```
' VB
Dim compStream As _
    New GZipStream(sourceFile, CompressionMode.Decompress)
```

```
// C#
GZipStream compStream =
    new GZipStream(sourceFile, CompressionMode.Decompress);
```

In addition, you need to change the way you process the file to read from the compression stream instead of from the source file and write out to the file directly instead of through the compression stream:

```
' VB
Dim theByte As Integer = compStream.ReadByte()
While theByte <> -1
    destFile.WriteByte(CType(theByte, Byte))
    theByte = compStream.ReadByte()
End While
```

```
// C#
int theByte = compStream.ReadByte();
while (theByte != -1)
{
    destFile.WriteByte((byte)theByte);
    theByte = compStream.ReadByte();
}
```

In either case (compression or decompression), the compression stream is meant to wrap the stream that contains (or will contain) compressed data. Whether you read or write compressed data is completely dependent on whether you are compressing or decompressing.

Lab: Compress and Decompress an Existing File

In this lab, you will create a simple console application that will read a file from the file system and compress it into a new file. If you encounter a problem completing an exercise, the completed projects are available on the companion CD in the Code folder.

▶ **Exercise 1: Compressing an Existing File**

In this exercise, you will compress an existing file into a new compressed file.

1. Create a new console application named CompressionDemo.

2. Add an *Imports* (or a *using* statement in C#) for the *System.IO* and *System.IO.Compression* namespaces into the new project.

3. Create a new static method (or a shared one for Visual Basic) named *Compress-File* that takes two strings: *inFilename* and *outFilename*. The method signature should look something like this:

```vb
' VB
Shared Sub CompressFile(ByVal inFilename As String, _
                        ByVal outFilename As String)
End Sub
```

```csharp
// C#
static void CompressFile(string inFilename,
                         string outFilename)
{
}
```

4. Inside this method, open a *FileStream* object (named *sourceFile*) by opening the file specified in the *inFilename*.

5. Create a new *FileStream* object (named *destFile*) by creating a new file specified in the *outFilename*.

6. Create a new *GZipStream* object (named *compStream*), specifying the *destFile* as the stream to write the compressed data to. Also specify that this will be a compression stream. Your code might look something like this:

```vb
' VB
Dim compStream As _
    New GZipStream(destFile, CompressionMode.Compress)
```

```csharp
// C#
GZipStream compStream =
    new GZipStream(destFile, CompressionMode.Compress);
```

7. Stream the data in the source file into the compression stream one byte at a time. Your code might look something like this:

```vb
' VB
Dim buffer(sourceFile.Length) As Byte
    sourceFile.Read(buffer, 0, buffer.Length)
    compStream.Write(buffer, 0, buffer.Length)
```

```
// C#
const int buf_size = 4096;
byte[] buffer = new byte[buf_size];
int bytes_read = 0;
do
{
    bytes_read = sourceFile.Read(buffer,0,buf_size);
    compStream.Write(buffer,0,bytes_read);
} while (bytes_read != 0);
```

8. Close the all the streams before exiting the method.

9. In the *Main* method of the new console project, call the *CompressFile* method
   with an existing file and a new file name (typically ending the source file with
   .gz). The call might look something like this:

```
' VB
CompressFile("c:\boot.ini", "c:\boot.ini.gz")
```

```
// C#
CompressFile(@"c:\boot.ini", @"c:\boot.ini.gz");
```

NOTE   Using a small file may result in the compressed file being larger than the original
because of the overhead of compression. If you use a larger file, the size of the overhead will
not cause such a pallor on the size of the resulting file

---

10. Build the project and resolve any errors. Verify that the console application cre-
    ated the new compressed file by manually checking the compressed file in the
    file system. The file should read as gibberish in a text editor (such as NotePad).

▶ **Exercise 2: Uncompressing the New File**

In this exercise, you will open the file you created in Exercise 1 and uncompress the
file into a new file.

1. Open the CompressionDemo project you created in Exercise 1.

2. Create a new static method (or a shared one for Visual Basic) named *Decompress-
   File* that takes two strings: *inFileName* and *outFileName*. The method signature
   should look something like this:

```
' VB
Shared Sub DecompressFile(ByVal inFilename As String, _
                          ByVal outFilename As String)
End Sub
```

```
// C#
static void DecompressFile(string inFilename,
                           string outFilename)
{
}
```

3. Inside this method, open a *FileStream* object (named *sourceFile*) by opening the file
   specified in the *inFilename*, which will be the compressed file you wrote in Exercise 1.

4. Create a new *FileStream* object (named *destFile*) by creating a new file specified in the *outFilename*.

5. Create a new *GZipStream* object (named *compStream*), specifying the *sourceFile* as the stream to read the compressed data from. Also specify that this will be a decompression stream. Your code might look something like this:

```
' VB
Dim compStream As _
    New GZipStream(sourceFile, CompressionMode.Decompress)
End Sub

// C#
GZipStream compStream =
    new GZipStream(sourceFile, CompressionMode.Decompress);
```

6. Stream the data in the compression file into the destination file one byte at a time. Your code might look something like this:

```
' VB
Dim theByte As Integer = compStream.ReadByte()
While theByte <> -1
    destFile.WriteByte(CType(theByte, Byte))
    theByte = compStream.ReadByte()
End While

// C#
int theByte = compStream.ReadByte();
while (theByte != -1)
{
    destFile.WriteByte((byte)theByte);
    theByte = compStream.ReadByte();
}
```

7. Close the all the streams before exiting the method.

8. In the *Main* method of the new console project, call the *UncompressFile* method and pass it the file name of the compressed file you created in Exercise 1 and the name of a file that will receive the uncompressed data. The call might look something like this:

```
' VB
DecompressFile("c:\boot.ini.gz", "c:\boot.ini.test")

// C#
DecompressFile(@"c:\boot.ini.gz", @"c:\boot.ini.test");
```

9. Build the project and resolve any errors. Verify that the console application creates the new uncompressed file by opening it with NotePad. Compare the file's contents to the original file to see whether they are identical.

Lesson Summary

- The compression stream classes (*GZipStream* and *DeflateStream*) can be used to compress or decompress any data up to 4 GB.

- The compression stream classes are used to wrap another stream into which the compressed data will be stored.

Lesson Review

You can use the following questions to test your knowledge of the information in Lesson 3, "Compressing Streams." The questions are also available on the companion CD if you prefer to review them in electronic form.

NOTE Answers

Answers to these questions and explanations of why each answer choice is right or wrong are located in the "Answers" section at the end of the book.

---

1. When compressing data with the *DeflateStream* class, how do you specify a stream into which to write compressed data?

   A. Set the *BaseStream* property with the destination stream, and set the *CompressionMode* property to *Compression*.

   B. Specify the stream to write into when the *DeflateStream* object is created (for example, in the constructor).

   C. Use the *Write* method of the *DeflateStream* class.

   D. Register for the *BaseStream* event of the *DeflateStream* class.

2. What types of data can a *GZipStream* compress? (Choose all that apply.)

   A. Any file

   B. Any data

   C. Any data less than 4 GB in size

   D. Any file no larger than 4 GB in size

Lesson 4: Working with Isolated Storage

As we are becoming more and more aware of, giving programs unfettered access to a computer is not a great idea. The emergence of spyware, malware, and viruses tells us that working in the sandbox of limited security is a better world for most users. Unfortunately, many programs still need to save some sort of state data about themselves. The way to do this can be as innocuous as storing data in a cache. To bridge the needs of applications to save data and the desire of administrators and users to use more limited security settings, the .NET Framework supports the concept of *isolated storage*.

After this lesson, you will be able to:

- Access isolated storage for storage of program data by using the *IsolatedStorageFile* class.
- Create files and folders in isolated storage by using the *IsolatedStorageFileStream* class.
- Access different stores within isolated storage on a per-user and per-machine basis using the *IsolatedStorageFile* class.

Estimated lesson time: 15 minutes

What Is Isolated Storage?

Running code with limited privileges has many benefits given the presence of predators who are foisting viruses and spyware on your users. The .NET Framework has several mechanisms for dealing with running as least-privileged users. Because most applications have to deal with storing some of their state in a persistent way (without resorting to databases or other means), it would be nice to have a place to store information that was safe to use without having to test whether the application has enough rights to save data to the hard drive. That solution is what isolated storage is designed to provide.

By using isolated storage to save your data, you will have access to a safe place to store information without needing to resort to having users grant access to specific files or folders in the file system. The main benefit of using isolated storage is that your application will run regardless of whether it is running under partial, limited, or full-trust.

NOTE .NET 2.0

In .NET 2.0, there are new types of applications that are meant to be deployed and installed from Web pages called "Click-Once applications" or, sometimes, "Smart-client applications." These new types of applications are meant to solve deployment of applications across a company or enterprise.

MORE INFO   **Click-Once applications**

For more information on Click-Once applications, please see *http://msdn2.microsoft.com/en-us/library/142dbbz4.aspx.*

The *IsolatedStorageFile* Class

The *IsolatedStorageFile* class provides the basic functionality to create files and folders in isolated storage. Table 2-34 shows the most important *IsolatedStorageFile* static/shared methods.

Table 2-34   *IsolatedStorageFile* Static/Shared Methods

Name	Description
GetMachineStoreForApplication	Retrieves a machine-level store for the Click-Once application that called
GetMachineStoreForAssembly	Retrieves a machine-level store for the assembly that called
GetMachineStoreForDomain	Retrieves a machine-level store for the *AppDomain* within the current assembly that called
GetStore	Retrieves stores whose scope is based on the *IsolatedStorageScope* enumerator
GetUserStoreForApplication	Retrieves a user-level store for the Click-Once application that called
GetUserStoreForAssembly	Retrieves a user-level store for the assembly that called
GetUserStoreForDomain	Retrieves a user-level store for the *AppDomain* within the current assembly that called

Table 2-35 shows the most important *IsolatedStorageFile* properties.

Table 2-35   *IsolatedStorageFile* Properties

Name	Description
ApplicationIdentity	The Click-Once application's identity that scopes the isolated storage
AssemblyIdentity	The assembly's identity that scopes the isolated storage

Table 2-35 *IsolatedStorageFile* Properties

Name	Description
CurrentSize	The current size of the data stored in this isolated storage
DomainIdentity	The identity of the *AppDomain* that scopes the isolated storage
MaximumSize	The maximum storage size for this isolated storage
Scope	The *IsolatedStorageScope* enumeration value that describes the scope of this isolated storage

Table 2-36 shows the most important *IsolatedStorageFile* methods.

Table 2-36 *IsolatedStorageFile* Methods

Name	Description
Close	Closes an instance of a store
CreateDirectory	Creates a directory within the store
DeleteDirectory	Deletes a directory within the store
DeleteFile	Deletes a file within the store
GetDirectoryNames	Gets a list of directory names within the store that match a directory mask
GetFileNames	Gets a list of file names within the store that match a file mask
Remove	Removes the entire store from the current system

How to Create a Store

Before you can save data in isolated storage, you must determine how to scope the data you want in your store. For most applications, you will want to choose one of the following two methods:

- **Assembly/Machine**   This method creates a store to keep information that is specific to the calling assembly and the local machine. This method is useful for creating application-level data.

- **Assembly/User**   This method creates a store to keep information that is specific to the calling assembly and the current user. This method is useful for creating user-level data.

Creating an assembly/machine-level store is accomplished by calling the *IsolatedStorageFile* class's *GetMachineStoreForAssembly* method, as shown here:

```
' VB
Dim machineStorage as IsolatedStorageFile = _
    IsolatedStorageFile.GetMachineStoreForAssembly()
```

```
// C#
IsolatedStorageFile machineStorage =
    IsolatedStorageFile.GetMachineStoreForAssembly();
```

This isolated storage store is specific to the assembly that is calling it, whether that is the main executable in a Microsoft Windows Forms project or a dynamic-link library (DLL) that is part of a larger project.

Creating an assembly/user-level store is similar, but the method is named *GetUserStoreForAssembly*, as shown in this example:

```
' VB
Dim userStorage as IsolatedStorageFile = _
    IsolatedStorageFile.GetUserStoreForAssembly()
```

```
// C#
IsolatedStorageFile userStorage =
    IsolatedStorageFile.GetUserStoreForAssembly();
```

The store in this case is scoped to the specific user that is executing the assembly. If you need to specify the user for the store, you will need to use impersonation (which is covered in Chapter 12).

NOTE Application-level store

For Click-Once deployed applications, isolated storage also supports an application-level store that supports both a machine-level store and a user-level store. Application level stores work only within Click-Once applications because the executing assembly has its own evidence that might or might not be valid for local applications.

MORE INFO Isolated storage

For more information about isolated storage, see the following sources:

■ "Introduction to Isolated Storage" by Microsoft Corporation (available online at *http://msdn.microsoft .com/library/default.asp?url=/library/en-us/cpguide/html/cpconintroductiontoisolatedstorage.asp*).

■ *Windows Forms Programming in C#/VB.NET* by Chris Sells (Addison-Wesley, 2004). Read Chapter 11, pages 426–430, "Application Settings," for an explanation of how different types of stores affect users and roaming users.

The *IsolatedStorageFileStream* Class

The *IsolatedStorageFileStream* class encapsulates a stream that is used to read, write, and create files in isolated storage. This class derives from the *FileStream* class, so its usage after creation is almost identical to the *FileStream* class. Table 2-37 shows the most important *IsolatedStorageFileStream* properties.

Table 2-37   *IsolatedStorageFileStream* **Properties**

Name	Description
CanRead	Determines whether the stream supports reading. (Inherited from the *Stream* class.)
CanSeek	Determines whether the stream supports seeking. (Inherited from the *Stream* class.)
CanTimeout	Determines whether the stream can time out. (Inherited from the *Stream* class.)
CanWrite	Determines whether the stream can be written to. (Inherited from the *Stream* class.)
Handle	Gets the stream's underlying file handle. (Inherited from the *FileStream* class.)
Length	Gets the length (in bytes) of the stream. (Inherited from the *Stream* class.)
Name	Gets the name of the file. (Inherited from the *FileStream* class.)
Position	Gets or sets the virtual cursor for determining where in the stream the current position is. The value of *Position* cannot be greater than the stream's length. (Inherited from the *Stream* class.)
ReadTimeout	Gets or sets the stream's timeout for read operations. (Inherited from the *Stream* class.)
WriteTimeout	Gets or sets the stream's timeout for write operations. (Inherited from the *Stream* class.)

Table 2-38 shows the most important *IsolatedStorageFileStream* methods.

Table 2-38   *IsolatedStorageFileStream* **Methods**

Name	Description
Close	Closes the stream and releases any resources associated with it. (Inherited from the *Stream* class.)
Flush	Clears any buffers within the stream and forces changes to be written to the underlying system or device. (Inherited from the *Stream* class.)
Lock	Prevents other processes from changing all or part of the file. (Inherited from the *FileStream* class.)
Read	Performs a sequential read of a specified number of bytes from the current position and updates the position to the end of the read upon completion of the operation. (Inherited from the *Stream* class.)
ReadByte	Performs the read of a single byte and updates the position by moving it by one. This method is identical to calling *Read* to read a single byte. (Inherited from the *Stream* class.)
Seek	Sets the position within the stream. (Inherited from the *Stream* class.)
SetLength	Specifies the length of the stream. Will truncate the stream if the new length is less than the old length and will expand the stream if the reverse is true. (Inherited from the *Stream* class.)
Unlock	Allows other processes to change all or part of the underlying file. (Inherited from the *FileStream* class.)
Write	Writes information to the stream as a number of bytes and updates the current position to reflect the new write position. (Inherited from the *Stream* class.)
WriteByte	Writes a single byte to the stream and updates the position. This method is identical to calling *Write* with a single byte. (Inherited from the *Stream* class.)

Reading and Writing Data to Isolated Storage

Creating data within isolated storage is just like writing any other data into the file system, with the exception that you must use the *IsolatedStorageFileStream* class. You create a new *IsolatedStorageFileStream* object by creating a new instance of the class, specifying a relative file name and including a store object to specify which store to include it within. The following code snippet provides an example:

```
' VB
Dim userStore as IsolatedStorageFile = _
    IsolatedStorageFile.GetUserStoreForAssembly()

Dim userStream As IsolatedStorageFileStream = New _
    IsolatedStorageFileStream("UserSettings.set", _
                              FileMode.Create, _
                              userStore)

// C#
IsolatedStorageFile userStore =
    IsolatedStorageFile.GetUserStoreForAssembly();

IsolatedStorageFileStream userStream =
    new IsolatedStorageFileStream("UserSettings.set",
                                  FileMode.Create,
                                  userStore);
```

After creating a store, you can create a file stream by specifying the file name, the *FileMode* to use in opening or creating the file, and the store object you created. Once you have an instance of the *IsolatedStorageFileStream* class, working with it is identical to working with any file stream (like we did in Lesson 2). This is because *IsolatedStorageFileStream* derives from *FileStream*. The following code snippet provides an example:

```
' VB
Dim userWriter As StreamWriter = New StreamWriter(userStream)
userWriter.WriteLine("User Prefs")
userWriter.Close()

// C#
StreamWriter userWriter = new StreamWriter(userStream);
userWriter.WriteLine("User Prefs");
userWriter.Close();
```

In this example, you use a standard *StreamWriter* object to write data into your stream. Again, once you have the *userStream* object, working with it is identical to working with any file in the file system.

Preparing to read the data back is as simple as creating a stream object by opening the file instead of creating it, as shown here:

```
' VB
Dim userStream As IsolatedStorageFileStream = New _
    IsolatedStorageFileStream("UserSettings.set", _
                              FileMode.Open, _
                              userStore)
```

```
// C#
IsolatedStorageFileStream userStream =
    new IsolatedStorageFileStream("UserSettings.set",
                                  FileMode.Open,
                                  userStore);
```

By simply changing the *FileMode* to *Open*, you can open the file instead of creating a new one. Unlike the application programming interface (API) for files stored arbitrarily in the file system, the API for files in Isolated Storage does not support checking for the existence of a file directly like *File.Exists* does. Instead, you need to ask the store for a list of files that match a particular file mask. If it is found, you can open the file, as shown in this example:

```
' VB
Dim files() As String =  userStore.GetFileNames("UserSettings.set")
If files.Length = 0 Then
    Console.WriteLine("No data saved for this user")
Else
    '...
End If
```

```
// C#
string[] files = userStore.GetFileNames("UserSettings.set");
if (files.Length == 0)
{
    Console.WriteLine("No data saved for this user");
}
else
{
    // ...
}
```

You can use the *GetFileNames* method of the *IsolatedStorageFile* class to get a list of files that match your file name (or other file masks such as **.set*). This replacement is adequate to test for the existence of the file before trying to read, delete, or replace the file.

How to Use Directories in Isolated Storage

You are not limited to storing data as just a set of files in isolated storage; instead, you are also allowed to create directories to store data within. Before you can create files in a directory, you must call the *CreateDirectory* method of the *IsolatedStorageFile* class, as shown here:

```
' VB
userStore.CreateDirectory("SomeDir")

Dim userStream As IsolatedStorageFileStream =  New _
    IsolatedStorageFileStream("SomeDir\UserSettings.set", _
                          FileMode.Create, _
                          userStore)

// C#
userStore.CreateDirectory("SomeDir");

IsolatedStorageFileStream userStream = new
    IsolatedStorageFileStream(@"SomeDir\UserSettings.set",
                          FileMode.Create,
                          userStore);
```

In this example, you create the directory before you try to create a new file in that directory. If you don't create the directory first, you will get a path-parsing exception.

Directories are treated much like files in that to test for their existence, you must use a method that returns an array of strings that match a mask. The *GetDirectoryNames* method of the *IsolatedStorageFile* class allows you to find an existing directory before you try to create it:

```
' VB
Dim directories() As String = _
    userStore.GetDirectoryNames("SomeDir")

If directories.Length = 0 Then
    userStore.CreateDirectory("SomeDir")
End If

// C#
string[] directories =
    userStore.GetDirectoryNames("SomeDir");

if (directories.Length == 0)
{
    userStore.CreateDirectory("SomeDir");
}
```

By getting the directory names that match your name, you can test to see whether the directory exists and create it only if it was not already created.

The *IsolatedStorageFilePermission* Class

The *IsolatedStorageFilePermission* class encapsulates the permission that can be granted to code to allow it to access isolated storage. Table 2-39 shows the most important *IsolatedStorageFilePermission* properties.

Table 2-39   *IsolatedStorageFilePermission* **Properties**

Name	Description
UsageAllowed	Gets or sets the types of usage allowed.
UserQuota	Gets or sets the overall size of storage allowed per user

Permitting Isolated Storage

Before an assembly (or application) can make use of isolated storage, it must be granted permission to do so. To make sure any code you are working with will have the sufficient permissions, you will need to demand that permission. This task can be accomplished by annotating your class or method with *IsolatedStorageFilePermission*, as seen here:

```vb
' VB
<IsolatedStorageFilePermission(SecurityAction.Demand)> _
Class Program
    ' ...
End Class
```

```csharp
// C#
[IsolatedStorageFilePermission(SecurityAction.Demand)]
class Program
{
    // ...
}
```

IsolatedStorageFilePermission is used to ensure that any calls to work with isolated storage within this class will succeed. If your code does not have the permissions to access isolated storage, including this attribute will allow administrators to better understand what assemblies need this permission and allow them to add the permission if needed.

This permission also supports several properties that can be used to modify how isolated storage is used, as shown in this example:

```
' VB
<IsolatedStorageFilePermission(SecurityAction.Demand, _
    UserQuota:=1024, _
    UsageAllowed:=IsolatedStorageContainment.AssemblyIsolationByUser)> _
Class Program
    ' ...
End Class

// C#
[IsolatedStorageFilePermission(SecurityAction.Demand,
    UserQuota=1024,
    UsageAllowed=IsolatedStorageContainment.AssemblyIsolationByUser)]
class Program
{
    // ...
}
```

Adding *UserQuota* and *UsageAllowed* describes to the security system how this code intends to use isolated storage.

Lab: Store and Retrieve Data from Isolated Storage

In this lab, you will create a new file in isolated storage and then read the file back from isolated storage. If you encounter a problem completing an exercise, the completed projects are available on the companion CD in the Code folder.

▶ **Exercise 1: Creating a File in Isolated Storage**

In this exercise, you will create a new file in isolated storage.

1. Create a new console application named IsolatedStorageDemo.

2. Add an *Imports* (or a *using* statement in C#) for the *System.IO* and *System.IO.IsolatedStorage* namespaces into the new project.

3. In the *Main* method of the new project, create a new instance of the *IsolatedStorageFile* class named *userStore* that is scoped to the current user and assembly. Your code might look something like this:

```
' VB
Dim userStore as IsolatedStorageFile = _
    IsolatedStorageFile.GetUserStoreForAssembly()

// C#
IsolatedStorageFile userStore =
    IsolatedStorageFile.GetUserStoreForAssembly();
```

4. Create a new instance of the *IsolatedStorageFileStream* object, passing in the name *UserSettings.set* and the new store, as shown in this example:

```
' VB
Dim userStream as IsolatedStorageFileStream = new _
    IsolatedStorageFileStream("UserSettings.set", _
                              FileMode.Create, _
                              userStore)
// C#
IsolatedStorageFileStream userStream = new
    IsolatedStorageFileStream("UserSettings.set",
                              FileMode.Create,
                              userStore);
```

5. Use a *StreamWriter* to write some data into the new stream, and close the writer when finished. Your code might look something like this:

```
' VB
Dim userWriter as new StreamWriter(userStream)
userWriter.WriteLine("User Prefs")
userWriter.Close()

// C#
StreamWriter userWriter = new StreamWriter(userStream);
userWriter.WriteLine("User Prefs");
userWriter.Close();
```

6. Build the project, and resolve any errors. Verify that the console application created the new file by checking the file in the file system. The file will exist in a directory under C:\Documents and Settings\<*user*>\Local Settings\Application Data\IsolatedStorage. This directory is a cache directory, so you will find some machine-generated directory names that might seem like gibberish. You should find the file if you dig deeper into the directory called AssemFiles.

▶ **Exercise 2: Reading a File in Isolated Storage**

In this exercise, you will read the file you created in Exercise 1.

1. Open the project you created in Exercise 1 (IsolatedStorageDemo).

2. After the code from Exercise 1, add code to check whether the file exists in the store and show a console message if no files were found. Your code might look something like this:

```
' VB
Dim files() As String = userStore.GetFileNames("UserSettings.set")
If files.Length = 0 Then
    Console.WriteLine("No data saved for this user")
End If
```

```
// C#
string[] files = userStore.GetFileNames("UserSettings.set");
if (files.Length == 0)
{
    Console.WriteLine("No data saved for this user.");
}
```

3. If the file was found, create a new *IsolatedStorageFileStream* object that opens the file you created in Exercise 1. Create a *StreamReader* to read all the text in the file into a new local string variable. Your code might look something like this:

```
' VB
userStream = New _
    IsolatedStorageFileStream("UserSettings.set", FileMode.Open, userStore)
Dim userReader As StreamReader =  New StreamReader(userStream)
Dim contents As String =  userReader.ReadToEnd()
```

```
// C#
userStream = new
    IsolatedStorageFileStream("UserSettings.set",
                             FileMode.Open, userStore);
StreamReader userReader = new StreamReader(userStream);
string contents = userReader.ReadToEnd();
```

4. Add a line to the console that shows the string you created from the *Stream-Reader*.

5. Build the project and resolve any errors. Verify that the console application shows the contents of the file on the command line.

Lesson Summary

- The *IsolatedStorageFile* class can be used to access safe areas to store data for assemblies and users.

- The *IsolatedStorageFileStream* class can be used to read and write data into these safe stores.

- The *IsolatedStorageFileStream* class derives from the *FileStream* class, so any files the class creates can be used like any other file in the file system.

- The *IsolatedStorageFilePermission* class can be used to make sure the code has adequate permissions to act upon isolated storage.

Lesson Review

You can use the following questions to test your knowledge of the information in Lesson 4, "Working with Isolated Storage." The questions are also available on the companion CD if you prefer to review them in electronic form.

1. What methods can be used to create a new *IsolatedStorageFile* object? (Choose all that apply.)

   A. *IsolatedStorageFile.GetStore*

   B. *IsolatedStorageFile.GetMachineStoreForAssembly*

   C. *IsolatedStorageFile.GetUserStoreForAssembly*

   D. *IsolatedStorageFile* constructor

2. An *IsolatedStorageFileStream* object can be used like any other *FileStream* object.

   A. True

   B. False

Chapter Review

To further practice and reinforce the skills you learned in this chapter, you can perform the following tasks:

- Review the chapter summary.
- Review the list of key terms introduced in this chapter.
- Complete the case scenarios. These scenarios set up real-world situations involving the topics of this chapter and ask you to create a solution.
- Complete the suggested practices.
- Take a practice test.

Chapter Summary

- The *FileSystemInfo* classes (*FileInfo* and *DirectoryInfo*) can be used to navigate the file system and get information about files and directories, including size, time stamps, names, attributes, and so on.
- The *File* class provides a jumping-off point to creating or opening files in the file system.
- The *FileStream* class can be used to stream data into or out of the file system.
- The *StreamReader* and *StreamWriter* classes are instrumental in dealing with moving text-oriented data into and out of streams, including *FileStream*s, *MemoryStream*s, and *IsolatedStorageFileStream*s.
- The .NET Framework supports two classes for compressing data: the *GZip-Stream* class and the *DeflateStream* class.
- Isolated storage provides a safe place to keep data about a specific assembly, user, or application. Because isolated storage requires so few security rights, it is the best way to store data without having to grant an application with permissive rights to a user's system.

Key Terms

Do you know what these key terms mean? You can check your answers by looking up the terms in the glossary at the end of the book.

- deflate
- file system

- isolated storage
- gzip

Case Scenarios

In the following case scenarios, you will apply what you've learned about files and directories. You can find answers to these questions in the "Answers" section at the end of this book.

Case Scenario 1: Saving User Settings

You are a newly hired developer for a large insurance company. Your manager asks you to add a user-preferences dialog to an existing Windows Forms application. Your manager also informs you that the users will not be running as administrators on their own machines, but as limited users. The dialog is to be added to a sales lead application, and users often share computers. It is very important that sales people cannot view each other's leads.

Questions

Answer the following questions for your manager.

1. At a high level, describe how you would store the information for the users.
2. How would that design change if you needed to compress the preference data to help limit the size of the data?

Case Scenario 2: Monitoring Old Servers

You are a developer working for a large IT organization. It has a large number of systems that are supposed to be brought offline in the next month. Your manager has heard that the file servers are still being used by some users, but she is having trouble finding out who is saving data to the servers. She asks you to write a small application she can install on those servers that will send her an e-mail message whenever a new file is saved or created on the server.

Interviews

Following is a list of company personnel interviewed and their statements:

- **IT Manager**   "I am sure that some users are still using those servers without knowing it. If we could monitor those servers for a week so that I can migrate those users to our new file servers, we could save a lot of money in upkeep costs."

■ **Development Manager** "One of our developers tried to write this file-monitoring app several weeks ago, but he ultimately gave up. He was keeping a list of all files in the system and scanning the system every five minutes, and it was taking too long."

Questions

Answer the following questions for your manager.

1. What type of application will you create to address the IT department's need?
2. How will you monitor the file servers?
3. How will you deal with the Development Manager's concern about performance?

Suggested Practices

To help you successfully master the objectives covered in this chapter, complete the following tasks.

Create a File Searcher Application

For this task, you should complete at least Practices 1 and 2. For additional experience with the compression streams, please complete Practice 3.

■ **Practice 1** Create an application that will search a drive for a particular file.
■ **Practice 2** Add code to view the file by using the *FileStream* class to show the file in a text window.
■ **Practice 3** Finally, add a feature to compress a file when it is found.

Create a Simple Configuration Storage

For this task, you should complete at least Practices 1 and 2. To understand how user and machine-level data differ in isolated storage, complete Practice 3 as well.

■ **Practice 1** Create a Windows Forms application that allows users to save data and store it in isolated storage.
■ **Practice 2** Test the Windows Forms application by running it under different user accounts.
■ **Practice 3** Modify the application to store some machine-level data to see whether that data is the same for all users.

Take a Practice Test

The practice tests on this book's companion CD offer many options. For example, you can test yourself on just one exam objective, or you can test yourself on all the 70-536 certification exam content. You can set up the test so that it closely simulates the experience of taking a certification exam, or you can set it up in study mode so that you can look at the correct answers and explanations after you answer each question.

MORE INFO   Practice tests

For details about all the practice test options available, see the "How to Use the Practice Tests" section in this book's Introduction.

Chapter 3

Searching, Modifying, and Encoding Text

Processing text is one of the most common programming tasks. User input is typically in text format, and it might need to be validated, sanitized, and reformatted. Often, developers need to process text files generated from a legacy system to extract important data. These legacy systems often use nonstandard encoding techniques. Additionally, developers might need to output text files in specific formats to input data into a legacy system.

This chapter describes how to use regular expressions to validate input, reformat text, and extract data. Additionally, this chapter describes different encoding types used by text files.

Exam objectives in this chapter:

- Enhance the text handling capabilities of a .NET Framework application (refer *System.Text* namespace), and search, modify, and control text in a .NET Framework application by using regular expressions. (Refer *System.RegularExpressions* namespace.)
    - ❑ *StringBuilder* class
    - ❑ *Regex* class
    - ❑ *Match* class and *MatchCollection* class
    - ❑ *Group* class and *GroupCollection* class
    - ❑ Encode text by using *Encoding* classes
    - ❑ Decode text by using *Decoding* classes
    - ❑ *Capture* class and *CaptureCollection* class

Lessons in this chapter:

143

Before You Begin

To complete the lessons in this chapter, you should be familiar with Microsoft Visual Basic or C# and be comfortable performing the following tasks:

- Create a console application in Microsoft Visual Studio using Visual Basic or C#.
- Add references to system class libraries to a project.
- Read and write to files and streams.

Lesson 1: Forming Regular Expressions

Developers frequently need to process text. For example, you might need to process input from a user to remove or replace special characters. Or you might need to process text that has been output from a legacy application to integrate your application with an existing system. For decades, UNIX and Perl developers have used a complex but efficient technique for processing text: regular expressions.

A regular expression is a set of characters that can be compared to a string to determine whether the string meets specified format requirements. You can also use regular expressions to extract portions of the text or to replace text. To make decisions based on text, you can create regular expressions that match strings consisting entirely of integers, strings that contain only lowercase letters, or strings that match hexadecimal input. You can also extract key portions of a block of text, which you could use to extract the state from a user's address or image links from an HTML page. Finally, you can update text using regular expressions to change the format of text or remove invalid characters.

> **After this lesson, you will be able to:**
> - Use regular expressions to determine whether a string matches a specific pattern.
> - Use regular expressions to extract data from a text file.
> - Use regular expressions to reformat text data.
>
> **Estimated lesson time: 45 minutes**

How to Use Regular Expressions for Pattern Matching

To enable yourself to test regular expressions, create a console application named TestRegExp that accepts two strings as input and determines whether the first string (a regular expression) matches the second string. The following console application, which uses the *System.Text.RegularExpressions* namespace, performs this check using the static *System.Text.RegularExpressions.Regex.IsMatch* method and displays the results to the console:

```
' VB
Imports System.Text.RegularExpressions

Namespace TestRegExp
    Class Class1
        <STAThread> _
        Shared  Sub Main(ByVal args() As String)
            If Regex.IsMatch(args(1),args(0)) Then
                Console.WriteLine("Input matches regular expression.")
```

```
            Else
                Console.WriteLine("Input DOES NOT match regular expression.")
            End If
        End Sub
    End Class
End Namespace

// C#
using System.Text.RegularExpressions;

namespace TestRegExp
{
    class Class1
    {
        [STAThread]
        static void Main(string[] args)
        {
            if (Regex.IsMatch(args[1], args[0]))
                Console.WriteLine("Input matches regular expression.");
            else
                Console.WriteLine("Input DOES NOT match regular expression.");
        }
    }
}
```

Next, run the application by determining whether the regular expression "^\d{5}$" matches the string "12345" or "1234". The regular expression won't make sense now, but it will by the end of the lesson. Your output should resemble the following:

```
C:\>TestRegExp ^\d{5}$ 1234
Input DOES NOT match regular expression.

C:\>TestRegExp ^\d{5}$ 12345
Input matches regular expression.
```

As this code demonstrates, the *Regex.IsMatch* method compares a regular expression to a string and returns *true* if the string matches the regular expression. In this example, "^\d{5}$" means that the string must be exactly five numeric digits. As shown in Figure 3-1, the carat ("^") represents the start of the string, "\d" means numeric digits, "{5}" indicates five sequential numeric digits, and "$" represents the end of the string.

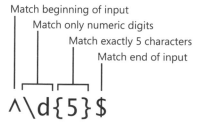

Match beginning of input
Match only numeric digits
Match exactly 5 characters
Match end of input

^\d{5}$

Figure 3-1   Analysis of a regular expression

If you remove the first character from the regular expression, you drastically change the meaning of the pattern. The regular expression "\d{5}$" will still match valid five-digit numbers, such as "12345". However, it will also match the input string "abcd12345" or "drop table customers – 12345". In fact, the modified regular expression will match any input string that ends in any five-digit number.

IMPORTANT **Include the leading carat**

When validating input, forgetting the leading carat can expose a security vulnerability. Use peer code reviews to limit the risk of human error.

When validating input, always begin regular expressions with a "^" character and end them with "$". This system ensures that input exactly matches the specified regular expression and does not merely *contain* matching input.

Regular expressions can be used to match complex input patterns, too. The following regular expression matches e-mail addresses:

```
^([\w-\.]+)@((\[[0-9]{1,3}\.[0-9]{1,3}\.[0-9]{1,3}\.)|((\[\w-]+\.)+))
([a-zA-Z]{2,4}|[0-9]{1,3})(\]?)$
```

Regular expressions are an extremely efficient way to check user input; however, using regular expressions has the following limitations:

- **Regular expressions are difficult to create unless you are extremely familiar with the format.**   If you have years of Perl programming experience, you won't have any problem using regular expressions in C# code. However, if you have a background in Visual Basic scripting, the cryptic format of regular expressions will initially seem completely illogical.

- **Creating regular expressions *can* be confusing, but reading regular expressions definitely is.**   There is a good chance that other programmers will overlook errors in regular expressions when performing a peer code review. The more complex the regular expression, the greater the chance that the structure of the expression contains an error that will be overlooked.

The sections that follow describe these and other aspects of regular expression pattern matching in more detail. As you read through these sections, experiment with different types of regular expressions using the TestRegExp application.

MORE INFO   **Regular expressions**

Entire books have been written about regular expressions, and this lesson can only scratch the surface. The information provided in this lesson should be sufficient for the exam. However, if you would like to learn more about the advanced features of regular expressions, read "Regular Expression Language Elements" in the .NET Framework General Reference at *http://msdn.microsoft.com/library/ en-us/cpgenref/html/cpconRegularExpressionsLanguageElements.asp.*

How to Use Match Simple Text

The simplest use of regular expressions is to determine whether a string matches a pattern. For example, the regular expression "abc" matches the strings "abc", "abcde", or "yzabc" because each of the strings contains the regular expression. No wildcards are necessary.

How to Match Text in Specific Locations

If you want to match text beginning at the first character of a string, start the regular expression with a "^" symbol. For example, the regular expression "^abc" matches the strings "abc" and "abcde", but it does not match "yzabc". To match text that ends at the last character of a string, place a "$" symbol at the end of the regular expression. For example, the regular expression "abc$" matches "abc" and "yzabc", but it does not match "abcde". To exactly match a string, include both "^" and "$". For example, "^abc$" only matches "abc" and does not match "abcde" or "yzabc".

When searching for words, use "\b" to match a word boundary. For example, "car\b" matches "car" or "tocar" but not "carburetor". Similarly, "\B" matches a nonword boundary and can be used to ensure that a character appears in the middle of a word. For example, "car\B" matches "carburetor" but not "tocar".

NOTE   **Confused?**

If regular expressions seem cryptic, that's because they are. Unlike almost everything else in the .NET Framework, regular expressions rely heavily on special characters with meanings that no human being could ever decipher on his or her own. The reason for this is simple: Regular expressions originated in the UNIX world during a time when memory and storage were extremely limited and developers had to make every single character count. Because of this, you should always comment regular expressions. As hard as they can be to create, reading another developer's regular expressions is almost impossible.

Table 3-1 lists characters you can use to cause your regular expression to match a specific location in a string. Of these, the most important to know are "^" and "$".

Table 3-1 Characters that Match Location in Strings

Character	Description
^	Specifies that the match must begin at either the first character of the string or the first character of the line. If you are analyzing multiline input, the ^ will match the beginning of any line.
$	Specifies that the match must end at either the last character of the string, the last character before \n at the end of the string, or the last character at the end of the line. If you are analyzing multiline input, the $ will match the end of any line.
\A	Specifies that the match must begin at the first character of the string (and ignores multiple lines).
\Z	Specifies that the match must end at either the last character of the string or the last character before \n at the end of the string (and ignores multiple lines).
\z	Specifies that the match must end at the last character of the string (and ignores multiple lines).
\G	Specifies that the match must occur at the point where the previous match ended. When used with *Match.NextMatch*, this arrangement ensures that matches are all contiguous.
\b	Specifies that the match must occur on a boundary between \w (alphanumeric) and \W (nonalphanumeric) characters. The match must occur on word boundaries, which are the first or last characters in words separated by any nonalphanumeric characters.
\B	Specifies that the match must not occur on a \b boundary.

Notice that regular expressions are case-sensitive, even in Visual Basic. Often, capitalized characters have the opposite meaning of lowercase characters.

Many regular expression codes begin with a backslash. When developing in C#, you should begin every regular expression with an @ so that backslashes are treated literally. Do this even if your regular expression does not contain a backslash, because it will reduce the risk of adding a very difficult-to-find bug if you edit the regular expression later. For example:

```
// C#
Regex.IsMatch("pattern", @"\Apattern\Z")
```

Exam Tip   Don't even try to memorize every regular expression code. Sure, it would impress the UNIX crowd at the office, but for the exam you only need to know the most commonly used codes, which this book calls out in examples.

How to Match Special Characters

You can match special characters in regular expressions. For example, \t represents a tab, and \n represents a newline. The special characters shown in Table 3-2 might not appear in user input or the average text file; however, they might appear if you are processing output from a legacy or UNIX system.

Table 3-2   Character Escapes Used in Regular Expressions

Character	Description
\a	Matches a bell (alarm) \u0007.
\b	In a regular expression, \b denotes a word boundary (between \w and \W characters) except within a [] character class, where \b refers to the backspace character. In a replacement pattern, \b always denotes a backspace.
\t	Matches a tab \u0009.
\r	Matches a carriage return \u000D.
\v	Matches a vertical tab \u000B.
\f	Matches a form feed \u000C.
\n	Matches a new line \u000A.
\e	Matches an escape \u001B.
\040	Matches an ASCII character as octal (up to three digits); numbers with no leading zero are backreferences if they have only one digit or if they correspond to a capturing group number. For example, the character \040 represents a space.

Table 3-2   Character Escapes Used in Regular Expressions

Character	Description
\x20	Matches an ASCII character using hexadecimal representation (exactly two digits).
\cC	Matches an ASCII control character—for example, \cC is control-C.
\u0020	Matches a Unicode character using hexadecimal representation (exactly four digits).
\	When followed by a character that is not recognized as an escaped character, matches that character. For example, * represents an asterisk (rather than matching repeating characters), and \\ represents a single backslash.

How to Match Text Using Wildcards

You can also use regular expressions to match repeated characters. The "*" symbol matches the preceding character zero or more times. For example, "to*n" matches "ton", "tooon", or "tn". The "+" symbol works similarly, but it must match one or more times. For example, "to+n" matches "ton" or "tooon", but not "tn".

To match a specific number of repeated characters, use "{n}" where n is a digit. For example, "to{3}n" matches "tooon" but not "ton" or "tn". To match a range of repeated characters, use "{min,max}". For example, "to{1,3}n" matches "ton" or "tooon" but not "tn" or "toooon". To specify only a minimum, leave the second number blank. For example, "to{3,}n" requires three or more consecutive "o" characters.

To make a character optional, use the "?" symbol. For example, "to?n" matches "ton" or "tn", but not "tooon". To match any single character, use ".". For example, "to.n" matches "totn" or "tojn" but not "ton" or "tn".

To match one of several characters, use brackets. For example, "to[ro]n" would match "toon" or "torn" but not "ton" or "toron". You can also match a range of characters. For example, "to[o-r]n" matches "toon", "topn", "toqn", or "torn" but would not match "toan" or "toyn".

Table 3-3 summarizes the regular expression characters used to match multiple characters or a range of characters.

Table 3-3   Wildcard and Character Ranges Used in Regular Expressions

Character	Description
*	Matches the preceding character or subexpression zero or more times. For example, "zo*" matches "z" and "zoo". The "*" character is equivalent to "{0,}".
+	Matches the preceding character or subexpression one or more times. For example, "zo+" matches "zo" and "zoo", but not "z". The "+" character is equivalent to "{1,}".
?	Matches the preceding character or subexpression zero or one time. For example, "do(es)?" matches the "do" in "do" or "does". The ? character is equivalent to "{0,1}".
{n}	The n is a non-negative integer. Matches exactly n times. For example, "o{2}" does not match the "o" in "Bob" but does match the two "o"s in "food".
{n,}	The n is a non-negative integer. Matches at least n times. For example, "o{2,}" does not match the "o" in "Bob" and does match all the "o"s in "foooood". The sequence "o{1,}" is equivalent to "o+". The sequence "o{0,}" is equivalent to "o*".
{n,m}	The m and n are non-negative integers, where "n <= m". Matches at least n and at most m times. For example, "o{1,3}" matches the first three "o"s in "fooooood". "o{0,1}" is equivalent to "o?". Note that you cannot put a space between the comma and the numbers.
?	When this character immediately follows any of the other quantifiers (*, +, ?, {n}, {n,}, {n,m}), the matching pattern is nongreedy. A nongreedy pattern matches as little of the searched string as possible, whereas the default greedy pattern matches as much of the searched string as possible. For example, in the string "oooo", "o+?" matches a single "o", whereas "o+" matches all "o"s.
.	Matches any single character except "\n". To match any character including the "\n", use a pattern such as "[\s\S]".
x|y	Matches either x or y. For example, "z|food" matches "z" or "food". "(z|f)ood" matches "zood" or "food".

Table 3-3   **Wildcard and Character Ranges Used in Regular Expressions**

Character	Description
[xyz]	A character set. Matches any one of the enclosed characters. For example, "[abc]" matches the "a" in "plain".
[a-z]	A range of characters. Matches any character in the specified range. For example, "[a-z]" matches any lowercase alphabetic character in the range "a" through "z".

Regular expressions also provide special characters to represent common character ranges. You could use "[0-9]" to match any numeric digit, or you can use "\d". Similarly, "\D" matches any non-numeric digit. Use "\s" to match any white-space character, and use "\S" to match any non-white-space character. Table 3-4 summarizes these characters.

Table 3-4   **Characters Used in Regular Expressions**

Character	Description
\d	Matches a digit character. Equivalent to "[0-9]".
\D	Matches a nondigit character. Equivalent to "[^0-9]".
\s	Matches any white-space character, including Space, Tab, and form-feed. Equivalent to "[\f\n\r\t\v]".
\S	Matches any non-white-space character. Equivalent to "[^ \f\n\r\t\v]".
\w	Matches any word character, including underscore. Equivalent to "[A-Za-z0-9_]".
\W	Matches any nonword character. Equivalent to "[^A-Za-z0-9_]".

To match a group of characters, surround the characters with parentheses. For example, "foo(loo){1,3}hoo" would match "fooloohoo" and "foolooloooloohoo" but not "foohoo" or "foololohoo". Similarly, "foo(loo|roo|)hoo" would match either "fooloohoo" or "fooroohoo". You can apply any wildcard or other special character to a group of characters.

You can also name groups to refer to the matched data later. To name a group, use the format "(?<*name*>*pattern*)". For example, the regular expression "foo(?<mid>loo|roo)hoo" would match "fooloohoo". Later, you could reference the group "mid" to retrieve "loo". If you used the same regular expression to match "fooroohoo", "mid" would contain "roo".

How to Match Using Backreferences

Backreferencing uses named groups to allow you to search for other instances of characters that match a wildcard. Backreferences provide a convenient way to find repeating groups of characters. They can be thought of as a shorthand instruction to match the same string again.

For example, the regular expression (?<char>\w)\k<char>, using named groups and backreferencing, searches for adjacent paired characters. When applied to the string "I'll have a small coffee," it finds matches in the words "I'll", "small", and "coffee". The metacharacter \w finds any single-word character. The grouping construct (?<char>) encloses the metacharacter to force the regular expression engine to remember a subexpression match (which, in this case, will be any single character) and save it under the name "char". The backreference construct \k<char> causes the engine to compare the current character to the previously matched character stored under "char". The entire regular expression successfully finds a match wherever a single character is the same as the preceding character.

To find repeating whole words, you can modify the grouping subexpression to search for any group of characters preceded by a space instead of simply searching for any single character. You can substitute the subexpression \w+, which matches any group of characters, for the metacharacter \w and use the metacharacter \s to match a space preceding the character group. This yields the regular expression (?<char>\s\w+)\k<char>, which finds any repeating whole words such as " the the" but also matches other repetitions of the specified string, as in the phrase "the theory."

To verify that the second match is on a word boundary, add the metacharacter \b after the repeat match. The resulting regular expression, (?<char>\s\w+)\k<char>\b, finds only repeating whole words that are preceded by white space.

A backreference refers to the most recent definition of a group (the definition most immediately to the left when matching left to right). Specifically, when a group makes multiple captures, a backreference refers to the most recent capture. For example, (?<1>a)(?<1>\1b)* matches aababb, with the capturing pattern (a)(ab)(abb). Looping quantifiers do not clear group definitions.

If a group has not captured any substring, a backreference to that group is undefined and never matches. For example, the expression \1() never matches anything, but the expression ()\1 matches the empty string.

Table 3-5 lists optional parameters that add backreference modifiers to a regular expression.

Table 3-5   Backreference Parameters

Backreference construct	Definition
\number	Backreference. For example, (\w)\1 finds doubled word characters.
\k<name>	Named backreference. For example, (?<char>\w)\k<char> finds doubled word characters. The expression (?<43>\w)\43 does the same. You can use single quotes instead of angle brackets—for example, \k'char'.

How to Specify Regular Expression Options

You can modify a regular expression pattern with options that affect matching behavior. Regular expression options can be set in one of two basic ways: they can be specified in the *options* parameter in the *Regex(pattern, options)* constructor, where options is a bitwise OR combination of *RegexOptions* enumerated values, or they can be set within the regular expression pattern using the inline (?imnsx-imnsx:) grouping construct or (?imnsx-imnsx) miscellaneous construct.

In inline option constructs, a minus sign (–) before an option or set of options turns off those options. For example, the inline construct (?ix–ms) turns on the *IgnoreCase* and *IgnorePatternWhitespace* options and turns off the *Multiline* and *Singleline* options. All regular expression options are turned off by default.

Table 3-6 lists the members of the *RegexOptions* enumeration and the equivalent inline option characters. Note that the options *RightToLeft* and *Compiled* apply only to an expression as a whole and are not allowed inline. (They can be specified only in the options parameter to the *Regex* constructor.) The options *None* and *ECMAScript* are not allowed inline.

Table 3-6 Regular Expression Options

RegexOption member	Inline character	Description
None	N/A	Specifies that no options are set.
IgnoreCase	i	Specifies case-insensitive matching.
Multiline	m	Specifies multiline mode. Changes the meaning of ^ and $ so that they perform matching at the beginning and end, respectively, of any line, not just at the beginning and end of the whole string.
ExplicitCapture	n	Specifies that the only valid captures are explicitly named or numbered groups of the form (?<*name*>...). This allows parentheses to act as noncapturing groups without the syntactic clumsiness of (?:...).
Compiled	N/A	Specifies that the regular expression will be compiled to an assembly. Generates Microsoft intermediate language (MSIL) code for the regular expression; yields faster execution at the expense of startup time.
Singleline	s	Specifies single-line mode. Changes the meaning of the period character (.) so that it matches every character (instead of every character except \n).
IgnorePattern-Whitespace	x	Specifies that unescaped white space is excluded from the pattern, and enables comments following a number sign (#). Note that white space is never eliminated from within a character class.

Table 3-6   **Regular Expression Options**

RegexOption member	Inline character	Description
RightToLeft	N/A	Specifies that the search moves from right to left instead of from left to right. A regular expression with this option moves to the left of the starting position instead of to the right. (Therefore, the starting position should be specified as the end of the string instead of the beginning.) This option cannot be specified in midstream, which is a limitation designed to prevent the possibility of crafting regular expressions with infinite loops. However, the (?<) lookbehind constructs provide something similar that can be used as a subexpression.
		RightToLeft changes the search direction only. It does not reverse the substring that is searched for. The lookahead and lookbehind assertions do not change: lookahead looks to the right; lookbehind looks to the left.
ECMAScript	N/A	Specifies that *ECMAScript*-compliant behavior is enabled for the expression. This option can be used only in conjunction with the *IgnoreCase* and *Multiline* flags. Use of *ECMAScript* with any other flags results in an exception.
CultureInvariant	N/A	Specifies that cultural differences in language are ignored.

Consider the following three-line text file:

```
abc
def
ghi
```

If this text file is copied to the *s String*, the following method returns *false* because "def" is not at both the beginning and end of the string:

```
Regex.IsMatch(s, "^def$")
```

But the following method returns *true* because the *RegexOptions.Multiline* option enables the "^" symbol to match the beginning of a line (rather than the entire string), and it enables the "$" symbol to match the end of a line:

```
Regex.IsMatch(s, "^def$", RegexOptions.Multiline)
```

How to Extract Matched Data

Besides simply determining whether a string matches a pattern, you can extract information from a string. For example, if you are processing a text file that contains "Company Name: Contoso, Inc.", you could extract just the company name using a regular expression.

To match a pattern and capture the match, follow these steps:

1. Create a regular expression, and enclose in parentheses the pattern to be matched.
2. Create an instance of the *System.Text.RegularExpressions.Match* class using the static *Regex.Match* method.
3. Retrieve the matched data by accessing the elements of the *Match.Groups* array.

For example, the following code sample extracts the company name from the input and displays it to the console:

```
' VB
Dim input As String = "Company Name: Contoso, Inc."
Dim m As Match = Regex.Match(input, "Company Name: (.*$)")
Console.WriteLine(m.Groups(1))

// C#
string input = "Company Name: Contoso, Inc.";
Match m = Regex.Match(input, @"Company Name: (.*$)");
Console.WriteLine(m.Groups[1]);
```

Running this console application (which requires the *System.Text.RegularExpressions* namespace) displays "Contoso, Inc.". This example demonstrates that with very little code, you can perform complex text extraction using regular expressions. Note that this example uses unnamed groups, which the runtime automatically numbers starting at 1.

The following example searches an input string and prints out all the href="..." values and their locations in the string. It does this by constructing a compiled *Regex* object and then using a *Match* object to iterate through all the matches in the string. In this example, the metacharacter \s matches any space character, and \S matches any non-space character.

```vb
' VB
Sub DumpHrefs(inputString As String)
    Dim r As Regex
    Dim m As Match

    r = New Regex("href\s*=\s*(?:""(?<1>[^""]*)""|(?<1>\S+))", _
        RegexOptions.IgnoreCase Or RegexOptions.Compiled)

    m = r.Match(inputString)
    While m.Success
        Console.WriteLine("Found href " & m.Groups(1).Value _
            & " at " & m.Groups(1).Index.ToString())
        m = m.NextMatch()
    End While
End Sub
```

```csharp
// C#
void DumpHrefs(String inputString)
{
    Regex r;
    Match m;

    r = new Regex("href\\s*=\\s*(?:\"(?<1>[^\"]*)\")\"|(?<1>\\S+))",
        RegexOptions.IgnoreCase|RegexOptions.Compiled);
    for (m = r.Match(inputString); m.Success; m = m.NextMatch())
    {
        Console.WriteLine("Found href " + m.Groups[1] + " at "
            + m.Groups[1].Index);
    }
}
```

You can also call the *Match.Result* method to reformat extracted substrings. The following code example uses *Match.Result* to extract a protocol and port number from a URL. For example, "http://www.contoso.com:8080/letters/readme.html" would return "http:8080".

```vb
' VB
Function Extension(url As String) As String
    Dim r As New Regex("^(?<proto>\w+)://[^/]+?(?<port>:\d+)?/", _
        RegexOptions.Compiled)
    Return r.Match(url).Result("${proto}${port}")
End Function
```

```csharp
// C#
String Extension(String url)
{
    Regex r = new Regex(@"^(?<proto>\w+)://[^/]+?(?<port>:\d+)?/",
        RegexOptions.Compiled);
    return r.Match(url).Result("${proto}${port}");
}
```

How to Replace Substrings Using Regular Expressions

You can also use regular expressions to perform replacements far more complex than is possible with the *String.Replace* method. The following code example uses the static *Regex.Replace* method to replace dates in the *mm/dd/yy* format with dates in the *dd-mm-yy* format:

```
' VB
Function MDYToDMY(input As String) As String
    Return Regex.Replace(input, _
        "\b(?<month>\d{1,2})/(?<day>\d{1,2})/(?<year>\d{2,4})\b", _
            "${day}-${month}-${year}")
End Function

// C#
String MDYToDMY(String input)
{
    return Regex.Replace(input,
        "\\b(?<month>\\d{1,2})/(?<day>\\d{1,2})/(?<year>\\d{2,4})\\b",
        "${day}-${month}-${year}");
}
```

This example demonstrates the use of named backreferences within the replacement pattern for *Regex.Replace*. Here, the replacement expression ${day} inserts the substring captured by the group (?<day>...).

The following code example uses the static *Regex.Replace* method to strip invalid characters from a string. You can use the *CleanInput* method defined here to strip potentially harmful characters that have been entered into a text field in a form that accepts user input. *CleanInput* returns a string after stripping out all nonalphanumeric characters except @, - (a dash), and . (a period).

```
' VB
Function CleanInput(strIn As String) As String
    ' Replace invalid characters with empty strings.
    Return Regex.Replace(strIn, "[^\w\.@-]", "")
End Function

// C#
String CleanInput(string strIn)
{
    // Replace invalid characters with empty strings.
    return Regex.Replace(strIn, @"[^\w\.@-]", "");
}
```

Character escapes and substitutions are the only special constructs recognized in a replacement pattern. All the syntactic constructs described in the following sections are allowed only in regular expressions; they are not recognized in replacement patterns. For example, the replacement pattern a*${txt}b inserts the string "a*" followed by the substring matched by the txt capturing group, if any, followed by the string "b". The * character is not recognized as a metacharacter within a replacement pattern. Similarly, $ patterns are not recognized within regular expression matching patterns. Within regular expressions, $ designates the end of the string.

Table 3-7 shows how to define named and numbered replacement patterns.

Table 3-7   Character Escapes Used in Substitutions

Character	Description
$number	Substitutes the last substring matched by group number *number* (decimal).
${name}	Substitutes the last substring matched by a (?<name>) group.
$$	Substitutes a single "$" literal.
$&	Substitutes a copy of the entire match itself.
$`	Substitutes all the text of the input string before the match.
$'	Substitutes all the text of the input string after the match.
$+	Substitutes the last group captured.
$_	Substitutes the entire input string.

How to Use Regular Expressions to Constrain String Input

When building security into your application, regular expressions are the most efficient way to validate user input. If you build an application that accepts a five-digit number from a user, you can use a regular expression to ensure that the input is exactly five characters long and that each character is a number from 0 through 9. Similarly, when prompting a user for her first and last name, you can check her input with a regular expression and throw an exception when the input contains numbers, delimiters, or any other nonalphabetic character.

Unfortunately, not all input is as easy to describe as numbers and e-mail addresses. Names and street addresses are particularly difficult to validate because they can contain a wide variety of characters from international alphabets unfamiliar to you. For example, O'Dell, Varkey Chudukatil, Skjønaa, Craciun, and McAskill-White are all legitimate last names. Programmatically filtering these examples of valid input from malicious input such as "1' DROP TABLE PRODUCTS –" (a SQL injection attack) is difficult.

One common approach is to instruct users to replace characters in their own names. For example, users who normally enter an apostrophe or a hyphen in their names could omit those characters. Users with letters that are not part of the standard Roman alphabet could replace letters with the closest similar Roman character. Although this system allows you to more rigorously validate input, it requires users to sacrifice the accurate spelling of their names—something many people take very personally.

As an alternative, you can perform as much filtering as possible on the input, and then clean the input of any potentially malicious content. Most input validation should be pessimistic and allow only input that consists entirely of approved characters. However, input validation of real names might need to be optimistic and cause an error only when specifically denied characters exist. For example, you could reject a user's name if it contained one of the following characters: !, @, #, $, %, ^, *, (), <, >. All these characters are unlikely to appear in a name but likely to be used in an attack. Microsoft Visual Studio .NET provides the following regular expression to match valid names: "[a-zA-Z'`-Ã,Â´\s]{1,40}".

Real World

Tony Northrup

I'm often stubborn to a fault. For many years, I simply refused to learn regular expressions. Regular expressions were the UNIX way of doing things, and I was a Windows guy.

Recently, I reviewed some code I wrote several years back when I was still being stubborn. I had written dozens of lines of code to check the validity of text data that could have been written with a singular regular expression. That doesn't bother me in itself, because sometimes writing more code improves readability. However, in this case, the text checking had gotten so complex that it contained bugs.

I rewrote the code using regular expressions, and it not only fixed the bugs, but it simplified the code. So, for your own sake, don't ignore regular expressions just because they seem overly complex. Dive in, spend a few hours working with them, and you won't regret it.

Lab: Create a *Regex* Expression Evaluator

In this lab, you process an array of strings to distinguish valid phone numbers and Zip Codes. Then you will reformat the phone numbers. If you encounter a problem completing an exercise, the completed projects are available on the companion CD in the Code folder.

▶ **Exercise 1: Distinguish Between a Phone Number and a Zip Code**

In this exercise, you write code to distinguish between a phone number, a Zip Code, and invalid data.

1. Copy either the Visual Basic or C# version of the Chapter03\Lesson1-Exercise1 folder from the companion CD to your hard disk, and open the solution file.

2. Using one line of code, complete the *IsPhone* method so that it returns *true* if any of the following formats are provided:

    ❑ (555)555-1212

    ❑ (555) 555-1212

    ❑ 555-555-1212

    ❑ 5555551212

    Though many different regular expressions would work, the *IsPhone* method you write could look like this:

```
' VB
Function IsPhone(ByVal s As String) As Boolean
    Return Regex.IsMatch(s, "^\(?\d{3}\)?[\s\-]?\d{3}\-?\d{4}$")
End Function
```

```
// C#
static bool IsPhone(string s)
{
    return Regex.IsMatch(s, @"^\(?\d{3}\)?[\s\-]?\d{3}\-?\d{4}$");
}
```

Each component of this regular expression matches a required or optional part of a phone number:

- ■ ^ Matches the beginning of the string.

- ■ \(? Optionally matches an opening parenthesis. The parenthesis is preceded with a backslash, because the parenthesis is a special character in regular expressions. The following question mark makes the parenthesis optional.

- **\d{3}**   Matches exactly three numeric digits.

- **\)?**   Optionally matches a closing parenthesis. The parenthesis is preceded with a backslash because the parenthesis is a special character in regular expressions. The following question mark makes the parenthesis optional.

- **[\s\-]?**   Matches either a space ("\s") or a hyphen ("\-") separating the area code from the rest of the phone number. The following question mark makes the space or hyphen optional.

- **\d{3}**   Matches exactly three numeric digits.

- **\-?**   Optionally matches a hyphen.

- **\d{4}$**   Requires that the string end with four numeric digits.

3. Using one line of code, complete the *IsZip* method so that it returns *true* if any of the following formats are provided:

   - ❑ 01111

   - ❑ 01111-1111

Though many different regular expressions would work, the *IsZip* method you write could look like this:

```
' VB
Function IsZip(ByVal s As String) As Boolean
    Return Regex.IsMatch(s, "^\d{5}(\-\d{4})?$")
End Function
```

```
// C#
static bool IsZip(string s)
{
    return Regex.IsMatch(s, @"^\d{5}(\-\d{4})?$");
}
```

Each component of this regular expression matches a required or optional part of a Zip Code:

- **^**   Matches the beginning of the string.

- **\d{5}**   Matches exactly five numeric digits.

- **(\-\d{4})?**   Optionally matches a hyphen followed by exactly four numeric digits. Because the expression is surrounded by parentheses and followed by a question mark, the expression is considered optional.

- **$**   Matches the end of the string.

4. Build and run the project. The output should match the following:

```
(555)555-1212 is a phone number
(555) 555-1212 is a phone number
555-555-1212 is a phone number
5555551212 is a phone number
01111 is a zip code
01111-1111 is a zip code
47 is unknown
111-11-1111 is unknown
```

If the output you get does not match the output just shown, adjust your regular expressions as needed.

▶ **Exercise 2: Reformat a String**

In this exercise, you must reformat phone numbers into a standard (###) ###-#### format.

1. Open the project you created in Exercise 1.

2. Add a method named *ReformatPhone* that returns a string and accepts a single string as an argument. Using regular expressions, accept phone-number data provided in one of the formats used in Exercise 1, and reformat the data into the (###) ###-#### format. Though many different regular expressions would work, the *ReformatPhone* method you write could look like this:

```
' VB
Function ReformatPhone(ByVal s As String) As String
    Dim m As Match = Regex.Match(s, "^\(?(\d{3})\)?[\s\-]?(\d{3})\-?(\d{4})$")
    Return String.Format("({0}) {1}-{2}", m.Groups(1), m.Groups(2), m.Groups(3))
End Function
```

```
// C#
static string ReformatPhone(string s)
{
    Match m = Regex.Match(s, @"^\(?(\d{3})\)?[\s\-]?(\d{3})\-?(\d{4})$");
    return String.Format("({0}) {1}-{2}", m.Groups[1], m.Groups[2], m.Groups[3]);
}
```

Notice that this regular expression almost exactly matches that used in the *IsPhone* method. The only difference is that each of the \d{n} expressions is surrounded by parentheses. This places each of the sets of numbers into a separate group that can be easily formatted using *String.Format*.

3. Change the *Main* method so that it writes *ReformatPhone(s)* in the *foreach* loop instead of simply s. For example, the *foreach* loop should now look like this:

```
' VB
For Each s As String In input
```

```
        If IsPhone(s) Then
            Console.WriteLine(ReformatPhone(s) + " is a phone number")
        Else
            If IsZip(s) Then
                Console.WriteLine(s + " is a zip code")
            Else
                Console.WriteLine(s + " is unknown")
            End If
        End If
Next

// C#
foreach (string s in input)
{
    if (IsPhone(s)) Console.WriteLine(ReformatPhone(s) + " is a phone number");
    else if (IsZip(s)) Console.WriteLine(s + " is a zip code");
    else Console.WriteLine(s + " is unknown");
}
```

4. Build and run the project. The output should match the following:

```
(555) 555-1212 is a phone number
(555) 555-1212 is a phone number
(555) 555-1212 is a phone number
(555) 555-1212 is a phone number
01111 is a zip code
01111-1111 is a zip code
47 is unknown
111-11-1111 is unknown
```

Notice that each of the phone numbers has been reformatted even though they were initially in four different formats. If your output does not match the output just shown, adjust your regular expressions as needed.

Lesson Summary

- Regular expressions enable you to determine whether text matches almost any type of format. Regular expressions support dozens of special characters and operators. The most commonly used are "^" to match the beginning of a string, "$" to match the end of a string, "?" to make a character optional, "." to match any character, and "*" to match a repeated character.

- To match data using a regular expression, create a pattern using groups to specify the data you need to extract, call *Regex.Match* to create a *Match* object, and then examine each of the items in the *Match.Groups* array.

- To reformat text data using a regular expression, call the static *Regex.Replace* method.

Lesson Review

You can use the following questions to test your knowledge of the information in Lesson 1, "Forming Regular Expressions." The questions are also available on the companion CD if you prefer to review them in electronic form.

NOTE **Answers**

Answers to these questions and explanations of why each answer choice is right or wrong are located in the "Answers" section at the end of the book.

---

1. You are writing an application to update absolute hyperlinks in HTML files. You have loaded the HTML file into a *String* named s. Which of the following code samples best replaces "http://" with "https://"?

    A.
    ```
    ' VB
    s = Regex.Replace(s, "http://", "https://")

    // C#
    s = Regex.Replace(s, "http.//", "https://");
    ```

    B.
    ```
    ' VB
    s = Regex.Replace(s, "https://", "http://")

    // C#
    s = Regex.Replace(s, "https://", "http://");
    ```

    C.
    ```
    ' VB
    s = Regex.Replace(s, "http://", "https://", RegexOptions.IgnoreCase)

    // C#
    s = Regex.Replace(s, "http://", "https://", RegexOptions.IgnoreCase);
    ```

    D.
    ```
    ' VB
    s = Regex.Replace(s, "https://", "http://", RegexOptions.IgnoreCase)

    // C#
    s = Regex.Replace(s, "https://", "http://", RegexOptions.IgnoreCase);
    ```

2. You are writing an application to process data contained in a text form. Each file contains information about a single customer. The following is a sample form:

    ```
    First Name: Tom
    Last Name: Perham
    ```

```
Address: 1 Pine St.
City: Springfield
State: MA
Zip: 01332
```

You have read the form data into the *String* variable *s*. Which of the following code samples correctly stores the data portion of the form in the *fullName*, *address*, *city*, *state*, and *zip* variables?

A.

```vb
' VB
Dim p As String = "First Name: (?<firstName>.*$)\n" + _
    "Last Name: (?<lastName>.*$)\n" + _
    "Address: (?<address>.*$)\n" + _
    "City: (?<city>.*$)\n" + _
    "State: (?<state>.*$)\n" + _
    "Zip: (?<zip>.*$)"
Dim m As Match = Regex.Match(s, p, RegexOptions.Multiline)
Dim fullName As String = m.Groups("firstName").ToString + " " +
m.Groups("lastName").ToString
Dim address As String = m.Groups("address").ToString
Dim city As String = m.Groups("city").ToString
Dim state As String = m.Groups("state").ToString
Dim zip As String = m.Groups("zip").ToString
```

```csharp
// C#
string p = @"First Name: (?<firstName>.*$)\n" +
    @"Last Name: (?<lastName>.*$)\n" +
    @"Address: (?<address>.*$)\n" +
    @"City: (?<city>.*$)\n" +
    @"State: (?<state>.*$)\n" +
    @"Zip: (?<zip>.*$)";
Match m = Regex.Match(s, p, RegexOptions.Multiline);
string fullName = m.Groups["firstName"] + " " + m.Groups["lastName"];
string address = m.Groups["address"].ToString();
string city = m.Groups["city"].ToString();
string state = m.Groups["state"].ToString();
string zip = m.Groups["zip"].ToString();
```

B.

```vb
Dim p As String = "First Name: (?<firstName>.*$)\n" + _
    "Last Name: (?<lastName>.*$)\n" + _
    "Address: (?<address>.*$)\n" + _
    "City: (?<city>.*$)\n" + _
    "State: (?<state>.*$)\n" + _
    "Zip: (?<zip>.*$)"
Dim m As Match = Regex.Match(s, p)
Dim fullName As String = m.Groups("firstName").ToString + " " +
m.Groups("lastName").ToString
Dim address As String = m.Groups("address").ToString
Dim city As String = m.Groups("city").ToString
```

```
Dim state As String = m.Groups("state").ToString
Dim zip As String = m.Groups("zip").ToString

// C#
string p = @"First Name: (?<firstName>.*$)\n" +
    @"Last Name: (?<lastName>.*$)\n" +
    @"Address: (?<address>.*$)\n" +
    @"City: (?<city>.*$)\n" +
    @"State: (?<state>.*$)\n" +
    @"Zip: (?<zip>.*$)";
Match m = Regex.Match(s, p);
string fullName = m.Groups["firstName"] + " " + m.Groups["lastName"];
string address = m.Groups["address"].ToString();
string city = m.Groups["city"].ToString();
string state = m.Groups["state"].ToString();
string zip = m.Groups["zip"].ToString();
```

C.

```
Dim p As String = "First Name: (?<firstName>.*$)\n" + _
    "Last Name: (?<lastName>.*$)\n" + _
    "Address: (?<address>.*$)\n" + _
    "City: (?<city>.*$)\n" + _
    "State: (?<state>.*$)\n" + _
    "Zip: (?<zip>.*$)"
Dim m As Match = Regex.Match(s, p, RegexOptions.Multiline)
Dim fullName As String = m.Groups("<firstName>").ToString + " " +
m.Groups("<lastName>").ToString
Dim address As String = m.Groups("<address>").ToString
Dim city As String = m.Groups("<city>").ToString
Dim state As String = m.Groups("<state>").ToString
Dim zip As String = m.Groups("<zip>").ToString

// C#
string p = @"First Name: (?<firstName>.*$)\n" +
    @"Last Name: (?<lastName>.*$)\n" +
    @"Address: (?<address>.*$)\n" +
    @"City: (?<city>.*$)\n" +
    @"State: (?<state>.*$)\n" +
    @"Zip: (?<zip>.*$)";
Match m = Regex.Match(s, p, RegexOptions.Multiline);
string fullName = m.Groups["<firstName>"] + " " + m.Groups["<lastName>"];
string address = m.Groups["<address>"].ToString();
string city = m.Groups["<city>"].ToString();
string state = m.Groups["<state>"].ToString();
string zip = m.Groups["<zip>"].ToString();
```

D.

```
Dim p As String = "First Name: (?<firstName>.*$)\n" + _
    "Last Name: (?<lastName>.*$)\n" + _
    "Address: (?<address>.*$)\n" + _
    "City: (?<city>.*$)\n" + _
    "State: (?<state>.*$)\n" + _
    "Zip: (?<zip>.*$)"
```

```
Dim m As Match = Regex.Match(s, p)
Dim fullName As String = m.Groups("<firstName>").ToString + " " + m.Groups("<last
Name>").ToString
Dim address As String = m.Groups("<address>").ToString
Dim city As String = m.Groups("<city>").ToString
Dim state As String = m.Groups("<state>").ToString
Dim zip As String = m.Groups("<zip>").ToString

// C#
string p = @"First Name: (?<firstName>.*$)\n" +
    @"Last Name: (?<lastName>.*$)\n" +
    @"Address: (?<address>.*$)\n" +
    @"City: (?<city>.*$)\n" +
    @"State: (?<state>.*$)\n" +
    @"Zip: (?<zip>.*$)";
Match m = Regex.Match(s, p);
string fullName = m.Groups["<firstName>"] + " " + m.Groups["<lastName>"];
string address = m.Groups["<address>"].ToString();
string city = m.Groups["<city>"].ToString();
string state = m.Groups["<state>"].ToString();
string zip = m.Groups["<zip>"].ToString();
```

3. Which of the following regular expressions matches the strings "zoot" and "zot"?

    A. z(oo)+t

    B. zo*t$

    C. $zo*t

    D. ^(zo)+t

4. Which of the following strings match the regular expression "^a(mo)+t.*z$"? (Choose all that apply.)

    A. amotz

    B. amomtrewz

    C. amotmoz

    D. atrewz

    E. amomomottothez

Lesson 2: Encoding and Decoding

Every string and text file is encoded using one of many different encoding standards. Most of the time, the .NET Framework handles the encoding for you automatically. However, there are times when you might need to manually control encoding and decoding, such as when:

- Interoperating with legacy or UNIX systems
- Reading or writing text files in other languages
- Creating HTML pages
- Manually generating e-mail messages

This lesson describes common encoding techniques and shows you how to use them in .NET Framework applications.

After this lesson, you will be able to:

- Describe the importance of encoding, and list common encoding standards.
- Use the *Encoding* class to specify encoding formats, and convert between encoding standards.
- Programmatically determine which code pages the .NET Framework supports.
- Create files using a specific encoding format.
- Read files using unusual encoding formats.

Estimated lesson time: 30 minutes

Understanding Encoding

Although it was not the first encoding type, American Standard Code for Information Interchange (ASCII) is still the foundation for existing encoding types. ASCII assigned characters to 7-bit bytes using the numbers 0 through 127. These characters included English uppercase and lowercase letters, numbers, punctuation, and some special control characters. For example, 0x21 is "!", 0x31 is "1", 0x43 is "C", 0x63 is "c", and 0x7D is "}".

While ASCII was sufficient for most English-language communications, ASCII did not include characters used in non-English alphabets. To enable computers to be used in non-English-speaking locations, computer manufacturers made use of the remaining values—128 through 255—in an 8-bit byte. Over time, different locations assigned unique characters to values greater than 127. Because different locations might have different characters assigned to a single value, transferring documents between different languages created problems.

To help reduce these problems, American National Standards Institute (ANSI) defined standardized *code pages* that had standard ASCII values for 0 through 127, and language-specific values for 128 through 255. A code page is a list of selected character codes (characters represented as code points) in a certain order. Code pages are usually defined to support specific languages or groups of languages that share common writing systems. Windows code pages contain 256 code points and are zero-based.

If you've ever received an e-mail message or seen a Web page that seemed to have box characters or question marks where letters should appear, you have witnessed an encoding problem. Because people create Web pages and e-mails in many different languages, each must be tagged with an encoding type. For example, an e-mail might include one of the following headers:

```
Content-Type: text/plain; charset=ISO-8859-1
Content-Type: text/plain; charset="Windows-1251"
```

"ISO-8859-1" corresponds to code page 28591, "Western European (ISO)". If it had specified "ISO-8859-7", it could have contained characters from the "Greek (ISO)" code page, number 28597. Similarly, HTML Web pages typically include a meta tag such as one of the following:

```
<meta http-equiv="Content-Type" content="text/html; charset=iso-8859-1">
<meta http-equiv="Content-Type" content="text/html; charset=utf-8">
```

More and more, ASCII and ISO 8859 encoding types are being replaced by Unicode. Unicode is a massive code page with tens of thousands of characters that support most languages and scripts, including Latin, Greek, Cyrillic, Hebrew, Arabic, Chinese, and Japanese (and many other scripts).

Unicode itself does not specify an encoding type; however, there are several standards for encoding Unicode. The .NET Framework uses Unicode UTF-16 (Unicode Transformation Format, 16-bit encoding form) to represent characters. In some cases, the .NET Framework uses UTF-8 internally. The *System.Text* namespace provides classes that allow you to encode and decode characters. *System.Text* encoding support includes the following encodings:

- **Unicode UTF-32 encoding** Unicode UTF-32 encoding represents Unicode characters as sequences of 32-bit integers. You can use the *UTF32Encoding* class to convert characters to and from UTF-32 encoding.

- **Unicode UTF-16 encoding** Unicode UTF-16 encoding represents Unicode characters as sequences of 16-bit integers. You can use the *UnicodeEncoding* class to convert characters to and from UTF-16 encoding.

- **Unicode UTF-8 encoding** Unicode UTF-8 uses 8-bit, 16-bit, 24-bit, and up to 48-bit encoding. Values 0 through 127 use 8-bit encoding and exactly match ASCII values, providing some degree of interoperability. Values from 128 through 2047 use 16-bit encoding and provide support for Latin, Greek, Cyrillic, Hebrew, and Arabic alphabets. Values 2048 through 65535 use 24-bit encoding for Chinese, Japanese, Korean, and other languages that require large numbers of values. You can use the *UTF8Encoding* class to convert characters to and from UTF-8 encoding.

- **ASCII encoding** ASCII encoding encodes the Latin alphabet as single 7-bit ASCII characters. Because this encoding only supports character values from U+0000 through U+007F, in most cases it is inadequate for internationalized applications. You can use the *ASCIIEncoding* class to convert characters to and from ASCII encoding.

- **ANSI/ISO Encodings** The *System.Text.Encoding* class provides support for a wide range of ANSI/ISO encodings.

MORE INFO Unicode

For more information about Unicode, see The Unicode Standard at *http://www.unicode.org*

Using the Encoding Class

You can use the *System.Text.Encoding.GetEncoding* method to return an encoding object for a specified encoding. You can use the *Encoding.GetBytes* method to convert a Unicode string to its byte representation in a specified encoding. The following code example uses the *Encoding.GetEncoding* method to create a target encoding object for the Korean code page. The code calls the *Encoding.GetBytes* method to convert a Unicode string to its byte representation in the Korean encoding. The code then displays the byte representations of the strings in the Korean code page.

```
' VB
' Get Korean encoding
Dim e As Encoding = Encoding.GetEncoding("Korean")

' Convert ASCII bytes to Korean encoding
Dim encoded As Byte()
encoded = e.GetBytes("Hello, world!")

' Display the byte codes
Dim i As Integer
For i = 0 To encoded.Length - 1
    Console.WriteLine("Byte {0}: {1}", i, encoded(i))
Next i
```

```
// C#
// Get Korean encoding
Encoding e = Encoding.GetEncoding("Korean");

// Convert ASCII bytes to Korean encoding
byte[] encoded;
encoded = e.GetBytes("Hello, world!");

// Display the byte codes
for (int i = 0; i < encoded.Length; i++)
    Console.WriteLine("Byte {0}: {1}", i, encoded[i]);
```

This code sample demonstrates how to convert text to a different code page; however, you would not normally convert an English-language phrase into a different code page. In most code pages, the code points 0 through 127 represent the same ASCII characters. This allows for continuity and legacy code. The code points 128 through 255 differ significantly between code pages. Because the sample code translated the ASCII phrase, "Hello, world!" (which consists entirely of ASCII bytes falling in the range of code points from 0 through 127), the translated bytes in the Korean code page exactly match the original ASCII bytes.

MORE INFO   Code pages

For a list of all supported code pages, see the "Encoding Class" topic at *http://msdn2.microsoft.com/en-us/library/system.text.encoding(VS.80).aspx.*

How to Examine Supported Code Pages

To examine all supported code pages in the .NET Framework, call *Encoding.GetEncodings*. This method returns an array of *EncodingInfo* objects. The following code sample displays the number, official name, and friendly name of the .NET Framework code bases:

```
' VB
Dim ei As EncodingInfo() = Encoding.GetEncodings
For Each e As EncodingInfo In ei
    Console.WriteLine("{0}: {1}, {2}", e.CodePage, e.Name, e.DisplayName)
Next

// C#
EncodingInfo[] ei = Encoding.GetEncodings();
foreach (EncodingInfo e in ei)
    Console.WriteLine("{0}: {1}, {2}", e.CodePage, e.Name, e.DisplayName);
```

How to Specify the Encoding Type when Writing a File

To specify the encoding type when writing a file, use an overloaded *Stream* constructor that accepts an *Encoding* object. For example, the following code sample creates several files with different encoding types:

```vb
' VB
Dim swUtf7 As StreamWriter = New StreamWriter("utf7.txt", False, Encoding.UTF7)
swUtf7.WriteLine("Hello, World!")
swUtf7.Close

Dim swUtf8 As StreamWriter = New StreamWriter("utf8.txt", False, Encoding.UTF8)
swUtf8.WriteLine("Hello, World!")
swUtf8.Close

Dim swUtf16 As StreamWriter = New StreamWriter("utf16.txt", False, Encoding.Unicode)
swUtf16.WriteLine("Hello, World!")
swUtf16.Close

Dim swUtf32 As StreamWriter = New StreamWriter("utf32.txt", False, Encoding.UTF32)
swUtf32.WriteLine("Hello, World!")
swUtf32.Close
```

```csharp
// C#
StreamWriter swUtf7 = new StreamWriter("utf7.txt", false, Encoding.UTF7);
swUtf7.WriteLine("Hello, World!");
swUtf7.Close();

StreamWriter swUtf8 = new StreamWriter("utf8.txt", false, Encoding.UTF8);
swUtf8.WriteLine("Hello, World!");
swUtf8.Close();

StreamWriter swUtf16 = new StreamWriter("utf16.txt", false, Encoding.Unicode);
swUtf16.WriteLine("Hello, World!");
swUtf16.Close();

StreamWriter swUtf32 = new StreamWriter("utf32.txt", false, Encoding.UTF32);
swUtf32.WriteLine("Hello, World!");
swUtf32.Close();
```

If you run the previous code sample, you will notice that the four different files each have different file sizes: the UTF-7 file is 19 bytes, the UTF-8 file is 18 bytes, the UTF-16 file is 32 bytes, and the UTF-32 file is 64 bytes. If you open each of the files in Notepad, the UTF-8 and UTF-16 files display correctly. However, the UTF-7 and UTF-32 files display incorrectly. All the files were correctly encoded; however, Notepad is not capable of correctly reading UTF-7 and UTF-32 files.

NOTE   Choosing an encoding type

If you are not sure which encoding type to use when creating a file, simply accept the default by not specifying an encoding type. The .NET Framework will choose UTF-16.

How to Specify the Encoding Type when Reading a File

Typically, you do not need to specify an encoding type when reading a file. The .NET Framework automatically decodes most common encoding types. However, you can specify an encoding type using an overloaded *Stream* constructor, as the following sample shows:

```
' VB
Dim fn As String = "file.txt"
Dim sw As StreamWriter = New StreamWriter(fn, False, Encoding.UTF7)
sw.WriteLine("Hello, World!")
sw.Close

Dim sr As StreamReader = New StreamReader(fn, Encoding.UTF7)
Console.WriteLine(sr.ReadToEnd)
sr.Close
```

```
// C#
string fn = "file.txt";
StreamWriter sw = new StreamWriter(fn, false, Encoding.UTF7);
sw.WriteLine("Hello, World!");
sw.Close();

StreamReader sr = new StreamReader(fn, Encoding.UTF7);
Console.WriteLine(sr.ReadToEnd());
sr.Close();
```

Unlike most Unicode encoding types, the unusual UTF-7 encoding type in the previous code sample does require you to explicitly declare it when reading a file. If you run the following code, which does not specify the UTF-7 encoding type when reading the file, it will be read incorrectly and will display the wrong result:

```
' VB
Dim fn As String = "file.txt"
Dim sw As StreamWriter = New StreamWriter(fn, False, Encoding.UTF7)
sw.WriteLine("Hello, World!")
sw.Close

Dim sr As StreamReader = New StreamReader(fn)
Console.WriteLine(sr.ReadToEnd)
sr.Close
```

```
// C#
string fn = "file.txt";
```

```
StreamWriter sw = new StreamWriter(fn, false, Encoding.UTF7);
sw.WriteLine("Hello, World!");
sw.Close();

StreamReader sr = new StreamReader(fn);
Console.WriteLine(sr.ReadToEnd());
sr.Close();
```

Lab: Read and Write an Encoded File

In this lab, you will convert a text file from one encoding type to another. If you encounter a problem completing an exercise, the completed projects are available on the companion CD in the Code folder.

▶ **Exercise: Convert a Text File to a Different Encoding Type**

In this exercise, you convert a text file to UTF-7.

1. Use Visual Studio 2005 to create a blank console application.

2. Write code to read the C:\boot.ini file, and then write it to a file named boot-utf7.txt using the UTF-7 encoding type. For example, the following code (which requires the *System.IO* namespace) would work:

```
' VB
Dim sr As StreamReader = New StreamReader("C:\boot.ini")
Dim sw As StreamWriter = New StreamWriter("boot-utf7.txt", False, Encoding.UTF7)
sw.WriteLine(sr.ReadToEnd)
sw.Close()
sr.Close()

// C#
StreamReader sr = new StreamReader(@"C:\boot.ini");
StreamWriter sw = new StreamWriter("boot-utf7.txt", false, Encoding.UTF7);
sw.WriteLine(sr.ReadToEnd());
sw.Close();
sr.Close();
```

3. Run your application, and open the boot-utf7.txt file in Notepad. If the file was translated correctly, Notepad will display it with some invalid characters because Notepad does not support the UTF-7 encoding type.

Lesson Summary

■ Encoding standards map byte values to characters. ASCII is one of the oldest, most widespread encoding standards; however, it provides very limited support for non-English languages. Today, various Unicode encoding standards provide multilingual support.

- The *System.Text.Encoding* class provides static methods for encoding and decoding text.

- Call *Encoding.GetEncodings* to retrieve a list of supported code pages.

- To specify the encoding type when writing a file, use an overloaded *Stream* constructor that accepts an *Encoding* object.

- You do not typically need to specify an encoding type when reading a file. However, you can specify an encoding type by using an overloaded *Stream* constructor that accepts an *Encoding* object.

Lesson Review

You can use the following questions to test your knowledge of the information in Lesson 2, "Encoding and Decoding." The questions are also available on the companion CD if you prefer to review them in electronic form.

NOTE   Answers

Answers to these questions and explanations of why each answer choice is right or wrong are located in the "Answers" section at the end of the book.

---

1. Which of the following encoding types would yield the largest file size?

    A. UTF-32

    B. UTF-16

    C. UTF-8

    D. ASCII

2. Which of the following encoding types support Chinese? (Choose all that apply.)

    A. UTF-32

    B. UTF-16

    C. UTF-8

    D. ASCII

3. You need to decode a file encoded in ASCII. Which of the following decoding types would yield correct results? (Choose all that apply.)

    A. Encoding.UTF32

    B. Encoding.UTF16

    C. Encoding.UTF8

    D. Encoding.UTF7

4. You are writing an application that generates summary reports nightly. These reports will be viewed by executives in your Korea office and must contain Korean characters. Which of the following encoding types should you use?

    A. iso-2022-kr

    B. x-EBCDIC-KoreanExtended

    C. x-mac-korean

    D. UTF-16.

Chapter Review

To further practice and reinforce the skills you learned in this chapter, you can perform the following tasks:

- Review the chapter summary.
- Review the list of key terms introduced in this chapter.
- Complete the case scenarios. These scenarios set up real-world situations involving the topics of this chapter and ask you to create a solution.
- Complete the suggested practices.
- Take a practice test.

Chapter Summary

- Regular expressions have roots in UNIX and Perl, and they can seem complicated and unnatural to .NET Framework developers. However, regular expressions are extremely efficient and useful for validating text input, extracting text data, and reformatting data.
- In the past decade, the most commonly used encoding standard for text files has gradually shifted from ASCII to Unicode. Unicode itself supports several different encoding standards. While the .NET Framework uses the UTF-16 encoding standard by default, you can specify other encoding standards to meet interoperability requirements.

Key Terms

Do you know what these key terms mean? You can check your answers by looking up the terms in the glossary at the end of the book.

- code page
- regular expression
- Unicode

Case Scenarios

In the following case scenarios, you will apply what you've learned about how to validate input using regular expressions and how to process text files with different encoding types. You can find answers to these questions in the "Answers" section at the end of this book.

Case Scenario 1: Validating Input

Your organization, Northwind Traders, is creating a Web-based application to allow customers to enter their own contact information into your database. As a new employee, you are assigned a simple task: create the front-end interface and prepare the user input to be stored in a database. You begin by interviewing several company personnel and reviewing the technical requirements.

Interviews

Following is a list of company personnel interviewed and their statements:

- **IT Manager**   "This is your first assignment, so I'm starting you out easy. Slap together a Web page that takes user input. That should take you, what, five minutes?"

- **Database Developer**   "Just drop the input into strings named "*companyName*", "*contactName*", and "*phoneNumber*". It's going into a SQL back-end database, but I'll write that code after you're done. Oh, the "*companyName*" can't be longer than 40 characters, "*contactName*" is limited to 30 characters, and "*phoneNumber*" is limited to 24 characters."

- **Chief Security Officer**   "This is not as easy an assignment as it seems. This page is going to be available to the unwashed public on the Internet, and there are lots of black hats out there. We've gotten some negative attention in the press recently for our international trade practices. Specifically, we've irritated a couple of groups with close ties to hacker organizations. Just do your best to clean up the input, because you're going to see some malicious junk thrown at you."

Technical Requirements

Create an ASP.NET application that accepts the following pieces of information from users and validates it rigorously:

- Company name
- Contact name
- Phone number

Questions

Answer the following questions for your manager:

1. How can you constrain the input before you write any code?
2. How can you further constrain the input by writing code?

Case Scenario 2: Processing Data from a Legacy Computer

You are an application developer working for Humongous Insurance. Recently, management decided to begin the process of migrating from a legacy system (nicknamed "Mainframe") to custom-built .NET Framework applications. As part of the kickoff meeting for the migration project, your manager asks you questions about how you will handle various challenges.

Questions

Answer the following questions for your manager:

1. Mainframe stores its data in a database; however, the raw data itself isn't accessible to us unless we can find a programmer who knows how to write code for that system. We can output the data we need in text-based reports, however. Is it possible to parse the text reports to extract just the data, without the labels and formatting? How would you do that, and which classes and methods would you use?

2. Mainframe's reports are in ASCII format. Can you handle that ASCII? If so, how?

Suggested Practices

To help you successfully master the exam objectives presented in this chapter, complete the following tasks.

Enhance the Text Handling Capabilities of a .NET Framework Application, and Search, Modify, and Control Text Within a .NET Framework Application by Using Regular Expressions

For this task, you should complete at least Practices 1 through 4. If you want a better understanding of how to specify encoding types, complete Practice 5 as well.

- **Practice 1** Write a console application that reads your C:\boot.ini file and displays just the timeout.

- **Practice 2** Write a console application that processes your %windir%\WindowsUpdate.log file and displays the time, date, and exit code for any rows that list an exit code.

- **Practice 3** Write a Windows Forms application that accepts a name, address, and phone number from a user. Add a Submit button that uses regular expressions to validate the input.

- **Practice 4** Write a console application that reads the %windir%\Windows-Update.log file, changes the date format to mm-dd-yy, and writes the output to a second file.

- **Practice 5** Write a console application with a method that reads the %windir%\WindowsUpdate.log file and writes the output to a second file using an encoding type provided in a parameter. Compare the file sizes of each encoding type.

Take a Practice Test

The practice tests on this book's companion CD offer many options. For example, you can test yourself on just one exam objective, or you can test yourself on all the 70-536 certification exam content. You can set up the test so that it closely simulates the experience of taking a certification exam, or you can set it up in study mode so that you can look at the correct answers and explanations after you answer each question.

MORE INFO Practice tests

For details about all the practice test options available, see the "How to Use the Practice Tests" section in this book's Introduction.

Chapter 4
Collections and Generics

Collections—classes used for grouping and managing related objects that allow you to iterate over those objects—are one of the most basic tools in any developer's toolchest. They allow you to store, look up, and iterate over collections of objects. Collections take over where arrays end. Arrays are useful, but without the richness of collections most applications would never get off the ground.

Exam objectives in this chapter:
- Manage a group of associated data in a .NET Framework application by using collections. (Refer *System.Collections* namespace)
  - *ArrayList* class
  - Collection interfaces
  - Iterators
  - *Hashtable* class
  - *CollectionBase* class and *ReadOnlyCollectionBase* class
  - *DictionaryBase* class and *DictionaryEntry* class
  - *Comparer* class
  - *Queue* class
  - *SortedList* class
  - *BitArray* class
  - *Stack* class
- Manage data in a .NET Framework application by using specialized collections. (Refer *System.Collections.Specialized* namespace)
  - Specialized *String* classes
  - Specialized *Dictionary*
  - *NameValueCollection* class
  - *CollectionsUtil*
  - *BitVector32* structure and *BitVector32.Section* structure

■ Improve type safety and application performance in a .NET Framework application by using generic collections. (Refer *System.Collections.Generic* namespace)

    ❑ Collection.Generic interfaces

    ❑ Generic *Dictionary*

    ❑ Generic *Comparer* class and Generic *EqualityComparer* class

    ❑ Generic *KeyValuePair* structure

    ❑ Generic *List* class, Generic List.Enumerator structure, and Generic *SortedList* class

    ❑ Generic *Queue* class and Generic Queue.Enumerator structure

    ❑ Generic *SortedDictionary* class

    ❑ Generic *LinkedList*

    ❑ Generic Stack class and Generic Stack.Enumerator structure

Lessons in this chapter:

Before You Begin

To complete the lessons in this chapter, you should be familiar with Microsoft Visual Basic or C# and comfortable with the following tasks:

■ Create a console application in Microsoft Visual Studio using Visual Basic or C#.

■ Add references to system class libraries to a project.

Real World

Shawn Wildermuth

Collections are the bedrock of most applications you will write as a developer. Practically every application I have ever developed has used collections extensively. For example, I have used collections to store lists of e-mail messages that I am ready to process in an e-mail system I wrote some years ago.

Lesson 1: Collecting Data Items

Computers are naturally good at dealing with large amounts of data. In your daily work as a developer, you will find it necessary to store data in an orderly way. The .NET Framework supports dealing with data in this way by providing a wide range of collections to store your data in. For every collection job, the .NET Framework supplies a solution.

After this lesson, you will be able to:

- Create a collection.
- Add and remove items from a collection.
- Iterate over items in a collection

Estimated lesson time: 15 minutes

Types of Collections

The .NET Framework's *System.Collections* namespace supports several types of collections. These collections are classes that support the gathering of information in an orderly way. Your challenge will be to discern the right collection to use in a specific instance. Table 4-1 shows the most frequently used collections in the *System.Collections* namespace and what they are used for.

Table 4-1   Types of Collections

Name	Description
ArrayList	A simple resizeable, index-based collection of objects
SortedList	A sorted collection of name/value pairs of objects
Queue	A first-in, first-out collection of objects
Stack	A last-in, first-out collection of objects
Hashtable	A collection of name/value pairs of objects that allows retrieval by name
BitArray	A compact collection of *Boolean* values
StringCollection	A simple resizeable collection of strings
StringDictionary	A collection of name/values pairs of strings that allows retrieval by name

Table 4-1   **Types of Collections**

Name	Description
ListDictionary	An efficient collection to store small lists of objects
HybridDictionary	A collection that uses a *ListDictionary* for storage when the number of items in the collection is small, and then migrates the items to a *Hashtable* for large collections
NameValueCollection	A collection of name/values pairs of strings that allows retrieval by name or index

All these collections are used in a variety of situations. The first four lessons of this chapter will explain how to use these collections, as well as when to use which collection. For the balance of Lesson 1, we will use the *ArrayList* collection to store and retrieve objects. *ArrayList* is the most basic of all the collections.

Adding and Removing Items

The *ArrayList* class is a simple, unordered container for objects of any type. Adding items to and removing items from the collection is very straightforward.

ArrayList supports two methods for adding items to the collection: *Add* and *AddRange*. The *Add* method allows you to add a single object to the collection. You can use the *Add* method to store any object in .NET. Here are some examples of code that adds objects of different types to an *ArrayList*:

```
' VB
Dim coll As New ArrayList()

' Add individual items to the collection
Dim s As String = "Hello"
coll.Add(s)
coll.Add("hi")
coll.Add(50)
coll.Add(New Object())

// C#
ArrayList coll = new ArrayList();

// Add individual items to the collection
string s = "Hello";
coll.Add(s);
coll.Add("hi");
coll.Add(50);
coll.Add(new object());
```

Notice that you can add objects that exist as variables or are created inline to the *Add* method. You can even add value types (such as the number '*50*' in the preceding example). Value types can be stored in collections, but first they need to be wrapped in an object reference, a process referred to as *boxing*.

MORE INFO Boxing

To understand boxing better, see Eric Gunnerson's *"Nice Box. What's in it?"* article from MSDN Online: *http://msdn.microsoft.com/library/default.asp?url=/library/en-us/dncscol/html/csharp02152001.asp*

In addition to supporting the *Add* method, the *ArrayList* supports the *AddRange* method to add a range of items, usually from an array or another collection. The following code provides an example:

```
' VB
Dim anArray() As String = {"more", "or", "less"}
coll.AddRange(anArray)

Dim anotherArray() As Object = {New Object(), New ArrayList()}
coll.AddRange(anotherArray)

// C#
string[] anArray =
    new string[] { "more", "or", "less" };
coll.AddRange(anArray);

object[] anotherArray =
    new object[] { new object(), new ArrayList() };
coll.AddRange(anotherArray);
```

The *AddRange* method supports adding a range of items from any object that supports the *ICollection* interface (which includes all arrays, *ArrayList* objects, and most collections discussed in this chapter).

The *Add* and *AddRange* methods add items to the end of the collection. Because Array-Lists are dynamic collections, they also support inserting objects into them at specific positions. To accomplish this task, an *ArrayList* also supports the *Insert* and *InsertRange* methods. The following code provides an example:

```
' VB
coll.Insert(3, "Hey All")

Dim moreStrings() As String = {"goodnight", "see ya"}
coll.InsertRange(4, moreStrings)
```

```
// C#
coll.Insert(3, "Hey All");

string[] moreStrings =
    new string[] { "goodnight", "see ya" };
coll.InsertRange(4, moreStrings);
```

In addition to the *Insert* and *Add* methods, you can also use the indexer to set a specific object in the collection, as shown in the following code:

```
' VB
coll(3) = "Hey All"
```

```
// C#
Coll[3] = "Hey All";
```

Note that using the indexer is not the same as using the *Insert* method, as it sets the item at that specific location in the collection by overwriting the old object at that position rather than just inserting an object.

Finally, the *ArrayList* supports removing items from the collection. Three methods support removing items: *Remove*, *RemoveAt*, and *RemoveRange*. The *Remove* method will remove a specific object from the collection. There is no indication if *Remove* failed to find the item to remove. In other words, if the item is not found in the collection, *Remove* will return without throwing an exception. The *Remove* method is demonstrated in the following example:

```
' VB
coll.Add("Hello")
coll.Remove("Hello")
```

```
// C#
coll.Add("Hello");
coll.Remove("Hello");
```

In contrast, the *RemoveAt* method removes an item at a particular index within the collection. In addition, the *RemoveRange* method supports removing a range of indexes from the collection all at once. Both methods are demonstrated here:

```
' VB
' Removes first item in ArrayList
coll.RemoveAt(0)
' Removes first four items in ArrayList
coll.RemoveRange(0, 4)
```

```
// C#
// Removes first item in ArrayList
coll.RemoveAt(0);
// Removes first four items in ArrayList
coll.RemoveRange(0, 4);
```

The *ArrayList* class also supports some other methods that are useful in adding objects to and removing objects from the collection:

- The *Clear* method is used to empty a collection of all its items.

- The *IndexOf* method is used to determine the index of a particular item in the collection.

- The *Contains* method is used to test whether a particular object exists in the collection.

By using these methods, you can perform more complex adding and removing of items within the collection, as shown in this example:

```vb
' VB
Dim myString As String = "My String"
If coll.Contains(myString) Then
    Dim index As Integer = coll.IndexOf(myString)
    coll.RemoveAt(index)
Else
    coll.Clear()
End If
```

```csharp
// C#
string myString = "My String";
if (coll.Contains(myString))
{
    int index = coll.IndexOf(myString);
    coll.RemoveAt(index);
}
else
{
    coll.Clear();
}
```

You can now manipulate the objects in the collection, but how do you get them out of the collection?

Iterating Over Items

A collection is not very useful unless you can walk through the items in it. Luckily, the *ArrayList* (like most collections in this chapter) supports several ways to iterate over its contents. The *ArrayList* supports a numeric indexer that allows you to write simple code, such as the following, to show the items in order (much like you can with an array):

```vb
' VB
Dim x As Integer
For  x = 0 To coll.Count - 1  Step + 1
    Console.WriteLine(coll(x))
Next
```

```
// C#
for (int x = 0; x < coll.Count; ++x)
{
    Console.WriteLine(coll[x]);
}
```

By using the *ArrayList*'s *Count* property and indexer, you can simply walk through the collection. The *ArrayList* also supports the *IEnumerable* interface to allow the use of an *Enumerator* to access the list. The *IEnumerable* interface dictates that the class supports the *GetEnumerator* method that returns an *IEnumerator* interface. In turn, the *IEnumerator* interface provides a simple mechanism for iterating in a forward direction. Details of the *IEnumerator* interface can be seen in Table 4-2 (which shows properties) and 4-3 (which shows methods).

Table 4-2   *IEnumerator* Properties

Name	Description
Current	Gets the current item in the collection being enumerated

Table 4-3   *IEnumerator* Methods

Name	Description
MoveNext	Moves to the next item in the collection. The return value of the method is used to determine whether the enumerator has reached the end of the collection.
Reset	Sets the enumerator to before the first item in the collection to allow *MoveNext* to be called to get the first item in the collection.

Using the *IEnumerator* interface allows you to walk through the list of objects in an ordered way, as seen in this example:

```
' VB
Dim enumerator As IEnumerator = coll.GetEnumerator()
While enumerator.MoveNext()
    Console.WriteLine(enumerator.Current)
End While

// C#
IEnumerator enumerator = coll.GetEnumerator();
while (enumerator.MoveNext())
{
    Console.WriteLine(enumerator.Current);
}
```

This example shows the simple pattern of getting an enumerator from the collection and using the *MoveNext* call to walk through the list. Accessing the *Current* property from the enumerator returns the current item in the list.

Both Visual Basic and C# support a language-level construct for doing this same enumeration in a more simplified manner: *foreach*. By using the *foreach* construct, you can enumerate a whole list, as the following example shows:

```vb
' VB
For Each item As Object In coll
    Console.WriteLine(item)
Next item
```

```csharp
// C#
foreach (object item in coll)
{
    Console.WriteLine(item);
}
```

The *foreach* construct specifies that you are enumerating the *coll* object and creating an *item* object for each item in the collection. This construct relies on the *IEnumerable* interface. It can be used on any collection that supports the *IEnumerable* interface. One of the benefits of this iteration scheme is that if you have a collection of some known types, you can specify the type in the *foreach* construct to save some time in casting from objects, as you can see in this code snippet:

```vb
' VB
Dim newColl As New ArrayList()
newColl.Add("Hello")
newColl.Add("Goodbye")

For Each item as String In  newColl
    Console.WriteLine(item)
Next item
```

```csharp
// C#
ArrayList newColl = new ArrayList();
newColl.Add("Hello");
newColl.Add("Goodbye");

foreach (string item in newColl)
{
    Console.WriteLine(item);
}
```

Because you know that all the items in the collection are strings, you can specify *string* as the type of the items to iterate over. If the collection had an item that was not a string, the .NET Framework would throw a casting exception.

Consistent Interfaces in Collections

As mentioned in the previous section, the *IEnumerable* interface is used to provide a common way to iterate over a collection. In addition, the .NET Framework supports another important interface that should be implemented in the application programming interface (API) of a collection class. This interface is called the *ICollection* interface, and it derives from the *IEnumerable* interface. This means that every collection that supports the *ICollection* interface must also support the *IEnumerable* interface.

The purpose of this interface is to ensure that every collection supports a common way of getting the items in a collection, as well as a way to copy the collection to an *Array* object. The *ICollection* interface's most important properties and methods are shown in Table 4-4 and Table 4-5, respectively.

Table 4-4   *ICollection* **Properties**

Name	Description
Count	Gets the number of items currently in the collection
IsSynchronized	Gets an indicator of whether the collection is thread safe
SyncRoot	Gets an object that can be used to synchronize the collection

Table 4-5   *ICollection* **Methods**

Name	Description
CopyTo	Copies the contents of a collection into an *Array*

For simple list collections (such as *ArrayList*), the .NET Framework supports another interface that is used to expose lists of items. This interface is called the *IList* interface and derives directly from the *ICollection* interface. If a class supports the *IList* interface, it must also support the *ICollection* and *IEnumerable* interfaces. This consistency of interfaces simplifies the way we work with collections in general.

Most of the *IList* interface should look familiar to you at this point. In the "Adding and Removing Items" section earlier in the chapter, most of these properties and methods were covered as part of the *ArrayList* class. The *IList* interface's most important properties and methods are shown in Table 4-6 and Table 4-7, respectively.

Table 4-6 *IList* **Properties**

Name	Description
IsFixedSize	Gets an indicator of whether this collection can be resized
IsReadOnly	Gets an indicator of whether a collection can be changed
Item	Gets or sets the item at a specific index in the collection

Table 4-7 *IList* **Methods**

Name	Description
Add	Adds an item to the collection
Clear	Clears the collection of all items
Contains	Tests whether a specific item is contained in the collection
IndexOf	Finds an item in the collection, and returns the index of the item
Insert	Adds an item at a specific index in the collection
Remove	Removes the first occurrence of the specified object in the collection
RemoveAt	Removes an item at a specific index in the collection

Sorting Items

The *ArrayList* supports a method to sort a collection's items. To sort items within an *ArrayList*, simply call the *Sort* method of the *ArrayList* like so:

```
' VB
coll.Sort()
```

```
// C#
coll.Sort();
```

The *Sort* method works by using the *Comparer* class to do the comparison. The *Comparer* class is a default implementation that supports the *IComparer* interface. This interface dictates that you implement a single method called *Compare* that takes two objects (for example, *a* and *b*) and returns an integer that represents the result of the comparison. The result is interpreted as shown in Table 4-8.

Table 4-8 *Compare* Results

Value	Condition
Less than zero	The left-hand object is less than the right-hand object.
Zero	The objects are equal.
More than zero	The left-hand object is more than the right-hand object.

The *Sort* method allows you to specify an *IComparer* object to use instead of the default. For example, instead of using the *Comparer* class you could specify a case-insensitive comparison using the *CaseInsensitiveComparer* like so:

```
' VB
coll.Sort(new CaseInsensitiveComparer())
```

```
// C#
coll.Sort(new CaseInsensitiveComparer());
```

Writing your own comparer is relatively simple because it only requires you to implement the *Compare* method of the *IComparer* interface. For example, if you wanted to do the comparison in reverse (resulting in a collection sorted in descending order), you could write a quick comparer class like so:

```
' VB
Public Class DescendingComparer
    Implements IComparer

    Private _comparer As New CaseInsensitiveComparer()

        Public Function Compare(x As Object, y As Object) As Integer _
            Implements IComparer

        ' Reversing the compared objects to
        ' get descending comparisons
        Return _comparer.Compare(y, x)

    End Function
End Class
```

```
// C#
public class DescendingComparer : IComparer
{
    CaseInsensitiveComparer _comparer = new CaseInsensitiveComparer();

    public int Compare(object x, object y)
    {
        // Reversing the compared objects to
        // get descending comparisons
        return _comparer.Compare(y, x);
    }
}
```

This class implements the *IComparer* interface. In our *Compare* method, we are simply reversing the left-hand and right-hand comparisons to get the comparison in the opposite (or descending) order.

Then we can use this new comparison object in sorting our collection in descending order:

```
' VB
coll.Sort(new DescendingComparer())
```

```
// C#
coll.Sort(new DescendingComparer());
```

Lab: Sort a Table of Strings

In this lab, you will create a collection of strings and sort them. If you encounter a problem completing an exercise, the completed projects are available on the companion CD in the Code folder.

▶ **Exercise 1: Create a Collection of Strings and Sort Them**

In this exercise, you will create a new console application that creates a simple collection, adds several strings, and displays them in the console window. You will then sort the collection and show the items in the collection in the console window in the new order.

1. Create a new console application called BasicCollection.

2. In the main code file, include (or import for Visual Basic) the *System.Collections* namespace.

3. In the *Main* method of the project, create a new instance of the *ArrayList* class.

4. Add four strings to the new collection, "*First*", "*Second*", "*Third*", and "*Fourth*".

5. Iterate over the collection, and show each item in the console window on a separate line.

6. Next call the *Sort* method on the collection to sort its items.

7. Iterate over the collection again, and show each item in the console window to confirm that the order is now different. Your resulting code might look something like this:

```
' VB
Imports System.Collections

Class Program
```

```
        Public Overloads Shared Sub Main(ByVal args() As String)

            Dim myList As New ArrayList()
            myList.Add("First")
            myList.Add("Second")
            myList.Add("Third")
            myList.Add("Fourth")

            For Each item as String In myList
              Console.WriteLine("Unsorted: {0}", item)
            Next item

            ' Sort using the standard comparer
            myList.Sort()

            For Each item as String In myList
              Console.WriteLine("  Sorted: {0}", item)
            Next item

        End Sub
    End Class

    // C#
    using System.Collections;

    class Program
    {
        static void Main(string[] args)
        {
            ArrayList myList = new ArrayList();
            myList.Add("First");
            myList.Add("Second");
            myList.Add("Third");
            myList.Add("Fourth");

            foreach (string item in myList)
            {
                Console.WriteLine("Unsorted: {0}", item);
            }

            // Sort using the standard comparer
            myList.Sort();

            foreach (string item in myList)
            {
                Console.WriteLine("  Sorted: {0}", item);
            }
        }
    }
```

8. Build the project, and resolve any errors. Verify that the console application success-
    fully shows items in the console window, both unsorted at first and then sorted
    alphabetically .

Lesson Summary

- The .NET Framework supports a variety of collection classes that can be used in different circumstances.

- The *ArrayList* is a simple collection of unordered items.

- The *Add* and *AddRange* methods of the *ArrayList* are used to add items to an *ArrayList*.

- The *Insert* and *InsertRange* methods of the *ArrayList* are used to insert items into specific places in a collection.

- The *Remove*, *RemoveAt*, and *RemoveRange* methods of the *ArrayList* are used to delete items from a collection.

- The indexer of the *ArrayList* can be used to iterate over a collection.

- The *IEnumerable* and *IEnumerator* interfaces can be used to enumerate through a collection as well.

- The *foreach* construct in Visual Basic and C# use the *IEnumerable* interface to concisely iterate over a collection.

Lesson Review

You can use the following questions to test your knowledge of the information in Lesson 1, "Collecting Data Items." The questions are also available on the companion CD if you prefer to review them in electronic form.

NOTE Answers

Answers to these questions and explanations of why each answer choice is right or wrong are located in the "Answers" section at the end of the book.

---

1. Which of the following *ArrayList* methods can be used to determine whether an item exists in the collection? (Choose all that apply.)

    A. *Remove*

    B. *Contains*

    C. *IndexOf*

    D. *Count*

2. What is the *Comparer* class used for? (Choose all that apply.)

    A. To compare two objects, usually for sorting

    B. To test whether two variables are referencing the same object

    C. To sort an *ArrayList* in the *ArrayList.Sort* method

    D. To provide a default implementation of the *IComparer* interface

Lesson 2: Working with Sequential Lists

Not all collections are created equal. At times, it makes more sense to deal with a list of objects as a sequential list of items rather than accessing them individually.

After this lesson, you will be able to:

- Create and use a first-in, first-out (FIFO) collection
- Create and use a last-in, first-out (LIFO) collection.

Estimated lesson time: 10 minutes

What Are Sequential Lists?

Often collections are simply a set of objects that need to be dealt with in an orderly way. For example, you might create a class that accepts objects to perform some work against. Depending on the specific requirements, you are likely to need to access the objects just one at a time and process them. Having access to items in the middle of the list has very little use for your class.

Instead of using a collection such as *ArrayList*, you can use two other classes exposed by the .NET Framework, whose job it is to store data as a list and simply allow access to those objects as they are needed. The *Queue* and *Stack* classes are meant to be used to store data in a sequential basis.

The *Queue* Class

The *Queue* class is a collection for dealing with first-in, first-out (FIFO) handling of sequential objects. The interface to the *Queue* class is very simple: it supports putting items into the queue and pulling them out.

The *Queue* class works quite differently than the *ArrayList* shown in Lesson 1. Specifically, accessing and removing items from the collection were two different operations in the *ArrayList*. The *Queue* combines these operations in the *Dequeue* method. The operations are combined primarily because the *Queue* class is meant to be used to create lists of objects to work with in some way. As its name suggests, the *Queue* treats objects like customers in line at the bank. It cares only about who is next and where to add people at the end of the line.

The most important properties and methods of the *Queue* class are shown in Table 4-9 and Table 4-10, respectively.

Table 4-9 *Queue* Properties

Name	Description
Count	Gets the number of items in the queue

Table 4-10 *Queue* Methods

Name	Description
Dequeue	Retrieves an item from the front of the queue, removing it at the same time
Enqueue	Adds an item to the end of the queue
Peek	Retrieves the first item from the queue without actually removing it

Working with the *Queue* class is very straightforward. Once you have an instance of the class, you can use the *Enqueue* method to add items to the queue and the *Dequeue* method to remove items from the list, as demonstrated in this short example:

```
' VB
Dim q As New Queue()
q.Enqueue("An item")
Console.WriteLine(q.Dequeue())
```

```
// C#
Queue q = new Queue();
q.Enqueue("An item");
Console.WriteLine(q.Dequeue());
```

The *Queue* class allows you to add duplicates items and null values, so you cannot test the result of the *Dequeue* or *Peek* method to see whether the *Queue* is empty. To do that, you can check the *Count* property to see whether the collection is empty. For example, if you add items to the *Queue* and want to remove them and show them in the console, you could write code like the following:

```
' VB
Dim q As New Queue()

q.Enqueue("First")
q.Enqueue("Second")
q.Enqueue("Third")
q.Enqueue("Fourth")

While q.Count > 0
  Console.WriteLine(q.Dequeue())
End While
```

```
// C#
Queue q = new Queue();

q.Enqueue("First");
q.Enqueue("Second");
q.Enqueue("Third");
q.Enqueue("Fourth");

while (q.Count > 0)
{
    Console.WriteLine(q.Dequeue());
}
```

Because the *Queue* is a FIFO collection, the preceding example will produce the following display order in the console window:

```
First
Second
Third
Fourth
```

There are times when being able to look at the next item without actually removing it is a good idea. Imagine if you had some code that could work with certain types of objects. If you were to *Dequeue* it and then find out that someone else had to handle it, you could put it back into the queue, but it would lose its place in line. That is where the *Peek* method comes in, as shown in this example:

```
' VB
If TypeOf q.Peek() Is String Then
    Console.WriteLine(q.Dequeue())
End If
```

```
// C#
if (q.Peek() is String)
{
    Console.WriteLine(q.Dequeue());
}
```

At times, the type of sequential collection you need is not first-in, first-out, but last-in, first-out. That is where the *Stack* class comes in.

The *Stack* Class

In contrast to the *Queue* class, the *Stack* class is a last-in, first-out (LIFO) collection. The interface to the *Stack* class is also very simple: it supports pushing items into the stack and popping them out.

As you can probably guess from its name, the *Stack* class most closely exemplifies a stack of cards. As you take cards from the stack, you can pull a card off the top but not dig down into the stack to get a card. The most important properties and methods of the *Stack* class are shown in Table 4-11 and Table 4-12, respectively.

Table 4-11 *Stack* Properties

Name	Description
Count	Gets the number of items in the stack

Table 4-12 *Stack* Methods

Name	Description
Pop	Retrieves an item from the top of the stack, removing it at the same time
Push	Adds an item to the top of the stack
Peek	Retrieves the top item from the stack without removing it

Working with the *Stack* class is similar to working with the *Queue* class, but instead of enqueuing and dequeuing, you are pushing onto and popping off of the stack. Once you have an instance of the class, you use the *Push* method to add items to the stack and the *Pop* method to remove items from the stack, as shown in this short example:

```vb
' VB
Dim s as new Stack()
s.Push("An item")
Console.WriteLine(s.Pop())
```

```csharp
// C#
Stack s = new Stack();
s.Push("An item");
Console.WriteLine(s.Pop());
```

As with the *Queue* class, you can add duplicates and null values, so you cannot test the result of the *Pop* or *Peek* method to see whether the *Stack* is empty. For example, if you add items to the *Stack* and want to remove them and show them in the console, you could write code like the following:

```vb
' VB
Dim s As New Stack()

s.Push("First")
s.Push("Second")
s.Push("Third")
s.Push("Fourth")
```

```
While s.Count > 0
    Console.WriteLine(s.Pop())
End While

// C#
Stack s = new Stack();

s.Push("First");
s.Push("Second");
s.Push("Third");
s.Push("Fourth");

while (s.Count > 0)
{
    Console.WriteLine(s.Pop());
}
```

Because the *Stack* is a LIFO collection, the order of the results of this code are reversed from what we saw earlier in the *Queue* class example:

```
Fourth
Third
Second
First
```

Exam Tip Discerning a *Queue* from a *Stack* is simple if you think of them as their real-world counterparts. Queues are lines to the movie theatre; stacks are paperwork on your desk. You never get to go first when others are in line before you at a movie theatre, and you probably always grab the sheet on the top of a stack of papers.

Lab: Building FIFO and LIFO Lists

In this lab, you will create a queue and a stack and show their data to the console. If you encounter a problem completing an exercise, the completed projects are available on the companion CD in the Code folder.

▶ **Exercise 1: Create and Use a Queue**

In this exercise, you will create a queue, add items to it, and empty the queue to the console window.

1. Create a new console application called SequentialCollections.

2. In the main code file, include (or import for Visual Basic) the *System.Collections* namespace.

3. In the *Main* method of the project, create a new instance of the *Queue* class.

4. Add four strings to the new collection: *"First"*, *"Second"*, *"Third"*, and *"Fourth"*.

5. Empty the queue, one item at a time, using the *Count* property to test whether the collection is empty. Your resulting code might look something like this:

```vb
' VB
Imports System.Collections

Class Program

    Public Shared Sub Main(ByVal args() As String)

        Dim queue As New Queue()

        queue.Enqueue("First")
        queue.Enqueue("Second")
        queue.Enqueue("Third")
        queue.Enqueue("Fourth")

        While queue.Count > 0
            Dim obj As Object = queue.Dequeue()
          Console.WriteLine("From Queue: {0}", obj)
        End While

    End Sub
End Class
```

```csharp
// C#
using System.Collections;

class Program
{
    static void Main(string[] args)
    {
        Queue queue = new Queue();

        queue.Enqueue("First");
        queue.Enqueue("Second");
        queue.Enqueue("Third");
        queue.Enqueue("Fourth");

        while (queue.Count > 0)
        {
            object obj = queue.Dequeue();
            Console.WriteLine("From Queue: {0}", obj);
        }
    }
}
```

6. Build the project, and resolve any errors. Verify that the console application successfully runs and shows the items in the queue, in first-in, first-out order.

▶ **Exercise 2: Create and Use a Stack**

In this exercise, you will create a stack, add items to it, and empty the stack to the console window.

1. Open the console application you created in Exercise 1, called Sequential-Collections.

2. After the *Queue* code, create a new instance of the *Stack* class.

3. Add four strings to the stack: *"First"*, *"Second"*, *"Third"*, and *"Fourth"*.

4. Empty the queue, one item at a time, using the *Count* property to test whether the collection is empty. Your resulting code might look something like this:

```
' VB
Dim stack As New Stack()

stack.Push("First")
stack.Push("Second")
stack.Push("Third")
stack.Push("Fourth")

While stack.Count > 0
    Dim obj As Object = stack.Pop()
    Console.WriteLine("From Stack: {0}", obj)
End While

// C#
Stack stack = new Stack();

stack.Push("First");
stack.Push("Second");
stack.Push("Third");
stack.Push("Fourth");

while (stack.Count > 0)
{
    object obj = stack.Pop();
    Console.WriteLine("From Stack: {0}", obj);
}
```

5. Build the project, and resolve any errors. Verify that the console application successfully runs and shows that the items in the stack are in reverse order of the queue's items (that is, in last-in, first-out order).

Lesson Summary

- The .NET Framework supports the *Queue* and *Stack* classes to provide collections that represent sequential lists of items.

- The *Queue* is a first-in, first-out (FIFO) collection.

- The *Queue* class supports the *Enqueue* and *Dequeue* methods for adding and removing items from the collection.

- The *Stack* is a last-in, first-out (LIFO) collection.

- The *Stack* class supports the *Push* and *Pop* methods for adding and removing items, respectively, from the collection.

- Both sequential collection classes support *Peek* for viewing the next item in the collection without removing it.

Lesson Review

You can use the following questions to test your knowledge of the information in Lesson 2, "Working with Sequential Lists." The questions are also available on the companion CD if you prefer to review them in electronic form.

NOTE Answers

Answers to these questions and explanations of why each answer choice is right or wrong are located in the "Answers" section at the end of the book.

---

1. What does the *Dequeue* method of the *Queue* class do? (Choose all that apply.)

    A. Retrieves an item from the front of the collection

    B. Adds an item to the collection

    C. Removes the first item from the collection

    D. Clears the collection

2. In what order does a *Stack* retrieve items as you use its *Pop* method?

    A. Random order

    B. First-in, first-out

    C. Last-in, first-out

    D. Last-in, last-out

Lesson 3: Working with Dictionaries

At the other end of the spectrum from sequential lists are dictionaries. Dictionaries are collections that are meant to store lists of key/value pairs to allow lookup of values based on a key.

After this lesson, you will be able to:

- Use a *Hashtable* to create a simple list of unique items.
- Use a *SortedList* to sort a list of objects.
- Work with *DictionaryEntry* objects to store name/value pairs.
- Enumerate dictionaries and know how to use *DictionaryEntry*.
- Understand the *IEqualityComparison* interface to provide uniqueness to Hashtables.
- Use the *HybridDictionary* to store name/value pairs in a very efficient way.
- Use the *OrderedDictionary* to store name/value pairs in a way that preserves the order of adding them to the collection.

Estimated lesson time: 30 minutes

Using a *Dictionary*

The *Dictionary* classes supported by the .NET Framework are used to map a key to a value. Essentially, they exist to allow you to create lookup tables that can map arbitrary keys to arbitrary values. In the most basic case, the *Hashtable* class is used to do this mapping of key/value pairs. For example, assume that you needed to map e-mail addresses to the full name of some user. You could use a *Hashtable* to store this mapping, as seen in this code snippet:

```
' VB
Dim emailLookup As New Hashtable()

' Add method takes a key (first parameter)
' and a value (second parameter)
emailLookup.Add("sbishop@contoso.com", "Bishop, Scott")

' The indexer is functionally equivalent to Add
emailLookup("sbishop@contoso.com") = "Bishop, Scott"

// C#
Hashtable emailLookup = new Hashtable();
```

```
// Add method takes a key (first parameter)
// and a value (second parameter)
emailLookup.Add("sbishop@contoso.com", "Bishop, Scott");

// The indexer is functionally equivalent to Add
emailLookup["sbishop@contoso.com"] = "Bishop, Scott";
```

Unlike the previous types of collections, dictionaries always expect two pieces of information to add them to the collection: a key and a value. This example shows us two ways to add items to our collection. First the *Add* method will allow us to add an item by specifying the key/value pair. In addition, you can use the indexer to specify a key/value pair by specifying the key in the indexer and assigning to it the value that you want the key to point to.

Retrieving objects from a dictionary is simple as well. To access data once it has been added to the dictionary (here, a *Hashtable*), you simply call the indexer with the key you are looking for:

```
' VB
Console.WriteLine(emailLookup("sbishop@contoso.com"))
```

```
// C#
Console.WriteLine(emailLookup["sbishop@contoso.com"]);
```

Because dictionaries are made for looking up key/value pairs, it is not a surprise that iterating through the objects in a dictionary is not all that straightforward. For example, assume that you've created a *Hashtable* and want to iterate over all the values. The code for accomplishing this task might look like this:

```
' VB
Dim emailLookup As New Hashtable()

emailLookup("sbishop@contoso.com") = "Bishop, Scott"
emailLookup("chess@contoso.com") = "Hess, Christian"
emailLookup("djump@contoso.com") = "Jump, Dan"

For Each name as Object In emailLookup
    Console.WriteLine(name)
Next name

// C#
Hashtable emailLookup = new Hashtable();

emailLookup["sbishop@contoso.com"] = "Bishop, Scott";
emailLookup["chess@contoso.com"] = "Hess, Christian";
emailLookup["djump@contoso.com"] = "Jump, Dan";
```

```
foreach (object name in emailLookup)
{
    Console.WriteLine(name);
}
```

You might expect this to show you the names of each person in the *emailLookup* variable. What is actually written to the console is this:

```
System.Collections.DictionaryEntry
System.Collections.DictionaryEntry
System.Collections.DictionaryEntry
```

Why does this happen? It happens because you are actually iterating through the entries in the *Dictionary* object, not the keys or the values. If you wanted this code to write out the names of all the users, you could change the iterator to work with these *DictionaryEntry* objects, like so:

```
' VB
For Each entry as DictionaryEntry In emailLookup
    Console.WriteLine(entry.Value)
Next entry

// C#
foreach (DictionaryEntry entry in emailLookup)
{
    Console.WriteLine(entry.Value);
}
```

A *DictionaryEntry* object is simply a container containing a *Key* and a *Value*. So getting the items out is as simple as doing the iteration, but you must retrieve the *Value* or *Key* as necessary for your needs.

All dictionary classes (including the *Hashtable*) support the *IDictionary* interface. The *IDictionary* interface derives from the *ICollection* interface. The *IDictionary* interface's most important properties and methods are explained in Table 4-13 and Table 4-14, respectively.

Table 4-13 *IDictionary* **Properties**

Name	Description
IsFixedSize	Gets an indicator of whether this collection can be resized
IsReadOnly	Gets an indicator of whether a collection can be changed
Item	Gets or sets the item at a specific element in the collection

Table 4-13 *IDictionary* Properties

Name	Description
Keys	Gets an *ICollection* object containing a list of the keys in the collection
Values	Gets an *ICollection* object containing a list of the values in the collection

Table 4-14 *IDictionary* Methods

Name	Description
Add	Adds a key/value pair to the collection.
Clear	Removes all items in the collection.
Contains	Tests whether a specific key is contained in the collection.
GetEnumerator	Returns an *IDictionaryEnumerator* object for the collection. This method is different from the method with the same name in the *IEnumerable* interface that returns an *IEnumerator* interface.
Remove	Removes the item in the collection that corresponds to a specific key.

The *IDictionary* interface is somewhat like the *IList* interface from Lesson 1, but it does not allow access to items by index, only by key. This interface gives access to the list of keys and values directly as collections of objects. This design is useful if you need to iterate over either of these lists separately.

Earlier in this section, you saw how to iterate over the names in an e-mail list by using the *DictionaryEntry* object that is returned by the iterator. You also could iterate over those values by iterating through the *Values* property instead, as seen in this example:

```
' VB
For Each name as Object In emailLookup.Values
    Console.WriteLine(name)
Next name
```

```
// C#
foreach (object name in emailLookup.Values)
{
```

```
    Console.WriteLine(name);
}
```

In addition to the *IDictionary* interface, the *Hashtable* supports two methods that allow for testing for the existence of keys and values. These methods are shown in Table 4-15.

Table 4-15 *Hashtable* **Methods**

Name	Description
ContainsKey	Determines whether the collection contains a specific key
ContainsValue	Determines whether the collection contains a specific value

Understanding Equality

The *Hashtable* class is a specific type of dictionary class that uses an integer value (called a hash) to aid in the storage of its keys. The *Hashtable* class uses the hash to speed up the searching for a specific key in the collection. Every object in .NET derives from the *Object* class. This class supports the *GetHashCode* method, which returns an integer that uniquely identifies the object.

Why does the fact that the *Hashtable* class is storing a hash value matter to you the developer? The *Hashtable* allows only unique hashes of values, not unique values. If you try to store the same key twice, the second call replaces the first call, as shown in this example:

```
' VB
Dim duplicates As New Hashtable()

duplicates("First") = "1st"
duplicates("First") = "the first"

Console.WriteLine(duplicates.Count) ' 1

// C#
Hashtable duplicates = new Hashtable();

duplicates["First"] = "1st";
duplicates["First"] = "the first";

Console.WriteLine(duplicates.Count); // 1
```

The *duplicates* collection stores only one item in this example because the hash of *"First"* is the same as *"First"*. The *String* class overrides the *GetHashCode* method of *Object* to get this behavior. It expects two strings with the same text to be equal even though they are different instances. This is how the *Hashtable* class tests for equality, by testing the hash code of the objects. This approach is likely what you would want (and expect) in most instances.

The .NET Framework doesn't always understand equality as we do, however. For example, imagine you created a simple class called *Fish* that holds the name of the fish like so:

```
' VB
Public Class Fish
    Private name As String

    Public Sub New(theName As String)
        name = theName
    End Sub
End Class

// C#
public class Fish
{
    string name;
    public Fish(string theName)
    {
        name = theName;
    }
}
```

Now if we create two instance of the *Fish* class with the same name, the *Hashtable* treats them as different objects, as shown in the following code:

```
' VB
Dim duplicates As New Hashtable()

Dim key1 As New Fish("Herring")
Dim key2 As New Fish("Herring")

duplicates(key1) = "Hello"
duplicates(key2) = "Hello"

Console.WriteLine(duplicates.Count)

// C#
Hashtable duplicates = new Hashtable();

Fish key1 = new Fish("Herring");
Fish key2 = new Fish("Herring");

duplicates[key1] = "Hello";
duplicates[key2] = "Hello";

Console.WriteLine(duplicates.Count); // 2
```

Why are there two items in the collection that have the same name? The *duplicates* collection stores two items in this example because the *Object* class's implementation of *GetHashCode* creates a hash that is likely to be unique for each instance of a class. You could override the *GetHashCode* in the *Fish* class to try and let the *Hashtable* know they are equal, like so:

```
' VB
Public Overrides Function GetHashCode() As Integer
    Return name.GetHashCode()
End Function
```

```
// C#
public override int GetHashCode()
{
    return name.GetHashCode();
}
```

If you return the hash of the fish's name, the two instances of the fish will have the same hash code. But is that enough for the *Hashtable* to determine they are identical objects? Unfortunately, no. If the *Hashtable* finds two objects with the same hash, it calls their *Equals* method to see whether the two objects are in fact equal. Again, the default implementation of *Object.Equals* will return *false* if the two objects are two different instances of the same class. So we need to also add an override of the *Equals* method to our *Fish* class:

```
' VB
Public Overrides Function Equals(ByVal obj As Object) As Boolean
    Dim otherFish As Fish = obj as Fish
    If otherFish Is Nothing Then
        Return False
    End If
    Return otherFish.name = name
End Function
```

```
// C#
public override bool Equals(object obj)
{
    Fish otherFish = obj as Fish;
    if (otherFish == null) return false;
    return otherFish.name == name;
}
```

Here we can test to see whether the other object is also a *Fish* and, if so, compare the name to test whether the two objects are equal. Only then will the *Hashtable* class be able to determine whether two keys are identical.

Using the *IEqualityComparer* Interface

In addition to being able to change your classes to provide equality, you might find it necessary to provide equality outside the class. For example, assume that you want to store keys in the *Hashtable* as strings but need to ignore the case of the string. Changing the string class to support this or creating your own *String* class that is case insensitive would be a painful solution. This situation is where the *Hashtable*'s ability to use a class that calculates equality comes in.

The *Hashtable* class supports a constructor that can accept an instance of the *IEquality-Comparer* interface as an argument. Much like the *IComparer* interface shown in Lesson 1 that allowed you to sort collections, the *IEqualityComparer* interface supports two methods: *GetHashCode* and *Equals*. These methods allow the comparer class to handle equality for objects instead of relying on the objects to supply them. For example, the following code creates a simple case-insensitive comparer so that you can make your string keys case insensitive:

```vb
' VB
Public Class InsensitiveComparer
    Implements IEqualityComparer
    Dim _comparer As CaseInsensitiveComparer = _
        New CaseInsensitiveComparer()

    Public Function GetHashCode(ByVal obj As Object) As Integer _
        Implements IEqualityComparer
        Return obj.ToString().ToLowerInvariant().GetHashCode()
    End Function

    Public Shadows Function Equals(ByVal x As Object, ByVal y As Object) _
        As Boolean Implements IEqualityComparer
        If _comparer.Compare(x,y) = 0 Then
            Return True
        Else
            Return False
        End If
    End Function
End Class
```

```csharp
// C#
public class InsensitiveComparer : IEqualityComparer
{
    CaseInsensitiveComparer _comparer = new CaseInsensitiveComparer();

    public int GetHashCode(object obj)
    {
        return obj.ToString().ToLowerInvariant().GetHashCode();
    }
```

```
    public new bool Equals(object x, object y)
    {
        if (_comparer.Compare(x, y) == 0)
        {
            return true;
        }
        else
        {
            return false;
        }
    }
}
```

In this new class, you are implementing the *IEqualityComparer* interface to provide hash codes and equality comparisons. Note that this class uses the built-in *CaseInsensitiveComparer* to do the actual *Equals* comparison. In addition, the *GetHash-Code* takes the object passed in and converts it to lowercase letters before getting the hashcode. This process is what takes the case sensitivity out of the hash-code creation. Now when you create a *Hashtable,* you can tell it to use this class to do the comparisons:

```
' VB
Dim dehash As Hashtable = New Hashtable(New InsensitiveComparer())

dehash("First") = "1st"
dehash("Second") = "2nd"
dehash("Third") = "3rd"
dehash("Fourth") = "4th"
dehash("fourth") = "4th"

Console.WriteLine(dehash.Count) ' 4

// C#
Hashtable dehash = new Hashtable(new InsensitiveComparer());

dehash["First"] = "1st";
dehash["Second"] = "2nd";
dehash["Third"] = "3rd";
dehash["Fourth"] = "4th";
dehash["fourth"] = "4th";

Console.WriteLine(dehash.Count); // 4
```

Because you are using this case-insensitive equality object in creating the *Hashtable,* you end up with only four items in the collection. It treats *"Fourth"* and *"fourth"* as identical.

The *Hashtable* is a great class for creating lookup tables, but there are times when what you really need is to sort one set of items by some key value. When you iterate over the *Hashtable* class, it returns the items in the order of their hash value. That order is not practical for most situations. The *SortedList* is a dictionary class that supports sorting.

Using the *SortedList* Class

Although the *SortedList* class is definitely a dictionary class, it shares some of its behavior with how simple lists work. This means that you can (and will probably) access items stored in the *SortedList* in order. For example, you use a *SortedList* to sort a simple list of items like so:

```
' VB
Dim sort As SortedList = New SortedList()
sort("First") = "1st"
sort("Second") = "2nd"
sort("Third") = "3rd"
sort("Fourth") = "4th"
sort("fourth") = "4th"

For Each entry as DictionaryEntry In sort
    Console.WriteLine("{0} = {1}", entry.Key, entry.Value)
Next

// C#
SortedList sort = new SortedList();
sort["First"] = "1st";
sort["Second"] = "2nd";
sort["Third"] = "3rd";
sort["Fourth"] = "4th";
sort["fourth"] = "4th";

foreach (DictionaryEntry entry in sort)
{
    Console.WriteLine("{0} = {1}", entry.Key, entry.Value);
}
```

This code results in a simple sorting of our objects:

```
First = 1st
fourth = 4th
Fourth = 4th
Second = 2nd
Third = 3rd
```

You can see from the *foreach* iterator in the preceding code snippet that the *SortedList* is still a dictionary class (as evidenced by *DictionaryEntry*). In addition to having the same interface that all dictionary classes have, the *SortedList* class supports additional properties to allow access of keys and values by index number. Table 4-16 and

Table 4-17 show the properties and methods, respectively, of *SortedList* (not including the *IDictionary* interface members).

Table 4-16 *SortedList* Properties

Name	Description
Capacity	Gets or sets the number of items currently allocated for the collection. This is the total number of currently allocated slots for items, not the number of items in the collection. (*Count* will give you the number of items in the collection.)

Table 4-17 *SortedList* Methods

Name	Description
ContainsKey	Determines whether the collection contains a specific key
ContainsValue	Determines whether the collection contains a specific value
GetByIndex	Retrieves the value at a specific index in the collection
GetKey	Retrieves the key at a specific index in the collection
GetKeyList	Retrieves an ordered list of the keys.
GetValueList	Retrieves a list of values.
IndexOfKey	Gets the index of a key in the collection
IndexOfValue	Gets the index of the first occurrence of the specified value in the collection
RemoveAt	Removes a specific value in the collection by index
SetByIndex	Replaces a value at a specific index in the collection
TrimToSize	Used to free unused capacity in the collection

As you can see by these tables, *SortedList* adds a number of methods for accessing data by index number. The class supports retrieving both keys and values by index, and it also supports looking them up to retrieve their index. Because this class is sorted, the index of an item can change as items are added or deleted.

You can use the same process you learned in Lesson 1 to sort a collection in *SortedList*. Instead of requiring you to call *Sort* in order to sort items, *SortedList* performs sorting as items are added. With that in mind, you can specify an *IComparer* when creating the

SortedList so that you can control the way the sorting happens. If you borrow the *DescendingComparer* class that was discussed in Lesson 1, you can change the code to include the *DescendingComparer* class, like so:

```vb
' VB
Dim sort As SortedList =  New SortedList(New DescendingComparer())
sort("First") = "1st"
sort("Second") = "2nd"
sort("Third") = "3rd"
sort("Fourth") = "4th"

Dim enTry
For Each entry As DictionaryEnTry In sort
    Console.WriteLine("{0} = {1}", entry.Key, entry.Value)
Next
```

```csharp
// C#
SortedList sort = new SortedList(new DescendingComparer());
sort["First"] = "1st";
sort["Second"] = "2nd";
sort["Third"] = "3rd";
sort["Fourth"] = "4th";

foreach (DictionaryEntry entry in sort)
{
    Console.WriteLine("{0} = {1}", entry.Key, entry.Value);
}
```

Now the sorting is in descending order (remember that the order is alphabetical by the name, not the number):

```
Third = 3rd
Second = 2nd
Fourth = 4th
First = 1st
```

Specialized Dictionaries

There are times when the standard dictionaries (*SortedList* and *Hashtable*) have limitations, either functional limitations or performance-related ones. To bridge that gap, the .NET Framework supports three other dictionaries: *ListDictionary*, *HybridDictionary*, and *OrderedDictionary*.

ListDictionary

The *Hashtable* class is a very efficient collection in general. The only issue with the *Hashtable* class is that it requires a bit of overhead, and for small collections (fewer than ten elements) the overhead can impede performance. That is where the *List-Dictionary* comes in. It is implemented as a simple array of items underneath the hood, so it is very efficient for small collections of items. The *ListDictionary* class has the same interface as the *Hashtable* class, so it can be used as a drop-in replacement. To demonstrate, here is the example used with *Hashtable* earlier. This time, however, we're using *ListDictionary*. Note that none of the code is different except for the construction of the object:

```vb
' VB
Dim emailLookup As New ListDictionary()

emailLookup("sbishop@contoso.com") = "Bishop, Scott"
emailLookup("chess@contoso.com") = "Hess, Christian"
emailLookup("djump@contoso.com") = "Jump, Dan"

For Each entry as DictionaryEntry In emailLookup
    Console.WriteLine(entry.Value)
Next name
```

```csharp
// C#

ListDictionary emailLookup = new ListDictionary ();

emailLookup["sbishop@contoso.com"] = "Bishop, Scott";
emailLookup["chess@contoso.com"] = "Hess, Christian",
emailLookup["djump@contoso.com"] = "Jump, Dan";

foreach (DictionaryEntry entry in emailLookup)
{
    Console.WriteLine(entry.Value);
}
```

HybridDictionary

As you saw in the discussion of *ListDictionary*, there are some inefficiencies in *Hashtable* for small collections. However, if you use *ListDictionary* for larger lists it is not efficient at all. In general, this means that if you know your collection is small, use a *ListDictionary*; if your collection is large, use a *Hashtable*. But what if you just do not know how large your collection is? That is where the *HybridDictionary* comes in. It is implemented as a *ListDictionary* and only when the list becomes too large does it convert itself into a *Hashtable* internally. The *HybridDictionary* is best used in situations where some lists are small and others are very large.

As with the *ListDictionary*, the interface is identical to the *Hashtable*, so it is an in-place replacement, as shown in the following code snippets:

```vb
' VB
Dim emailLookup As New HybridDictionary()

emailLookup("sbishop@contoso.com") = "Bishop, Scott"
emailLookup("chess@contoso.com") = "Hess, Christian"
emailLookup("djump@contoso.com") = "Jump, Dan"
```

```
For Each entry as DictionaryEntry In emailLookup
    Console.WriteLine(entry.Value)
Next name

// C#
HybridDictionary emailLookup = new HybridDictionary ();

emailLookup["sbishop@contoso.com"] = "Bishop, Scott";
emailLookup["chess@contoso.com"] = "Hess, Christian";
emailLookup["djump@contoso.com"] = "Jump, Dan";

foreach (DictionaryEntry entry in emailLookup)
{
    Console.WriteLine(entry.Value);
}
```

OrderedDictionary

There are times when you want the functionality of the *Hashtable* but you need to control the order of the elements in the collection. When you add items to a *Hashtable*, two things are true: there is no way to access the elements by index; and if you use an enumerator to get around that limitation, the items are ordered by their hash value. You could use a *SortedList*, but that assumes that you want the items sorted in the order provided by the keys. Perhaps there is just an ordinal order?

To accommodate you when you need a fast dictionary but also need to keep the items in an ordered fashion, the .NET Framework supports the *OrderedDictionary*. An *OrderedDictionary* is much like a *Hashtable* except that it has extra methods and properties—as seen in Table 4-18 and Table 4-19, respectively—to allow access to the items by index.

Table 4-18 *OrderedDictionary* Extra Properties

Name	Description
Item	Overloaded to support access by index

Table 4-19 *OrderedDictionary* Extra Methods

Name	Description
Insert	Inserts a key/value pair at a specific index in the collection
RemoveAt	Removes a key/value pair at a specific index in the collection

These additions to the interface of the class allow it to deal with the collection as if the class were a mix of an *ArrayList* and a *Hashtable*.

Lab: Create a Lookup Table

In this lab, you create a lookup table to replace numbers with their string representations. If you encounter a problem completing an exercise, the completed projects are available on the companion CD in the Code folder.

▶ **Exercise 1: Create a Lookup Table**

In this exercise, you will create a lookup table for a series of numbers, parse through the digits of a string, and display the numbers in the console.

1. Create a new console application called DictionaryCollections.

2. In the main code file, include (or import for Visual Basic) the *System.Collections* namespace.

3. In the *Main* method of the project, create a new instance of the *Hashtable* class.

4. Add items into the new instance of the *Hashtable* class where the key is a string containing the numbers zero through nine, and the value is the spelled-out name of the numbers zero through nine.

5. Next create a string variable with a series of numbers in it.

6. Go through the string, one character at a time using a *foreach* construct.

7. Within the *foreach*, create a new string from the character variable you created in the *foreach* loop.

8. Check to see whether the *Hashtable* contains the key of the single character string.

9. If it does, get the value for the key from the *Hashtable* and show it in the console. Your code might look something like this:

```vb
' VB
Imports System.Collections

Class Program
    Shared  Sub Main(ByVal args() As String)
        Dim lookup As Hashtable =  New Hashtable()

        lookup("0") = "Zero"
        lookup("1") = "One"
        lookup("2") = "Two"
        lookup("3") = "Three"
        lookup("4") = "Four"
```

```
        lookup("5") = "Five"
        lookup("6") = "Six"
        lookup("7") = "Seven"
        lookup("8") = "Eight"
        lookup("9") = "Nine"

        Dim ourNumber As String =  "888-555-1212"

        For Each c as Char In ourNumber
            Dim digit As String =  c.ToString()
            If lookup.ContainsKey(digit) Then
                Console.WriteLine(lookup(digit))
            End If
        Next
    End Sub
End Class

// C#
using System.Collections;

class Program
{
    static void Main(string[] args)
    {
        Hashtable lookup = new Hashtable();

        lookup["0"] = "Zero";
        lookup["1"] = "One";
        lookup["2"] = "Two";
        lookup["3"] = "Three";
        lookup["4"] = "Four";
        lookup["5"] = "Five";
        lookup["6"] = "Six";
        lookup["7"] = "Seven";
        lookup["8"] = "Eight";
        lookup["9"] = "Nine";

        string ourNumber = "888-555-1212";

        foreach (char c in ourNumber)
        {
            string digit = c.ToString();
            if (lookup.ContainsKey(digit))
            {
                Console.WriteLine(lookup[digit]);
            }
        }
    }
}
```

10. Build the project, and resolve any errors. Verify that the console application successfully spells out all the digits in the number you specified.

Lesson Summary

- The *IDictionary* interface provides the basic calling convention for all *Dictionary* collections.

- The *Hashtable* class can be used to create lookup tables.

- You can use a *DictionaryEntry* object to get at the key and value of an object in a *Dictionary* collection.

- The *SortedList* can be used to create list of items that can be sorted by a key.

- The *IEqualityComparer* can be used to construct hash values and compare two arbitrary objects for equality.

Lesson Review

You can use the following questions to test your knowledge of the information in Lesson 3, "Working with Dictionaries." The questions are also available on the companion CD if you prefer to review them in electronic form.

NOTE Answers

Answers to these questions and explanations of why each answer choice is right or wrong are located in the "Answers" section at the end of the book.

1. When adding a key to a *Hashtable*, what methods can be called on the key to determine whether the key is unique? (Choose all that apply.)

    A. *GetType*

    B. *GetHashCode*

    C. *ToString*

    D. *Equals*

2. Which of the following statements is true?

    A. You can pass an instance of a class that supports the *IEqualityComparer* interface when you construct a *Hashtable* to change the way keys are evaluated for uniqueness.

    B. You can assign an *IEqualityComparer* object to an existing *Hashtable*.

    C. You cannot use an *IEqualityComparer* with a *Hashtable*.

    D. A *Hashtable* implements *IEqualityComparer*.

Lesson 4: Using Specialized Collections

The first three lessons in this chapter introduced a series of collections that can be used to store any object in .NET. Although these are valuable tools, using them can often lead to you having to cast objects when you retrieve them from the collections. The .NET Framework supports a new namespace called *System.Collections.Specialized* that includes collections that are meant to work with specific types of data.

After this lesson, you will be able to:

- Use the *BitArray* and *BitVector32* classes to deal with sets of *Boolean* values.
- Use the *StringCollection* and *StringDictionary* classes to store collections of strings.
- Use the *NameValueCollection* to store name/value pairs in a type-safe way.

Estimated lesson time: 30 minutes

Working with Bits

In many situations, you will need to deal with data in sets of *Boolean* expressions. One of the most common needs is to have a list of bits that can be either on or off. Two classes in the .NET Framework simplify working with collections of bits: *BitArray* and *BitVector32*.

The *BitArray* class is a resizeable collection that can store *Boolean* values. In addition to being resizeable, it supports common bit-level operations such as and, not, or, and exclusive-or (*Xor*).

The *BitVector32* structure is a slightly different beast than a *BitArray*. The purpose of the *BitVector32* structure is to aid in manipulating bits in a 32-bit integer. The *BitVector32* is not a resizeable collection at all. Instead, it is fixed at 32 bits so that it can manipulate the individual bits of a 32-bit integer.

How to Use a *BitArray*

The *BitArray* is a traditionally resizeable collection, but not a dynamically resizing one. When you create a new instance of the *BitArray* class, you must specify the size of the collection. Once the new instance has been created, you can change the size by changing the *Length* property. Unlike other collections, *BitArray* does not support *Add* or *Remove*. This support is missing because each value in a *BitArray* can be only *true* or *false*, so the idea of adding or removing does not really apply.

Once you create an instance of the *BitArray* class, it will have a collection of *Boolean* values with the default value of *false*. To set individual bits, you use the indexer like so:

```vb
' VB
Dim bits As BitArray =  New BitArray(3)
bits(0) = False
bits(1) = True
bits(2) = False
```

```csharp
// C#
BitArray bits = new BitArray(3);
bits[0] = false;
bits[1] = true;
bits[2] = false;
```

The real power of the *BitArray* is in its ability to perform *Boolean* operations on two *BitArray* objects (of the same size). To create two *BitArray* objects and perform an exclusive-or operation on them, follow these steps:

1. Create an instance of the *BitArray* class, specifying the size that you need.

2. Set some values of the individual bits.

3. Repeat steps 1 and step 2 to create a second *BitArray* that is the same size as the first one.

4. Call the *Xor* method on the first *BitArray*, supplying the second *BitArray*. Doing this will produce a new *BitArray* with the results of the *Xor* operation. Your code should look something like this:

```vb
' VB
Dim bits As BitArray =  New BitArray(3)
bits(0) = False
bits(1) = True
bits(2) = False

Dim moreBits As BitArray =  New BitArray(3)
morebits(0) = True
morebits(1) = True
morebits(2) = False

Dim xorBits As BitArray =  bits.Xor(moreBits)

For Each bit as Boolean In xorBits
    Console.WriteLine(bit)
Next
```

```csharp
// C#
BitArray bits = new BitArray(3);
bits[0] = false;
bits[1] = true;
bits[2] = false;
```

```
BitArray moreBits = new BitArray(3);
morebits[0] = true;
morebits[1] = true;
morebits[2] = false;

BitArray xorBits = bits.Xor(moreBits);

foreach (bool bit in xorBits)
{
    Console.WriteLine(bit);
}
```

How to Use a *BitVector32* for Bit Masks

The *BitVector32* structure is very useful for managing individual bits in a larger number. The *BitVector32* stores all its data as a single 32-bit integer. All operations on the *BitVector32* actually change the value of the integer within the structure. At any time, you can retrieve the stored integer by calling the structure's *Data* property.

The *BitVector32* structure allows you to create bit masks in sequential order by calling its static (or shared, in Visual Basic) method *CreateMask*. Calling the *CreateMask* method without any parameters creates a mask for the first bit in the structure. Calling it subsequently, supplying the last mask created, will create the next bit mask. These masks can be used with the *BitVector32* structure's indexer to set or get values at that specific bit.

An example will help clarify the process. Assume that you need to set the value of the first three bits in some 32-bit integer. Use these steps to create bit masks, set values, and get values for those bits:

1. Create an instance of the *BitVector32* structure, specifying a zero for the initial value to make sure all the bits are clear.

2. Create a mask for the first bit by calling the *BitVector32.CreateMask* method without any parameters.

3. Create the next bit mask by calling the *BitVector32.CreateMask* method, but include the last bit mask as a parameter to tell it to create the next mask.

4. Repeat steps 1 through 3 until you have three bit masks. Your code should look like this:

```
' VB
Dim vector As BitVector32 = New BitVector32(0)

Dim firstBit As Integer = BitVector32.CreateMask()
Dim secondBit As Integer = BitVector32.CreateMask(firstBit)
Dim thirdBit As Integer = BitVector32.CreateMask(secondBit)
```

```
// C#
BitVector32 vector = new BitVector32(0);

int firstBit = BitVector32.CreateMask();
int secondBit = BitVector32.CreateMask(firstBit);
int thirdBit = BitVector32.CreateMask(secondBit);
```

5. Now set the first and second bits to *true* by using the indexer like so:

```
' VB
Vector(firstBit) = True
vector(secondBit) = True
```

```
// C#
vector[firstBit] = true;
vector[secondBit] = true;
```

6. Write the *BitVector32*'s *Data* property to the console window to confirm that the value is now 3 (1 for the first bit plus 2 for the second bit equals 3).

```
' VB
Console.WriteLine("{0} should be 3", vector.Data)
```

```
// C#
Console.WriteLine("{0} should be 3", vector.Data);
```

7. If you write the whole structure (not the *Data* property) to the console window, it will show you which bits are turned on:

```
' VB
Console.WriteLine(vector)
' BitVector32{00000000000000000000000000000011}
```

```
// C#
Console.WriteLine(vector);
// BitVector32{00000000000000000000000000000011}
```

8. Next create a new *BitVector32* object and set its initial value to 4 (which should turn on bit 3 and turn off bits 1 and 2).

9. Then get each of the first three bits as *Boolean* values using the indexer of the *BitVector32*. You can use the masks you created for the first three bits; they are not specific to an instance of a *BitVector32* because the structure always stores 32 bits. Your code should look like this:

```
' VB
Dim NewVector As BitVector32 =  New BitVector32(4)

Dim bit1 As Boolean =  NewVector(firstBit)
Dim bit2 As Boolean =  NewVector(secondBit)
Dim bit3 As Boolean =  NewVector(thirdBit)

' bit1 = false, bit2 = false, bit3 = true
```

```
// C#
BitVector32 newVector = new BitVector32(4);

bool bit1 = newVector[firstBit];
bool bit2 = newVector[secondBit];
bool bit3 = newVector[thirdBit];

// bit1 = false, bit2 = false, bit3 = true
```

Understanding Binary Math

The *BitVector32* structure is designed to simplify use of binary math to use individual bits of information within a larger number. To fully understand how the *BitVector32* structure works, though, you will need to understand how binary math works.

Inside of computer memory, each piece of data is stored as a series of switches that can be either on or off. To store numbers as a set of switches, each number requires a certain amount of these switches. These "switches" are referred to as bits. For example, an unsigned byte is an 8-bit number and can store numbers from zero through 255. This process works because each bit of the number represents 2 to the power of its digit (starting with zero; the bits are numbered right-to-left). So if the first digit is on, it is 2^0, or 1. The second digit is 2^1, or 2, and so on. So if an unsigned byte has all 8 bits filled in, it can be represented by this equation: $1 + 2 + 4 + 8 + 16 + 32 + 64 + 128 = 255$. For example, to store the number 5, digits 0 and 2 are turned on (00000101), which can be expressed as $(2^0) + (2^2) = 1 + 4 = 5$.

Numbers with 8 bits are not large enough to worry about. The *BitVector32* structure is used because as the numbers grow the bit arrangement becomes more and more confusing. For example, the last digit in an unsigned 32-bit integer is quite large (2,147,483,648). Complicating matters even more is the fact that the *BitVector32* actually works with an unsigned integer, so the last digit is actually $-(2^{31})$, which deals with the negative range of a signed 32-bit integer. The purpose of a *BitVector32* is to hide the numbers behind the scenes so that you can deal with the bits as just indexes of the number.

How to Use a *BitVector32* for Bit Packing

Although *BitVector32* is a very useful structure for dealing with individual bits, it also supports bit packing. Bit packing can be defined as taking several smaller numbers and packing them into one large number. Bit packing is often done to decrease storage of especially small numbers.

For example, you might have three numbers to store that are fairly small. The first number might have a maximum value of 10, the second a maximum value of 50, and the third a maximum value of 500. You could store these as three *Int16s* but you'd be wasting space. Instead, you should use a *BitVector32* to store all three values in a single 32-bit number.

BitVector32 allows you to create sections of the structure that will be used to store numbers of certain sizes. So before you begin, you will need to create the sections. You do this in much the same way as you create masks, but you need to specify the largest number that the section can store. So if you use the earlier example of 10, 50, and 500, you would create the sections like so:

```vb
' VB
Dim firstSection As BitVector32.Section = _
    BitVector32.CreateSection(10)
Dim secondSection As BitVector32.Section = _
    BitVector32.CreateSection(50, firstSection)
Dim thirdSection As BitVector32.Section = _
    BitVector32.CreateSection(500, secondSection)
```

```csharp
// C#
BitVector32.Section firstSection =
    BitVector32.CreateSection(10);
BitVector32.Section secondSection =
    BitVector32.CreateSection(50, firstSection);
BitVector32.Section thirdSection =
    BitVector32.CreateSection(500, secondSection);
```

Like the *CreateMask*, the *CreateSection* uses the last section to determine where to "pack" the new number.

Once you have the sections, you can set and get them using the indexer and the new section variables, as shown here:

```vb
' VB
Dim packedBits As BitVector32 =  New BitVector32(0)

packedBits(firstSection) = 10
packedBits(secondSection) = 1
packedBits(thirdSection) = 192

Console.WriteLine(packedBits(firstSection))
Console.WriteLine(packedBits(secondSection))
Console.WriteLine(packedBits(thirdSection))
```

```
// C#
BitVector32 packedBits = new BitVector32(0);

packedBits[firstSection] = 10;
packedBits[secondSection] = 1;
packedBits[thirdSection] = 192;

Console.WriteLine(packedBits[firstSection]);
Console.WriteLine(packedBits[secondSection]);
Console.WriteLine(packedBits[thirdSection]);
```

After you have worked with the sections, you can get the *BitVector32*'s *Data* property to keep the underlying number that contains the three numbers packed into it:

```
' VB
Console.WriteLine(packedBits.Data)
' 1966314

Console.WriteLine(packedBits)
' BitVector32{00000000000000110000000000011010}

// C#
Console.WriteLine(packedBits.Data);
// 1966314

Console.WriteLine(packedBits);
// BitVector32{00000000000000110000000000011010}
```

You could do the math to figure out that the number 1966314 can store 10, 1, and 192, but the *BitVector32* can do it for you with much less work.

Collecting Strings

Probably the most common type of object that you need to store in a collection are strings. To accommodate this need, the .NET Framework supports two specialized collections that are strongly typed to store strings: *StringCollection* and *StringDictionary*.

The *StringCollection* Class

The *StringCollection* is a simple dynamically sized collection (such as *ArrayList*) that can only store strings. But *StringCollection* is still just a collection like the others mentioned in this chapter, so working with it is virtually identical to using an *ArrayList*, as seen in this example:

```
' VB
Dim coll As New StringCollection()

coll.Add("First")
coll.Add("Second")
```

```
coll.Add("Third")
coll.Add("Fourth")
coll.Add("fourth")
' coll.Add(50); <- Doesn't compile...not a string

Dim theString As String =  coll(3)
' No longer need to
' string theString = (string) coll[3];

// C#
StringCollection coll = new StringCollection();

coll.Add("First");
coll.Add("Second");
coll.Add("Third");
coll.Add("Fourth");
coll.Add("fourth");
// coll.Add(50); <- Doesn't compile...not a string

string theString = coll[3];
// No longer need to
// string theString = (string) coll[3];
```

The lines that add the strings to the collection look just like the earlier examples using the *ArrayList*. The only difference is that adding a nonstring generates a compilation error. (See the commented-out line.) In addition, when retrieving the string, you no longer are working with objects but with strings. This cuts down on the need to cast when retrieving elements.

The *StringDictionary* Class

The *StringDictionary* is a strongly typed version of the dictionary collections shown in Lesson 3. This means that you can use it just like a *Hashtable*, except that both the keys and values must be strings:

```
' VB
Dim dict As New StringDictionary()

dict("First") = "1st"
dict("Second") = "2nd"
dict("Third") = "3rd"
dict("Fourth") = "4th"
dict("fourth") = "fourth"
' dict[50] = "fifty"; <- Won't compile...not a string

Dim converted As String =  dict("Second")
' No casting needed

// C#
StringDictionary dict = new StringDictionary();
```

```
dict["First"] = "1st";
dict["Second"] = "2nd";
dict["Third"] = "3rd";
dict["Fourth"] = "4th";
dict["fourth"] = "fourth";
// dict[50] = "fifty"; <- Won't compile...not a string

string converted = dict["Second"];
// No casting needed
```

It is important to understand that the keys are case insensitive by default for *String-Dictionary* objects, so the keys *"Fourth"* and *"fourth"* are equivalent.

Case-Insensitive Collections

As you saw earlier in this chapter, you can control comparison or equality by using the *IComparer* and *IEqualityComparer* interfaces. One of the most common uses for these interfaces is to create case-insensitive dictionary collections. Because this is such a common use, the .NET Framework has a *CollectionsUtil* class that supports creating *Hashtable* and *SortedList* objects that are case insensitive. Using it is as easy as calling *CreateCaseInsensitiveHashtable* or *CreateCaseInsensitiveSortedList*. The following code snippet provides an example:

```
' VB
Dim inTable As Hashtable = _
    CollectionsUtil.CreateCaseInsensitiveHashtable()
inTable("hello") = "Hi"
inTable("HELLO") = "Heya"
Console.WriteLine(inTable.Count) ' 1

Dim inList As SortedList = _
    CollectionsUtil.CreateCaseInsensitiveSortedList()
inList("hello") - "Hi"
inList("HELLO") = "Heya"
Console.WriteLine(inList.Count) ' 1

// C#
Hashtable inTable =
    CollectionsUtil.CreateCaseInsensitiveHashtable();
inTable["hello"] = "Hi";
inTable["HELLO"] = "Heya";
Console.WriteLine(inTable.Count); // 1

SortedList inList =
    CollectionsUtil.CreateCaseInsensitiveSortedList();
inList["hello"] = "Hi";
inList["HELLO"] = "Heya";
Console.WriteLine(inList.Count); // 1
```

Culture-Invariant Collections

The default behavior for collections is to use the thread's current culture. This means that comparisons are dependent on the rules of the current culture. Comparisons are used both when making sure objects are unique within collections as well as when ordering items in sorted collections (or when inserting items into sorted collections such as *SortedList*).

Depending on your specific needs, it might be important to do the comparisons in a culture-invariant way, without regard to the current culture or any culture. This situation arises with Web applications and applications that need to store information across cultures. What would you expect to happen if you stored a list that had English, Spanish, Hebrew, and Farsi keys? How would you expect the ordering to occur. In most of these cases, you should create collections that are not affected by (invariant with regard to) the current culture. Unlike case-insensitive collections, *CollectionsUtil* methods cannot be used to create your collections. Instead, you must specify the new collection with new instances of a *StringComparer* object that performs a case-sensitive string comparison using the word comparison rules of the invariant culture. For example, you might want to create a new *Hashtable* and *SortedList* with both case insensitivity and invariant culture. Your code should look like this:

```
' VB
Dim hash As Hashtable = New Hashtable( _
    StringComparer.InvariantCulture)

Dim list As SortedList = New SortedList( _
    StringComparer.InvariantCultureIgnoreCase)

// C#
Hashtable hash = new Hashtable(
    StringComparer.InvariantCulture);
SortedList list = new SortedList(
    StringComparer.InvariantCultureIgnoreCase);
```

The *NameValueCollection* Class

Finally, there is a specialized type of class called a *NameValueCollection*. At first glance, it looks like this class and a *StringDictionary* are similar because both allow you to add keys and values that are strings. However, there are some specific differences: it allows multiple values per key and values can be retrieved by index as well as key.

With the *NameValueCollection* class, you can store multiple values per key. You do this with the *Add* method. To retrieve all the values for a particular key, you can use the *GetValues* method like so:

```
' VB
Dim nv As NameValueCollection =  New NameValueCollection()

nv.Add("Key", "Some Text")
nv.Add("Key", "More Text")

Dim s As String
For Each s In nv.GetValues("Key")
    Console.WriteLine(s)
Next
' Some Text
' More Text

// C#
NameValueCollection nv = new NameValueCollection();

nv.Add("Key", "Some Text");
nv.Add("Key", "More Text");

foreach (string s in nv.GetValues("Key"))
{
    Console.WriteLine(s);
}
// Some Text
// More Text
```

When you add identical keys with the *Add* method, you can then access the values by calling *GetValues* and supplying the key. When you list all the values, it will display both items you added with the same key.

Interestingly, the *Add* method and the indexer have different behaviors. For example, if you add two items with the indexer and use the same key, you retain only the last value you added. This behavior is the same as it is with the other dictionaries discussed in Lesson 3. For example, if you add values with the indexer and with the *Add* method, you can see the difference in behavior:

```
' VB
nv("First") = "1st"
nv("First") = "FIRST"

nv.Add("Second", "2nd")
nv.Add("Second", "SECOND")

Console.WriteLine(nv.GetValues("First").Length)
' 1
```

```
Console.WriteLine(nv.GetValues("Second").Length)
' 2

// C#
nv["First"] = "1st";
nv["First"] = "FIRST";

nv.Add("Second", "2nd");
nv.Add("Second", "SECOND");

Console.WriteLine(nv.GetValues("First").Length);
// 1

Console.WriteLine(nv.GetValues("Second").Length);
// 2
```

Finally, the other difference between using the *NameValueCollection* and the *String-Dictionary* is that you can retrieve items by key index. So when you ask the *Name-ValueCollection* to return a specific index's value, it returns the value of that key. If the key has more than one value, it returns it as a comma-delimited list:

```
' VB
Dim nv As NameValueCollection = New NameValueCollection()

nv.Add("First", "1st")
nv.Add("Second", "2nd")
nv.Add("Second", "Not First")

Dim x As Integer
For  x = 0 To  nv.Count- 1  Step   + 1
    Console.WriteLine(nv(x))
Next
' 1st
' 2nd,Not First

// C#
NameValueCollection nv = new NameValueCollection();

nv.Add("First", "1st");
nv.Add("Second", "2nd");
nv.Add("Second", "Not First");

for (int x = 0; x < nv.Count; ++x)
{
    Console.WriteLine(nv[x]);
}
// 1st
// 2nd,Not First
```

Lab: A Case-Insensitive, Localizable Lookup Table

In this lab, you will create a localizable lookup table. If you encounter a problem completing an exercise, the completed projects are available on the companion CD in the Code folder.

▶ **Exercise 1: Create a *ListCollection***

In this exercise, you will create a lookup table for country names. The keys will be in Spanish.

1. Create a new console application called LookupCollections.

2. In the main code file, include (or import for Visual Basic) the *System.Collections*, *System.Collections.Specialized*, and *System.Globalization* namespaces.

3. In the *Main* method of the project, create a new instance of the *ListDictionary* class, specifying case insensitive and culture invariant.

4. Add three lookups to the collection, specifying "Estados Unidos" for "United States", "Canadá" for "Canada", and "España" for "Spain.

5. Write out to the console the values for the Spanish versions of Spain and Canada. Your code should look something like this:

```
'VB
Imports System.Globalization
Imports System.Collections
Imports System.Collections.Specialized

Class Program
    Shared  Sub Main(ByVal args() As String)

        ' Make the dictionary case insensitive
        Dim list as New ListDictionary( _
           New CaseInsensitiveComparer(CultureInfo.InvariantCulture))

        ' Add some items
        list("Estados Unidos") = "United States of America"
        list("Canadá") = "Canada"
        list("España") = "Spain"

        ' Show the results
        Console.WriteLine(list("españa"))
        Console.WriteLine(list("CANADÁ"))

        Console.Read()

    End Sub

End Class
```

```csharp
// C#
using System.Globalization;
using System.Collections;
using System.Collections.Specialized;

class Program
{
    static void Main(string[] args)
    {

        // Make the dictionary case insensitive
        ListDictionary list = new ListDictionary(
          new CaseInsensitiveComparer(CultureInfo.InvariantCulture));

        // Add some items
        list["Estados Unidos"] = "United States of America";
        list["Canadá"] = "Canada";
        list["España"] = "Spain";

        // Show the results
        Console.WriteLine(list["españa"]);
        Console.WriteLine(list["CANADÁ"]);

        Console.Read();
    }
}
```

6. Build the project, and resolve any errors. Verify that the console application successfully shows both Spain and Canada.

Lesson Summary

■ The *BitArray* class and the *BitVector32* structure can both be used to perform bit-wise operations on a series of *Boolean* values.

■ The *StringCollection* and *StringDictionary* classes are type-safe classes for storing strings.

■ You can create case-insensitive versions of *Hashtable* and *SortedList* objects using the *CollectionsUtil* class.

■ *NameValueCollection* is a useful class for storing more than one value per key in a name/value collection.

Lesson Review

You can use the following questions to test your knowledge of the information in Lesson 4, "Using Specialized Collections." The questions are also available on the companion CD if you prefer to review them in electronic form.

1. What types of collections can be made from the *CollectionsUtil* class? (Choose all that apply.)

   A. Case-insensitive *StringDictionary*

   B. Culture-invariant *Hashtable*

   C. Case-insensitive *Hashtable*

   D. Case-insensitive *SortedList*

2. What types of objects can stored as a *Value* in *StringDictionary*?

   A. Strings

   B. Objects

   C. Arrays of strings

   D. Any .NET Types

Lesson 5: Generic Collections

Prior to Lesson 4, only collections that worked with instances of the *Object* class were discussed. If you wanted to retrieve a specific type of object, you needed to cast that object to its real type. In Lesson 4, you saw some common specialized collections for working with well-known types such as strings. But adding a couple of specialized collections does not solve most problems with type safety and collections. That is where generic collections come in.

After this lesson, you will be able to:

- Create and work with type-safe lists
- Create and work with type-safe queues
- Create and work with type-safe stacks
- Create and work with type-safe dictionaries
- Create and work with type-safe linked list collections

Estimated lesson time: 20 minutes

How Generics Work

Programming is about solving problems. Sometimes the need to solve a particular problem is common to a lot of situations. For example, the need to collect an ordered list of items is a very common problem. Inside the .NET Framework, the *ArrayList* class attempts to solve this problem. Because *ArrayList* does not know what kind of objects users might want to store, it simply stores instances of the *Object* class. Everything in .NET can be represented as an object; therefore, an *ArrayList* can store any type of object. Problem solved, right?

Although collections of objects does solve this problem, it introduces new ones. For example, if you wanted to store a collection of integers, you could write code like the following:

```vb
' VB
Dim myInts As New ArrayList()

myInts.Add(1)
myInts.Add(2)
myInts.Add(3)

For Each i as Object In myInts
    Dim number As Integer = CType(i, Integer)
Next
```

```
// C#
ArrayList myInts = new ArrayList();

myInts.Add(1);
myInts.Add(2);
myInts.Add(3);

foreach (Object i in myInts)
{
    int number = (int)i;
}
```

All is good; you can create a collection and add integers to it. You can get your integers out of the collection by casting them from the *Object* that your collection returns. But what if you added a line like the following one:

```
' VB
myInts.Add("4")
```

```
// C#
myInts.Add("4");
```

This will compile fine, but in your *foreach* loop it will throw an exception because the 4 is a string and not an integer. Dealing with such minor exceptions is troublesome. It would be better if you could deal with the collection so that it can store only integers. You could write a new class that has this behavior, as shown in the following code snippet:

```
' VB
Public Class IntList
    Implements ICollection
    Implements IEnumerable

    Private _innerList As ArrayList =  New ArrayList()

    Public Sub Add(ByVal number As Integer)
        _innerList.Add(number)
    End Sub

    Default Public ReadOnly Property Item(index As Integer) As Integer
        Get
            Return CType(_innerList(index), Integer)
        End Get
    End Property

    #region ICollection Members
    ' NOTE: ICollection Members are not shown here for brevity.
    '       You will need to implement ICollection on your own collections
    #End Region
```

```
    #region IEnumerable Members
    ' NOTE: IEnumerable Members are not shown here for brevity.
    '       You will need to implement IEnumerable on your own collections
    #End Region
End Class
```

```csharp
// C#
public class IntList : ICollection, IEnumerable
{
    private ArrayList _innerList = new ArrayList();

    public void Add(int number)
    {
        _innerList.Add(number);
    }

    public int this[int index]
    {
        get
        {
            return (int)_innerList[index];
        }
    }

    #region ICollection Members
    // NOTE: ICollection Members are not shown here for brevity.
    //       You will need to implement ICollection on your own collections
    #endregion

    #region IEnumerable Members
    // NOTE: IEnumerable Members are not shown here for brevity.
    //       You will need to implement IEnumerable on your own collections
    #endregion
}
```

To summarize, you create a new collection that supports the basic collection interfaces (*ICollection* and *IEnumerable*). You use an *ArrayList* to actually do the collecting of items. Finally, you make an *Add* method and an indexer that are strongly typed to integers. Now you can use this class like so:

```vb
' VB
Dim myIntegers As New IntList()

myIntegers.Add(1)
myIntegers.Add(2)
myIntegers.Add(3)
' myIntegers.Add("4") does not compile!

For Each i As Object In myIntegers
    Dim number As Integer = CType(i , Integer) ' Never throws an exception
Next
```

```csharp
// C#
IntList myIntegers = new IntList();

myIntegers.Add(1);
myIntegers.Add(2);
myIntegers.Add(3);
// myIntegers.Add("4"); does not compile!

foreach (Object i in myIntegers)
{
    int number = (int)i; // Never throws an exception
}
```

This works great. You get a compile error if someone tries to add something that is not an integer to your class. Your *foreach* code will never throw an exception because you never let anything except for integers into the collection. Problem solved, right?

It's a great solution, but it took a lot of work. It would be great if you could write a collection class and just specify in the class what type you want to use. Luckily, you can with generic types.

Generic types are types that take other type names to define them as a type. Instead of creating a collection that is strongly typed to a specific type, let's write a quick collection that can use any type:

```vb
' VB
Public Class MyList(Of T)
    Implements ICollection
    Implements IEnumerable

    Private _innerList As ArrayList =  New ArrayList()

    Public Sub Add(ByVal val As T)
        _innerList.Add(val)
    End Sub

    Default Public ReadOnly Property Item(index As Integer) As T
        Get
            Return CType(_innerList(index), T)
        End Get
    End Property

    #region ICollection Members
    ' ...
    #End Region

    #region IEnumerable Members
    ' ...
    #End Region
End Class
```

```
// C#
public class MyList<T> : ICollection, IEnumerable
{
    private ArrayList _innerList = new ArrayList();

    public void Add(T val)
    {
        _innerList.Add(val);
    }

    public T this[int index]
    {
        get
        {
            return (T)_innerList[index];
        }
    }

    #region ICollection Members
    // ...
    #endregion

    #region IEnumerable Members
    // ...
    #endregion
}
```

This class is identical to the collection created earlier in the chapter, but instead of making it a collection of integers, we'll use a generic type parameter **T**. In every place that we had integers, we'll now put the parameter **T**. This **T** is replaced with the type name during compilation. So we can use this class to create collections that are strongly typed to any valid .NET type, as shown in the following example:

```
' VB
Dim myIntList As new MyList(Of Integer)()
myIntList.Add(1)
' myIntList.Add("4") does not compile!

Dim myStringList As new MyList(Of String)()
myStringList.Add("1")
' myStringList.Add(2) does not compile!

// C#
MyList<int> myIntList = new MyList<int>();
myIntList.Add(1);
// myIntList.Add("4"); does not compile!

MyList<String> myStringList = new MyList<String>();
myStringList.Add("1");
// myStringList.Add(2); // does not compile!
```

When you use this generic class, you simply have to include the generic parameter (the name of a type) in the creation of the instance. The first example creates the integer collection we wanted, but the same generic class can also create a string collection or a collection of any type in .NET, even your own.

Generics are used in different places within the .NET Framework, but the generics you will see most often are generic collection classes. Note that you won't need to create your own generic list collection—the generic collection classes in the framework already have one...and many more.

Improving Safety and Performance

In the .NET Framework, generic equivalents exist for most of the classes already discussed in this chapter. In addition, several new collections exist that are available only as generic types. This section will provide examples of how to use each one of these types. Table 4-20 lists the types discussed, along with a mapping to their generic type equivalents.

Table 4-20   Equivalent Generic Types

Type	Generic Type
ArrayList	List<>
Queue	Queue<>
Stack	Stack<>
Hashtable	Dictionary<>
SortedList	SortedList<>
ListDictionary	Dictionary<>
HybridDictionary	Dictionary<>
OrderedDictionary	Dictionary<>
SortedDictionary	SortedDictionary<>
NameValueCollection	Dictionary<>
DictionaryEntry	KeyValuePair<>

Table 4-20   Equivalent Generic Types

Type	Generic Type
StringCollection	*List<String>*
StringDictionary	*Dictionary<String>*
N/A	*LinkedList<>*

As you can see from Table 4-20, most classes you have learned how to use in this chapter have a generic equivalent. The only collection type that is new is the *LinkedList* class, which will be covered shortly.

The Generic *List* Class

The generic *List* class is used to create simple type-safe ordered lists of objects. For example, if you wanted to have a list of integers, you would create a *List* object specifying the integer type for the generic parameter. Once you create an instance of the generic *List* class, you can then perform the following actions:

- You can use *Add* to add items into the *List*, but the items must match the type specified in the generic type parameter of the *List*.

- You can also use the indexer syntax to retrieve items of the *List* type.

- You can also use the *foreach* syntax to iterate over the list. This example stores integers in the *List*:

```vb
' VB
Dim intList As new List(Of Integer)()

intList.Add(1)
intList.Add(2)
intList.Add(3)

Dim number as Integer = intList(0)

For Each i as Integer in intList
    Console.WriteLine(i)
Next

// C#
List<int> intList = new List<int>();

intList.Add(1);
intList.Add(2);
```

```
intList.Add(3);
int number = intList[0];

foreach (int i in intList)
{
    Console.WriteLine(i);
}
```

The generic *List* class is as simple to use as the *ArrayList*, but type-safe based on the generic type parameter. As we saw Lesson 1, we can sort a *List* by calling the *Sort* method. It is no different for the generic *List* class, but there is a new overload worth mentioning. The *Sort* method on the generic *List* class supports a generic delegate.

What are generic delegates? They are just like generic classes or structures, but generic parameters are used only to define the calling convention of the delegate. For example, the *Sort* method of the generic *List* class takes a generic *Comparison* delegate. The generic *Comparison* delegate is defined like so:

```
' VB
public delegate int Comparison<T> (
    T x,
    T y
)

// C#
public delegate int Comparison<T> (
    T x,
     T y
)
```

Assume that you want to sort a *List* in reverse order. You could write an entire *Comparer* class to do this. Or you can make it easy on yourself and just write a method that matches the generic delegate, as shown here:

```
' VB
Shared Function ReverseIntComparison(ByVal x As Integer, _
                                     ByVal y As Integer) As Integer
    Return y - x
End Function

// C#
static int ReverseIntComparison(int x, int y)
{
    return y - x;
}
```

Notice that this method is not generic itself, but it matches up with the generic *Comparison* delegate. (Your *List* is composed of integers, so your *Comparison* must use integers for the two parameters.) This consistency allows you to call the sort function with your method to call for each comparison:

```
' VB
intList.Sort(ReverseIntComparison)
```

```
// C#
intList.Sort(ReverseIntComparison);
```

This approach is a lot easier than writing a whole *Comparison* class for seldom-used comparisons.

Generic *Queue* and *Stack* Classes

These generic classes are type-safe versions of the *Queue* and *Stack* classes discussed in Lesson 2. To use these collections, simply create new instances of them supplying the generic type parameter of the type to hold in the *Queue* or *Stack*. To use a generic *Queue* type, you can create an instance of the *Queue* class and do either of the following actions:

- You can use *Enqueue* to add items into the *Queue*, but the items must match the type specified in the generic type parameter of the *Queue*.

- You can also use *Dequeue* to retrieve items of the *Queue* type. This example stores strings in the *Queue*:

  ```
  ' VB
  Dim que as new Queue(Of String)()
  que.Enqueue("Hello")
  dim queued as String = que.Dequeue()
  ```

  ```
  // C#
  Queue<String> que = new Queue<String>();
  que.Enqueue("Hello");
  String queued = que.Dequeue();
  ```

A generic *Stack* type is just as simple to use. You can create an instance of the *Stack* class and perform either of the following actions:

- You can use *Push* to add items to the *Stack*, but the items must match the type specified in the generic type parameter of the *Stack*.

- You can also use *Pop* to retrieve items of the *Stack* type. For example, this *Stack* stores integers:

  ```
  ' VB
  Dim serials As new Stack(Of Integer)()
  serials.Push(1)
  Dim serialNumber As Integer = serials.Pop()
  ```

```
// C#
Stack<int> serials = new Stack<int>();
serials.Push(1);
int serialNumber = serials.Pop();
```

Generic *Dictionary* Class

The generic *Dictionary* class most closely resembles the *Hashtable*, *ListDictionary*, and *HybridDictionary* classes. The generic *Dictionary* class is unlike the generic *List*, *Stack*, and *Queue* classes in that it is used to store a key/value pair in a collection. To allow this, you will need to specify two generic type parameters when you create an instance of the generic *Dictionary* class. To use a generic *Dictionary* type, you can follow these steps:

1. Create an instance of the generic *Dictionary* class, specifying the type of the key and the type of the values to store in the *Dictionary*.

2. You can use indexer syntax to add or retrieve items in the *Dictionary*, but the types of these items' keys and values must match the types specified in the generic type parameters of the *Dictionary*. This example stores integers as the keys and strings as the values of the *Dictionary*:

```
' VB
Dim dict = New Dictionary(Of Integer, String)()
dict(3) = "Three"
dict(4) = "Four"
dict(1) = "One"
dict(2) = "Two"
Dim str as String = dict(3)

// C#
Dictionary<int, string> dict = new Dictionary<int, string>();
dict[3] = "Three";
dict[4] = "Four";
dict[1] = "One";
dict[2] = "Two";
String str = dict[3];
```

This example shows how to use an integer for the key in the *Dictionary* and how to use a string for the contents. One important difference between the generic *Dictionary* class and its nongeneric counterparts is that it does not use a *DictionaryEntry* object to hold the key/value pair. So when you retrieve individual objects or iterate over the collection, you will need to work with a new generic type called a *KeyValuePair*.

The generic *KeyValuePair* class takes two types just like the generic *Dictionary* class. Ordinarily, you will not create instances of this type; instead, you will return them from generic *Dictionary* classes. For example, if you iterate over a *Dictionary* object, the enumerator returns a *KeyValuePair* tied to the name key and value types specified in the *Dictionary* type. You can iterate over items in a generic *Dictionary* class by following these steps:

1. Create a *foreach* loop, specifying a generic *KeyValuePair* class as the type of object to be returned in each iteration. The types specified in the *KeyValuePair* must match the types used in the original *Dictionary*.

2. Inside the *foreach* block, you can use the *KeyValuePair* to retrieve the keys and values with properties called *Key* and *Value*, respectively. This example continues the *Dictionary* example shown earlier:

```vb
' VB
For Each i as KeyValuePair(Of Integer, String) in dict
    Console.WriteLine("{0} = {1}", i.Key, i.Value)
Next
```

```csharp
// C#
foreach (KeyValuePair<int, string> i in dict)
{
    Console.WriteLine("{0} = {1}", i.Key, i.Value);
}
```

The generic *Dictionary* class retains the order in which the items were added to the list.

Generic *SortedList* and *SortedDictionary* Classes

The generic *SortedList* and *SortedDictionary* classes are like the generic *Dictionary* class, with the exception that it maintains its items sorted by the key of the collection. To use a *SortedList*, follow these steps:

1. Create an instance of *SortedList*, specifying the key and value generic type parameters.

2. You can use indexer syntax to add or retrieve items in the *SortedList*, but the types of these items' keys and values must match the types specified in the generic type parameters of the *SortedList*.

3. Create a *foreach* loop, specifying a generic *KeyValuePair* class as the type of object to be returned in each iteration. The types specified in the *KeyValuePair* must match the types used in the original *SortedList*.

4. Inside the *foreach* block, you can use the *KeyValuePair* to retrieve the keys and values with properties called *Key* and *Value*, respectively. This example stores integers as the keys and strings as the values of the *SortedList*:

```vb
' VB
Dim sortList As new SortedList(Of String, Integer)()
sortList("One") = 1
sortList("Two") = 2
sortList("Three") = 3
```

```
For Each i as KeyValuePair(Of String, Integer) in sortList
    Console.WriteLine(i)
Next

// C#
SortedList<string, int> sortList = new SortedList<string, int>();
sortList["One"] = 1;
sortList["Two"] = 2;
sortList["Three"] = 3;

foreach (KeyValuePair<string, int> i in sortList)
{
    Console.WriteLine(i);
}
```

The use of the *SortedDictionary* is identical. To use a *SortedDictionary*, follow these steps:

1. Create an instance of *SortedDictionary*, specifying the key and value generic type parameters.

2. You can use indexer syntax to add or retrieve items in the *SortedDictionary*, but the types of these items' keys and values must match the types specified in the generic type parameters of the *SortedDictionary*.

3. Create a *foreach* loop, specifying a generic *KeyValuePair* class as the type of object to be returned in each iteration. The types specified in the *KeyValuePair* must match the types used in the original *SortedDictionary*.

4. Inside the *foreach* block, you can use the *KeyValuePair* to retrieve the keys and values with properties called *Key* and *Value*, respectively. This example stores integers as the keys and strings as the values of the *SortedDictionary*:

```
' VB
Dim sortedDict as new SortedDictionary(Of String, Integer)()
sortedDict("One") = 1
sortedDict("Two") = 2
sortedDict("Three") = 3

For Each KeyValuePair(Of string, int) i in sortedDict
    Console.WriteLine(i)
Next

// C#
SortedDictionary<string, int> sortedDict =
    new SortedDictionary<string, int>();
sortedDict["One"] = 1;
sortedDict["Two"] = 2;
sortedDict["Three"] = 3;
```

```
foreach (KeyValuePair<string, int> i in sortedDict)
{
    Console.WriteLine(i);
}
```

Generic *LinkedList* Class

The generic *LinkedList* class is a type of collection that is new to .NET, though the concept is well worn and tested. In fact, I remember writing a *LinkedList* in college. The idea behind a linked list is a set of items that are linked to each other. From each item, you can navigate to the next or previous item without having to have access to the collection itself. This is very useful when you are passing objects around that need to know about their siblings.

Table 4-21 and Table 4-22 show the interface to the generic *LinkedList* class:

Table 4-21 *LinkedList* **Properties**

Name	Description
Count	Gets the number of nodes in *LinkedList*
First	Gets the first node in *LinkedList*
Last	Gets the last node in *LinkedList*

Table 4-22 *LinkedList* **Methods**

Name	Description
AddAfter	Adds a new node after an existing node in *LinkedList*
AddBefore	Adds a new node before an existing node in *LinkedList*
AddFirst	Adds a new node at the beginning of *LinkedList*
AddLast	Adds a new node at the end of *LinkedList*
Clear	Removes all nodes from *LinkedList*
Contains	Tests to see whether a value is contained within *LinkedList*
CopyTo	Copies the entire *LinkedList* to an *Array*
Find	Locates the first node containing the specified value
FindLast	Locates the last node containing the specified value

Table 4-22 *LinkedList* **Methods**

Name	Description
Remove	Removes the first occurrence of a value or node from *LinkedList*
RemoveFirst	Removes the first item from *LinkedList*
RemoveLast	Removes the last item from *LinkedList*

A *LinkedList* contains a collection of *LinkedListNode* objects. When working with a *LinkedList*, you will be primarily getting and walking down the nodes. The properties of the generic *LinkedListNode* class are detailed in Table 4-23.

Table 4-23 *LinkedListNode* **Properties**

Name	Description
List	Gets the *LinkedList* that the node belongs to
Next	Gets the next node in the *LinkedList*
Previous	Gets the previous node in the *LinkedList*
Value	Gets the value contained in the node.

One peculiarity of the generic *LinkedList* class is that the implementation of the enumerator (*ILinkedListEnumerator*) allows for enumeration of the values of the list without using *LinkedListNode* objects. This behavior is unlike the generic *Dictionary* type, where the enumerator returns a generic *KeyValuePair* object. The difference exists because *LinkedListNode* objects can be used to walk the list of items, but only one piece of data is in each node. Therefore, there is no need to return the nodes during enumeration.

To use a *LinkedList*, you can create an instance of the *LinkedList* class, specifying the type to be stored as values in the list, then you can perform any of the following actions:

- You can use the *AddFirst* and *AddLast* methods to add items to the beginning and end of the list, respectively. The *AddFirst* and *AddLast* methods return a *LinkedListNode* if you are simply specifying the value in these methods.

- You can also use the *AddBefore* and *AddAfter* methods to add values in the middle of the list. To use these methods, you need to have access to a *LinkedListNode* at which you want to add values before or after.

■ You can also use the *foreach* construct to iterate over the values in the *LinkedList*. Note that the type you can enumerate are the values, not the nodes of the list. This example stores strings in the *LinkedList*:

```vb
' VB
Dim links As new LinkedList(Of String)()
Dim first as LinkedListNode(Of String) = links.AddLast("First")
Dim last as LinkedListNode(Of String) = links.AddFirst("Last")
Dim second as LinkedListNode(Of String) = links.AddBefore(last, "Second")
links.AddAfter(second, "Third")

For Each s As String In links
    Console.WriteLine(s)
Next
```

```csharp
// C#
LinkedList<String> links = new LinkedList<string>();
LinkedListNode<string> first = links.AddLast("First");
LinkedListNode<string> last = links.AddFirst("Last");
LinkedListNode<string> second = links.AddBefore(last, "Second");
links.AddAfter(second, "Third");

foreach (string s in links)
{
    Console.WriteLine(s);
}
```

Generic Collection Class Structure

Much like nongeneric collections, there are different parts of the way that the generic collections work that are common across different generic collections. These commonalities include the use of generic collection interfaces, generic enumerators, and generic comparisons.

Generic Collection Interfaces

In nongeneric collections, a set of interfaces define a consistent interface across collections. These interfaces include *IEnumerable*, *ICollection*, *IList*, and so on. Although generic collections implement these interfaces, they also support generic versions of these same interfaces, as shown in the following example:

```vb
' VB
Dim stringList As New List(Of String)

' ...

Dim theList As IList = CType(stringList, IList)
Dim firstItem As Object = theList(0)
```

```csharp
// C#
List<String> stringList = new List<String>();

// ...

IList theList = (IList)stringList;
object firstItem = theList[0];
```

The nongeneric *IList* interface is supported by the generic *List* collection. But in addition, there is a generic *IList* interface that can be used to get data from the interface in a type-safe way, like so:

```vbnet
' VB
Dim typeSafeList As IList(Of String) = CType(stringList, IList(Of String))
Dim firstString As String = typeSafeList(0)
```

```csharp
// C#
IList<String> typeSafeList = (IList<String>) stringList;
String firstString = typeSafeList[0];
```

This is the same for *ICollection*, *IDictionary*, *IEnumerable*, and so on. In general, if you are working with generic collections but also want to work with the interfaces instead of the specific class, you should use the generic version of the interface to support type safety.

Generic Collection Enumerators

The generic collections that are shown in this lesson all support iterating over the values in the collection. To facilitate iteration, each collection supports its own generic nested *Enumerator* structure. This enumerator structure is specialized to the same type's parent class. If you need to use the actual enumerator instead of the *foreach* construct, you can get the enumerator by calling the *GetEnumerator* method like so:

```vbnet
' VB
Dim stringList As New List(Of String) ()

' ...

Dim e As List(Of String).Enumerator = stringList.GetEnumerator

While e.MoveNext
    ' Typesafe Access to the current item
    Dim s As String = e.Current
End While
```

```
// C#
List<string> stringList = new List<string>();

// ...

List<string>.Enumerator e = stringList.GetEnumerator();

while (e.MoveNext())
{
    // Typesafe Access to the current item
    string s = e.Current;
}
```

By using the *Enumerator* structure, you can get at the current item in the generic collection in a type-safe way. All the generic collections support this *Enumerator* structure.

Generic Comparisons

In earlier lessons, we saw that we could use the *IComparer* and *IEqualityComparer* interfaces to provide for comparison operations for sorting and comparison actions in our collections. For the generic collections, there are generic versions of these interfaces. In cases when you need to write your own implementations of the *IComparer* and *IEqualityComparer* interfaces, generic base classes can do much of the work for you. These classes are the generic *Comparer* class and generic *EqualityComparer* class. If you need to implement your own comparison logic, you would inherit from these base classes, implement any abstract methods and override any default behavior that you need, as shown in the following example:

```
' VB
Class MyComparer(Of T)
    Inherits Comparer(Of T)

    Public Overrides Function Compare(ByVal x As T, ByVal y As T) _
                                      As Integer
      Return (x.GetHashCode - y.GetHashCode)
    End Function
End Class

// C#
class MyComparer<T> : Comparer<T>
{

    public override int Compare(T x, T y)
    {
        return x.GetHashCode() - y.GetHashCode();
    }
}
```

Writing Your Own Collections

The collection interfaces mentioned in this chapter (for example, *IList and ICollection*) can be used to implement your own collections. You can start from scratch and write your own collections that implement these interfaces, and the rest of the .NET Framework will recognize your classes as collections.

Much of the work required to write your collections is common to many collections. The .NET Framework exposes several base classes to wrap up this common behavior:

- *CollectionBase*
- *ReadOnlyCollectionBase*
- *DictionaryBase*

These base classes can be used as the basis of a collection of your own. The *CollectionBase* class supports the *IList*, *IEnumerable*, and *ICollection* interfaces. Inheriting from *CollectionBase* will allow you to have a collection that already supports these interfaces. You would use the *CollectionBase* class whenever you need a simple collection of items with some specific behavior that you do not find in the built-in collections.

Like the *CollectionBase* class, the *ReadOnlyCollectionBase* supports the *IList*, *IEnumerable*, and *ICollection* interfaces. The big difference in the *ReadOnlyCollectionBase* is that it does not support changing the collection from outside the class. This class is ideal when you need your own collection that is read-only to the users of the collection.

Unlike the *CollectionBase* and *ReadOnlyCollectionBase* classes, the *DictionaryBase* implements the *IDictionary*, *IEnumerable*, and *ICollection* interfaces. The *DictionaryBase* class would be used if you need to implement your own keyed collection.

Before .NET 2.0, it would be common to create your own collections using these interfaces in order to create type-safe collections. Now that generics are available, it is preferable to use the generic collections if your only requirement is a type-safe collection.

Lab: Create and Use a Generic Collection

In this lab, you create a generic *Dictionary* to hold country calling codes and the full name of the country. If you encounter a problem completing an exercise, the completed projects are available on the companion CD in the Code folder.

▶ **Exercise 1: Create a Generic Collection to Store State Data**

In this exercise, you create a generic *Dictionary* to hold calling codes with their full names.

1. Create a new console application called GenericCollections.

2. In the *Main* method of the project, create a new instance of the generic *Dictionary* class, specifying the key to be an integer and the value to be a string.

3. Add items to the collection using country codes for the keys and country names as the values.

4. Try to add strings for the keys of the country codes to make sure that the *Dictionary* is type safe. If they fail to compile, remove them in code or comment them out.

5. Write out to the console of one of your country codes using the indexer syntax of the *Dictionary*.

6. Iterate over the collection, and write out the country code and name of the country for each *KeyValuePair* in the *Dictionary*. Your code might look something like this:

```
' VB
Class Program

    Public Overloads Shared Sub Main()

        Dim countryLookup As New Dictionary(Of Integer, String)()

        countryLookup(44) = "United Kingdom"
        countryLookup(33) = "France"
        countryLookup(31) = "Netherlands"
        countryLookup(55) = "Brazil"
        'countryLookup["64"] = "New Zealand";

        Console.WriteLine("The 33 Code is for: {0}", countryLookup(33))

        For Each item As KeyValuePair(Of Integer, String) In countryLookup
            Dim code As Integer = item.Key
            Dim country As String = item.Value
            Console.WriteLine("Code {0} = {1}", code, country)
        Next
```

```
            Console.Read()
        End Sub
End Class

// C#
class Program
{
    static void Main(string[] args)
    {
        Dictionary<int, String> countryLookup =
            new Dictionary<int, String>();

        countryLookup[44] = "United Kingdom";
        countryLookup[33] = "France";
        countryLookup[31] = "Netherlands";
        countryLookup[55] = "Brazil";
        //countryLookup["64"] = "New Zealand";

        Console.WriteLine("The 33 Code is for: {0}", countryLookup[33]);

        foreach (KeyValuePair<int, String> item in countryLookup)
        {
            int code = item.Key;
            string country = item.Value;
            Console.WriteLine("Code {0} = {1}", code, country);
        }

        Console.Read();
    }
}
```

7. Build the project, and resolve any errors. Verify that the console application successfully shows all the countries added.

Lesson Summary

- Generic collections can be used to create more type-safe and potentially faster versions of their nongeneric counterparts.

- The generic *List*, *Dictionary*, *Queue*, *Stack*, *SortedList*, and *SortedDictionary* classes are type-safe versions of the collections that were discussed in Lessons 1 through 3.

- The new *LinkedList* generic class is a collection for storing items that know about their own relationship in the list, and it allows for iteration without having access to the collection itself.

Lesson Review

You can use the following questions to test your knowledge of the information in Lesson 5, "Generic Collections." The questions are also available on the companion CD if you prefer to review them in electronic form.

NOTE **Answers**

Answers to these questions and explanations of why each answer choice is right or wrong are located in the "Answers" section at the end of the book.

---

1. What kind of object does the generic *Dictionary* enumerator return?

    A. *Object*

    B. Objects of the generic class *KeyValuePair*

    C. *Key*

    D. *Value*

2. Where can you add items to a *LinkedList*? (Choose all that apply.)

    A. At the beginning of the *LinkedList*

    B. Before any specific node

    C. After any specific node

    D. At the end of the *LinkedList*

    E. At any numeric index in the *LinkedList*

Chapter Review

To further practice and reinforce the skills you learned in this chapter, you can perform the following tasks:

- Review the chapter summary.
- Review the list of key terms introduced in this chapter.
- Complete the case scenarios. These scenarios set up real-world situations involving the topics of this chapter and ask you to create a solution.
- Complete the suggested practices.
- Take a practice test.

Chapter Summary

- An *ArrayList* is the most basic of the collections, allowing you to keep an ordered list of objects.
- The *Queue* and *Stack* collections allow you to store sequential lists of items.
- Dictionaries can be used to keep key/value pairs of items for quick lookups.
- There are specialized collections to allow you to collect strings and *Boolean* values and to create string-only lookup tables.
- Generic collections are a mechanism for creating type-safe collections without writing all your own collection classes.

Key Terms

Do you know what these key terms mean? You can check your answers by looking up the terms in the glossary at the end of the book.

- collection
- generic type
- iteration

Case Scenarios

In the following case scenarios, you will apply what you've learned about how to use collections. You can find answers to these questions in the "Answers" section at the end of this book.

Case Scenario 1: Use an *ArrayList* to Store Status Codes

You are a developer for an IT deparment in a large company. You write small applications that help users view orders in the system. Your boss tells you that you need to add a status code field to an existing application. She says that the status codes are static and there are going to be at least five, although that number might change later.

Questions

Answer the following questions for your manager.

1. How are you going to store the status codes for use on the form?

2. If status codes need to be sorted differently for different users, is that a problem?

Case Scenario 2: Select the Correct Collection

You are a developer working for a small real estate business. You wrote a small application that allows the company to keep track of current listings. You are informed by your manager that the company has just been purchased by a larger company. Your manager wants the current application to be modified to keep a list of all the current sales people.

Interviews

Following is a list of company personnel interviewed and their statements:

- **Your Manager**   "We are unsure how many new sales people we have, but we need to be able to use a sales code and the full name of the sales person on different parts of the application."

- **Sales Person**   "Currently the application does not show the listing agent responsible. But if adding this behavior is going to slow down the application, we can live without it."

Questions

Answer the following questions for your manager:

1. Which collection will you use, knowing that the size of the list will change and might be either small or large?

2. How will showing the listing agent affect the performance of your application?

Case Scenario 3: Rewrite to Use a Type-Safe Collection

You are a lead developer in a large banking company. The IT department you work for has a lot of junior developers. One of the junior developers wrote a collection to keep a list of all the bank account activity for a year. Different developers are using it and having some trouble with run-time errors because an *ArrayList* is used to store all the activity.

Interviews

Following is a list of company personnel interviewed and their statements:

- **Your Manager**   "We need to change that collection to help our staff develop their applications faster and the applications themselves need to be more reliable."

- **Junior Programmer**   "When I use the collection, I try to add activity and some-times I accidentally add the wrong type of object into the collection. Since it compiles fine, we do not hear of a problem until one of the tellers has the application crash."

Questions

Answer the following questions for your manager.

1. How will you re-implement this collection to solve these issues?
2. Will the new collection be slower than the current one?

Suggested Practices

To help you successfully master the objectives covered in this chapter, complete the following tasks.

Use the Generic Collections

For this task, you should complete at least Practices 1 and 2. For a more in-depth understanding of generic collections you should also complete Practice 3.

Practice 1

- Create a new *ArrayList* object.
- Add some objects to it of different types.

Practice 2

- Create a generic *List* of a specific type.

- Add some objects of the right and wrong types.

- See how it works differently in each situation.

Practice 3

- Create a generic *Dictionary* object.

- Add several items to it.

- Iterate over the items, and see how the generic *KeyValuePair* class works.

Compare *Dictionary* Classes

For this task, you should complete at least Practice 1. If you want to see how large collections work, you should also complete Practices 2 and 3.

Practice 1

- Create *Hashtable*, *ListDictionary*, and *HybridDictionary* objects.

- Store five objects in each dictionary.

- Test the speed of lookups with the different dictionaries, and see how they differ based on the size of the store list.

Practice 2

- Change the objects you created in Practice 1 to store 100 objects, and see whether the results are similar.

Practice 3

- Change the objects you created in Practice 1 to store 10,000 objects, and see whether the results are similar.

Take a Practice Test

The practice tests on this book's companion CD offer many options. For example, you can test yourself on just one exam objective, or you can test yourself on all the 70-536 certification exam content. You can set up the test so that it closely simulates the experience of taking a certification exam, or you can set it up in study mode so that you can look at the correct answers and explanations after you answer each question.

MORE INFO   Practice tests

For details about all the practice test options available, see the "How to Use the Practice Tests" section in this book's Introduction.

Chapter 5
Serialization

Many applications need to store or transfer data stored in objects. To make these tasks as simple as possible, the .NET Framework includes several serialization techniques. These techniques convert objects into binary, Simple Object Access Protocol (SOAP), or XML documents that can be easily stored, transferred, and retrieved. This chapter discusses how to implement serialization using the tools built into the .NET Framework and how to implement serialization to meet custom requirements.

Exam objectives in this chapter:
- Serialize or deserialize an object or an object graph by using runtime serialization techniques. (Refer *System.Runtime.Serialization* namespace.)
  - Serialization interfaces.
  - Serialization attributes.
  - *SerializationEntry* structure and *SerializationInfo* class.
  - *ObjectManager* class.
  - *Formatter* class, *FormatterConverter* class, and *FormatterServices* class.
  - *StreamingContext* structure.
- Control the serialization of an object into XML format by using the *System.Xml.Serialization* namespace.
  - Serialize and deserialize objects into XML format by using the *XmlSerializer* class.
  - Control serialization by using serialization attributes.
  - Implement XML Serialization interfaces to provide custom formatting for XML serialization.
  - Delegates and event handlers are provided by the *System.Xml.Serialization* namespace.

- Implement custom serialization formatting by using the Serialization Formatter classes.

  ❑ *SoapFormatter* class. (Refer *System.Runtime.Serialization.Formatters.Soap* namespace.)

  ❑ *BinaryFormatter* class (Refer *System.Runtime.Serialization.Formatters.Binary* namespace.)

Lessons in this chapter:

Before You Begin

To complete the lessons in this chapter, you should be familiar with Microsoft Visual Basic or C# and be comfortable with the following tasks:

- Create a console application in Microsoft Visual Studio using Visual Basic or C#.
- Add references to system class libraries to a project.
- Write to files and stream objects.

Lesson 1: Serializing Objects

When you create an object in a .NET Framework application, you probably never think about how the data is stored in memory. You shouldn't have to—the .NET Framework takes care of that for you. However, if you want to store the contents of an object to a file, send an object to another process, or transmit it across the network, you do have to think about how the object is represented because you will need to convert it to a different format. This conversion is called *serialization.*

After this lesson, you will be able to:

- Choose between binary, SOAP, XML, and custom serialization.
- Serialize and deserialize objects using the standard libraries.
- Create classes that can be serialized and deserialized.
- Change the standard behavior of the serialization and deserialization process.
- Implement custom serialization to take complete control of the serialization process.

Estimated lesson time: 45 minutes

What Is Serialization?

Serialization, as implemented in the *System.Runtime.Serialization* namespace, is the process of serializing and deserializing objects so that they can be stored or transferred and then later re-created. *Serializing* is the process of converting an object into a linear sequence of bytes that can be stored or transferred. *Deserializing* is the process of converting a previously serialized sequence of bytes into an object.

Real World

Tony Northrup

Serialization can save a lot of development time. Before serialization was available, I had to write custom code just to store or transfer information. Of course, this code tended to break when I made changes elsewhere to the application. Nowadays, with the .NET Framework, I can store and transfer data with just a couple of lines of code. In fact, I rarely find the need to modify the default serialization behavior—it just works.

Basically, if you want to store an object (or multiple objects) in a file for later retrieval, you store the output of serialization. The next time you want to read the objects, you call the deserialization methods, and your object is re-created exactly as it had been previously. Similarly, if you want to send an object to an application running on another computer, you establish a network connection, serialize the object to the stream, and then deserialize the object on the remote application. Teleportation in science fiction is a good example of serialization (though teleportation is not currently supported by the .NET Framework).

NOTE Serialization behind the scenes

Windows relies on serialization for many important tasks, including Web services, remoting, and copying items to the clipboard.

How to Serialize an Object

At a high level, the steps for serializing an object are as follows:

1. Create a stream object to hold the serialized output.

2. Create a *BinaryFormatter* object (located in *System.Runtime.Serialization.Formatters .Binary*).

3. Call the *BinaryFormatter.Serialize* method to serialize the object, and output the result to the stream.

At the development level, serialization can be implemented with very little code. The following console application—which requires the *System.IO*, *System.Runtime.Serialization*, and *System.Runtime.Serialization.Formatters.Binary* namespaces—demonstrates this:

```
' VB
Dim data As String = "This must be stored in a file."


' Create file to save the data to
Dim fs As FileStream = New FileStream("SerializedString.Data", _
FileMode.Create)

' Create a BinaryFormatter object to perform the serialization
Dim bf As BinaryFormatter = New BinaryFormatter

' Use the BinaryFormatter object to serialize the data to the file
bf.Serialize(fs, data)

' Close the file
fs.Close
```

```csharp
// C#
string data = "This must be stored in a file.";

// Create file to save the data to
FileStream fs = new FileStream("SerializedString.Data", FileMode.Create);

// Create a BinaryFormatter object to perform the serialization
BinaryFormatter bf = new BinaryFormatter();

// Use the BinaryFormatter object to serialize the data to the file
bf.Serialize(fs, data);

// Close the file
fs.Close();
```

If you run the application and open the SerializedString.Data file in Notepad, you'll see the contents of the string you stored surrounded by binary information (which appears as garbage in Notepad), as shown in Figure 5-1. The .NET Framework stored the string as ASCII text and then added a few more binary bytes before and after the text to describe the data for the deserializer.

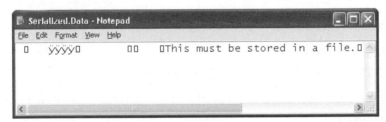

Figure 5-1   Serialized objects can be stored as files but are not text files.

If you just needed to store a single string in a file, you wouldn't need to use serialization—you could simply write the string directly to a text file. Serialization becomes useful when storing more complex information, such as the current date and time. As the following code sample demonstrates, serializing complex objects is as simple as serializing a string:

```vb
' VB
' Create file to save the data to
Dim fs As FileStream = New FileStream("SerializedDate.Data", _
FileMode.Create)

' Create a BinaryFormatter object to perform the serialization
Dim bf As BinaryFormatter = New BinaryFormatter

' Use the BinaryFormatter object to serialize the data to the file
bf.Serialize(fs, System.DateTime.Now)
```

```
' Close the file
fs.Close()

// C#
// Create file to save the data to
FileStream fs = new FileStream("SerializedDate.Data", FileMode.Create);

// Create a BinaryFormatter object to perform the serialization
BinaryFormatter bf = new BinaryFormatter();

// Use the BinaryFormatter object to serialize the data to the file
bf.Serialize(fs, System.DateTime.Now);

// Close the file
fs.Close();
```

How to Deserialize an Object

Deserializing an object allows you to create a new object based on stored data. Essentially, deserializing restores a saved object. At a high level, the steps for deserializing an object are as follows:

1. Create a stream object to read the serialized output.

2. Create a *BinaryFormatter* object.

3. Create a new object to store the deserialized data.

4. Call the *BinaryFormatter.Deserialize* method to deserialize the object, and cast it to the correct type.

At the code level, the steps for deserializing an object are easy to implement. The following console application—which requires the *System.IO*, *System.Runtime.Serialization*, and *System.Runtime.Serialization.Formatters.Binary* namespaces—demonstrates how to read and display the serialized string data saved in an earlier example:

```
' VB
' Open file to read the data from
Dim fs As FileStream = New FileStream("SerializedString.Data", _
FileMode.Open)

' Create a BinaryFormatter object to perform the deserialization
Dim bf As BinaryFormatter = New BinaryFormatter

' Create the object to store the deserialized data
Dim data As String = ""

' Use the BinaryFormatter object to deserialize the data from the file
data = CType(bf.Deserialize(fs),String)
```

```
' Close the file
fs.Close

' Display the deserialized string
Console.WriteLine(data)

// C#
// Open file to read the data from
FileStream fs = new FileStream("SerializedString.Data", FileMode.Open);

// Create a BinaryFormatter object to perform the deserialization
BinaryFormatter bf = new BinaryFormatter();

// Create the object to store the deserialized data
string data = "";

// Use the BinaryFormatter object to deserialize the data from the file
data = (string) bf.Deserialize(fs);

// Close the file
fs.Close();

// Display the deserialized string
Console.WriteLine(data);
```

Deserializing a more complex object, such as *DateTime*, works exactly the same. The following code sample displays the day of the week and the time stored by a previous code sample:

```
' VB
' Open file to read the data from
Dim fs As FileStream = New FileStream("SerializedDate.Data", FileMode.Open)

' Create a BinaryFormatter object to perform the deserialization
Dim bf As BinaryFormatter = New BinaryFormatter

' Create the object to store the deserialized data
Dim previousTime As DateTime = New DateTime

' Use the BinaryFormatter object to deserialize the data from the file
previousTime = CType(bf.Deserialize(fs),DateTime)

' Close the file
fs.Close

' Display the deserialized time
Console.WriteLine(("Day: " _
    + (previousTime.DayOfWeek + (", Time: " _
    + previousTime.TimeOfDay.ToString))))
```

```csharp
// C#
// Open file to read the data from
FileStream fs = new FileStream("SerializedDate.Data", FileMode.Open);

// Create a BinaryFormatter object to perform the deserialization
BinaryFormatter bf = new BinaryFormatter();

// Create the object to store the deserialized data
DateTime previousTime = new DateTime();

// Use the BinaryFormatter object to deserialize the data from the file
previousTime = (DateTime) bf.Deserialize(fs);

// Close the file
fs.Close();

// Display the deserialized time
Console.WriteLine("Day: " + previousTime.DayOfWeek + ", _
    Time: " + previousTime.TimeOfDay.ToString());
```

As these code samples demonstrate, storing and retrieving objects requires only a few lines of code, no matter how complex the object is.

NOTE   **The inner workings of deserialization**

Within the runtime, deserialization can be a complex process. The runtime proceeds through the deserialization process sequentially, starting at the beginning and working its way through to the end. The process gets complicated if an object in the serialized stream refers to another object.

If an object references another object, the *Formatter* (discussed in more detail in Lesson 3) queries the *ObjectManager* to determine whether the referenced object has already been deserialized (a backward reference), or whether it has not yet been deserialized (a forward reference). If it is a backward reference, the *Formatter* immediately completes the reference. However, if it is a forward reference, the *Formatter* registers a *fixup* with the *ObjectManager*. A fixup is the process of finalizing an object reference after the referenced object has been deserialized. Once the referenced object is deserialized, *ObjectManager* completes the reference.

How to Create Classes That Can Be Serialized

You can serialize and deserialize custom classes by adding the *Serializable* attribute to the class. This is important to do so that you, or other developers using your class, can easily store or transfer instances of the class. Even if you do not immediately need serialization, it is good practice to enable it for future use.

If you are satisfied with the default handling of the serialization, no other code besides the *Serializable* attribute is necessary. When your class is serialized, the runtime serializes all members, including private members.

NOTE Security concerns with serialization

Serialization can allow other code to see or modify object instance data that would otherwise be inaccessible. Therefore, code performing serialization requires the *SecurityPermission* attribute (from the *System.Security.Permissions* namespace) with the *SerializationFormatter* flag specified. Under default policy, this permission is not given to Internet-downloaded or intranet code; only code on the local computer is granted this permission. The *GetObjectData* method should be explicitly protected either by demanding the *SecurityPermission* attribute with the *SerializationFormatter* flag specified, as illustrated in the sample code in Lesson 3, or by demanding other permissions that specifically help protect private data. For more information about code security, refer to Chapter 12, "User and Data Security."

You can also control serialization of your classes to improve the efficiency of your class or to meet custom requirements. The sections that follow discuss how to customize how your class behaves during serialization.

How to Disable Serialization of Specific Members

Some members of your class, such as temporary or calculated values, might not need to be stored. For example, consider the following class, *ShoppingCartItem*:

```vb
' VB
<Serializable()> Class ShoppingCartItem
    Public productId As Integer
    Public price As Decimal
    Public quantity As Integer
    Public total As Decimal

    Public Sub New(ByVal _productID As Integer, ByVal _price As Decimal, _
        ByVal _quantity As Integer)
        MyBase.New
        productId = _productID
        price = _price
        quantity = _quantity
        total = (price * quantity)
    End Sub
End Class
```

```csharp
// C#
[Serializable]
class ShoppingCartItem
{
    public int productId;
    public decimal price;
    public int quantity;
    public decimal total;
```

```
public ShoppingCartItem(int _productID, decimal _price, int _quantity)
{
    productId = _productID;
    price = _price;
    quantity = _quantity;
    total = price * quantity;
}
}
```

The *ShoppingCartItem* includes three members that must be provided by the application when the object is created. The fourth member, *total*, is dynamically calculated by multiplying the price and quantity. If this class were serialized as-is, the total would be stored with the serialized object, wasting a small amount of storage. To reduce the size of the serialized object (and thus reduce storage requirements when writing the serialized object to a disk, and bandwidth requirements when transmitting the serialized object across the network), add the *NonSerialized* attribute to the *total* member:

```
' VB
<NonSerialized()> Public total As Decimal
```

```
// C#
[NonSerialized] public decimal total;
```

Now, when the object is serialized, the *total* member will be omitted. Similarly, the *total* member will not be initialized when the object is deserialized. However, the value for *total* must still be calculated before the deserialized object is used.

To enable your class to automatically initialize a nonserialized member, use the *IDeserializationCallback* interface, and then implement *IDeserializationCallback .OnDeserialization*. Each time your class is deserialized, the runtime will call the *IDeserializationCallback.OnDeserialization* method after deserialization is complete. The following example shows the *ShoppingCartItem* class modified to not serialize the *total* value, and to automatically calculate the value upon deserialization:

```
' VB
<Serializable()> Class ShoppingCartItem
    Implements IDeserializationCallback

    Public productId As Integer
    Public price As Decimal
    Public quantity As Integer
    <NonSerialized()> Public total As Decimal

    Public Sub New(ByVal _productID As Integer, ByVal _price As Decimal, _
        ByVal quantity As Integer)
        MyBase.New
        productId = _productID
        price = _price
```

```
        quantity = _quantity
        total = (price * quantity)
    End Sub

    Sub IDeserializationCallback_OnDeserialization(ByVal sender As Object)
        Implements IDeserializationCallback.OnDeserialization
        ' After deserialization, calculate the total
        total = (price * quantity)
    End Sub
End Class
// C#
[Serializable]
class ShoppingCartItem : IDeserializationCallback {
    public int productId;
    public decimal price;
    public int quantity;
    [NonSerialized] public decimal total;
    public ShoppingCartItem(int _productID, decimal _price, int _quantity)
    {
        productId = _productID;
        price = _price;
        quantity = _quantity;
        total = price * quantity;
    }
    void IDeserializationCallback.OnDeserialization(Object sender)
    {
        // After deserialization, calculate the total
        total = price * quantity;
    }
}
```

With *OnDeserialization* implemented, the *total* member is now properly defined and available to applications after the class is deserialized.

How to Provide Version Compatibility

You might have version compatibility issues if you ever attempt to deserialize an object that has been serialized by an earlier version of your application. Specifically, if you add a member to a custom class and attempt to deserialize an object that lacks that member, the runtime will throw an exception. In other words, if you add a member to a class in version 3.1 of your application, it will not be able to deserialize an object created by version 3.0 of your application.

To overcome this limitation, you have two choices:

- Implement custom serialization, as described in Lesson 3, that is capable of importing earlier serialized objects.

- Apply the *OptionalField* attribute to newly added members that might cause version compatibility problems.

The *OptionalField* attribute does not affect the serialization process. During deserialization, if the member was not serialized, the runtime will leave the member's value as *null* rather than throwing an exception. The following example shows how to use the *OptionalField* attribute:

```
' VB
<Serializable()> Class ShoppingCartItem
    Implements IDeserializationCallback

    Public productId As Integer
    Public price As Decimal
    Public quantity As Integer
    <NonSerialized()> Public total As Decimal
    <OptionalField()> Public taxable As Boolean
```

```
// C#
[Serializable]
class ShoppingCartItem : IDeserializationCallback
{
    public int productId;
    public decimal price;
    public int quantity;
    [NonSerialized] public decimal total;
    [OptionalField] public bool taxable;
```

If you need to initialize optional members, either implement the *IDeserializationCallback* interface as described in the "How to Disable Serialization of Specific Members" section earlier in this lesson, or respond to serialization events, as described in Lesson 3.

NOTE   .NET 2.0

The .NET Framework 2.0 is capable of deserializing objects that have unused members, so you can still have the ability to deserialize an object if it has a member that has been removed since serialization. This behavior is different from .NET Framework 1.0 and 1.1, which threw an exception if additional information was found in the serialized object.

Best Practices for Version Compatibility

To ensure proper versioning behavior, follow these rules when modifying a custom class from version to version:

- Never remove a serialized field.
- Never apply the *NonSerializedAttribute* attribute to a field if the attribute was not applied to the field in a previous version.
- Never change the name or type of a serialized field.

- When adding a new serialized field, apply the *OptionalFieldAttribute* attribute.

- When removing a *NonSerializedAttribute* attribute from a field that was not serializable in a previous version, apply the *OptionalFieldAttribute* attribute.

- For all optional fields, set meaningful defaults using the serialization callbacks unless *0* or *null* as defaults are acceptable.

Choosing a Serialization Format

The .NET Framework includes two methods for formatting serialized data in the *System .Runtime.Serialization* namespace, both of which implement the *IRemotingFormatter* interface:

- **BinaryFormatter**   Located in the *System.Runtime.Serialization.Formatters.Binary* namespace, this formatter is the most efficient way to serialize objects that will be read by only .NET Framework–based applications.

- **SoapFormatter**   Located in the *System.Runtime.Serialization.Formatters.Soap* namespace, this XML-based formatter is the most reliable way to serialize objects that will be transmitted across a network or read by non–.NET Framework applications. *SoapFormatter* is more likely to successfully traverse firewalls than *BinaryFormatter*.

In summary, you should choose *BinaryFormatter* only when you know that all clients opening the serialized data will be .NET Framework applications. Therefore, if you are writing objects to the disk to be read later by your application, *BinaryFormatter* is perfect. Use *SoapFormatter* when other applications might read your serialized data and when sending data across a network. *SoapFormatter* also works reliably in situations where you could choose *BinaryFormatter*, but the serialized object can consume three to four times more space.

While *SoapFormatter* is XML-based, it is primarily intended to be used by SOAP Web services. If your goal is to store objects in an open, standards-based document that might be consumed by applications running on other platforms, the most flexible way to perform serialization is to choose XML serialization. Lesson 2 in this chapter discusses XML serialization at length.

How to Use *SoapFormatter*

To use *SoapFormatter*, add a reference to the *System.Runtime.Serialization.Formatters .Soap.dll* assembly to your project. (Unlike *BinaryFormatter*, it is not included by default.) Then write code exactly as you would to use *BinaryFormatter*, but substitute the *SoapFormatter* class for the *BinaryFormatter* class.

While writing code for *BinaryFormatter* and *SoapFormatter* is very similar, the serialized data is very different. The following example is a three-member object serialized with *SoapFormatter* that has been slightly edited for readability:

```
<SOAP-ENV:Envelope xmlns:xsi="http://www.w3.org/2001/XMLSchema-instance">
    <SOAP-ENV:Body>
        <a1:ShoppingCartItem id="ref-1">
            <productId>100</productId>
            <price>10.25</price>
            <quantity>2</quantity>
        </a1:ShoppingCartItem>
    </SOAP-ENV:Body>
</SOAP-ENV:Envelope>
```

NOTE .NET 2.0

SoapFormatter does not support serialization compatibility between versions of the .NET Framework. Serialization between versions 1.1 and 2.0 types in the Framework often fails. *BinaryFormatter* does provide compatibility between versions.

How to Control SOAP Serialization

Binary serialization is intended for use only by .NET Framework–based applications. Therefore, there is rarely a need to modify the standard formatting. However, SOAP serialization is intended to be read by a variety of platforms. Additionally, you might need to serialize an object to meet specific requirements, such as predefined SOAP attribute and element names.

You can control the formatting of a SOAP serialized document by using the attributes listed in Table 5-1.

Table 5-1 Soap Serialization Attributes

Attribute	Applies to	Specifies
SoapAttribute	Public field, property, parameter, or return value	The class member will be serialized as an XML attribute.
SoapElement	Public field, property, parameter, or return value	The class will be serialized as an XML element.
SoapEnum	Public field that is an enumeration identifier	The element name of an enumeration member.

Table 5-1 Soap Serialization Attributes

Attribute	Applies to	Specifies
SoapIgnore	Public properties and fields	The property or field should be ignored when the containing class is serialized.
SoapInclude	Public derived class declarations and public methods for Web Services Description Language (WSDL) documents	The type should be included when generating schemas (to be recognized when serialized).

SOAP serialization attributes function similarly to XML serialization attributes. For more information about XML serialization attributes, refer to the "How to Control XML Serialization" section in Lesson 2 of this chapter.

Guidelines for Serialization

Keep the following guidelines in mind when using serialization:

- When in doubt, mark a class as *Serializable*. Even if you do not need to serialize it now, you might need serialization later. Or another developer might need to serialize a derived class.

- Mark calculated or temporary members as *NonSerialized*. For example, if you track the current thread ID in a member variable, the thread ID is likely to not be valid upon deserialization. Therefore, you should not store it.

- Use *SoapFormatter* when you require portability. Use *BinaryFormatter* for greatest efficiency.

Lab: Serialize and Deserialize Objects

In this lab, you modify a class to enable efficient serialization and then update an application to perform serialization and deserialization of that class. If you encounter a problem completing an exercise, the completed projects are available on the companion CD in the Code folder.

▶ **Exercise 1: Make a Class Serializable**

In this exercise, you modify a custom class so that developers can easily store it to the disk for later retrieval or transfer it across a network to another .NET Framework application.

1. Copy the Chapter05\Lesson1-Serialize-People folder from the companion CD to your hard disk, and open either the C# version or the Visual Basic version of the Serialize-People project.

2. Examine the *Person* class. What changes do you need to make so that the *Person* class is serializable?

   You must add the *Serializable* attribute.

3. Add the *System.Runtime.Serialization* namespace to the class.

4. Add the *Serializable* attribute to the *Person* class, and then build the project to ensure it compiles correctly.

▶ **Exercise 2: Serialize an Object**

In this exercise, you write code to store an object to the disk using the most efficient method possible.

1. Open the Serialize-People project you modified in Exercise 1.

2. Add the *System.IO*, *System.Runtime.Serialization* and *System.Runtime.Serialization .Formatters.Binary* namespaces to the file containing Main.

3. Add code to the *Serialize* method to serialize the *sp* object to a file in the current directory named *Person.dat*. Your code could look like the following:

```
' VB
Private Sub Serialize(ByVal sp As Person)
    ' Create file to save the data to
    Dim fs As FileStream = New FileStream("Person.Dat", FileMode.Create)

    ' Create a BinaryFormatter object to perform the serialization
    Dim bf As BinaryFormatter = New BinaryFormatter

    ' Use the BinaryFormatter object to serialize the data to the file
    bf.Serialize(fs, sp)

    ' Close the file
    fs.Close()
End Sub

// C#
private static void Serialize(Person sp)
{
    // Create file to save the data to
    FileStream fs = new FileStream("Person.Dat", FileMode.Create);

    // Create a BinaryFormatter object to perform the serialization
    BinaryFormatter bf = new BinaryFormatter();
```

```
        // Use the BinaryFormatter object to serialize the data to the file
        bf.Serialize(fs, sp);

        // Close the file
        fs.Close();
    }
```

4. Build the project, and resolve any errors.

5. Open a command prompt to the build directory, and then test the application by running the following command:

```
Serialize-People Tony 1923 4 22
```

6. Examine the serialized data by opening the file your application produced to verify that the name you entered was successfully captured. The date and age information are contained in the serialized data as well; however, they are less easy to interpret in Notepad.

▶ **Exercise 3: Deserialize an Object**

In this exercise, you must read an object from the disk that has been serialized by using *BinaryFormatter*.

1. Open the Serialize-People project you modified in Exercises 1 and 2.

2. Add code to the *Deserialize* method in the main program to deserialize the *dsp* object from a file in the default directory named *Person.dat*. Your code could look like the following:

```
' VB
Private Function Deserialize() As Person
    Dim dsp As Person = New Person

    ' Open file to read the data from
    Dim fs As FileStream = New FileStream("Person.Dat", FileMode.Open)

    ' Create a BinaryFormatter object to perform the deserialization
    Dim bf As BinaryFormatter = New BinaryFormatter

    ' Use the BinaryFormatter object to deserialize the data from the file
    dsp = CType(bf.Deserialize(fs), Person)

    ' Close the file
    fs.Close()

    Return dsp
End Function

// C#
private static Person Deserialize()
{
    Person dsp = new Person();
```

```
    // Open file to read the data from
    FileStream fs = new FileStream("Person.Dat", FileMode.Open);

    // Create a BinaryFormatter object to perform the deserialization
    BinaryFormatter bf = new BinaryFormatter();

    // Use the BinaryFormatter object to deserialize the data from the file
    dsp = (Person)bf.Deserialize(fs);

    // Close the file
    fs.Close();

    return dsp;
}
```

3. Build the project, and resolve any errors.

4. Open a command prompt to the build directory, and then run the following command with no command-line parameters:

   ```
   Serialize-People
   ```

   Note that the *Serialize-People* command displays the name, date of birth, and age of the previously serialized *Person* object.

▶ **Exercise 4: Optimize a Class for Deserialization**

In this exercise, you modify a class to improve the efficiency of serialization.

1. Open the Serialize-People project you modified in Exercises 1, 2, and 3.

2. Modify the *Person* class to prevent the age member from being serialized. To do this, add the *NonSerialized* attribute to the member, as the following code demonstrates:

   ```
   ' VB
   <NonSerialized()> Public age As Integer
   ```

   ```
   // C#
   [NonSerialized] public int age;
   ```

3. Build and run the project with no command-line parameters. Note that the *Serialize-People* command displays the name and date of birth of the previously serialized *Person* object. However, the age is displayed as zero.

4. Modify the *Person* class to implement the *IDeserializationCallback* interface, as the following code snippet demonstrates:

   ```
   ' VB
   <Serializable()> Public Class Person
       Implements IDeserializationCallback
   ```

```
// C#
namespace Serialize_People
{
    [Serializable]
    class Person : IDeserializationCallback
```

5. Add the *IDeserializationCallback.OnDeserialization* method to the *Person* class. Your code could look like the following:

```
' VB
Sub IDeserializationCallback_OnDeserialization(ByVal sender As Object) _
    Implements IDeserializationCallback.OnDeserialization
    ' After deserialization, calculate the age
    CalculateAge()
End Sub
```

```
// C#
void IDeserializationCallback.OnDeserialization(Object sender)
{
    // After deserialization, calculate the age
    CalculateAge();
}
```

6. Build and run the project with no command-line parameters. Note that the *Serialize-People* command displays the name, date of birth, and age of the previously serialized *Person* object. The age displays properly this time because it is calculated immediately after deserialization.

Lesson Summary

- Serialization is the process of converting information into a byte stream that can be stored or transferred.

- To serialize an object, first create a stream object. Then create a *BinaryFormatter* object and call the *BinaryFormatter.Serialize* method. To deserialize an object, follow the same steps but call the *BinaryFormatter.Deserialize* method.

- To create a class that can be serialized, add the *Serializable* attribute. You can also use attributes to disable serialization of specific members.

- *SoapFormatter* provides a less efficient, but more interoperable, alternative to the *BinaryFormatter* class.

- To use *SoapFormatter*, follow the same process as you would for *BinaryFormatter*, but use the *System.Runtime.Serialization.Formatters.Soap.SoapFormatter* class.

- You can control *SoapFormatter* serialization by using attributes to specify the names of serialized elements and to specify whether a member is serialized as an element or an attribute.

- It is a good practice to make all classes serializable even if you do not immediately require serialization. You should disable serialization for calculated and temporary members.

Lesson Review

You can use the following questions to test your knowledge of the information in Lesson 1, "Serializing Objects." The questions are also available on the companion CD if you prefer to review them in electronic form.

NOTE   Answers

Answers to these questions and explanations of why each answer choice is right or wrong are located in the "Answers" section at the end of the book.

---

1. Which of the following are required to serialize an object? (Choose all that apply.)

    A. An instance of *BinaryFormatter* or *SoapFormatter*

    B. File permissions to create temporary files

    C. Internet Information Services

    D. A stream object

2. Which of the following attributes should you add to a class to enable it to be serialized?

    A. *ISerializable*

    B. *Serializable*

    C. *SoapInclude*

    D. *OnDeserialization*

3. Which of the following attributes should you add to a member to prevent it from being serialized by *BinaryFormatter*?

    A. *NonSerialized*

    B. *Serializable*

    C. *SerializationException*

    D. *SoapIgnore*

4. Which of the following interfaces should you implement to enable you to run a method after an instance of your class is deserialized?

    A. *IFormatter*

    B. *ISerializable*

    C. *IDeserializationCallback*

    D. *IObjectReference*

Lesson 2: XML Serialization

XML is a standardized, text-based document format for storing application-readable information. Just as HTML provided a text-based standard for formatting human-readable documents, XML provides a standard that can be easily processed by computers. XML can be used to store any type of data, including documents (the latest version of Microsoft Office stores documents using XML), pictures, music, binary files, and database information.

The .NET Framework includes several libraries for reading and writing XML files, including the *System.Xml.Serialization* namespace. *System.Xml.Serialization* provides methods for converting objects, including those based on custom classes, to and from XML files. With XML serialization, you can write almost any object to a text file for later retrieval with only a few lines of code. Similarly, you can use XML serialization to transmit objects between computers through Web services—even if the remote computer is not using the .NET Framework.

***

After this lesson, you will be able to:

- Serialize and deserialize objects using XML serialization.
- Customize serialization behavior of custom classes to meet specific requirements, such as an XML schema.
- Serialize a dataset.

Estimated lesson time: 40 minutes

***

Why Use XML Serialization?

Use XML serialization when you need to exchange an object with an application that might not be based on the .NET Framework, and you do not need to serialize any private members. XML serialization provides the following benefits over standard serialization:

- **Greater interoperability**   XML is a text-based file standard, and all modern development environments include libraries for processing XML files. Therefore, an object that is serialized by using XML can be easily processed by an application written for a different operating system in a different development environment.

- **More administrator-friendly**   Objects serialized by using XML can be viewed and edited by using any text editor, including Notepad. If you are storing objects in files, this gives administrators the opportunity to view and edit the XML file. This can be useful for customizing your application, troubleshooting problems, and developing new applications that interoperate with your existing application.

- **Better forward-compatibility**   Objects serialized by using XML are self-describing and easily processed. Therefore, when the time comes to replace your application, the new application will have an easier time processing your serialized objects if you use XML.

Additionally, you must use XML serialization any time you need to conform to a specific XML schema or control how an object is encoded. XML cannot be used for every situation, however. Specifically, XML serialization has the following limitations:

- XML serialization can serialize only public data. You cannot serialize private data.

- You cannot serialize object graphs; you can use XML serialization only on objects.

How to Use XML to Serialize an Object

At a high level, the steps for serializing an object are as follows:

1. Create a stream, *TextWriter*, or *XmlWriter* object to hold the serialized output.

2. Create an *XmlSerializer* object (in the *System.Xml.Serialization* namespace) by passing it the type of object you plan to serialize.

3. Call the *XmlSerializer.Serialize* method to serialize the object and output the results to the stream.

At the code level, these steps are similar to standard serialization. The following console application—which requires using *System.IO* and *System.Xml.Serialization* namespaces—demonstrates the simplicity:

```
' VB
' Create file to save the data to
Dim fs As FileStream = New FileStream("SerializedDate.XML", _
    FileMode.Create)

' Create an XmlSerializer object to perform the serialization
Dim xs As XmlSerializer = New XmlSerializer(GetType(DateTime))

' Use the XmlSerializer object to serialize the data to the file
xs.Serialize(fs, System.DateTime.Now)

' Close the file
fs.Close

// C#
// Create file to save the data to
FileStream fs = new FileStream("SerializedDate.XML", FileMode.Create);
```

```
// Create an XmlSerializer object to perform the serialization
XmlSerializer xs = new XmlSerializer(typeof(DateTime));

// Use the XmlSerializer object to serialize the data to the file
xs.Serialize(fs, System.DateTime.Now);

// Close the file
fs.Close();
```

When run, the application produces a text file similar to the following:

```
<?xml version="1.0" ?>
<dateTime>2005-12-05T16:28:11.0533408-05:00</dateTime>
```

Compared with the serialized *DateTime* object created in Lesson 1, XML serialization produces a very readable, easily edited file.

How to Use XML to Deserialize an Object

To deserialize an object, follow these steps:

1. Create a stream, *TextReader*, or *XmlReader* object to read the serialized input.

2. Create an *XmlSerializer* object (in the *System.Xml.Serialization* namespace) by passing it the type of object you plan to deserialize.

3. Call the *XmlSerializer.Deserialize* method to deserialize the object, and cast it to the correct type.

The following code sample deserializes an XML file containing a *DateTime* object and displays that object's day of the week and time.

```
' VB
' Open file to read the data from
Dim fs As FileStream = New FileStream("SerializedDate.XML", FileMode.Open)

' Create an XmlSerializer object to perform the deserialization
Dim xs As XmlSerializer = New XmlSerializer(GetType(DateTime))

' Use the XmlSerializer object to deserialize the data from the file
Dim previousTime As DateTime = CType(xs.Deserialize(fs),DateTime)

' Close the file
fs.Close

' Display the deserialized time
Console.WriteLine(("Day: " _
    + (previousTime.DayOfWeek + (", Time: " _
    + previousTime.TimeOfDay.ToString))))
```

```
// C#
// Open file to read the data from
FileStream fs = new FileStream("SerializedDate.XML", FileMode.Open);

// Create an XmlSerializer object to perform the deserialization
XmlSerializer xs = new XmlSerializer(typeof(DateTime));

// Use the XmlSerializer object to deserialize the data from the file
DateTime previousTime = (DateTime)xs.Deserialize(fs);

// Close the file
fs.Close();

// Display the deserialized time
Console.WriteLine("Day: " + previousTime.DayOfWeek + ",
    Time: " + previousTime.TimeOfDay.ToString());
```

How to Create Classes that Can Be Serialized by Using XML Serialization

To create a class that can be serialized by using XML serialization, you must perform the following tasks:

- Specify the class as public.
- Specify all members that must be serialized as *public*.
- Create a parameterless constructor.

Unlike classes processed with standard serialization, classes do not have to have the *Serializable* attribute to be processed with XML serialization. If there are private or protected members, they will be skipped during serialization.

How to Control XML Serialization

If you serialize a class that meets the requirements for XML serialization but does not have any XML serialization attributes, the runtime uses default settings that meet many people's requirements. The names of XML elements are based on class and member names, and each member is serialized as a separate XML element. For example, consider the following simple class:

```
' VB
Public Class ShoppingCartItem
    Public productId As Int32
    Public price As Decimal
    Public quantity As Int32
    Public total As Decimal
```

```
    Public Sub New()
        MyBase.New
    End Sub
End Class

// C#
public class ShoppingCartItem
{
    public Int32 productId;
    public decimal price;
    public Int32 quantity;
    public decimal total;

    public ShoppingCartItem()
    {
    }
}
```

Serializing an instance of this class with sample values creates the following XML (which has been slightly simplified for readability):

```
<?xml version="1.0" ?>
<ShoppingCartItem>
    <productId>100</productId>
    <price>10.25</price>
    <total>20.50</total>
    <quantity>2</quantity>
</ShoppingCartItem>
```

If you are defining the XML schema, this might be sufficient. However, if you need to create XML documents that conform to specific standards, you might need to control how the serialization is structured. You can do this using the attributes listed in Table 5-2.

Table 5-2   XML Serialization Attributes

Attribute	Applies to	Specifies
XmlAnyAttribute	Public field, property, parameter, or return value that returns an array of *XmlAttribute* objects	When deserializing, the array will be filled with *XmlAttribute* objects that represent all XML attributes unknown to the schema.
XmlAnyElement	Public field, property, parameter, or return value that returns an array of *XmlElement* objects	When deserializing, the array is filled with *XmlElement* objects that represent all XML elements unknown to the schema.

Table 5-2   XML Serialization Attributes

Attribute	Applies to	Specifies
XmlArray	Public field, property, parameter, or return value that returns an array of complex objects	The members of the array will be generated as members of an XML array.
XmlArrayItem	Public field, property, parameter, or return value that returns an array of complex objects	The derived types that can be inserted into an array. Usually applied in conjunction with *XmlArrayAttribute*.
XmlAttribute	Public field, property, parameter, or return value	The member will be serialized as an XML attribute.
XmlChoice-Identifier	Public field, property, parameter, or return value	The member can be further disambiguated by using an enumeration.
XmlElement	Public field, property, parameter, or return value	The field or property will be serialized as an XML element.
XmlEnum	Public field that is an enumeration identifier	The element name of an enumeration member.
XmlIgnore	Public properties and fields	The property or field should be ignored when the containing class is serialized. This functions similarly to the *NonSerialized* standard serialization attribute.
XmlInclude	Public derived class declarations and return values of public methods for Web Services Description Language (WSDL) documents	The class should be included when generating schemas (to be recognized when serialized).

Table 5-2   XML Serialization Attributes

Attribute	Applies to	Specifies
XmlRoot	Public class declarations	Controls XML serialization of the attribute target as an XML root element. Use the attribute to further specify the namespace and element name.
XmlText	Public properties and fields	The property or field should be serialized as XML text.
XmlType	Public class declarations	The name and namespace of the XML type.

You could use these attributes to make a serialized class conform to specific XML requirements. For example, consider the attributes required to make the following three changes to the serialized XML document:

- Change the *ShoppingCartItem* element name to *CartItem*.

- Make *productId* an attribute of *CartItem*, rather than a separate element.

NOTE **Attributes and elements in XML**

In XML, an element can contain other elements, much like an object can have members. Elements can also have attributes, which describe the element, just as a property can describe an object in the .NET Framework. When examining an XML document, you can recognize attributes because they appear within an element's < > brackets. Examine the differences between the two examples in this section to understand the distinction.

- Do not include the total in the serialized document.

To make these changes, modify the class with attributes as shown:

```vb
' VB
<XmlRoot("CartItem")> Public Class ShoppingCartItem
    <XmlAttribute()>  Public productId As Int32
    Public price As Decimal
    Public quantity As Int32
    <XmlIgnore()> Public total As Decimal

    Public Sub New()
        MyBase.New
    End Sub
End Class
```

```
// C#
[XmlRoot ("CartItem")]
public class ShoppingCartItem
{
    [XmlAttribute] public Int32 productId;
    public decimal price;
    public Int32 quantity;
    [XmlIgnore] public decimal total;

    public ShoppingCartItem()
    {
    }
}
```

This would result in the following XML file, which meets the specified requirements:

```
<?xml version="1.0" ?>
<CartItem productId="100">
    <price>10.25</price>
    <quantity>2</quantity>
</CartItem>
```

Although attributes will enable you to meet most XML serialization requirements, you can take complete control over XML serialization by implementing the *IXmlSerializable* interface in your class. For example, you can separate data into bytes instead of buffering large data sets, and also avoid the inflation that occurs when the data is encoded using Base64 encoding. To control the serialization, implement the *ReadXml* and *WriteXml* methods to control the *XmlReader* and *XmlWriter* classes used to read and write the XML.

How to Conform to an XML Schema

Typically, when two different applications are going to exchange XML files, the developers work together to create an XML schema file. An XML schema defines the structure of an XML document. Many types of XML schema already exist, and whenever possible, you should leverage an existing XML schema.

MORE INFO XML schemas

For more information about XML schemas, visit *http://www.w3.org/XML/Schema*.

If you have an XML schema, you can run the XML Schema Definition tool (Xsd.exe) to produce a set of classes that are strongly typed to the schema and annotated with attributes. When an instance of such a class is serialized, the generated XML adheres to the XML schema. This is a simpler alternative to using other classes in the .NET Framework, such as the *XmlReader* and *XmlWriter* classes, to parse and write an XML stream.

To generate a class based on a schema, follow these steps:

1. Create or download the XML schema .*xsd* file on your computer.

2. Open a Visual Studio 2005 Command Prompt.

3. From the Visual Studio 2005 Command Prompt, run *Xsd.exe schema.xsd /classes /language:[CS | VB]*. For example, to create a new class based on a schema file named C:\schema\library.xsd, you would run the following command:

```
' VB
xsd C:\schema\library.xsd /classes /language:VB
```

```
// C#
xsd C:\schema\library.xsd /classes /language:CS
```

4. Open the newly created file (named *Schema*.CS or *Schema*.VB), and add the class to your application.

When you serialize the newly created class, it will automatically conform to the XML schema. This makes it simple to create applications that interoperate with standards-based Web services.

MORE INFO Conforming to the XML schema

For more information about conforming to the XML Schema, read "XML Schema Part 0: Primer" at *http://www.w3.org/TR/2001/REC-xmlschema-0-20010502/* and "Using Schema and Serialization to Leverage Business Logic" by Eric Schmidt at *http://msdn.microsoft.com/library/en-us/dnexxml/html/xml04162001.asp*.

How to Serialize a *DataSet*

Besides serializing an instance of a public class, an instance of a *DataSet* object can also be serialized, as shown in the following example:

```
' VB
Private Sub SerializeDataSet(filename As String)
    Dim ser As XmlSerializer = new XmlSerializer(GetType(DataSet))
    ' Creates a DataSet; adds a table, column, and ten rows.
    Dim ds As DataSet = new DataSet("myDataSet")
    Dim t As DataTable = new DataTable("table1")
    Dim c As DataColumn = new DataColumn("thing")
    t.Columns.Add(c)
    ds.Tables.Add(t)
    Dim r As DataRow
    Dim i As Integer
    for i = 0 to 10
        r = t.NewRow()
```

```
        r(0) = "Thing " &  i
        t.Rows.Add(r)
    Next
    Dim writer As TextWriter = new StreamWriter(filename)
    ser.Serialize(writer, ds)
    writer.Close()
End Sub

// C#
private void SerializeDataSet(string filename){
    XmlSerializer ser = new XmlSerializer(typeof(DataSet));

    // Creates a DataSet; adds a table, column, and ten rows.
    DataSet ds = new DataSet("myDataSet");
    DataTable t = new DataTable("table1");
    DataColumn c = new DataColumn("thing");
    t.Columns.Add(c);
    ds.Tables.Add(t);
    DataRow r;
    for(int i = 0; i<10;i++){
        r = t.NewRow();
        r[0] = "Thing " + i;
        t.Rows.Add(r);
    }
    TextWriter writer = new StreamWriter(filename);
    ser.Serialize(writer, ds);
    writer.Close();
}
```

Similarly, you can serialize arrays, collections, and instances of an *XmlElement* or *XmlNode* class. Although this is useful, it does not provide the same level of control that you would have if the data were stored in custom classes. Alternatively, you could use the *DataSet.WriteXml*, *DataSet.ReadXML*, and *DataSet.GetXml* methods.

Lab: Using XML Serialization

In this lab, you will update an application that currently uses *BinaryFormatter* serialization to use XML serialization. If you encounter a problem completing an exercise, the completed projects are available on the companion CD in the Code folder.

▶ **Exercise: Replacing Binary Serialization with XML Serialization**

In this exercise, you upgrade a project to support storing data using open standards-based XML serialization.

1. Copy the Chapter05\Lesson2-Serialize-People folder from the companion CD to your hard disk, and open either the C# version or the Visual Basic version of the Serialize-People project.

2. Add the *System.Xml.Serialization* namespace to the main program.

3. Rewrite the *Serialization* method to use XML serialization instead of binary serialization. Name the temporary file Person.xml. Your code could look like the following:

```vb
' VB
Private Sub Serialize(ByVal sp As Person)
    ' Create file to save the data to
    Dim fs As FileStream = New FileStream("Person.XML", FileMode.Create)

    ' Create an XmlSerializer object to perform the serialization
    Dim xs As XmlSerializer = New XmlSerializer(GetType(Person))

    ' Use the XmlSerializer object to serialize the data to the file
    xs.Serialize(fs, sp)

    ' Close the file
    fs.Close
End Sub
```

```csharp
// C#
private static void Serialize(Person sp)
{
    // Create file to save the data to
    FileStream fs = new FileStream("Person.XML", FileMode.Create);

    // Create an XmlSerializer object to perform the serialization
    XmlSerializer xs = new XmlSerializer(typeof(Person));

    // Use the XmlSerializer object to serialize the data to the file
    xs.Serialize(fs, sp);

    // Close the file
    fs.Close();
}
```

4. Rewrite the *Deserialization* method to use XML deserialization instead of binary deserialization. Your code could look like the following:

```vb
' VB
Private Function Deserialize() As Person
    Dim dsp As Person = New Person

    ' Create file to save the data to
    Dim fs As FileStream = New FileStream("Person.XML", FileMode.Open)

    ' Create an XmlSerializer object to perform the deserialization
    Dim xs As XmlSerializer = New XmlSerializer(GetType(Person))

    ' Use the XmlSerializer object to deserialize the data to the file
    dsp = CType(xs.Deserialize(fs), Person)
```

```
      ' Close the file
      fs.Close()
      Return dsp
End Function

// C#
private static Person Deserialize()
{
    Person dsp = new Person();

    // Create file to save the data to
    FileStream fs = new FileStream("Person.XML", FileMode.Open);

    // Create an XmlSerializer object to perform the deserialization
    XmlSerializer xs = new XmlSerializer(typeof(Person));

    // Use the XmlSerializer object to deserialize the data to the file
    dsp = (Person)xs.Deserialize(fs);

    // Close the file
    fs.Close();
    return dsp;
}
```

5. Build the project, and resolve any errors.

6. Open a command prompt to the build directory, and then run the following command:

   ```
   Serialize-People Tony 1923 4 22
   ```

   What exception message do you receive, and why?

   You see the message "Invalid parameters. Serialize_People.Person is inaccessible due to its protection level. Only public types can be processed." The error occurs because the *Person* class is not marked as public.

7. Edit the person class, and mark it as public. Then rebuild the project, and run the following command again:

   ```
   Serialize-People Tony 1923 4 22
   ```

8. Examine the serialized data to verify that the information you provided on the command line was successfully captured. Why does the age appear in the serialized file even though the age member has the *NonSerialized* attribute?

   The *NonSerialized* attribute applies to binary serialization, but it does not affect XML serialization.

9. Now run the command with no parameters to verify that deserialization works properly.

Lesson Summary

- XML serialization provides the interoperability to communicate with different platforms and the flexibility to conform to an XML schema.

- XML serialization cannot be used to serialize private data or object graphs.

- To serialize an object, first create a stream, *TextWriter*, or *XmlWriter*. Then create an *XmlSerializer* object and call the *XmlSerializer.Serialize* method. To deserialize an object, follow the same steps but call the *XmlSerializer.Deserialize* method.

- To create a class that can be serialized, specify the class and all members as public, and create a parameterless constructor.

- You can control XML serialization by using attributes. Attributes can change the names of elements, serialize members as attributes rather than elements, and exclude members from serialization.

- Use the Xsd.exe tool to create a class that will automatically conform to an XML schema when serialized.

- Datasets, arrays, collections, and instances of an *XmlElement* or *XmlNode* class can all be serialized with *XmlSerializer*.

Lesson Review

You can use the following questions to test your knowledge of the information in Lesson 2, "XML Serialization." The questions are also available on the companion CD if you prefer to review them in electronic form.

NOTE Answers

Answers to these questions and explanations of why each answer choice is right or wrong are located in the "Answers" section at the end of the book.

---

1. Which of the following are requirements for a class to be serialized with XML serialization? (Choose all that apply.)

    A. The class must be public.

    B. The class must be private.

    C. The class must have a parameterless constructor.

    D. The class must have a constructor that accepts a *SerializationInfo* parameter.

2. Which of the following attributes would you use to cause a member to be serialized as an attribute, rather than an element?

   A. *XmlAnyAttribute*

   B. *XMLType*

   C. *XMLElement*

   D. *XMLAttribute*

3. Which tool would you use to help you create a class that, when serialized, would produce an XML document that conformed to an XML schema?

   A. Xsd.exe

   B. Xdcmake.exe

   C. XPadsi90.exe

   D. Xcacls.exe

4. Which of the following attributes should you add to a member to prevent it from being serialized by XML serialization?

   A. *XMLType*

   B. *XMLIgnore*

   C. *XMLElement*

   D. *XMLAttribute*

Lesson 3: Custom Serialization

Custom serialization is the process of controlling the serialization and deserialization of a type. By controlling serialization, it is possible to ensure serialization compatibility, which is the ability to serialize and deserialize between versions of a type without breaking the core functionality of the type. For example, in the first version of a type, there might be only two fields. In the next version of a type, several more fields are added. Yet the second version of an application must be able to serialize and deserialize both types. This lesson describes how to control serialization by implementing your own serialization classes.

After this lesson, you will be able to:

- Implement the *ISerializable* interface to take control over how a class is serialized.
- Respond to serialization events to run code at different stages of the serialization process.
- Write code that adjusts serialization and deserialization according to the context.
- Describe the role of *IFormatter*.

Estimated lesson time: 30 minutes

How to Implement Custom Serialization

Serialization in the .NET Framework is very flexible and can be customized to meet most development requirements. In some circumstances, you might need complete control over the serialization process.

You can override the serialization built into the .NET Framework by implementing the *ISerializable* interface and applying the *Serializable* attribute to the class. This is particularly useful in cases where the value of a member variable is invalid after deserialization, but you need to provide the variable with a value to reconstruct the full state of the object. In addition, you should not use default serialization on a class that is marked with the *Serializable* attribute and has declarative or imperative security at the class level or on its constructors. Instead, these classes should always implement the *ISerializable* interface.

Implementing *ISerializable* involves implementing the *GetObjectData* method and a special constructor that is used when the object is deserialized. The runtime calls *GetObjectData* during serialization, and the serialization constructor during deserialization. The compiler will warn you if you forget to implement *GetObjectData*, but if you forget to implement the special constructor, you won't notice a problem until runtime when you receive a serialization exception.

When the runtime calls *GetObjectData* during serialization, you are responsible for populating the *SerializationInfo* object provided with the method call. Simply add the variables to be serialized as name/value pairs using the *AddValue* method, which internally creates *SerializationEntry* structures to store the information. Any text can be used as the name. You have the freedom to decide which member variables are added to the *SerializationInfo* object, provided that sufficient data is serialized to restore the object during deserialization. When the runtime calls your serialization constructor, simply retrieve the values of the variables from *SerializationInfo* using the names used during serialization.

The following sample code, which uses the *System.Runtime.Serialization* and *System .Security.Permissions* namespaces, shows how to implement *ISerializable*, the serialization constructor, and the *GetObjectData* method:

```vb
' VB
<Serializable()> Class ShoppingCartItem
    Implements ISerializable

    Public productId As Int32
    Public price As Decimal
    Public quantity As Int32
    <NonSerialized()> Public total As Decimal

    ' The standard, non-serialization constructor
    Public Sub New(ByVal _productID As Integer, ByVal _price As Decimal, _
ByVal _quantity As Integer)
        MyBase.New()
        productId = _productID
        price = _price
        quantity = _quantity
        total = (price * quantity)
    End Sub

    ' The following constructor is for deserialization
    Protected Sub New(ByVal info As SerializationInfo, _
        ByVal context As StreamingContext)
        MyBase.New()
        productId = info.GetInt32("Product ID")
        price = info.GetDecimal("Price")
        quantity = info.GetInt32("Quantity")
        total = (price * quantity)
    End Sub
```

```vbnet
    ' The following method is called during serialization
        <SecurityPermissionAttribute(SecurityAction.Demand, _
        SerializationFormatter:=True)> _
        Public Overridable Sub _
        GetObjectData(ByVal info As SerializationInfo, _
        ByVal context As StreamingContext) _
        Implements System.Runtime.Serialization.ISerializable.GetObjectData
        info.AddValue("Product ID", productId)
        info.AddValue("Price", price)
        info.AddValue("Quantity", quantity)
    End Sub

    Public Overrides Function ToString() As String
        Return (productId + (": " _
                    + (price + (" x " _
                    + (quantity + (" = " + total))))))
    End Function
End Class
```

```csharp
// C#
[Serializable]
class ShoppingCartItem : ISerializable
{
    public Int32 productId;
    public decimal price;
    public Int32 quantity;
    [NonSerialized]
    public decimal total;

    // The standard, non-serialization constructor
    public ShoppingCartItem(int _productID, decimal _price, int _quantity)
    {
        productId = _productID;
        price = _price;
        quantity = _quantity;
        total = price * quantity;
    }

    // The following constructor is for deserialization
    protected ShoppingCartItem(SerializationInfo info,
        StreamingContext context)
    {
        productId = info.GetInt32("Product ID");
        price = info.GetDecimal("Price");
        quantity = info.GetInt32("Quantity");
        total = price * quantity;
    }

    // The following method is called during serialization
    [SecurityPermissionAttribute(SecurityAction.Demand,
        SerializationFormatter=true)]
    public virtual void GetObjectData(SerializationInfo info,
        StreamingContext context)
```

```
    {
        info.AddValue("Product ID", productId);
        info.AddValue("Price", price);
        info.AddValue("Quantity", quantity);
    }

    public override string ToString()
    {
        return productId + ": " + price + " x " + quantity + " = " + total;
    }
}
```

In this example, *SerializationInfo* does much of the work of serialization and deserialization. The construction of a *SerializationInfo* object requires an object whose type implements the *IFormatterConverter* interface. *BinaryFormatter* and *SoapFormatter* always construct an instance of the *System.Runtime.Serialization.FormatterConverter* type, without giving you the opportunity to use a different *IFormatterConverter* type. *FormatterConverter* includes methods for converting values between core types, such as converting a *Decimal* to a *Double*, or a signed integer to an unsigned integer.

IMPORTANT   Reducing security risks by using data validation

You must perform data validation in your serialization constructor and throw a *SerializationException* if invalid data is provided. The risk is that an attacker could use your class but provide fake serialization information in an attempt to exploit a weakness. You should assume that any calls made to your serialization constructor are initiated by an attacker, and allow the construction only if all the data provided is valid and realistic. For more information about code security, refer to Chapter 12, "User and Data Security."

Responding to Serialization Events

The .NET Framework 2.0 supports binary serialization events when using the *Binary-Formatter* class. These events call methods in your class when serialization and deserialization take place. There are four serialization events:

- **Serializing**   This event is raised just before serialization takes place. Apply the *OnSerializing* attribute to the method that should run during this event.

- **Serialized**   This event is raised just after serialization takes place. Apply the *OnSerialized* attribute to the method that should run during this event.

- **Deserializing**   This event is raised just before deserialization takes place. Apply the *OnDeserializing* attribute to the method that should run during this event.

- *Deserialized*   This event is raised just after deserialization takes place and after *IDeserializationCallback.OnDeserialization* has been called. You should use *IDeserializationCallback.OnDeserialization* instead when formatters other than *BinaryFormatter* might be used. Apply the *OnDeserialized* attribute to the method that should run during this event.

The sequence of these events is illustrated in Figure 5-2.

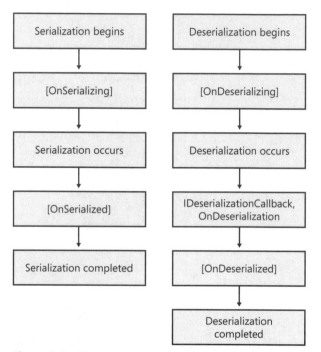

Figure 5-2   You can use serialization events to run methods during different phases of the serialization and deserialization process.

Using these events is the best and easiest way to control the serialization process. The methods do not access the serialization stream but instead allow you to alter the object before and after serialization, or before and after deserialization. The attributes can be applied at all levels of the type inheritance hierarchy, and each method is called in the hierarchy from the base to the most derived. This mechanism avoids the complexity and any resulting issues of implementing the *ISerializable* interface by giving the responsibility for serialization and deserialization to the most derived implementation.

For a method to respond to one of these events, it must meet these requirements:

- Accept a *StreamingContext* object as a parameter

- Return void

- Have the attribute that matches the event you want to intercept

The following example demonstrates how to create an object that responds to serialization events. In your own code, you can respond to as many or as few events as you want. Additionally, you can apply the same serialization event to multiple methods, or apply multiple events to a single method.

```vb
' VB
<Serializable()> Class ShoppingCartItem
    Public productId As Int32
    Public price As Decimal
    Public quantity As Int32
    Public total As Decimal

    <OnSerializing()> _
    Private Sub CalculateTotal(ByVal sc As StreamingContext)
        total = (price * quantity)
    End Sub

    <OnDeserialized()> _
    Private Sub CheckTotal(ByVal sc As StreamingContext)
        If (total = 0) Then
            CalculateTotal(sc)
        End If
    End Sub
End Class
```

```csharp
// C#
[Serializable]
class ShoppingCartItem
{
    public Int32 productId;
    public decimal price;
    public Int32 quantity;
    public decimal total;

    [OnSerializing]
    void CalculateTotal(StreamingContext sc)
    {
        total = price * quantity;
    }

    [OnDeserialized]
    void CheckTotal(StreamingContext sc)
    {
        if (total == 0) { CalculateTotal(sc); }
    }
}
```

Events are supported only for *BinaryFormatter* serialization. For *SoapFormatter* or custom serialization, you are limited to using the *IDeserializationCallback* interface, as discussed in Lesson 1 of this chapter.

How to Change Serialization Based on Context

Typically, when you serialize an object, the destination does not matter. In some circumstances, however, you might want to serialize and deserialize an object differently depending on the destination. For example, you should typically not serialize members that contain information about the current process, because that information might be invalid when the object is deserialized. However, that information would be useful if the object is going to be deserialized by the same process. Alternatively, if the object is useful only if deserialized by the same process, you might choose to throw an exception if you knew the destination was a different process.

The *StreamingContext* structure can provide information about the destination of a serialized object to classes that implement the *ISerializable* interface. *StreamingContext* is passed to both *GetObjectData* and an object's serialization constructor. The *Streaming-Context* structure has two properties:

- **Context** A reference to an object that contains any user-desired context information.
- **State** A set of bit flags indicating the source or destination of the objects being serialized/deserialized. The flags are:
  - ❑ *CrossProcess* The source or destination is a different process on the same machine.
  - ❑ *CrossMachine* The source or destination is on a different machine.
  - ❑ *File* The source or destination is a file. Don't assume that same process will deserialize the data.
  - ❑ *Persistence* The source or destination is a store such as a database, file, or other. Don't assume that same process will deserialize the data.
  - ❑ *Remoting* The source or destination is remoting to an unknown location. The location might be on the same machine but might also be on another machine.
  - ❑ *Other* The source or destination is unknown.
  - ❑ *Close* The object graph is being cloned. The serialization code might assume that the same process will deserialize the data and it is therefore safe to access handles or other unmanaged resources.

❏ *CrossAppDomain*   The source or destination is a different *AppDomain*.

❏ *All*   The source or destination might be any of the above contexts. This is the default context.

To make context decisions during serialization and deserialization, implement the *ISerialization* interface in your class. For serialization, inspect the *StreamingContext* structure passed to your object's *GetObjectData* method. For deserialization, inspect the *StreamingContext* structure passed to your object's serialization constructor.

If you are serializing or deserializing an object and want to provide context information, modify the *IFormatter.Context StreamingContext* property before calling the formatter's *Serialize* or *Deserialize* methods. This property is implemented by both the *BinaryFormatter* and *SoapFormatter* classes. When you construct a formatter, the formatter automatically sets the *Context* property to *null* and the *State* property to *All*.

How to Create a Custom Formatter

To create a custom formatter, implement the *IFormatter* or *IGenericFormatter* interface. Both *BinaryFormatter* and *SoapFormatter* implement the *IFormatter* interface. The *FormatterServices* class provides static methods (including *GetObjectData*) to aid with the implementation of a formatter.

NOTE .NET 2.0

Although *IFormatter* was available beginning with .NET 1.1, *IGenericFormatter* is new with .NET 2.0.

MORE INFO Custom Formatters

Very few people will need to implement custom formatters. Therefore, this book covers them at a very high level. For detailed information about custom formatters, read "Format Your Way to Success with the .NET Framework Versions 1.1 and 2.0" at *http://msdn.microsoft.com/msdnmag/issues/04/10/AdvancedSerialization/default.aspx*.

Lab: Implement Custom Serialization

In this lab, you will modify a class to override the default serialization and take control over which members are serialized. If you encounter a problem completing an exercise, the completed projects are available on the companion CD in the Code folder.

▶ **Exercise: Update a Class to Use Custom Serialization**

In this exercise, you will update a class to improve the efficiency of serialization while maintaining complete control over how data is stored and retrieved.

1. Copy the Chapter05\Lesson3-Serialize-People folder from the companion CD to your hard disk, and open either the C# version or the Visual Basic version of the Serialize-People project.

2. Add the *System.Runtime.Serialization* namespace to the *Person* class.

3. Add the *Serializable* attribute to the *Person* class, and then build the project to ensure it compiles correctly.

4. Modify the *Person* class so that it implements *ISerializable*.

5. Add the *GetObjectData* method, which accepts a *SerializationInfo* object and a *StreamingContext* object, and adds items to be serialized to the *SerializationInfo* object. Add the *name* and *dateOfBirth* variables to the *SerializationInfo* object, but do not add the age variable. Your code could look like the following:

```
' VB
Public Overridable Sub GetObjectData(ByVal info As SerializationInfo, _
    ByVal context As StreamingContext) _

Implements System.Runtime.Serialization.ISerializable.GetObjectData
    info.AddValue("Name", name)
    info.AddValue("DOB", dateOfBirth)
End Sub
```

```
// C#
public virtual void GetObjectData(SerializationInfo info,
    StreamingContext context)
{
    info.AddValue("Name", name);
    info.AddValue("DOB", dateOfBirth);
}
```

6. Add the serialization constructor, which accepts a *SerializationInfo* object and a *StreamingContext* object, and then initializes member variables using the contents of the *SerializationInfo* object. Use the same element names you used in the previous step. After you have deserialized all variables, call the *CalculateAge* method to initialize the age variables. Your code could look like the following:

```
' VB
Public Sub New(ByVal info As SerializationInfo, _
    ByVal context As StreamingContext)
    name = info.GetString("Name")
```

```
        dateOfBirth = info.GetDateTime("DOB")
        CalculateAge
    End Sub

    // C#
    public Person(SerializationInfo info, StreamingContext context)
    {
        name = info.GetString("Name");
        dateOfBirth = info.GetDateTime("DOB");
        CalculateAge();
    }
```

7. Build the project, and resolve any errors.

8. Open a command prompt to the build directory, and then run the following command:

   ```
   Serialize-People Tony 1923 4 22
   ```

9. Now run the command with no parameters to verify that deserialization works properly.

Lesson Summary

- You can implement *ISerialization* to perform custom serialization.

- *BinaryFormatter* provides four events that you can use to control parts of the serialization process: *OnSerializing*, *OnSerialized*, *OnDeserializing*, and *OnDeserialized*.

- The *StreamingContext* class, an instance of which is provided to methods called during serialization events, gives you information about the origin or planned destination of the serialization process. The method performing serialization must specify this information for it to be useful.

- Though few developers will require total control over serialization, you can implement the *IFormatter* or *IGenericFormatter* interfaces to create custom formatters.

Lesson Review

You can use the following questions to test your knowledge of the information in Lesson 3, "Custom Serialization." The questions are also available on the companion CD if you prefer to review them in electronic form.

NOTE Answers

Answers to these questions and explanations of why each answer choice is right or wrong are located in the "Answers" section at the end of the book.

---

1. Which parameters must a constructor accept if the class implements *ISerializable*? (Choose all that apply.)

   A. *SerializationInfo*

   B. *Formatter*

   C. *StreamingContext*

   D. *ObjectManager*

2. Which event would you use to run a method immediately before deserialization occurs?

   A. *OnSerializing*

   B. *OnDeserializing*

   C. *OnSerialized*

   D. *OnDeserialized*

3. Which event would you use to run a method immediately after serialization occurs?

   A. *OnSerializing*

   B. *OnDeserializing*

   C. *OnSerialized*

   D. *OnDeserialized*

4. Which of the following are requirements for a method that is called in response to a serialization event? (Choose all that apply.)

   A. Accept a *StreamingContext* object as a parameter.

   B. Accept a *SerializationInfo* object as a parameter.

   C. Return void.

   D. Return a *StreamingContext* object.

Chapter Review

To further practice and reinforce the skills you learned in this chapter, you can do any of the following tasks:

- Review the chapter summary.
- Review the list of key terms introduced in this chapter.
- Complete the case scenarios. These scenarios set up real-world situations involving the topics of this chapter and ask you to create a solution.
- Complete the suggested practices.
- Take a practice test.

Chapter Summary

- Serialization outputs an object as a series of bytes, whereas deserialization reads a serialized object and defines the value of an object. Most custom classes can be serialized by simply adding the *Serializable* attribute. In some cases, you might be able to improve efficiency or provide for changes to the structure of classes by modifying your class to change the default serialization behavior.

- XML serialization provides a way to store and transfer objects using open standards. XML serialization can be customized to fit the exact requirements of an XML schema, making it simple to convert objects into XML documents and back into objects.

- Custom serialization is required in situations where classes contain complex information, significant changes have occurred to the structure of a class between different versions, and where you need complete control over how information is stored. You can perform custom serialization by implementing the *ISerializable* interface or by responding to serialization events.

Key Terms

Do you know what these key terms mean? You can check your answers by looking up the terms in the glossary at the end of the book.

- BinaryFormatter
- deserialization
- serialization

- SoapFormatter
- XML (eXtensible Markup Language)

Case Scenarios

In the following case scenarios, you will apply what you've learned about how to implement and apply serialization, as well as how to upgrade applications that make use of serialization. You can find answers to these questions in the "Answers" section at the end of this book.

Case Scenario 1: Choosing a Serialization Technique

You are an application developer for City Power & Light. For the last year, you and your team have been creating a distributed .NET Framework solution to replace the antiquated system that currently accounts for electrical usage and distributes bills to customers. You have created components for monitoring electrical usage, and you are at the stage of development when you need to transmit usage information to the billing system. Your manager asks you to interview key people and then come to his office to answer his questions about your design choices.

Interviews

Following is a list of company personnel interviewed and their statements:

- **Billing System Development Manager**   "I've already got my guy working on this, and he has built methods with .NET that accept your *Usage* object classes and add billing information to the database. So we just need you to create those objects and send them over the internal network to us."
- **Network Manager**   "All the accounting and billing servers are on the same subnet, so you don't have to worry about your network traffic going through any firewalls. I would like you to try and minimize the bandwidth used—we have millions of accounts, and that subnet is close to being saturated already."

Questions

Answer the following questions for your manager:

1. Which serialization method will you use?
2. What changes will you need to make to your class to enable serialization?
3. About how many lines of code will you need to write to perform the serialization?

Case Scenario 2: Serializing Between Versions

You are an application developer working for Humongous Insurance. Recently, you have launched version 1.0 of Incident, an application based on .NET 1.1 that tracks insurance events throughout their life cycle.

With the successful launch of version 1.0 of Incident, you have begun development of Incident 2.0. Incident 2.0 is based on the .NET 2.0. During a planning meeting, your manager asks you questions about how Incident 2.0 will handle the upgrade process during deployment.

Questions

Answer the following questions for your manager:

1. In Incident 1.0, I know you save some user preferences, such as window position, to a file by serializing your *Preferences* object using *BinaryFormatter*. Will you be able to directly deserialize those settings in Incident 2.0 if you don't make any changes to the *Preferences* class?

2. We have some feature requests that will require you to add more preferences. If you add more members to the *Preferences* class, will you still be able to directly deserialize those settings in Incident 2.0? If so, what special accommodations will you need to make?

3. The IT department has requested we switch to using XML-based configuration files so that they can more easily edit them. How could you deserialize the existing binary-formatted object, while serializing an XML object?

Suggested Practices

To help you successfully master the "Implementing serialization and input/output functionality in a .NET Framework application" exam objective, complete the following tasks.

Serialize or Deserialize an Object or an Object Graph by Using Runtime Serialization Techniques

For this task, you should complete at least Practices 1 and 2. If you want a better understanding of how serialization can be used in the real world and you have the resources needed to do Practice 3, complete it as well.

- **Practice 1** Using the last custom class you created as part of your job, modify it so that it can be serialized. Then write an application to serialize and deserialize it using *BinaryFormatter*. Examine the serialized data. Then modify the application to use *SoapFormatter*. Examine the serialized data.

- **Practice 2** Examine the class you used in Practice 1 and, if possible, identify a member that does not need to be serialized. Modify your class so that the member will not be serialized, but will be automatically defined upon deserialization.

- **Practice 3** Write a client/server application to transfer an object between two networked computers using serialization and deserialization.

Control the Serialization of an Object into XML Format by Using the *System.Xml.Serialization* Namespace

For this task, you should complete all three practices to gain experience using XML serialization with real-world classes and schema.

- **Practice 1** Write an application that uses XML serialization to serialize and deserialize the last class you created as part of your job.

- **Practice 2** Examine the class you used in Practice 1 and, if possible, identify a member that does not need to be serialized. Use an attribute to modify your class so that the member will not be serialized.

- **Practice 3** Find an XML schema on the Internet and create a class that, when serialized, conforms to that XML schema. Create the class using two different techniques: manually and with Xsd.exe.

Implement Custom Serialization Formatting by Using the Serialization Formatter Classes

For this task, you should complete at least Practices 1 and 2. If you want in-depth knowledge of the serialization process, complete Practice 3 as well.

- **Practice 1** Using the last custom class you created as part of your job, modify it so that it implements *ISerialization* and can be successfully serialized and deserialized. Examine the member classes to determine whether you can optimize serialization by omitting calculated values.

- **Practice 2** Create a class that provides methods for all four *BinaryFormatter* serialization events.

- **Practice 3** Implement the *IFormatter* interface to create a custom formatter. Use it during serialization and deserialization to understand the formatter's role in serialization.

Take a Practice Test

The practice tests on this book's companion CD offer many options. For example, you can test yourself on just one exam objective, or you can test yourself on all the 70-536 certification exam content. You can set up the test so that it closely simulates the experience of taking a certification exam, or you can set it up in study mode so that you can look at the correct answers and explanations after you answer each question.

MORE INFO Practice tests

For details about all the practice test options available, see the "How to Use the Practice Tests" section in this book's Introduction.

Chapter 6
Graphics

You can use graphics to enhance the user interface of your applications, generate graphical charts and reports, and edit or create images. The .NET Framework includes tools that allow you to draw lines, shapes, patterns, and text. This chapter discusses how to create graphics and images using the classes in the *System.Drawing* namespace.

Exam objectives in this chapter:

- Enhance the user interface of a .NET Framework application by using the *System .Drawing* namespace.

  - Enhance the user interface of a .NET Framework application by using brushes, pens, colors, and fonts.

  - Enhance the user interface of a .NET Framework application by using graphics, images, bitmaps, and icons.

  - Enhance the user interface of a .NET Framework application by using shapes and sizes.

Lessons in this chapter:

Before You Begin

To complete the lessons in this chapter, you should be familiar with Microsoft Visual Basic or C# and be comfortable with the following tasks:

- Create a Windows Forms application in Microsoft Visual Studio using Visual Basic or C#.

- Write to files and streams.

Lesson 1: Drawing Graphics

You can use the .NET Framework to enhance the user interface by drawing lines, circles, and other shapes. With just a couple of lines of code, you can display these graphics on a form or other Windows Forms control.

After this lesson, you will be able to:

- Describe the members of the *System.Drawing* namespace.
- Control the location, size, and color of controls.
- Draw lines, empty shapes, and solid shapes.
- Customize pens and brushes to enhance graphics.

Estimated lesson time: 60 minutes

The *System.Drawing* Namespace

The .NET Framework includes the *System.Drawing* namespace to enable you to create graphics from scratch or modify existing images. With the *System.Drawing* namespace, you can do the following:

- Add circles, lines, and other shapes to the user interface dynamically.
- Create charts from scratch.
- Edit and resize pictures.
- Change the compression ratios of pictures saved to disk.
- Crop or zoom pictures.
- Add copyright logos or text to pictures.

This lesson will focus on drawing graphics. Lesson 2 covers working with images, and Lesson 3 describes how to format text.

Table 6-1 lists the most important classes in the *System.Drawing* namespace, which you can use to build objects used for creating and editing images.

Table 6-1 *System.Drawing* Classes

Class	Description
Bitmap	Encapsulates a GDI+ bitmap, which consists of the pixel data for a graphics image and its attributes. A *Bitmap* object is an object used to work with images defined by pixel data. This is the class you will use when you need to load or save images.

Table 6-1 *System.Drawing* Classes

Class	Description
Brush	Classes derived from this abstract base class, described in the "How to Fill Shapes" section, define objects used to fill the interiors of graphical shapes such as rectangles, ellipses, pies, polygons, and paths.
Brushes	Brushes for all the standard colors. This class cannot be inherited. Use this class to avoid creating an instance of a *Brush* class.
ColorConverter	Converts colors from one data type to another. Access this class through the *TypeDescriptor*.
ColorTranslator	Translates colors to and from GDI+ *Color* structures. This class cannot be inherited.
Font	Defines a particular format for text, including font face, size, and style attributes. This class cannot be inherited.
FontConverter	Converts *Font* objects from one data type to another. Access the *FontConverter* class through the *TypeDescriptor* object.
FontFamily	Defines a group of type faces having a similar basic design and certain variations in styles. This class cannot be inherited.
Graphics	Encapsulates a GDI+ drawing surface. This class cannot be inherited. You will use this class any time you need to draw lines, draw shapes, or add graphical text to a control or image.
Icon	Represents a Microsoft Windows icon, which is a small bitmap image used to represent an object. Icons can be thought of as transparent bitmaps, although their size is determined by the system.
IconConverter	Converts an *Icon* object from one data type to another. Access this class through the *TypeDescriptor* object.
Image	An abstract base class that provides functionality for the *Bitmap* and *Metafile* descended classes.
ImageAnimator	Animates an image that has time-based frames.
ImageConverter	*ImageConverter* is a class that can be used to convert *Image* objects from one data type to another. Access this class through the *TypeDescriptor* object.

Table 6-1   *System.Drawing* **Classes**

Class	Description
ImageFormat-Converter	*ImageFormatConverter* is a class that can be used to convert colors from one data type to another. Access this class through the *TypeDescriptor* object.
Pen	Defines an object used to draw lines, curves, and arrows. This class cannot be inherited.
Pens	Pens for all the standard colors. This class cannot be inherited. Use this class to avoid creating an instance of a *Pen* class.
PointConverter	Converts a *Point* object from one data type to another. Access this class through the *TypeDescriptor* object.
Rectangle-Converter	Converts rectangles from one data type to another. Access this class through the *TypeDescriptor* object.
Region	Describes the interior of a graphics shape composed of rectangles and paths. This class cannot be inherited.
SizeConverter	The *SizeConverter* class is used to convert from one data type to another. Access this class through the *TypeDescriptor* object.
SolidBrush	Defines a brush of a single color. Brushes are used to fill graphics shapes, such as rectangles, ellipses, pies, polygons, and paths. This class cannot be inherited.
StringFormat	Encapsulates text layout information (such as alignment and line spacing), display manipulations (such as ellipsis insertion and national digit substitution), and *OpenType* features. This class cannot be inherited.
SystemBrushes	Each property of the *SystemBrushes* class is a *SolidBrush* object that is the color of a Windows display element.
SystemColors	Each property of the *SystemColors* class is a *Color* structure that is the color of a Windows display element.
SystemFonts	Specifies the fonts used to display text in Windows display elements.

Table 6-1 *System.Drawing* **Classes**

Class	Description
SystemIcons	Each property of the *SystemIcons* class is an *Icon* object for Windows systemwide icons. This class cannot be inherited.
SystemPens	Each property of the *SystemPens* class is a *Pen* object that is the color of a Windows display element and that is a width of 1.
TextureBrush	Each property of the *TextureBrush* class is a *Brush* object that uses an image to fill the interior of a shape. This class cannot be inherited.
ToolboxBitmap-Attribute	You can apply a *ToolboxBitmapAttribute* to a control so that containers, such as Microsoft Visual Studio Form Designer, can retrieve an icon that represents the control. The bitmap for the icon can be in a file by itself or embedded in the assembly that contains the control.
	The size of the bitmap that you embed in the control's assembly (or store in a separate file) should be 16 by 16. The *GetImage* method of a *ToolboxBitmapAttribute* object can return the small 16-by-16 image or a large 32-by-32 image that it creates by scaling the small image.

Of these classes, you will use *Graphics* the most often because it provides methods for drawing to the display device. The *Pen* class is used to draw lines and curves, while classes derived from the abstract class *Brush* are used to fill the interiors of shapes. Additionally, you should be familiar with the *PictureBox* class, which you can use in Windows Forms applications to display an image as part of the user interface. The *System.Drawing* namespace includes the structures shown in Table 6-2.

Table 6-2 *System.Drawing* **Structures**

Class	Description
CharacterRange	Specifies a range of character positions within a string.
Color	Represents a color.
Point	Represents an ordered pair of integer x and y coordinates that defines a point in a two-dimensional plane.

Table 6-2 *System.Drawing* **Structures**

Class	Description
PointF	Represents an ordered pair of floating point x and y coordinates that defines a point in a two-dimensional plane.
Rectangle	Stores a set of four integers that represent the location and size of a rectangle. For more advanced region functions, use a *Region* object.
RectangleF	Stores a set of four floating-point numbers that represent the location and size of a rectangle. For more advanced region functions, use a *Region* object.
Size	Stores an ordered pair of integers, typically the width and height of a rectangle.
SizeF	Stores an ordered pair of floating-point numbers, typically the width and height of a rectangle.

The most important of these structures—the structures you'll use most often—are *Color*, *Point*, *Rectangle*, and *Size*.

How to Specify the Location and Size of Controls

One of the simplest and most common uses for the *System.Drawing* namespace is specifying the location of controls in a Windows Forms application. This process can be useful to create forms that dynamically adjust based on user input.

To specify a control's location, create a new *Point* structure by specifying the coordinates relative to the upper-left corner of the form, and use the *Point* to set the control's *Location* property. The related *PointF* structure accepts coordinates as floating points, rather than integers, but *PointF* cannot be used to specify the location of GUI controls. For example, to move a button to the upper-left corner of a form, exactly 10 pixels from the top and left sides, you would use the following code:

```
' VB
button1.Location = New Point(10, 10)
```

```
// C#
button1.Location = new Point(10, 10);
```

> **NOTE**   **Graphics samples require a Windows Forms application**
>
> Most of this book relies on console applications for samples. However, this chapter uses Windows Forms applications to easily display graphics.

As an alternative to using *Point*, you could perform the same function using the *Left* and *Top* or *Right* and *Bottom* properties of a control. However, this requires two lines of code, as the following example illustrates:

```
' VB
button1.Left = 10
button1.Top = 10

// C#
button1.Left = 10;
button1.Top = 10;
```

You can specify the size of a control just as simply as you specify the location. The following code demonstrates how to specify the size using the *Size* class:

```
' VB
button1.Size = New Size(30, 30)

// C#
button1.Size = new Size(30, 30);
```

How to Specify the Color of Controls

You can specify a control's color using the *Color* structure. The simplest way to specify a color is to use one of the predefined properties located within *System.Drawing.Color*, as the following example demonstrates:

```
' VB
Button1.ForeColor = Color.Red
Button1.BackColor = Color.Blue

// C#
button1.ForeColor = Color.Red;
button1.BackColor = Color.Blue;
```

If you need to specify a custom color, use the static *Color.FromArgb* method. The method has several overloads, so you can specify the color by using a single byte, by specifying the red, green, and blue levels, or by using other information.

The following example illustrates how to specify color by providing three integers, for red, green, and blue:

```
' VB
Button1.ForeColor = Color.FromArgb(10, 200, 200)
Button1.BackColor = Color.FromArgb(200, 5, 5)

// C#
button1.ForeColor = Color.FromArgb(10, 200, 200);
button1.BackColor = Color.FromArgb(200, 5, 5);
```

How to Draw Lines and Shapes

To draw on a form or control, follow these high-level steps:

1. Create a *Graphics* object by calling the *System.Windows.Forms.Control.CreateGraphics* method.
2. Create a *Pen* object.
3. Call a member of the *Graphics* class to draw on the control using the *Pen*.

Drawing begins with the *System.Drawing.Graphics* class. To create an instance of this class, you typically call a control's *CreateGraphics* method. Alternatively, as discussed in Lesson 2, you can create a *Graphics* object based on an *Image* object if you want to be able to save the picture as a file. Once you create the graphics object, you have many methods you can call to perform the drawing:

- *Clear*   Clears the entire drawing surface, and fills it with a specified color.
- *DrawEllipse*   Draws an ellipse or circle defined by a bounding rectangle specified by a pair of coordinates, a height, and a width. The ellipse will touch the edges of the bounding rectangle.
- *DrawIcon* and *DrawIconUnstretched*   Draws the image represented by the specified icon at the specified coordinates, with or without scaling the icon.
- *DrawImage, DrawImageUnscaled,* and *DrawImageUnscaledAndClipped*   Draws the specified *Image* object at the specified location, with or without scaling or cropping the image.
- *DrawLine*   Draws a line connecting the two points specified by the coordinate pairs.
- *DrawLines*   Draws a series of line segments that connect an array of *Point* structures.

- ■ *DrawPath*   Draws a series of connected lines and curves.

- ■ *DrawPie*   Draws a pie shape defined by an ellipse specified by a coordinate pair, a width, a height, and two radial lines. Note that the coordinates you supply with DrawPie specify the upper left corner of an imaginary rectangle that would form the pie's boundaries; the coordinates do not specify the pie's center.

- ■ *DrawPolygon*   Draws a shape with three or more sides as defined by an array of *Point* structures.

- ■ *DrawRectangle*   Draws a rectangle or square specified by a coordinate pair, a width, and a height.

- ■ *DrawRectangles*   Draws a series of rectangles or squares specified by *Rectangle* structures.

- ■ *DrawString*   Draws the specified text string at the specified location with the specified *Brush* and *Font* objects.

To use any of these methods, you must provide an instance of the *Pen* class. Typically, you specify the *Pen* class's color and width in pixels with the constructor. For example, the following code draws a 7-pixel wide red line from the upper left corner (1, 1) to a point near the middle of the form (100, 100), as shown in Figure 6-1. To run this code, create a Windows Forms application and add the code to a method run during the form's *Paint* event:

```
' VB
' Create a graphics object from the form
Dim g As Graphics = Me.CreateGraphics

' Create a pen object with which to draw
Dim p As Pen = New Pen(Color.Red, 7)

' Draw the line
g.DrawLine(p, 1, 1, 100, 100)

// C#
// Create a graphics object from the form
Graphics g = this.CreateGraphics();

// Create a pen object with which to draw
Pen p = new Pen(Color.Red, 7);

// Draw the line
g.DrawLine(p, 1, 1, 100, 100);
```

Figure 6-1   Use *Graphics.DrawLine* to create straight lines

Similarly, the following code draws a blue pie shape with a 60-degree angle, as shown in Figure 6-2:

```vb
' VB
Dim g As Graphics = Me.CreateGraphics
Dim p As Pen = New Pen(Color.Blue, 3)

g.DrawPie(p, 1, 1, 100, 100, -30, 60)
```

```csharp
// C#
Graphics g = this.CreateGraphics();
Pen p = new Pen(Color.Blue, 3);

g.DrawPie(p, 1, 1, 100, 100, -30, 60);
```

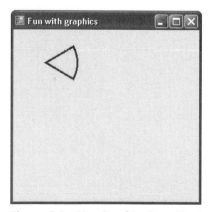

Figure 6-2   Use *Graphics.DrawPie* to create pie shapes

Graphics.DrawLines, *Graphics.DrawPolygon*, and *Graphics.DrawRectangles* accept arrays as parameters to allow you to create more complex shapes. For example, the following code draws a purple, five-sided polygon, as shown in Figure 6-3:

```vb
' VB
Dim g As Graphics = Me.CreateGraphics
Dim p As Pen = New Pen(Color.MediumPurple, 2)

' Create an array of points
Dim points As Point() = New Point() {New Point(10, 10), _
    New Point(10, 100), _
    New Point(50, 65), _
    New Point(100, 100), _
    New Point(85, 40)}

' Draw a shape defined by the array of points
g.DrawPolygon(p, points)
```

```csharp
// C#
Graphics g = this.CreateGraphics();
Pen p = new Pen(Color.MediumPurple, 2);

// Create an array of points
Point[] points = new Point[]
    {new Point(10, 10),
        new Point(10, 100),
        new Point(50, 65),
        new Point(100, 100),
        new Point(85, 40)};

// Draw a shape defined by the array of points
g.DrawPolygon(p, points);
```

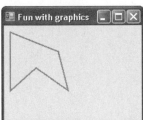

Figure 6-3   Use *Graphics.DrawPolygon* to create shapes made of multiple lines

NOTE   **Horizontal, and then vertical**

When you pass coordinates to any .NET Framework method, you will pass the horizontal (X) coordinate first, and then the vertical (Y) coordinate second. In a 100-by-100 pixel image, 0,0 is the upper left corner; 100,0 is the upper right corner; 0, 100 is the lower left corner; and 100,100 is the lower right corner.

How to Customize Pens

Besides controlling the color and size of a pen, which are specified in the *Pen* constructor, you can also control the pattern and endcaps. The endcaps are the ends of the line, and you can use them to create arrows and other special effects.

By default, pens draw solid lines. To draw a dotted line, create an instance of the *Pen* class, and then set the *Pen.DashStyle* property to one of these values: *DashStyle.Dash*, *DashStyle.DashDot*, *DashStyle.DashDotDot*, *DashStyle.Dot*, or *DashStyle.Solid*. The following code, which requires the *System.Drawing.Drawing2D* namespace, demonstrates each of these pen styles and creates the result shown in Figure 6-4:

```
' VB
Dim g As Graphics = Me.CreateGraphics
Dim p As Pen = New Pen(Color.Red, 7)

p.DashStyle = DashStyle.Dot
g.DrawLine(p, 50, 25, 400, 25)

p.DashStyle = DashStyle.Dash
g.DrawLine(p, 50, 50, 400, 50)

p.DashStyle = DashStyle.DashDot
g.DrawLine(p, 50, 75, 400, 75)

p.DashStyle = DashStyle.DashDotDot
g.DrawLine(p, 50, 100, 400, 100)

p.DashStyle = DashStyle.Solid
g.DrawLine(p, 50, 125, 400, 125)

// C#
Graphics g = this.CreateGraphics();
Pen p = new Pen(Color.Red, 7);

p.DashStyle = DashStyle.Dot;
g.DrawLine(p, 50, 25, 400, 25);

p.DashStyle = DashStyle.Dash;
g.DrawLine(p, 50, 50, 400, 50);

p.DashStyle = DashStyle.DashDot;
g.DrawLine(p, 50, 75, 400, 75);

p.DashStyle = DashStyle.DashDotDot;
g.DrawLine(p, 50, 100, 400, 100);

p.DashStyle = DashStyle.Solid;
g.DrawLine(p, 50, 125, 400, 125);
```

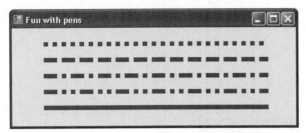

Figure 6-4   The *Pen* class provides several dash styles

You can also use the *Pen.DashOffset* and *Pen.DashPattern* properties to define a custom dash pattern.

To control the endcaps and create arrows or callouts, modify the *Pen.StartCap* and *Pen.EndCap* properties using the *LineCap* enumeration. The following code demonstrates most of the pen cap styles and creates the result shown in Figure 6-5:

```vb
' VB
Dim g As Graphics = Me.CreateGraphics
Dim p As Pen = New Pen(Color.Red, 10)

p.StartCap = LineCap.ArrowAnchor
p.EndCap = LineCap.DiamondAnchor
g.DrawLine(p, 50, 25, 400, 25)

p.StartCap = LineCap.SquareAnchor
p.EndCap = LineCap.Triangle
g.DrawLine(p, 50, 50, 400, 50)

p.StartCap = LineCap.Flat
p.EndCap = LineCap.Round
g.DrawLine(p, 50, 75, 400, 75)

p.StartCap = LineCap.RoundAnchor
p.EndCap = LineCap.Square
g.DrawLine(p, 50, 100, 400, 100)

// C#
Graphics g = this.CreateGraphics();
Pen p = new Pen(Color.Red, 10);

p.StartCap = LineCap.ArrowAnchor;
p.EndCap = LineCap.DiamondAnchor;
g.DrawLine(p, 50, 25, 400, 25);

p.StartCap = LineCap.SquareAnchor;
p.EndCap = LineCap.Triangle;
g.DrawLine(p, 50, 50, 400, 50);
```

```
p.StartCap = LineCap.Flat;
p.EndCap = LineCap.Round;
g.DrawLine(p, 50, 75, 400, 75);

p.StartCap = LineCap.RoundAnchor;
p.EndCap = LineCap.Square;
g.DrawLine(p, 50, 100, 400, 100);
```

Figure 6-5   The *Pen* class provides options for startcaps and endcaps

How to Fill Shapes

For most of the *Draw* methods, the *Graphics* class also has *Fill* methods that draw a shape and fill in the contents. These methods work exactly like the *Draw* methods, except they require an instance of the *Brush* class instead of the *Pen* class. The *Brush* class is abstract, so you must instantiate one of the child classes:

- **System.Drawing.Drawing2D.HatchBrush**   Defines a rectangular brush with a hatch style, a foreground color, and a background color

- **System.Drawing.Drawing2D.LinearGradientBrush**   Encapsulates a brush with a linear gradient that provides a visually appealing, professional-looking fill

- **System.Drawing.Drawing2D.PathGradientBrush**   Provides similar functionality to *LinearGradientBrush*; however, you can define a complex fill pattern that fades between multiple points

- **System.Drawing.SolidBrush**   Defines a brush of a single color

- **System.Drawing.TextureBrush**   Defines a brush made from an image that can be tiled across a shape, like a wallpaper design

For example, the following code draws a solid maroon, five-sided polygon, as shown in Figure 6-6:

```vb
' VB
Dim g As Graphics = Me.CreateGraphics
Dim b As Brush = New SolidBrush(Color.Maroon)
Dim points As Point() = New Point() {New Point(10, 10), New Point(10, 100), _
    New Point(50, 65), New Point(100, 100), New Point(85, 40)}
```

```
g.FillPolygon(b, points)

// C#
Graphics g = this.CreateGraphics();
Brush b = new SolidBrush(Color.Maroon);
Point[] points = new Point[]
    {new Point(10, 10),
        new Point(10, 100),
        new Point(50, 65),
        new Point(100, 100),
        new Point(85, 40)};

g.FillPolygon(b, points);
```

Figure 6-6　Use the *Brush* class with the various *Graphics.Fill* methods to draw solid objects

You can draw filled objects with an outline by first calling the *Graphics* class *Fill* method, and then calling the *Graphics* class *Draw* method. For example, the following code draws a polygon with an outline and a fill pattern, as shown in Figure 6-7:

```
' VB
Dim g As Graphics = Me.CreateGraphics
Dim p As Pen = New Pen(Color.Maroon, 2)
Dim b As Brush = New LinearGradientBrush(New Point(1, 1), New Point(100, 100), _
    Color.White, Color.Red)
Dim points As Point() = New Point() {New Point(10, 10), _
    New Point(10, 100), _
    New Point(50, 65), _
    New Point(100, 100), _
    New Point(85, 40)}

g.FillPolygon(b, points)
g.DrawPolygon(p, points)

// C#
Graphics g = this.CreateGraphics();
Pen p = new Pen(Color.Maroon, 2);
Brush b = new LinearGradientBrush(new Point(1,1), new Point(100,100),
    Color.White, Color.Red);
Point[] points = new Point[]
    {new Point(10, 10),
        new Point(10, 100),
        new Point(50, 65),
```

```
        new Point(100, 100),
        new Point(85, 40)};

g.FillPolygon(b, points);
g.DrawPolygon(p, points);
```

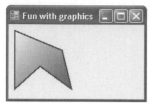

Figure 6-7   Combine *Graphics.Fill* with *Graphics.Draw* methods to create solid objects with outlines

You can use the same techniques to draw on controls, such as buttons or the instances of the *PictureBox* class. If you need to fill an entire *Graphics* object with a single color, call the *Graphics.Clear* method.

Lab: Create a Method to Draw a Pie Chart

In this lab, you create a method to draw a pie chart, and then improve that method to make the pie chart more visually appealing. If you encounter a problem completing an exercise, the completed projects are available on the companion CD in the Code folder.

▶ **Exercise 1: Draw a Pie Chart**

In this exercise, you write a method that draws a pie chart given an array of data and a *Size* structure. At this point, simple black lines will suffice.

1. Copy the Chapter06\Lesson1-Exercise1-PieChart folder from the companion CD to your hard disk, and open either the C# version or the Visual Basic version of the PieChart project.

2. Examine the form. The form has a single *PictureBox* named chart that is bound to all four sides of the form. Notice that the *Paint* event calls the *Draw* method.

3. Examine the *Draw* method. This method includes sample data that will be passed as parameters to the *drawPieChart* method you will complete. Notice that the *drawPieChart* method returns an *Image* object, which is used to define the chart *PictureBox*.

4. Examine the *PieChartElement* class. This simple class contains information to describe a single section of your pie chart.

5. Examine the *drawPieChart* method. It receives two parameters: an *ArrayList* containing only *PieChartElement* objects, and a *Size* structure.

6. Complete the *drawPieChart* method. First, define a *Bitmap* object to be returned, create a *Graphics* object from the *Bitmap* object, and then return the *Bitmap* object. For example, the following code would work:

```
' VB
Dim bm As Bitmap = New Bitmap(s.Width, s.Height)
Dim g As Graphics = Graphics.FromImage(bm)

' TODO: Draw pie chart in g
Return bm

// C#
Bitmap bm = new Bitmap(s.Width, s.Height);
Graphics g = Graphics.FromImage(bm);

// TODO: Draw pie chart in g
return bm;
```

7. At this point, the project will compile, but no pie chart is drawn. Before you can create a pie chart from the *PieChartElement* objects in the *ArrayList*, you must determine how many degrees each element uses. To do that, you must calculate the total of all the *PieChartElement.value* objects. For example, the following code would work:

```
' VB
' Calculate total value of all rows
Dim total As Single = 0

For Each e As PieChartElement In elements
    If e.value < 0 Then
        Throw New ArgumentException("All elements must have positive values")
    End If
    total += e.value
Next

// C#
// Calculate total value of all rows
float total = 0;

foreach (PieChartElement e in elements)
{
    if (e.value < 0)
    {
        throw new ArgumentException("All elements must have positive values");
    }
    total += e.value;
}
```

8. Now you should define the rectangle that the pie chart will consume based on the *Size* structure passed to the method as a parameter. The following code would work, and it provides a sufficient buffer on all sides of the image:

```
' VB
' Define the rectangle that the pie chart will use
Dim rect As Rectangle = New Rectangle(1, 1, s.Width - 2, s.Height - 2)
```

```
// C#
// Define the rectangle that the pie chart will use
Rectangle rect = new Rectangle(1, 1, s.Width - 2, s.Height - 2);
```

9. Next, define a *Pen* object with which to draw the pie chart. This can be a simple, black, one-pixel pen:

```
' VB
Dim p As Pen = New Pen(Color.Black, 1)
```

```
// C#
Pen p = new Pen(Color.Black, 1);
```

10. Finally, create a *foreach* loop that calculates the degrees for each pie chart section, and draws the pie charts. There are many ways to do this, such as the following code:

```
' VB
' Draw the first section at 0 degrees
Dim startAngle As Single = 0

' Draw each of the pie shapes
For Each e As PieChartElement In elements
    ' Calculate the degrees that this section will consume,
    ' based on the percentage of the total
    Dim sweepAngle As Single = (e.value / total) * 360

    ' Draw the pie shape
    g.DrawPie(p, rect, startAngle, sweepAngle)

    ' Calculate the angle for the next pie shape by adding
    ' the current shape's degrees to the previous total.
    startAngle += sweepAngle
Next
```

```
// C#
// Draw the first section at 0 degrees
float startAngle = 0;

// Draw each of the pie shapes
foreach (PieChartElement e in elements)
{
    // Calculate the degrees that this section will consume,
    // based on the percentage of the total
    float sweepAngle = (e.value / total) * 360;
```

```
// Draw the pie shape
g.DrawPie(p, rect, startAngle, sweepAngle);

// Calculate the angle for the next pie shape by adding
// the current shape's degrees to the previous total.
startAngle += sweepAngle;
}
```

11. Run the application, and fix any errors. Resize the form, and notice that the pie chart is automatically resized; the *Paint* event calls the *Draw* method when you resize the form.

▶ **Exercise 2: Improve the Appearance of the Pie Chart**

In this exercise, you improve the project you created in Exercise 1 to make the pie chart more visually appealing. Specifically, you will fill in each section with a different color and enable anti-aliasing to smooth the lines.

1. Copy the Chapter06\Lesson1-Exercise2-PieChart folder from the companion CD to your hard disk, and open either the C# version or the Visual Basic version of the PieChart project. Alternatively, you can continue working from the project you created in Exercise 1.

2. First, in the *drawPieChart* method, create an array containing the colors you want to use in your pie chart. You will assign the colors sequentially, so do not place similar colors after each other. For the sake of simplicity, throw an exception if the pie chart has more elements than you have colors in your array. For example:

```
' VB
Dim colors As Color() = {Color.Red, Color.Orange, Color.Yellow, Color.Green, _
    Color.Blue, Color.Indigo, Color.Violet, Color.DarkRed, Color.DarkOrange, _
    Color.DarkSalmon, Color.DarkGreen, Color.DarkBlue, Color.Lavender, _
    Color.LightBlue, Color.Coral}

If elements.Count > colors.Length Then
    Throw New ArgumentException("Pie chart must have " + _
        colors.Length.ToString() + " or fewer elements")
End If

// C#
Color[] colors = { Color.Red, Color.Orange, Color.Yellow, Color.Green,
    Color.Blue, Color.Indigo, Color.Violet, Color.DarkRed,
    Color.DarkOrange, Color.DarkSalmon, Color.DarkGreen,
    Color.DarkBlue, Color.Lavender, Color.LightBlue, Color.Coral };

if (elements.Count > colors.Length)
{
    throw new ArgumentException("Pie chart must have " +
        colors.Length.ToString() + " or fewer elements");
}
```

NOTE Keeping it simple

For the sake of keeping the exercise focused, some aspects of this project are not exactly as you would design them in the real world. For example, you would typically want to give the calling application the option of specifying colors for different sections, which could be done by adding a *Color* object to the *PieChartElement* class. Additionally, elements such as catching exceptions, validating input, and asserting are omitted from the examples.

---

3. You will need to track the color in use. Before the *foreach* loop, initialize an integer to zero to act as a counter:

```
' VB
Dim colorNum As Integer = 0

// C#
int colorNum = 0;
```

4. Within the *foreach* loop, add two lines: one to create a new *Brush* object, and a second to call the *Graphics.FillPie* method. Call *Graphics.FillPie* immediately before you call *Graphics.DrawPie* so that the outline is drawn over the filled pie. The following code example uses the *LinearGradientBrush* class, which requires adding the *System.Drawing.Drawing2D* namespace to the project:

```
' VB
' Draw the first section at 0 degrees
Dim startAngle As Single = 0
Dim colorNum As Integer = 0

' Draw each of the pie shapes
For Each e As PieChartElement In elements
    ' Create a brush with a nice gradient
    Dim b As Brush = New LinearGradientBrush(rect, colors(colorNum), Color.White, 45)
    colorNum += 1

    ' Calculate the degrees that this section will consume,
    ' based on the percentage of the total
    Dim sweepAngle As Single = (e.value / total) * 360

    ' Draw the filled-in pie shapes
    g.FillPie(b, rect, startAngle, sweepAngle)

    ' Draw the pie shape
    g.DrawPie(p, rect, startAngle, sweepAngle)

    ' Calculate the angle for the next pie shape by adding
    ' the current shape's degrees to the previous total.
    startAngle += sweepAngle
Next
```

```csharp
// C#
// Draw the first section at 0 degrees
float startAngle = 0;
int colorNum = 0;

// Draw each of the pie shapes
foreach (PieChartElement e in elements)
{
    // Create a brush with a nice gradient
    Brush b = new LinearGradientBrush(rect, colors[colorNum++], Color.White, (float)45
);

    // Calculate the degrees that this section will consume,
    // based on the percentage of the total
    float sweepAngle = (e.value / total) * 360;

    // Draw the filled-in pie shapes
    g.FillPie(b, rect, startAngle, sweepAngle);

    // Draw the pie shape outlines
    g.DrawPie(p, rect, startAngle, sweepAngle);

    // Calculate the angle for the next pie shape by adding
    // the current shape's degrees to the previous total.
    startAngle += sweepAngle;
}
```

5. Now, run the application. Experiment with different brush types to find the one that is most appealing. Notice that the lines appear a bit jagged; you can make the lines appear smoother by setting *Graphics.SmoothingMode*, as the following line demonstrates:

```vb
' VB
g.SmoothingMode = SmoothingMode.HighQuality
```

```csharp
// C#
g.SmoothingMode = SmoothingMode.HighQuality;
```

Lesson Summary

- The *System.Drawing* namespace provides tools for drawing graphics and editing existing images. The most useful classes are *Graphics*, *Image*, and *Bitmap*.

- Use the *Point* and *Size* classes to specify the location and size of controls.

- The *System.Drawing.Color* structure provides predefined properties for common colors.

- To draw lines and shapes, create an instance of the *Graphics* class, create a *Pen* object, and then call one of the *Graphics* member methods to draw a line or a shape using the *Pen* instance.

- Pens can be customized by adding endcaps or changing the line pattern to various combinations of dots and dashes.

- To draw solid shapes, create an instance of the *Graphics* class, create a *Brush* object, and then call one of the *Graphics* member methods to draw the shape using the *Brush* instance.

Lesson Review

You can use the following questions to test your knowledge of the information in Lesson 1, "Drawing Graphics." The questions are also available on the companion CD if you prefer to review them in electronic form.

NOTE   Answers

Answers to these questions and explanations of why each answer choice is right or wrong are located in the "Answers" section at the end of the book.

---

1. Which of the following methods would you use to draw a square with a solid color?

    A. *Graphics.DrawLines*

    B. *Graphics.DrawRectangle*

    C. *Graphics.DrawPolygon*

    D. *Graphics.DrawEllipse*

    E. *Graphics.FillRectangle*

    F. *Graphics.FillPolygon*

    G. *Graphics.FillEllipse*

2. Which of the following methods would you use to draw an empty triangle?

    A. *Graphics.DrawLines*

    B. *Graphics.DrawRectangle*

    C. *Graphics.DrawPolygon*

    D. *Graphics.DrawEllipse*

    E. *Graphics.FillRectangle*

    F. *Graphics.FillPolygon*

    G. *Graphics.FillEllipse*

3. Which of the following classes is required to draw an empty circle? (Choose all that apply.)

    A. *System.Drawing.Graphics*

    B. *System.Drawing.Pen*

    C. *System.Drawing.Brush*

    D. *System.Drawing.Bitmap*

4. Which of the following brush classes would you use to create a solid rectangle that is red at the top and gradually fades to white towards the bottom?

    A. *System.Drawing.Drawing2D.HatchBrush*

    B. *System.Drawing.Drawing2D.LinearGradientBrush*

    C. *System.Drawing.Drawing2D.PathGradientBrush*

    D. *System.Drawing.SolidBrush*

    E. *System.Drawing.TextureBrush*

5. What type of line would the following code sample draw?

```
' VB
Dim g As Graphics = Me.CreateGraphics
Dim p As Pen = New Pen(Color.Red, 10)

p.StartCap = LineCap.Flat
p.EndCap = LineCap.ArrowAnchor
g.DrawLine(p, 50, 50, 400, 50)

// C#
Graphics g = this.CreateGraphics();
Pen p = new Pen(Color.Red, 10);

p.StartCap = LineCap.Flat;
p.EndCap = LineCap.ArrowAnchor;
g.DrawLine(p, 50, 50, 400, 50);
```

    A. An arrow pointing up

    B. An arrow pointing down

    C. An arrow pointing left

    D. An arrow pointing right

Lesson 2: Working with Images

Often developers need to display, create, or modify images. The .NET Framework provides tools to work with a variety of image formats, enabling you to perform many common image-editing tasks.

After this lesson, you will be able to:

- Describe the purpose of the *Image* and *Bitmap* classes.
- Display pictures in forms or *PictureBox* objects.
- Create a new picture, add lines and shapes to the picture, and save it as a file.

Estimated lesson time: 30 minutes

The *Image* and *Bitmap* Classes

The *System.Drawing.Image* abstract class gives you the ability to create, load, modify, and save images such as .BMP files, .JPG files, and .TIF files. Some useful things you can do with the *Image* class include:

- Create a drawing or chart, and save the results as an image file.
- Use text (as described in Lesson 3) to add copyright information or a watermark to a picture.
- Resize JPEG images so that they consume less space and can be downloaded faster.

The *Image* class is abstract, but you can create instances of the classing using the *Image.FromFile* (which accepts a path to an image file as a parameter) and *Image.FromStream* (which accepts a *System.IO.Stream* object as a parameter) methods. You can also use two classes that inherit *Image*: *System.Drawing.Bitmap* for still images, and *System.Drawing.Imaging.Metafile* for animated images.

Bitmap is the most commonly used class for working with new or existing images. The different constructors allow you to create a *Bitmap* from an existing *Image*, file, or stream, or to create a blank bitmap of a specified height and width. *Bitmap* contains two particularly useful methods that *Image* lacks:

- **GetPixel**   Returns a *Color* object describing a particular pixel in the image. A pixel is a single colored dot in the image, consisting of a red, green, and blue component.
- **SetPixel**   Sets a pixel to the specified color.

However, more complex image editing requires you to create a *Graphics* object by calling *Graphics.FromImage*.

How to Display Pictures

To display an image that is saved to the disk in a form, load it with *Image.FromFile* and create a *PictureBox* control, and then use the *Image* to define *PictureBox.BackgroundImage*. The following sample code (which requires a form with an instance of *PictureBox* named *pictureBox1*) demonstrates this process:

```vb
' VB
Dim I As Image = Image.FromFile("C:\windows\gone fishing.bmp")
PictureBox1.BackgroundImage = I
```

```csharp
// C#
Image i = Image.FromFile(@"C:\windows\gone fishing.bmp");
pictureBox1.BackgroundImage = i;
```

Similarly, the following code accomplishes the same thing using the *Bitmap* class:

```vb
' VB
Dim B As Bitmap = Image.FromFile("C:\windows\gone fishing.bmp")
PictureBox1.BackgroundImage = B
```

```csharp
// C#
Bitmap b = new Bitmap(@"C:\windows\gone fishing.bmp");
pictureBox1.BackgroundImage = b;
```

Alternatively, you can display an image as the background for a form or control by using the *Graphics.DrawImage* method. This method has 30 overloads, so you have a wide variety of options for how you specify the image location and size. The following code uses this method to set an image as the background for a form, no matter what the dimensions of the form are:

```vb
' VB
Dim Bm As Bitmap = New Bitmap("C:\WINDOWS\Web\Wallpaper\Azul.jpg")
Dim G As Graphics = Me.CreateGraphics
G.DrawImage(Bm, 1, 1, Me.Width, Me.Height)
```

```csharp
// C#
Bitmap bm = new Bitmap(@"C:\WINDOWS\Web\Wallpaper\Azul.jpg");
Graphics g = this.CreateGraphics();
g.DrawImage(bm, 1, 1, this.Width, this.Height);
```

How to Create and Save Pictures

To create a new, blank picture, create an instance of the *Bitmap* class with one of the constructors that does not require an existing image. You can then edit it using the *Bitmap.SetPixel* method, or you can call *Graphics.FromImage* and edit the image using the *Graphics* drawing methods.

To save a picture, call *Bitmap.Save*. This method has several easy-to-understand over-loads. Two of the overloads accept a parameter of type *System.Drawing.Imaging.Image-Format*, for which you should provide one of the following properties to describe the file type: Bmp, Emf, Exif, Gif, Icon, Jpeg, MemoryBmp, Png, Tiff, or Wmf. Jpeg is the most common format for photographs, and Gif is the most common format for charts, screen shots, and drawings.

For example, the following code creates a blank 600-by-600 *Bitmap*, creates a *Graphics* object based on the *Bitmap*, uses the *Graphics.FillPolygon* and *Graphics.DrawPolygon* methods to draw a shape in the *Bitmap*, and then saves it to a file named bm.jpg in the current directory. This code can run as a console application, and it requires the *System.Drawing.Drawing2D* and *System.Drawing.Imaging* namespaces.

```vb
' VB
Dim Bm As Bitmap = New Bitmap(600, 600)
Dim G As Graphics = Graphics.FromImage(bm)

Dim B As Brush = New LinearGradientBrush(New Point(1, 1), New Point(600, 600), _
    Color.White, Color.Red)
Dim Points As Point() = New Point() {New Point(10, 10), _
    New Point(77, 500), _
    New Point(590, 100), _
    New Point(250, 590), _
    New Point(300, 410)}

G.FillPolygon(B, Points)
Bm.Save("bm.jpg", ImageFormat.Jpeg)
```

```csharp
// C#
Bitmap bm = new Bitmap(600, 600);
Graphics g = Graphics.FromImage(bm);

Brush b = new LinearGradientBrush(new Point(1, 1), new Point(600, 600),
    Color.White, Color.Red);
Point[] points = new Point[]
    {new Point(10, 10),
        new Point(77, 500),
        new Point(590, 100),
        new Point(250, 590),
        new Point(300, 410)};

g.FillPolygon(b, points);
bm.Save("bm.jpg", ImageFormat.Jpeg);
```

To edit an existing image, simply change the *Bitmap* constructor in the previous example to load a picture.

How to Use Icons

Icons are transparent bitmaps of specific sizes that are used by Windows to convey status. The .NET Framework provides standard 40-by-40 system icons as properties of the *SystemIcons* class, including icons for exclamation, information, and question.

The simplest way to add an icon to a form or image is to call the *Graphics.DrawIcon* or *Graphics.DrawIconUnstretched* methods. The following code produces the result shown in Figure 6-8:

```
' VB
Dim G As Graphics = Me.CreateGraphics
G.DrawIcon(SystemIcons.Question, 40, 40)

// C#
Graphics g = this.CreateGraphics();
g.DrawIcon(SystemIcons.Question, 40, 40);
```

Figure 6-8 *SystemIcons* provides access to common icons that you can use to convey status

You can also edit system icons or load saved icons using the constructors built into the *Icon* class. Once you create an instance of the *Icon* class, call *Icon.ToBitmap* to create a *Bitmap* object that can be edited.

Lab: Save a Pie Chart as a Picture

In this lab, you write code to save a *Bitmap* object to the disk as a JPEG file. If you encounter a problem completing an exercise, the completed projects are available on the companion CD in the Code folder.

▶ **Exercise: Save a Pie Chart as a Picture**

In this exercise, you add code to save a pie chart picture to the disk as a file.

1. Copy the Chapter06\Lesson2-Exercise1-PieChart folder from the companion CD to your hard disk, and open either the C# version or the Visual Basic version of the PieChart project.

2. Add code to the *saveButton_Click* method to prompt the user for a filename, and write the pie chart to disk. For simplicity, always save the picture as a JPEG file. The following code, which requires the *System.Drawing.Imaging* namespace, is an example of how to do this:

```
' VB
' Display the Save dialog
Dim saveDialog As SaveFileDialog = New SaveFileDialog
saveDialog.DefaultExt = ".jpg"
saveDialog.Filter = "JPEG files (*.jpg)|*.jpg;*.jpeg|All files (*.*)|*.*"

If Not (saveDialog.ShowDialog = DialogResult.Cancel) Then
    ' Save the image to the specified file in JPEG format
    chart.Image.Save(saveDialog.FileName, ImageFormat.Jpeg)
End If

// C#
// Display the Save dialog
SaveFileDialog saveDialog = new SaveFileDialog();
saveDialog.DefaultExt = ".jpg";
saveDialog.Filter = "JPEG files (*.jpg)|*.jpg;*.jpeg|All files (*.*)|*.*";

if (saveDialog.ShowDialog() != DialogResult.Cancel)
{
    // Save the image to the specified file in JPEG format
    chart.Image.Save(saveDialog.FileName, ImageFormat.Jpeg);
}
```

3. Run and test the application to verify that it works properly and that you can view the saved file.

Lesson Summary

- The *Image* and *Bitmap* classes enable you to edit or create pictures, and save the results as a file.

- To display a picture in a Windows Forms assembly, load the picture into an instance of the *Image* or *Bitmap* class, create an instance of the *PictureBox* control, and then use the *Image* or *Bitmap* object to define the *PictureBox.BackgroundImage* property.

- To create and save a picture, create a *Bitmap* object, edit it using a *Graphics* object, and then call the *Bitmap.Save* method.

- To display an icon, call the *Graphics.DrawIcon* or *Graphics.DrawIconUnstretched* methods using one of the properties of the *SystemIcons* class.

Lesson Review

You can use the following questions to test your knowledge of the information in Lesson 2, "Working with Images." The questions are also available on the companion CD if you prefer to review them in electronic form.

NOTE Answers

Answers to these questions and explanations of why each answer choice is right or wrong are located in the "Answers" section at the end of the book.

---

1. Which of the following classes could you use to display a JPEG image from an existing file in a form? (Choose all that apply.)

   A. *System.Drawing.Image*

   B. *System.Drawing.Bitmap*

   C. *System.Drawing.Imaging.Metafile*

   D. *System.Windows.Forms.PictureBox*

2. How can you draw a black border around a JPEG image that you have saved to disk, and then save the updated image back to the disk?

   A. Create a *Graphics* object by loading the JPEG image from disk. Draw the border by calling *Graphics.DrawRectangle*. Finally, save the updated image by calling *Graphics.Save*.

   B. Create a *Bitmap* object by loading the JPEG image from disk. Draw the border by calling *Bitmap.DrawRectangle*. Finally, save the updated image by calling *Bitmap.Save*.

   C. Create a *Bitmap* object by loading the JPEG image from disk. Create a *Graphics* object by calling *Graphics.FromImage*. Draw the border by calling *Graphics.DrawRectangle*. Finally, save the updated image by calling *Bitmap.Save*.

   D. Create a *Bitmap* object by loading the JPEG image from disk. Create a *Graphics* object by calling *Bitmap.CreateGraphics*. Draw the border by calling *Graphics.DrawRectangle*. Finally, save the updated image by calling *Bitmap.Save*.

3. Which format should you choose to save a photograph that could be opened by a wide variety of applications?

   A. *ImageFormat.Bmp*

   B. *ImageFormat.Gif*

   C. *ImageFormat.Jpeg*

   D. *ImageFormat.Png*

4. Which format should you choose to save a pie chart that could be opened by a wide variety of applications?

   A. *ImageFormat.Bmp*

   B. *ImageFormat.Gif*

   C. *ImageFormat.Jpeg*

   D. *ImageFormat.Png*

Lesson 3: Formatting Text

Developers often add text to images to label objects or create reports. This lesson describes how to add formatted text to images.

> **After this lesson, you will be able to:**
> - Describe the process of creating the objects required to add text to images.
> - Create *Font* objects to meet your requirements for type, size, and style.
> - Use *Graphics.DrawString* to annotate images with text.
> - Control the formatting of text.
>
> **Estimated lesson time: 30 minutes**

How to Add Text to Graphics

You can add text to images by creating an instance of the *Graphics* class, in the same way that you add solid objects. At a high level, you follow these steps:

1. Create a *Graphics* object, as discussed in Lessons 1 and 2.
2. Create a *Font* object.
3. Optionally, create a *Brush* object.
4. Call *Graphics.DrawString* and specify the location for the text.

> ### Real World
>
> *Tony Northrup*
>
> When I'm not coding, I'm taking pictures. I sell photos on the Web to cover the outrageous cost of my camera equipment. Unfortunately, while they have digital rights management (DRM) for music and video, nobody has really figured out DRM for pictures. So, until someone develops a good image DRM system, your best bet is to add obtrusive watermarks and visible copyright notifications to images published on the Web. This won't stop someone from copying your pictures and violating the copyright, but the copyright text does make the pictures more difficult to use.

How to Create a *Font* Object

The *Font* class offers 13 different constructors. The simplest way to create a *Font* object is to pass the font family name (as a string), font size (as an integer or float), and font style (a *System.Drawing.FontStyle* property). For example, the following constructor creates an Arial 12-point bold font:

```
' VB
Dim F As Font = New Font("Arial", 12, FontStyle.Bold)
```

```
// C#
Font f = new Font("Arial", 12, FontStyle.Bold);
```

You can also create a new *Font* object using a *FontFamily*, as the following code shows:

```
' VB
Dim Ff As FontFamily = New FontFamily("Arial")
Dim F As Font = New Font(Ff, 12)
```

```
// C#
FontFamily ff = new FontFamily("Arial");
Font f = new Font(ff, 12);
```

If you need to read the font type from a string, you can use the *FontConverter* class. This is not the preferred method, however, because using a string to describe a font is less reliable. (It's less reliable because the compiler cannot detect errors or typos.) Therefore, you won't discover an error in the font name until a run time *Argument-Exception* is thrown. The following example creates an Arial 12-point font:

```
' VB
Dim Converter As FontConverter = New FontConverter
Dim F As Font = CType(converter.ConvertFromString("Arial, 12pt"), Font)
```

```
// C#
FontConverter converter = new FontConverter();
Font f = (Font)converter.ConvertFromString("Arial, 12pt");
```

How to Write Text

After you create a *Font* object, you need to create a *Brush* object (as described in Lesson 1) to define how the text will be filled. Alternatively, you can simply provide a *System.Drawing.Brushes* property to avoid creating a *Brush* object. To finally add the text to the image, call *Graphics.DrawString*. The following code draws text on the current form and produces the result shown in Figure 6-9:

```
' VB
Dim G As Graphics = Me.CreateGraphics
Dim F As Font = New Font("Arial", 40, FontStyle.Bold)
```

```
G.DrawString("Hello, World!", F, Brushes.Blue, 10, 10)

// C#
Graphics g = this.CreateGraphics();
Font f = new Font("Arial", 40, FontStyle.Bold);
g.DrawString("Hello, World!", f, Brushes.Blue, 10, 10);
```

Figure 6-9 Call *Graphics.DrawString* to add text to a *Graphics* object.

Of course, it's much easier to add text to a form using *Label* objects. However, *Graphics.DrawString* also enables you to add text to *Images* and *Bitmaps*. This is useful for adding visible copyright information to a picture, adding timestamps to images, and annotating charts.

How to Control the Formatting of Text

The .NET Framework gives you control over the alignment and direction of text using the *StringFormat* class. After creating and configuring a *StringFormat* object, you can provide it to the *Graphics.DrawString* method to control how text is formatted. The most important members of the *StringFormat* class are:

- **Alignment** Gets or sets horizontal text alignment. Possible options are
    - ❑ **StringAlignment.Center** Horizontally centers text
    - ❑ **StringAlignment.Near** Aligns text to the left
    - ❑ **StringAlignment.Far** Aligns text to the right
- **FormatFlags** Gets or sets a *StringFormatFlags* enumeration that contains formatting information. Possible options for *StringFormatFlags* are
    - ❑ **DirectionRightToLeft** Text is displayed from right to left.
    - ❑ **DirectionVertical** Text is vertically aligned.
    - ❑ **DisplayFormatControl** Control characters such as the left-to-right mark are shown in the output with a representative glyph.
    - ❑ **FitBlackBox** Parts of characters are allowed to overhang the string's layout rectangle. By default, characters are repositioned to avoid any overhang.
    - ❑ **LineLimit** Only entire lines are laid out in the formatting rectangle. By default, layout continues until the end of the text or until no more lines are visible as a result of clipping, whichever comes first. Note that the default

settings allow the last line to be partially obscured by a formatting rectangle that is not a whole multiple of the line height. To ensure that only whole lines are seen, specify this value and be careful to provide a formatting rectangle at least as tall as the height of one line.

❑ *MeasureTrailingSpaces* Includes the trailing space at the end of each line. By default, the boundary rectangle returned by the *MeasureString* method excludes the space at the end of each line. Set this flag to include that space in measurement.

❑ *NoClip* Overhanging parts of glyphs, and unwrapped text reaching outside the formatting rectangle are allowed to show. By default, all text and glyph parts reaching outside the formatting rectangle are clipped.

❑ *NoFontFallback* Fallback to alternate fonts for characters not supported in the requested font is disabled. Any missing characters are displayed with the fonts-missing glyph, usually an open square.

❑ *NoWrap* Text wrapping between lines when formatting within a rectangle is disabled. This flag is implied when a point is passed instead of a rectangle, or when the specified rectangle has a zero line length.

■ *LineAlignment* Gets or sets vertical text alignment. Possible options are

❑ *StringAlignment.Center* Vertically centers text

❑ *StringAlignment.Near* Aligns text to the top

❑ *StringAlignment.Far* Aligns text to the bottom

■ *Trimming* Gets or sets the *StringTrimming* enumeration for this *StringFormat* object. Possible options are

❑ *Character* Specifies that the text is trimmed to the nearest character.

❑ *EllipsisCharacter* Specifies that the text is trimmed to the nearest character, and an ellipsis is inserted at the end of a trimmed line.

❑ *EllipsisPath* The center is removed from trimmed lines and replaced by an ellipsis. The algorithm keeps as much of the last slash-delimited segment of the line as possible.

❑ *EllipsisWord* Specifies that text is trimmed to the nearest word, and an ellipsis is inserted at the end of a trimmed line.

❑ *None* Specifies no trimming.

❑ *Word* Specifies that text is trimmed to the nearest word.

The following code demonstrates the use of the *StringFormat* class and produces the output shown in Figure 6-10:

```vb
' VB
Dim G As Graphics = Me.CreateGraphics

' Construct a new Rectangle
Dim R As Rectangle = New Rectangle(New Point(40, 40), New Size(80, 80))

' Construct 2 new StringFormat objects
Dim F1 As StringFormat = New StringFormat(StringFormatFlags.NoClip)
Dim F2 As StringFormat = New StringFormat(f1)

' Set the LineAlignment and Alignment properties for
' both StringFormat objects to different values
F1.LineAlignment = StringAlignment.Near
f1.Alignment = StringAlignment.Center
f2.LineAlignment = StringAlignment.Center
f2.Alignment = StringAlignment.Far
f2.FormatFlags = StringFormatFlags.DirectionVertical

' Draw the bounding rectangle and a string for each
' StringFormat object
G.DrawRectangle(Pens.Black, R)
G.DrawString("Format1", Me.Font, Brushes.Red, CType(R, RectangleF), F1)
G.DrawString("Format2", Me.Font, Brushes.Red, CType(R, RectangleF), F2)

// C#
Graphics g = this.CreateGraphics();

// Construct a new Rectangle.
Rectangle r = new Rectangle(new Point(40, 40), new Size(80, 80));

// Construct 2 new StringFormat objects
StringFormat f1 = new StringFormat(StringFormatFlags.NoClip);
StringFormat f2 = new StringFormat(f1);

// Set the LineAlignment and Alignment properties for
// both StringFormat objects to different values.
f1.LineAlignment = StringAlignment.Near;
f1.Alignment = StringAlignment.Center;
f2.LineAlignment = StringAlignment.Center;
f2.Alignment = StringAlignment.Far;
f2.FormatFlags = StringFormatFlags.DirectionVertical;

// Draw the bounding rectangle and a string for each
// StringFormat object.
g.DrawRectangle(Pens.Black, r);
g.DrawString("Format1", this.Font, Brushes.Red, (RectangleF)r, f1);
g.DrawString("Format2", this.Font, Brushes.Red, (RectangleF)r, f2);
```

Figure 6-10   Use *StringFormat* to control alignment and direction of text

Lab: Add Text to an Image

In this lab, you add a copyright logo to a picture before writing it to the disk, and you update a pie chart to display a legend. If you encounter a problem completing an exercise, the completed projects are available on the companion CD in the Code folder.

▶ **Exercise 1: Add a Copyright Notice to a Picture**

1. Copy the Chapter06\Lesson3-Exercise1-PieChart folder from the companion CD to your hard disk, and open either the C# version or the Visual Basic version of the PieChart project. Alternatively, you can continue working from the project you created in Lesson 2.

2. Without modifying the chart *PictureBox*, add a copyright notice to the saved image. The notice should say "Copyright 2006, Contoso, Inc." and appear in the upper left corner. The following code could replace the previous contents of the *if* statement:

```vb
' VB
If Not (saveDialog.ShowDialog = DialogResult.Cancel) Then
    ' Define the Bitmap, Graphics, Font, and Brush for copyright logo
    Dim bm As Bitmap = CType(chart.Image, Bitmap)
    Dim g As Graphics = Graphics.FromImage(bm)
    Dim f As Font = New Font("Arial", 12)
    Dim b As Brush = New SolidBrush(Color.White)

    ' Add the copyright text
    g.DrawString("Copyright 2006, Contoso, Inc.", f, b, 5, 5)

    ' Save the image to the specified file in JPEG format
    chart.Image.Save(saveDialog.FileName, ImageFormat.Jpeg)
End If

// C#
if (saveDialog.ShowDialog() != DialogResult.Cancel)
{
    // Define the Bitmap, Graphics, Font, and Brush for copyright logo
    Bitmap bm = (Bitmap)chart.Image;
```

```
Graphics g = Graphics.FromImage(bm);
Font f = new Font("Arial", 12);
Brush b = new SolidBrush(Color.White);

// Add the copyright text
g.DrawString("Copyright 2006, Contoso, Inc.", f, b, 5, 5);

// Save the image to the specified file in JPEG format
bm.Save(saveDialog.FileName, ImageFormat.Jpeg);
}
```

3. Run the application, and save a picture. Notice that the copyright notice is difficult to read where it overlaps the picture. One way to resolve this is to draw text with a contrasting color behind the string, and offset by one pixel in each direction. For example, the following code adds a black background to the white copyright text:

```
' VB
' Define the Bitmap, Graphics, Font, and Brush for copyright logo
Dim bm As Bitmap = CType(chart.Image, Bitmap)
Dim g As Graphics = Graphics.FromImage(bm)
Dim f As Font = New Font("Arial", 12)

' Create the foreground text brush
Dim b As Brush = New SolidBrush(Color.White)

' Create the background text brush
Dim bb As Brush = New SolidBrush(Color.Black)

' Add the copyright text background
Dim ct As String = "Copyright 2006, Contoso, Inc."
g.DrawString(ct, f, bb, 4, 4)
g.DrawString(ct, f, bb, 4, 6)
g.DrawString(ct, f, bb, 6, 4)
g.DrawString(ct, f, bb, 6, 6)

' Add the copyright text foreground
g.DrawString(ct, f, b, 5, 5)

' Save the image to the specified file in JPEG format
chart.Image.Save(saveDialog.FileName, ImageFormat.Jpeg)

// C#
// Define the Bitmap, Graphics, Font, and Brush for copyright logo
Bitmap bm = (Bitmap)chart.Image;
Graphics g = Graphics.FromImage(bm);
Font f = new Font("Arial", 12);

// Create the foreground text brush
Brush b = new SolidBrush(Color.White);
```

```
// Create the backround text brush
Brush bb = new SolidBrush(Color.Black);

// Add the copyright text background
string ct = "Copyright 2006, Contoso, Inc.";
g.DrawString(ct, f, bb, 4, 4);
g.DrawString(ct, f, bb, 4, 6);
g.DrawString(ct, f, bb, 6, 4);
g.DrawString(ct, f, bb, 6, 6);

// Add the copyright text foreground
g.DrawString(ct, f, b, 5, 5);

// Save the image to the specified file in JPEG format
bm.Save(saveDialog.FileName, ImageFormat.Jpeg);
```

4. Re-run the application, and save the picture again. Notice that where the copyright text overlaps the pie chart, the text has a black background, which makes it easy to read.

▶ **Exercise 2: Add a Legend to the Pie Chart**

In this exercise, you modify the *drawPieChart* method created in previous exercises to split the image into two parts. The left half will display the pie chart, and the right half will display a legend showing the color of each pie chart segment, the name of that segment, and the value.

1. Copy the Chapter06\Lesson3-Exercise2-PieChart folder from the companion CD to your hard disk, and open either the C# version or the Visual Basic version of the PieChart project. Alternatively, you can continue working from the project you created in Exercise 1.

2. First, modify the *drawPieChart* method so that the pie chart consumes only the left half of the image. The following modification accomplishes this:

```
' VB
' Define the rectangle that the pie chart will use
' Use only half the width to leave room for the legend
Dim rect As Rectangle = New Rectangle(1, 1, (s.Width/2) - 2, s.Height - 2)

// C#
// Define the rectangle that the pie chart will use
// Use only half the width to leave room for the legend
Rectangle rect = new Rectangle(1, 1, (s.Width/2) - 2, s.Height - 2);
```

3. Next, in the right half of the image, draw a black box with a white background. The following code shows one way to do this:

```
' VB
' Define the rectangle that the legend will use
Dim lRectCorner As Point = New Point((s.Width / 2) + 2, 1)
```

```
Dim lRectSize As Size = New Size(s.Width - (s.Width / 2) - 4, s.Height - 2)
Dim lRect As Rectangle = New Rectangle(lRectCorner, lRectSize)

' Draw a black box with a white background for the legend.
Dim lb As Brush = New SolidBrush(Color.White)
Dim lp As Pen = New Pen(Color.Black, 1)
g.FillRectangle(lb, lRect)
g.DrawRectangle(lp, lRect)

// C#
// Define the rectangle that the legend will use
Point lRectCorner = new Point((s.Width / 2) + 2, 1);
Size lRectSize = new Size(s.Width - (s.Width / 2) - 4, s.Height - 2);
Rectangle lRect = new Rectangle(lRectCorner, lRectSize);

// Draw a black box with a white background for the legend.
Brush lb = new SolidBrush(Color.White);
Pen lp = new Pen(Color.Black, 1);
g.FillRectangle(lb, lRect);
g.DrawRectangle(lp, lRect);
```

4. Calculate values required to draw each legend item, including:

- ❑ Number of vertical pixels for each legend item
- ❑ Width of the legend box
- ❑ Height of the legend box
- ❑ Buffer space between legend elements
- ❑ Left border of the legend text
- ❑ Width of the legend text

The following code demonstrates one way to do this:

```
' VB
' Determine the number of vertical pixels for each legend item
Dim vert As Integer = (lRect.Height - 10) / elements.Count

' Calculate the width of the legend box as 20% of the total legend width
Dim legendWidth As Integer = lRect.Width / 5

' Calculate the height of the legend box as 75% of the legend item height
Dim legendHeight As Integer = CType((vert * 0.75), Integer)

' Calculate a buffer space between elements
Dim buffer As Integer = CType((vert - legendHeight), Integer) / 2

' Calculate the left border of the legend text
Dim textX As Integer = lRectCorner.X + legendWidth + buffer * 2

' Calculate the width of the legend text
Dim textWidth As Integer = lRect.Width - (lRect.Width / 5) - (buffer * 2)
```

```csharp
// C#
// Determine the number of vertical pixels for each legend item
int vert = (lRect.Height - 10) / elements.Count;

// Calculate the width of the legend box as 20% of the total legend width
int legendWidth = lRect.Width / 5;

// Calculate the height of the legend box as 75% of the legend item height
int legendHeight = (int) (vert * 0.75);

// Calculate a buffer space between elements
int buffer = (int)(vert - legendHeight) / 2;

// Calculate the left border of the legend text
int textX = lRectCorner.X + legendWidth + buffer * 2;

// Calculate the width of the legend text
int textWidth = lRect.Width - (lRect.Width / 5) - (buffer * 2);
```

5. Finally, loop through the *PieChartElements* objects and draw each legend element. The following example shows a separate *foreach* loop for simplicity; however, for efficiency, this should be combined with the existing *foreach* loop:

```vb
' VB
' Start the legend five pixels from the top of the rectangle
Dim currentVert As Integer = 5
Dim legendColor As Integer = 0

For Each e As PieChartElement In elements
    ' Create a brush with a nice gradient
    Dim thisRect As Rectangle = New Rectangle(lRectCorner.X + buffer, _
        currentVert + buffer, legendWidth, legendHeight)
    Dim b As Brush = New LinearGradientBrush(thisRect, _
        colors(System.Math.Min(System.Threading.Interlocked.Increment(legendColor), _
        legendColor - 1)), Color.White, CType(45, Single))

    ' Draw the legend box fill and border
    g.FillRectangle(b, thisRect)
    g.DrawRectangle(lp, thisRect)

    ' Define the rectangle for the text
    Dim textRect As RectangleF = New Rectangle(textX, currentVert + buffer, _
        textWidth, legendHeight)

    ' Define the font for the text
    Dim tf As Font = New Font("Arial", 12)

    ' Create the foreground text brush
    Dim tb As Brush = New SolidBrush(Color.Black)

    ' Define the vertical and horizontal alignment for the text
    Dim sf As StringFormat = New StringFormat
```

```
    sf.Alignment = StringAlignment.Near
    sf.LineAlignment = StringAlignment.Center

    ' Draw the text
    g.DrawString(e.name + ": " + e.value.ToString(), tf, tb, textRect, sf)

    ' Increment the current vertical location
    currentVert += vert
Next

// C#
// Start the legend five pixels from the top of the rectangle
int currentVert = 5;
int legendColor = 0;

foreach (PieChartElement e in elements)
{
    // Create a brush with a nice gradient
    Rectangle thisRect = new Rectangle(lRectCorner.X + buffer,
        currentVert + buffer, legendWidth, legendHeight);
    Brush b = new LinearGradientBrush(thisRect, colors[legendColor++],
        Color.White, (float)45);

    // Draw the legend box fill and border
    g.FillRectangle(b, thisRect);
    g.DrawRectangle(lp, thisRect);

    // Define the rectangle for the text
    RectangleF textRect = new Rectangle(textX, currentVert + buffer,
        textWidth, legendHeight);

    // Define the font for the text
    Font tf = new Font("Arial", 12);

    // Create the foreground text brush
    Brush tb = new SolidBrush(Color.Black);

    // Define the vertical and horizontal alignment for the text
    StringFormat sf = new StringFormat();
    sf.Alignment = StringAlignment.Near;
    sf.LineAlignment = StringAlignment.Center;

    // Draw the text
    g.DrawString(e.name + ": " + e.value, tf, tb, textRect, sf);

    // Increment the current vertical location
    currentVert += vert;
}
```

6. Run the application to verify that it works. With the legend added, more of the copyright text now overlaps with the pie chart, demonstrating the effectiveness of the black background.

Lesson Summary

- To add text to graphics, create a *Graphics* object, create a *Font* object, optionally create a *Brush* object, and then call the *Graphics.DrawString* method.

- To create a *Font* object, pass the font family name, font size, and font style.

- Write text by calling the *Graphics.DrawString* method. The *DrawString* method requires a *Font* object, a *Brush* object that specifies the color of the text, and the location to draw the text.

- Use the *StringFormat* class to control the formatting of text. You can use this class to change the direction of the text, or to change the alignment of text.

Lesson Review

You can use the following questions to test your knowledge of the information in Lesson 3, "Formatting Text." The questions are also available on the companion CD if you prefer to review them in electronic form.

NOTE Answers

Answers to these questions and explanations of why each answer choice is right or wrong are located in the "Answers" section at the end of the book.

---

1. What are the steps for adding text to an image?

   A. Create a *Graphics* object and a *string* object. Then call *string.Draw*.

   B. Create a *Graphics* object, a *Font* object, and a *Brush* object. Then call *Graphics .DrawString*.

   C. Create a *Graphics* object, a *Font* object, and a *Pen* object. Then call *Graphics .DrawString*.

   D. Create a *Bitmap* object, a *Font* object, and a *Brush* object. Then call *Bitmap .DrawString*.

2. Which of the following is a class would you need to create an instance of to specify that a string should be centered when drawn?

   A. *StringFormat*

   B. *StringAlignment*

   C. *FormatFlags*

   D. *LineAlignment*

3. Which of the following commands would cause a string to be flush left?

   A. *StringFormat.LineAlignment = Near*

   B. *StringFormat.LineAlignment = Far*

   C. *StringFormat.Alignment = Near*

   D. *StringFormat.Alignment = Far*

Chapter Review

To further practice and reinforce the skills you learned in this chapter, you can complete the following tasks:

- Review the chapter summary.
- Review the list of key terms introduced in this chapter.
- Complete the case scenarios. These scenarios set up real-world situations involving the topics of this chapter and ask you to create solutions.
- Complete the suggested practices.
- Take a practice test.

Chapter Summary

- To draw graphics, create two objects: a *Pen* object and a *Graphics* object. Use the *Pen* object to define the color and width of the drawing. The *Graphics* object exposes methods for drawing lines and shapes. To fill in shapes, use a *Brush* object with a *Graphics* object.
- To work with images, use the *Image* and *Bitmap* classes. To edit images, create a *Graphics* object based on the *Image* or *Bitmap* object.
- To add text to an image or graphic, create *Font* and *Brush* objects. Then call *Graphics.DrawString*. To format the text, use the *StringFormat* class.

Key Terms

Do you know what these key terms mean? You can check your answers by looking up the terms in the glossary at the end of the book.

- Bitmap
- Brush
- Graphics
- Pen

Case Scenarios

In the following case scenarios, you will apply what you've learned in this chapter. You can find answers to these questions in the "Answers" section at the end of this book.

Case Scenario 1: Choosing Graphics Techniques

You are an internal application developer for Contoso, Inc. You and your team are responsible for an internal application that Contoso uses for order tracking and inventory management. Recently, a person in the Public Relations group asked your manager to discuss changes that are necessary to the look and feel of your internal applications. Your manager delegated the discussion to you.

Interviews

Following is a list of company personnel interviewed and their statements:

- **Public Relations Representative** "We are in the process of re-inventing our corporate image. There are many elements to our new image, including pictures, the use of specific color and fonts, and logos. For consistent branding both internally and externally, everything we produce must conform to these standards. Specifically, on our internal application, I'd like to show a splash screen that displays a photo of our corporate headquarters with our logo in the upper left corner. When the program loads, I'd like the logo to appear in the upper left corner. Additionally, all fonts in the application should be Arial 12. Oh, Legal is still in the process of approving our logo, so that's likely to change. I can provide you with the current logo and the picture of our headquarters in .JPEG format."

- **IT Manager** "These PR guys will change the logo and picture about a dozen times before they decide what they want to use, so I'd suggest storing the pictures as files in the installation directory and loading them dynamically with the application. I wouldn't take anything for granted, including the size of the images."

Questions

Answer the following questions for your manager:

1. The photo of the headquarters is 6 megapixels, and it's way too big for the splash screen. How can you resize it?

2. How can you display the corporate logo over the photo of the corporate headquarters?

3. If the size of the corporate logo changes, how can you ensure it doesn't cover the entire photo of the headquarters and consumes only the upper left corner of the picture?

4. How can you change the fonts used throughout the application?

Case Scenario 2: Creating Simple Charts

You are a developer in the IT department of Fabrikam, Inc. Recently, you released version 1.0 of Sales, an internal application used by the sales team to track orders. Sales replaced their previous paper-based tracking methods, and everyone on the Sales team has been pleased with the application.

Now the Vice President of Sales would like to discuss feature requests for the next version of your application.

Interviews

Following is a list of company personnel interviewed and their statements:

- **Vice President, Sales** "The sales-tracking application you wrote is great, and it has really improved the efficiency of our sales organization. Now that we have this data stored in a database, I'd like the ability to access it to provide more insight into how different sales teams are performing over time. I want to be able to see either a line graph or a bar chart showing sales performance for each quarter of the year, with each team's performance in a different color. I also need to be able to save the graph so I can add it to a presentation I have to give before the board of directors."

Questions

Answer the following questions for your manager:

1. What type of control will you use to display a chart in a Windows Forms application?
2. What method will you use to draw a line graph?
3. What method will you use to draw a bar graph?
4. How will you save the chart to a file?

Suggested Practices

To help you successfully master the "Enhance the user interface of a .NET Framework application by using the *System.Drawing* namespace" exam objective, complete the following tasks.

Enhance the User Interface of a .NET Framework Application by Using Brushes, Pens, Colors, and Fonts

For this task, you should complete at least Practices 1 through 3 to gain experience using brushes, colors, and fonts. If you want in-depth knowledge of using pens, complete Practice 4 as well.

- **Practice 1** Create a Windows Forms application to demonstrate the different *Graphics.SmoothingMode* techniques available. Draw a circle, and display the name of the current *SmoothingMode*. Every five seconds, redraw the circle, and display the new *SmoothingMode*. Examine the edges of the circle with the different *SmoothingMode* settings.

- **Practice 2** Draw a solid circle on a form, and change the color every two seconds while displaying the name of the color at the bottom of the form.

- **Practice 3** Draw a solid circle on a form, and change the brush every five seconds while displaying the name of the brush at the bottom of the form.

- **Practice 4** Create an application that uses the *Pen.DashOffset* and *Pen.DashPattern* properties to define a custom dash pattern.

Enhance the User Interface of a .NET Framework Application by Using Graphics, Images, Bitmaps, and Icons

For this task, you should complete all three practices to gain experience working with images in real-world scenarios.

- **Practice 1** Create a Windows Forms application to allow you to browse pictures saved on your computer.

- **Practice 2** Create an application that creates 80-by-80-pixel thumbnails for all images saved in a folder.

- **Practice 3** Create an application that reads images from one folder, adds a copyright logo to the picture, and saves the images in a second folder.

Enhance the User Interface of a .NET Framework Application by Using Shapes and Sizes

For this task, you should complete at least Practices 1 and 2. If you want in-depth knowledge of drawing shapes, complete Practice 3 as well.

■ **Practice 1**   Create an application that allows you to draw polygons by clicking on a form. Each time the user clicks on the form, add a new point to the polygon at the location clicked.

■ **Practice 2**   Add a series of randomly generated rectangles to an array, and then call *Graphics.DrawRectangles* to display them.

■ **Practice 3**   Create a method to draw a bar graph that is similar in function to the *DrawPieChart* method used in this chapter.

Take a Practice Test

The practice tests on this book's companion CD offer many options. For example, you can test yourself on just one exam objective, or you can test yourself on all the 70-536 certification exam content. You can set up the test so that it closely simulates the experience of taking a certification exam, or you can set it up in study mode so that you can look at the correct answers and explanations after you answer each question.

MORE INFO   **Practice tests**

For details about all the practice test options available, see the "How to Use the Practice Tests" section in this book's Introduction.

Chapter 7
Threading

Threading is an important concept in software development. The basic concept behind threading is to perform multiple operations concurrently. Each of these operations can be thought of as a separate thread of logic. Most operations have downtime, where an operation is waiting for something else to happen (for example, waiting for a response from a Web server or waiting for a resource to become available). With threading, you can have the processor or processors of a machine continue to do other work during that time.

It's becoming more common to run code on machines that have multiple processors. When you write an application that does not use threading, your application is wasting these extra processors. By using the threading system in the .NET Framework, you can create robust and reliable multithreaded applications.

Exam objectives in this chapter:
- Develop multithreaded .NET Framework applications. (Refer *System.Threading* namespace)
  - ❏ *Thread* class
  - ❏ *ThreadPool* class
  - ❏ *ThreadStart* delegate and *ParameterizedThreadStart* delegate
  - ❏ *Timeout* class, *Timer* class, *TimerCallback* delegate, *WaitCallback* delegate, *WaitHandle* class, and *WaitOrTimerCallback* delegate
  - ❏ *ThreadExceptionEventArgs* class and *ThreadExceptionEventHandler* class
  - ❏ *ThreadState* enumeration and *ThreadPriority* enumeration
  - ❏ *ReaderWriterLock* class
  - ❏ *AutoResetEvent* class and *ManualResetEvent* class
  - ❏ *IAsyncResult* Interface (Refer *System* namespace)
  - ❏ *EventWaitHandle* class, *RegisteredWaitHandle* class, *SendOrPostCallback* delegate, and *IOCompletionCallback* delegate

❑ *Interlocked* class, *NativeOverlapped* structure, and *Overlapped* class

❑ *ExecutionContext* class, *HostExecutionContext* class, *HostExecutionContext-Manager* class, and *ContextCallback* delegate

❑ *LockCookie* structure, *Monitor* class, *Mutex* class, and *Semaphore* class

---

Real World

Shawn Wildermuth

I have used the threading system in .NET in many projects I have worked on. Whether I was using it to queue up work with the *ThreadPool* to speed up a long-running process or to run a background thread in a Microsoft Windows Forms application to enable better usability for an application, threading has been a crucial tool in my toolbox.

Lessons in this chapter:

Before You Begin

To complete the lessons in this chapter, you should be familiar with Microsoft Visual Basic or C# and be comfortable with the following tasks:

- Create a console application in Microsoft Visual Studio using Visual Basic or C#.
- Add references to system class libraries to a project.
- Create text files.
- Add events to the event log.

Lesson 1: Creating Threads

Threads are the basis of high-performance applications. In the .NET Framework, the *System.Threading* namespace contains the types that are used to create and manage multiple threads in an application.

After this lesson, you will be able to:

- Create threads to do work concurrently.
- Start and join threads.
- Abort threads.
- Use critical regions.

Estimated lesson time: 20 minutes

Simple Threads

To start working with threads, you must become acquainted with the *Thread* class. This class exemplifies a single thread. The *Thread* class is used to create and start threads. The *Thread* class's most important properties and methods are described in Table 7-1 and Table 7-2, respectively.

Table 7-1 *Thread* Properties

Name	Description
IsAlive	Gets a value indicating that the current thread is currently executing.
IsBackground	Gets or sets whether the thread runs as a background thread.
IsThreadPoolThread	Gets whether this thread is a thread in the thread pool.
ManagedThreadId	Gets a number to identify the current thread. Not the same as the operating system's thread ID.
Name	Gets or sets a name associated with the thread.
Priority	Gets or sets the priority of the thread.
ThreadState	Gets the *ThreadState* value for the thread.

Table 7-2   *Thread* Methods

Name	Description
Abort	Raises a *ThreadAbortException* on the thread to indicate that the thread should be aborted.
Interrupt	Raises a *ThreadInterruptedException* when a thread is in a blocked state (*ThreadState.WaitSleepJoin*). If the thread never blocks, the interruption never happens.
Join	Blocks the calling thread until the thread terminates.
Resume	Deprecated. Do not use.
Start	Sets a thread to be scheduled for execution.
Suspend	Deprecated. Do not use.

In addition to the properties and methods of an instance of a thread, the *Thread* class also has static properties and methods. These are detailed in Table 7-3 and Table 7-4.

Table 7-3   Static *Thread* Properties

Name	Description
CurrentContext	Gets the current *ThreadContext* object related to the current thread
CurrentPrincipal	Gets and sets the user associated with the current thread
CurrentThread	Gets the current running thread

Table 7-4   Static *Thread* Methods

Name	Description
BeginCriticalRegion	Used to notify the host that code to be executed cannot be aborted safely. Aborting a thread between a *BeginCriticalRegion* and *EndCriticalRegion* might leave an *AppDomain* in an unsafe state.
EndCriticalRegion	Used to notify the host that you have reached the end of a critical region.

Table 7-4 Static *Thread* Methods

Name	Description
GetDomain	Gets the *AppDomain* associated with the current running thread.
GetDomainID	Gets a unique identifier for the *AppDomain* associated with the currently running thread.
ResetAbort	Cancels an *Abort* request for the currently running thread.
Sleep	Blocks the current thread for a certain amount of time. Relinquishes execution to other threads to allow them to do work.
SpinWait	Blocks the current thread for a certain number of iterations. Does not relinquish execution to other threads.
VolatileRead	Reads the latest version of a field value regardless of which processor in a multiprocessor environment wrote the value.
VolatileWrite	Writes a field value immediately to ensure it is available to all processors.

In addition to the *Thread* class, the *ThreadState* enumeration is crucial in understanding how to work with *Thread* objects. Table 7-5 details the values in the *ThreadState* enumeration.

Table 7-5 *ThreadState* Enumeration

Name	Description
Aborted	The thread has stopped.
AbortRequested	The thread has been requested to abort, but the abort is still pending and has not received the *ThreadAbortException*.
Background	The thread is running as a background thread.
Running	The thread has started.
Stopped	The thread has stopped.
StopRequested	The thread is being requested to stop. For internal use only.

Table 7-5 *ThreadState* Enumeration

Name	Description
Suspended	The thread has been suspended. Supported for backward compatibility, but because *Suspend/Resume* should not be used, this state should not be used either.
SuspendedRequested	The thread has been requested to suspend. Supported for backward compatibility, but because *Suspend/Resume* should not be used, this state should not be used either.
Unstarted	The thread has been created, but the *Thread.Start* method has not been called.
WaitSleepJoin	The thread is blocked as a call to *Monitor.Wait*, *Thread.Sleep*, or *Thread.Join*.

Creating a Thread

To create and start a new thread, follow these steps:

1. Create a method that takes no arguments and does not return any data (for example, use the *void* return type for C#). This method should look something like this:

```vb
' VB
Shared  Sub SimpleWork()
    Console.WriteLine("Thread: {0}", Thread.CurrentThread.ManagedThreadId)
End Sub
```

```csharp
// C#
static void SimpleWork()
{
    Console.WriteLine("Thread: {0}", Thread.CurrentThread.ManagedThreadId);
}
```

2. Create a new *ThreadStart* delegate, and specify the method created in step 1.

3. Create a new *Thread* object, specifying the *ThreadStart* object created in step 2.

4. Call *Thread.Start* to begin execution of the new thread. Your code will end up looking something like this:

```vb
' VB
Dim operation As New ThreadStart(SimpleWork)
```

```
' Creates, but does not start, a new thread
Dim theThread As New Thread(operation)

' Starts the work on a new thread
theThread.Start()

// C#
ThreadStart operation = new ThreadStart(SimpleWork);

// Creates, but does not start, a new thread
Thread theThread = new Thread(operation);

// Starts the work on a new thread
theThread.Start();
```

When the *Start* method is called, the *SimpleWork* method is called on a new thread and the thread executes until the method completes. In this example, our *SimpleWork* method writes the phrase "In Thread#" and shows the *ManagedThreadId* property. This property is a numeric number assigned to every thread. Later on, we will use this value to see what work is being done on which thread.

Using Multiple Threads

A more likely scenario than this simple case is one in which you'll want to create multiple threads to do work. For example, we can change the example just shown to create multiple threads and start them all on the same work:

```
' VB
Dim operation As New ThreadStart(SimpleWork)

For x As Integer = 1 To 5
    ' Creates, but does not start, a new thread
    Dim theThread As New Thread(operation)

    ' Starts the work on a new thread
    theThread.Start()
Next

// C#
ThreadStart operation = new ThreadStart(SimpleWork);

for (int x = 1; x <= 5; ++x)
{
    // Creates, but does not start, a new thread
    Thread theThread = new Thread(operation);

    // Starts the work on a new thread
    theThread.Start();
}
```

This executes the work on five separate threads, as concurrently as your particular machine is capable of doing. If we implement this change, we should get five separate threads all writing out their own thread ID to the console window:

```
Thread: 3
Thread: 4
Thread: 5
Thread: 6
Thread: 7
```

We see consecutive thread numbers because the work we are doing in *SimpleWork* is very quick. Let's change our work to something a little more lengthy so that we can see the threads working concurrently:

```vb
' VB
Shared Sub SimpleWork()
    For x As Integer = 1 To 10
        Console.WriteLine("Thread: {0}", _
            Thread.CurrentThread.ManagedThreadId)

        ' Slow down thread and let other threads work
        Thread.Sleep(10)
    Next
End Sub
```

```csharp
// C#
static void SimpleWork()
{
    for (int x = 1; x <= 10; ++x)
    {
        Console.WriteLine("Thread: {0}",
            Thread.CurrentThread.ManagedThreadId);

        // Slow down thread and let other threads work
        Thread.Sleep(10);
    }
}
```

In this new version of *SimpleWork*, we are writing out our thread identifier 10 times. In addition, we are using *Thread.Sleep* to slow down our execution. The *Thread.Sleep* method allows us to specify a time in milliseconds to let other threads perform work. On every thread, we are allowing 10 milliseconds for the other threads to write their own data to the console. To see how this works, we can change our *SimpleWork* method to write out the iteration it is working on:

```
Thread: 3
Thread: 4
Thread: 5
Thread: 6
Thread: 7
```

```
Thread: 3
Thread: 4
Thread: 5
Thread: 6
Thread: 7
```

Doing this allows us to perform operations as concurrently as our hardware will allow.

NOTE **Threading and processors**

Creating multithreaded applications used to be the domain of the server-side developer. This is no longer the case. With the inclusion of hyperthreading and dual-core processors on the desktop and in the laptop, most applications will find threading useful.

As our work increases and the time it takes to complete each thread becomes longer, we will need to determine how to make our main thread (the one that the thread creation code exists on) wait until all the work is complete. This is where the *Thread.Join* method comes in.

Using *Thread.Join*

More often than not, you will need your application to wait for a thread to complete execution. To accomplish this, the *Thread* class supports the *Join* method:

```
' VB
theThread.Join()
```

```
// C#
theThread.Join();
```

The *Join* method tells the system to make your application wait until the thread has completed. Of course, in this simple case you do not really need a second thread because you are just waiting for it to complete anyway. A better example is for us to have five threads that all do some work and to wait for them. When we are working with multiple threads, our programming task is a bit more complicated, as we need to wait for all our threads. We can do this by keeping a reference to all our threads and calling *Join* on each of the threads to wait for the threads to complete, one at a time, as demonstrated in the following code:

```
' VB
Dim operation As ThreadStart = New ThreadStart(SomeWork)
Dim theThreads(5) as Thread

For x As Integer = 0 To 4
    ' Creates, but does not start, a new thread
    theThreads(x) = New Thread(operation)
```

```
        ' Starts the work on a new thread
        theThreads(x).Start()
Next

' Wait for each thread to complete
For Each t As Thread In theThreads
        t.Join()
Next

// C#
ThreadStart operation = new ThreadStart(SomeWork);
Thread[] theThreads = new Thread[5];

for (int x = 0; x < 5; ++x)
{
        // Creates, but does not start, a new thread
        theThreads[x] = new Thread(operation);

        // Starts the work on a new thread
        theThreads[x].Start();
}

// Wait for each thread to complete
foreach (Thread t in theThreads)
{
        t.Join();
}
```

By storing the threads in an array, we can wait for each of the *Threads* one at a time. As each thread completes, the *Join* method will return and we can continue.

Thread Priority

The *Thread* class supports the setting or getting of the priority of a thread using the *ThreadPriority* enumeration. The *ThreadPriority* enumeration consists of the values detailed in Table 7-6.

Table 7-6   *ThreadPriority* Enumeration Values

Name	Description
Highest	The highest priority
AboveNormal	Higher priority than *Normal*
Normal	The default priority
BelowNormal	Lower than *Normal*
Lowest	The lowest priority

Threads are scheduled based on this enumeration. In most cases, you will want to use the default (*Normal*). Deciding to use threads that have lower thread priority can cause the operation system to starve a thread more than you might expect, or if you use higher priorities (especially *Highest*), you can starve the system. Although it is necessary to use non-*Normal* thread priorities at times, make this decision with much caution. Increasing the performance of a system simply by increasing thread priority is not likely to help in the long term, as other starved threads tend to back up and cause unexpected consequences.

Passing Data to Threads

In each of the earlier examples, we were using the *ThreadStart* delegate, which takes no parameters. In most real-world use of threading, you will need to pass information to individual threads. To do this, you need to use a new delegate called *ParameterizedThreadStart*. This delegate specifies a method signature with a single parameter of type *Object* and returns nothing. The following code snippet provides an example:

```vb
' VB
Shared Sub WorkWithParameter(ByVal o As Object)
    Dim info As String = CType(o, String)

    For x = 0 To 9
        Console.WriteLine("{0}: {1}", info, _
            Thread.CurrentThread.ManagedThreadId)

        ' Slow down thread and let other threads work
        Thread.Sleep(10)
    Next
End Sub
```

```csharp
// C#
static void WorkWithParameter(object o)
{
    string info = (string) o;
    for (int x = 0; x < 10; ++x)
    {
        Console.WriteLine("{0}: {1}", info,
            Thread.CurrentThread.ManagedThreadId);

        // Slow down thread and let other threads work
        Thread.Sleep(10);
    }
}
```

This is a method that takes a single *Object* parameter (and therefore can be a reference to any object). To use this as the starting point of a thread call, you can create a *ParameterizedThreadStart* delegate to point at this new method and use the *Thread.Start* method's overload that takes a single object parameter. The following code snippet provides an example:

```
' VB
ParameterizedThreadStart operation = _
    New ParameterizedThreadStart(WorkWithParameter)

' Creates, but does not start, a new thread
Dim theThread As Thread =  New Thread(operation)

' Starts the work on a new thread
theThread.Start("Hello")

' A Second Thread with a different parameter
Dim NewThread As New Thread(operation)
NewThread.Start("Goodbye")

// C#
ParameterizedThreadStart operation =
    new ParameterizedThreadStart(WorkWithParameter);

// Creates, but does not start, a new thread
Thread theThread = new Thread(operation);

// Starts the work on a new thread
theThread.Start("Hello");

// A Second Thread with a different parameter
Thread newThread = new Thread(operation);
newThread.Start("Goodbye");
```

Be aware that because the *WorkWithParameter* method takes an object, *Thread.Start* could be called with any object instead of the string it expects. Being careful in choosing your starting method for a thread to deal with unknown types is crucial to good threading code. Instead of blindly casting the method parameter into our string, it is a better practice to test the type of the object, as shown in the following example:

```
' VB
Dim info As String =  o as String

If info Is Nothing Then
    Throw InvalidProgramException("Parameter for thread must be a string")
End If

// C#
string info = o as string;

if (info == null)
{
    throw new InvalidProgramException("Parameter for thread must be a string");
}
```

Stopping Threads

Controlling threads in your applications often requires that you be able to stop threads. The primary mechanism for stopping threads is to use the *Thread.Abort* method. When the *Thread.Abort* method is called, the threading system prepares to throw a *ThreadAbortException* in the thread. Whether the exception is caught or not, the thread is stopped after it is thrown. The following code snippet provides an example:

```vb
' VB
Dim NewThread As Thread = New Thread(New ThreadStart(AbortThisThread))

NewThread.Start()
NewThread.Abort()

Shared Sub AbortThisThread()
    ' Setting data
    SomeClass.IsValid = True
    SomeClass.IsComplete = True

    ' Write the object to the console
    SomeClass.WriteToConsole()
End Sub
```

```csharp
// C#
Thread newThread = new Thread(new ThreadStart(AbortThisThread));

newThread.Start();
newThread.Abort();

static void AbortThisThread()
{
    // Setting data
    SomeClass.IsValid = true;
    SomeClass.IsComplete = true;

    // Write the object to the console
    SomeClass.WriteToConsole();
}
```

Because the *AbortThisThread* method never catches the *ThreadAbortException*, this thread stops at the line currently executing when the main thread calls *Abort* to kill the thread. This is a problem because the thread system doesn't know where it can safely kill the thread. Aborting the thread in the wrong place in the code could leave data in an inconsistent state. For example, if the *ThreadAbortException* is thrown between the setting of the *IsValid* and *IsComplete* properties, the *SomeClass* object might be left in an inconsistent state. If the *ThreadAbortException* is thrown after the code writes the properties but before the code calls the *WriteToConsole* method, our object will be consistent. It will just never write itself out to the console.

To solve the problem of leaving objects or the *AppDomain* in an inconsistent state, the *Thread* class has two important static methods: *BeginCriticalRegion* and *EndCriticalRegion*. We can add calls to these methods to tell the threading system that it can abort this thread, just not within this critical region. The following code snippet provides an example:

```vb
' VB
Shared Sub AbortThisThread()
    ' Setting data
    Thread.BeginCriticalRegion()
    SomeClass.IsValid = True
    SomeClass.IsComplete = True
    Thread.EndCriticalRegion()

    ' Write the object to the console
    SomeClass.WriteToConsole()
End Sub
```

```csharp
// C#
static void AbortThisThread()
{
    // Setting data
    Thread.BeginCriticalRegion();
    SomeClass.IsValid = true;
    SomeClass.IsComplete = true;
    Thread.EndCriticalRegion();

    // Write the object to the console
    SomeClass.WriteToConsole();
}
```

The idea behind a critical region is to provide a region of code that must be executed as if it were a single statement. Any attempt to abort a thread while it is within a critical region will have to wait until after the critical region is complete. At that point, the thread will be aborted, throwing the *ThreadAbortException*. The difference between a thread with and without a critical region is illustrated in Figure 7-1.

NOTE   .NET 2.0

A major change to threading in the 2.0 version of the .NET Framework is that the *Thread.Suspend* and *Thread.Resume* methods have been retired (and marked as obsolete). To suspend and resume threads, you must use thread synchronization methods, as described in Lesson 2.

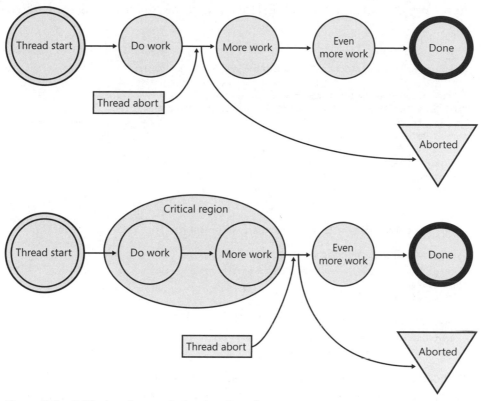

Figure 7-1 Critical regions and aborting threads

Execution Context

Each thread has data associated with it, and that data is usually propagated to new threads. This data includes security information (the *IPrincipal* and thread identity), the localization settings (the culture the thread is running in), and transaction information from *System.Transactions*. To access the current execution context, the *ExecutionContext* class supplies static methods to control the flow of context information.

By default, the execution context flows to helper threads, but it does so at a cost. If you want to stop the flow of the context information (increasing performance, but losing the current security, culture, and transaction context information), you can use the *ExecutionContext* class. To suppress the context, you call *ExecutionContext.SuppressFlow*;

to restore the context, you call *ExecutionContext.RestoreFlow*—as shown in the following code:

```vb
' VB
Dim flow As AsyncFlowControl = ExecutionContext.SuppressFlow()

' New thread does not get the execution context
Dim thread As Thread = New Thread(New ThreadStart(SomeWork))
thread.Start()
thread.Join()

' Restore the flow
ExecutionContext.RestoreFlow()
' could also flow.Undo()
```

```csharp
// C#
AsyncFlowControl flow = ExecutionContext.SuppressFlow();

// New thread does not get the execution context
Thread thread = new Thread(new ThreadStart(SomeWork));
thread.Start();
thread.Join();

// Restore the flow
ExecutionContext.RestoreFlow();
// could also flow.Undo();
```

You can also call the static *Run* method of *ExecutionContext*, which allows you to execute arbitrary code on the current thread and specify the context information to use. To use the *Run* method, you need to get a copy of an execution context. You can use *ExecutionContext.Capture* to retrieve the current context. Then you can call *Run*, specifying the context to use and a *ContextCallback* delegate with a method to run within the specified context. The following code snippet provides an example:

```vb
' VB

' Get the Current Context
Dim ctx As ExecutionContext = ExecutionContext.Capture()

' Run the ContextCalled method
ExecutionContext.Run(ctx, New ContextCallback(ContextCalled), Nothing)
```

```csharp
// C#

// Get the Current Context
ExecutionContext ctx = ExecutionContext.Capture();

// Run the ContextCalled method
ExecutionContext.Run(ctx, new ContextCallback(ContextCalled), null);
```

NOTE Host-specific context

If the *AppDomainManager* class has a reference to a valid *HostExecutionContextManager* object (in the *AppDomainManager* class's *HostExecutionContextManager* property), then the runtime will also flow a separate execution context, called the *HostExecutionContext*, with every thread. Much as with *ExecutionContext*, you can *Capture* or *Revert* data in the *HostExecutionContext*, but only the host (the code that creates the *AppDomain*) can determine if it needs this additional execution context.

Lab: Use the *Thread* Class to Demonstrate Multithreading

In this lab, you create a simple application that counts from 1 to 10 and shows each iteration in the console window. If you encounter a problem completing an exercise, the completed projects are available on the companion CD in the Code folder.

▶ **Exercise: Create Multiple Threads**

In this exercise, you create a simple console application and start two threads simultaneously.

1. Create a new console application, and call it SimpleThreadingDemo.

2. Create a new static method called *Counting*.

3. In the new class, add a *using* statement (or the *Imports* statement for Visual Basic) to the *System.Threading* namespace.

4. In the new method, create a *for* loop that counts from 1 to 10.

5. Within the new *for* loop, write out the current count and the *ManagedThreadId* for the current thread.

6. After writing out to the console, sleep the current thread for 10 milliseconds.

7. Go back to the *Main* method, and create a new *ThreadStart* delegate that points to the *Counting* method.

8. Now create two threads, each pointing to the *Counting* method.

9. Start both threads.

10. Join both threads to ensure that the application doesn't complete until the threads are done. Your code should look something like this:

```
' VB
Imports System.Threading

Class Program

    Public Overloads Shared Sub Main()
```

```vb
            Dim starter As ThreadStart =  New ThreadStart(AddressOf Counting)
            Dim first As Thread =  New Thread(starter)
            Dim second As Thread =  New Thread(starter)

            first.Start()
            second.Start()

            first.Join()
            second.Join()

            Console.Read()
        End Sub

    Shared  Sub Counting()
        Dim i As Integer
        For  i = 1 To  10 Step  i + 1
            Console.WriteLine("Count: {0} - Thread: {1}", _
                i, Thread.CurrentThread.ManagedThreadId)
            Thread.Sleep(10)
        Next
    End Sub
End Class
```

```csharp
// C#
using System;
using System.Collections.Generic;
using System.Text;

using System.Threading;

class Program
{
    static void Main(string[] args)
    {
        ThreadStart starter = new ThreadStart(Counting);
        Thread first = new Thread(starter);
        Thread second = new Thread(starter);

        first.Start();
        second.Start();

        first.Join();
        second.Join();

        Console.Read();
    }

    static void Counting()
    {
        for (int i = 1; i <= 10; i++)
        {
```

```
            Console.WriteLine("Count: {0} - Thread: {1}",
                i, Thread.CurrentThread.ManagedThreadId);
            Thread.Sleep(10);
        }
    }
}
```

11. Build the project, and resolve any errors. Verify that the console application successfully shows the threads running concurrently. You can determine this by checking whether each thread's counts are intermingled with those of other threads. The exact nature of the intermingling is dependent on the type of hardware you have. A single processor machine will be very ordered, but a multiprocessor (or multicore) machine will be somewhat random.

Lesson Summary

- To perform work concurrently, use the *Thread* class.

- To start thread execution, use the *Thread* class's *Start* method.

- To wait on threads to complete, use the *Thread* class's *Join* method.

- To cancel execution of a thread, use the *Thread* class's *Abort* method

- To share data across threads, use the *ExecutionContext* class.

Lesson Review

You can use the following questions to test your knowledge of the information in Lesson 1, "Creating Threads." The questions are also available on the companion CD if you prefer to review them in electronic form.

NOTE Answers

Answers to these questions and explanations of why each answer choice is right or wrong are located in the "Answers" section at the end of the book.

---

1. What type of object is required when starting a thread that requires a single parameter?

    A. *ThreadStart* delegate

    B. *ParameterizedThreadStart* delegate

    C. *SynchronizationContext* class

    D. *ExecutionContext* class

2. What method stops a running thread?

   A. *Thread.Suspend*

   B. *Thread.Resume*

   C. *Thread.Abort*

   D. *Thread.Join*

Lesson 2: Sharing Data

The most challenging part of working with threads is sharing data between multiple threads. Once you start to work with multiple threads in an application, you become responsible for the protection of any shared data that can be accessed from multiple threads. Lucky for us that the .NET Framework makes that very straightforward.

After this lesson, you will be able to:

- Use the *Interlocked* class to perform atomic operations.
- Use the C# *lock* or the Visual Basic *SyncLock* syntax to lock data.
- Use the *Monitor* class to lock data.
- Use a *ReaderWriterLock* to lock data.
- Use a *Mutex* to synchronize threads.
- Use a *Semaphore* to throttle threads.
- Use an *Event* to signal threads.

Estimated lesson time: 40 minutes

Avoiding Collisions

Before threading became available, you could expect that any access of data was being done by one object at a time. Now that we have entered the multithreaded world, we have to deal with the fact that multiple threads might be interrogating our objects simultaneously. This causes problems in some deceptive ways. For example, consider the following class:

```
' VB
Public Class Counter
    Public Shared Count As Integer
End Class

// C#
public class Counter
{
    public static int Count;
}
```

The *Counter* class contains a static field called *Count* that allows direct access to a number of items in the collection. We could write a simple method that adds to that count a large number of times, like so:

```
' VB
Shared  Sub UpdateCount()
    Dim x As Integer
```

```
    For  x = 1 To  10000
        Counter.Count = Counter.Count + 1
    Next
End Sub

// C#
static void UpdateCount()
{
    for (int x = 1; x <= 10000; ++x)
    {
        Counter.Count = Counter.Count + 1;
    }
}
```

No matter how many times we run this *UpdateCount*, we should always add 10,000 to the number in the count. It seems logical then that if we use threads to run this method, we should just get 10,000 multiplied by the number of threads in our count. For instance, this threading code could run 10 threads to update the counts:

```
' VB
Dim starter As New ThreadStart(UpdateCount)

Dim threads() As Thread =  New Thread(10) {}
Dim x As Integer
For x = 0 To 9
    threads(x) = New Thread(starter)
    threads(x).Start()
Next

' Wait for them to complete
For x = 0 To 9
    threads(x).Join()
Next

' Show to the console the total count
' Should be 10 * 10,000 = 100,000
Console.WriteLine("Total: {0}", Counter.Count)

// C#
ThreadStart starter = new ThreadStart(UpdateCount);

Thread[] threads = new Thread[10];
for (int x = 0; x < 10; ++x)
{
    threads[x] = new Thread(starter);
    threads[x].Start();
}

// Wait for them to complete
for (int x = 0; x < 10; ++x)
{
    threads[x].Join();
}
```

```
// Show to the console the total count
// Should be 10 * 10,000 = 100,000
Console.WriteLine("Total: {0}", Counter.Count);
```

If you are working with a single processor without Hyper-Threading support, this code will probably always work as expected. But if you run this code several times on a multiprocessor or Hyper-Threaded machine, you will see that sometimes the resulting number is less than the 100,000 expected. Why?

This happens because of the way that updating the *Count* field works on the processor. On most computers, this code resolves into three steps:

1. Load the value into a register inside the processor.

2. Increment (or decrement) the value in the register.

3. Copy the value from the register back to memory.

The problem is that in threaded code all these three steps are treated as atomic operations. As shown in Figure 7-2, two threads could each read the values from memory and at the same time update them with the same updated value. This is why the code just shown loses some counts.

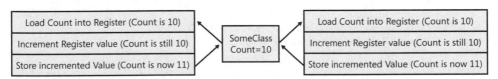

Figure 7-2 Incrementing values on multiple threads

What if we used a different syntax? We could format our code as follows instead:

```
' VB
Counter.Count = Counter.Count + 1
' or
Counter.Count += 1

// C#
Counter.Count++;
// or
Counter.Count += 1;
```

Our change does not matter because the compiled code still needs to perform the three operations shown earlier. How do you solve this issue? You can use the *Interlocked* class to perform the incrementing operation. The *Interlocked* class is detailed in Table 7-7.

Table 7-7   *Interlocked* Static Methods

Name	Description
Add	Adds two integers as an atomic operation. Can be used for subtraction by adding a negative integer.
Decrement	Subtracts one from a value as an atomic operation.
Exchange	Swaps two values as an atomic operation.
Increment	Adds one to a value as an atomic operation.
Read	Reads a 64-bit number as an atomic operation. Required for 32-bit systems because 64-bit numbers are represented as two pieces of information.

We can change our *UpdateCount* method to use the *Interlocked* class to solve the threading issue like so:

```
' VB
Shared  Sub UpdateCount()
    Dim x As Integer
    For  x = 1 To 10000
        ' Counter.Count = Counter.Count + 1;
        Interlocked.Increment(Counter.Count)
    Next
End Sub
```

```
// C#
static void UpdateCount()
{
    for (int x = 1; x <= 10000; ++x)
    {
        // Counter.Count = Counter.Count + 1;
        Interlocked.Increment(ref Counter.Count);
    }
}
```

NOTE Volatile data

The *Thread* class (as well as the C# compiler) supports volatile reading from and writing to fields. The idea behind volatile reads and writes is to prevent the caching of data within a CPU from causing data inconsistencies in your threaded applications. Instead of using the *Thread*'s *VolatileRead* and *VolatileWrite* methods (or the volatile keyword in C#), use the *Interlocked* class's methods or other high-level synchronization discussed in this lesson. Using these strategies will ensure that you have the correct behavior regardless of what CPU or memory model your software runs on.

MORE INFO   Thread synchronization

Thread synchronization is a complex topic that has many subtle interactions on different environments. Please see *CLR via C#*, *Second Edition*, by Jeffrey Richter (Microsoft Press, 2006), specifically pages 622-629, to understand the nuances of thread synchronization.

By using the *Interlocked.Increment* method and passing in a reference to the value you want to increment, you are guaranteed that the increment operation is atomic, so your problem goes away. The main problem with the *Interlocked* class is that it works with a small set of .NET types. What if you need to synchronize access to your own classes or treat larger pieces of code as atomic? How do you ensure that other types of code are protected from multiple thread access? Synchronization locks address all these issues.

Synchronization Locks

The purpose of synchronization locks is to allow you to synchronize access to objects in .NET. If we change our *Counter* class example to calculate two different counts (a simple count, and a count of whenever our counter is an even number), our code would look like this:

```
' VB
Public Class Counter
    Dim _count As Integer =  0
    Dim _evenCount As Integer =  0

    Public ReadOnly Property Count() As Integer
        Get
            Return _count
        End Get
    End Property

    Public ReadOnly Property EvenCount() As Integer
        Get
            Return _evenCount
        End Get
    End Property

    Public Sub UpdateCount()
        Interlocked.Increment(_count)
        If Count % 2 = 0 Then ' An even number
            Interlocked.Increment(_evenCount)
        End If
    End Sub
End Class
```

```csharp
// C#
public class Counter
{
    int _count = 0;
    int _evenCount = 0;

    public int Count
    {
        get { return _count; }
    }

    public int EvenCount
    {
        get { return _evenCount; }
    }

    public void UpdateCount()
    {
        Interlocked.Increment(ref _count);
        if (Count % 2 == 0) // An even number
        {
            Interlocked.Increment(ref _evenCount);
        }
    }
}
```

We can now use this class in a modified version of our earlier code:

```vb
' VB
Dim count As New Counter()

ParameterizedThreadStart starter = New _
    ParameterizedThreadStart(UpdateCount)
Dim threads() As New Thread(10) {}

Dim x As Integer
For  x = 0 To 9
    threads(x) = New Thread(starter)
    threads(x).Start(count)
Next

' Wait for them to complete
Dim x As Integer
For  x = 0 To 9
    threads(x).Join()
Next

' Show to the console the total count and accesses
Console.WriteLine("Total: {0} - EvenCount: {1}", _
    count.Count, count.EvenCount)

Shared  Sub UpdateCount(ByVal param As Object)
```

```vb
    Dim count As Counter = CType(param, Counter)

    Dim x As Integer
    For  x = 1 To 10000
        ' Add two to the count
        count.UpdateCount()
    Next
End Sub
```

```csharp
// C#
Counter count = new Counter();

ParameterizedThreadStart starter = new
    ParameterizedThreadStart(UpdateCount);
Thread[] threads = new Thread[10];

for (int x = 0; x < 10; ++x)
{
    threads[x] = new Thread(starter);
    threads[x].Start(count);
}

// Wait for them to complete
for (int x = 0; x < 10; ++x)
{
    threads[x].Join();
}

// Show to the console the total count and accesses
Console.WriteLine("Total: {0} - EvenCount: {1}",
    count.Count, count.EvenCount);

static void UpdateCount(object param)
{
    Counter count = (Counter)param;

    for (int x = 1; x <= 10000; ++x)
    {
        // Add two to the count
        count.UpdateCount();
    }
}
```

As before, we create 10 threads to add counts for us, but in this case we are sharing one instance of the *Counter* class. When we run this code, our simple count is always right, but occasionally our count of the even values is wrong. This is because two threads can come in and update the simple counts right after each other so that the line that checks whether the count is even or odd can miss an even count. Even though each of the incrementing operations is thread-safe, as a unit the two operations are not.

To solve this problem, you can use the synchronization locks. In C#, you would use the *lock* keyword, and in Visual Basic it is the *SyncLock* keyword. We can change our *Counter* class to use a synchronization lock to solve this problem like so:

```vb
' VB
Public Sub UpdateCount()
    SyncLock Me
        _count = _count + 1
        If Count % 2 = 0 Then ' An even number
            _evenCount = _evenCount + 1
        End If
    End SyncLock
End Sub
```

```csharp
// C#
public void UpdateCount()
{
    lock (this)
    {
        _count = _count + 1;
        if (Count % 2 == 0) // An even number
        {
          _evenCount = _evenCount + 1;
        }
    }
}
```

By replacing the *Interlocked* class code with a synchronization lock, we can ensure that only one thread at a time can enter the locked section of code. The lock requires you to specify an object to use as the lock's identifier. For code that manipulates several pieces of data within a class, you can use the current instance of the class (*this* in C#, and *Me* in Visual Basic).

The synchronization lock works by blocking other threads from access to the code while a thread is inside the lock. For example, the first thread will cause this piece of code to be locked based on the instance of the class. The second thread will wait until the first thread exits the lock before it enters the lock, and so on for additional threads.

Even though using the keywords in Visual Basic and C# are often the easiest ways to create synchronization locks, you might need to have more control over the way you are creating a lock. Underneath the covers, the synchronization locks are just using the *Monitor* class to perform the synchronization. Table 7-8 shows a listing of the most important static methods of the *Monitor* class.

Table 7-8 *Monitor* **Static Methods**

Name	Description
Enter	Creates an exclusive lock on a specified object
Exit	Releases an exclusive lock on a specified object
TryEnter	Attempts to create an exclusive lock on a specified object; optionally supports a timeout value on acquiring the lock
Wait	Releases an exclusive lock, and blocks the current thread until it can re-acquire the lock

We could get the identical behavior from the *Monitor* by changing our code to look like this:

```
' VB
Public Sub UpdateCount()
    Monitor.Enter(Me)
    Try
        _count = _count + 1
        If Count % 2 = 0 Then 'An even number
            _evenCount = _evenCount + 1
        End If
    Finally
        Monitor.Exit(Me)
    End Try
End Sub

// C#
public void UpdateCount()
{
    Monitor.Enter(this);
    try
    {
        _count = _count + 1;
        if (Count % 2 == 0) // An even number
        {
            _evenCount = _evenCount + 1;
        }
    }
    finally
    {
        Monitor.Exit(this);
    }
}
```

Although synchronization locks will solve many thread synchronization problems, they can introduce a problem known as deadlocks.

Understanding Deadlocks

A deadlock is a case where two pieces of code are trying to access the same objects but are blocking each other from getting at the resources. The following code snippet provides an example:

```vb
' VB
Class Deadlocker
    Dim ResourceA As Object =  New Object()
    Dim ResourceB As Object =  New Object()

    Public Sub First()
        SyncLock ResourceA
            SyncLock ResourceB
                Console.WriteLine("First")
            End SyncLock
        End SyncLock
    End Sub

    Public Sub Second()
        SyncLock ResourceB
            SyncLock ResourceA
                Console.WriteLine("Second")
            End SyncLock
        End SyncLock
    End Sub
End Class
```

```csharp
// C#
class Deadlocker
{
    object ResourceA = new Object();
    object ResourceB = new Object();

    public void First()
    {
        lock (ResourceA)
        {
            lock (ResourceB)
            {
                Console.WriteLine("First");
            }
        }
    }

    public void Second()
    {
        lock (ResourceB)
        {
            lock (ResourceA)
            {
```

```
            Console.WriteLine("Second");
        }
    }
  }
}
```

If we call this class like so:

```
' VB
Dim deadlock As New Deadlocker()

Dim firstStart As New ThreadStart(deadlock.First)
Dim secondStart As New ThreadStart(deadlock.Second)

Dim first As New Thread(firstStart)
Dim second As New Thread(secondStart)

first.Start()
second.Start()

first.Join()
second.Join()

// C#
Deadlocker deadlock = new Deadlocker();

ThreadStart firstStart = new ThreadStart(deadlock.First);
ThreadStart secondStart = new ThreadStart(deadlock.Second);

Thread first = new Thread(firstStart);
Thread second = new Thread(secondStart);

first.Start();
second.Start();

first.Join();
second.Join();
```

The deadlock happens like this:

1. First thread starts and locks ResourceA.

2. Second thread starts and locks ResourceB.

3. First thread blocks waiting for ResourceB to be freed.

4. Second thread blocks waiting for ResourceA to be freed.

5. The application stops in its tracks.

At this point in the explanation, it would be great to be able to tell you that there is some magic class to help you avoid deadlocks. There isn't. Deadlocks are a matter of careful development and detection. Other than being very careful in locking objects with the *Monitor* class, you can also use the following methods to deal with some deadlocking objects:

- Use *Monitor.TryEnter* with timeouts to allow deadlocking situations to recover or retry instead of getting stuck.

- Reduce the amount of code you have locked to reduce the time that a resource is locked.

BEST PRACTICES   Waiting forever

Instead of using overly long millisecond timeouts for infinite timeouts (where you are willing to wait as long as it takes), you should use the *Timeout* class's static *Infinite* property.

Other Synchronization Methods

Although the *Monitor* class is a useful (and lightweight) tool for developing threaded software, other synchronizing mechanisms have their own uses. In this section, you will learn about each of these synchronization objects, including the following:

- *ReaderWriterLock* class
- Synchronization with Windows kernel objects
  - ❏ *Mutex* class
  - ❏ *Semaphore* class
  - ❏ *AutoResetEvent* class
  - ❏ *ManualResetEvent* class

ReaderWriterLock class   The purpose of the *ReaderWriterLock* is to differentiate between the two classes of code that can use certain resources. By using the *ReaderWriterLock*, you can lock access to readers and writers separately. The *ReaderWriterLock* allows multiple readers to access the data at the same time, but only a single writer can get a lock on the data. All readers must release their locks before a writer can get a lock on the data. The *ReaderWriterLock* class's properties and methods are detailed in Table 7-9 and Table 7-10, respectively.

Table 7-9   *ReaderWriterLock* Properties

Name	Description
IsReaderLockHeld	Gets an indicator showing whether a reader has a lock
IsWriterLockHeld	Gets an indicator showing whether a writer has a lock

Table 7-10 *ReaderWriterLock* Methods

Name	Description
AcquireReaderLock	Gets a reader lock within a specified time. If a lock cannot be granted within the timeout period, an application exception is thrown.
AcquireWriterLock	Gets a writer lock within a specified time. If a lock cannot be granted within the timeout period, an application exception is thrown.
DowngradeFromWriterLock	Converts a writer lock to a reader lock.
ReleaseReaderLock	Frees a reader lock.
ReleaseWriterLock	Frees a writer lock.
UpgradeToWriterLock	Upgrades a reader lock to a writer lock.

To acquire a reader lock, follow these steps:

1. Create an instance of the *ReaderWriterLock* class to be shared across any threads.

2. Create a *try/catch* block (catching an *ApplicationException*). This *try/catch* block will be used to catch the exception if the acquisition of the reader lock reaches the timeout.

3. Inside the *try/catch* block, acquire the reader lock by calling *ReaderWriter-Lock.AcquireReaderLock*.

4. After acquiring the reader lock, create a *try/finally* block to hold any read code.

5. Do any work you need, but only read any thread-safe data within the *try* part of the *try/finally* block.

6. In the *finally* part of the *try/finally* block, release the reader lock with *ReaderWrit-erLock.ReleaseReaderLock*.

For example, if you wanted to read a value out to the console, you could use a reader lock to access it, like so:

```
' VB
Dim rwLock As New ReaderWriterLock()
Dim counter As Integer =  0

Try
    rwLock.AcquireReaderLock(100)
```

```
        Try
            Console.WriteLine(counter)
        Finally
            rwLock.ReleaseReaderLock()
        End Try
Catch
    Console.WriteLine("Failed to get a Reader Lock")
End Try

// C#
ReaderWriterLock rwLock = new ReaderWriterLock();
int counter = 0;

try
{
    rwLock.AcquireReaderLock(100);

    try
    {
        Console.WriteLine(counter);
    }
    finally
    {
        rwLock.ReleaseReaderLock();
    }
}
catch (ApplicationException)
{
    Console.WriteLine("Failed to get a Reader Lock");
}
```

For times when you need to change data, you will need a writer lock. To acquire a writer lock, follow these steps:

1. Create an instance of the *ReaderWriterLock* class to be shared across any threads.

2. Create a *try/catch* block (catching an *ApplicationException*). This *try/catch* block will be used to catch the exception if the acquisition of the writer lock reaches the timeout.

3. Inside the *try/catch* block, acquire the writer lock by calling *ReaderWriterLock* *.AcquireWriterLock*.

4. After acquiring the writer lock, create a *try/finally* block to hold any writing code.

5. Do any work you need within the *try* part of the *try/finally* block.

6. In the *finally* part of the *try/finally* block, release the writer lock with *ReaderWriter-Lock.ReleaseWriterLock*.

For example, if you wanted to changes values, you could use a writer lock to allow you to change it safely:

```vb
' VB
Dim rwLock As New ReaderWriterLock()
Dim counter As Integer =  0

Try
    rwLock.AcquireWriterLock(1000)

    Try
        Interlocked.Increment(counter)
    Finally
        rwLock.ReleaseWriterLock()
    End Try
Catch
    Console.WriteLine("Failed to get a Writer Lock")
End Try
```

```csharp
// C#
ReaderWriterLock rwLock = new ReaderWriterLock();
int counter = 0;

try
{
    rwLock.AcquireWriterLock(1000);

    try
    {
        Interlocked.Increment(ref counter);
    }
    finally
    {
        rwLock.ReleaseWriterLock();
    }
}
catch (ApplicationException)
{
    Console.WriteLine("Failed to get a Writer Lock");
}
```

The *ReaderWriterLock* is designed to work with two classes of locks, readers and writers. To further facilitate the usefulness of these locks, the *ReaderWriterLock* also support upgrading a read lock to a write lock and returning back to a read lock. It performs these two tasks with the *UpgradeToWriterLock* and *DowngradeFromWriterLock* methods, respectively. These methods need to be used in tandem, much like *Monitor.Enter* and *Monitor.Exit* methods. The *UpgradeToWriterLock* method returns a *LockCookie* object. This *LockCookie* is a structure that the *ReaderWriterLock* uses to allow the writer lock to be downgraded when you are done writing to the locked data. The following code snippet provides an example:

```
' VB
Try
    Dim cookie As LockCookie =  rwLock.UpgradeToWriterLock(1000)
    counter = counter + 1
    rwLock.DowngradeFromWriterLock( cookie)
Catch
    ' Could not get a lock, so ignore the writing portion
End Try
```

```
// C#
try
{
    LockCookie cookie = rwLock.UpgradeToWriterLock(1000);
    counter++;
    rwLock.DowngradeFromWriterLock(ref cookie);
}
catch (ApplicationException)
{
    // Could not get a lock, so ignore the writing portion
}
```

Note that the *UpgradeToWriterLock* call requires a timeout value and might fail to acquire the writer lock within the specified time (like any acquisition of a writer lock). Conversely, the *DowngradeFromWriterLock* method requires no timeout because it is releasing the writer lock and reinstituting the reader lock that was acquired before the lock was upgraded.

Synchronization with Windows Kernel Objects   At the operating-system level, there are three kernel objects—*Mutex*, *Semaphore*, and *Event*—whose job is to allow you to perform thread synchronization. Although these kernel objects provide powerful synchronization facilities, they are heavyweight objects. For example, using a *Mutex* to synchronize your threads instead of a *Monitor* is about 33 times slower (as pointed out by Jeffrey Richter in his book *CLR via C#*, mentioned earlier in this chapter). Even though these kernel objects come with additional overhead, they allow you to perform synchronization tasks that are impossible with the *Monitor* and *ReaderWriterLock* classes:

- A *Mutex* allows synchronization (like a lock) across *AppDomain* and process boundaries.

- A *Semaphore* is used to throttle access to a resource to a set number of threads.

- An *Event* provides a way to notify to multiple threads (across *AppDomain* and process boundaries) that some event has occurred.

Each of these synchronization objects is represented by classes in the .NET Framework (*Mutex*, *Semaphore*, *AutoResetEvent*, and *ManualResetEvent*). These classes all derive from a common class called a *WaitHandle*. The *WaitHandle* class's most important properties and methods are detailed in Table 7-11 and Table 7-12, respectively.

Table 7-11   *WaitHandle* Property

Name	Description
Handle	Gets or sets the kernel object's native system handle

Table 7-12   *WaitHandle* Methods

Name	Description
Close	Releases all resources used by the current kernel object
WaitOne	Blocks the current thread until the kernel object is signaled

Mutex *class*   The purpose of the *Mutex* class is to provide a locking mechanism, and it works in much the same way as the *Monitor* class. The major difference is that the *Mutex* class can lock data across *AppDomain* and process boundaries. To use a *Mutex*, follow these steps:

1. Create an instance of the *Mutex* class to be shared across any threads:

    ```
    ' VB
    Dim m As New Mutex()

    // C#
    Mutex m = new Mutex();
    ```

2. Inside a new thread, create an *if* statement calling the *Mutex* class's *WaitOne* method to wait until the lock is available:

    ```
    ' VB
    If m.WaitOne(1000, False) Then
    End If

    // C#
    if (m.WaitOne(1000, false)) // wait 1 second for lock
    {
    }
    ```

3. Create a *try/finally* block inside the *if* statement block.

4. Inside the *try* portion of the *try/finally* block, do the work you need to do while having exclusive access to the *Mutex* object.

5. In the *finally* part of the *try/finally* block, release the *Mutex* by calling *Mutex.ReleaseMutex*:

```
' VB
Try
    ' Some Work
Finally
    m.ReleaseMutex()
End Try
```

```
// C#
try
{
    // Some Work
}
finally
{
    m.ReleaseMutex();
}
```

6. Optionally, create an *else* block after the *if* statement block to deal with not getting the lock:

```
' VB
Else
    ' React to not getting the resource (e.g. retrying
    ' or notifying the user).
End If
```

```
// C#
}
else
{
    // React to not getting the resource (e.g. retrying
    // or notifying the user).
}
```

In most cases, you will want to create the *Mutex* with a well-known name so that you can get the *Mutex* across *AppDomain* and/or process boundaries. If you create it with a name, you can use the *Mutex*'s static *OpenExisting* method to get a *Mutex* that has already been created. The following code snippet provides an example:

```
' VB
Dim theMutex As Mutex = Nothing

Try
    theMutex = Mutex.OpenExisting("MYMUTEX")
Catch ex as WaitHandleCannotBeOpenedException
    ' Cannot open the mutex because it doesn't exist
End Try
```

```
' Create it if it doesn't exist
If theMutex Is Nothing Then
    theMutex = New Mutex(False, "MYMUTEX")
End If

// C#
Mutex theMutex = null;

try // Try and open the Mutex
{
    theMutex = Mutex.OpenExisting("MYMUTEX");
}
catch (WaitHandleCannotBeOpenedException)
{
    // Cannot open the mutex because it doesn't exist
}

// Create it if it doesn't exist
if (theMutex == null)
{
    theMutex = new Mutex(false, "MYMUTEX");
}
```

You need to use a *try/catch* block when attempting to open an existing *Mutex* because instead of returning a null, a *WaitHandleCannotBeOpenedException* is thrown instead. Using a named *Mutex* is a common way to synchronize data across process boundaries. The first process to try to open the *Mutex* will end up creating it, and all other processes will simply get the one created by the first process.

Semaphore *class*   The *Semaphore* class is used to throttle usage of some resource. Specifically, a *Semaphore* creates a kernel object that supports a certain number of valid slots at once. When the slots are filled, the remaining code will block until a slot is made available by another thread releasing the slot.

NOTE .NET 2.0

The *Semaphore* class is new in the .NET Framework 2.0.

Creating a new instance of the *Semaphore* class allows you to specify the current number of used slots and the number of maximum slots. The following code snippet provides an example:

```
' VB
Dim theSemaphore As New Semaphore(0, 10)

// C#
Semaphore theSemaphore = new Semaphore(0, 10);
```

Most operations after creation of the *Semaphore* are just like the operations shown earlier for the *Mutex* class. The one major difference is that when you release the *Semaphore* you can specify how many slots you want to release, as shown in the following example:

```
' VB
theSemaphore.Release(5)

// C#
theSemaphore.Release(5);
```

In addition, as with the *Mutex* class, you can specify a name that can be used to create and open shared semaphores across *AppDomain* and process boundaries. The following code snippet provides an example:

```
' VB
Dim theSemaphore As Semaphore = Nothing

Try ' Try and open the Semaphore
    theSemaphore = Semaphore.OpenExisting("THESEMAPHORE")
Catch ex as WaitHandleCannotBeOpenedException
    ' Cannot open the Semaphore because it doesn't exist
End Try

' Create it if it doesn't exist
If theSemaphore Is Nothing Then
    theSemaphore = New Semaphore(0, 10, "THESEMAPHORE")
End If

// C#
Semaphore theSemaphore = null;

try // Try and open the Semaphore
{
    theSemaphore = Semaphore.OpenExisting("THESEMAPHORE");
}
catch (WaitHandleCannotBeOpenedException)
{
    // Cannot open the Semaphore because it doesn't exist
}

// Create it if it doesn't exist
if (theSemaphore == null)
{
    theSemaphore = new Semaphore(0, 10, "THESEMAPHORE");
}
```

Event *class*   Events are a type of kernel object that has two states, on and off. These states allow threads across an application to wait until an event is signaled to do something specific. There are two types of events: auto reset and manual reset. When an auto reset event is signaled, the first object waiting for the event turns it back to a non-signaled state. This behavior is similar to that of a *Mutex*. Conversely, a manual reset event allows all threads that are waiting for it to become unblocked until something manually resets the event to a nonsignaled state.

These events are represented as the *AutoResetEvent* and *ManualResetEvent* classes in the .NET Framework. Both of these classes inherit from a common *EventWaitHandle* class (which itself inherits from the *WaitHandle* class).

NOTE .NET 2.0

EventWaitHandle, AutoResetEvent, and *ManualResetEvent* classes are new in the .NET Framework 2.0.

Creating a new instance of an event class allows you to specify the signal state of the event, as shown in the following example:

```
' VB
Dim autoEvent As New AutoResetEvent(true)
Dim manualEvent As New ManualResetEvent(false)
```

```
// C#
AutoResetEvent autoEvent = new AutoResetEvent(true);
ManualResetEvent manualEvent = new ManualResetEvent(false);
```

The *EventWaitHandle* class supports two new methods that are specific to working with events: *Set* and *Reset*. These methods are used to switch the event on and off, as shown in the following example:

```
' VB
autoEvent.Set()
manualEvent.Reset()
```

```
// C#
autoEvent.Set();
manualEvent.Reset();
```

Like the other kernel objects, events allow you to specify a name that can be used to create and open them across *AppDomain* and process boundaries. The support for named events is at the *EventWaitHandle* level. When creating or opening a named event, you will need to deal with *EventWaitHandle* instead of the *AutoResetEvent* and *ManualResetEvent* classes. When creating a new *EventWaitHandle* object, you not only specify the signal state, but also the type of event needed. For example, you can use the following code to create or open a named event:

```
' VB
Dim theEvent As EventWaitHandle = Nothing
```

```
Try
    theEvent = EventWaitHandle.OpenExisting("THEEVENT")
Catch ex as WaitHandleCannotBeOpenedException
    ' Cannot open the AutoResetEvent because it doesn't exist
End Try

' Create it if it doesn't exist
If theEvent Is Nothing Then
    theEvent = New EventWaitHandle(False, _
        EventResetMode.AutoReset, "THEEVENT")
End If

// C#
EventWaitHandle theEvent = null;

try // Try and open the Event
{
    theEvent = EventWaitHandle.OpenExisting("THEEVENT");
}
catch (WaitHandleCannotBeOpenedException)
{
    // Cannot open the AutoResetEvent because it doesn't exist
}

// Create it if it doesn't exist
if (theEvent == null)
{
    theEvent = new EventWaitHandle(false,
        EventResetMode.AutoReset, "THEEVENT");
}
```

Lab: Use a *Mutex* to Create a Single-Instance Application

In this lab, you create a simple console application in which you will use a *Mutex* to ensure there is only one instance of the application running at any point. If you encounter a problem completing an exercise, the completed projects are available on the companion CD in the Code folder.

1. Create a new console application called *SingleInstance*.

2. In the main code file, include (or import for Visual Basic) *System.Threading*.

3. In the *Main* method of the console application, create a local *Mutex* variable and assign it a null (or Nothing in Visual Basic).

4. Create a constant string to hold the name of the shared *Mutex*. Make the value "RUNMEONCE".

5. Create a *try/catch* block.

6. Inside the *try* section of the *try/catch* block, call the *Mutex.OpenExisting* method, using the constant string defined in step 4 as the name of the *Mutex*. Then assign the result to the *Mutex* variable created in step 2.

7. For the *catch* section of the *try/catch* block, catch a *WaitHandleCannotBeOpenedException* to determine that the named *Mutex* doesn't exist.

8. Next, test the *Mutex* variable created in step 2 for null (or Nothing in Visual Basic) to see whether the *Mutex* could be found.

9. If the *Mutex* was not found, create the *Mutex* with the constant string from step 4.

10. If the *Mutex* was found, close the *Mutex* variable and exit the application. Your final code might look something like this:

```vb
' VB
Imports System.Threading

Class Program

    Public Overloads Shared Sub Main()
        Dim oneMutex As Mutex = Nothing
        Const MutexName As String = "RUNMEONLYONCE"

        Try ' Try and open the Mutex
            oneMutex = Mutex.OpenExisting(MutexName)
        Catch ex as WaitHandleCannotBeOpenedExccption
            ' Cannot open the mutex because it doesn't exist
        End Try

        ' Create it if it doesn't exist
        If oneMutex Is Nothing Then
            oneMutex = New Mutex(True, MutexName)
        Else
            ' Close the mutex and exit the application
            ' because we can only have one instance
            oneMutex.Close()
            Return
        End If

        Console.WriteLine("Our Application")
        Console.Read()
    End Sub

End Class
```

```csharp
// C#
using System.Threading;

class Program
{
    static void Main(string[] args)
    {
        Mutex oneMutex = null;
        const string MutexName = "RUNMEONLYONCE";
```

```
            try // Try and open the Mutex
            {
                oneMutex = Mutex.OpenExisting(MutexName);
            }
            catch (WaitHandleCannotBeOpenedException)
            {
                // Cannot open the mutex because it doesn't exist
            }

            // Create it if it doesn't exist
            if (oneMutex == null)
            {
                oneMutex = new Mutex(true, MutexName);
            }
            else
            {
                // Close the mutex and exit the application
                // because we can only have one instance
                oneMutex.Close();
                return;
            }

            Console.WriteLine("Our Application");
            Console.Read();
        }
    }
```

11. Build the project, and resolve any errors. Verify that only one instance of the application can be run at once.

Lesson Summary

- To perform atomic math operations, use the *Interlocked* class.

- To lock data, use the C# *lock* or the Visual Basic *SyncLock* syntax.

- To lock data with a synchronization object, use the *Monitor* class.

- To lock data where multiple readers can access data at once but one writer at a time can change data, use a *ReaderWriterLock*.

- To synchronize threads across AppDomains or process boundaries, use a *Mutex*.

- To throttle threads with a resource-based synchronization object, use a *Semaphore*.

- To signal threads across AppDomains or process boundaries, use an *Event*.

Lesson Review

You can use the following questions to test your knowledge of the information in Lesson 2, "Sharing Data." The questions are also available on the companion CD if you prefer to review them in electronic form.

NOTE Answers

Answers to these questions and explanations of why each answer choice is right or wrong are located in the "Answers" section at the end of the book.

---

1. Assuming there is not a writer lock in place, how many readers can simultaneously read data with a *ReaderWriterLock*?

   A. 0

   B. 1

   C. 10

   D. Unlimited

2. Which of the following can be used to synchronize threads across *AppDomain* and process boundaries? (Choose all that apply)

   A. *Monitor* class

   B. *Mutex* class

   C. *Semaphore* class

   D. C#'s *lock* or Visual Basic's *SyncLock* keyword

Lesson 3: The Asynchronous Programming Model

Through much of the .NET Framework, it is possible to perform tasks in a nonlinear way. By using the Asynchronous Programming Model (APM) defined through the .NET Framework, you can make your applications perform better, be more responsive, and use the resources of the system they are running on to the fullest extent.

After this lesson, you will be able to:

- Understand the Asynchronous Programming Model (APM).
- Use the *ThreadPool* class.
- Use the *Timer* class.
- Use the *IAsyncResult* interface to perform asynchronous calls.
- Understand how exceptions work in the APM.

Estimated lesson time: 40 minutes

Understanding Asynchronous Programming

Asynchronous programming is simply allowing some portions of code to be executed on separate threads. This is referred to as the Asynchronous Programming Model (APM). Throughout the .NET Framework, many classes support using the APM by supplying *BeginXXX* and *EndXXX* versions of methods. For example, the *FileStream* class has a *Read* method that reads data from the stream. To support the APM model, it also supports *BeginRead* and *EndRead* methods. This pattern of using *BeginXXX* and *EndXXX* methods allows you to execute methods asynchronously, as shown in the following example:

```vb
' VB
Dim buffer() As Byte =  New Byte(100) {}

Dim filename as String = _
    String.Concat(Environment.SystemDirectory, "\\mfc71.pdb")

FileStream strm = New FileStream(filename, _
    FileMode.Open, FileAccess.Read, FileShare.Read, 1024, _
    FileOptions.Asynchronous)

' Make the asynchronous call
Dim result As IAsyncResult = _
    strm.BeginRead(buffer, 0, buffer.Length, Nothing, Nothing)

' Do some work here while you wait
```

```vb
' Calling EndRead will block until the Async work is complete
Dim numBytes As Integer = strm.EndRead(result)

' Don't forget to close the stream
strm.Close()

Console.WriteLine("Read {0} Bytes", numBytes)
Console.WriteLine(BitConverter.ToString(buffer))
```

```csharp
// C#
byte[] buffer = new byte[100];

string filename =
    string.Concat(Environment.SystemDirectory, "\\mfc71.pdb");

FileStream strm = new FileStream(filename,
    FileMode.Open, FileAccess.Read, FileShare.Read, 1024,
    FileOptions.Asynchronous);

// Make the asynchronous call
IAsyncResult result = strm.BeginRead(buffer, 0, buffer.Length, null, null);

// Do some work here while you wait

// Calling EndRead will block until the Async work is complete
int numBytes = strm.EndRead(result);

// Don't forget to close the stream
strm.Close();

Console.WriteLine("Read {0} Bytes", numBytes);
Console.WriteLine(BitConverter.ToString(buffer));
```

To understand how this works, let's take a look at the *FileStream.Read* method signature:

```vb
' VB
Function Read(ByVal array() As Byte, _
            ByVal offset As Integer, _
            ByVal count As Integer) As Integer
```

```csharp
// C#
int Read(byte[] array, int offset, int count);
```

The *BeginRead* looks much like the *Read* method:

```vb
' VB
Function BeginRead(ByVal array() As Byte, _
                ByVal offset As Integer, _
                ByVal numBytes As Integer, _
                ByVal userCallback As AsyncCallback, _
                ByVal stateObject As Object) As IAsyncResult
```

```
// C#
IAsyncResult BeginRead(byte[] array, int offset, int numBytes,
    AsyncCallback userCallback, object stateObject);
```

The differences include that it returns an *IAsyncResult* instead of the number of bytes read and that two parameters are added to the method signature to support APM. These two parameters will be explained later in the section that describes the callback style of handling APM.

The *EndRead* method is meant to end the asynchronous operation:

```
' VB
Function EndRead(ByVal asyncResult As IAsyncResult) As Integer
```

```
// C#
int EndRead(IAsyncResult asyncResult);
```

At the end of the operation, you will call the *EndRead* with the *IAsyncResult* object and it will return the bytes read. The *BeginRead* method, therefore, handles the data going into the asynchronous operation, and the *EndRead* handles returning data from the asynchronous operation.

There needs to be a way to do the asynchronous operation and know when or where to call the *EndXXX* methods. That is where rendezvous techniques come in.

Rendezvous Models

There are three styles of programming with the APM to deal with handling the end of the call in an asynchronous call: wait-until-done, polling, and callback. Let's look at each of these.

Wait-Until-Done Model   The wait-until-done model allows you to start the asynchronous call and perform other work. Once the other work is done, you can attempt to end the call and it will block until the asynchronous call is complete. The following code snippet provides an example:

```
' VB
Dim buffer() As Byte = New Byte(100) {}

Dim filename as String = _
    String.Concat(Environment.SystemDirectory, "\\mfc71.pdb")

FileStream strm = New FileStream(filename, _
    FileMode.Open, FileAccess.Read, FileShare.Read, 1024, _
    FileOptions.Asynchronous)
```

```
' Make the asynchronous call
strm.Read(buffer, 0, buffer.Length)

Dim result As IAsyncResult =  _
    strm.BeginRead(buffer, 0, buffer.Length, Nothing, Nothing)

' Do some work here while you wait

' Calling EndRead will block until the Async work is complete

Dim numBytes As Integer =  strm.EndRead(result)

' Don't forget to close the stream
strm.Close()

Console.WriteLine("Read {0} Bytes", numBytes)
Console.WriteLine(BitConverter.ToString(buffer))

// C#
byte[] buffer = new byte[100];

string filename =
    string.Concat(Environment.SystemDirectory, "\\mfc71.pdb");

FileStream strm = new FileStream(filename,
    FileMode.Open, FileAccess.Read, FileShare.Read, 1024,
    FileOptions.Asynchronous);


// Make the asynchronous call
strm.Read(buffer, 0, buffer.Length);
IAsyncResult result = strm.BeginRead(buffer, 0, buffer.Length, null, null);

// Do some work here while you wait

// Calling EndRead will block until the Async work is complete
int numBytes = strm.EndRead(result);

// Don't forget to close the stream
strm.Close();

Console.WriteLine("Read {0} Bytes", numBytes);
Console.WriteLine(BitConverter.ToString(buffer));
```

When the *BeginRead* call is made, null (or Nothing in Visual Basic) values are specified for the callback and state objects. Because we are not going to be using a callback, they are unnecessary. After some work is performed, the code calls the *EndRead* method, and this will block the thread until the asynchronous call is done.

Polling Model   The polling method is similar, with the exception that the code will poll the *IAsyncResult* to see whether it has completed. The following code snippet provides an example:

```vb
' VB
Dim buffer() As Byte =  New Byte(100) {}

Dim filename as String = _
    String.Concat(Environment.SystemDirectory, "\\mfc71.pdb")

FileStream strm = New FileStream(filename, _
    FileMode.Open, FileAccess.Read, FileShare.Read, 1024, _
    FileOptions.Asynchronous)

' Make the asynchronous call
Dim result As IAsyncResult = _
    strm.BeginRead(buffer, 0, buffer.Length, Nothing, Nothing)

' Poll testing to see if complete
While Not result.IsCompleted
    ' Do more work here if the call isn't complete
    Thread.Sleep(100)
End While

' Finished, so we can call EndRead and it will return without blocking
Dim numBytes As Integer = strm.EndRead(result)

' Don't forget to close the stream
strm.Close()

Console.WriteLine("Read {0} Bytes", numBytes)
Console.WriteLine(BitConverter.ToString(buffer))

// C#
byte[] buffer = new byte[100];

string filename =
    string.Concat(Environment.SystemDirectory, "\\mfc71.pdb");

FileStream strm = new FileStream(filename,
    FileMode.Open, FileAccess.Read, FileShare.Read, 1024,
    FileOptions.Asynchronous);

// Make the asynchronous call
IAsyncResult result = strm.BeginRead(buffer, 0, buffer.Length, null, null);

// Poll testing to see if complete
while (!result.IsCompleted)
{
    // Do more work here if the call isn't complete
    Thread.Sleep(100);
}
```

```
// Finished, so we can call EndRead and it will return without blocking
int numBytes = strm.EndRead(result);

// Don't forget to close the stream
strm.Close();

Console.WriteLine("Read {0} Bytes", numBytes);
Console.WriteLine(BitConverter.ToString(buffer));
```

By calling the *IsCompleted* property on the *IAsyncResult* object returned by the *Begin-Read*, we can continue to do work as necessary until the operation is complete.

Callback Model   The callback model requires that we specify a method to callback on and include any state that we need in the callback method to complete the call. The callback model can be seen in the following example:

```
' VB
Shared buffer() As Byte =  New Byte(100) {}

Shared  Sub TestCallbackAPM()
    Dim filename as String = _
        String.Concat(Environment.SystemDirectory, "\\mfc71.pdb")

    FileStream strm = New FileStream(filename, _
        FileMode.Open, FileAccess.Read, FileShare.Read, 1024, _
        FileOptions.Asynchronous)

    ' Make the asynchronous call
    IAsyncResult result = strm.BeginRead(buffer, 0, buffer.Length, _
        New AsyncCallback(CompleteRead), strm)
End Sub

// C#
static byte[] buffer = new byte[100];

static void TestCallbackAPM()
{
    string filename =
        string.Concat(Environment.SystemDirectory, "\\mfc71.pdb");

    FileStream strm = new FileStream(filename,
        FileMode.Open, FileAccess.Read, FileShare.Read, 1024,
        FileOptions.Asynchronous);

    // Make the asynchronous call
    IAsyncResult result = strm.BeginRead(buffer, 0, buffer.Length,
        new AsyncCallback(CompleteRead), strm);
}
```

In this model, we are creating a new *AsyncCallback* delegate, specifying a method to call (on another thread) when the operation is complete. In addition, we are specifying some object that we might need as the state of the call. For this example, we are sending the stream object in because we will need to call *EndRead* and close the stream.

The method that we create to be called at the end of the call would look somewhat like this:

```vb
' VB
Shared  Sub CompleteRead(ByVal result As IAsyncResult)
    Console.WriteLine("Read Completed")

    Dim strm As FileStream = CType(result.AsyncState, FileStream)

    ' Finished, so we can call EndRead and it will return without blocking
    Dim numBytes As Integer = strm.EndRead(result)

    ' Don't forget to close the stream
    strm.Close()

    Console.WriteLine("Read {0} Bytes", numBytes)
    Console.WriteLine(BitConverter.ToString(buffer))
End Sub
```

```csharp
// C#
static void CompleteRead(IAsyncResult result)
{
    Console.WriteLine("Read Completed");

    FileStream strm = (FileStream) result.AsyncState;

    // Finished, so we can call EndRead and it will return without blocking
    int numBytes = strm.EndRead(result);

    // Don't forget to close the stream
    strm.Close();

    Console.WriteLine("Read {0} Bytes", numBytes);
    Console.WriteLine(BitConverter.ToString(buffer));
}
```

Note that instead of holding on to the *IAsyncResult*, the preceding code is passing it in as a parameter of the callback method. We can then retrieve the *FileStream* object that we passed in as state. From there, everything is identical to the other models.

Exceptions and APM

When you are using the APM, there might be operations that throw exceptions during the asynchronous processing of a request. To allow for this, the exceptions are actually thrown during the *EndXXX* call. The exception is not thrown at the moment the exception happens. (If it were, how would you catch it?) If you need to handle any exceptions, you need to do it at the time the *EndXXX* call is made. For example, we could change the *EndRead* call from the preceding example to catch and report any *IOExceptions* that were thrown, like so:

```vb
' VB
Dim numBytes As Integer =  0
Try
    numBytes = strm.EndRead(result)
Catch
    Console.WriteLine("An IO Exception occurred")
End Try
```

```csharp
// C#
int numBytes = 0;
try
{
    numBytes = strm.EndRead(result);
}
catch (IOException)
{
    Console.WriteLine("An IO Exception occurred");
}
```

Windows Forms Application Exception Handling

In Windows Forms applications, when an exception is thrown anywhere in the application (on the main thread or during asynchronous calls), a standard dialog box is shown to users to inform them about the exception and the process is killed. As the application developer, you have the opportunity to determine how to handle this situation. You do this by registering for the *ThreadException* event on the *Application* class. To handle these exceptions, you would register for this event like so:

```vb
' VB
AddHandler Application.ThreadException, _
    AddressOf Me.Application_ThreadException
Application.Run(New Form1)

Private Shared Sub Application_ThreadException(ByVal sender As Object, _
    ByVal e As ThreadExceptionEventArgs)
        MessageBox.Show(String.Format("{0}", e.Exception))
End Sub
```

```csharp
// C#
Application.ThreadException += new
    ThreadExceptionEventHandler(Application_ThreadException);
Application.Run(new Form1());
```

```
static void Application_ThreadException(object sender,
                                          ThreadExceptionEventArgs e)
{
    MessageBox.Show(string.Format("{0}", e.Exception));
}
```

The *ThreadExceptionEventHandler* delegate specifies the calling convention of the event handler, whereas the *ThreadExceptionEventArgs* class holds the exception that was called.

MORE INFO   APM

For more information on the APM, see Jeffrey Richter's book, *CLR via C#*, *Second Edition* (Microsoft Press, 2006), specifically pages 599–620.

Using the *ThreadPool*

Earlier in this chapter, you learned how to create your own threads to perform asynchronous programming. In many cases, creating your own thread is not necessary or suggested. The threading system in .NET supports a built-in thread pool that can be used in many situations where you might expect to create your own threads. For example, let's take the same code we used in Lesson 1 to perform some work on a thread:

```vb
' VB
Shared Sub WorkWithParameter(ByVal o As Object)
    Dim info As String = CType(o, String)

    For x = 0 To 9
        Console.WriteLine("{0}: {1}", info, _
            Thread.CurrentThread.ManagedThreadId)

        ' Slow down thread and let other threads work
        Thread.Sleep(10)
    Next
End Sub
```

```csharp
// C#
static void WorkWithParameter(object o)
{
    string info = (string) o;
    for (int x = 0; x < 10; ++x)
    {
        Console.WriteLine("{0}: {1}", info,
            Thread.CurrentThread.ManagedThreadId);
```

```
        // Slow down thread and let other threads work
        Thread.Sleep(10);
    }
}
```

Instead of creating a new thread and controlling it, we can use the *ThreadPool* to do this work by using its *QueueUserWorkItem* method:

```
' VB
Dim workItem As New WaitCallback(WorkWithParameter)
If Not ThreadPool.QueueUserWorkItem(workItem,"ThreadPooled") Then
    Console.WriteLine("Could not queue item")
End If
```

```
// C#
WaitCallback workItem = new WaitCallback(WorkWithParameter);
if (!ThreadPool.QueueUserWorkItem(workItem, "ThreadPooled"))
{
    Console.WriteLine("Could not queue item");
}
```

This is not a shortcut to creating a thread for you, but instead .NET maintains a set of threads that can be reused in your application. This pool of threads is faster because the threads in it are reused as necessary, saving expensive setup costs. In addition, it helps throttle the number of threads that are running at any one time in a process by queuing up work to be performed. As threads are available, the thread pool posts the new work to the thread.

The *ThreadPool* class supports methods not only for queuing up work items, but also for managing the *ThreadPool*. The most important methods of the *ThreadPool* class are detailed in Table 7-13.

Table 7-13 *ThreadPool* Static Methods

Name	Description
GetAvailableThreads	Returns the number of threads that are available to use in the pool.
GetMaxThreads	Returns the maximum number of threads this process's *ThreadPool* can support.
GetMinThreads	Returns the minimum number of threads that are created at any time. This represents the number of prebuilt threads for use in the thread pool.

Table 7-13   *ThreadPool* Static Methods

Name	Description
QueueUserWorkItem	Adds a piece of work to the thread pool to be executed by an available thread.
RegisterWaitForSingleObject	Allows a callback to be issued for a specific *WaitHandle* when that *WaitHandle* is signaled.
SetMaxThreads	Sets the maximum number of threads in this process's thread pool.
SetMinThreads	Sets the minimum number of threads created in the thread pool.
UnsafeQueueNativeOverlapped	Used to queue asynchronous File I/O Completion Ports, using the *Overlapped* and *NativeOverlapped* structures. See Chapter 13, "Interoperation," for more information.
UnsafeQueueUserWorkItem	Queues a work item for a thread for high-performance scenarios. Does not propagate the call stack or execution context information to the new thread.
UnsafeRegisterWaitForSingleObject	Allows a callback to be issued for a specific *WaitHandle* when that *WaitHandle* is signaled. For use in high-performance scenarios. Does not propagate the call stack or execution context information to the new thread.

Limiting the Number of Threads in a *ThreadPool*

The *ThreadPool* class supports static methods for setting the number of minimum and maximum threads in the thread pool. In most circumstances, the number of threads in the pool is set at optimum numbers. If you find that your application is being constrained by the threads in the thread pool, you can set the limits yourself. Changing these numbers affects the current process only.

There are two types of situations where you will want to change the thread pool thread limits: thread starvation, and startup thread speed.

In a thread-starvation scenario, your application is using the thread pool but is being hampered because you have too many work items and you are reaching the maximum number of threads in the pool. To set the high watermark of threads for your application, you can simply use *ThreadPool.SetMaxThreads* like so:

```vb
' VB
Dim threads As Integer
Dim completionPorts As Integer

' Get the maximum number of threads from the ThreadPool
ThreadPool.GetMaxThreads(threads, completionPorts)

' Set it and bump up the number
ThreadPool.SetMaxThreads(threads + 10, completionPorts + 100)
```

```csharp
// C#
int threads;
int completionPorts;

// Get the maximum number of threads from the ThreadPool
ThreadPool.GetMaxThreads(out threads, out completionPorts);

// Set it and bump up the number
ThreadPool.SetMaxThreads(threads + 10, completionPorts + 100);
```

First this code gets the maximum number of threads and completion ports from the *ThreadPool*. A completion ports is a special kernel-level thread object that is used to do asynchronous file I/O operations. Typically there are many more completion ports than the number of managed threads. Next you can set the thread numbers simply by specifying the new ceiling values you want to use.

In cases where the startup costs of using the thread pool are expensive, increasing the minimum number of threads can improve performance. The minimum number of threads dictates how many threads are created immediately and set to wait for new work to do. Typically, the *ThreadPool* limits the number of new threads to be created during the running of a process to two per second. If your applications need more threads created faster, you can increase this size. Changing the minimum number of threads is similar to changing the maximum number of threads:

```vb
' VB
Dim threads As Integer
Dim completionPorts As Integer

' Get the number of threads from the ThreadPool
ThreadPool.GetMinThreads(threads, completionPorts)
```

```
' Set it and bump up the number
ThreadPool.SetMinThreads(threads + 10, completionPorts + 100)

// C#
int threads;
int completionPorts;

// Get the number of threads from the ThreadPool
ThreadPool.GetMinThreads(out threads, out completionPorts);

// Set it and bump up the number
ThreadPool.SetMinThreads(threads + 10, completionPorts + 100);
```

This code is identical to the previous example, except it uses the *GetMinThreads* and *SetMinThreads* methods.

ThreadPool and *WaitHandle*

In Lesson 2, you learned that all kernel-level synchronization objects (*Mutex*, *Semaphore*, and *Event*) use *WaitHandle* as their base class. The thread pool also provides a mechanism to use threads in the pool to wait on these handles and fire off callbacks to methods when the *WaitHandles* are signaled. This is done by calling the *Thread-Pool.RegisterWaitForSingleObject*, as shown in the following example:

```
' VB

' Create a Mutex and own it to begin with
Dim mutex As New Mutex(True)

' Register for a notification
ThreadPool.RegisterWaitForSingleObject(mutex, _
    New WaitOrTimerCallback(MutexHasFired), Nothing, Time.Infinite, True)

' Signal the mutex to cause the thread to fire
mutex.ReleaseMutex()

// C#

// Create a Mutex and own it to begin with
Mutex mutex = new Mutex(true);

// Register for a notification
ThreadPool.RegisterWaitForSingleObject(mutex,
    new WaitOrTimerCallback(MutexHasFired), null, Timeout.Infinite, true);

// Signal the mutex to cause the thread to fire
mutex.ReleaseMutex();
```

The *RegisterWaitForSingleObject* method takes the *WaitHandle* object, as well as a delegate that points to a method that takes an object (that represents the thread state specified in the method call), and a Boolean value that indicates whether the timeout has been reached instead of the *WaitHandle* being signaled. The *MutexHasFired* callback method might look something like this:

```vb
' VB
Shared Sub MutexHasFired(ByVal state As Object, ByVal timedOut As Boolean)
    If timedOut = True Then
        Console.WriteLine("Mutex Timed out")
    Else
        Console.WriteLine("Mutex got signaled")
    End If
End Sub
```

```csharp
// C#
static void MutexHasFired(object state, bool timedOut)
{
    if (timedOut)
    {
        Console.WriteLine("Mutex Timed out");
    }
    else
    {
        Console.WriteLine("Mutex got signaled");
    }
}
```

The *SynchronizationContext* Class

Writing asynchronous code in different environment presents different problems. Threading models in Windows Forms are different than threading models in ASP.NET. A Windows Forms threading model prefers that any user interface code runs directly on the main "user interface" thread. Contrast this with ASP.NET, where most work is done inside a thread pool so that asynchronous calls can happen on any thread in that pool. To deal with these different threading models, the .NET Framework supports the *SynchronizationContext* class, which allows you to write code without knowing the threading model of the particular application.

To use the *SynchronizationContext* class, you would first get an instance of the *SynchronizationContext* class by calling the static *Current* property of the *SynchronizationContext* class. Once you have an instance of the *SynchronizationContext* class, you can take either of the following actions:

■ Call the *SynchronizationContext* class's *Send* method to call some code. Calling *Send* will execute the code (perhaps on a separate thread), but will block until the executing code completes until returning.

```vb
' VB
Dim ctx As SynchronizationContext = SynchronizationContext.Current

' Send Executes the code synchronously
ctx.Send(AddressOf RunMe, "Hi")
```

```csharp
// C#
SynchronizationContext ctx = SynchronizationContext.Current;

// Send Executes the code synchronously
ctx.Send(RunMe, "Hi");
```

■ Call the *SynchronizationContext* class's *Post* method to call some code. Calling *Post* is more like fire-and-forget in that it queues up the request and returns immediately if possible.

```vb
' VB
Dim ctx As SynchronizationContext = SynchronizationContext.Current

' Post Executes the code asynchronously
ctx.Post(AddressOf RunMe, "Hi")
```

```csharp
// C#
SynchronizationContext ctx = SynchronizationContext.Current;

// Post Executes the code asynchronously
ctx.Post(RunMe, "Hi");
```

Depending on the particular threading model, both the *Send* and *Post* methods might not return immediately. If executing the code asynchronously is not supported (like in the Windows Forms threading model), both methods will run the code and return after execution.

The *Send* and *Post* methods do not return any sort of object on which you can wait on or get a return value (such as the *IAsyncResult* interface we were using in the earlier examples). The *SynchronizationContext* class is useful if you need to execute some arbitrary code but not act on the results on that code.

Using *Timer* Objects

A *Timer* is a basic object that will fire off an asynchronous call to a method based on time. *Timer* objects are exemplified by the *Timer* class in the *System.Threading* namespace. When you create a *Timer*, you specify a *TimerCallback* delegate that points to the method you want to run when the *Timer* fires. In addition, you specify how long until the *Timer* starts (with zero indicating immediately) and how long between *Timer* firings. For example, you can create a *Timer* that will fire a *TimerTick* method every second, starting immediately, like this:

```
' VB
Dim tm As Timer = New Timer(New TimerCallback(TimerTick), _
                            Nothing, 0, 1000)

Shared  Sub TimerTick(ByVal state As Object)
    Console.WriteLine("Tick")
End Sub

// C#
Timer tm = new Timer(new TimerCallback(TimerTick), null, 0, 1000);

static void TimerTick(object state)
{
    Console.WriteLine("Tick");
}
```

The *Timer* class also supports a *Change* method that allows you to re-specify when the *Timer* fires and the time interval between the ticks:

```
' VB
Dim tm As Timer =  New Timer(New TimerCallback(TimerTick), _
                            Nothing, 0, 1000)
' Using Infinite to specify to stop the timer for now
tm.Change(Time.Infinite, 1000)

// C#
Timer tm = new Timer(new TimerCallback(TimerTick), null, 0, 1000);
// Using Infinite to specify to stop the timer for now
tm.Change(Timeout.Infinite, 1000);
```

NOTE   *Timer* **classes**

The three *Timer* classes are:

- **System.Threading.Timer**   This is the class discussed in this lesson.
- **System.Windows.Forms.Timer**   This timer class fires events on the same thread as the Form using the WM_TIMER window message. The *System.Windows.Forms.Timer* timer is not related to the *System.Threading.Timer* timer we use in this lesson.
- **System.Timers.Timer**   A wrapper around the *System.Threading.Timer* to support dropping it on various Visual Studio design surfaces.

Lab: Use the *ThreadPool* to Queue Work Items

In this lab, you will create an application that uses the thread pool to queue up meth-ods to call on separate threads. If you encounter a problem completing an exercise, the completed projects are available on the companion CD in the Code folder.

1. Create a blank console application with the name ThreadPoolDemo.

2. Include (or import for Visual Basic) the *System.Threading* namespace.

3. Create a new method to simply display some text. Call it *ShowMyText*. Accept one parameter of type object, and call it *state*.

4. Create a new string variable inside the *ShowMyText* method, and cast the *state* parameter to a string while storing it in the new text variable.

5. Inside the *ShowMyText* method, write out the *ManagedThreadId* of the current thread and write the new string out to the console.

6. In the *Main* method of the console application, create a new instance of the *WaitCallback* delegate that refers to the *ShowMyText* method.

7. Use the *ThreadPool* to queue up several calls to the *WaitCallback* delegate, speci-fying different strings as the object state. Your code might look something like this:

```
' VB
Imports System.Threading

Class Program
    Shared  Sub Main(ByVal args() As String)
        Dim callback As WaitCallback = _
            New WaitCallback(AddressOf ShowMyText)

        ThreadPool.QueueUserWorkItem(callback, "Hello")
        ThreadPool.QueueUserWorkItem(callback, "Hi")
        ThreadPool.QueueUserWorkItem(callback, "Heya")
        ThreadPool.QueueUserWorkItem(callback, "Goodbye")

        Console.Read()
    End Sub

    Shared  Sub ShowMyText(ByVal state As Object)
        Dim myText As String = CType(state, String)

        Console.WriteLine("Thread: {0} - {1}", _
            Thread.CurrentThread.ManagedThreadId, myText)

    End Sub
End Class
```

```csharp
// C#
using System.Threading;

class Program
{
    static void Main(string[] args)
    {
        WaitCallback callback = new WaitCallback(ShowMyText);

        ThreadPool.QueueUserWorkItem(callback, "Hello");
        ThreadPool.QueueUserWorkItem(callback, "Hi");
        ThreadPool.QueueUserWorkItem(callback, "Heya");
        ThreadPool.QueueUserWorkItem(callback, "Goodbye");

        Console.Read();
    }

    static void ShowMyText(object state)
    {
        string myText = (string)state;

        Console.WriteLine("Thread: {0} - {1}",
            Thread.CurrentThread.ManagedThreadId, myText);
    }
}
```

8. Build the project, and resolve any errors. Verify that the console application successfully shows each of the calls to the *ShowMyText* methods out to the console. Note that some of the work items may be executed on different threads.

Lesson Summary

- The Asynchronous Programming Model (APM) can improve the user experience by allowing multiple operations to happen concurrently, at the same time improving the responsiveness of an application.

- To perform asynchronous operations without the overhead of the *Thread* class, use the *ThreadPool* class.

- To create periodically reoccurring calls, use the *Timer* class.

- To retrieve the result of an asynchronous operation, use *IAsyncResult* interface.

- Be prepared to catch exceptions when completing an asynchronous operation (usually with the *EndXXX* method).

Lesson Review

You can use the following questions to test your knowledge of the information in Lesson 3, "The Asynchronous Programming Model." The questions are also available on the companion CD if you prefer to review them in electronic form.

1. What method of the *ThreadPool* class is used to have the *ThreadPool* run some specified code on threads from the pool? (Choose all that apply.)

   A. *ThreadPool.RegisterWaitForSingleObject*

   B. *ThreadPool.QueueUserWorkItem*

   C. *ThreadPool.UnsafeRegisterWaitForSingleObject*

   D. *ThreadPool.UnsafeQueueUserWorkItem*

2. How do you temporarily stop a *Timer* from firing?

   A. Call *Dispose* on the *Timer*.

   B. Call *Timer.Change*, and set the time values to *Timeout.Infinite*.

   C. Let the *Timer* object go out of scope.

   D. Call *Timer.Change*, and set the time values to zero.

Chapter Review

To further practice and reinforce the skills you learned in this chapter, you can perform the following tasks:

- Review the chapter summary.
- Review the list of key terms introduced in this chapter.
- Complete the case scenarios. These scenarios set up real-world situations involving the topics of this chapter and ask you to create a solution.
- Complete the suggested practices.
- Take a practice test.

Chapter Summary

- The *Thread* class can be used to create multiple paths for simultaneous execution in your own applications.
- Using the *lock* (*SyncLock* in Visual Basic) keyword will allow you to write thread-safe access to your code's data.
- You must be careful in writing thread-safe code to avoid deadlock situations.
- The *ReaderWriterLock* class can be used to write thread-safe code that is less prone to allowing only a single thread at a time to access its data.
- The *WaitHandle* derived classes (*Mutex*, *Semaphore*, and *Event* classes) exemplify Windows operating-system-level synchronization objects.
- Much of the .NET Framework supports the Asynchronous Programming Model (APM) to allow for asynchronous execution of code without having to directly deal with the *ThreadPool* or *Threads*.
- The *ThreadPool* is a convenient class that enables fast creation of threads for queuing up code to run as well as for waiting for *WaitHandle* derived objects.
- *Timers* are useful objects for firing off code on separate threads at specific intervals.

Key Terms

Do you know what these key terms mean? You can check your answers by looking up the terms in the glossary at the end of the book.

- Asynchronous Programming Model
- thread
- Windows kernel objects

Case Scenarios

In the following case scenarios, you will apply what you've learned about the topics of this chapter. You can find answers to these questions in the "Answers" section at the end of this book.

Case Scenario 1: Improving Server Processing

You work for a small Internet start-up company. As one of their programmers, you created a simple application that reads data from a database once a week and sends out e-mails to registered users of the main Web site. The company has been doing well and has a large database of users (more than 100,000). Now that the number of registered users has increased dramatically, your tool is taking far too long to send out the e-mails. Your manager needs you to make it much faster.

Interviews

Following is a list of company personnel interviewed and their statements:

- **IT Department Head**   "We've noticed that when we run your application on our server it is not consuming much CPU time. Most of one CPU is taken up, but the other three CPUs are completely unused."

Questions

Answer the following questions for your manager:

1. Why is the current application not using all the CPUs?
2. How do you plan to solve the performance issue?
3. How do you know that your application won't use too many threads and bring a machine to a halt?

Case Scenario 2: Multiple Applications

You are a developer for a small development company that specializes in instrument-monitoring software. Your company creates a series of applications that each monitor a different set of instruments. Unfortunately, most of these instruments still use interfaces to the system that can have only one process read the interface at a time. Your manager needs you to create a plan to ensure only one of the company's applications can access the interface at a time.

Questions

Answer the following questions for your manager:

1. How can you synchronize the applications to access the interface one at a time?
2. How will this impact the performance of the applications?

Suggested Practices

To help you successfully master the objectives covered in this chapter, complete the following tasks.

Create a *ThreadPool* Application

For this task, you should complete at least Practices 1 and 2. You can complete Practice 3 for a more in-depth understanding of the *ThreadPool*.

Practice 1

- Create a test application that writes data out to the console, including the thread that the code is using.
- Use the *ThreadPool* to queue up 20 instances of the data-writing code.
- Note how many threads are used and how often they are reused from the pool (by observing the *ManagedThreadId* being used on different instances of the code).

Practice 2

- Show the minimum and maximum size of the *ThreadPool* by calling the *Thread-Pool.GetMinThreads* and *ThreadPool.GetMaxThreads* methods.
- Change the minimum and maximum number of the *ThreadPool*'s threads by decreasing and increasing the threads using the *ThreadPool.SetMinThreads* and *ThreadPool.SetMaxThreads* methods.
- Run the application with different settings to see how the thread pool operates differently.

Practice 3

■ Take the application to different CPU configurations (single CPU, Hyper-Threaded CPU, and multiple CPUs), and see how the thread pool operates differently and how the minimum and maximum number of threads is different on different CPU platforms.

Take a Practice Test

The practice tests on this book's companion CD offer many options. For example, you can test yourself on just one exam objective, or you can test yourself on all the 70-536 certification exam content. You can set up the test so that it closely simulates the experience of taking a certification exam, or you can set it up in study mode so that you can look at the correct answers and explanations after you answer each question.

MORE INFO   Practice tests

For details about all the practice test options available, see the "How to Use the Practice Tests" section in this book's Introduction.

Chapter 8
Application Domains and Services

This chapter covers two distinct topics: application domains and services. Application domains enable you to call external assemblies with the optimal efficiency and security. Services are a special type of assembly that runs in the background, presents no user interface, and is controlled by using special tools. This chapter discusses how to create and configure application domains, and how to develop and install services.

Exam objectives in this chapter:
- Create a unit of isolation for common language runtime in a .NET Framework application by using application domains. (Refer *System* namespace.)
    - Create an application domain.
    - Unload an application domain.
    - Configure an application domain.
    - Retrieve setup information from an application domain.
    - Load assemblies into an application domain.
- Implement, install, and control a service. (Refer *System.ServiceProcess* namespace.)
    - Inherit from *ServiceBase* class
    - *ServiceController* class and *ServiceControllerPermission* class
    - *ServiceInstaller* and *ServiceProcessInstaller* class
    - *SessionChangeDescription* structure and *SessionChangeReason* enumeration

Lessons in this chapter:

Before You Begin

To complete the lessons in this chapter, you should be familiar with Microsoft Visual Basic or C# and be comfortable with the following tasks:

- Create a console application in Microsoft Visual Studio using Visual Basic or C#.
- Add references to system class libraries to a project.
- Create text files.
- Add events to the event log.

Lesson 1: Creating Application Domains

Developers often need to run an external assembly. However, running an external assembly can lead to inefficient resource usage and security vulnerabilities. The best way to manage these risks is to create an application domain and call the assembly from within the protected environment.

After this lesson, you will be able to:

- Describe the purpose of an application domain.
- Write code that makes use of the *AppDomain* class.
- Create an application domain.
- Launch an assembly within an application domain.
- Unload the application domain.

Estimated lesson time: 20 minutes

What Is an Application Domain?

An *application domain* is a logical container that allows multiple assemblies to run within a single process but prevents them from directly accessing other assemblies' memories. Application domains offer many of the features of a process, such as separate memory spaces and access to resources. However, application domains are more efficient than processes, enabling multiple assemblies to be run in separate application domains without the overhead of launching separate processes. Figure 8-1 shows how a single process can contain multiple application domains.

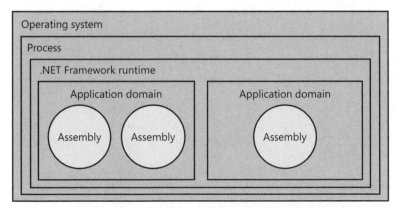

Figure 8-1   Application domains keep assemblies separate within a single process

---

IMPORTANT   Contrasting application domains and processes

The .NET Framework runtime manages application domains, whereas the operating system manages processes.

The best example of application domains in use is Internet Information Services (IIS) 5.0's ASP.NET worker process, implemented by Aspnet_wp.exe. If 10 people visit an ASP.NET Web site simultaneously, ASP.NET will create a separate application domain for each user. Essentially, ASP.NET runs 10 separate instances of the assembly.

Each instance of the assembly can store a property called *userName* without any concern that other instances will be able to access or overwrite the contents of the property. This same effect could be achieved by launching the same assembly in 10 separate processes, but switching between the processes would consume processor time, thus decreasing performance.

Most of the time, you will rely on the existing run-time hosts to automatically create application domains for your assemblies. Examples of run-time hosts built into Microsoft Windows are ASP.NET, Internet Explorer (which creates a single application domain for all assemblies from a specific Web site), and the operating system. You can configure the behavior of these application domains by using friendly tools such as the Internet Information Services Manager and the .NET Framework Configuration tool.

However, just as Aspnet_wp.exe creates application domains to isolate multiple instances of an assembly, you can create your own application domains to call assemblies with little risk that the assembly will take any action or access any resources that you have not specifically permitted. Figure 8-2 shows how an assembly can host application domains.

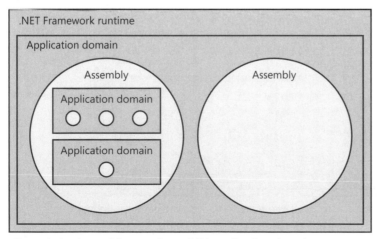

Figure 8-2   Assemblies can host child application domains.

Besides isolating an assembly for security reasons, you can use application domains to improve reliability and efficiency:

- **Reliability**   Use application domains to isolate tasks that might cause a process to terminate. If the state of the application domain that's executing a task becomes unstable, the application domain can be unloaded without affecting the process. This technique is important when a process must run for long periods without restarting. You can also use application domains to isolate tasks that should not share data.

- **Efficiency**   If an assembly is loaded into the default application domain, the assembly cannot be unloaded from memory while the process is running. However, if you open a second application domain to load and execute the assembly, the assembly is unloaded when that application domain is unloaded. Use this technique to minimize the working set of long-running processes that occasionally use large dynamic-link libraries (DLLs).

The *AppDomain* Class

Application domains are implemented in the .NET Framework using the *System.App-Domain* class. To use an application domain, create an instance of the *AppDomain* class, and then execute an assembly within that domain. Table 8-1 shows the *App-Domain* properties.

Table 8-1   *AppDomain* Properties

Name	Description
ActivationContext	Gets the activation context for the current application domain.
ApplicationIdentity	Gets the identity of the application in the application domain.
ApplicationTrust	Gets information describing permissions granted to an application and whether the application has a trust level that allows it to run.
BaseDirectory	Gets the base directory that the assembly resolver uses to probe for assemblies.
CurrentDomain	Gets the current application domain for the current *Thread*. This property allows you to analyze the current domain to determine context or verify permissions.

Table 8-1 *AppDomain* Properties

Name	Description
DomainManager	Gets the domain manager that was provided by the host when the application domain was initialized.
DynamicDirectory	Gets the directory that the assembly resolver uses to probe for dynamically created assemblies.
Evidence	Gets the *Evidence* associated with this application domain that is used as input to the security policy. For more information about evidence, refer to Chapter 11, "Application Security."
FriendlyName	Gets the friendly name of this application domain. For domains created by the .NET Framework, this friendly name takes the form "*ProjectName*.vshost.exe". You must specify the friendly name when you create application domains programmatically.
Id	Gets an integer that uniquely identifies the application domain within the process.
RelativeSearchPath	Gets the path relative to the base directory where the assembly resolver should probe for private assemblies.
SetupInformation	Gets the application domain configuration information for this instance.
ShadowCopyFiles	Gets an indication whether all assemblies loaded in the application domain are shadow copied.

Table 8-2 shows the most important *AppDomain* public methods.

Table 8-2 *AppDomain* Methods

Name	Description
ApplyPolicy	Returns the assembly display name after a policy has been applied.
CreateComInstanceFrom	Creates a new instance of a specified COM type.

Table 8-2 *AppDomain* Methods

Name	Description
CreateDomain	Creates a new application domain. Use this method instead of an *AppDomain* constructor.
CreateInstance	Creates a new instance of a specified type defined in a specified assembly.
CreateInstanceAndUnwrap	Creates a new instance of a specified type.
CreateInstanceFrom	Creates a new instance of a specified type defined in the specified assembly file.
CreateInstanceFromAndWrap	Creates a new instance of a specified type defined in the specified assembly file.
DefineDynamicAssembly	Defines a dynamic assembly in the current application domain.
DoCallBack	Executes the code in another application domain that is identified by the specified delegate.
ExecuteAssembly	Executes the assembly contained in the specified file.
ExecuteAssemblyByName	Executes an assembly.
GetAssemblies	Gets the assemblies that have been loaded into the execution context of this application domain.
GetCurrentThreadId	Gets the current thread identifier.
GetData	Gets the value stored in the current application domain for the specified name.
InitializeLifetimeService	Overridden. Gives the *AppDomain* an infinite lifetime by preventing a lease from being created.
IsDefaultAppDomain	Returns a value that indicates whether the application domain is the default application domain for the process.

Table 8-2   *AppDomain* **Methods**

Name	Description
IsFinalizingForUnload	Indicates whether this application domain is unloading, and the objects it contains are being finalized by the common language runtime.
Load	Loads an *Assembly* into this application domain.
ReflectionOnlyGetAssemblies	Returns the assemblies that have been loaded into the reflection-only context of the application domain.
SetAppDomainPolicy	Establishes the security policy level for this application domain.
SetData	Assigns a value to an application domain property.
SetDynamicBase	Establishes the specified directory path as the location where dynamically generated files are stored and accessed.
SetPrincipalPolicy	Specifies how principal and identity objects should be attached to a thread if the thread attempts to bind to a principal while executing in this application domain.
SetShadowCopyFiles	Turns on shadow copying.
SetShadowCopyPath	Establishes the specified directory path as the location of assemblies to be shadow copied.
SetThreadPrincipal	Sets the default principal object to be attached to threads if they attempt to bind to a principal while executing in this application domain.
Unload	Unloads the specified application domain.

How to Create an Application Domain

To create an application domain, call one of the overloaded *AppDomain.CreateDomain* methods. At a minimum, you must provide a name for the new application domain. The following code demonstrates this process:

```
' VB
Dim d As AppDomain = AppDomain.CreateDomain("NewDomain")

Console.WriteLine("Host domain: " + AppDomain.CurrentDomain.FriendlyName)
Console.WriteLine("Child domain: " + d.FriendlyName)

// C#
AppDomain d = AppDomain.CreateDomain("NewDomain");

Console.WriteLine("Host domain: " + AppDomain.CurrentDomain.FriendlyName);
Console.WriteLine("Child domain: " + d.FriendlyName);
```

As the previous code sample demonstrated, you can access the application domain your assembly is currently running in (which was probably automatically created by the .NET Framework) by accessing *AppDomain.CurrentDomain*.

How to Load Assemblies in an Application Domain

Creating a new application domain and launching an assembly within that domain is as simple as creating an instance of the *System.AppDomain* class with a friendly name, and then calling the *ExecuteAssembly* method, as the following code demonstrates:

```
' VB
Dim d As AppDomain = AppDomain.CreateDomain("NewDomain")
d.ExecuteAssembly("Assembly.exe")

// C#
AppDomain d = AppDomain.CreateDomain("NewDomain");
d.ExecuteAssembly("Assembly.exe");
```

The *AppDomain.ExecuteAssembly* method has overloads that allow you to pass command-line arguments, too. As an alternative to providing the complete path to the assembly, you can add a reference to the assembly and then run it by name using the *AppDomain.ExecuteAssemblyByName* method, as the following code demonstrates:

```
' VB
Dim d As AppDomain = AppDomain.CreateDomain("NewDomain")
d.ExecuteAssemblyByName("Assembly")

// C#
AppDomain d = AppDomain.CreateDomain("NewDomain");
d.ExecuteAssemblyByName("Assembly");
```

Calling an assembly in this manner provides isolation for the assembly but does not take advantage of the huge power and flexibility built into application domains. Lesson 2 discusses configuring application domains in more detail.

How to Unload an Application Domain

One of the advantages of loading assemblies in new application domains is that you can unload the application domain at any time, freeing up resources. To unload a domain and any assemblies within the domain, call the static *AppDomain.Unload* method:

```
' VB
Dim d As AppDomain = AppDomain.CreateDomain("NewDomain")
AppDomain.Unload(d)
```

```
// C#
AppDomain d = AppDomain.CreateDomain("NewDomain");
AppDomain.Unload(d);
```

Individual assemblies or types cannot be unloaded.

Lab: Creating Domains and Loading Assemblies

In this lab, you create an application domain and then load an assembly using two different techniques: by filename and by reference. If you encounter a problem completing an exercise, the completed projects are available on the companion CD in the Code folder.

▶ **Exercise 1: Load an Assembly by Filename**

In this exercise, you create an application domain and use it to run an assembly that displays your Boot.ini file.

1. Copy the Chapter08\Lesson1-ShowBootIni folder from the companion CD to your hard disk, and open either the C# version or the Visual Basic version of the project.

2. Build and run the ShowBootIni console application to verify it works properly. If it does properly display your Boot.ini file, modify the application to display any text file.

3. Create a new console application named AppDomainDemo.

4. In your new console application, write code to create an *AppDomain* object. For example, the following code would work:

```
' VB
Dim d As AppDomain = AppDomain.CreateDomain("NewDomain")

// C#
AppDomain d = AppDomain.CreateDomain("New Domain");
```

5. Next, write code to run the *ShowBootIni* assembly within the newly created *App-Domain* by explicitly providing the full path to the file. For example, the following code would work, but it will need to be adjusted to reflect where you saved the executable file:

```
' VB
d.ExecuteAssembly("ShowBootIni.exe")

// C#
d.ExecuteAssembly("ShowBootIni.exe");
```

6. Build the project, and resolve any errors. Verify that the console application successfully calls the *ShowBootIni.exe* assembly and that it displays the text file successfully.

▶ **Exercise 2: Load an Assembly by Assembly Name**

In this exercise, you modify the console application you created in Exercise 1 to run an assembly based on the assembly name rather than the file name.

1. Open the AppDomainDemo project you created in Exercise 1.

2. Add a reference to the *ShowBootIni* assembly.

3. Modify the call to the *AppDomain.ExecuteAssembly* method to call *AppDomain .ExecuteAssemblyByName* instead. For example, you might use the following code:

```
' VB
Dim d As AppDomain = AppDomain.CreateDomain("NewDomain")
d.ExecuteAssemblyByName("ShowBootIni")

// C#
AppDomain d = AppDomain.CreateDomain("New Domain");
d.ExecuteAssemblyByName("ShowBootIni");
```

4. Build the project, and resolve any errors. Verify that the console application successfully calls the *ShowBootIni.exe* assembly and that it displays the text file successfully.

Lesson Summary

- An application domain is a logical container that allows multiple assemblies to run within a single process but prevents them from directly accessing other assemblies' memories. Create an application domain any time you want to launch an assembly.

- The *AppDomain* class contains methods for defining privileges, folders, and other properties for a new application domain; launching an assembly; and unloading an application domain.

- To create an *AppDomain* class, call the static *AppDomain.CreateDomain* method. *AppDomain* does not have any traditional constructors.

- To load an assembly in an application domain, create an instance of the *App-Domain* class, and then call the *AppDomain.ExecuteAssembly* method.

- To unload an application domain, call the *AppDomain.Unload* static method.

Lesson Review

You can use the following questions to test your knowledge of the information in Lesson 1, "Creating Application Domains." The questions are also available on the companion CD if you prefer to review them in electronic form.

NOTE   Answers

Answers to these questions and explanations of why each answer choice is right or wrong are located in the "Answers" section at the end of the book.

---

1. Which of the following are valid reasons to create an application domain? (Choose all that apply.)

    A. It is the only way to launch a separate process.

    B. You can remove the application domain to free up resources.

    C. Application domains improve performance.

    D. Application domains provide a layer of separation and security.

2. Which of the following are valid ways to run an assembly within an application domain? (Choose all that apply.)

    A. *AppDomain.CreateDomain*

    B. *AppDomain.ExecuteAssembly*

    C. *AppDomain.ExecuteAssemblyByName*

    D. *AppDomain.ApplicationIdentity*

3. Which command would you use to close the application domain in the following code sample?

```
' VB
Dim d As AppDomain = AppDomain.CreateDomain("New Domain")
d.ExecuteAssemblyByName("MyAssembly")

// C#
AppDomain d = AppDomain.CreateDomain("New Domain");
d.ExecuteAssemblyByName("MyAssembly");
```

    A. *d.DomainUnload()*

    B. *d = null*

    C. *d.Unload()*

    D. *AppDomain.Unload(d)*

Lesson 2: Configuring Application Domains

You can configure application domains to create customized environments for assemblies. The most important application of modifying the default settings for an application domain is restricting permissions to reduce the risks associated with security vulnerabilities. When configured ideally, an application domain not only provides a unit of isolation, but it limits the damage that attackers can do if they successfully exploit an assembly.

After this lesson, you will be able to:

■ Launch assemblies in an application domain with limited privileges.

■ Configure application domain properties to control folder locations and other settings.

Estimated lesson time: 25 minutes

How to Use an Application Domain to Launch Assemblies with Limited Privileges

Restricting the permissions of an application domain can greatly reduce the risk that an assembly you call will perform some malicious action. Consider the following scenario: You purchase an assembly from a third party and use the assembly to communicate with a database. An attacker discovers a security vulnerability in the third-party assembly and uses it to configure a spyware application to start automatically. To the user, the security vulnerability is your fault, because your application trusted the third-party assembly and ran it with privileges sufficient to install software.

Now consider the same scenario using an application domain with limited privileges: An attacker discovers a security vulnerability in the third-party assembly. However, when the attacker attempts to exploit the vulnerability to write files to the local hard disk, the file I/O request is rejected because of insufficient privileges. While the security vulnerability still exists, the limited privileges assigned to the application domain prevented it from being exploited.

In this example, launching assemblies with limited privileges is an example of *defense-in-depth*. Defense-in-depth is the security principal of providing multiple levels of protection so that you are still protected in the event of a vulnerability. Defense-in-depth is particularly important when calling external code, because external code might have vulnerabilities that you are not aware of, cannot prevent, and cannot fix.

The sections that follow describe how to use evidence to configure application domains. There are several other ways to control the permissions granted to an assembly. For more information about code access security, refer to Chapter 11.

How to Provide Host Evidence for an Assembly

When you create an application domain and launch assemblies, you have complete control over the host *evidence*. Evidence is the information that the runtime gathers about an assembly to determine which code groups the assembly belongs to. The code groups, in turn, determine the assembly's privileges. Common forms of evidence include the folder or Web site the assembly is running from and digital signatures.

By assigning evidence to an assembly, you can control the permissions that will be assigned to the assembly. To provide evidence for an assembly, first create a *System.Security.Policy.Evidence* object, and then pass it as a parameter to the application domain's overloaded *ExecuteAssembly* method.

When you create an *Evidence* object with the constructor that requires two object arrays, you must provide one array that represents host evidence, and a second one that provides assembly evidence. Either of the arrays can be null, and unless you have specifically created an assembly evidence class, you will probably assign only the host evidence property. It might seem odd that *Evidence* takes generic object arrays instead of strongly typed *Evidence* objects. However, evidence can be *anything*: a string, an integer, or a custom class. So even if you are using the evidence types built into the .NET Framework, you will have to add them to an object array.

MORE INFO   Evidence

For more information about evidence, refer to Chapter 11.

The simplest way to control the permissions assigned to an assembly in an application domain is to pass Zone evidence by using a *System.Security.Policy.Zone* object and the *System.Security.SecurityZone* enumeration. The following code demonstrates using the *Evidence* constructor that requires two object arrays by creating a *Zone* object, adding it to an object array named *hostEvidence*, and then using the object array to create an *Evidence* object named *internetEvidence*. Finally, that *Evidence* object is passed to the application domain's *ExecuteAssembly* method along with the filename of the assembly. The following code sample, which requires the *System.Security* and *System.Security .Policy* namespaces, demonstrates this process:

```vb
' VB
Dim hostEvidence As Object() = {New Zone (SecurityZone.Internet)}
Dim internetEvidence As Evidence = New Evidence (hostEvidence, Nothing)
Dim myDomain As AppDomain = AppDomain.CreateDomain("MyDomain")
myDomain.ExecuteAssembly("SecondAssembly.exe", internetEvidence)
```

```csharp
// C#
object [] hostEvidence = {new Zone(SecurityZone.Internet)};
Evidence internetEvidence = new Evidence(hostEvidence, null);
AppDomain myDomain = AppDomain.CreateDomain("MyDomain");
myDomain.ExecuteAssembly("SecondAssembly.exe", internetEvidence);
```

The result is that the specified assembly will run in an isolated application domain with only the permission set granted to the *Internet_Zone* code group. When the application domain launches the assembly, the runtime analyzes the evidence provided. Because the evidence matches the Internet zone, the runtime assigns it to the *Internet_Zone* code group, which in turn assigns the extremely restrictive Internet permission set.

IMPORTANT Controlling evidence

Running an assembly using the *Internet_Zone* code group is useful for maximizing application security because the assembly has its permissions restricted as if it came from the Internet. But the assembly isn't necessarily coming from the Internet—it can be stored on the same folder as the running assembly. Essentially, you are providing false evidence to the runtime. Providing evidence to the runtime can also be used to grant an assembly *more* permissions than it would normally receive, which is a powerful capability. To control this capability, restrict the *SecurityPermission .ControlEvidence* permission as discussed in Chapter 11.

How to Provide Host Evidence for an Application Domain

You can also provide evidence for entire application domains. The technique is similar to providing evidence for a new assembly, and it uses an overload of the *AppDomain.CreateDomain* method that accepts an *Evidence* object, as the following code sample (which requires the *System.Security* and *System.Security.Policy* namespaces) demonstrates:

```vb
' VB
Dim hostEvidence As Object() =  {New Zone (SecurityZone.Internet)}
Dim appDomainEvidence As Evidence = New Evidence (hostEvidence, Nothing)
Dim d As AppDomain = AppDomain.CreateDomain("MyDomain", appDomainEvidence)
d.ExecuteAssembly("SecondAssembly.exe")
```

```
// C#
object [] hostEvidence = {new Zone(SecurityZone.Internet)};
Evidence appDomainEvidence = new Evidence(hostEvidence, null);
AppDomain d = AppDomain.CreateDomain("MyDomain", appDomainEvidence);
d.ExecuteAssembly("SecondAssembly.exe");
```

How to Configure Application Domain Properties

You can provide the common language runtime with configuration information for a new application domain using the *AppDomainSetup* class. When creating your own application domains, the most important property is *ApplicationBase*. The other *AppDomainSetup* properties are used mainly by run-time hosts to configure a particular application domain. Changing the properties of an *AppDomainSetup* instance does not affect any existing *AppDomain*. It can affect only the creation of a new *AppDomain*, when the *CreateDomain* method is called with the *AppDomainSetup* instance as a parameter.

Table 8-3 shows the most useful *AppDomainSetup* properties.

Table 8-3   *AppDomainSetup* Properties

Name	Description
ActivationArguments	Gets or sets data about the activation of an application domain.
ApplicationBase	Gets or sets the name of the root directory containing the application. When the runtime needs to satisfy a type request, it probes for the assembly containing the type in the directory specified by the *ApplicationBase* property.
ApplicationName	Gets or sets the name of the application.
ApplicationTrust	Gets or sets an object containing security and trust information.
ConfigurationFile	Gets or sets the name of the configuration file for an application domain.
DisallowApplication- BaseProbing	Specifies whether the application base path and private binary path are probed when searching for assemblies to load.

Table 8-3 *AppDomainSetup* Properties

Name	Description
DisallowBinding-Redirects	Gets or sets a value indicating whether an application domain allows assembly binding redirection.
DisallowCode-Download	Gets or sets a value indicating whether HTTP download of assemblies is allowed for an application domain. The default value is false, which is not secure for services (discussed in Lesson 3, "Creating Windows Services"). To help prevent services from downloading partially trusted code, set this property to true.
DisallowPublisher-Policy	Gets or sets a value indicating whether the publisher policy section of the configuration file is applied to an application domain.
DynamicBase	Gets or sets the base directory where the directory for dynamically generated files is located.
LicenseFile	Gets or sets the location of the license file associated with this domain.
LoaderOptimization	Specifies the optimization policy used to load an executable.
PrivateBinPath	Gets or sets the list of directories under the application base directory that are probed for private assemblies.

To apply these properties to an application domain, create and configure an *AppDomainSetup* object, and pass it (along with an *Evidence* object) to the *AppDomain .CreateDomain* method. The following code sample demonstrates this process:

```
' VB
' Construct and initialize settings for a second AppDomain
Dim ads As AppDomainSetup = New AppDomainSetup
ads.ApplicationBase = "file://" + System.Environment.CurrentDirectory
ads.DisallowBindingRedirects = False
ads.DisallowCodeDownload = True
ads.ConfigurationFile = _
    AppDomain.CurrentDomain.SetupInformation.ConfigurationFile

' Create the second AppDomain
Dim d As AppDomain = AppDomain.CreateDomain("New Domain", Nothing, ads)
```

```
// C#
// Construct and initialize settings for a second AppDomain.
AppDomainSetup ads = new AppDomainSetup();
ads.ApplicationBase = "file://" + System.Environment.CurrentDirectory;
ads.DisallowBindingRedirects = false;
ads.DisallowCodeDownload = true;
ads.ConfigurationFile =
    AppDomain.CurrentDomain.SetupInformation.ConfigurationFile;

// Create the second AppDomain
AppDomain d = AppDomain.CreateDomain("New Domain", null, ads);
```

To examine the properties for the current application domain, use the *AppDomain .CurrentDomain.SetupInformation* object, as the following code sample demonstrates:

```
' VB
Dim ads As AppDomainSetup = AppDomain.CurrentDomain.SetupInformation
Console.WriteLine(ads.ApplicationBase)
Console.WriteLine(ads.ApplicationName)
Console.WriteLine(ads.DisallowCodeDownload)
Console.WriteLine(ads.DisallowBindingRedirects)

// C#
AppDomainSetup ads = AppDomain.CurrentDomain.SetupInformation;
Console.WriteLine(ads.ApplicationBase);
Console.WriteLine(ads.ApplicationName);
Console.WriteLine(ads.DisallowCodeDownload);
Console.WriteLine(ads.DisallowBindingRedirects);
```

Lab: Control Application Domain Privileges

In this lab, you create an application domain with reduced privileges to reduce the security risks of running an external assembly. If you encounter a problem completing an exercise, the completed projects are available on the companion CD in the Code folder.

▶ **Exercise: Load an Assembly with Restricted Privileges**

In this exercise, you load an assembly without granting it privileges to read system files.

1. Copy the Chapter08\Lesson2-Exercise1-AppDomainDemo folder from the companion CD to your hard disk, and open either the C# version or the Visual Basic version of the project.

2. Add the *System.Security* and *System.Security.Policy* namespaces to your project.

3. Prior to the creation of the *AppDomain* object, create an *Evidence* object containing the Internet security zone. The following code would work:

```vb
' VB
' Create an Evidence object for the Internet zone
Dim safeZone As Zone = New Zone(SecurityZone.Internet)
Dim hostEvidence As Object() = {New Zone(SecurityZone.Internet)}
Dim e As Evidence = New Evidence(hostEvidence, Nothing)
```

```csharp
// C#
// Create an Evidence object for the Internet zone
Zone safeZone = new Zone(SecurityZone.Internet);
object[] hostEvidence = { new Zone(SecurityZone.Internet) };
Evidence e = new Evidence(hostEvidence, null);
```

4. Modify the call to the *AppDomain.CreateDomain* method to provide the evidence object you created. For example:

```vb
' VB
' Create an AppDomain
Dim d As AppDomain = AppDomain.CreateDomain("NewDomain", e)
```

```csharp
// C#
// Create an AppDomain.
AppDomain d = AppDomain.CreateDomain("New Domain", e);
```

5. Build and run the AppDomainDemo console application. This time, when your assembly attempts to run *ShowBootIni*, the runtime will throw a *SecurityException*. The application domain you created is in the Internet zone, which lacks privileges to read the Boot.ini file. If the assembly contained a security vulnerability or deliberately malicious code, providing restrictive evidence for the application domain could have prevented a security compromise such as a virus or spyware infection.

Lesson Summary

- The simplest way to use an application domain to launch an assembly with limited privileges is to specify a restricted zone, such as the Internet zone, as evidence.

- To configure an application domain's properties, create an instance of the *AppDomainSetup* class. Then use the instance when creating the application domain.

Lesson Review

You can use the following questions to test your knowledge of the information in Lesson 2, "Configuring Application Domains." The questions are also available on the companion CD if you prefer to review them in electronic form.

1. How does the runtime use evidence when creating an application domain?

    A. To determine the priority at which the process should run

    B. To identify the author of the assembly

    C. To determine which privileges the assembly should receive

    D. To track the actions of the assembly for audit purposes

2. Which of the following code samples runs an assembly as if it were located on the Internet? (Choose all that apply.)

    A.

    ```
    ' VB
    Dim hostEvidence As Object() =  {New Zone (SecurityZone.Internet)}
    Dim e As Evidence = New Evidence (hostEvidence, Nothing)
    Dim d As AppDomain = AppDomain.CreateDomain("MyDomain", e)
    d.ExecuteAssembly("Assembly.exe")

    // C#
    object [] hostEvidence = {new Zone(SecurityZone.Internet)};
    Evidence e = new Evidence(hostEvidence, null);
    AppDomain d = AppDomain.CreateDomain("MyDomain", e);
    d.ExecuteAssembly("Assembly.exe");
    ```

    B.

    ```
    ' VB
    Dim hostEvidence As Object() =  {New Zone (SecurityZone.Internet)}
    Dim d As AppDomain = AppDomain.CreateDomain("MyDomain")
    Dim e As Evidence = New Evidence (hostEvidence, Nothing)
    d.Evidence = e
    d.ExecuteAssembly("Assembly.exe")

    // C#
    object [] hostEvidence = {new Zone(SecurityZone.Internet)};
    AppDomain d = AppDomain.CreateDomain("MyDomain");
    Evidence e = new Evidence(hostEvidence, null);
    d.Evidence = e;
    d.ExecuteAssembly("Assembly.exe");
    ```

C.

```vb
' VB
Dim myDomain As AppDomain = AppDomain.CreateDomain("MyDomain")
myDomain.ExecuteAssembly("Assembly.exe", New Zone (SecurityZone.Internet))
```

```csharp
// C#
AppDomain myDomain = AppDomain.CreateDomain("MyDomain");
myDomain.ExecuteAssembly("Assembly.exe", new Zone(SecurityZone.Internet));
```

D.

```vb
' VB
Dim e As Evidence = New Evidence
e.AddHost(New Zone (SecurityZone.Internet))
Dim myDomain As AppDomain = AppDomain.CreateDomain("MyDomain")
myDomain.ExecuteAssembly("Assembly.exe", e)
```

```csharp
// C#
Evidence e = new Evidence();
e.AddHost(new Zone(SecurityZone.Internet));
AppDomain myDomain = AppDomain.CreateDomain("MyDomain");
myDomain.ExecuteAssembly("Assembly.exe", e);
```

3. How can you set the base directory for an application in an application domain?

   A. Create an instance of the *AppDomain* class, and then set the *Dynamic-Directory* property.

   B. Create an instance of the *AppDomain* class, and then set the *BaseDirectory* property.

   C. Create an instance of the *AppDomainSetup* class, and then set the *Dynamic-Base* property. Pass the *AppDomainSetup* object to the *AppDomain* constructor.

   D. Create an instance of the *AppDomainSetup* class, and then set the *Application-Base* property..

4. You need to notify the user if your assembly is running without the ability to use HTTP to download assemblies. How can you determine whether you have that permission?

   A. Examine *AppDomain.CurrentDomain.SetupInformation.DisallowCodeDownload*.

   B. Examine *AppDomain.CurrentDomain.DisallowCodeDownload*.

   C. Examine *AppDomain.CurrentDomain.SetupInformation.DisallowPublisherPolicy*.

   D. Examine *AppDomain.CurrentDomain.DisallowPublisherPolicy*.

Lesson 3: Creating Windows Services

Creating services enables you to run an assembly in the background, without any interaction from the user. Services are perfect when you want to continuously monitor something, when your assembly needs to listen for incoming network connections, or when you need to launch your assembly before the user logs on. Because of their unique nature, services require special security and installation considerations.

After this lesson, you will be able to:

- Describe the purpose of a service.
- Create a service project in Visual Studio.
- Specify properties for a service.
- Install a service manually.
- Create a setup project for a service.
- Start and manage a service using tools built into Windows.

Estimated lesson time: 45 minutes

What Is a Windows Service?

Windows services are processes that run in the background, without a user interface, and in their own user session. Services can be automatically started when the computer starts, even if a user does not log on. Therefore, services are an ideal way to implement an application that should be running constantly and does not need to interact with the user. Windows has dozens of services built-in, including Server (which shares folders on the network), Workstation (which connects to shared folders), and World Wide Web Publishing (which serves Web pages).

NOTE **Creating Windows services in different versions of Visual Studio**

The Windows Service template and associated functionality is not available in the Standard Edition of Visual Studio.

Service applications function differently from other project types in several ways:

- The compiled executable file that a service application project creates must be installed before the project can function in a meaningful way. You cannot debug or run a service application by pressing F5 or F11; you cannot immediately run a service or step into its code. Instead, you must install and start your service, and then attach a debugger to the service's process.

MORE INFO   Debugging services

For more information about debugging services, see "Debugging Windows Service Applications" at *http://msdn.microsoft.com/library/en-us/vbcon/html/vbtskdebuggingserviceapplications.asp.*

- Unlike you do with some types of projects, you must create installation components for service applications. The installation components install and register the service on the server and create an entry for your service with the Windows Services Control Manager.

- The *Main* method for your service application must issue the Run command for the services your project contains. The *Run* method loads the services into the Services Control Manager on the appropriate server. If you use the Windows Services project template, this method is written for you automatically.

- Windows Service applications run in a different window station than the interactive station of the logged-on user. A window station is a secure object that contains a Clipboard, a set of global atoms, and a group of desktop objects. Because the station of the Windows service is not an interactive station, dialog boxes raised from within a Windows service application will not be seen and might cause your program to stop responding. Similarly, error messages should be logged in the Windows event log rather than raised in the user interface.

- Windows service applications run in their own security context and are started before the user logs into the Windows computer on which they are installed. You should plan carefully what user account to run the service within; a service running under the system account has more permissions and privileges than a user account. The more privileges your service has, the more damage attackers can do if they successfully exploit a security vulnerability in your service. Therefore, you should run your service with the fewest privileges possible to minimize potential damage.

Real World

Tony Northrup

I started using the .NET Framework as soon as betas of the first version were available. However, earlier versions did not support creating services with the .NET Framework. I didn't want to revert to another development environment, so I relied on hacks to enable .NET assemblies to run in the background. Typically, I would create a console application, and then use Scheduled Tasks to configure it to start automatically under a special user account. This system enabled the process to run continuously in the background, but the technique was difficult to manage because I couldn't use the Services snap-in to start or stop the service.

How to Create a Service Project

At a high level, you follow these steps to create a service project:

1. Create a project using the Windows Service application template, as shown in Figure 8-3. This template creates a class for you that inherits from *ServiceBase* and writes much of the basic service code, such as the code to start the service.

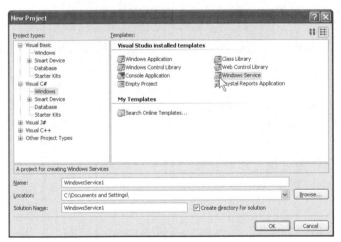

Figure 8-3   Visual Studio includes the Windows Service application template.

2. Write the code for the *OnStart* and *OnStop* procedures, and override any other methods that you want to redefine.

3. Add the necessary installers for your service application. By default, a class containing two or more installers is added to your application when you click the Add Installer link: one to install the process, and one for each of the associated services your project contains.

4. Build your project.

5. Create a setup project to install your service, and then install it.

6. Use the Services snap-in to start your service.

The sections that follow describe how to implement these capabilities at the code level.

How to Implement a Service

After you create your service project in Visual Studio, follow these steps to implement the service:

1. In the properties for your designer, modify the *ServiceBase.ServiceName* property. Every service must have a unique name; therefore, it is very important to change this setting. *ServiceName* is not the friendly name you will see in the Services snap-in. Instead, *ServiceName* is used by the operating system to identify the service and can be used to programmatically identify the service. For example, you can start a service from the command line by running Net Start *ServiceName*.

2. Add code to the *OnStart* method to set up whatever polling or monitoring your service requires. Note that *OnStart* does not actually do the monitoring. The *OnStart* method must return to the operating system once the service's operation has begun. It must not loop forever or block. To set up a simple polling mechanism, you can use the *System.Timers.Timer* component. In the *OnStart* method, you would set parameters on the component, and then you would set the *Enabled* property to true. The timer would then raise events in your code periodically, at which time your service could do its monitoring. Refer to Lab Exercise 1, later in this lesson, for an example.

3. Add code to the *OnStop* method to perform any actions required for your service to stop.

4. Optionally, override the *OnPause*, *OnContinue*, and *OnShutdown* methods. *OnPause* is called when a user pauses your service from the Services snap-in (a rare event). *OnContinue* is called when a service resumes from a paused state. Finally, *OnShutdown* is called when a computer shuts down. If you do override these methods, set *ServiceBase.CanPauseAndContinue* or *ServiceBase.CanShutdown* to true.

How to Create an Install Project for a Service

Unlike with other applications, you cannot simply run a service executable file. This limitation prevents you from running and debugging the application directly from the Visual Studio development environment. Services must be installed prior to running. The .NET Framework provides the *ServiceInstaller* and *ServiceProcessInstaller* classes for this purpose. Use *ServiceInstaller* to define the service description, display name, service name, and start type. Use *ServiceProcessInstaller* to define the service account settings.

In practice, you will not need to write code that uses the *ServiceInstaller* and *Service-ProcessInstaller* classes because Visual Studio will automatically generate the code. To create a service installer using Visual Studio, you follow these steps:

1. In Visual Studio, open the design view for your service. Right-click the designer, and then click Add Installer. Visual Studio creates a *ProjectInstaller* component.

2. Set the *StartType* property for the *ProjectInstaller ServiceInstaller* component to one of the following values:
    ❑ **Automatic** The service still start automatically after the computer starts, whether or not a user logs in.
    ❑ **Manual (the default)** A user must manually start the service.
    ❑ **Disabled** The service does not start automatically, and users cannot start the service without first changing the startup type.

3. Set the *Description* and *DisplayName* properties for the *ServiceInstaller* component.

4. Specify the security context for your service by setting the *Account* property for the *ProjectInstaller ServiceProcessInstaller* component to one of the following values:
    ❑ **LocalService** Runs in the context of an account that acts as a nonprivileged user on the local computer, and presents anonymous credentials to any remote server. Use *LocalService* to minimize security risks.
    ❑ **NetworkService** Enables the service to authenticate to another computer on the network. This authentication is not required for anonymous connections, such as most connections to a Web server.
    ❑ **LocalSystem** The service runs with almost unlimited privileges and presents the computer's credentials to any remote server. Using this account type presents a severe security risk; any vulnerabilities in your application could be exploited to take complete control of the user's computer.

❑ *User* **(the default)**   Causes the system to prompt for a valid user name and password when the service is installed (unless you set values for both the *Username* and *Password* properties of your *ServiceProcessInstaller* instance).

5. Define your service project's startup object. Right-click the project in Solution Explorer and then click Properties. In the Project Designer, on the Application tab, select your service project from the Startup Object list.

6. Now build your project.

At this point, you can manually install the service using the InstallUtil tool or create a setup project that will provide a wizard-based installation interface and a Windows Installer (MSI) package. The sections that follow discuss each of these two options.

How to Install a Service Manually

After you implement and build your service, you can install it manually. To install a service manually, run InstallUtil.exe from the command line with your service's name as a parameter. To install your service, run InstallUtil *yourservice.exe*. To uninstall your service, run InstallUtil /u *yourservice.exe*.

How to Build a Setup Project for a Service

1. Add a Setup Project to your current solution, as shown in Figure 8-4.

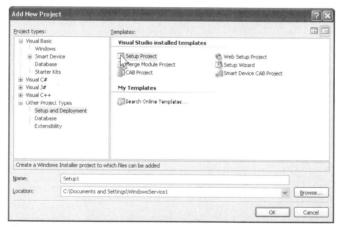

Figure 8-4   Adding a setup project simplifies deploying services.

2. Add the output from your service project to your setup project by following these steps:

   A. Right-click your setup project in Solution Explorer, click Add, and then click Project Output.

    B. In the Add Project Output Group dialog box, select your service project from the Project list, select Primary Output, and then click OK.

  3. Finally, add a custom action to install the service executable file by following these steps:

    A. Right-click your setup project in Solution Explorer, click View, and then click Custom Actions.

    B. In the Custom Actions editor, right-click Custom Actions and then click Add Custom Action.

    C. In the Select Item In Project dialog box, select the Application Folder, and then select Primary Output From *your service project name*, as shown in Figure 8-5. Click OK. The primary output is added to all four nodes of the custom actions: Install, Commit, Rollback, and Uninstall.

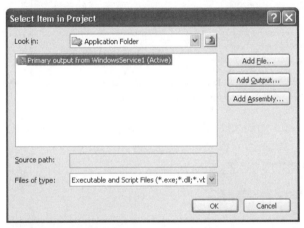

Figure 8-5 Creating a setup project for a service requires special considerations

    D. In Solution Explorer, right-click your setup project and then click Build. The service setup build folder now includes a Setup.exe file to interactively install the service and an MSI file for automatic deployment of the service.

After installation, you can uninstall the service using the standard methods: manually, from the Add or Remove Programs tool, or automatically using Windows Installer (MSI) tools.

How to Manage and Control a Service

After you install a service, you need to start it. If you set the service startup type to Automatic, rebooting the computer will cause the service to start. If the service startup type is set to Manual, or you want to start the service without restarting the computer, you use the Services snap-in:

1. While logged on as an administrator or another user account with privileges to manage services, click Start, right-click My Computer, and then click Manage.

2. Expand Services And Applications, and then click Services.

3. In the right pane, right-click your service and then click Start, as shown in Figure 8-6.

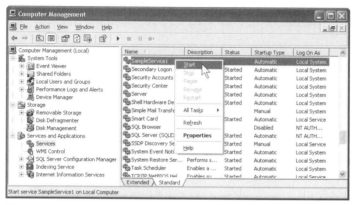

Figure 8-6   Start services from the Services snap-in.

You can use the same process to stop, pause, resume, or restart your service. To change the service startup type or user account, right-click the service and then click Properties, as shown in Figure 8-7.

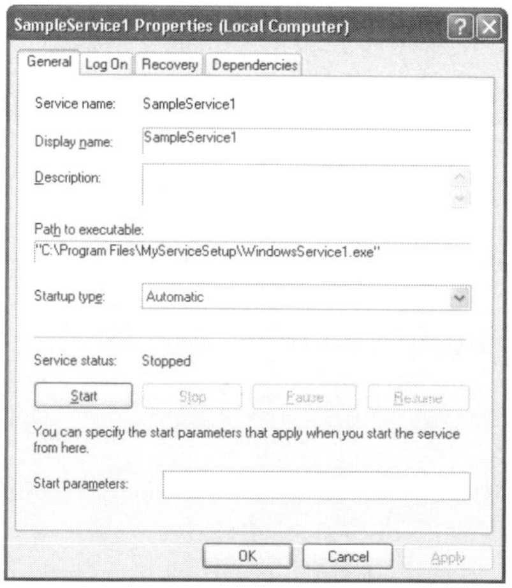

Figure 8-7   Configure service startup type and user account after setup by viewing the service properties dialog box.

You can also control services from the command line by using the Net command with the format Net Start *ServiceName* or Net Stop *ServiceName*.

To control services from an assembly, use the *System.ServiceProcess.ServiceController* class. This class gives you the ability to connect to a service on the local computer or a remote computer, examine the service's capabilities, and start, stop, pause, or resume the service. The following code sample, which requires both the *System.ServiceProcess* (which you must manually add a reference to in Visual Studio) and *System.Threading* namespaces, demonstrates this process:

```
' VB
' Connect to the Server service
Dim sc As ServiceController = New ServiceController("Server")

' Stop the service
sc.Stop()

' Wait two seconds before starting the service
Thread.Sleep(2000)

' Start the service
sc.Start()

// C#
// Connect to the Server service
ServiceController sc = new ServiceController("Server");

// Stop the service
sc.Stop();

// Wait two seconds before starting the service
Thread.Sleep(2000);

// Start the service
sc.Start();
```

Lab: Create, Install, and Start a Service to Monitor a Web Site

In this lab, you create a service project using Visual Studio, and write code to log the status of a Web page every 10 seconds. Then you create a setup project for the service. Finally, you install and start the service.

▶ **Exercise 1: Create a Service to Monitor a Web Site**

In this exercise, you create and build a Windows service that will check a Web site every 10 seconds and write a message to a log file indicating whether the Web site returned a page successfully.

1. Using Visual Studio, create a project using the Windows Service application template. Name the project MonitorWebSite.

2. Using the service designer view, change the Name and the ServiceName to MonitorWebSite. Set the *CanPauseAndContinue* and *CanShutdown* properties to True.

3. Add the *System.Timers*, *System.IO*, and *System.Net* namespaces to the project.

4. Within the *MonitorWebSite* class, create a *Timer* object. For example, the following code would work:

```
' VB
Private t As Timer = Nothing
```

```
// C#
private Timer t = null;
```

5. Within the *MonitorWebSite* constructor (in Visual Basic, the *New* method is located in Service1.Designer.VB), configure the timer to call a method every 10 seconds, as the following code demonstrates:

```
' VB
t = New Timer(10000)
AddHandler t.Elapsed, New System.Timers.ElapsedEventHandler(AddressOf _
    Me.t_Elapsed)
```

```
// C#
t = new Timer(10000);
t.Elapsed += new ElapsedEventHandler(t_Elapsed);
```

6. Add code to the *OnStart* method to enable and start the timer, as demonstrated here:

```
' VB
t.Start()
```

```
// C#
t.Start();
```

7. Add code to the *OnStop* method to stop the timer, as the following sample demonstrates:

```
' VB
t.Stop()
```

```
// C#
t.Stop();
```

8. Override the *OnPause*, *OnContinue*, and *OnShutdown* methods, and add code to start and stop the timer, as demonstrated here:

```
' VB
Protected Overrides Sub OnContinue()
    t.Start()
End Sub
```

```
Protected Overrides Sub OnPause()
    t.Stop()
End Sub

Protected Overrides Sub OnShutdown()
    t.Stop()
End Sub

// C#
protected override void OnContinue()
{
    t.Start();
}

protected override void OnPause()
{
    t.Stop();
}

protected override void OnShutdown()
{
    t.Stop();
}
```

9. In the method you specified for the *ElapsedEventHandler*, write the code to check the Web site and write the current time and status code to a text file. Add an event to the event log if you experience an exception, because services lack a user interface to easily communicate the exception information to the user. The following code demonstrates this:

```
' VB
Protected Sub t_Elapsed(ByVal sender As System.Object, _
    ByVal e As System.Timers.ElapsedEventArgs)

    Try
        ' Send the HTTP request
        Dim url As String = "http://www.microsoft.com"
        Dim g As HttpWebRequest = CType(WebRequest.Create(url), _
            HttpWebRequest)
        Dim r As HttpWebResponse = CType(g.GetResponse, HttpWebResponse)

        ' Log the response to a text file
        Dim path As String = _
            AppDomain.CurrentDomain.SetupInformation.ApplicationBase + _
            "log.txt"
        Dim tw As TextWriter = New StreamWriter(path, True)
        tw.WriteLine(DateTime.Now.ToString + " for " + url + ": " + _
            r.StatusCode.ToString)
        tw.Close()

        ' Close the HTTP response
        r.Close()
```

```
      Catch ex As Exception
          System.Diagnostics.EventLog.WriteEntry("Application", _
              "Exception: " + ex.Message.ToString)
      End Try
  End Sub

  // C#
  void t_Elapsed(object sender, ElapsedEventArgs e)
  {
      try
      {
          // Send the HTTP request
          string url = "http://www.microsoft.com";
          HttpWebRequest g = (HttpWebRequest)WebRequest.Create(url);
          HttpWebResponse r = (HttpWebResponse)g.GetResponse();

          // Log the response to a text file
          string path =
              AppDomain.CurrentDomain.SetupInformation.ApplicationBase +
              "log.txt";
          TextWriter tw = new StreamWriter(path, true);
          tw.WriteLine(DateTime.Now.ToString() + " for " + url +
              ": " + r.StatusCode.ToString());
          tw.Close();

          // Close the HTTP response
          r.Close();
      }
      catch (Exception ex)
      {
          System.Diagnostics.EventLog.WriteEntry("Application",
              "Exception: " + ex.Message.ToString());
      }
  }
```

10. Build the project and resolve any problems that appear. Note that you cannot yet run the service because you have not created an installer.

▶ **Exercise 2: Create a Service Installer**

In this exercise, you create an installer for the project you created in Exercise 1.

1. Add an installer to your service project.

2. Set the installer properties as:

   ■ *StartType*   Automatic.

   ■ *Description*   "Logs responses from Microsoft.com".

   ■ *DisplayName*   "Web Site Monitor".

   ■ *Account*   *LocalSystem*. Note that using *LocalSystem* is not typically recommended; however, this project requires access to write a text file to the file system, which *LocalSystem* provides. A more secure method would be to create a custom user account with only the necessary privileges; however, this would distract from the purpose of this exercise.

3. Define the service project as the startup object if you have not yet defined it.

4. Add a Setup Project to your solution, and then add the output from your service project to your setup project.

5. Add a custom action to install the service executable file in the application folder.

6. Build your setup project.

▶ **Exercise 3: Install, Start, and Manage the Service**

In this exercise, you install and manage the project you created in Exercises 1 and 2.

1. Launch the Setup.exe that you created in Exercise 2, and install the service with the default settings.

2. Launch Computer Management, and select the Services node.

3. Right-click your Web Site Monitor service, and then select Start. Notice that the Services snap-in shows the Name and Description you provided in Exercise 2.

4. Wait 30 seconds, and then open the text file that your service logs request responses to. Verify that it is successfully querying the Web server and writing the results to the text file.

5. Pause the service, wait 30 seconds, and verify that it no longer adds information to the log file.

6. Resume the service, wait 30 seconds, and verify that it continues adding information to the log file.

7. Stop the service by opening a command line and running the command "net stop monitorwebsite".

8. Finally, uninstall the service by re-running Setup.exe.

Lesson Summary

- A Windows service is a process that runs in the background, without a user interface, in its own user session.

- To create a Windows service, use Visual Studio to create a project using the Windows Service application template. Then write the code for the *OnStart* and *OnStop* procedures, and override any other methods that you want to redefine.

Add the necessary installers for your service application. Finally, create a setup project to install your service.

- To implement a service, specify the service name, description, and startup type. Then override the *OnStart*, *OnStop*, *OnPause*, *OnContinue*, and *OnShutdown* procedures as necessary.

- To create an install project for a service, first define the properties of a *ServiceInstaller* object to specify the service description, display name, service name, and start type. Then define the properties of a *ServiceProcessInstaller* to specify the service account settings. At this point, you can manually install the service, or build a setup project for the service.

- To manually control a service, you can use the Net command-line tool or the Services snap-in. Alternatively, you can use the *System.ServiceProcess.ServiceController* class to control a service from an assembly.

Lesson Review

You can use the following questions to test your knowledge of the information in Lesson 3, "Creating Windows Services." The questions are also available on the companion CD if you prefer to review them in electronic form.

NOTE Answers

Answers to these questions and explanations of why each answer choice is right or wrong are located in the "Answers" section at the end of the book.

---

1. Which account type should you choose to minimize security risks?

    A. *LocalService*

    B. *NetworkService*

    C. *LocalSystem*

    D. *User*

2. Which account type should you choose to minimize the possibility of problems caused by overly restrictive permissions on the local computer?

    A. *LocalService*

    B. *NetworkService*

    C. *LocalSystem*

    D. *User*

3. Which of the following are valid ways to install a service on a computer? (Choose all that apply.)

    A. Add a shortcut to your assembly to the user's Startup group.

    B. Use InstallUtil to install your service.

    C. Configure Scheduled Tasks to launch your assembly upon startup.

    D. Use Visual Studio to create an installer for your service.

4. Which tools can you use to change the user account for a service after the service is installed?

    A. My Computer

    B. Computer Management

    C. Net

    D. Microsoft .NET Framework 2.0 Configuration

Chapter Review

To further practice and reinforce the skills you learned in this chapter, you can complete the following tasks:

- Review the chapter summary.
- Review the list of key terms introduced in this chapter.
- Complete the case scenarios. These scenarios set up real-world situations involving the topics of this chapter and ask you to create a solution.
- Complete the suggested practices.
- Take a practice test.

Chapter Summary

- Application domains are logical containers that allow multiple assemblies to run within a single process without being able to directly access each other's memories. Application domains offer separate memory spaces and access to resources without the overhead of creating a second process.

- When you create a new application domain, you can control many aspects of that application domain's configuration. Most importantly, you can restrict the privileges of assemblies running within the application domain by providing evidence when creating the application domain or when launching the process.

- Services run in the background, without providing an interface to the user. Creating a service is different from creating other types of applications because you cannot directly run a service executable file. Instead, you must manually install the service or create a setup project for the service. Other considerations unique to services include startup type, account type, and management tools.

Key Terms

Do you know what these key terms mean? You can check your answers by looking up the terms in the glossary at the end of the book.

- application domain
- assembly evidence
- defense-in-depth

- evidence
- *LocalService*
- *LocalSystem*
- *NetworkService*
- service

Case Scenarios

In the following case scenarios, you will apply what you've learned about how to use application domains and services. You can find answers to these questions in the "Answers" section at the end of this book.

Case Scenario 1: Creating a Testing Tool

You are a developer for the Baldwin Museum of Science. Your end users run your application from various locations. Because the .NET Framework runtime assigns different permission sets based on the assembly's location, your assembly is often running in a partially trusted environment. This situation has caused problems for your end users. Your manager asks you to interview key company personnel and to then come to her office to answer some questions. Your manager needs you to create an application that creates an application domain and launches an assembly in the new application domain using Internet zone permissions to enable more realistic testing procedures.

Interviews

Following is a list of company personnel interviewed and their statements:

- **Customer Support Manager** "We're getting a lot of calls from customers who want to deploy our app from a Web server. It seems like this doesn't work for some reason, though. Users end up getting different errors. From the way they describe the errors, it seems like the application crashes at different times depending on whether the application is launched from the public Internet or the user's local intranet. Right now we just tell them to copy it to their local computers and run it, and that seems to solve the problem. The IT people don't like this work-around, though, and want to know why we can't make it work from a Web server."

- **Development Manager** "I talked to the Customer Support Manager, and it sounds like users are having problems because of code access security restrictions. We need to start testing our application in different zones so that we can identify problems when permissions are restricted. Do me a favor, and write an application that allows our Quality Assurance team to run our application in different zones."

Questions

Answer the following questions:

1. At a high level, describe how you would create the application.

2. Create an application that creates an application domain and launches the *CASDemands* assembly in the new application domain using Internet zone permissions.

Case Scenario 2: Monitoring a File

You are an application developer working for the IT department of Humongous Insurance. You just released a project that you've been working on for months. The IT manager has decided to use your spare time by having you create a tool to help the systems administrators maintain the integrity of the desktop computers in your organization.

Interviews

Following is a list of company personnel interviewed and their statements:

- **IT Manager** "Thanks to the most recent round of application updates produced by your team, all of our applications support XML-based configuration files. This is great, because it allows our most advanced users to tweak configuration settings. However, we noticed that one of our users made a change that disabled the application's built-in security features. I want users to be able to make some changes, but I want to be notified if they change the configuration setting that controls the security features. File auditing isn't precise enough, because it notifies me when the user makes any change to the configuration file. I need to be able to deploy the service using our Systems Management Server infrastructure, so please provide an MSI file."

- **Development Manager** "We don't need to prevent users from making changes, and I don't know how we could do that anyway without blocking all access to the configuration file. We just need to add an event to the event log if we detect that the user changes the security settings in the configuration file. After the event is added to the event log, the IT department's event management infrastructure will notify an administrator who can address the problem. We need to create the event immediately after the user saves the change, however, so running a process nightly will not be sufficient."

Questions

Answer the following questions for your manager:

1. What type of application will you create to address the IT department's need?
2. How will you address the need to deploy the application using an MSI file?
3. What startup type will you specify?
4. What account type will you specify?

Suggested Practices

To help you successfully master the objectives covered in this chapter, complete the following tasks.

Create a Unit of Isolation for the Common Language Runtime Within a .NET Framework Application by Using Application Domains

For this task, you should complete both practices.

■ **Practice 1**   Create an assembly that mimics malware by reading a file from the current user's My Documents folder and then connecting to a Web server. Then create a second assembly that specifies evidence to create a restrictive application domain for the malware assembly and prevents it from reading the user's personal information.

■ **Practice 2**   Create an assembly that allocates large amounts of memory. Run the assembly, and use the Performance snap-in to monitor the assembly's memory usage. Then create a second assembly that launches the first assembly in an application domain and then unloads the application domain. Monitor the assembly's memory usage to verify that the resources are deallocated.

Implement, Install, and Control a Service

For this task, you should complete at least Practice 1. If you want a better understanding of the challenges involved with implementing services in the real world, complete Practices 2 and 3 as well.

- **Practice 1** Create a service that listens for incoming network connections, and use the InstallUtil tool to install the service. Once you have verified that it works properly, use the InstallUtil tool to uninstall the service.

- **Practice 2** Create a service that performs the tasks described in Case Scenario 2 earlier in this chapter.

- **Practice 3** Modify the service you created in Exercises 1 and 2 of Lesson 3 so that it runs using the LocalService account. Identify the privileges that the LocalService account requires to enable the service to function correctly. Create a new user account with only the necessary privileges, and configure the service to run under the new user account.

Take a Practice Test

The practice tests on this book's companion CD offer many options. For example, you can test yourself on just one exam objective, or you can test yourself on all the 70-536 certification exam content. You can set up the test so that it closely simulates the experience of taking a certification exam, or you can set it up in study mode so that you can look at the correct answers and explanations after you answer each question.

MORE INFO   Practice tests

For details about all the practice test options available, see the "How to Use the Practice Tests" section in this book's Introduction.

Chapter 9
Installing and Configuring Applications

This chapter covers two distinct topics: installing applications and configuring applications. Because it is impossible to know exactly which user settings will be necessary for any given installation, making your application configurable ensures that making such changes will be trivial. Furthermore, creating a seamless, reversible installation is not just an option in today's marketplace, it's a mandate. Moreover, the installation will have a major impact on how customers initially view your application. Therefore, ensuring that the process is easy, intuitive, and thorough is a prerequisite for today's professional applications.

Exam objectives in this chapter:
- Embed configuration management functionality into a .NET Framework application. (Refer *System.Configuration* namespace)
  - *Configuration* class and *ConfigurationManager* class
  - *ConfigurationElement* class, *ConfigurationElementCollection* class, and *ConfigurationElementProperty* class
  - *ConfigurationSection* class, *ConfigurationSectionCollection* class, *ConfigurationSectionGroup* class and *ConfigurationSectionGroupCollection* class
  - Implement *ISettingsProviderService* interface
  - Implement *IApplicationSettingsProvider* interface
  - *ConfigurationValidatorBase* class
- Create a custom Microsoft Windows Installer for the .NET Framework components by using the *System.Configuration.Install* namespace, and configure the .NET Framework applications by using configuration files, environment variables, and the .NET Framework Configuration tool (Mscorcfg.msc).
  - *Installer* class
  - Configure which runtime version a .NET Framework application should use
  - Configure where the runtime should search for an assembly
  - Configure the location of an assembly and which version of the assembly to use

❑ Direct the runtime to use the DEVPATH environment variable when you search for assemblies

❑ *AssemblyInstaller* class

❑ *ComponentInstaller* class

❑ Configure a .NET Framework application by using the .NET Framework Configuration tool (Mscorcfg.msc)

❑ *ManagedInstallerClass* class

❑ *InstallContext* class

❑ *InstallerCollection* class

❑ *InstallEventHandler* delegate

❑ Configure concurrent garbage collection

❑ Register remote objects by using configuration files

Lessons in this chapter:

Before You Begin

To complete the lessons in this chapter, you should be familiar with Microsoft Visual Basic or C# and be comfortable with the following tasks:

■ Create a console or Winforms application in Microsoft Visual Studio using Visual Basic or C#.

■ Direct output to the debug window or the console window.

■ Set a breakpoint in the debugger.

■ Step into a code segment.

■ Step over a code segment.

■ Step through a code segment.

■ Have a basic understanding of a configuration file.

■ Have a basic understanding of XML document structure.

Real World

William Ryan

The task of software configuration in the recent past was far different than what it entails today. Not long ago, there wasn't a *System.Configuration* namespace, and there wasn't a Windows Registry or isolated storage either. Even with the advent of .NET Framework, creating and customizing an application's configuration was typically quite a chore. When writing my first production .NET application, I spent well over six hours creating the configuration files, creating the classes to handle those files, and testing the code. Just to get a comparative baseline, I rewrote the configuration elements of that same application using the new tools provided with Visual Studio. The task that took me over six hours to complete back then was now accomplished in under 15 minutes!

Lesson 1: Configuration Settings

With respect to application development, there are few absolutes. Instead of "always do it this way" or "this way is always best" approaches, developers are confronted with tradeoffs. Some decisions are more straightforward than others, but most involve tradeoffs nonetheless. Making accurate assessments of the costs of the benefits and costs associated with the tradeoffs is absolutely critical to delivering quality products on time and on budget.

One area that tends toward the absolute, however, is the avoidance of hard-coding variables. Hard-coding variables introduces multiple challenges. Although there are certainly times when hard-coding is advisable, as a general rule it's best to avoid that practice.

The .NET Framework gives developers an ample tool set to avoid hard-coding and makes it relatively simple to greatly enhance the flexibility of your application. To fully understand the value of the tools available in .NET Framework 2.0, it is worth mentioning how .NET applications had to be configured in previous versions of the Framework.

Prior to .NET Framework 2.0, developers had two ways to handle configuration. The first approach was to simply put all settings in the *appSettings* section of the configuration file. This strategy provided the benefit of simplicity, but that simplicity came at the cost of having to deal with those settings in a non–object-oriented way. The other way was to define custom configuration settings sections in the configuration file and build the corresponding classes to consume those settings. This approach allowed developers to deal with configuration settings in a fully object-oriented way, but that functionality came at the cost of having to write a lot of code—code that was often monotonous and time-consuming to write. It wasn't uncommon for a developer who was dealing with nontrivial applications to spend nearly two hours creating and testing custom configuration sections in the previous versions of the Framework. Using the new tools available in .NET Framework 2.0, developers can use the latter approach to configure even a complex application in just a few minutes, because now all that monotonous code is written for you.

With this in mind, the primary benefits of using .NET configuration are as follows:

- It allows you to set and retain settings without having to know what those settings will be in advance.

- It allows you to handle your configuration settings in an intuitive object-oriented manner.

■ It allows you to read and write settings without dependence on the Windows registry. This will make your application much less intrusive to security and network administrators (because there will not be a need to modify or grant privileges to the Windows registry). It will also help ensure cross-platform compatibility. (Other operating systems, such as Linux and Mac OS, don't have a registry.)

After this lesson, you will be able to:
■ Manipulate common settings.
■ Manipulate application settings.
■ Retrieve specific settings.
■ Register remote components.

Estimated lesson time: 45 minutes

Configuration in .NET Framework 2.0

The *System.Configuration* namespace serves as the repository of all the classes that developers use to manage configuration.

NOTE   Code samples require a reference to the *System.Configuration* namespace.

All the code samples in this lesson assume that the *System.Configuration* namespace has been imported. This can be accomplished by specifying *Imports System.Configuration* at the top of a class or module in Visual Basic or specifying *using System.Configuration* in C#. It might also be necessary to add a reference to the System.Configuration.dll assembly through the Visual Studio menu by clicking Project, clicking Add Reference, selecting the .NET tab, and selecting *System.Configuration*.

This namespace is quite comprehensive and provides both general-purpose and specific types for just about every conceivable configuration scenario.

NOTE   .NET 2.0

The *ConfigurationManager* class first came to being in Microsoft's Enterprise Library. It has since become a member of the .NET Framework and replaces many of the existing approaches to manipulating configuration data.

At the top of the logical hierarchy within the *System.Configuration* namespace are the *Configuration* and *ConfigurationManager* classes.

Chapter 9 Installing and Configuring Applications

When using any of the objects discussed in this chapter (or any that are members of the *System.Configuration* namespace), fully qualified object names will need to be used or importing the *System.Configuration* namespace will need to be done. This is accomplished by adding Imports System.Configuration at the top of a Visual Basic module or class or using System.Configuration in a C# class.

These two classes have an intuitive synergy that becomes evident when you use them. Also, it's worth noting that neither class has a constructor specified. Table 9-1 and Table 9-2 show the most important class definitions of the *Configuration* and *Configuration Manager* classes, respectively. Pay close attention to the class definitions of each class—you'll see why shortly.

Table 9-1 *Configuration* **Properties and Methods**

Name	Description
AppSettings	This property gets the *AppSettingsSection* object configuration section that applies to this *Configuration* object
ConnectionStrings	This property gets the *ConnectionStringsSection* object configuration section that applies to this *Configuration* object
EvaluationContext	This property gets the *ContextInformation* object configuration section that applies to this *Configuration* object
FilePath	This property gets the physical path to the configuration file represented by this *Configuration* object
GetSection	This method returns the specified *ConfigurationSection* object
GetSectionGroup	This method returns the specified *ConfigurationSectionGroup* object
HasFile	This property indicates whether a configuration file exists for the resource represented by the configuration object
NamespaceDeclared	This property gets or sets a value indicating whether the configuration file has an XML namespace
RootSectionGroup	This property gets the *ConfigurationSectionGroup* for this *Configuration* object

Table 9-1 *Configuration* **Properties and Methods**

Name	Description
Save	This method writes the configuration settings contained within this *Configuration* object to the current XML configuration file
SaveAs	This method writes the configuration settings contained within this *Configuration* object to the specified XML configuration file

Table 9-2 *Configuration* **Properties and Methods**

Name	Description
AppSettings	Gets the *AppSettingsSection* data for the current application's default configuration
ConnectionStrings	Gets the *ConnectionStringsSection* data for the current application's default configuration
GetSection	Retrieves a specified configuration section for the current application's default configuration
OpenExeConfiguration	Opens the specified client configuration as a *System.Configuration.Configuration* object
OpenMachine-Configuration	Opens the Machine Configuration file on the current computer as a *System.Configuration.Configuration* object
OpenMappedExe-Configuration	Opens the specified client configuration as a *System.Configuration.Configuration* object using the specified file mapping and user level
OpenMappedMachine-Configuration	Opens the specified machine configuration file as a *System.Configuration.Configuration* object using the specified file mapping.

Two things should be evident at this point. First, both classes have two identical properties (*AppSettings* and *ConnectionStrings*). Second, each of the properties of the *ConfigurationManager* class returns *Configuration* objects. These facts should give you some hint as to how these two classes interact. To retrieve configuration settings, follow these steps:

1. Declare a *Configuration* object.

2. Use the various methods in *ConfigurationManager* with the "Open" prefix to open the application's or machine's configuration file. The following code demonstrates this:

```
'VB
Dim cs As Configuration = _
    ConfigurationManager.OpenExeConfiguration(ConfigurationUserLevel.None)
// C#
Configuration cs =
    ConfigurationManager.OpenExeConfiguration(ConfigurationUserLevel.None);

' VB
Dim cs As Configuration = ConfigurationManager.OpenMachineConfiguration()
// C#
Configuration cs = ConfigurationManager.OpenMachineConfiguration();

' VB
Dim myMap As New ExeConfigurationFileMap
    myMap.ExeConfigFilename = "DBConnectionStringDemo.exe.config"
Dim cs As Configuration = _
    ConfigurationManager.OpenMappedExeConfiguration(myMap, _
    ConfigurationUserLevel.None)

// C#
ExeConfigurationFileMap myMap = new ExeConfigurationFileMap();
    myMap.ExeConfigFilename = @"DBConnectionStringDemo.exe.config";
Configuration cs =
    ConfigurationManager.OpenMappedExeConfiguration(myMap,
    ConfigurationUserLevel.None);

'VB
Dim myMap As New ExeConfigurationFileMap
myMap.ExeConfigFilename = "DBConnectionStringDemo.exe.config"

Dim cs As Configuration = _
    ConfigurationManager.OpenMappedMachineConfiguration(myMap)

// C#
ExeConfigurationFileMap myMap = new ExeConfigurationFileMap();
myMap.ExeConfigFilename = @"DBConnectionStringDemo.exe.config";

Configuration cs =
    ConfigurationManager.OpenMappedMachineConfiguration(myMap);
```

These methods are all very similar and ultimately serve a similar purpose—namely, to open a configuration file and return the values it contains to a *Configuration* object. The first and third methods are used for opening application-specific configuration files, whereas the second and the fourth methods are used to open a given machine's configuration file. Opening and reading configuration information using the *ConfigurationManager* class, as the preceding examples illustrate, is fairly intuitive, but a few areas need further clarification.

The first area that might need explanation is the *ConfigurationUserLevel* enumeration. Details of the *ConfigurationUserLevel* enumeration are provided in Table 9-3.

Table 9-3 *ConfigurationUserLevel* **Enumeration**

Name	Description
None	Gets the *System.Configuration.Configuration* object that applies to *all* users
PerUserRoaming	Gets the roaming *System.Configuration.Configuration* object that applies to the *current* user
PerUserRoaming-AndLocal	Gets the local *System.Configuration.Configuration* object that applies to the *current* user

The main issue to be aware of is that the default setting here is *None*, which might appear counterintuitive to some.

The next issue that might need elaboration involves the *ExeConfigurationFileMap* object or "File Map." Not surprisingly, if you want to use a mapped file, the runtime needs some mechanism to inform it that you want to do so, as well as a mechanism for telling it where that file can be found. This process is facilitated through the *ExeConfigFilename* property.

When you call either the *OpenMappedExeConfiguration* or *OpenMappedMachineConfiguraton* method, you're informing the runtime of your intention to use a mapped file. The constructor requires this, so the only other minimum requirement is to specify a file location. The consuming application will need adequate permissions to access this file, so you'll need to ensure that the file exists and that you have permission to access it.

MORE INFO   **Permissions and declarative security**

Managing permissions is an essential part of creating secure .NET Framework applications. The subject of permissions and both declarative and imperative security is covered in depth in Chapter 11. Additional information is available on MSDN at *http://msdn.microsoft.com/library/ default.asp?url=/library/en-us/cpguide/html/cpconPermissions.asp*.

In addition to ensuring that the user has permissions to access the file, you will need to verify the location of the file. If you specify an empty string or blank for the *ExeConfigFilename* property, the runtime will throw an *ArgumentException*. Figure 9-1 shows the output of an attempt to set the *ExeConfigFilename* property to *String.Empty*.

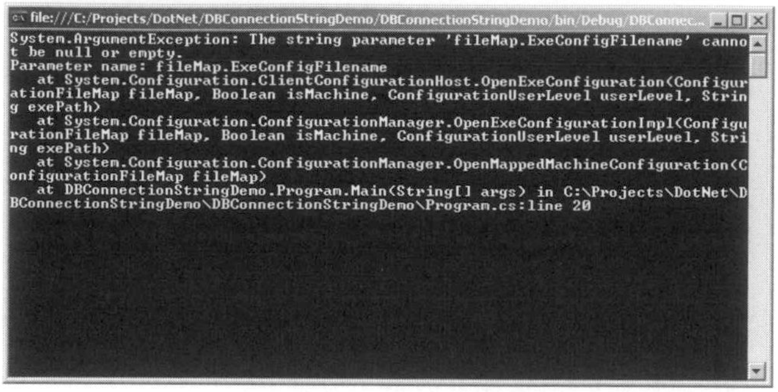

Figure 9-1   Attempting to set *ExeConfigFilename* to an empty string

Unfortunately, if you set the *ExeConfigFilename* to a file that is nonexistent, the runtime will not stop you from doing so (until later when you have null values when you expected something else). You can avoid this mistake by ensuring that you have a valid file before setting this property. You can implement whatever control flow logic you want, but for the sake of clarity we'll use a debug assertion here to verify the file's existence:

```
'VB
Dim cs As Configuration = ConfigurationManager.OpenMachineConfiguration()
Debug.Assert(File.Exists(ExeFileName), _
    "The mapped file or path is missing or incorrect!")
myMap.ExeConfigFilename = ExeFileName
```

```
// C#
ExeConfigurationFileMap myMap = new ExeConfigurationFileMap();
String ExeFileName = @"DBConnectionString.exe.config";
Debug.Assert(File.Exists(ExeFileName),
    "The mapped file or path is missing or incorrect!");
myMap.ExeConfigFilename = ExeFileName;
```

Common Settings

The term *common settings* refers to a few areas that determine how applications run. An example of this functionality is configuring an application to run under a specific version of the .NET Framework. For example, you might build an application with a given version of the Framework but choose to run it with a different one. To be able to do this, you must specify the *supportedRuntime* version in the startup section. If you wanted to run your application under the 1.1 version of the Framework, you'd enter the following code in the configuration section of the application or Web configuration file:

```
<?xml version ="1.0"?>
<configuration>
   <startup>
      <supportedRuntime version="v1.1.4322" />
   </startup>
</configuration>
```

However, there might be instances where the version you want to run under isn't present on the machine. There are strict rules that are followed under these circumstances:

- If the version of the Framework that the application was built with is present, that version will be used by the application.

- If the version of the Framework that the application was built with isn't present and nothing is specified in the *supportedRuntime* version tag, the application will run under the latest version of the Framework that is available on the machine. So it would run under .NET Framework 2.0 if that was the only version present, even if the application was built under the 1.x versions.

- If the version of the Framework that the application was built with isn't present but the configuration file specifies a *supportedRuntime* tag, the .NET Framework will use the specified runtime version although the specified version must be present on the computer.

These rules are intuitive. If you don't have the right version of the runtime that an application needs and you don't specify a different version, the runtime will do it's best to run the application. If the runtime can't run the assembly with the available version, you have a problem.

Another common scenario involves using a shared assembly and verifying that it works with multiple applications. Installing this given assembly to the global assembly cache (GAC) and uninstalling it from the GAC can be cumbersome. To accommodate this task, there is a specific variable called the DEVPATH that can be configured. To take advantage of this, two things need to be done:

1. Add an environment variable named DEVPATH that points to the location of the assembly.

2. Set the *developmentMode* value to *true*. The following code snippet shows how to do this:

```
<configuration>
   <runtime>
      <developmentMode developerInstallation="true"/>
   </runtime>
</configuration>
```

Another common task entails specifying where a certain version of an assembly is located. You can do this by using the .NET Framework 2.0 Configuration tool (which is covered in depth in Lesson 3) or by manually editing the machine configuration file. There is a specific element, *codeBase*, that allows you to specify both the location and version of an assembly so that when the runtime is loaded, it will use what you have specified. The following code provides an example of how to accomplish this:

```
<configuration>
   <runtime>
      <assemblyBinding xmlns="schemaname">
         <dependentAssembly>
            <assemblyIdentity name="myprogram"
            publicKeyToken="xxxxxxxxx" culture="en-us" />
            <codeBase version="x.0.0.0"
            href="http://www.adatum.com/myprogram.dll"/>
         </dependentAssembly>
      </assemblyBinding>
   </runtime>
</configuration>
```

Other common settings are configuration values that are already defined for you by the .NET Framework. They comprise two primary sections, *connectionStrings* and *appSettings*. In many ways, these configuration values are used identically to any other configuration component; however, they do contain some nuances that give them distinct advantages over other items. Because they are treated differently than other settings, they have a predefined location in the configuration file where they need to be placed. The following code snippet shows an example of a configuration file that includes both an *appSettings* and a *connectionStrings* section:

```
<?xml version="1.0" encoding="utf-8" ?>
<configuration>
   <appSettings>
      <add key="Foo" value="Hello World!"/>
   </appSettings>
   <connectionStrings>
      <clear/>
      <add name="AdventureWorksString"
      providerName="System.Data.SqlClient"
      connectionString="Data Source=localhost;
      Initial Catalog=AdventureWorks; Integrated Security=true"/>
   </connectionStrings>
</configuration>
```

The preceding code creates one *appSettings* element and one *connectionStrings* value. The *appSettings* value is named *Foo* and contains the literal *"Hello World"*. The *connectionStrings* value is named *AdventureWorksString* and contains a connection string that can be used to connect to a SQL Server database.

The approach to using an *appSettings* section is straightforward. You specify a key, which is a name that you'll use to uniquely identify that setting so that it can be retrieved, and you specify a value. The sole purpose of the key is to provide a human-readable means by which you can retrieve a given value. In this example, the word *Foo* might be a bit cryptic, so a better example might be *CompanyName*. By reading the configuration file, most anyone should be able to figure out what a key named *CompanyName* refers to. Although the *ConfigurationSettings* class is obsolete, the *AppSettings* property is still a part of it for backward compatibility. There are additional ways, however, to reference it under .NET Framework 2.0. The following code illustrates a simple example of how to retrieve an AppSettings value.

```
' VB
Dim HelloWorldVariable = ConfigurationSettings.AppSettings("Foo")
```

```
// C#
String HelloWorldVariable = ConfigurationSettings.AppSettings["Foo"];
```

NOTE The meaning of "obsolete"

While the word "obsolete" has a general meaning, it also has a precise meaning in the .NET Framework. Many methods, properties, and objects that are deprecated and therefore considered obsolete are still retained in the Framework to provide backward compatibility. Technically speaking, you can still use them without causing your application to break. However, obsolete items are not guaranteed to remain supported and good programming practice dictates that you avoid them unless there's a compelling reason not to. Also, using an obsolete item will result in a compiler warning. Depending on your build configuration, this might stop your application from compiling.

However, as noted, the *AppSettings* property is considered obsolete and will result in a compiler warning. The correct way to use *AppSettings* is to access it through the *ConfigurationManager* object rather than through the *ConfigurationSettings* object. The following code shows the .NET Framework 2.0 method for retrieving *AppSettings*:

```
'VB
Dim AllAppSettings As NameValueCollection = ConfigurationManager.AppSettings
Console.WriteLine(AllAppSettings("Foo"))
Console.WriteLine(AllAppSettings(0))
```

```
// C#
NameValueCollection AllAppSettings = ConfigurationManager.AppSettings;
Console.WriteLine(AllAppSettings["Foo"]);
Console.WriteLine(AllAppSettings[0]);
```

To use *AppSettings*, you need to declare an instance of the *NameValueCollection* object and set it to the *AppSettings* property of the *ConfigurationManager* object. After doing this, you can access the value using either an index-based or a string-based lookup. In this example, only one *AppSettings* variable is defined. This variable contains the value *"Hello World"* and a key of *"Foo"*. Assuming it to be the only item in the collection, the *AppSettings* variable occupies the collection's first (0th) index. Also, each value in *AppSettings* is of type *System.String*, so there is no need to cast the value to its corresponding type.

There is one other nuance that needs to be mentioned. You might have an instance where you need to walk through or enumerate your *AppSettings* value as opposed to referencing it specifically. The *AppSettings* class implements the *IEnumerable* interface (requiring the *System.Collections* namespace) and, because of this, you can enumerate the collection the same way you would any other object with an *Enumerator*. You simply declare an *IEnumerator* object and set it to the result of the *GetEnumerator* method of the *Keys* property of your *AppSettings* instance. From there, you walk through the collection calling the *MoveNext* method. The following code illustrates enumerating the values in the *AppSettings* section:

```
'VB
Dim AllAppSettings As NameValueCollection = _
    ConfigurationManager.AppSettings
Dim SettingsEnumerator As IEnumerator = AllAppSettings.Keys.GetEnumerator
Dim Counter As Int32 = 0
While SettingsEnumerator.MoveNext
    Console.WriteLine("Item: {0}  Value: {1}", _
    AllAppSettings.Keys(Counter), AllAppSettings(Counter))
End While
```

```
// C#
NameValueCollection AllAppSettings =
    ConfigurationManager.AppSettings;
Int32 Counter = 0;
IEnumerator SettingsEnumerator = AllAppSettings.Keys.GetEnumerator();
while (SettingsEnumerator.MoveNext())
    {
    Console.WriteLine("Item: {0}  Value: {1}", AllAppSettings.Keys[Counter],
    AllAppSettings[Counter]);
    }
```

Using the *ConnectionStrings* component is slightly more involved, but doing so is still intuitive and easy. Because many current applications entail interacting with a database in some fashion or another, the developers of the Framework decided that they needed to provide an elegant and secure way to store database connection strings. If you hard-code the connection string, you'll greatly decrease the flexibility of the application because you need to change the connection string and redeploy your application each time a server name changes or you make any substantive change to it. Storing the connection string in a configuration file gives you much more flexibility because you can simply edit the file and change the settings if you change or add a server.

In the previous versions of the Framework, no real distinction was made between a connection string and any other string. A major enhancement with respect to configuration in.NET Framework 2.0 is support for strong typing (although there were other reasons that strong typing was added). This improved configuration capability includes a specific provision to accommodate the provider type. (See the *System.Data* namespace for more information.)

CAUTION   **Connection string security considerations**

Connection strings (and all other sensitive information) should be encrypted or hashed wherever possible. Storing a database connection string in plain-text (human readable) form can present a huge security vulnerability and should be avoided if possible.

A common misconception is that if you are using a Windows trust to authenticate your application against a database, there is no need to encrypt this. Although this might be the case in some circumstances, it is not true in others. Depending on the sophistication of the attacker, critical details might be revealed even though using Windows Authentication minimizes how much an attacker can discern. In cases where Windows Authentication is not used, it is very dangerous to store a connection string in plain text because an attacker can easily discern both a username and a password to access the database. As such, it is strongly advised that you encrypt or hash this information.

MORE INFO   **Encryption and hashing**

Encryption and hashing are discussed in depth in Chapter 12, "User and Data Security," and such techniques should be employed unless security is not an issue.

In the previous versions of the Framework, no real distinction was made between a connection string and any other string. A major enhancement with respect to configuration in .NET Framework 2.0 is support for strong typing (although there were other reasons that strong typing was added). This improved configuration capability includes a specific provision to accommodate the provider type. (See the *System.Data* namespace for more information.)

By default, you can access the *ConnectionStrings* property almost identically to how you access *AppSettings*. The primary difference is that instead of using a *NameValue-Collection* object, you use a *ConnectionStringSettingsCollection* object in conjunction with the *ConnectionStringSettings* object. First we'll look at what the configuration file settings will need to look like. For the sake of thoroughness, this configuration file hosts the following libraries: *SqlClient*, *OracleClient*, *OleDb*, and *Odbc*:

```xml
<?xml version="1.0" encoding="utf-8" ?>
<configuration>
   <connectionStrings>
      <clear/>
      <add name="AdventureWorksString"
         providerName="System.Data.SqlClient"
         connectionString="Data Source=localhost;Initial
         Catalog=AdventureWorks; Integrated Security=true"/>
      <add name="MarsEnabledSqlServer2005String"
         providerName="System.Data.SqlClient"
         connectionString=
         "Server=Aron1;Database=
         pubs;Trusted_Connection=True;MultipleActiveResultSets=true" />
      <add name="OdbcConnectionString"
         providerName="System.Data.Odbc"
```

```
        connectionString=
        "Driver={Microsoft Access Driver (*.mdb)};Dbq=C:\adatabase.mdb;
        Uid=Admin;Pwd=R3m3emberToUseStrongPasswords;"/>
      <add name="AccessConnectionString"
        providerName="System.Data.OleDb"
        connectionString="Provider=Microsoft.Jet.OLEDB.4.0;
        Data Source=\PathOrShare\mydb.mdb;
        User Id=admin;Password=Rememb3rStr0ngP4sswords;" />
      <add name="OracleConnectionString"
        providerName="System.Data.OracleClient"
        connectionString="Data Source=MyOracleDB;Integrated Security=yes;" />
    </connectionStrings>
</configuration>
```

To configure each of the preceding data libraries (OleDb, SqlClient, OracleClient, Odbc), do the following:

1. Specify the *Clear* element to eliminate any existing connection strings.

2. For each connection string (for example, *SqlClient*, *OracleClient*, and so on), add a *Name* element. This element allows the value to be referenced by name without the developer having to remember indices.

3. Specify a *providerName* attribute for each of the *Name* elements (for example, *System.Data.OracleClient*).

4. Specify a *connectionString* attribute with the appropriate connection string to connect to the data source.

In the example just shown, for each library type, I've added a specific connection string that corresponds to it. For the *SqlClient* library, I added two different connection strings just to illustrate that there's no problem associated with doing so. The second *SqlClient* connection string differs from the first mainly in that it enabled multiple active result sets (MARS).

Now that you have the values set in the configuration file, here's how to access them:

```
'VB
Dim MySettings As ConnectionStringSettingsCollection = _
   ConfigurationManager.ConnectionStrings
If Not MySettings Is Nothing Then
   Dim sb As New StringBuilder
   Dim individualSettings As ConnectionStringSettings

   For Each individualSettings In MySettings
      sb.Append("Full Connection String: " & _
         individualSettings.ConnectionString)
      sb.Append("Provider Name: " & individualSettings.ProviderName)
      sb.Append("Section Name: " & individualSettings.Name)
   Next

   Console.WriteLine(sb.ToString)
End If
```

```csharp
// C#
ConnectionStringSettingsCollection MySettings =
    ConfigurationManager.ConnectionStrings;

if (MySettings != null)
    {
    StringBuilder sb = new StringBuilder();
    foreach (ConnectionStringSettings individualSettings in MySettings)
        {
        sb.Append("Full Connection String: " +
            individualSettings.ConnectionString + "\r\n");
        sb.Append("Provider Name: " + individualSettings.ProviderName + "\r\n");
        sb.Append("Section Name: " + individualSettings.Name + "\r\n");
        }
    Console.WriteLine(sb.ToString());
    }
```

To summarize what the preceding code does, it creates an instance of the *Connection-StringSettingsCollection* class and then sets it to the result of the *Configuration-Manager*'s *ConnectionStrings* property. Three properties are of particular importance: *Name*, *ProviderName*, and *ConnectionString*. Of the three, *ConnectionString* is probably the most important because it's the one you'll need to create or instantiate a new *Connection* object. The following code (which requires the *System.Data*, *System. Data.SqlClient*, *System .Data.OracleClient*, *System.Data.OleDB*, and *System.Data.Odbc* namespaces) may be added to the *foreach* loop of the preceding code snippets to create a connection based on the values of those properties:

```vb
'VB
Dim MyConnection As IDbConnection
Select Case individualSettings.ProviderName
    Case "System.Data.SqlClient"
        MyConnection = New SqlConnection(individualSettings.ConnectionString)
    Case "System.Data.OracleClient"
        MyConnection = New OracleConnection(individualSettings.ConnectionString)
    Case "System.Data.OleDb"
        MyConnection = New OleDbConnection(individualSettings.ConnectionString)
    Case "System.Data.Odbc"
        MyConnection = New OdbcConnection(individualSettings.ConnectionString)
End Select
```

```csharp
// C#
IDbConnection MyConnection = null;
switch (individualSettings.ProviderName)
    {
    case "System.Data.SqlClient":
        MyConnection = new SqlConnection(individualSettings.ConnectionString);
        break;
    case "System.Data.OracleClient":
        MyConnection = new OracleConnection(individualSettings.ConnectionString);
        break;
    case "System.Data.OleDb":
        MyConnection = new OleDbConnection(individualSettings.ConnectionString);
        break;
```

```
case "System.Data.Odbc":
  MyConnection = new OdbcConnection(individualSettings.ConnectionString);
  break;
}
```

Although the preceding code illustrates how to retrieve different types of connection strings stored in a configuration file, typical applications don't use multiple database providers. A more typical scenario is using just one database or using multiple databases of the same type—for example, multiple SQL Server databases. As such, if you know what you are looking for, iterating a collection is unnecessary and possibly ambiguous. Accordingly, you might want to directly retrieve the connection string for the provider that you know exists. There are two ways to accomplish this. The first approach is to use the section name of the section accessing the library type, as shown here:

```
' VB
Dim MySettings As ConnectionStringSettings = _
  ConfigurationManager.ConnectionStrings("AdventureWorksString")
If Not MySettings Is Nothing Then
  Dim MyConnection As New SqlConnection(MySettings.ConnectionString)
  Console.WriteLine(MySettings.ConnectionString)
End If

// C#
ConnectionStringSettings MySettings =
  ConfigurationManager.ConnectionStrings["AdventureWorksString"];

if (MySettings != null)
  {
  SqlConnection cn = new SqlConnection(MySettings.ConnectionString);
  Console.WriteLine(MySettings.ConnectionString);
  }
```

The second approach entails using the index that corresponds to the item's position in the *ConnectionStrings* collection, as shown here:

```
'VB
Dim MySettings As ConnectionStringSettings = _
  ConfigurationManager.ConnectionStrings(0)
If Not MySettings Is Nothing Then
  Dim MyConnection As New SqlConnection(MySettings.ConnectionString)
  Console.WriteLine(MySettings.ConnectionString)
End If

// C#
ConnectionStringSettings MySettings =
  ConfigurationManager.ConnectionStrings[0];

if (MySettings != null)
  {
  SqlConnection cn = new SqlConnection(MySettings.ConnectionString);
  Console.WriteLine(MySettings.ConnectionString);
  }
```

Similarly, if you had multiple databases of the same type (and again, we'll use the example of SQL Server), you can enumerate the values by type and then load them accordingly. In the following example, the configuration file supplies two connection strings for SQL Server databases, *AdventureWorksString* and *MarsEnabledSqlServer2005String*. So we can look for the type (*System.Data.SqlClient*) and respond accordingly.

```vb
'VB
Dim MyTypeSettings As ConnectionStringSettingsCollection = _
    ConfigurationManager.ConnectionStrings
If Not MyTypeSettings Is Nothing Then
    For Each typeSettings As ConnectionStringSettings In MyTypeSettings
        If typeSettings.ProviderName = "System.Data.SqlClient" Then
            Dim MyConnection As New _
                SqlConnection(typeSettings.ConnectionString)
            Console.WriteLine("Connection String: " & _
                typeSettings.ConnectionString)
        End If
    Next
End If
```

```csharp
// C#
ConnectionStringSettingsCollection MyTypeSettings =
    ConfigurationManager.ConnectionStrings;
if (MyTypeSettings != null)
    {
    foreach (ConnectionStringSettings typeSettings in MyTypeSettings)
        {
        if (typeSettings.ProviderName == "System.Data.SqlClient")
            {
            SqlConnection MyConnection = new
                SqlConnection(typeSettings.ConnectionString);
            Console.WriteLine("Connection String " +
                typeSettings.ConnectionString);
            }
        }
    }
```

The previous example illustrates using the *ConfigurationManager* class, which is the primary mechanism for retrieving and storing configuration information in Winforms or console applications (or more generally, in any application that is not a Web application). Although this methodology will work in ASP.NET applications, different mechanisms can and should be used to retrieve these values in a Web application. The main usage difference between Winforms and Web applications is that Web applications should employ the *WebConfigurationManager* to manage configuration information as opposed to the *ConfigurationManager*. Although this statement is a bit of an oversimplification, it is safe to say that the *WebConfigurationManager* class is identical for all intents and purposes to the *ConfigurationManager* class with three exceptions:

- The *WebConfigurationManager* class has a *GetWebApplicationSection* method that the *ConfigurationManager* class does not have. This method will retrieve an entire

ConfigurationSection from a web.config file. This method is the functional equivalent of the *GetSection* method of the *ConfigurationManager* class.

- The *OpenMappedExeConfiguration* method of the *ConfigurationManager* is replaced with the *OpenMappedWebConfiguration* method of the *WebConfigurationManager* class.

- The OpenExeConfiguration method of the ConfigurationManager is replaced with the OpenWebConfiguration method of the WebConfigurationManager class.

The examples earlier in this lesson that referenced the various *Open*-prefixed methods of the *ConfigurationManager* class will still work with the *WebConfigurationManager* class, with the previous noted exceptions. Moreover, class usage is virtually identical. The following example shows basic usage of the *WebConfigurationManager* to loop through multiple connection string entries and illustrates how they can be retrieved. The following configuration file will be used for both the Visual Basic and C# examples.

NOTE   The *WebConfigurationManager* class belongs to the *System.Web.Configuration* namespace.

The *WebConfigurationManager* class is not a member of the *System.Configuration* namespace as you might have expected. Instead, it belongs to the *System.Web.Configuration* namespace. To use the following examples, please include a reference to the *System.Web.Configuration* namespace, as well as the *System.Collections* namespace.

```
Configuration File:
<?xml version="1.0"?>
<configuration>
   <appSettings/>
   <connectionStrings>
      <clear/>
      <add name="AdventureWorksString"
         providerName="System.Data.SqlClient"
         connectionString="Data Source=localhost;Initial
            Catalog=AdventureWorks; Integrated Security=true"/>
      <add name="MarsEnabledSqlServer2005String"
         providerName="System.Data.SqlClient"
         connectionString="Server=Aron1;Database=pubs;Trusted_Connection=True;
         MultipleActiveResultSets=true" />
      <add name="OdbcConnectionString"
         providerName="System.Data.Odbc"
         connectionString="Driver={Microsoft Access Driver
            (*.mdb)};Dbq=C:\mydatabase.mdb;Uid=Admin;Pwd=;"/>
      <add name="AccessConnectionString"
         providerName="System.Data.OleDb"
         connectionString="Provider=Microsoft.Jet.OLEDB.4.0;
         Data Source=\somepath\mydb.mdb;User Id=admin;Password=;" />
      <add name="OracleConnectionString"
         providerName="System.Data.OracleClient"
         connectionString="Data Source=MyOracleDB;Integrated Security=yes;" />
   </connectionStrings>
```

```
    <system.web>
       <!-- -->
          <compilation debug="true"/>
       <!-- -->
          <authentication mode="Windows"/>
       <!-- -->
    </system.web>
</configuration>
```

```vb
'VB
Private Const CONNECTIONSTRING As String = "connectionStrings"
Protected Sub Page_Load(ByVal sender As Object, ByVal e As System.EventArgs) _
   Handles Me.Load
   Dim ConnectionStringsSection As ConnectionStringsSection = _
      CType(WebConfigurationManager.GetSection(CONNECTIONSTRING), _
      ConnectionStringsSection)

   Dim ConnectionStrings As ConnectionStringSettingsCollection = _
      ConnectionStringsSection.ConnectionStrings

   Dim ConnectionStringsEnumerator As System.Collections.IEnumerator = _
      ConnectionStrings.GetEnumerator

   Dim i As Int32 = 0
   Response.Write("[Display the connectionStrings]:<BR>")
   While ConnectionStringsEnumerator.MoveNext
      Dim ConnectionStringName As String = ConnectionStrings(i).Name
      Response.Write(String.Format("Name: {0}  Value: {1} <BR>", _
      ConnectionStringName, ConnectionStrings(ConnectionStringName)))
      i += 1
   End While
End Sub
```

```csharp
// C#
private const String CONNECTIONSTRINGS = "connectionStrings";
protected void Page_Load(object sender, EventArgs e)
   {
   ConnectionStringsSection ConnectionStringsSection =
      WebConfigurationManager.GetSection(CONNECTIONSTRINGS)
      as ConnectionStringsSection;

   ConnectionStringSettingsCollection ConnectionStrings =
      ConnectionStringsSection.ConnectionStrings;

   //Make sure you use the System.Collections IEnumerator vs. the
   //System.Collections.Generic IEnumerator, it will take additional
   //work to get the latter one to workq
   System.Collections.IEnumerator ConnectionStringsEnumerator =
      ConnectionStrings.GetEnumerator();

   // Loop through the collection and
   // display the connectionStrings key, value pairs.
   Int32 i = 0;
   Response.Write("[Display the connectionStrings]:<BR>");
   while (ConnectionStringsEnumerator.MoveNext())
      {
```

```
        String ConnectionStringName = ConnectionStrings[i].Name;
        Response.Write(String.Format("Name: {0} Value: {1} <BR>",
        ConnectionStringName, ConnectionStrings[ConnectionStringName]));

        i++;
    }
}
```

Application Settings

Application settings are configuration values that apply to the application as a whole rather than being pegged to a specific user. Typical candidates for this type of value include database connection strings (which we'll cover in depth in the lab at the end of this section), Web service URLs, remoting settings, and the like. Again, one of the main benefits of using application settings is that you can store and retrieve your application's settings in an object-oriented, strongly typed fashion. The best way to understand how this works is to take a look at the actual implementation. In this instance, an application setting named WebServiceUrl is added to a project so that we can use it in the application. It's created in a class called *SampleSettings*. The sections in boldface type refer specifically to the relevant sections:

```
<?xml version="1.0" encoding="utf-8" ?>
<configuration>
    <configSections>
        <sectionGroup name="userSettings"
            type="System.Configuration.UserSettingsGroup, System,
            Version=2.0.0.0, Culture=neutral, PublicKeyToken=b77a5c561934e089" >
                <section name="WindowsApplication2.SampleSettings"
                    type="System.Configuration.ClientSettingsSection, System,
                    Version=2.0.0.0, Culture=neutral,
                        PublicKeyToken=b77a5c561934e089"
                        allowExeDefinition="MachineToLocalUser" />
        </sectionGroup>
        <sectionGroup name="applicationSettings"
            type="System.Configuration.ApplicationSettingsGroup, System,
            Version=2.0.0.0, Culture=neutral, PublicKeyToken=b77a5c561934e089" >
                <section name="WindowsApplication2.SampleSettings"
                    type="System.Configuration.ClientSettingsSection, System,
                    Version=2.0.0.0, Culture=neutral,
                        PublicKeyToken=b77a5c561934e089" />
        </sectionGroup>
    </configSections>
    <userSettings>
        <WindowsApplication2.SampleSettings />
    </userSettings>
    <applicationSettings>
        <WindowsApplication2.SampleSettings>
            <setting name="WebServiceUrl" serializeAs="String">
                <value>http://www.adatum.com/myservice.asmx</value>
            </setting>
        </WindowsApplication2.SampleSettings>
    </applicationSettings>
</configuration>
```

There are two ways to get here, although one is vastly simpler than the other. The first is to write this out by hand. This approach is highly discouraged because configuration files demand extreme precision. Issues such as capitalization and extraneous spaces can cause the application to misbehave. The other method is to use the *Settings* class and take advantage of the designer. This approach is a much better choice overall. The most straightforward way to use the designer is to simply add a new project item of type Settings File to your project, as shown in Figure 9-2.

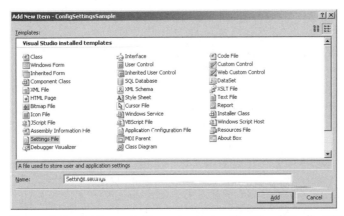

Figure 9-2   Adding a *Settings* class using the Visual Studio 2005 integrated development environment (IDE)

After you give the file a friendly name, the IDE will present you with a designer that allows you to create and manage your settings. The Settings dialog box will allow you to create and rename your settings, set the scope of each of them, select the type for each of them, and specify a default value, as shown in Figure 9-3.

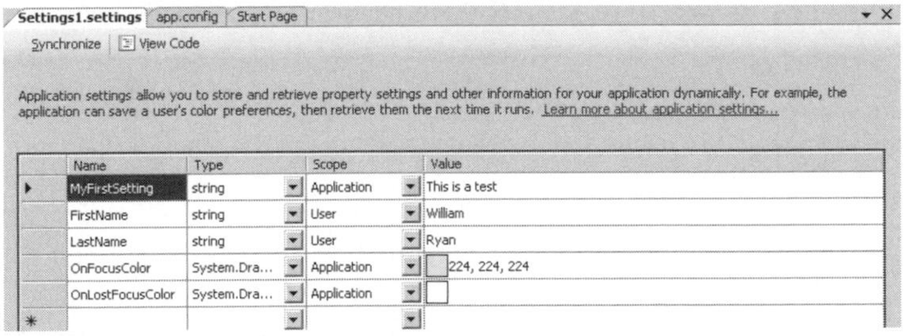

Figure 9-3   The Visual Studio 2005 Application Settings Designer

The Application Settings Designer saves the developer a tremendous amount of time. Another benefit is that it relieves the developer from having to know all the nuances of each specification. (After all, even the most astute developer would probably stumble trying to remember the specific *PublicKeyToken* for a given class.) Another benefit is the support for strong typing and designer support. Using the designer, you can select from all available .NET Framework type options (for instance, *System.Drawing .Color*) without having to remember them or type them out. The Application Settings Designer will also provide the specific designers for whatever type you choose. Again, it's a lot easier to select a color after seeing it on a grid than trying to remember what the *RGB* arguments are for it.

The corresponding class property (and it's worth mentioning here that this would have had to be coded by hand in previous versions) is provided:

```
'VB
<Global.System.Configuration.ApplicationScopedSettingAttribute(), _
    Global.System.Diagnostics.DebuggerNonUserCodeAttribute(), _
    Global.System.Configuration.DefaultSettingValueAttribute _
    ("http://www.adatum.com/myservice.asmx")> _
Public ReadOnly Property WebServiceUrl() As String
    Get
        Return CType(Me("WebServiceUrl"),String)
    End Get
End Property
```

```
//C#
[global::System.Configuration.ApplicationScopedSettingAttribute()]
[global::System.Diagnostics.DebuggerNonUserCodeAttribute()]
[global::System.Configuration.DefaultSettingValueAttribute
("http://www.adatum.com/myservice.asmx")]
public string WebServiceUrl
    {
    get
        {
            return ((string)(this["WebServiceUrl"]));
        }
    }
```

Now all you need to use this setting is the following:

```
'VB
Dim mySettings as new SampleSettings()
Debug.WriteLine(mySettings.WebServiceUrl)
```

```
// C#
SampleSettings mySettings = new SampleSettings();
Debug.WriteLine(mySettings.WebServiceUrl);
```

The last mechanism provided for storing and retrieving custom settings is the *Application-SettingsBase*. Note that in the preceding example where the designer is used, this is the methodology that Visual Studio is using. Similar to the previous example, *Application-SettingsBase* contains an internal *Key/Value* collection that you reference by key. All that needs to be done to use this class is to inherit from *ApplicationSettingsBase* and then decorate each property that maps to a configuration setting value with either the *UserScopedSettings* attribute or the *ApplicationScopedSettings* attribute.

```vb
'VB
Public Class AppSettingsHelper
   Inherits ApplicationSettingsBase
   <UserScopedSetting()> _
      Public Property Key() As String
      Get
         Return CType(Me("Key"), String)
      End Get
      Set(ByVal value As String)
         Me("Key") = value
      End Set
   End Property
   <ApplicationScopedSetting()> _
      Public Property SettingValues() As String
      Get
         Return CType(Me("SettingValue"), String)
      End Get
      Set(ByVal value As String)
         Me("SettingValue") = value
      End Set
   End Property
End Class
```

```csharp
// C#
class AppSettingsHelper : ApplicationSettingsBase
   {
   [UserScopedSetting()]
   public String Key
      {
      get { return (this["Key"] as String); }
      set { this["Key"] = value;}
      }
   [ApplicationScopedSetting()]
   public String SettingValue
      {
      get { return (this["SettingValue"] as String); }
      set { this["SettingValue"] = value; }
      }
   }
```

The last area that remains to be discussed here with respect to configuration is configuring remote components. Few areas benefit from configuration as much as remoting. If configuration with remoting is used correctly, you will gain multiple benefits. The first benefit is that you can add assemblies without having to recompile and redeploy your application. In a world where downtime can be devastating, this factor alone justifies using this approach. However, there are other benefits as well. You can change where assemblies are hosted without having to recompile and redeploy. For the same reason just mentioned, this is a major benefit. Let's use an example to help illuminate the benefits here.

Assume that you have a traditional three-tier application with a presentation layer, business layer, and data access layer. Assume further that all three layers run on the same machine. It all works well, but due to a growing user base the application starts to perform sluggishly. This result isn't all that surprising because every part of the application is running on the same machine. If you don't use remoting, not a lot can be done other than buying more powerful hardware. This solution is expensive, and it's impractical because users might not appreciate the downtime.

If you use remoting, you can move the assemblies to other machines to spread out the load. However, if you registered your components in code, you'll have to recompile the assemblies with the new references and locations and redeploy. In a zero-downtime environment, this might not be a viable option and all the benefits of remoting are effectively whittled away. However, if you use remoting and configuration, you can simply copy the assemblies to the new machine or machines and change the configuration file. Without even restarting Internet Information Services (IIS), your application can consume the assemblies on new machines.

Similarly, let's say that you need to modify one of the components and you wanted to add some new assemblies. Using either remoting or configuration, you'd be in the same position that I first mentioned. However, using remoting *and* configuration, the solution is as easy as adding the files to a given machine and making the appropriate entries in the configuration file. Although this might sound enticing already, the real beauty of this approach isn't evident until you actually see it in action. The following code is all that is needed to register a component as a server:

```
<system.runtime.remoting>
   <application name ="MyApplication">
      <service>
        <wellknown type="FullyQualifiedName,AssemblyName" mode="Singleton"
           objectUri="MyClass.rem"
      </service>
   </application>
</system.runtime.remoting>
```

Essentially, all that's required is specifying the fully qualified object name and assembly, the type of object (Singleton, Single Call), and the Uniform Resource Identifier (URI). If you plan on hosting the assembly in IIS, be aware that you need to use the *.rem* extension.

It's just as simple to configure the client application to consume the assembly. The only difference is that the mode doesn't need to be specified and the URI needs to point to the virtual directory and port of the machine that the object is to be hosted on. So assuming that you are hosting it on your local machine on port 5000, the configuration for the client would look like the following example:

```
<system.runtime.remoting>
  <application name ="MyClientApplication">
    <service>
      <well known type="FullyQualifiedName, AssemblyName"
        url="http://localhost:5000/MyClass.rem"
    </service>
  </application>
</system.runtime.remoting>
```

Lab: Get a Database Connection String

In this lab, you create a configuration file and store a database connection string in it. If you encounter a problem completing an exercise, the completed projects are available on the companion CD in the Code folder.

▶ **Exercise: Retrieve a Connection String from a Configuration File**

In this exercise, you create an entry in a configuration file to store a connection string to a SQL Server database and then write client code to retrieve it.

1. Open Visual Studio 2005. Select File, New, Project, and then select your language of choice. Select the Windows project type, and choose Console Application. You will see a dialog box like the one shown in Figure 9-4.

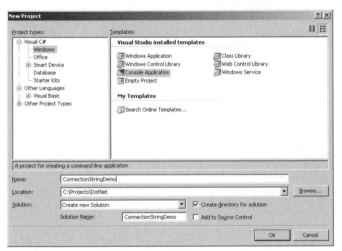

Figure 9-4   Create a new console application

2. Name the project ConnectionStringDemo.

3. Now select Project, Add New Item, and then choose Application Configuration File, as shown in Figure 9-5.

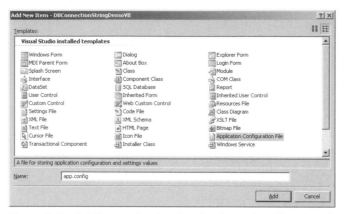

Figure 9-5 Adding an Application Configuration File using the Visual Studio 2005 IDE

4. In the resulting XML file app.config, add a configuration section named *<connectionStrings>*. Next add sections named *AdventureWorksString* and *MarsEnabledSqlServer2005String*. Set the *providerName* for each section to *"System.Data.SqlClient"*.

```
<connectionStrings>
   <clear/>
   <add name="AdventureWorksString"
      providerName="System.Data.SqlClient"
      connectionString="Data Source=localhost;Initial Catalog=AdventureWorks;
      Integrated Security=true"/>
   <add name="MarsEnabledSqlServer2005String"
      providerName="System.Data.SqlClient"
      connectionString="Server=Aron1;Database=pubs;
      Trusted_Connection=True;MultipleActiveResultSets=true" />
</connectionStrings>
```

5. Add each connection string exactly as it appears in the preceding code, except that the *connectionStrings* attribute value must appear all on one line.

6. Create a class called *DemoConnectionStringHandler* by selecting Project, Add New Item, and then Add Class. Name it DemoConnectionStringHandler.cs or DemoConnectionStringHandler.vb, depending on your language of choice.

7. Add project references as necessary to the *System.Configuration.dll*, *System.Data.SqlClient.dll*, *System.Data.OleDb.dll*, *System.Data.Odbc.dll* and *System.Data.OracleClient.dll* assemblies. Do this by right-clicking your project and selecting Add Reference. On the .NET tab, add each of the libraries just mentioned. Now add each of the methods provided in the following code::

```
'VB
Imports System.Diagnostics
Imports System.Configuration
Imports System.Data
Imports System.Data.SqlClient
```

```vbnet
Imports System.Data.OleDb
Imports System.Data.Odbc
Imports System.Data.OracleClient
Imports System.Text

Public Enum RetrievalType
    ByName = 0
    ByProviderType = 1
End Enum

Public Class DemoConnectionStringHandler

    Public Shared Sub GetSpecificConnectionString(ByVal type As _
        RetrievalType, ByVal typeOrName As String)
        If typeOrName Is Nothing Or typeOrName = String.Empty Then
            Throw New ArgumentException("Name cannot be empty", "TypeOrName")
        End If
        Select Case type
            Case RetrievalType.ByName
                Dim MySettings As ConnectionStringSettings = _
                    ConfigurationManager.ConnectionStrings(typeOrName)
                If Not MySettings Is Nothing Then
                        Console.WriteLine(MySettings.ConnectionString)
                End If
            Case RetrievalType.ByProviderType
                Dim MyTypeSettings As ConnectionStringSettingsCollection = _
                    ConfigurationManager.ConnectionStrings
                If Not MyTypeSettings Is Nothing Then
                    For Each typeSettings As ConnectionStringSettings In _
                        MyTypeSettings
                        If typeSettings.ProviderName = typeOrName Then
                            Console.WriteLine("Connection String: " & _
                                typeSettings.ConnectionString)
                        End If
                    Next
                End If
        End Select
    End Sub
    Public Shared Sub GetAllConnectionStrings()
    Dim MySettings As ConnectionStringSettingsCollection = _
        ConfigurationManager.ConnectionStrings

    If Not MySettings Is Nothing Then
        Dim sb As New StringBuilder
        Dim individualSettings As ConnectionStringSettings

        For Each individualSettings In MySettings
            sb.Append("Full Connection String: " & _
            individualSettings.ConnectionString & Environment.NewLine)
            sb.Append("Provider Name: " & _
            individualSettings.ProviderName & Environment.NewLine)
            sb.Append("Section Name: " & individualSettings.Name &  Environment.NewLine)

        Next
        Console.WriteLine(sb.ToString)
    End If
    End Sub
End Class

// C#
using System;
using System.Data;
```

```csharp
using System.Collections.Generic;
using System.Text;
using System.Configuration;
using System.Diagnostics;
using System.Data.SqlClient;
using System.Data.OleDb;
using System.Data.OracleClient;
using System.Data.Odbc;
namespace ConnectionStringDemo
    {
    public enum RetrievalType
        {
        ByName = 0,
        ByProviderType = 1
        }
    class DemoConnectionStringHandler
        {
        private String _MyValue;
        public String MyValue
            {
            get { return this._MyValue; }
            set { this._MyValue = value; }
            }
        public static void GetSpecificConnectionString(RetrievalType type,
            String typeOrName)
            {
            if (typeOrName == string.Empty || typeOrName == null)
                {
                throw new ArgumentException("Name cannot be empty", "typeOrname");
                }
            switch (type)
                {
                case RetrievalType.ByName:
                    ConnectionStringSettings MySettings =
                    ConfigurationManager.ConnectionStrings[typeOrName];
                    Debug.Assert(MySettings != null,
        "The name does not appear to exist, verify it in the configuration file");
                    if (MySettings != null)
                        {
                        Console.WriteLine(MySettings.ConnectionString);
                        }
                    break;
                case RetrievalType.ByProviderType:
                    ConnectionStringSettingsCollection MyTypeSettings =
                    ConfigurationManager.ConnectionStrings;
                    Debug.Assert(MyTypeSettings != null,
                    "Type does not appear to be present.");
                    if (MyTypeSettings != null)
                        {
                        foreach (ConnectionStringSettings typeSettings in
                            MyTypeSettings)
                            {
                            if (typeSettings.ProviderName == typeOrName)
                                {
                                SqlConnection MyConnection = new
                                    SqlConnection(typeSettings.ConnectionString);
                                Console.WriteLine("Connection String " +
                                    typeSettings.ConnectionString);
                                }
                            }
```

```
                }
            break;
        }
    }
    public static void GetAllConnectionStrings()
        {
        ConnectionStringSettingsCollection MySettings =
            ConfigurationManager.ConnectionStrings;
        Debug.Assert(MySettings != null);
//Should fail if no values
//are present
        if (MySettings != null)
            {
            StringBuilder sb = new StringBuilder();
            foreach (ConnectionStringSettings individualSettings in
                MySettings)
                {
                sb.Append("Full Connection String: " +
                    individualSettings.ConnectionString + "\r\n");
                sb.Append("Provider Name: " +
                    individualSettings.ProviderName + "\r\n");
                sb.Append("Section Name: " +
                    individualSettings.Name + "\r\n");
                }
            Console.WriteLine(sb.ToString());
            }
    }
  }
}
```

8. Select the Program.cs file if you're using C# or Module1.vb if you're using Visual Basic. Add the following code to the *Main* method:

```
' VB
DemoConnectionStringHandler.GetAllConnectionStrings()
Console.ReadLine()
```

```
// C#
DemoConnectionStringHandler.GetAllConnectionStrings();
Console.ReadLine();
```

9. Press the F5 key or choose Build, Build Solution, and then run the application. The output should look similar to that shown in Figure 9-6.

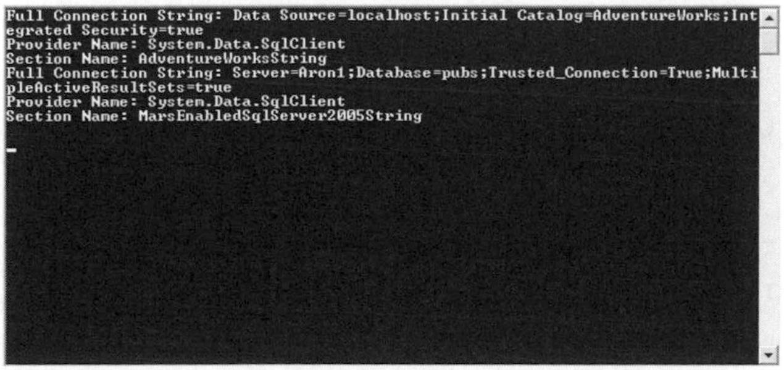

Figure 9-6   Console output from the *GetAllConnectionStrings* method

10. Select the Program.cs file if you're using C# or Module1.vb if you're using Visual Basic. Add the following lines of code to the *Main* method:

```
'VB
DemoConnectionStringHandler. _
    GetSpecificConnectionString(RetrievalType.ByName, "AdventureWorksString")
DemoConnectionStringHandler. _
    GetSpecificConnectionString(RetrievalType.ByName, _
    "MarsEnabledSqlServer2005String")
DemoConnectionStringHandler. _
    GetSpecificConnectionString(RetrievalType.ByProviderType, _
    "System.Data.SqlClient")
Console.ReadLine()

// C#
DemoConnectionStringHandler.GetSpecificConnectionString(RetrievalType.ByName,
    "AdventureWorksString");
DemoConnectionStringHandler.GetSpecificConnectionString(RetrievalType.ByName,
    "MarsEnabledSqlServer2005String");
DemoConnectionStringHandler.
    GetSpecificConnectionString(RetrievalType.ByProviderType,
    "System.Data.SqlClient");
Console.ReadLine();
```

11. Press the F5 key or select Build, Build Solution, and then run the application. The output should look like that shown in Figure 9-7.

Figure 9-7 Console output from the *GetAllConnectionStrings* and *GetSpecificConnectionString* methods

Lesson Summary

- The *System.Configuration* namespace is the primary vehicle for configuring .NET applications.

- The *codeBase* element is used to tell the .NET runtime which version of the .NET Framework to use.

- The *ConfigurationManager* class provides two default properties for storing configuration information, *AppSettings* and *ConnectionStrings*.

- The *appSettings* section of a configuration file can be used to store custom settings.

- Database connection strings should be accessed by using the *ConnectionStrings* property of the *ConfigurationManager* class.

- Leaving a connection string visible in plain text poses a huge security vulnerability. For security reasons, all connection strings should be encrypted.

- .NET remoting can be set up through configuration files. Adding a *<System.Runtime .Remoting>* section to the configuration file allows access to this.

Lesson Review

You can use the following questions to test your knowledge of the information in Lesson 1, "Configuration Settings." The questions are also available on the companion CD if you prefer to review them in electronic form.

NOTE Answers

Answers to these questions and explanations of why each answer choice is right or wrong are located in the "Answers" section at the end of the book.

---

1. Which code segment shows the best way to retrieve the *"Foo"* value of the following configuration file?

   ```xml
   <?xml version="1.0" encoding="utf-8" ?>
   <configuration>
     <appSettings>
       <add key="Foo" value="Hello World!"/>
     </appSettings>
   </configuration>
   ```

   A.

   ```
   NameValueCollection AllAppSettings = ConfigurationManager.AppSettings;
   Console.WriteLine(AllAppSettings["Hello World!"]);
   ```

   B.

   ```
   Console.WriteLine(ConfigurationSettings.AppSettings["Foo"]);
   ```

   C.

   ```
   NameValueCollection AllAppSettings = ConfigurationManager.AppSettings;
   Console.WriteLine(AllAppSettings[5]);
   ```

   D.

   ```
   NameValueCollection AllAppSettings = ConfigurationManager.AppSettings;
   Console.WriteLine(AllAppSettings["Foo"]);
   ```

2. What will happen if you try to use the following section of code to store a connection string?

```xml
<?xml version="1.0" encoding="utf-8" ?>
<configuration>
  <SqlConnectionStrings>
    <clear/>
    <add name="AdventureWorksString"
      providerName="System.Data.SqlClient"
      connectionString="Data Source=localhost;Initial
      Catalog=AdventureWorks;
      Integrated Security=true"/>
  </ SqlConnectionStrings >
</configuration>
```

A. There is no problem with this file, and the connection string values can be retrieved without any issues.

B. The *<clear/>* tag is unnecessary because there is only one connection string, and this tag will cause the file not to parse.

C. As long as you use the *SqlConnectionStrings* property of the *Configuration-Manager* object, it will retrieve the value correctly.

D. There is no predefined property for *SqlConnectionStrings*, so the file will not process correctly. If *SqlConnectionStrings* were changed to *connectionStrings*, everything would work properly.

3. Which of the following objects or interfaces is the best solution to provide customized configuration manipulation?

A. *IConfigurationSectionHandler*

B. *ConfigurationValidatorBase*

C. *IConfigurationSystem*

D. *ApplicationSettingsBase*

Lesson 2: Creating an Installer

Although it is possible to use Microsoft Windows Installer and the corresponding Setup and Deployment projects in Visual Studio 2005, it is sometimes necessary to include custom functionality that isn't provided out of the box by the Setup and Deployment projects. In these cases you should create custom installers, using the *Installer* class. The custom installers can then be used as part of and Setup and Deployment project or installed by using the InstallUtil.exe command-line tool.

After this lesson, you will be able to:

- Use the base installer.
- Commit an installation.
- Roll back an installation.

Estimated lesson time: 25 minutes

Using Base Installer

The primary tool that the .NET Framework gives developers to install applications is the *Installer* class. At a high level, the main reasons for using installers are as follows:

- They give your application a professional look and feel. Although this certainly wasn't always the case, all quality professional applications contain installers.

- They simplify what a user needs to do to use your product. The harder it is for users to get up and running with your product, the less likely they are to actually use it.

- They allow you to specify settings that the application needs to run (such as Web service URLs or database locations), and they allow you to set registry keys, make desktop shortcuts, and use many other such features that greatly enhance the user experience.

- They provide a mechanism for users to remove your application without leaving unwanted remnants (for example, files, images, or registry entries) on their machines.

The *Installer* class is the base class you use to create custom installers. There are also two specific predefined installers in the Framework that you can use, *AssemblyInstaller* and *ComponentInstaller*. We'll get back to those shortly. To be able to use the *Installer* class to meet your application's needs, it's necessary to understand how it works. The following steps must be followed to create and use a class derived from the *Installer* class:

1. Derive a class from the *Installer* class.

2. Override the *Install*, *Commit*, *Rollback*, and *Uninstall* methods.

3. Add the *RunInstallerAttribute* to your derived class, and set the *runInstaller* parameter to *true*.

4. Put your derived class in the assembly with your application to install.

5. Invoke the installers. For example, you can use the Installer Tool, InstallUtil.exe, or the *AssemblyInstaller* or *ComponentInstaller* class programmatically.

MORE INFO   *Installer* class

More information about the *Installer* class can be found at *http://msdn2.microsoft.com/en-US/library/system.configuration.install.installer(VS.80).aspx*.

Although most of this is straightforward, the last step needs some explanation. There are many ways to invoke your installers—for example, by using the InstallUtil.exe utility. The *Installer* class has an *Installers* property, which returns an instance of the *Installer-Collection*. This property is useful because it allows you to add multiple installers to a single assembly so that different isolated tasks can be run.

The next item you need to be aware of is the process of what happens when you start an installation. The first step is that the *Install* method is called, which commences the installation. If no error conditions are found, the *Commit* method is called at the end of the installation. The word "commit" has a special meaning for those familiar with the database and transactional worlds, and its meaning is the same here. Everything succeeds or fails as a group. And because installations are transactional in this sense, you won't have the problem of a partially installed application. This arrangement is a huge benefit. Think of a typical large application Microsoft Office. Imagine that the installation was 99 percent complete and then failed. If it wasn't transactional, you'd have many files and registry entries left on your machine that would be of no use. This alone would seriously clutter your machine. So Office is polite enough to restore the machine's state if an installation isn't successful, thereby cleaning up the mess it made. Classes that derive from *Installer* extend this courtesy as well. However, a trigger needs to be set to indicate that the installation was successful, and therefore, no cleanup is necessary. The mechanism to accomplish this is the *Commit* method.

Similarly, if you decide that you no longer want an application on a machine, there is an *Uninstall* method. This method allows users to simply remove the application and restore the computer's state, as opposed to manually looking through the application and deleting files and registry entries.

To facilitate the *Commit* method, the class has a delegate called the *Install-EventHandler*. Let's take a look at the specific implementations. To implement an installer, reference as necessary, import the *System, System.Collections, System.ComponentModel,* and *System.Configuration.Install* namespaces, and follow these steps:

1. Create a class that inherits from the *Installer* class and is marked with the *RunInstallerAttribute* attribute, passing True for the *runInstaller* parameter:

```
' VB
<System.ComponentModel.RunInstallerAttribute(True)>_
Public Class CustomInstaller
    Inherits Installer
End Class

// C#
namespace CustomInstaller
{
    [System.ComponentModel.RunInstaller(true)]
    public class CustomInstaller : Installer
    {
    }
}
```

2. Override each of the four main methods (*Install, Commit, Rollback,* and *Uninstall*) and wire up the *Committed* and *Committing* events in the constructor:

```
' VB
Public Sub New()
  MyBase.New()
  ' Wire up the Committed event.
  AddHandler Me.Committed, AddressOf CustomInstaller_Committed
  ' Wire up the Committing event.
  AddHandler Me.Committing, AddressOf CustomInstaller_Committing
End Sub

' Event handler for Committing event.
Private Sub CustomInstaller_Committing(ByVal sender As Object, _
  ByVal e As InstallEventArgs)

  'Committing event occurred
End Sub

' Event handler for Committed event.
Private Sub CustomInstaller_Committed(ByVal sender As Object, _
  ByVal e As InstallEventArgs)

  ' Committed event occurred
End Sub

' Overriden Install method.
Public Overrides Sub Install(ByVal savedState As IDictionary)
  MyBase.Install(savedState)
End Sub

' Overriden Commit method.
Public Overrides Sub Commit(ByVal savedState As IDictionary)
```

```
    MyBase.Commit(savedState)
End Sub

' Overriden Rollback method.
Public Overrides Sub Rollback(ByVal savedState As IDictionary)
  MyBase.Rollback(savedState)
End Sub

' Overriden Uninstall method.
Public Overrides Sub Uninstall(ByVal savedState As IDictionary)
  MyBase.Uninstall(savedState)
End Sub

// C#
public CustomInstaller() : base()
{
  // Wire up the Committed event.
  this.Committed +=
    new InstallEventHandler(CustomInstaller_Committed);
  // Wire up the Committing event.
  this.Committing +=
    new InstallEventHandler(CustomInstaller_Committing);
}

// Event handler for Committing event.
private void CustomInstaller_Committing(object sender, InstallEventArgs e)
{
 //Committing event occurred
}

// Event handler for Committed event.
private void CustomInstaller_Committed(object sender, InstallEventArgs e)
{
 //Committed event occurred
}

// Overriden Install method.
public override void Install(IDictionary savedState)
{
  base.Install(savedState);
}

// Overriden Commit method.
public override void Commit(IDictionary savedState)
{
  base.Commit(savedState);
}

// Overriden Rollback method.
public override void Rollback(IDictionary savedState)
{
  base.Rollback(savedState);
}

// Overriden Uninstall method.
public override void Uninstall(IDictionary savedState)
{
  base.Uninstall(savedState);
}
```

Committing an Installation

At each juncture, all we are doing is overriding the base class's implementation and putting in our own. The only other noteworthy item is that within the constructor of the class, an *InstallEventHandler* delegate is being added and it's being wired to the *Committed* and *Committing* events. Because those are both events, they differ from the methods in that there's no need to call the base class's implementation. After all, the base class doesn't know or care about such events and whether they ever happen.

Earlier I mentioned the *Installers* property. Let's revisit it for a second. You might have multiple installers that do multiple things. The more complex your installation, the more likely this is to be the case. In simple installs, there will be only one item in the collection. In other installs, there might be many. Let's examine how this works.

When the class derived from the *Installer* class is invoked, each item in the collection is iterated and the corresponding methods are called:

- If you had a successful install, the *Commit* method is called.
- If there was a failure, the *Rollback* method is called.
- If the application is being removed, the *Uninstall* method is called.

To launch an installer programmatically, either the *AssemblyInstaller* or *Component-Installer* class is used. To use either of them, two steps are necessary:

1. Create an instance of either object.
2. Call the method or methods corresponding to the actions that you want the installer to perform.

Again, this process is best illustrated by an example where the code is called from the Main procedure of a Console application:

```vb
'VB
Public Sub Main(ByVal args() As String)
  Dim actions As IDictionary = New Hashtable()

  Try
    'Create an instance of the AssemblyInstaller class.
    Dim customAssemblyInstaller As New _
      AssemblyInstaller("CustomInstaller.dll",args)
    'Use new install context
    customAssemblyInstaller.UseNewContext = True
    'Install the CustomInstaller assembly.
    customAssemblyInstaller.Install(actions)
    'Commit the installation of CustomInstaller assembly.
    customAssemblyInstaller.Commit(actions)
  Catch e As Exception
    Console.WriteLine(e.Message)
```

```
    End Try
End Sub

// C#
static void Main(string[] args)
{
  IDictionary actions = new Hashtable();

  try
  {
    // Create an instance of the AssemblyInstaller class.
    AssemblyInstaller customAssemblyInstaller = new
      AssemblyInstaller("CustomInstaller.dll", args);
    // Use new install context
    customAssemblyInstaller.UseNewContext = true;
    // Install the CustomInstaller assembly.
    customAssemblyInstaller.Install(actions);
    // Commit the installation of the CustomInstaller assembly.
    customAssemblyInstaller.Commit(actions);
  }
  catch (Exception e)
  {
    Console.WriteLine(e.Message);
  }
}
```

Rolling Back an Installation

In the previous example you installed an assembly, but you can just as easily uninstall an application by calling the *Uninstall* method instead of the *Install* class, as shown in this example:

```
'VB
Public Sub Main(ByVal args() As String)
  Dim actions As IDictionary = New Hashtable()
  Try
    'Create an instance of the AssemblyInstaller class.
    Dim customAssemblyInstaller As New _
      AssemblyInstaller("CustomInstaller.dll", args)
    'Use new install context
    customAssemblyInstaller.UseNewContext = True
    'Uninstall the CustomInstaller assembly.
    customAssemblyInstaller.Uninstall(actions)
    'Commit the uninstallation of CustomInstaller assembly.
    customAssemblyInstaller.Commit(actions)
  Catch e As Exception
    Console.WriteLine(e.Message)
  End Try
End Sub

// C#
static void Main(string[] args)
{
  IDictionary actions = new Hashtable();
```

```
try
{
  // Create an instance of the AssemblyInstaller class.
  AssemblyInstaller customAssemblyInstaller = new
    AssemblyInstaller("CustomInstaller.dll", args);
  // Use new install context
  customAssemblyInstaller.UseNewContext = true;
  // Uninstall the CustomInstaller assembly.
  customAssemblyInstaller.Uninstall(actions);
  // Commit the uninstallation of the CustomInstaller assembly.
  customAssemblyInstaller.Commit(actions);
}
catch (Exception e)
{
  Console.WriteLine(e.Message);
}
}
```

To uninstall the application programmatically, follow these steps:

1. Create a new *AssemblyInstaller* or *ComponentInstaller* object.

2. Specify the name of the assembly or application.

3. Call the *Uninstall* method.

To roll back an installation instead of uninstalling it, a similar methodology is used. Assuming the same facts as in the preceding example, all that is needed is a call to the *Rollback* method:

```
' VB
customAssemblyInstaller.Rollback(actions)
```

```
// C#
customAssemblyInstaller.Rollback(actions);
```

Lab: Set and Roll Back a Registry Key

In this lab, you create a custom installer that creates a Windows registry key and then rolls it back if the program is uninstalled. If you encounter a problem completing an exercise, the completed projects are available on the companion CD in the Code folder.

▶ **Exercise: Set and Roll Back a Registry Key**

In this exercise, you create a custom installer that creates or removes a Windows Registry key (depending on whether you install or uninstall the custom installer) by using the Installer Tool, InstallUtil.exe.

1. Copy the CustomInstaller.sln solution and associated project (CustomInstaller) from the companion CD, and open in Visual Studio 2005.

2. Open the *CustomInstaller.cs* or *CustomInstaller.vb* component file in Code view.

3. When the *CustomInstaller* class is installed it should create a new registry sub key named CustomKey, in the Software key of the HKEY_CURRENT_USER hive. Append the following code to the overridden *Install* method:

```
'VB
'Create new registry sub key
Registry.CurrentUser.CreateSubKey("Software\CustomKey")
```

```
// C#
// Create new registry sub key
Registry.CurrentUser.CreateSubKey(@"Software\CustomKey");
```

4. When the *CustomInstaller* class is uninstalled it should remove the registry sub key named CustomKey from the Software key of the HKEY_CURRENT_USER hive. Append the following code to the overridden *Uninstall* method:

```
'VB
'Remove registry sub key
Registry.CurrentUser.DeleteSubKey("Software\CustomKey")
```

```
// C#
// Remove registry sub key
Registry.CurrentUser.DeleteSubKey(@"Software\CustomKey");
```

5. Build the solution and fix any build errors.

6. Open a Visual Studio Command Prompt in the bin\Debug folder in which you have just built the CustomInstaller.dll.

7. Run the Installer Tool to install the CustomInstaller.dll assembly:

```
InstallUtil.exe CustomInstaller.dll
```

Log and state files have now been created in the bin\Debug folder.

8. Open the Registry Editor and check that HKEY_CURRENT_USER\Software\ CustomKey key has been created.

9. Run the Installer Tool to uninstall the CustomInstaller.dll assembly:

```
InstallUtil.exe /u CustomInstaller.dll
```

The state file has now been deleted from the bin\Debug folder, and the HKEY_CURRENT_USER\Software\CustomKey registry key has been removed.

Lesson Summary

- The *Installer* class provides a framework for creating custom installation packages for .NET applications.

- If an installation fails, the *Installer* will automatically undo any changes it has made. This includes changes to the file system, Start menu, Windows registry, and Desktop.

- The *Commit* method of the *Installer* class signals that the installation was successful and that changes can be persisted.

- The *Rollback* method of the *Installer* class signals that there was an error and that all modifications should be undone.

- The *Uninstall* method of the *Installer* class provides the primary mechanism for completely undoing an application installation after it has been successfully committed.

- The *AssemblyInstaller* and *ComponentInstaller* classes are used to programmatically install an assembly.

- The Installer Tool, InstallUtil.exe, can be used from the command line to install an assembly.

Lesson Review

You can use the following questions to test your knowledge of the information in Lesson 2, "Creating an Installer." The questions are also available on the companion CD if you prefer to review them in electronic form.

NOTE Answers

Answers to these questions and explanations of why each answer choice is right or wrong are located in the "Answers" section at the end of the book.

---

1. What base class should you derive from when creating custom installers?

    A. The *InstallContext* class

    B. The *InstallerCollection* class

    C. The *ManagedInstallerClass* class

    D. The *Installer* class

2. You want to create an installation that, in the event of failure, undoes everything it has done so far. Which of the following mechanisms accomplishes that task?

    A. The *Rollback* method of the *Installer* class

    B. The *Undo* method of the *Installer* class

    C. The *Clear* and *Rollback* methods of the *Installer* class

    D. The *Uninstall* method of the *Installer* class.

Lesson 3: Using the .NET Framework 2.0 Configuration Tool

The .NET Framework 2.0 Configuration tool is a powerful visual tool that enables developers to manage just about any aspect of configuration for an assembly. The .NET Framework 2.0 Configuration tool, which is installed with the .NET Framework SDK version 2.0, runs as a Microsoft Management Console snap-in and is available in all recent versions of Microsoft Windows including Windows 2000, Windows XP, and Windows Server 2003. Although it certainly has other implementations, the .NET Framework 2.0 Configuration tool primarily helps developers do three tasks:

- Configure and manage assemblies located in the GAC.
- Adjust the code access security policy.
- Adjust remoting services.

> **After this lesson, you will be able to:**
> - Launch the .NET Framework 2.0 Configuration tool for any version of the Framework installed on a machine.
> - Add an application to configure.
> - Change configuration settings for an application.
> - Restore configuration settings for an application.
>
> **Estimated lesson time: 15 minutes**

Browsing Configurations

The first thing necessary to use the tool is to open it. You can access it under Administrative Tools (.NET Framework *X.X* Configuration), or you can launch it from the SDK Command Prompt.

Figure 9-8 shows what the tool should look like.

You have the following options at this point:

- Manage The Assembly Cache
- Manage Configured Assemblies
- Configure Code Access Security Policy
- Adjust Remoting Services
- Manage Individual Applications

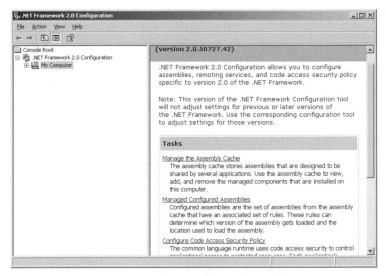

Figure 9-8   .NET Framework 2.0 Configuration tool

I'll go through each of these options and discuss what they do. The first option is Manage The Assembly Cache. The following actions can be taken by using this option:

- View List Of Assemblies In The Assembly Cache.

- Add An Assembly To The Assembly Cache.

By selecting View List Of Assemblies In The Assembly Cache, you'll be presented with everything available in the GAC.

Adding a strong-named assembly to the cache is just as simple. All you need to do is select Add An Assembly To The Assembly Cache and browse to a given assembly.

The next option is Manage Configured Assemblies. The following actions can be taken by using this option:

- View List Of Configured Assemblies.

- Configure An Assembly.

The last option that allows you to browse configurations is Manage Individual Applications. The only option here involves adding an application to configure. It's important to note that if you haven't added any assemblies using this tool, there might be no assemblies there other than the ones listed in the GAC.

Changing a Configuration

The process for changing a configuration is equally straightforward, as illustrated by the following steps:

1. Under the Configured Assemblies tree node, select Configure An Assembly.

2. A wizard will pop up asking you to select the location of the assembly.

3. Select the assembly you want to configure.

4. A dialog box like the one shown in Figure 9-9 will appear, allowing you to specify exactly what you want to do.

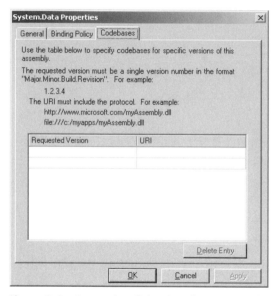

Figure 9-9   Properties dialog box for an assembly

On the Binding Policy tab, you can change the binding redirections. A typical use is switching from one release version to a newer one or vice versa.

On the Codebases tab, you can do the same. Here you can delete any given codebase or revert back to an earlier one by selecting it and clicking the Apply button.

Another area in which you might want to make changes is security settings. To manipulate them, follow these steps:

1. Open the .NET 2.0 Configuration tool, expand My Computer, and select the Runtime Security Policy node. Under this node, you can select multiple items to change—specifically the nodes Enterprise, Machine, and User.

2. Each of these nodes has a Code Groups section, a Permission Sets section, and a Policy Assemblies section. Choose whichever option you want to manipulate.

3. For each of the Enterprise, Machine, and User nodes, you can choose either to edit a code group's properties or add a child code group. The two main areas you can manipulate are the membership conditions and the permission sets. For example, you can change the Zone from Local Internet to My Computer. The screen to do this should look like Figure 9-10.

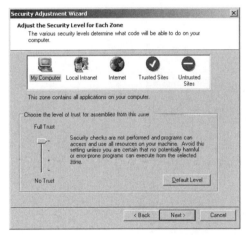

Figure 9-10   Security Adjustment Wizard, Adjust The Security Level For Each Zone page

There is a specific code group setting named *All_Code*. If you choose it, you'll see a dialog box informing you that "Code group grants all code full trust and forms the root of the code group tree." So this option could be used to easily bind *All_Code* evidence with a specific permission set. Editing permission sets is similar. You should see a dialog box similar to Figure 9-11 when you select the Permission Set tab.

Therefore, for each zone, you can view permission sets, change them, or do both. Let's walk through two common tasks, creating a permission set and creating a code group. To create a permission set, simply do the following:

1. Open the configuration tool and expand the My Computer, Runtime Security Policy, and Machine nodes.

2. Under the Machine node, right-click Permission Sets and select New. You should see a dialog box named Create Permission Set, as shown in Figure 9-12.

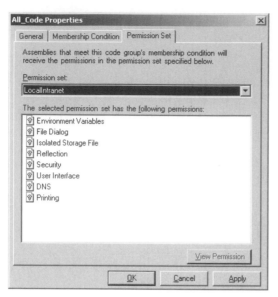

Figure 9-11 All_Code Properties - Permission Set tab

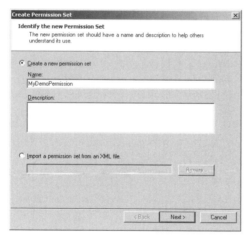

Figure 9-12 Create Permission Set dialog box

3. Select Create A New Permission Set, and type **MyDemoPermission** in the Name text box.

4. Click Next.

5. Select Registry from the Available Permissions list. You should see a dialog box similar to Figure 9-13.

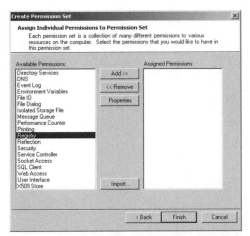

Figure 9-13   Available Permissions list of the Create Permission Set dialog box

6. Click the Add button. You should see a dialog box similar to Figure 9-14.

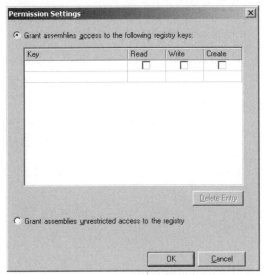

Figure 9-14   Permission Settings dialog box

7. Select the Read, Write, and Create permissions and insert the text **MyKeyValue** into the Key section, and click OK. You should see MyDemoPermission available in the Available Permissions section, when you click Finish.

To create a new code group, use the following steps:

1. Open the configuration tool, and expand the My Computer, Runtime Security Policy, Machine, and Code Groups nodes.

2. Right-click All Code, and select New. You should see a dialog box similar to the one shown in Figure 9-15.

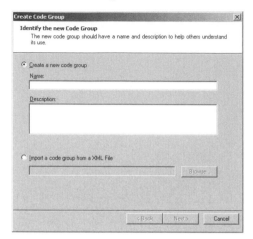

Figure 9-15   Create Code Group dialog box

3. In the Name text box, type **MyCodeGroup** and click Next.

4. When prompted to choose a condition type, choose the Application Directory option and click Next.

5. Choose MyDemoPermission, and click Next and Finish.

At this point, you've successfully created both a permission set and a code group. Another option is increasing an assembly's trust level. To accomplish this, do the following:

1. Open the configuration tool, and expand My Computer. Select the Runtime Security Policy node.

2. Select the Increase Assembly Trust option in the right pane.

From there, you'll be prompted to specify the assembly, and then you can make whatever changes you feel are necessary. If you've done everything correctly, you should see a dialog box similar to the one shown in Figure 9-16.

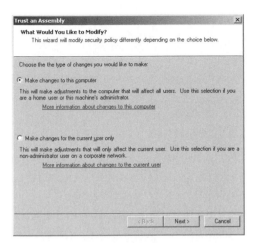

Figure 9-16   Trust An Assembly dialog box

Resetting a Configuration

There are multiple things you can reset in a configuration, with the most common being security settings. The easiest way to do this is to select the Runtime Security Policy node and choose the Reset All Policy Levels option.

CAUTION   **Resetting a configuration**

Reset a configuration only if you are sure it will not interfere with the operation of your computer. Resetting a configuration will reset all security policy features that have been set on your computer. Unless you are certain that resetting these values will not cause problems on your machine, you should take great caution when using this feature.

You'll get a confirmation box asking if you really want to do this, because once you do it you can't undo it. After selecting Reset All Policy Levels, you'll see the dialog box shown in Figure 9-17—don't click Yes unless you're sure you want to reset everything.

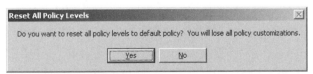

Figure 9-17   Verifying that you want to reset security settings

The other option involves an individual assembly. Once you've added an assembly, you can select its node and choose the Fix This Assembly option. The only catch to using this tool is that for it to work properly, the application had to run successfully at least once. Once the tool runs, it prompts you for a previous version to use; and once you select it, it will use that version, thereby undoing or restoring any changes that have been made. Again, this tool should be used with caution because if you reset a configuration, you will have a hard time retrieving those settings if that wasn't what you wanted.

Lab: Change and Restore Application Settings

In this lab, you will increase the trust of an application and subsequently reset it. You will use a strong-named version of the application created in the Lab exercise in Lesson 1 of this chapter, ConnectionStringDemo, to provide evidence used by the .NET Framework 2.0 Configuration tool when trusting. If you haven't done so already, copy the \Code\Chapter09\Lesson3\ConnectionStringDemo folder from the companion CD.

▶ **Exercise: Change and Restore Application Settings**

1. Select Start, Control Panel, Administrative Tools, and then .NET Framework 2.0 Configuration tool.

2. Select the Runtime Security Policy node, and select the Increase Assembly Trust option.

3. Select the Make Changes To This Computer option and click Next.

4. In the Trust An Assembly Wizard, on the Which Assembly Do You Want To Trust page, browse to and select the ConnectionStringDemo.exe assembly in the Chapter09\Lesson3\ConnectionStringDemo folder. Click Next.

5. On the Trust This Assembly Or All Assemblies From This Publisher? page, select This One Assembly, and click Next.

6. On the Choose The Minimum Level Of Trust For The Assembly page, select Full Trust, click Next, and then click Finish.

7. Expand the .NET Framework 2.0 Configuration and Applications nodes. If no assemblies are listed below the Applications node, click Add An Application To Configure, and select one of the assemblies you created in a previous exercise.

8. Select an assembly from the Applications node, and choose the Fix This Application option, which you can see in the .NET Framework 2.0 Configuration MMC snap-in shown in Figure 9-18.

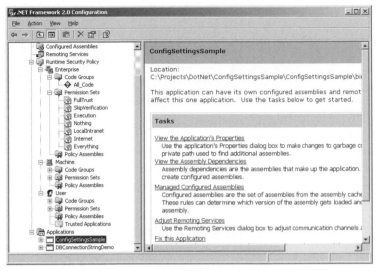

Figure 9-18   .NET Framework 2.0 Configuration tool

9. If there are existing configurations, you will be presented with each one, and you can choose which configuration you want to revert to. This will effectively undo any changes that have been made since then.

Lesson Summary

- You can use the .NET Framework 2.0 Configuration tool to visually manage the default configuration of an application, create custom code groups, create custom permission sets, and manage export policies.

- To view items in the GAC or to add items to it, use the Assembly Cache option under the My Computer setting of the .NET Framework Configuration tool.

- Code groups in .NET are named after the evidence they provide.

- All code groups must have unique names. Duplicate names will be disallowed by the tool.

- The *Enterprise* and *User* policies contain only a single code group, *All_Code*.

- To grant unrestricted permission to an application, use the *All_Code* code group in either the Enterprise or User groups.

- The *Machine* policy, unlike *Enterprise* and *User*, defaults to the Nothing permission set.

- To find permission sets in the *Machine* policy, you must use code groups, such as *My_Computer_Zone* or *Internet_Zone*.

Lesson Review

You can use the following questions to test your knowledge of the information in Lesson 3, "Using the .NET Framework 2.0 Configuration Tool." The questions are also available on the companion CD if you prefer to review them in electronic form.

NOTE Answers

Answers to these questions and explanations of why each answer choice is right or wrong are located in the "Answers" section at the end of the book.

---

1. What can be handled by using the .NET Framework 2.0 Configuration tool? (Choose all that apply.)

   A. View All running processes and manage their permission sets

   B. View All running services and manage their operation

   C. View All configured applications

   D. View All assemblies in the global assembly cache (GAC)

2. Which of the following items can be created by using the .NET Framework 2.0 Configuration tool?

   A. Permission sets

   B. Code sets

   C. Assembly sets

   D. Application sets

Lesson 4: Configuration Management

Configuration management, as its name implies, is the practice of controlling your application's configuration. Configuration management can entail performing tasks such as specifying which version of the runtime your application is supposed to use or telling your application what database it should connect to. Configuration management is inextricably intertwined with user satisfaction, so it must be handled well.

After this lesson, you will be able to:

■ Retrieve and store configuration settings.

■ Implement the interfaces in *System.Configuration*.

Estimated lesson time: 25 minutes

Getting and Storing Settings

The primary vehicle through which configuration settings are retrieved is the *ConfigurationManager* class. In the first lesson, we covered the various methods to open up configuration files, so please refer to that section if needed. Once you have successfully read in your configuration values, retrieving settings is straightforward. The following code shows the basic means of retrieval:

```
'VB
Dim AllAppSettings As NameValueCollection = ConfigurationManager.AppSettings
Console.WriteLine(AllAppSettings("MyFirstSetting"))
Console.WriteLine(AllAppSettings(0))

// C#
NameValueCollection AllAppSettings = ConfigurationManager.AppSettings;
Console.WriteLine(AllAppSettings["MyFirstSetting"]);
Console.WriteLine(AllAppSettings[0]);
```

Using the *AppSettings* property of the *ConfigurationManager* object, every value in the *appSettings* section of the configuration file is available. Assume that you have the following configuration file:

```
<appSettings>
    <add key="ApplicationName" value="Demo Application"/>
    <add key="ApplicationVersion" value="2.0.0.1"/>
    <add key="UserFirstName" value="John"/>
    <add key="UserLastName" value="Public"/>
</appSettings>
```

The value returned from the *AppSettings* property would be a collection with four objects. The keys of those objects would be *ApplicationName*, *ApplicationVersion*,

UserFirstName, and *UserLastName*. You can also reference them through their indices, so *ApplicationName* would be the 0th index, *ApplicationFirstName* would be the 1st, and so on.

The next way to retrieve values is through the *ConnectionStrings* property. The process for doing this was discussed in depth in the first lesson, so I won't repeat it here.

A final way to retrieve values is through the *GetSection* method of the *Configuration-Manager* object. Assume that you have the following configuration entry:

```
<configuration>
  <configSections>
    <sectionGroup name="MyFirstSectionGroup">
      <section name="MyFirstSection"
        type="ConnectionStringDemo.MyFirstSectionHandler, ConnectionStringDemo"/>
    </sectionGroup>
  </configSections>
  <MyFirstSectionGroup>
    <MyFirstSection>
      <Value>
        <Identifier>111</Identifier>
        <SettingValue>System.Data.SqlClient</SettingValue>
      </Value>
      <Value>
        <Identifier>112</Identifier>
        <SettingValue>System.Data.OleDb</SettingValue>
      </Value>
      <Value>
        <Identifier>113</Identifier>
        <SettingValue>System.Data.Odbc</SettingValue>
      </Value>
    </MyFirstSection>
  </MyFirstSectionGroup>
</configuration>
```

The first thing you need to do is declare in the *configSections* portion of the file that you intend to use a section group called *MyFirstSectionGroup* and a section called *MyFirst-Section*. Theoretically, you can have limitless section groups and sections in here, and it makes sense to have as many section groups and sections as units of isolation. It's not uncommon for large enterprise applications to have many section groups and multiple sections specified here. Now this can be retrieved as follows:

```
' VB
Dim vals As ValuesHandler = CType(ConfigurationManager. _
  GetSection("MyFirstSectionGroup/MyFirstSection"), ValuesHandler)

// C#
ValuesHandler vals = ConfigurationManager.GetSection(
  "MyFirstSectionGroup/MyFirstSection") as ValuesHandler;
```

The value returned is of type *Object*, so it will need to be cast to a specific object to be of much use. Doing this is discussed in the next section under the *IConfiguration-SectionHandler* topic.

Saving settings is even simpler. In the simplest form of saving settings, all you need to do is call the *Save* or *SaveAs* method of the *Configuration* object instance you're using. *Save* will add any sections you might have added or remove any sections you've removed, provided that you've set the *ForceSave* property of the *SectionInformation* property of the *ConfigurationSection* object to *true* and have saved the file in the *ApplicationName*.exe.config format. If you don't specify the *ForceSave* to be *true*, the values will be ignored when you choose either *Save* or *SaveAs* if they have not been modified. *SaveAs* behaves similarly to the *SaveAs* feature in other Windows applications; it will save the settings in a file that you specify.

Implementing Configuration Interfaces

Like most aspects of the Framework, the *System.Configuration* class has multiple interfaces that developers can implement to achieve precise functionality. Some of these interfaces, such as the *IConfigurationSectionHandler* interface, are meant to be used in general purpose libraries. Others, such as the *ISettingsProviderService* and *IApplicationSettingsProvider* interfaces, provide much more general-purpose functionality. The *ISettingsProviderService* interface, for example, is used almost exclusively for building design-time support for components or enhancing debuggers. It is of relatively limited use for most development scenarios.

There are times when you need a higher degree of granularity with your classes, and one of the best ways to get it is through the *System.Configuration.IConfigurationSectionHandler* interface. This interface has been deprecated in version 2.0 of the .NET Framework but it forms the basis for its replacement, the *ConfigurationSection* class. Although you are still free to use *IConfigurationSectionHandler*, it's preferable to use the new *ConfigurationSection* class and its supporting classes.

In the examples in the first lesson, we were manipulating two specific sections of the configuration file, the *appSettings* and *connectionStrings* settings. In addition to using those sections, you can add items to the *configSections* section of the configuration file. Such modifications can be done at the application-configuration level, the machine-configuration level, the Web-configuration level, or all three. This flexibility allows the developer to add multiple sections that are isolated from the others (as opposed to using the general-purpose *appSettings* section) and use a designated class to read those values. This is logically equivalent to what we did in the example in the preceding section.

One of the first tasks you need to perform to implement the *IConfigurationSection-Handler* interface is to create a *sectionGroup* object within the *configSections* section of the configuration file. *ConfigurationSection* objects are stored in the *Configuration-SectionCollection* collection, accessible using the *Sections* property of the *Configuration* object. A typical declaration will look like this:

```
<configSections>
  <sectionGroup name="MyFirstSectionGroup">
    <section name="MyFirstSection"
      type="ConnectionStringDemo.MyFirstSectionHandler, ConnectionStringDemo"/>
  </sectionGroup>
</configSections>
```

A similar grouping occurs with a *ConfigurationSectionGroup* and its corresponding *ConfigurationSectionGroupCollection* (which is merely a container for *Configuration-SectionGroup* objects). To manage them, the *Configuration* class is used:

```
'VB
Dim config As Configuration = _
    ConfigurationManager.OpenExeConfiguration(ConfigurationUserLevel.None)
Dim DemoGroups As ConfigurationSectionGroupCollection = config.SectionGroups

For Each groupName As String In DemoGroups.Keys
    Console.WriteLine(groupName)
Next

// C#
Configuration config =
    ConfigurationManager.OpenExeConfiguration(
    ConfigurationUserLevel.None);
ConfigurationSectionGroupCollection
    DemoGroups = config.SectionGroups;
foreach (String groupName in DemoGroups.Keys)
    {
    Console.WriteLine(groupName);
    }
```

When I mentioned earlier that editing and maintaining configuration files on your own can be a chore, I was referring precisely to an issue that often arises in a typical scenario like the one just shown. The specifics of this will be revealed shortly.

Notice that first we created a *configSections* group within the configuration file. Next, we declared that we were going to name our section *MyFirstSection*. After specifying a name, the type needs to be specified. To specify the type, you need to reference the fully qualified object name, followed by the assembly name. This task needs to be done with great caution because even minor typing errors can result in serious problems. In this example, we're just specifying one configuration section; however, there's theoretically no limit to how many we can add. In enterprise-level applications, it's not uncommon to find as many as 5 to 15 custom sections.

After the declaration is in place, the next step is creating the actual section. This needs to be placed outside of all other configuration elements. Therefore, a fictitious declaration and section could look like the following code snippet:

```
<configSections>
  <sectionGroup name="MyFirstSectionGroup">
    <section name="MyFirstSection"
      type="ConnectionStringDemo.MyFirstSectionHandler, ConnectionStringDemo"/>
  </sectionGroup>
</configSections>
<MyFirstSectionGroup>
  <MyFirstSection>
    <Value>
      <Identifier>111</Identifier>
      <SettingValue>System.Data.SqlClient</SettingValue>
    </Value>
    <Value>
      <Identifier>112</Identifier>
      <SettingValue>System.Data.OleDb</SettingValue>
    </Value>
    <Value>
      <Identifier>113</Identifier>
      <SettingValue>System.Data.Odbc</SettingValue>
    </Value>
  </MyFirstSection>
</MyFirstSectionGroup>
```

From here, there's a tremendous amount of flexibility in how to approach managing these settings, but at a minimum you need to implement the *IConfigurationSectionHandler* interface. Specifically, you can retrieve items by attribute, element, or any combination thereof. Fortunately, this is a simple interface to implement and it only requires that one method be implemented—namely, the *Create* method. With respect to implementation, though, there are an infinite number of ways to handle it. Let's use the example shown earlier where we were storing an *Identifier* and a *SettingValue*. This is a basic *Key/Value* pair, and it's used only for illustration. Now we need to create a class, which we'll name *MyFirstSectionHandler*, that implements the *IConfigurationSectionHandler* interface.

```
'VB
Public Function Create(ByVal parent As Object, _
  ByVal configContext As Object, _
  ByVal section As System.Xml.XmlNode) As Object _
  Implements System.Configuration.IConfigurationSectionHandler.Create

  Dim configValues As New Hashtable
  Dim root As XmlElement = CType(section, XmlElement)
  Dim tempValue As String = ""

  For Each parentNode As XmlNode In root.ChildNodes
    For Each childNode As XmlNode In parentNode.ChildNodes
      If childNode.Name = "Identifier" Then
        tempValue = childNode.InnerText
      End If
```

```
        If childNode.Name = "SettingValue" Then
          configValues(tempValue) = childNode.InnerText
        End If
      Next
    Next

    Dim myHandler As New ValuesHandler(configValues)
    Return myHandler
End Function

// C#
public object Create(object parent, object configContext, System.Xml.XmlNode section)
{
    Hashtable configValues = new Hashtable();
    XmlElement root = section as XmlElement;
    String tempValue = string.Empty;

    foreach (XmlNode parentNode in root.ChildNodes)
    {
        foreach (XmlNode childNode in parentNode.ChildNodes)
        {
            if (childNode.Name == "Identifier")
            {
                tempValue = childNode.InnerText;
            }

            if (childNode.Name == "SettingValue")
            {
                configValues[tempValue] = childNode.InnerText;
            }
        }
    }

    ValuesHandler myHandler = new ValuesHandler(configValues);

    return myHandler;
}
```

For convenience, we'll create another helper class that stores a *HashTable* object and provides a mechanism by which values can be retrieved from the table:

```
'VB
Public Class ValuesHandler
  Private customValue As Hashtable

  Public Sub New(ByVal configValues As Hashtable)
    Me.customValue = configValues
  End Sub

  Public Function GetValueFromKey(ByVal key As String) As String
    Return CType(Me.customValue(key), String)
  End Function
End Class

// C#
```

```
public class ValuesHandler
{
  private Hashtable customValue;

  public ValuesHandler(Hashtable configValues)
  {
    this.customValue = configValues;
  }

  public String GetValueFromKey(String key)
  {
    return this.customValue[key] as String;
  }
}
```

Now let's assume that we used a completely different methodology for the configuration file. For instance, instead of using element-based values, assume we were using attribute-based values. Our XML parsing routine would have to take this into account to populate the values. So, in effect, what happens inside the *Create* method is dependent on the XML you want to store in the configuration file and the corresponding object or objects you want to use to hold those values. The point to keep in mind is that this implementation is just an example and virtually any implementation you chose would be valid as long as the XML was valid and well formed.

At this point, everything is in place and the application is ready to consume these values. There are two primary methods to accomplish this. The first, *ConfigSettings .GetConfig* is obsolete and should be used with the same amount of caution one would apply to any obsolete method. The next one is the *ConfigurationManager*'s *GetSection* method:

```
' VB
Dim vals As ValuesHandler = CType(ConfigurationManager. _
  GetSection("MyFirstSectionGroup/MyFirstSection"), ValuesHandler)

// C#
ValuesHandler vals = ConfigurationManager.GetSection(
  "MyFirstSectionGroup/MyFirstSection") as ValuesHandler;
```

The key point with retrieval is to ensure that you specify the correct node or nodes. Although the nuances of XML parsing are out of the scope of this lesson, we need to specify the root region where the parsing should start. Whenever the class is initialized, it will call the *Create* method and parse the XML accordingly. Just for reference, here's the configuration snippet without the individual values:

```
<MyFirstSectionGroup>
  <MyFirstSection>
  </MyFirstSection>
</MyFirstSectionGroup>
```

MyFirstSectionGroup is the name of the section group, and that's where the processing begins. Via our call to *GetSection*, our code instructs the parser to start at MyFirstSection as the root node and begin processing from there.

In the .NET Framework 2.0, there are new ways to accomplish the same objectives, and fortunately, these new ways are much simpler to use and much more powerful. Assume for a moment that we wanted to create a *ConfigurationSection* named Chapter9Section. To create the declaration, the following should be done:

```
<configSections>
   <section name="Chapter9Section"
      type="Chapter9.Configuration.ConfigHandler, App_Code" />
</configSections>
```

Essentially, all we just did was add a custom *ConfigurationSection* to the *configSections* section of the configuration file, add a name to it, and then add the type. The first portion of the type section takes the fully qualified object name (*namespace.objectname*) a comma, and then the assembly name. This example used an ASP.NET 2.0 Web application that stored the class in the *App_Code* folder, so *App_Code* was used as the assembly name. So far, these are the same steps we would take to implement an *IConfiguration-SectionHandler* object. Keep in mind that the previous samples for the *IConfigurationSectionHandler* interface wrapped the section in a section group in the configuration file. This is optional, although recommended, much like using namespaces for your classes. However, in the following samples, you're working with a section only, not a section group.

The previous paragraph describes the declaration of the custom *ConfigurationSection*. Now it is necessary to implement it. For the sake of simplicity, we'll add a simple *ConfigurationSection* with two elements. Only one *ConfigurationSection* is being used in this example, although multiple *ConfigurationSections* can be used. When a *ConfigurationSection* is used, it is added to the *ConfigurationSectionCollection* and can be retrieved by a name or an index. Typically, as was done with *IConfigurationSectionHandler* objects, using the name to reference the section makes the most sense. (This is because it's a lot easier to remember something like "WebServiceSettings" than it is to remember that this was the ninth *ConfigurationSection*.)

A *ConfigurationSection* can be simple or as complex as you would like. Attributes can be used instead of elements, or multiple elements can be added. In short, you can use just about any combination that is necessary to accomplish a given objective. The following XML segment shows the code generated for our example (again, it simply shows a *ConfigurationSection* named "Chapter9Section" with a *ConfigurationElement* named "LastName" and a *ConfigurationElement* named "FirstName").

```
<Chapter9Section LastName="Ryan" FirstName="William"/>
```

You have seen how to set up a *ConfigurationSection* and add *ConfigurationSection* objects to the *ConfigurationSectionCollection,* but more needs to be done to use these objects. You can use the *ConfigurationSection* class as a base class from which to derive classes to consume these value. Following is a sample class named *ConfigHandler* that inherits from *ConfigurationSection*. It defines two properties, *FirstName* and *LastName,* that map to the *ConfigurationSection* just shown.

```vb
'VB
Namespace Chapter9.Configuration
  Public Class ConfigHandler
    Inherits ConfigurationSection

    <ConfigurationProperty("FirstName", IsRequired:=False, _
      DefaultValue:="NotGiven")> _
    Public Property FirstName() As String
      Get
        Return CType(Me("FirstName"), String)
      End Get
      Set(ByVal value As String)
        Me("FirstName") = value
      End Set
    End Property

    <ConfigurationProperty("LastName", IsRequired:=False, _
      DefaultValue:="NotGiven")> _
    Public Property LastName() As String
      Get
        Return CType(Me("LastName"), String)
      End Get
      Set(ByVal value As String)
        Me("LastName") = value
      End Set
    End Property
  End Class
End Namespace
```

```csharp
// C#
namespace Chapter9.Configuration
{
  public class ConfigHandler : ConfigurationSection
  {
    [ConfigurationProperty("LastName", IsRequired = false,
      DefaultValue = "NotGiven")]
    public String LastName
    {
      get
      {
        return (String) base["LastName"];
      }
      set
      {
```

```
      base["LastName"] = value;
    }
  }

  [ConfigurationProperty("FirstName", IsRequired = false, DefaultValue =
    "NotGiven")]
  public String FirstName
  {
    get
    {
      return (String) base["FirstName"];
    }
    set
    {
      base["FirstName"] = value;
    }
  }

  public ConfigHandler()
  {
  }
  }
}
```

Now, this class can be used to store and handle variables that map back to this class in the configuration file:

```
'VB
'Load configuration from web.config into configuration object
Dim Chapter9Config As System.Configuration.Configuration = _
  WebConfigurationManager.OpenWebConfiguration(Request.ApplicationPath)
'Retrieve the ChapterSection configuration section from
'configuration object
Dim Chapter9Section As Chapter9.Configuration.ConfigHandler = _
  CType(Chapter9Config.GetSection("Chapter9Section"), _
  Chapter9.Configuration.ConfigHandler)
'Output Chapter9Section configuration element attributes
Response.Write(Chapter9Section.FirstName)
Response.Write(Chapter9Section.LastName)

'Clear configuration sections from configuration object
Chapter9Config.Sections.Clear()
'Add new section
Chapter9Config.Sections.Add("Chapter9Section", Chapter9Section)
'Save to configuration file
Chapter9Config.Save()

// C#
// Load configuration from web.config into configuration object
Configuration Chapter9Config =
  WebConfigurationManager.OpenWebConfiguration(Request.ApplicationPath);
// Retrieve the ChapterSection configuration section from
// configuration object
Chapter9.Configuration.ConfigHandler Chapter9Section =
  (Chapter9.Configuration.ConfigHandler)
  Chapter9Config.GetSection("Chapter9Section");
```

```
// Output Chapter9Section configuration element attributes
Response.Write(Chapter9Section.FirstName);
Response.Write(Chapter9Section.LastName);

// Clear configuration sections from configuration object
Chapter9Config.Sections.Clear();
// Add new section
Chapter9Config.Sections.Add("Chapter9Section", Chapter9Section);
// Save to configuration file
Chapter9Config.Save();
```

By using the preceding code, you can read values directly from a custom *Configuration-Section* (provided it exists), write values to a custom *ConfigurationSection* (provided it exists) and create a custom *ConfigurationSection* if it doesn't yet exist.

Another useful interface used throughout the *System.Configuration* namespace is the *IApplicationSettingsProvider* interface. In the first lesson, we used the *ApplicationSettingsBase* class. The *ApplicationSettingsBase* class, among others, implements the *IApplicationSettingsProvider* interface. (As an aside, the *LocalFileSettingsProvider* class also implements *IApplicationSettingsProvider*.) This interface has three methods, which are described in Table 9-4.

Table 9-4 *IApplicationSettingsProvider* **Interface**

Name	Description
GetPreviousVersion	Returns the value of the specified settings property for the previous version of the same application.
Reset	Resets the application settings associated with the specified application to their default values.
Upgrade	Indicates to the provider that the application has been upgraded. This offers the provider an opportunity to upgrade its stored settings as appropriate.

This interface provides benefits that are consequently provided by all classes that implement the interface, such as the *ApplicationSettingsBase*. According to the MSDN Online documentation, those benefits include:

- Side-by-side execution of different versions of an application
- Retaining application settings when upgrading an application
- Resetting the application settings to their default values for the currently used version

While these benefits might or might not fit initial application deployments, the *Application-SettingsBase*, for instance, implements them and the functionality is there if you need it. There are a few other noteworthy items that differentiate this class from a class that implements the *IConfigurationSectionHandler* interface:

- Each property can be scoped at either the application or user level. You do not have this level of granularity with *IConfigurationSectionHandler* objects.

- Values that are scoped at the user level are stored differently than those scoped at the application level.

- If the *Application* attribute is used, an additional configuration file is created. This file follows the standard configuration naming convention with one alteration—it uses the computer's User Name and appends *.config* to the end of it. So if I was logged onto this machine as John Public, a separate configuration file would be created named JohnPublic.config.

- This is stored in a Windows Special Folder and can be accessed via the *Application* class through *Application.LocalUserAppDataPath*.

- Access is facilitated through the *LocalFileSettingsProvider* class.

By using strong typing, a great deal can be done to verify the validity of values in a configuration file. If you used an *IConfigurationSectionHandler* object, for instance, to populate an object containing an *Int32 Key* and a *String* value, you could detect that you were reading the value "Bill" instead of the number 1 and throw an exception. Strong type checking is one of the primary advantages that configuration files have over previous mechanisms. In many cases type verification will be necessary, but type checking alone might not provide the level of validation that an application demands. For example, suppose you wanted to host *Key/Value* pairs, but you wanted to ensure that the *Value* portions were valid US telephone numbers. Where and when you'd validate the phone numbers would rely heavily on the methodology you used. If you were using an *IConfigurationSectionHandler* object, you could have checks in the *Create* method that detected when you were reading a node that was supposed to contain a telephone number and run your validation against the value there.

The last interface that needs to be mentioned is the *IConfigurationSystem* interface. The MSDN Documentation specifies that this class is not meant to be used by developers. This is mainly to be used for designers of tools that have IDE support.

Lab: Read and Write Configuration Settings

In this lab, you create a configuration file and read those values. After reading values from the configuration file you'll learn how to write values to that configuration file. If you encounter a problem completing an exercise, the completed projects are available on the companion CD in the Code folder.

▶ **Exercise: Read and Write Configuration Settings**

In this exercise, you programmatically write a value to a configuration file.

1. Open Visual Studio 2005. Select File, New, Project, and then select your language of choice. Select the Console Application project type. Name the project ConfigSettingsDemo.

2. From the Visual Studio 2005 menu, select Project, Add New Item, Application Configuration File, and then click the Add button.

3. In Solution Explorer, right-click your project and choose Add Reference. On the .NET tab, scroll down to the *System.Configuration* assembly and select OK. If you do not explicitly add this reference, you will not be able to access the *Configuration-Manager* class.

4. Add the following code snippet to the configuration file:

```
<appSettings>
    <add key="Foo" value="Hello World!"/>
</appSettings>
```

5. Select the Program.cs file or the Module1.vb file in your application, and enter the following code at the top of the file:

```
' VB
Imports System.Collections.Specialized
Imports System.Collections
Imports System.Configuration

// C#
using System.Collections.Specialized;
using System.Collections;
using System.Configuration;
```

6. Add a new class to the project, named LabSection, that inherits from System.Configuration.ConfigurationSection as shown:

```
'VB
Public Class LabSection
  Inherits ConfigurationSection

End Class
```

```
// C#
public class LabSection : ConfigurationSection
{
}
```

7. Select either the Program.cs or Module1.vb file, and open it. Create a new method with no return type, and name it *WriteSettings*, as shown here:

```
'VB
Private Sub WriteSettings()
End Sub
```

```
// C#
private static void WriteSettings()
{}
```

8. Insert the following code into the method:

```
' VB
Try
  Dim labSec As ConfigurationSection
  Dim config As System.Configuration.Configuration = _
    ConfigurationManager.OpenExeConfiguration( _
    ConfigurationUserLevel.None)

  If config.Sections("LabSection") Is Nothing Then
    labSec = New LabSection()
    config.Sections.Add("LabSection", labSec)
    labSec.SectionInformation.ForceSave = True
    config.Save(ConfigurationSaveMode.Full)
  End If
Catch ex As ApplicationException
  Console.WriteLine(ex.ToString())
End Try
```

```
// C#
try
{
  ConfigurationSection labSec;
  // Get the current configuration file.
  System.Configuration.Configuration config = ConfigurationManager.
    OpenExeConfiguration(ConfigurationUserLevel.None);
  if (config.Sections["LabSection"] == null)
```

```
        {
            labSec = new LabSection();
            config.Sections.Add("LabSection", labSec);
            labSec.SectionInformation.ForceSave = true;
            config.Save(ConfigurationSaveMode.Full);
        }
    }
    catch (ApplicationException ex)
    {
        Console.WriteLine(ex.ToString());
    }
```

9. Insert the following code in the *Main* method:

   ```
   ' VB
   WriteSettings()

   // C#
   WriteSettings();
   ```

10. Open a command prompt and browse to the ...\ConfigSettingsDemo\bin\Debug folder. Run the ConfigSettingsDemo.exe program.

11. Open the configuration file, ConfigSettingsDemo.exe.config, in a text editor and verify that there is a configuration section named *LabSection*.

Lesson Summary

- The *IConfigurationSectionHandler* interface provides a mechanism to access customized sections of a configuration file.

- The *Create* method is the only implementation detail necessary to fulfill the *IConfigurationSectionHandler* contract.

- The *configSections* node of the configuration file is the main mechanism provided for implementing custom sections.

- *ConfigurationSection* objects can be used to programmatically add configuration sections, as opposed to manually entering them through the configuration file.

- To save any changes made to a *Configuration* object, use the *Save* method.

- If an alternate file is to be used for changes to a *Configuration* object, *SaveAs* facilitates this.

- The *ApplicationSettingsBase* class serves as wrapper to implement configurable application settings in .NET applications.

- All settings stored by an *ApplicationSettingsBase* class use the *LocalFileSettings-Provider* for storage.

Lesson Review

You can use the following questions to test your knowledge of the information in Lesson 4, "Configuration Management." The questions are also available on the companion CD if you prefer to review them in electronic form.

NOTE   Answers

Answers to these questions and explanations of why each answer choice is right or wrong are located in the "Answers" section at the end of the book.

---

1. Which methods of the *ConfigurationManager* class are valid ways to open a configuration file? (Choose all that apply.)

   A. *OpenExeConfiguration*

   B. *OpenMachineConfiguration*

   C. *OpenMappedExeConfiguration*

   D. *OpenMappedMachineConfiguration*

2. What method causes settings to be read from a section in the configuration file into an *IConfigurationSectionHandler* object?

   A. *Create*

   B. *ReadSection*

   C. *GetConfig*

   D. *GetAppSettings*

Chapter Review

To further practice and reinforce the skills you learned in this chapter, you can do any of the following tasks:

- Review the chapter summary.
- Review the list of key terms introduced in this chapter.
- Complete the case scenarios. These scenarios set up real-world situations involving the topics of this chapter and ask you to create a solution.
- Complete the suggested practices.
- Take a practice test.

Chapter Summary

- The *System.Configuration* namespace provides many tools that will help you configure your applications.
- There are two primary areas that configuration can manage: custom settings and built-in settings. Custom settings include things such as a customer name or the placement of a screen that the user has set. Built-in settings address issues such as which runtime version the application should use or provide a means by which you can retrieve specialized sections such as connection strings.
- Connection strings have a special place in many applications and, as such, a special tool exists for accessing them. In this chapter, we only addressed connection strings in plain text, but in real-world applications, you should never leave an unencrypted connection string in a configuration file.
- Any professional program should include an installer. By using the *Commit* method, you can tell the application that the installation was successful. If the installation is not successful, it should be undone using the *Rollback* method. To completely remove an application that you've installed, use the *Uninstall* method.
- To visually configure items, you can use the .NET Framework 2.0 Configuration tool. This will help you adjust items such as security policy or add assemblies to and manage the global assembly cache.

Key Terms

Do you know what these key terms mean? You can check your answers by looking up the terms in the glossary at the end of the book.

- application setting
- configuration management
- connection string
- .NET Framework 2.0 Configuration tool
- roll back
- uninstall

Case Scenario: Installing and Configuring a New Application

In the following case scenario, you will apply what you've learned in this chapter. You can find answers to these questions in the "Answers" section at the end of this book.

You are a developer for company where you're working on a large enterprise application that, after it is deployed, must minimize downtime. Your specifications have many requirements. The first requirement is that user settings, such as positions of windows, are saved. The next requirement is that all settings except secure ones need to be human readable and editable. If your program doesn't contain an editor, one needs to be provided. The application needs to have an installer, and in case of failure, it needs to be rolled back.

Interviews

Following is a list of company personnel interviewed and their statements:

- **IT Manager**   "The last developer who worked on this program thought my computer's registries were his own. Everything in the application read and wrote from the registry. This was totally unacceptable. After this deployment, I'm using group policy to lock down permissions, and if your application can't run without writing to my registry, we won't be using it. Also, it better have a good installer and if the install fails, undo itself."

■ **Programming Manager**   "I want everything configurable. I don't want to hear anything about "We hard-coded those settings in there." If there's a setting for it, I want it configurable because redeploying has been a major problem in the past."

Questions

Answer the following questions for your manager.

1. If the registry can't be used, what should be used instead?

2. Does anything else need to be handled in the installation?

Suggested Practices

To help you successfully master the objectives covered in this chapter, complete the following tasks.

Embed Configuration Management Functionality into a .NET Framework Application

For this task, you should complete at least Practices 1 and 2. If you want a better understanding of how the *System.Configuration* namespace works, complete Practices 3 and 4 as well. If you understand .NET remoting well enough, complete Practice 5.

■ **Practice 1**   Add connection strings to a configuration file for multiple provider types, including *SqlClient*, *OleDb*, *Odbc*, and *OracleClient*.

■ **Practice 2**   Create multiple application settings, and retrieve them using the *ConfigurationManager*.

■ **Practice 3**   Create a custom section in your configuration file, and either create a custom class derived from a base class or one that implements an interface such as *IConfigurationSectionHandler* to retrieve those settings.

■ **Practice 4**   Create an installer for your application that writes values to the registry or sets a desktop shortcut. Uninstall the application, and verify that everything is as it should be.

■ **Practice 5**   Create a remoting server, and use configuration files to register the components to both the client and the server.

Take a Practice Test

The practice tests on this book's companion CD offer many options. For example, you can test yourself on just one exam objective, or you can test yourself on all the 70-536 certification exam content. You can set up the test so that it closely simulates the experience of taking a certification exam, or you can set it up in study mode so that you can look at the correct answers and explanations after you answer each question.

MORE INFO Practice tests

For details about all the practice test options available, see the "How to Use the Practice Tests" section in this book's Introduction.

Chapter 10

Instrumentation

This chapter covers instrumentation in the .NET Framework 2.0. Instrumentation includes a large number of objectives, but all deal with logging and measuring what happens in an application.

Exam objectives in this chapter:

- Manage an event log by using the *System.Diagnostics* namespace.
    - ❑ Write to an event log.
    - ❑ Read from an event log.
    - ❑ Create a new event log.
- Manage system processes and monitor the performance of a .NET Framework application by using the diagnostics functionality of the .NET Framework 2.0 (Refer *System.Diagnostics* namespace).
    - ❑ Get a list of all running processes.
    - ❑ Retrieve information about the current process.
    - ❑ Get a list of all modules that are loaded by a process.
    - ❑ *PerformanceCounter* class, *PerformanceCounterCategory*, and *CounterCreationData* class.
    - ❑ Start a process both by using and by not using command-line arguments.
    - ❑ *StackTrace* class.
    - ❑ *StackFrame* class.
- Debug and trace a .NET Framework application by using the *System.Diagnostics* namespace.
    - ❑ *Debug* class and *Debugger* class.
    - ❑ *Trace* class, *CorrelationManager* class, *TraceListener* class, *TraceSource* class, *TraceSwitch* class, *XmlWriterTraceListener* class, *DelimitedListTraceListener* class, and *EventlogTraceListener* class.
    - ❑ *Debugger* attributes.

■ Embed management information and events into a .NET Framework application. (Refer *System.Management* namespace).

❑ Retrieve a collection of *Management* objects by using the *Management-ObjectSearcher* class and its derived classes.

❑ *ManagementQuery* class.

❑ Subscribe to management events by using the *ManagementEventWatcher* class.

Lessons in this chapter:

Before You Begin

To complete the lessons in this chapter, you should be familiar with Microsoft Visual Basic or C# and be comfortable with the following tasks:

■ Create a console application in Microsoft Visual Studio using Visual Basic or C#.

■ Add references to system class libraries to a project.

■ View Windows event logs.

Lesson 1: Logging Events

It's impossible to know in advance every situation that your application might encounter after it is deployed. You don't necessarily know, for instance, how much RAM a user's computer will have, so it's impossible to know when your application might run out of memory.

After this lesson, you will be able to:

- Create an event log.
- Read entries from and write entries to an event log.

Estimated lesson time: 20 minutes

Using Microsoft Windows Events and Logging Them

No matter how well written and tested an application is, chances are high that there will be a bug or some unexpected behavior. Moreover, users typically aren't developers and don't use the same terminology that developers are accustomed to. It's common to have users report problems using terminology that developers don't recognize or understand. This communication gap makes bug verification a difficult process. And even when a bug can be verified, the circumstances that caused it might remain unknown. This reality makes identifying and fixing bugs difficult and can cause serious delays in repairing them.

Later versions of Windows such as Windows 2000, Windows XP, and Windows Server 2003 provide a mechanism to let applications log things that happen to them. This feature has many benefits. By using the event log, developers can record certain aspects of the state of an application, including serious errors. Essentially, developers can record just about anything that they think might be useful after the application is deployed. The ability to review significant events makes it much easier for support people to diagnose issues. A summary of the benefits of using Windows events and logging them are as follows:

- Provide an easy mechanism to record specific items regarding an application's state

- Provide an easy mechanism to record situations that the developers consider to be out of the ordinary

- Provide an easy mechanism for users to check on the state of applications that are running

Figure 10-1 shows the Event Viewer in Windows XP.

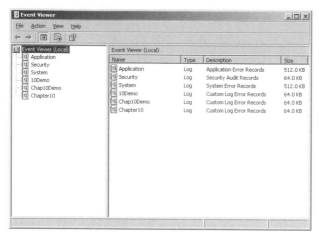

Figure 10-1   The Windows XP Event Viewer

The creators of the Framework gave developers multiple tools to create and manage event log entries. Although the event logging mechanism is elegant and simple, you should keep in mind the old cliché that states, "There's no such thing as a free lunch." Accordingly, a few points need to be made before any responsible instruction on the use of event logs can take place. The MSDN documentation (which can be found at *http://msdn2.microsoft.com/en-US/library/system.diagnostics.eventlog(VS.80).aspx*) includes the following caveats:

- Creating an *EventLog* object, writing to it, and passing it to code executing in a partial trust setting can be a huge security vulnerability. *EventLog* objects, including *EventLogEntry* objects and *EventLogEntryCollection* objects, should never be passed to less trusted code. This means *any* less trusted code, so it's important to be cognizant of the security context these objects are executing in.

- The *EventLogPermission* is required for many actions that use *EventLog* manipulation. Granting this permission to partially trusted code can open a serious security vulnerability. For example, mischievous code running in a partial trust environment with this permission granted could easily spoof other applications. It could, for example, shut down a critical antivirus or spyware-detection application yet make it appear as if it's still running. The potential for mischief is unlimited.

■ Reading and logging events are relatively resource intensive in terms of disk utilization, system processor time, and other resources. *EventLog* objects can also get filled up, at which point attempts to write to them will cause exceptions to be thrown. *EventLog* objects should be used as necessary, but judiciously as well.

CAUTION   Avoid *EventLog* objects in partial trust environments

Use of *EventLog* objects in a partial trust environment can cause serious security holes and should be avoided if at all possible.

With these warnings and caveats stated, let's look at the benefits of using *EventLog* objects.

Creating and Deleting an Event Log

To create an event log, the .NET Framework provides the *EventLog* class. If you're performing one or two actions against an event log, use its static methods. If you're performing several actions, create an instance of the *EventLog* class and perform the actions directly on the instance, whenever possible. To use the *EventLog* class, the *Source* property needs to be specified and a message needs to be written, as shown in the following code, which requires importing the *System.Diagnostics* namespace:

```
' VB
Dim DemoLog As New EventLog("Chap10Demo")
DemoLog.Source = "Chap10Demo"
DemoLog.WriteEntry("CreateEventLog called", EventLogEntryType.Information)
```

```
// C#
EventLog DemoLog = new EventLog("Chap10Demo");
    DemoLog.Source = "Chap10Demo";
    DemoLog.WriteEntry("CreateEventLog called", EventLogEntryType.Information);
```

In the sample code, a new event source named Chap10Demo is registered for your application with the Chap10Demo event log. Event sources are registered with an event log in the Windows Registry. After you create an *EventLog* object and specify its source (which, by the way, can all be done in one of the overloaded constructors), information about the object should be visible from the Windows Event Viewer. Figure 10-2 shows what should be in the *EventLog* after successful execution of this code.

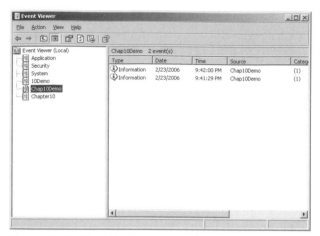

Figure 10-2   The Windows Event Viewer after the Chap10Demo event log has been created and written to

Deleting an event log is equally simple. You may want, for example, to delete the log that you just created as part of this exercise. To remove the demonstration log, use the *Delete* method of *EventLog* in code like the following:

```
' VB
EventLog.Delete("Chap10Demo")
```

```
// C#
EventLog.Delete("Chap10Demo");
```

Just be sure you don't delete a log with valuable information by using this method! An *InvalidOperationException* exception is thrown if the event log doesn't exist.

Writing to an Event Log

As you saw from the previous code samples, the *WriteEntry* method of the *EventLog* class is used to write an entry to an event log.

In the previous example, the *WriteEntry* method looks rather simple. However, there are 10 overloads for it. As is the case with many overloaded constructors, the minimal construction can be used and then you can set all necessary properties. Or you can specify all the information you need in the constructor. Although doing everything in the overload is typically considered more elegant and straightforward, you might encounter situations in which this approach won't work well with the rest of your code. For example, you might not know the rest of the values that you intend to record.

```
' VB
DemoLog.WriteEntry("CreateEventLog called", EventLogEntryType.Information)
```

```
// C#
DemoLog.WriteEntry("CreateEventLog called", EventLogEntryType.Information);
```

The following example shows how to use an overload to add an event ID:

```
' VB
DemoLog.WriteEntry("CreateEventLog called", EventLogEntryType.Information, 100)
```

```
// C#
DemoLog.WriteEntry("CreateEventLog called", EventLogEntryType.Information, 100);
```

In addition to reading custom logs, the *EventLog* object also gives developers the ability to read from and write to built-in event logs. The built-in logs are the Application, Security, and System logs. Even though you might have a specified log for your application, you might want to take advantage of the built-in logs. Assume for a second that you have an ASP.NET Web application that authenticates users. Assume further that you have code in place to detect attempted SQL injection attacks. Developers of an application can do little about attempted attacks (other than ensuring that the code prevents them from being successful), but security administrators will be very interested in this type of activity, even when it is unsuccessful. Therefore it makes sense to write such events to the built-in Security log, where security personnel will be sure to see it.

IMPORTANT   The meaning of "SQL injection attack"

SQL injection attacks are hack attempts made through an application that trusts user input. The attacker uses special characters to change the nature of the input in order to embed SQL-database commands. Depending on what an attacker is allowed to do, he or she might be able to completely take over the database, as well as destroy it.

Following are examples of how to write to the Application and System built-in logs. Remember that you must have permission to write to those logs. If you need to write to the Security event log, you must impersonate the LocalSystem account because it is the only account with write permission.

- Use the following code to write to the Application log:

```
' VB
Dim DemoLog As New EventLog("Application")
DemoLog.Source = "DemoApp"
DemoLog.WriteEntry("Written to Application Log", _
  EventLogEntryType.Information)
```

```
// C#
EventLog DemoLog = new EventLog("Application");
DemoLog.Source = "DemoApp";
DemoLog.WriteEntry("Written to Application Log",
  EventLogEntryType.Information);
```

- Use the following code to write to the System log:

```
' VB
Dim DemoLog As New EventLog("System")
DemoLog.Source = "DemoApp"
DemoLog.WriteEntry("A DemoService Restarted due to reboot", _
  EventLogEntryType.Information)
```

```
// C#
EventLog DemoLog = new EventLog("System");
DemoLog.Source = "DemoApp";
DemoLog.WriteEntry("A DemoService Restarted due to reboot",
  EventLogEntryType.Information);
```

If an event source, such as DemoApp, has already been registered with one event log
(which would be the case if you first run the code for writing to the Application event
log), then the code to write to the System event log will write to the Application, and
not the System event log. An event source can be registered only once and only to a
single event log.

Reading from an Event Log

At this point, an event log has been created and data has been written to it. The *Event-
Log* object has an *Entries* property. This property is an instance of the *EventLogEntry-
Collection* and contains *EventLogEntry* objects. After you have an instance of your
EventLog class, you can easily iterate through the log entries, as illustrated by the
following code:

```
' VB
Dim DemoLog As New EventLog()
DemoLog.Log = "Chap10Demo"

For Each DemoEntry As EventLogEntry In DemoLog.Entries
  Console.WriteLine(DemoEntry.Source & ": " & DemoEntry.Message)
Next
```

```
// C#
EventLog DemoLog = new EventLog();
DemoLog.Log = "Chap10Demo";

foreach (EventLogEntry DemoEntry in DemoLog.Entries)
{
  Console.WriteLine(DemoEntry.Source + ":" + DemoEntry.Message);
}
```

If the previous code was executed, you would see output resembling that shown in Figure 10-3.

Figure 10-3   Output from reading the Chap10Demo event log

The only real task left to address is clearing a log. The method for doing this is one of the simplest methods to use. All you need to do is call the *Clear* method of the *Event-Log* instance:

```
' VB
Dim DemoLog As New EventLog("Chap10Demo")
DemoLog.Source = "Chap10Demo"
DemoLog.Clear()
```

```
// C#
EventLog DemoLog = new EventLog("Chap10Demo");
DemoLog.Source = "Chap10Demo";
DemoLog.Clear();
```

If you use the *ReadEventLog* method just referenced in the previous section after calling *ClearEventLog*, you should see no log entries. If you see any entries—other than entries that might have been written by another piece of code in the interim—something has failed.

Lab: Create and Use an Application Event Log

In this lab, you'll create a custom event log and write entries to it. If you encounter a problem completing an exercise, the completed projects are available on the companion CD in the Code folder.

1. Open Visual Studio 2005.

2. Create a new console application in Microsoft Visual C# 2005 or Microsoft Visual Basic 2005. Visual Basic 2005 creates a module for you, along with an

empty *Main* procedure. Visual C# creates a *Program.cs* class for you with an empty *Main* procedure.

3. Open the *Module1.vb* or *Program.cs* file and import the *System.Diagnostics* namespace so that you will not be required to qualify declarations from this namespace later in your code.

4. Add the following code to check whether the Chap10DemoApplication event source is registered on the local machine (indicated by the period passed as the second parameter), and create it if not. Keep in mind that the event source could be registered with a different event log than the Application log you're trying to register it with. If this is true, the call to the *CreateEventSource* method will throw an exception.

```vb
' VB
If Not EventLog.SourceExists("Chap10DemoApplication", ".") Then
   EventLog.CreateEventSource("Chap10DemoApplication", "Application")
End If

Dim DemoLog As New EventLog("Application", ".", "Chap10DemoApplication")
DemoLog.WriteEntry("Entry written to Application Log", _
  EventLogEntryType.Information, 234, CType(3, Int16))
```

```csharp
// C#
if (!EventLog.SourceExists("Chap10DemoApplication", "."))
{
    EventLog.CreateEventSource("Chap10DemoApplication", "Application");
}

EventLog DemoLog = new EventLog("Application", ".", "Chap10DemoApplication");
DemoLog.WriteEntry("Entry written to Application Log",
EventLogEntryType.Information, 234, Convert.ToInt16(3));
```

5. Save and run your code. Then verify that the entry was written to the Application log.

6. To write to an event log on a remote machine, simply change the machine name from period (".") to the remote machine for which you have privileges to write to the event log.

Lesson Summary

- The Windows event log mechanism is a convenient tool for developers to record information that they think might be useful in the future to system administrators or users.

- There are myriad ways to log information, but the event log mechanism provides a clean, object-oriented way to handle this task.

- Use the *Source* property of the *EventLog* to define where the information is coming from.

- Use the *EventLogEntryType* to specify what type of entry the output will be.

- The primary object for interacting with the event log system is the *EventLog* class in the *System.Diagnostics* namespace.

- Although the *EventLog* class provides substantial functionality that is simple to use, it does have overhead in terms of resources. It should be used judiciously.

- Many security vulnerabilities can be raised when using *EventLog* objects. Therefore, you should avoid using them in partial trust environments and avoid passing such objects to a partial trust environment.

- To remove all the entries in an event log, use the *Clear* method.

- The *Message* property of the *EventLogEntry* is used to read back the information that was written to the *EventLog* object.

Lesson Review

You can use the following questions to test your knowledge of the information in Lesson 1, "Logging Events." The questions are also available on the companion CD if you prefer to review them in electronic form.

NOTE Answers

Answers to these questions and explanations of why each answer choice is right or wrong are located in the "Answers" section at the end of the book.

---

1. You need to log application state information for your application. The application will run in a Full Trust environment but will make calls to partial trust assemblies. Which statement best describes how this should be handled?

    A. Use the *EventLog* class as necessary.

    B. Use the *EventLog* class in assemblies that will have no contact with the partial trust assemblies.

    C. Avoid the use of *EventLog* class objects because the security risk is too high.

D. Use *EventLog* objects, but ensure that they are specific to this application. If they are used by a partial trust object, create a separate log for security reasons.

2. Which of the following considerations should be taken into account when using *EventLog* objects? (Choose all that apply.)

A. They can fill up if overused, so writing to them should be done judiciously.

B. They should be avoided in all partial trust environments.

C. They are potential resource hogs, so they should be used judiciously.

D. They are one of the safest mechanisms available to perform I/O operations, so they should be used wherever possible.

3. What method of the *EventLog* object should be used to clear an *EventLog*?

A. Call the *Clear* method for each item in the log.

B. Use *RemoveEntries* and then call the *Clear* method.

C. Use the *Clear* method.

D. Use the *ClearAll* method.

4. What method of the *EventLog* class should be used to delete an *EventLog* object?

A. Use the *ClearLog* method.

B. Use the *RemoveLog* method.

C. Use the *Delete* method.

D. Use the *DeleteLog* method.

5. Which types of messages can be written to an event log? (Choose all that apply.)

A. Error

B. Warning

C. Information

D. SuccessAudit

6. Which logs are available by default in the Windows event log mechanism? (Choose all that apply.)

A. Application

B. Security

C. System

D. Audit

Lesson 2: Debugging and Tracing

If, throughout the day, you were to stop by the desks of application developers I work with, you probably wouldn't see them writing code. Most of the time, you'd see them debugging their code and stepping through it. Debugging is absolutely critical to developing quality code, and being proficient at it can help developers be more productive and write higher quality code.

After this lesson, you will be able to:

- Write output.
- Debug attributes.
- Create trace listeners.
- Configure listeners.

Estimated lesson time: 20 minutes

Writing Output

As mentioned earlier, an important part of a developer's job is stepping through code and tracking bugs. Learning how to effectively use the tools available for this task is critical for many reasons. Effective use of these tools includes performing the following tasks:

- Verify that your code is doing what you expect it to.

- Use the *Debug* and *Debugger* classes so that your code can provide feedback to confirm that it is or is not working as planned. You use these classes because stepping through code in other ways is time consuming.

- Use tools that help to track down bugs after your application has been deployed.

The two foundational classes used for debugging, *Debugger* and *Debug,* are both in the *System.Diagnostics* namespace.

The *Debugger* Class

The *Debugger* class, which enables communication with a debugger application, is fairly straightforward. Although it has multiple members, a few in particular are of primary interest to developers. Those members are listed in Table 10-1.

Table 10-1   Members of the *Debugger* Class

Name	Description
Break	Signals a break to the debugger. This is an excellent tool for conditionally stopping the execution of the application.
IsAttached	Indicates whether the debugger is attached to a process already.
IsLogging	Indicates whether the *Debugger* is currently logging.
Launch	Launches a debugger, and attaches it to a process.
Log	Posts a message to the current debugger.

The *Break* method provides the equivalent of setting a breakpoint manually, but it allows you to do it conditionally and through code. Assume that you have a method named *ReturnMessage* that returns a *String* value. Assume further that a return value of *null* or *nothing* signals a problem for which you want to stop processing and break into the debugger. Your choice is to set a breakpoint manually or use the *Break* method. The two methods are functionally equivalent. The following code illustrates how to use the *Break* method. We assume that the method ReturnMessage() has been declared previously:

```
' VB
Dim MyMessage As String = ReturnMessage()

If MyMessage Is Nothing Then
    Debugger.Break()
End If

// C#
String MyMessage = ReturnMessage();

if (MyMessage == null)
{
    Debugger.Break();
}
```

This use of the *Break* method could yield results similar to those shown in the C# implementation in Figure 10-4.

Another important feature of the *Debugger* class is the *Log* method. Stated simply, the *Log* method posts information to the attached *Debugger* if one is present. If no *Debugger* is present, the result is effectively nothing.

```
using System;
using System.Collections.Generic;
using System.Text;
using System.Diagnostics;
namespace Debugging
{
    class Program
    {
        static void Main(string[] args)
        {
            String MyMessage = ReturnMessage();
            if (MyMessage == null)
            {
                Debugger.Break();
            }
        }
    }
}
```

Figure 10-4   Breaking into the CLR/Visual Studio .NET 2005 debugger via the *Debugger.Break* method

---

NOTE   **Build vs. Release build**

For the *Debugger* or *Debug* class to function, the build must be performed in Debug mode. If the build is done in any other mode, such as Release, the .NET runtime will effectively ignore any *Debug* or *Debugger* statements.

When you use the *Log* method, it directs the output to whatever *listener* objects are attached to the debugger. Listener objects will be discussed shortly, but for now it's only pertinent to understand that the *Log* method directs the output to a listener. To use the *Log* method, all you need to do is call it and indicate a level, category, and message. We'll begin with a simple listener, *DefaultTraceListener*. This listener, when attached, will take any *Log* methods and write them as text to the specified target. To keep things simple, we'll use the Output window as the specified target. To use this method, add a listener object and call the *Log* method. The following code illustrates this process:

```
' VB
Trace.Listeners.Clear()
Dim MyListener As New DefaultTraceListener
MyListener.TraceOutputOptions = TraceOptions.Callstack
Trace.Listeners.Add(MyListener)
Debugger.Log(1, "Test", "This is a test")
Console.ReadLine()

// C#
Trace.Listeners.Clear();
DefaultTraceListener MyListener = new DefaultTraceListener();
Trace.Listeners.Add(MyListener);
Debugger.Log(1, "Test", "This is a test");
Console.ReadLine();
```

All that we've done is cleared any existing *Listeners* from the *Listeners* collection, added a *DefaultTraceListener* object, and then sent some output to it. There are multiple overloads for the *DefaultTraceListener*, and we could just as easily have directed the output to a text file, for instance. If the listener is implemented correctly, you should see the text "This is a test" in the Output window.

NOTE   **Length of the *Category* parameter**

The *Category* parameter can be only 256 characters long. If your message exceeds that length, it will be truncated.

The *Debug* Class

Although the *Debugger* class is very useful, it essentially provides only two methods: *Break* and *Log*. Although the value of these methods should not be underestimated, there are times when you need more granularity. In those cases, the *Debug* class fits the bill quite well. Table 10-2 lists the most common methods of the *Debug* class that developers use.

Table 10-2   Methods of the *Debug* Class

Name	Description
Assert	Evaluates a condition, and displays a message if the condition evaluates to false.
Close	Flushes the output buffer and then calls the *Close* method on each of the attached listeners.
Fail	Outputs a failure message.
Flush	Flushes the output buffer, and causes buffered data to write to the *Listeners* collection.
Indent	Increments the indent level by one. This method is mainly useful for formatting purposes.
Print	Writes a message followed by a line terminator to the trace listeners in the *Listeners* collection.
Unindent	Opposite of the *Indent* method. Decrements the indent level by one unit.

Table 10-2   **Methods of the *Debug* Class**

Name	Description
Write	Writes information to attached *Debug* or *Trace* class listener objects in the *Listeners* collection.
WriteIf	Performs the same action as the *Write* method, but does so only if a specified condition is met.
WriteLine	Writes information to attached *Debug* or *Trace* class listener objects in the *Listeners* collection.
WriteLineIf	Performs the same action as the *WriteLine* method, but does so only if a specified condition is met.

The importance of the *Indent* and *Unindent* methods should not be trivialized, but because they are used specifically for formatting I won't discuss them in much detail.

Let's start with what I believe to be one of the most important methods of the *Debug* class, the *Assert* method.

Real World

William Ryan

When I present at .NET User Groups and Microsoft events, I typically incorporate items I view as important in my professional career, and few items are more important to me than the *Assert* method. Let me say this as unequivocally as I can: "Using assertions is critical to writing good code." Even if you write "good" code now, you can realize a notable improvement almost immediately by liberal use of the *Assert* statement. Many authors—including two of the foremost debugging experts in the world, John Robbins and Paul Kimmel—maintain this same position.

MORE INFO   The *Assert* method

For more information from these two experts, read *Debugging Applications for Microsoft .NET and Microsoft Windows* by John Robbins (Microsoft Press, 2001) and *Visual Basic .NET Power Coding* by Paul Kimmel (Addison-Wesley Professional, 2003).

The *Assert* Method

You might remember from earlier in the chapter that one of the benefits of using the *Debugger* and *Debug* classes is that they allow you to run your application and examine the output without having to manually step through your code. Stepping through the code is sometimes necessary, but when dealing with large enterprise applications, it's simply not feasible in many instances. It's next to impossible to step through 500,000 lines of code in a short amount of time. One of the best tools to help you do this in a time-efficient manner is the *Assert* method. You should load your code with *Debug.Assert* methods wherever you have a condition that will always be true or false. When the code evaluates, if the condition isn't true, it will break into the debugger automatically.

The main benefit to this approach is that you can verify that conditions you thought were true really are true. Often developers will check code into source control for a project, which ends up breaking other code. When you use *Assert* statements correctly, simply running the application will produce immediate notification of a problem.

Suppose that you used an *IConfigurationSectionHandler* object and someone deleted the entry in the configuration file. Without a *Debug* assertion, you might spend 20 minutes trying to track down the object before realizing that someone deleted it. An *Assert* statement could point you directly to the problem. Moreover, you can use highly detailed messages, which make finding the problem much quicker. Furthermore, when you build your application in Release mode, none of the *Debug* commands such as *Assert* statements are compiled in, so your application suffers no performance degradation by using them. This scenario gives you the best of both worlds: more efficient debugging with no negative impact on performance. Assume you had the following configuration file, but somehow each of the settings was deleted:

```
<appSettings>
    <add key="Foo" value="Hello World!"/>
    <add key="ApplicationName" value="Demo Application"/>
    <add key="ApplicationVersion" value="2.0.0.1"/>
    <add key="UserFirstName" value="John"/>
    <add key="UserLastName" value="Public"/>
</appSettings>
```

By using the following code (which requires the namespace references to *System.Configuration* and *System.Collections.Specialized* as well as to *System.Diagnostics*), you would know immediately if the setting "*Foo*" had been accidentally deleted:

```
' VB
Dim MySettings As NameValueCollection = ConfigurationManager.AppSettings
Debug.Assert(Not MySettings Is Nothing AndAlso Not MySettings("Foo") Is Nothing, _
```

```
   "There was a problem with either the configuration file or the Foo Setting")
 Console.WriteLine(MySettings("Foo"))

 // C#
  NameValueCollection MySettings = ConfigurationManager.AppSettings;
     Debug.Assert(MySettings != null && MySettings["Foo"] != null,
       "There was a problem with either the configuration file or the Foo Setting");
     Console.WriteLine(MySettings["Foo"]);
```

NOTE **.NET 2.0**

The *ConfigurationManager* class is new in .NET 2.0. It replaces the now-deprecated *Configuration-Settings* class.

If *"Foo"* has a value, execution will proceed as expected; but if it is missing or deleted, you will see a message similar to the one shown in Figure 10-5, which was generated by the C# example.

Figure 10-5 Output from a failed assertion

Similar to *Assert* is the *Fail* method. This method simply causes the *Debugger* to break at the offending line of code and output a failure message. The *Fail* method doesn't use an evaluation. To demonstrate how the *Fail* method works, assume the following code snippets:

```
' VB
Dim MySettings As NameValueCollection = ConfigurationManager.AppSettings

If MySettings("Foo") Is Nothing Then
   Debug.Fail("Configuration Setting 'Foo' is Missing")
End If

// C#
NameValueCollection MySettings = ConfigurationManager.AppSettings;

if (MySettings["Foo"] == null)
   Debug.Fail("Configuration Setting 'Foo' is Missing");
```

If the "Foo" section or value was missing, the C# code, for example, would generate the dialog box shown in Figure 10-6.

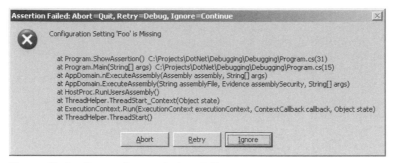

Figure 10-6   Output from a *Debug.Fail*

In each of these scenarios, the dialog box presents the following three options:

- **Abort**   Stops execution of the program totally.
- **Retry**   Attempts to execute the code block again. Unless something in the state has changed, the result will be the same as before.
- **Ignore**   Skips over the failure, and attempts to resume execution.

Next we'll cover the *Write*, *WriteIf*, *WriteLine*, and *WriteLineIf* methods. These methods are virtually identical, so they'll be discussed together.

The *Write* Method

To use the *Write* method, simply call it followed by whatever message you want sent to the Output window:

```
' VB
Debug.Write("WriteStatements() was reached")

// C#
Debug.Write("WriteStatements() was reached");
```

This code will cause the "WriteStatements() was reached" message to be sent to the Visual Studio Output window.

The *WriteIf* Method

The *WriteIf* method works identically to the *Write* method except that it writes output only if a condition is met. This behavior differs from *Write* only in the sense that it's conditional.

```
' VB
Dim s As String = Nothing
Debug.WriteIf(s Is Nothing, "Variable [s] is null")

// C#
String s = null;
Debug.WriteIf(s == null, "Variable [s] is null");
```

This code will cause the message "Variable [s] is null" to be sent to the Output window if, in fact, the variable is null.

Both the *WriteLine* and *WriteLineIf* methods work identically to these two methods except that they include a line terminator at the end. Other than the format, there's no difference in the behavior of these respective methods.

The *WriteLine* Method

To use the *WriteLine* method, simply call it followed by whatever message you want sent to the Output window:

```
' VB
Debug.WriteLine("WriteStatements() was reached")

// C#
Debug.WriteLine("WriteStatements() was reached");
```

This code will cause the "WriteStatements() was reached" message to be sent to the Output window.

The *WriteLineIf* Method

The *WriteIf* method works identically to the *WriteLine* method except that it writes output only if a condition is met. This behavior differs from *WriteLine* only in the sense that it's conditional.

```
' VB
Dim s As String = Nothing
Debug.WriteLineIf(s Is Nothing, "Variable [s] is null")

// C#
String s = null;
Debug.WriteLineIf(s == null, "Variable [s] is null");
```

This code will cause the message "Variable [s] is null" to be sent to the Output window if, in fact, the variable is null.

The *Print* Method

The *Print* method works similarly to the various write methods except that it writes output only to attached listener objects.

```
' VB
Debug.Print("PrintStatements() was reached")
```

```
// C#
Debug.Print("PrintStatements() was reached");
```

This code will cause the "PrintStatements() was reached" message to be sent to any attached listener objects.

The *Flush* Method

The *Flush* method is used to push any output to the attached *Listener* objects. It takes no parameters, and there's nothing more to calling it than simply calling it.

```
' VB
Debug.Flush()
```

```
// C#
Debug.Flush();
```

After calling *Flush*, everything in the output buffer is flushed and that data is forwarded to any attached *Listener* objects.

Debug Attributes

Debug attributes are provided by the .NET Framework to allow developers to declaratively specify how they want their application to behave. Attributes are used throughout the .NET Framework but are particularly helpful in debugging scenarios. If you want to set the state of an object, typically you have to create it and set some properties. But let's say that you knew a given method was working and you never wanted the debugger to step into it. Using traditional imperative methods, you'd actually have to step over it to tell the debugger to ignore it. This hardly makes any sense, does it? Doing this is the equivalent of me calling everyone I know to tell them I'm busy and please refrain from calling me, as opposed to simply turning off my phone. An attribute, on the other hand, describes a behavior, and callers of this object know in advance how to handle it. Because of this capability, attributes are particularly well suited to debugging scenarios.

In this section, we're going to discuss the following attributes:

- *DebuggerBrowsableAttribute*
- *DebuggerDisplayAttribute*
- *DebuggerHiddenAttribute*

- *DebuggerNonUserCodeAttribute*

- *DebuggerStepperBoundaryAttribute*

- *DebuggerStepThroughAttribute*

- *DebuggerTypeProxyAttribute*

- *DebuggerVisualizerAttribute*

Let's begin with a basic class that we can refer to before and after adding the attributes just mentioned. We'll create a simple class named *SoftwareCompany* that has three public properties (*CompanyName*, *CompanyCity*, and *CompanyState*) and three private variables (*_companyName*, *_companyCity*, and *_companyState*). We'll use an overloaded constructor that allows you to pass in each of these values, as demonstrated in the following code snippet:

```
' VB
Public Class SoftwareCompany
  Private _companyName As String
  Private _companyCity As String
  Private _companyState As String

  Public Property CompanyName() As String
    Get
      Return Me._companyName
    End Get
    Set(ByVal value As String)
      Me._companyName = value
    End Set
  End Property

  Public Property CompanyCity() As String
    Get
      Return Me._companyCity
    End Get
    Set(ByVal value As String)
      Me._companyCity = value
    End Set
  End Property

  Public Property CompanyState() As String
    Get
      Return Me._companyState
    End Get
    Set(ByVal value As String)
      Me._companyState = value
    End Set
  End Property

  Public Sub New(ByVal companyName As String, ByVal companyCity As String, _
    ByVal companyState As String)
```

```
    End Sub
End Class

// C#
class SoftwareCompany
{
    private String _companyName;
    private String _companyState;
    private String _companyCity;

    public String CompanyName
    {
      get
      {
        return _companyName;
      }
      set
      {
        _companyName = value;
      }
    }

    public String CompanyState
    {
      get
      {
        return _companyState;
      }
      set
      {
        _companyState = value;
      }
    }

    public String CompanyCity
    {
      get
      {
        return _companyCity;
      }
      set
      {
        _companyCity = value;
      }
    }

    public SoftwareCompany(String companyName, String companyState, String companyCity)
    {
      this._companyCity = companyCity;
      this._companyName = companyName;
      this._companyState = companyState;
    }
}
```

Now go to the main method of whichever language you're using and insert the following code:

```vb
' VB
Dim Company As New SoftwareCompany("A Datum", "Miami", "Florida")
```

```csharp
// C#
SoftwareCompany Company = new SoftwareCompany("A Datum", "Florida", "Miami");
```

Set a breakpoint on the line of code just shown, run the code, and then examine the Locals window after stepping over the line of code on which the breakpoint is set. You should see something approximating Figure 10-7.

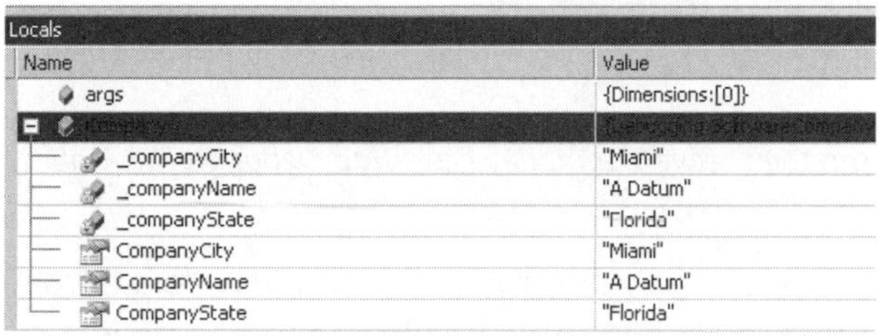

Figure 10-7   Locals window from the *SoftwareCompany* class

DebuggerBrowsableAttribute

Notice that you see each of the members of the class, including both private members (*_companyName*, *_companyCity*, and *_companyState*) and public members (*Company-Name*, *CompanyCity*, and *CompanyState*). Stop debugging, go back to the private members of the class, add the *DebuggerBrowsableAttribute*, and set the *DebuggerBrowsableState* to *never*. Your code, which references the *Sytems.Diagnostics* namespace, should look like the following:

CAUTION   DebuggerBrowsable not supported in Visual Basic

The following code in the Visual Basic example is provided solely so there is a Visual Basic counter-part for each C# example and vice versa. This attribute is not supported in Visual Basic; however, using it will not throw an exception or cause any other discernible problem. Visual Basic does support the *DebuggerDisplayAttribute*, which closely approximates the behavior of the *Debugger-Browsable* attribute.

```vb
' VB
<DebuggerBrowsable(DebuggerBrowsableState.Never)> _
Private _companyName As String
<DebuggerBrowsable(DebuggerBrowsableState.Never)> _
Private _companyCity As String
<DebuggerBrowsable(DebuggerBrowsableState.Never)> _
Private _companyState As String
```

```
// C#
[DebuggerBrowsable(DebuggerBrowsableState.Never)]
private String _companyName;
[DebuggerBrowsable(DebuggerBrowsableState.Never)]
private String _companyState;
[DebuggerBrowsable(DebuggerBrowsableState.Never)]
private String _companyCity;
```

Run the program again, and examine the output in the Locals window. You should see something similar to Figure 10-8.

Figure 10-8   Locals window from the *SoftwareCompany* class with *DebuggerBrowsable* attributes set

If everything was done correctly, the private variables (*_companyName*, *_companyState*, and *_companyCity*) should no longer be visible. In this example, we used the Never option on the *DebuggerBrowsableState* enumeration, but we had two other options, which are shown along with the Never option in Table 10-3.

Table 10-3   The *DebuggerBrowsableState* Enumeration

Name	Description
Never	Specifies that the element will never be visible
Collapsed	Shows the element, but shows it in a collapsed state
RootHidden	Does not display the root element, but displays the child elements if they are members of a collection or belong to an array

DebuggerDisplayAttribute

Just to get a baseline again, run the *SoftwareCompany* class, setting a breakpoint right after the constructor. If you use the code from the previous example, you should see output similar to that in Figure 10-9. (Note that the following image is based on C#. The output in Visual Basic will differ slightly.)

Figure 10-9   Locals window from the *SoftwareCompany* class

In the Value column of the Locals window for the Company local variable, you should see the value *Debugging.Software*. (*Debugging* is the namespace, so it might differ on your setup.) Stop debugging, modify the code by adding *DebuggerDisplayAttribute* on top of the *Class* definition, and add the parameters shown in the following code:

```vb
' VB
<DebuggerDisplay("CompanyName = {_companyName}, " & _
  "CompanyState = {_companyState}, CompanyCity{_companyCity}")> _
Public Class SoftwareCompany
```

```csharp
// C#
[DebuggerDisplay("CompanyName = {_companyName}, CompanyState = " +
  "{_companyState}, CompanyCity{_companyCity}")]
class SoftwareCompany
```

Here we have told the attribute to display the literal "*CompanyName*" and the private variable *_companyName*, display the literal "*CompanyState*" and the private variable *_companyState*, and finally display the literal "*CompanyCity*" followed by *_companyCity*. Now when the program is run, the output will be changed to something similar to the output shown in Figure 10-10. (Note that this image is based on C# and the output in Visual Basic will vary.)

Figure 10-10   Locals window from the *SoftwareCompany* class with *DebuggerDisplay* attributes set

All we did here was reference specific properties within the *SoftwareCompany* class. You can, however, reference any property of any of those properties. For example, instead of referencing the *_companyState* member, we could just as easily have referenced the *Length* property of the *_companyState* member. Similarly, let's say that we had a *Collection* property inside the *SoftwareCompany* class named *PhoneNumbers*. We could access the 0th index as follows:

```vb
' VB
<DebuggerDisplay("PhoneNumber = {PhoneNumbers(0)}, " & _
  "CompanyState = {_companyState}, CompanyCity{_companyCity}")> _
Public Class SoftwareCompany
```

```csharp
// C#
[DebuggerDisplay("PhoneNumber = {PhoneNumbers[0]}, " +
  "CompanyState = {_companyState}, CompanyCity{_companyCity}")]
public class SoftwareCompany
```

DebuggerHiddenAttribute

The purpose of the *DebuggerHiddenAttribute* class is simple: it stops a breakpoint from being set inside anything that it decorates. If a caller has a breakpoint set in it, when the class, method, or property that this attribute decorates is reached, it's simply ignored. And any attempts to set a breakpoint in the item it decorates will be ignored. The sole purpose of this class is to tell the debugger to ignore whatever it decorates, so there would be little value in showing an example.

DebuggerNonUserCodeAttribute

This attribute is similar to *DebuggerHiddenAttribute*. It's main purpose is to decorate code that is created from a designer, and therefore, it serves little purpose to a developer. Specifically, all the code that it decorates and it's associated types are not shown in the debugger, and the debugger will just step over it. Again, the primary purpose of this class is to tell the debugger to ignore whatever it decorates, so there's little value in an example.

DebuggerStepperBoundaryAttribute

This attribute is used within code that's wrapped in a *DebuggerNonUserCodeAttribute* section. Once this attribute is encountered, the debugger will stop in code decorated with this attribute and, when the next section of user code is encountered, will resume the behavior specified by the *DebuggerNonUserCodeAttribute*. You would use this attribute when something created by the designer contains one or more properties or methods of interest to you. It allows you to see the relevant portion of the code without having to view everything else.

DebuggerStepThroughAttribute

This attribute is similar to the previous two in that its main purpose is to signal to the *Debugger* that whatever code it's decorating should be stepped over and not shown in any of the debugging windows. This class is valuable when you are absolutely sure of the soundness of the code block it's decorating. For example, suppose you had a class that just initialized some properties or set default values and you were positive that no exception could be thrown from that code and/or that none of the values changed inside of it would ever be of interest to you. In Visual Basic .NET and Visual Basic 2005 every time you created a Winform for instance, this attribute is applied to the *Initialize-Component* method. This behavior was beneficial because having to step through or step over multiple statements that are simply performing initialization serves little purpose other than to consume time.

These last three attributes are similar and ultimately serve the same purpose. Unlike the *DebuggerHiddenAttribute* though, this attribute tells the *Debugger* to step over the code instead of hiding it from output.

DebuggerTypeProxyAttribute

This attribute allows you to override how a given type is shown and then specify how you want it shown. This attribute is typically used when you have an internal type and you want to take control over how it's displayed. In the following code sample (using the System.Diagnostics and System.Collections namespaces), the default way an *ArrayList* object is displayed in the debugger is modified:

```vb
' VB
<DebuggerTypeProxy(GetType(ArrayListDemo.MyDemoObject))> _
Public Class ArrayListDemo
  Inherits ArrayList

  Private ShouldIgnore As String = "The Debugger won't see this"

  Friend Class MyDemoObject
    Dim _myList As ArrayList
    Private ShouldIgnore As String = "The Debugger WILL see this"

    Public Sub New(ByVal myList As ArrayList)
      Me._myList = myList
    End Sub

    <DebuggerBrowsable(DebuggerBrowsableState.RootHidden)> _
    Public ReadOnly Property AllValues() As Object
      Get
        Dim o() As Object = New Object(Me._myList.Count) {}

        For x As Int32 = 0 To Me._myList.Count
          o(x) = Me._myList(x)
        Next

        Return o
      End Get
    End Property
  End Class
End Class
```

```csharp
// C#
[DebuggerTypeProxy(typeof(MyDemoObject))]
class ArrayListDemo : ArrayList
{
    public String ShouldIgnore = "The Debugger won't see this";

    internal class MyDemoObject
    {
      public String ShouldIgnore = "The Debugger WILL see this";

      private ArrayList _myList;

      public MyDemoObject(ArrayList myList)
```

```
      {
        this._myList = myList;
      }

      [DebuggerBrowsable(DebuggerBrowsableState.RootHidden)]
      public Object[] AllValues
      {
        get
        {
          Object[] o = new Object[this._myList.Count];

          for (Int32 x = 0; x < this._myList.Count; x++)
          {
            o[x] = this._myList[x];
          }

          return o;
        }
      }
    }
  }
}
```

So with this class, we are specifying that we don't want the default information for an *ArrayList* object and, instead, we're going to use a Proxy type—in this case, *MyDemoObject*. This attribute's main value stems from overriding what you'd normally see with your types, particularly when you have an internal class that you need displayed in a specific way.

DebuggerVisualizerAttribute

Visualizers are a new tool introduced with Visual Studio 2005. They afford a mechanism for you to see, much like with IntelliSense, all the properties of an object. (See the "Visualizers" topic at *http://msdn2.microsoft.com/en-us/library/e2zc529c.aspx*.) This attribute lets you tell the debugger that you have an associated visualizer for the given class.

NOTE .NET 2.0

The *DebuggerVisualizerAttribute* class is new in .NET 2.0.

This attribute has 12 overloads for the constructor, but in its simplest form, only the type needs to be specified. Assuming we have created a visualizer named *MyDemo-Visualizer*, we can associate it with any given class as follows:

```
' VB
<DebuggerVisualizer("MyDemoVisualizer")> _
Public Class SoftwareCompany
```

```
// C#
[DebuggerVisualizer("MyDemoVisualizer")]
class SoftwareCompany
```

Creating Trace Listeners

So far, we've focused on the output side of debugging. However, none of these methods have any value without being associated with a listener. Two primary instrumentation classes are provided by default: *Trace* and *Debug*. They are used almost identically, and the only substantive difference is within their physical implementation. *Trace* is implemented in both *Release* and *Debug* builds, whereas *Debug* is implemented only in *Debug* builds. Because we've discussed the *Debug* class in depth already, we'll now focus on the *Trace* class.

The *Trace* Class

Like the *Debug* class, the *Trace* class is mainly useful when a listener object is attached to it. Visual Studio 2005 has many listener objects built in, including *XmlTraceListener*, *DefaultTraceListener*, *DelimitedListTraceListener*, and *EventLogTraceListener*. A list of the most useful members is provided in Table 10-4.

Table 10-4   Members of the *Trace* Class

Name	Description
AutoFlush	Gets or sets whether output will be automatically flushed after every write operation
Close	Flushes the output buffer, and closes all associated listener objects
Fail	Emits an error message with the information you specify
Flush	Flushes the output buffer, and writes the output to all attached listener objects
Indent	Increments the current *IndentLevel* of trace output
IndentLevel	Gets or sets the *IndentLevel*
IndentSize	Gets or sets the number of spaces in an *Indent*
Listeners	Gets the collection of listeners that are monitoring trace output
Refresh	Refreshes the trace information

Table 10-4   Members of the *Trace* Class

Name	Description
TraceInformation	Writes an information message to all associated *Trace* class listener objects
TraceWarning	Writes a warning message to all associated *Trace* class listener objects
Unindent	Decrements the *IndentLevel*
UseGlobalLock	Gets whether a *GlobalLock* should be issued, and sets one if necessary
Write	Writes information about attached *Debug* or *Trace* class *Listener* objects in the *Listeners* collection
WriteIf	Performs the same actions as the *Write* method, but does so only if a specified condition is met
WriteLine	Writes information about attached *Debug* or *Trace* class *Listener* objects in the *Listeners* collection
WriteLineIf	Performs the same actions as the *WriteLine* method, but does so only if a specified condition is met

Because these members are identical to those discussed in the earlier section about the *Debug* class or they are self explanatory, let's move on.

The *TraceSource* Class

The *TraceSource* class provides a mechanism that enables the tracing of code execution as well as associating trace messages with their source. To use *TraceSource*, do the following:

1. Declare an instance of a *TraceSource* class.

2. Name the *TraceSource*.

3. Call the respective methods on it.

The following code demonstrates one use of *TraceSource*, where a *ConsoleTraceListener* object is added to the *TraceSource* object. By adding the switch (see the next section for more information), the message passed to the *TraceInformation* method is output to the attached listeners, in this case the console.

```vb
' VB
' Create ConsoleTraceLister object
Dim consoleTracer As New ConsoleTraceListener()
' Set up trace source for this app
Dim DemoTrace As New TraceSource("DemoApp")
' Add listener to trace source
DemoTrace.Listeners.Add(consoleTracer)
' Add source switch to source trace
DemoTrace.Switch = New SourceSwitch("DemoApp.Switch", "Information")
' Add source information indicating we're about
' to write to the console
DemoTrace.TraceInformation("Before writing to Console")
Console.WriteLine("Writing to the Console")
' Add source information indicating we have
' written to the console
DemoTrace.TraceInformation("After writing to Console")
```

```csharp
// C#
// Create ConsoleTraceLister object
ConsoleTraceListener consoleTracer = new ConsoleTraceListener();
// Set up trace source for this app
TraceSource DemoTrace = new TraceSource("DemoApp");
// Add listener to trace source
DemoTrace.Listeners.Add(consoleTracer);
// Add source switch to source trace
DemoTrace.Switch = new SourceSwitch("DemoApp.Switch", "Information");
// Add source information indicating we're about
// to write to the console
DemoTrace.TraceInformation("Before writing to Console");
Console.WriteLine("Writing to the Console");
// Add source information indicating we have
// written to the console
DemoTrace.TraceInformation("After writing to Console");
```

The *TraceSwitch* Class

The *TraceSwitch* class is used to dynamically alter behavior of the *Trace* class. For instance, you can alter the behavior for the *Trace* class to log the *TraceError*, *TraceWarning*, or *TraceInfo* properties. You can also specify, for example, that the log use verbose mode, in which everything is logged. This class provides all the functionality developers need to finely tailor tracing. Tracing can be turned on and off, for example. The levels can be changed. And as with most every other object in the *System.Diagnostics* namespace, switch objects can be manipulated by using code or a configuration file:

```xml
<configuration>
  <system.diagnostics>
    <switches>
      <add name="DemoApp.Switch" value="Information"/>
    </switches>
  </system.diagnostics>
</configuration>
```

```
' VB
Dim DemoTrace As New TraceSource("DemoApp")
DemoTrace.Switch.ShouldTrace(TraceEventType.Information)
DemoTrace.Switch.Level = SourceLevels.Information
DemoTrace.TraceInformation("This is a Test")

// C#
TraceSource DemoTrace = new TraceSource("DemoApp");
DemoTrace.Switch.ShouldTrace(TraceEventType.Information);
DemoTrace.Switch.Level = SourceLevels.Information;
DemoTrace.TraceInformation("This is a test");
```

Listener Objects

To be of value, the *Debug* and *Trace* classes depend on listener objects because, stated simply, output is valuable only if it can be analyzed. By default, Visual Studio attaches a listener object that, when written to, directs output to the Output window. The *Trace* and *Debug* classes both have a *Listeners* collection, which includes all the attached listener objects. One or more listener objects can be added to either the *Debug* or the *Trace* class and often are.

The *DefaultTraceListener* Class

Listeners can be added manually or through the configuration file. Let's go through the process of adding a listener object before moving on. First, we'll add a *DefaultTrace-Listener* through code. The *DefaultTraceListener* is attached to the Output window:

```
' VB
Trace.Listeners.Clear()
Trace.Listeners.Add(New DefaultTraceListener())
Trace.WriteLine("This is a test")

// C#
Trace.Listeners.Clear();
Trace.Listeners.Add(new DefaultTraceListener());
Trace.WriteLine("This is a test");
```

The result of the first two lines of code, which set up the tracing, can be accomplished by using a Configuration file entry:

```
<configuration>
  <system.diagnostics>
    <trace autoflush="true" indentsize="5" />
  </system.diagnostics>
</configuration>
```

The *TextWriterTraceListener* Class

The *TextWriterTraceListener* class is one of the simplest listener objects to use and simply directs output to a text file or stream. The *TextWriterTraceListener* class can be enabled by using either code or a configuration file. Following is an example of how you can enable the class by using code:

```vb
' VB
Trace.Listeners.Clear()
Trace.Listeners.Add(New TextWriterTraceListener("C:\output.txt"))
Trace.AutoFlush = True
Trace.WriteLine("This is a test")
```

```csharp
// C#
Trace.Listeners.Clear();
Trace.Listeners.Add(new TextWriterTraceListener(@"C:\output.txt"));
Trace.AutoFlush = true;
Trace.WriteLine("This is a test");
```

The same result can be accomplished using a configuration file:

```xml
<configuration>
  <system.diagnostics>
    <trace autoflush="true" indentsize="5">
      <listeners>
        <add name="DemoListener" type="System.Diagnostics.TextWriterTraceListener"
          initializeData="output.txt" />
        <remove name="Default" />
      </listeners>
    </trace>
  </system.diagnostics>
</configuration>
```

Although various listener objects might have different constructors, the same methodology is used to manage them.

The *XmlWriterTraceListener* Class

The *XmlWriterTraceListener* class forwards *Debug* or *Trace* information to a *TextWriter* object or *Stream* object.

NOTE Default filename behavior of the *XmlWriterTraceListener* class

If no name for the output file is specified, the .NET runtime uses a globally unique identifier (GUID) as a name.

XmlWriterTraceListener strongly resembles *TextWriterTraceListener,* so you might be inclined to ask, "Why use this class instead of *TextWriterTraceListener?*" The answer lies in the various attributes that this class provides. Table 10-5 shows many of these features.

NOTE .NET 2.0

The *XMLWriterTraceListener* class is new in .NET 2.0

Table 10-5   Attributes and Elements of the *XmlWriterTraceListener* Class

Name	Description
CallStack	Will display the runtime's call stack if the *CallStack* variable in *TraceOutputOptions* is set.
Computer	The name of the computer the application is running on.
Correlation	The *Correlation* object contained in the *CorrelationManager* object.
DataItem	Value contained in the *data* parameter of the *TraceData* method.
EventId	The event ID, if specified.
Execution	The execution type.
Level	Any integer value from 0 through 255. If a number greater than 255 is used, no exception will be thrown but *Level* will default to 255.
Message	The specific text message.
Source	The initiator of the message.
TimeCreated	The current time by default.
TimeStamp	The system time on the machine the application is running on if the *Timestamp* variable in *TraceOutputOptions* is set.
Type	The object's type.

With all this information, much of which is provided by default, this class provides quite a bit of enhanced functionality compared to the *TextWriterTraceListener* class. Let's look at how to enable an *XmlTraceListener*:

```
' VB
Trace.Listeners.Clear()
Trace.Listeners.Add(New XmlWriterTraceListener("C:\output.xml"))
Trace.AutoFlush = True
Trace.WriteLine("This is a test")

// C#
Trace.Listeners.Clear();
Trace.Listeners.Add(new XmlWriterTraceListener(@"C:\output.xml"));
Trace.AutoFlush = true;
Trace.WriteLine("This is a test");
```

This can also be configured using the following:

```xml
<?xml version="1.0" encoding="utf-8" ?>
  <configuration>
    <system.diagnostics>
      <trace autoflush="true" indentsize="5">
        <listeners>
          <add name="DemoListener" type="System.Diagnostics.XmlWriterTraceListener"
            initializeData="output.xml" />
          <remove name="Default" />
        </listeners>
      </trace>
    </system.diagnostics>
  </configuration>
```

After running this code snippet, the output should resemble that shown in Figure 10-11.

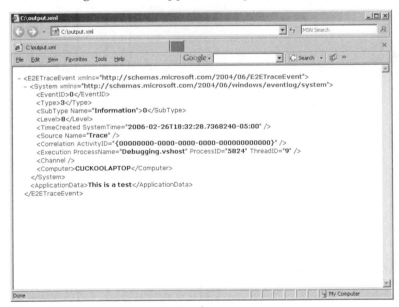

Figure 10-11   Output to output.xml

The *EventLogTraceListener* Class

Suppose you want to direct the application's output to an event log, which was covered in the previous lesson. Enabling an *EventLogTraceListener* can be accomplished by using either code or a configuration file. Following is an example of how you can enable the class by using code:

```
' VB
Trace.Listeners.Clear()
Trace.Listeners.Add(New EventLogTraceListener("Chapter10"))
Trace.AutoFlush = True
Trace.WriteLine("Something happened")

// C#
Trace.Listeners.Clear();
Trace.Listeners.Add(new EventLogTraceListener("Chapter10"));
Trace.AutoFlush = true;
Trace.WriteLine("Something happened");
```

The *DelimitedListTraceListener* Class

Now let's say that we wanted to enable a different type of listener—for example, a *DelimitedListTraceListener* that works similarly to the *TextWriterTraceListener*, except that it takes a delimited token and separates output with this token. Again, this behavior can be accomplished by using either code or a configuration file. Following is an example of how you can enable the class by using code:

```
' VB
Trace.Listeners.Clear()
Trace.Listeners.Add(New DelimitedListTraceListener ("C:\output.txt"))
Trace.AutoFlush = True
Trace.WriteLine("This is a test")

// C#
Trace.Listeners.Clear();
Trace.Listeners.Add(new DelimitedListTraceListener(@"C:\output.txt"));
Trace.AutoFlush = true;
Trace.WriteLine("This is a test");
```

Here is an equivalent configuration file (if you're using Visual Basic, remove one of the backslash characters from the path set for the value of the *initializeData* attribute):

```
<configuration>
  <system.diagnostics>
    <trace autoflush="true" indentsize="5">
      <listeners>
        <add name="DemoListener"
          type="System.Diagnostics.DelimitedListTraceListener"
```

```
            delimiter="|"
            initializeData="C:\\output.txt"/>
          <remove name="Default" />
        </listeners>
      </trace>
    </system.diagnostics>
</configuration>
```

The *CorrelationManager* Class

There are times where one application is managing multiple processes. The classic example is the ASP.NET process, which at any given time might be managing many different requests. The *CorrelationManager* class provides an easy-to-use mechanism to keep the requests isolated and unique.

Lab: Create and Use an Application Event Log

In this lab, you'll create an entry in the Event log by using the *EventLogTraceListener* class. If you encounter a problem completing an exercise, the completed projects are available on the companion CD in the Code folder.

1. Open Visual Studio 2005.

2. Create a new console application in Microsoft Visual C# 2005 or Microsoft Visual Basic 2005. Visual Basic 2005 creates a module for you, along with an empty *Main* procedure. Visual C# creates a *Program.cs* class for you with an empty *Main* procedure.

3. Import the *System* and *System.Diagnostics* namespaces so that you will not be required to qualify declarations from these namespaces later in your code.

4. Within the *Module.vb* or *Main.cs* class/module, add the following code:

```
' VB
Trace.Listeners.Clear()
Trace.AutoFlush = True
Trace.Listeners.Add(New EventLogTraceListener("Chap10Demo"))
Trace.Listeners.Add(MyListener)
Trace.WriteLine("This is a test")

// C#
Trace.Listeners.Clear();
Trace.AutoFlush = true;
Trace.Listeners.Add(new EventLogTraceListener("Chap10Demo"));
Trace.Listeners.Add(MyListener)
Trace.WriteLine("This is a test");
```

5. Compile and run the application by pressing the F5 key.

6. Open the event log, and verify that the output was written. If it was done correctly, the output should look like that shown in Figure 10-12.

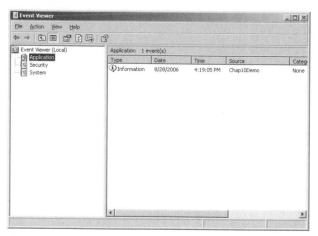

Figure 10-12   Event log entry from the *EventLogTraceListener* class

Lesson Summary

- The *Debug* and *Trace* classes are two of the primary tools developers can use to examine the execution of their applications while they run.

- The *Write*, *WriteLine*, *WriteIf*, and *WriteLineIf* methods all can be used to send output to attached listener objects.

- The *Assert* method of the *Debug* and *Trace* classes is one mechanism to test a condition of your code and receive feedback based on that evaluation.

- Listener objects are used as receptacles for *Debug* and *Trace* information.

- If no listener object is specified, the *DefaultTraceListener* is used.

- The *XmlTraceListener* can be used to output detailed information in XML format.

- The *TraceSource* class allows the developer to specify information about the source of the trace information

- The *TraceSwitch* allows the developer to manipulate virtually every aspect of the *TraceSource* class.

Lesson Review

You can use the following questions to test your knowledge of the information in Lesson 2, "Debugging and Tracing." The questions are also available on the companion CD if you prefer to review them in electronic form.

NOTE Answers

Answers to these questions and explanations of why each answer choice is right or wrong are located in the "Answers" section at the end of the book.

1. You need to ensure that the trace from one logical operation is isolated from that of other operations. How do you accomplish this objective?

    A. Use the *CorrelationManager* object to keep each trace isolated.

    B. Use a *TraceSwitch* to change the process's trace information.

    C. Use a different *TraceLevel* for each process.

    D. Specify a *Correlation* object, and use the *CorrelationManager* to control each instance of the correlation.

2. To use a specific visualizer object for a given class, which attribute should be used?

    A. *DebuggerDisplayAttribute*

    B. *DebuggerVisualizerAttribute*

    C. *DebuggerStepThroughAttribute*

    D. Use the *DebuggableAttribute*

Lesson 3: Monitoring Performance

No matter how well an application is designed, if it does not perform well it won't be well received by users. In fact, performance problems can sometimes be notably more problematic than traditional bugs because, unlike most bugs, performance problems are often quite difficult to correct. Here are some common performance problems:

- Slow or sluggish user interface (UI) responsiveness—for example, frozen screens or application locks

- Slow or sluggish network access

- Slow or sluggish database connectivity, response time, or both

- Slow or sluggish file input/output

Understanding how each of these areas works is critical to writing applications the perform well. However, once an application is deployed, life can get quite complicated. Assume that you wrote a Web application that did a lot of database access. Assume further that suddenly your company received a large influx of support calls complaining about performance. What would you do in response, and what would you tell your customers or your boss? If you can't isolate the problem, you're going to have a hard time fixing it. You'll inevitably end up searching in some wrong directions, all the while wasting precious time. Fortunately, the *System.Diagnostics* namespace provides all the tools necessary to avoid this ineffective approach to problem solving.

Real World

William Ryan

A few years ago, I worked at a company where the software manager had utter disdain for most programmatic details. He hated database normalization. He hated object-oriented design. Basically, he hated any answer other than, "Yes sir, that deadline won't be a problem." We did minimal testing as well (he hated testing too), but typically our applications performed well in our test cases. After our applications were deployed to customer sites, however, we'd start having problems with both bugs and performance. The software manager's immediate answer to any performance problem was to buy more RAM.

In one instance, we upgraded our application from 2 GB of RAM to 12 GB. This solution wasn't cheap. Unfortunately, the version of Microsoft SQL Server we were using supported only 2 GB of RAM—those extra 10 GBs were a total waste as far as our application was concerned. So our manager insisted that we upgrade the SQL

Server version. Once the new SQL Server was running and using all 12 GB, there was a slight performance gain but it was still unacceptable to the client.

Next our manager blamed the client's hardware: "We've got a Ferrari running on bicycle tires with this configuration." So he recommended the client get more hardware. At this point, the client already had spent over $20,000 more than they had planned, so they weren't budging on hardware. Our company, of course, had to absorb this additional cost. After the client had the new hardware in place, performance improved slightly but not enough to make a difference. Now the system was $40,000 over budget.

Next our manager blamed the network configuration: we couldn't use 100-MB pipes any more; we needed 1-GB pipes. After spending another $4,000, we had 1 GB of network bandwidth, but once again there was not enough benefit to fix the poor performance. Left with nothing else to point a finger at, our manager finally blamed Microsoft. Windows 2000 Server and SQL Server 2000 were the problem. After all, things ran a lot faster on old green-screen applications, and with all that new hardware, how could it not be Microsoft's fault?

The real problems all along were as follows:

- Bad data structures on the database (one of our tables had 255 columns and many others were close to this large)
- Excessive use of cursors, and cursors that were poorly written
- Single-threaded execution for everything

Had our manager bothered to diagnose the problem beforehand, a lot of time and money would have been saved. Had he bothered to diagnose the problem before finger-pointing, he might not have presided over a successful company's quick demise. The moral of the story: Before you start spending money or time fixing problems, make sure you thoroughly understand what the problems are.

After this lesson, you will be able to:
- Enumerate processes.
- Use performance counters.
- Start processing.
- Use the *StackTrace* and *StackFrame* objects.

Estimated lesson time: 20 minutes

An Overview of Processes

Before we move onto creating and manipulation processes, we must define what we mean by a process. The TechnoGeek definition would be something like: "A process is a memory slice that contains resources." A less jargony definition would be something to the effect of: "An isolated task performed by the operating system" or "an application that's being run." Therefore, a process owns one or more operating-system threads. It can also open private virtual addressing space that can only be managed by its own threads.

Most users aren't accustomed to working with processes. Instead, they typically work with applications. Microsoft Office Word, for example, is an application. Microsoft Office Outlook is another example of an application. Depending on what you're doing with either of these applications, they are probably managing multiple processes at any given time.

Technically (assuming a typical Intel-based 32-bit processor), a process is best described as a contiguous memory space of 4 GB. This measurement includes memory from 0x00000000 to 0xFFFFFFFF. This memory is secure and private, and it cannot be accessed by other processes. This configuration greatly enhances the stability and performance of Windows applications. Two things are noteworthy about how processes are managed:

- Windows allocates whatever memory resources are necessary for a process to operate, but nothing more. Traditional 32-bit machines have a maximum RAM allocation of 4 GB.
- The Virtual Memory manager saves chunks of RAM to disk as memory pages. These pages, by default, have a size of 4 KB.

The *Process* Class

An instance of the *Process* object can reference an operating-system process. The processes that this class can reference are as follows:

- One or more processes running on a local machine
- One or more processes running on a remote machine

Enumerating Processes

There are four primary methods to determine which processes are running at any given time or to identify specific processes: the *GetCurrentProcess* method, the *GetProcessById* method, the *GetProcessesByName* method, and the *GetProcesses* method.

The simplest of these four methods is the *GetCurrentProcess* method. This method associates a *Process* object with the currently active process and returns it. Since it takes no parameters, invoking it is trivial, as shown by this example (which depends on the *System.Diagnostics* namespace):

```vb
' VB
Dim ThisProcess As Process = Process.GetCurrentProcess()
Console.WriteLine("Current Process: " & ThisProcess.ToString)
```

```csharp
// C#
Process ThisProcess = Process.GetCurrentProcess();
Console.WriteLine("Current Process: " + ThisProcess.ToString());
```

Although this method is simple to use, it has limited usefulness. If you need to know about anything other than the currently running process, this method can't be of assistance.

The next method to enumerate processes is the *GetProcessById* method. This method does exactly what its name implies: it will take a process ID and return information about it if it's found. The second overload takes a process ID and a machine name and returns the information about the process. However, it's important to note that if the process is not found, an *ArgumentException* will be thrown. Therefore, care should be taken to respond gracefully unless you're certain that the process exists and, in the case of the second overload, that the machine specified exists. The following code snippet accepts a process identifier and returns information about it. (To run the code, substitute the name of your machine for the "machinename" string.)

```vb
' VB
'For illustration purposes, the number 2 is randomly chosen
Dim SpecificProcess As Process = Nothing
Try
    SpecificProcess = Process.GetProcessById(2)
    Console.WriteLine(SpecificProcess.ProcessName)
Catch Problem As ArgumentException
    Console.WriteLine(Problem.Message)
End Try
Try
    SpecificProcess = Process.GetProcessById(2, "machinename")
    Console.WriteLine(SpecificProcess.ProcessName)
Catch Problem As ArgumentException
    Console.WriteLine(Problem.Message)
End Try
```

```csharp
// C#
//For illustration purposes, the number 2 is randomly chosen
Process SpecificProcess = null;
try
{
```

```
      SpecificProcess = Process.GetProcessById(2);
      Console.WriteLine(SpecificProcess.ProcessName);
}
catch (ArgumentException Problem)
{
      Console.WriteLine(Problem.Message);
}
try
{
      SpecificProcess = Process.GetProcessById(2, "machinename");
      Console.WriteLine(SpecificProcess.ProcessName);
}
catch (ArgumentException Problem)
{
      Console.WriteLine(Problem.Message);
}
```

The methods just discussed return information about individual processes (in this example, whatever process has an identifier of 2). The following code will retrieve information about a process by using the process's name as an identifier (as opposed to using a numeric identifier as was done in the previous example):

```
' VB
Dim SpecificProcesses() As Process = Nothing
SpecificProcesses = Process.GetProcessesByName("explorer", "machinename")
For Each ThisProcess As Process In SpecificProcesses
   Console.WriteLine(ThisProcess.ProcessName)
Next

// C#
Process[] SpecificProcesses = null;
SpecificProcesses = Process.GetProcessesByName("explorer", "machinename");
  foreach (Process ThisProcess in SpecificProcesses)
  {
    Console.WriteLine(ThisProcess.ProcessName);
  }
```

The next method is the *GetProcesses* method. This method takes the name of a machine and returns all the processes running on that machine. *GetProcesses* can throw quite a few exceptions, each of which is listed here:

- *PlatformNotSupportedException*
- *ArgumentNullException*
- *InvalidOperationException*
- *Win32Exception*
- *ArgumentException*

Catching *ArgumentException* will result in all the preceding exception types being handled. Depending on the overall exception management strategy, this approach might or might not be desirable. The following code illustrates how to enumerate all the processes running on a machine.

```vb
' VB
Private Sub GetAllProcessWithoutMachineName()
  Dim AllProcesses() As Process = Nothing
  Try
    AllProcesses = Process.GetProcesses
    For Each Current As Process In AllProcesses
      Console.WriteLine(Current.ProcessName)
    Next
  Catch Problem As ArgumentException
    Console.WriteLine(Problem.Message)
  End Try
End Sub

Private Sub GetAllProcessWithMachineName()
  Dim AllProcesses() As Process = Nothing
  Try
    AllProcesses = Process.GetProcesses("machinename")
    For Each Current As Process In AllProcesses
      Console.WriteLine(Current.ProcessName)
    Next
  Catch Problem As ArgumentException
    Console.WriteLine(Problem.Message)
  End Try
End Sub
```

```csharp
// C#
private static void GetAllProcessesWithoutMachineName()
{
  Process[] AllProcesses = null;
  try
  {
    AllProcesses = Process.GetProcesses();
    foreach (Process Current in AllProcesses)
    {
      Console.WriteLine(Current.ProcessName);
    }
  }
  catch (ArgumentException Problem)
  {
    Console.WriteLine(Problem.Message);
  }
}

private static void GetAllProcessesWithMachineName()
{
  Process[] AllProcesses = null;
  try
```

```
{
  AllProcesses = Process.GetProcesses("machinename");
  foreach (Process Current in AllProcesses)
  {
    Console.WriteLine(Current.ProcessName);
  }
}
catch (ArgumentException Problem)
{
    Console.WriteLine(Problem.Message);
  }
}
```

Using Performance Counters

Because performance considerations can have a major impact on user acceptance of an application, being able to measure performance is critical. For example, if an abundance of support calls indicated that the application was sluggish, you'd want to follow some process to diagnose and troubleshoot the problem. The procedure for doing this is outlined in the following steps:

1. Create a baseline measurement of how the application should perform.

2. Verify and confirm that the problem exists.

3. Compare the baseline measurements to the current measurements.

4. Record each functional area where a disparity exists between the baseline performance and actual performance.

5. Examine the code that's running where the disparities exist.

6. Take corrective action.

Although the actual process will differ from company to company and developer to developer, the steps listed are fairly representative of the process. And the majority of these steps involve measuring actual performance.

To accomplish this measurement, the .NET Framework provides the *Performance-Counter* class.

CAUTION   .NET 2.0 *PerformanceCounter* security

In earlier versions of the .NET Framework, *PerformanceCounter* objects required Full Trust permissions to execute. In .NET 2.0, the *PerformanceCounterPermission* must be specifically granted. Unless there is a compelling reason to do so, the *PerformanceCounterPermission* should not be granted to assemblies that run in a partial trust context. If this permission is granted, an assembly can start and manipulate other system processes, which can create a huge surface area for an attack. In this respect, the *PerformanceCounter* class has security implications similar to the *EventLog* class.

PerformanceCounter objects allow for the collection and retrieval of data in a clean, object-oriented fashion. Values written to a *PerformanceCounter* object are stored in the Windows Registry and, as such, are dependent on the application running on the Windows platform.

This class can be used exclusively through code as well as through the *Performance-Counter* component, which allows developers to visually control *PerformanceCounter* objects at design time. To use this component, simply open the Components view of the Visual Studio 2005 Toolbox, select Performance Counter, and drag it onto a form. Figure 10-13 shows this view.

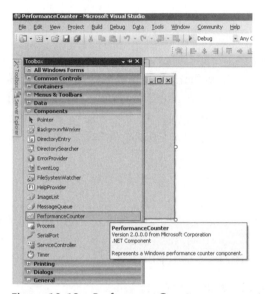

Figure 10-13   *PerformanceCounter* component in Visual Studio

*PerformanceCounter*s metaphorically are similar to file paths, which are identified by their names, their directories, or myriad other properties. The properties that identify a *PerformanceCounter* object are as follows:

- Computer Name
- Category Name
- Category Instance
- Counter Name

The properties of a *PerformanceCounter* component are shown in Figure 10-14.

Figure 10-14   Properties of a *PerformanceCounter* component

Windows has many built-in performance counters, which on their own can measure almost any resource that developers might be concerned with. These performance counters will vary based on what applications are installed on the machine. It's important to be aware of which counters are installed on your machine; otherwise, you might end up creating your own counters that duplicate functionality already available.

The *CounterCreationData* Class

The *CounterCreationData* class has one main purpose: it serves as a container object that holds all the pertinent properties that will be needed to create a *Performance-Counter* object. The *CounterCreationData* class has three properties that developers will want to manipulate. These properties are described in Table 10-6.

Table 10-6   Properties of the *CounterCreationData* Class

Name	Description
CounterHelp	Retrieves or sets a counter's friendly description
CounterName	Retrieves or sets a counter's name
CounterType	Retrieves or sets a counter's *PerformanceCounterType*

To create a new instance of the *CounterCreationData* class, do one of the following:

- Declare a new instance of the object, and set each property manually.
- Pass in all three properties to the second overloaded constructor.

The following code snippet demonstrates the first process listed:

```vb
' VB
Dim DemoCounterName As String = "DemoCounter"
Dim DemoData As New CounterCreationData()
DemoData.CounterName = DemoCounterName
DemoData.CounterHelp = "Training Demo Counter"
DemoData.CounterType = PerformanceCounterType.SampleCounter
```

```csharp
// C#
String DemoCounterName = "DemoCounter";
CounterCreationData DemoData = new CounterCreationData();
DemoData.CounterName = DemoCounterName;
DemoData.CounterHelp = "Training Demo Counter";
DemoData.CounterType = PerformanceCounterType.SampleCounter;
```

The following code snippet demonstrates the second process listed:

```vb
' VB
Dim DemoCounterName As String = "DemoCounter"
Dim DemoData As New CounterCreationData(DemoCounterName, _
  "Training Demo Counter", PerformanceCounterType.SampleCounter)
```

```csharp
// C#
String DemoCounterName = "DemoCounter";
CounterCreationData DemoData = new CounterCreationData(DemoCounterName,
  "Training Demo Counter", PerformanceCounterType.SampleCounter);
```

The *PerformanceCounterCategory* Class

The main purpose of the *PerformanceCounterCategory* class is to manage and manipulate *PerformanceCounter* objects and their categories. It contains the following five static methods, which allow a tremendous amount of control over performance categories:

- **Create**   Creates a *PerfomanceCounterCategory* class
- **Delete**   Deletes a *PerformanceCounterCategory* class
- **Exists**   Determines whether a *PerformanceCounterCategory* is already in existence
- **GetCategories**   Lists each of the *PerformanceCounterCategories* on a given machine
- **ReadCategory**   Reads all the counter and performance data associated with a given *PeformanceCategory*

To use the *Create* method, call the static *Create* method of the *PerformanceCounterCategory* class, passing in the *CategoryName*, *CategoryHelp*, *CategoryType*, *CounterName*, and *CounterHelp* values. Before attempting to call the *Create* method, the *Exists* method can be called to verify whether the category exists. (Obviously, if it does, there's no need to re-create it.). The following code checks to see if a given performance counter exists and if not, it creates it.

```
' VB
Dim DemoCategory As New PerformanceCounterCategory("DemoCategory")

If Not PerformanceCounterCategory.Exists("DemoCategory") Then
    PerformanceCounterCategory.Create("DemoCategory", _
      "Training Demo Category", PerformanceCounterCategoryType.SingleInstance, _
      "DemoCounter", "Training Counter Demo")
End If

// C#
PerformanceCounterCategory DemoCategory = new PerformanceCounterCategory("DemoCategory");

if (!PerformanceCounterCategory.Exists("DemoCategory"))
{
    PerformanceCounterCategory.Create("DemoCategory", "Training Demo Category",
    PerformanceCounterCategoryType.SingleInstance, "DemoCounter",
      "Training Counter Demo");
}
```

There is one thing to be careful of with this method. If the *Category* already exists, an *InvalidOperationException* will be thrown.

To delete a category, all that's needed is to call the *Delete* method of the *Performance-CounterCategory* and pass in the category name, like so:

```
' VB
If PerformanceCounterCategory.Exists("DemoCategory") Then
    PerformanceCounterCategory.Delete("DemoCategory\")
End If

// C#
if (PerformanceCounterCategory.Exists("DemoCategory"))
{
    PerformanceCounterCategory.Delete("DemoCategory");
}
```

The *GetCategories* method is the next method in the list, and it simply enables retrieval of all the *PerformanceCounterCategory* objects on a given machine. By default, it will refer to the *PerformanceCounterCategory* on the local machine; however, the constructor provides an overload that can specify another machine's name from which the *PerformanceCounterCategory* objects will be retrieved. Here is an example of using the *GetCategories* method:

```
' VB
Dim DemoCategories() As PerformanceCounterCategory = _
  PerformanceCounterCategory.GetCategories("machinename")

For Each ThisCategory As PerformanceCounterCategory In DemoCategories
  Console.WriteLine(ThisCategory.CategoryName)
Next
```

```
// C#
PerformanceCounterCategory[] DemoCategories =
  PerformanceCounterCategory.GetCategories("machinename");

  foreach (PerformanceCounterCategory ThisCategory in DemoCategories)
  {
    Console.WriteLine(ThisCategory.CategoryName);
  }
```

The final method on the list is the *ReadCategory* method. *ReadCategory* reads all the counter and performance object instance data that is associated with this category. This method returns an *InstanceDataCollectionCollection*. (Although the name looks peculiar, this is the actual object name.) The following code snippet shows how to use the *ReadCategory* method:

```
' VB
Dim DemoCounterCategory As New PerformanceCounterCategory(".NET CLR Data")
Dim DemoCollection As InstanceDataCollectionCollection = DemoCounterCategory.ReadCategory
```

```
// C#
PerformanceCounterCategory DemoCounterCategory = new PerformanceCounterCategory();
InstanceDataCollectionCollection DemoCollection = DemoCounterCategory.ReadCategory();
```

The *PerformanceCounter* Class

Each of the previous items were parts that, when used together, help provide a tremendous amount of information about *PerformanceCounter* objects. To illustrate what can be done with a *PerformanceCounter*, I'll present a common scenario: examining how many applications are running on an ASP.NET process. There is a predefined category named "ASP.NET" and a predefined counter named "Applications Running". Examine the following code:

```
' VB
Dim DemoCounter As New PerformanceCounter("ASP.NET", "Applications Running")
Dim Crlf As String = ControlChars.CrLf
Dim Builder As New StringBuilder()

Builder.Append("Counter Name: " & DemoCounter.CounterName & Crlf)
Builder.Append("Counter Type: " & DemoCounter.CounterType.ToString() & Crlf)
Builder.Append("Category Name: " & DemoCounter.CategoryName & Crlf)
Builder.Append("Instance Name: " & DemoCounter.InstanceName & Crlf)
Builder.Append("Machine Name: " & DemoCounter.MachineName & Crlf)

Console.WriteLine(Builder.ToString())

// C#
PerformanceCounter DemoCounter =
  new PerformanceCounter("ASP.NET", "Applications Running");
StringBuilder Builder = new StringBuilder();
```

```
Builder.Append("Counter Name:" + DemoCounter.CounterName + "\r\n");
Builder.Append("Counter Type:" + DemoCounter.CounterType.ToString() + "\r\n");
Builder.Append("Category Name:" + DemoCounter.CategoryName + "\r\n");
Builder.Append("Instance Name:" + DemoCounter.InstanceName + "\r\n");
Builder.Append("Machine Name:" + DemoCounter.MachineName + "\r\n");

Console.WriteLine(Builder.ToString());
```

When run, this code presents information about this specific *PerformanceCounter*.

Starting Processes

Many times there is a need to start external applications or processes from within your application. For instance, you might want to provide help for a user and start Internet Explorer, passing it a specific URL that provides useful information. There are two ways to start a process:

- Use without command-line arguments.
- Specify command-line arguments.

Each approach is described in the following sections.

Start Processes without Command-Line Arguments

For a simple process, all that's needed to start a process in .NET is to call the *Start* method of the *Process* class. The *Process* class's constructor has five overloads, three of which are for non–command-line scenarios.

NOTE   **Specifying command-line parameters to start a program**

The *Main* method of .NET applications has two overloaded constructors. The first of those takes no parameters. The second of those takes an array of *String* objects separated by a single space. Each of those values is considered a separate parameter. For example, the literal "This is a Test" passed into the *Main* method would evaluate to four different values: 'This', 'is', 'a', and 'Test'.

The first of those five overloads takes one parameter of type *ProcessStartInfo*. The *ProcessStartInfo* class has quite a few properties, which afford in-depth control over how a process is started. Because you can start many process types (for example, a console application, a Winforms application, and so on), the properties that are specified for each can differ substantially. For the sake of this discussion, we'll focus on the properties that correspond to the overloaded constructors. (Refer to the code named ProcessStartDemo in the Chapter 11 folder the companion CD.)

NOTE   **Use of the *ProcessStartInfo* class**

In many instances, you'll want to set many more properties than are provided in the constructors. To accomplish this, the *ProcessStartInfo* class must be used.

```vb
' VB
Dim Info as New ProcessStartInfo()
Info.FileName = Me.tbProcessName.Text
Process.Start(Info)
```

```csharp
// C#
ProcessStartInfo Info = new ProcessStartInfo();
Info.FileName = this.tbProcessName.Text;
Process.Start(Info);
```

This code creates an instance of the *ProcessStartInfo* class to start a specific process.

The second overload takes a single *String* parameter that corresponds to the name of the application. If the application is installed as a program, you can just use the application name. Otherwise, you need to specify the fully qualified file name.

```vb
' VB
Dim Info as New ProcessStartInfo()
Dim FileName As String = "C:\ProcessStartDemo.exe"
Process.Start(FileName)
```

```csharp
// C#
ProcessStartInfo Info = new ProcessStartInfo();
String FileName = @"C:\ProcessStartDemo.exe";
Process.Start(FileName);
```

The third overload takes a file name just like the one in the previous example, a *String* value corresponding to the user's logon user name, and a *System.Security.SecureString* corresponding to the user's logon password and the domain name.

```vb
' VB
Dim SecurePassword As New SecureString
For i As Int32 = 0 To Me.tbPassword.Text.Length - 1
    SecurePassword.AppendChar(Convert.ToChar(Me.tbPassword.Text(i)))
Next
Process.Start(Me.tbFileName.Text, Me.tbUserName.Text, SecurePassword, Me.tbDomain.Text)
```

```csharp
// C#
SecureString SecurePassword = new SecureString();
for (Int32 i = 0; i < this.tbPassword.Text.Length; i++)
{
    SecurePassword.AppendChar(Convert.ToChar(this.tbPassword.Text[i]));
}
Process.Start(this.tbFileName.Text, this.tbUserName.Text, SecurePassword,
  this.tbDomain.Text);
```

CAUTION *UseShellExecute*

If a username and password are specified, the *UseShellExecute* property must be set to *false*.

Start Processes with Command-Line Arguments

Specifying command-line arguments to start a process is similar to starting a process without them. The first example in the previous section illustrated using the *ProcessStartInfo* to start a process. The *ProcessStartInfo* class has an *Arguments* property that allows you to specify as many arguments as are needed. To specify them, simply insert each one with a space in between them. In the previous section, the *Arguments* property was not specified, which allowed the process to be started without any command-line arguments. To specify command-line arguments, use the following code, which needs the *System.Diagnostics* namespace:

```
' VB
Dim Info as New ProcessStartInfo()
Info.FileName = Me.tbProcessName.Text
Info.Arguments = "EACH OF THESE WORDS IS AN ARGUMENT"
Process.Start(Info)
```

```
// C#
ProcessStartInfo Info = new ProcessStartInfo();
Info.FileName = this.tbProcessName.Text;
Info.Arguments = "EACH OF THESE WORDS IS AN ARGUMENT " ;
Process.Start(Info);
```

If the *ProcessStartInfo* class is used, the only necessary step is to specify the *Arguments* property:

```
' VB
Dim Info As New ProcessStartInfo()
    Info.FileName = Me.tbUserName.Text
    If Me.tbArguments.Text <> String.Empty Then
      Info.Arguments = Me.tbArguments.Text
    End If
    If Me.tbUserName.Text <> String.Empty Then
      Dim SecurePassword As New System.Security.SecureString()
      For i As Int32 = 0 To Me.tbPassword.Text.Length - 1
        SecurePassword.AppendChar(Convert.ToChar(Me.tbPassword.Text(i)))
        Info.UseShellExecute = False
        Info.UserName = Environment.UserName
        Info.Password = SecurePassword
        Return
      Next i
    ElseIf tbPassword.Text <> String.Empty Then
      MessageBox.Show("If a UserName is provided, a Password must be provided as well")
    End If
    If Me.tbDomain.Text <> String.Empty Then
      Info.Domain = Me.tbDomain.Text
    End If
    If Me.tbProcessName.Text <> String.Empty Then
      Info.FileName = Me.tbProcessName.Text
      Process.Start(Info)
    End If
```

```
// C#
ProcessStartInfo Info = new ProcessStartInfo();
Info.FileName = this.tbProcessName.Text;
if (this.tbArguments.Text != string.Empty)
{
   Info.Arguments = this.tbArguments.Text;
}
if (this.tbUserName.Text != String.Empty)
{
   SecureString SecurePassword = new SecureString();
   for (Int32 i = 0; i < this.tbPassword.Text.Length; i++)
   {
     SecurePassword.AppendChar(Convert.ToChar(this.tbPassword.Text[i]));
   }
   //Set UseShellExecute to false if you specify a username
   Info.UseShellExecute = false;
   Info.UserName = Environment.UserName;
   Info.Password = SecurePassword;
}
else
{
   MessageBox.Show("If a UserName is provided, a Password must be provided as well");
   return;
}
if (this.tbDomain.Text != String.Empty){
Info.Domain = this.tbDomain.Text;
   }
if (this.tbProcessName.Text != string.Empty)
{
   Process.Start(Info);
}
```

The *StackTrace* and *StackFrame* Classes

The *StackTrace* class allows you to see the state of the .NET runtime's call stack at a given point in time. Although a full discussion of the call stack mechanism is beyond the scope of this discussion, we'll touch upon it briefly.

Each time a method is called, a *StackFrame* is added and pushed onto the stack. Each subsequent method is pushed onto the stack to be executed in last-in, first-out order. When there are no more methods to be called, each method is executed and popped (removed) from the stack. So by examining the *StackTrace* and vicariously its *Stack-Frames*, a tremendous amount of information about the state of the application can be discerned. However, the *StackFrame* class is intended to help support .NET Framework methods and is not intended to be used directly. A brief overview of the constructors of the *StackFrame* class is shown in Table 10-7.

Table 10-7 The *StackFrame* Class Constructors

Constructor	Available Parameters
StackTrace Constructor ()	[None]
StackTrace Constructor (Boolean)	fNeedFileInfo
StackTrace Constructor (Exception)	e
StackTrace Constructor (Int32)	skipFrames
StackTrace Constructor (StackFrame)	frame
StackTrace Constructor (Exception, Boolean)	e fNeedFileInfo
StackTrace Constructor (Exception, Int32)	e skipFrames
StackTrace Constructor (Int32, Boolean)	skipFrames fNeedFileInfo
StackTrace Constructor (Thread, Boolean)	targetThread fNeedFileInfo
StackTrace Constructor (Exception, Int32, Boolean)	e skipFrames fNeedFileInfo

Every time an exception is thrown by the .NET runtime, the *Exception* object's current *StackTrace* property is set to the current *StackTrace*. If the assembly where the exception is thrown has *Debug* symbols loaded, this information can be viewed. Examine the following code snippet:

```
' VB
Try
  Dim x as Int32 = 1
  x = x - 1
  Dim i as Int32 = 10 \ x
Catch Problem as ArithmeticException
   Debug.Assert(False, Problem.StackTrace)
End Try
```

```csharp
// C#
try
{
  Int32 x = 1;
  x--;
  Int32 i = 10 / x;
}
catch (DivideByZeroException Problem)
{
    Debug.Assert(false, Problem.StackTrace);
}
```

After the *Exception* object is caught, the code intentionally causes a *Debug* assertion to fail so that the *StackTrace* can be viewed. The resulting output will look like that shown in Figure 10-15.

Figure 10-15   Results from a *StackTrace* object

Lab: Monitoring Application Performance

In this lab, you create an application, add two *PerformanceCounter* objects to it, and monitor their values. If you encounter a problem completing an exercise, the completed projects are available on the companion CD in the Code folder.

1. Open Visual Studio 2005.

2. Select File, New, Project, Visual C#/ Visual Basic .NET, Windows, and then Console Application.

3. Type **PerformanceCounterDemo** in the Name text box, and press the OK button.

4. Select the Program.cs file in Visual C# or Module1.vb in Visual Basic.

5. Add the following code to the top of the Program.cs file or Module1.vb file:

```vbnet
' VB
Imports System.Diagnostics
Imports System.Timers
```

```csharp
// C#
using System.Diagnostics;
using System.Timers;
```

6. Create the following three private members: a *PerformanceCounter* object named *HeapCounter*, a *PerformanceCounter* object named *ExceptionCounter*, and a *Timer* object named *DemoTimer*. The following code demonstrates this:

```vb
' VB
Private HeapCounter As PerformanceCounter
Private ExceptionCounter As PerformanceCounter
Private DemoTimer As Timer
```

```csharp
// C#
private static PerformanceCounter HeapCounter = null;
private static PerformanceCounter ExceptionCounter = null;
private static Timer DemoTimer;
```

7. In the *Main* method, instantiate a new instance of *DemoTimer* and pass in the value 3000 to the overloaded constructor. Doing this will set the *Interval* property to 3000 milliseconds, or 3 seconds.

```vb
' VB
DemoTimer = New Timer(3000)
```

```csharp
// C#
DemoTimer = new Timer(3000);
```

8. Create an *EventHandler* for the *DemoTimer*'s *Elapsed* event, and name it *OnTick*:

```vb
' VB
Private Sub OnTick(ByVal source As Object, ByVal e As ElapsedEventArgs)

End Sub
```

```csharp
// C#
private static void OnTick(object source, ElapsedEventArgs e)
{

}
```

9. Go back to the *Main* method and wire up a handler for the *Elapsed* event:

```vb
' VB
AddHandler DemoTimer.Elapsed, AddressOf OnTick
```

```csharp
// C#
DemoTimer.Elapsed += new ElapsedEventHandler(OnTick);
```

10. Immediately after the previous line of code, set the *Enabled* property of the *DemoTimer* object to *true*:

```vb
' VB
DemoTimer.Enabled = True
```

```csharp
// C#
DemoTimer.Enabled = true;
```

11. Instantiate the *HeapCounter PerformanceCounter*, and set its *CategoryName* property to ".NET CLR Memory" and its *CounterName* property to "# Bytes in all Heaps" as illustrated in the following code snippet. Afterward, set the *InstanceName* property to "_Global_":

```
' VB
HeapCounter = New PerformanceCounter(".NET CLR Memory", "# Bytes in all Heaps")
HeapCounter.InstanceName = "_Global_"
```

```
// C#
HeapCounter = new PerformanceCounter(".NET CLR Memory", "# Bytes in all Heaps");
HeapCounter.InstanceName = "_Global_";
```

12. Follow the same steps to instantiate the *ExceptionCounter PerformanceCounter*, except set the *CounterName* property to "# of Exceps Thrown"

```
' VB
ExceptionCounter = New PerformanceCounter(".NET CLR Exceptions", "# of Exceps Thrown")
ExceptionCounter.InstanceName = "_Global_"
```

```
// C#
ExceptionCounter = new PerformanceCounter(".NET CLR Exceptions", "# of Exceps Thrown");
ExceptionCounter.InstanceName = "_Global_";
```

13. Add the following lines of code immediately afterward. The first line is for display purposes only, and the second will allow the application to continue running:

```
' VB
Console.WriteLine("Press [Enter] to Quit Program")
Console.ReadLine()
```

```
// C#
Console.WriteLine("Press [Enter] to Quit Program");
Console.ReadLine();
```

14. Add code to display the *NextValue* property of each of the *PerformanceCounter* objects in the console window in the *EventHandler*:

```
' VB
Console.WriteLine("# of Bytes in all Heaps : " & HeapCounter.NextValue().ToString())
Console.WriteLine("# of Framework Exceptions Thrown : " & _
    ExceptionCounter.NextValue().ToString())
```

```
// C#
Console.WriteLine("# of Bytes in all Heaps : " + HeapCounter.NextValue().ToString());
Console.WriteLine("# of Framework Exceptions Thrown : " +
    ExceptionCounter.NextValue().ToString());
```

15. Compile the application by selecting Build and then choosing Build Solution or by pressing the F5 key.

Lesson Summary

■ A process is an executing application, with a unique identifier to differentiate it from other processes. Processes are mechanisms that allow applications to run safely isolated from other applications.

■ The two primary classes for directing output from an application are *Debug* and *Trace*. The *Trace* class listener object is enabled by default in .NET applications. Listener objects are the mechanisms by which *Debug* and *Trace* output can be handled. The *XmlTextWriterListener* allows *Debug* and *Trace* output to be written with detailed information stored in predefined Xml attributes. The *Assert* method of both the *Debug* and *Trace* classes forces an examination of a condition, and based on the evaluation, it will let the application continue to run or break into the debugger. The *Break* method of the *Debugger* class causes an application's execution to stop at a specific breakpoint.

■ The *Start* method of the *Process* class allows applications to be started programmatically. The *GetProcesses* method of the *Process* class returns information about all running processes on a machine. If information about a specific process is needed (as opposed to general information about all processes), the *GetProcessByName* or *GetProcessById* methods should be used.

■ To pass values into the constructor of the *Main* method, command-line arguments can be specified.

■ The *StackTrace* object provides detailed information about the state of execution for a given application. *StackFrame* objects make up the *StackTrace* object. However, they are intended to support the .NET Framework and should not be used directly.

■ Because *String* objects are reference types, they pose a potential security vulnerability when used to store passwords. In the current version of the .NET Framework, the *SecureString* class is provided to manage sensitive data.

■ *PerformanceCounter* objects are mechanisms that allow specific measurement of an application's resource utilization.

Lesson Review

You can use the following questions to test your knowledge of the information in Lesson 3, "Monitoring Performance." The questions are also available on the companion CD if you prefer to review them in electronic form.

NOTE Answers

Answers to these questions and explanations of why each answer choice is right or wrong are located in the "Answers" section at the end of the book.

1. Which method will start an instance of Internet Explorer and specify the URL "http://www.microsoft.com" for it to navigate to?

    A. *Process.Start("iexplore.exe");*

    B. *Process.Start("InternetExplorer, http://www.microsoft.com");*

    C. *Process.Start("iexplore.exe", "http://www.microsoft.com");*

    D. *Process.Run("iexplore.exe", "http://www.microsoft.com");*

2. Assume that the following code was just run. Which answer illustrates how to specifically output the current *StackTrace* to the console window?

```
' VB
Try
  Dim x as Int32 = 1
  x = x - 1
  Dim i as Int32 = 10 / x
Catch Problem as ArithmeticException
'This is the code to fill in
End Try

// C#
try
{
  Int32 x = 1;
  x--;
  Int32 i = 10 / x;
}
catch (DivideByZeroException Problem)
{
  //This is the code to fill in
}
```

    A. *Debug.Assert(Problem.Message);*

    B. *Debug.Assert(false, Problem.ToString();*

    C. *Console.WriteLine(Problem.ToString());*

    D. *Console.WriteLine(Problem.StackTrace.ToString());*

3.   Which method is appropriate to specify a password when starting a process?

   A.   Use a *String* variable that contains the password.

   B.   Use an *Array* of type *Char*

   C.   Use an Array of type *String* coupled with an Integer reference to the password's index in the array.

   D.   Use a *SecureString* object.

Lesson 4: Detecting Management Events

The *System.Management* namespace provides a comprehensive set of tools to monitor and manage the system, devices, and applications via the Windows Management Instrumentation (WMI) technology.

After this lesson, you will be able to:

- Enumerate management objects.
- Create queues.
- Respond to events.

Estimated lesson time: 20 minutes

Enumerating Management Objects

At the core of the *System.Management* namespace is the *ManagementObjectSearcher* object, which can programmatically access resources through WMI. This mechanism is extremely easy to use because the syntax mimics that of Structured Query Language (SQL), which most developers are already familiar with. To execute a query using the *ManagementObjectSearcher*, the following steps need to be performed:

1. Declare an instance of the *ConnectionOptions* class, and set the *UserName* and *Password* properties.

2. Declare an instance of the *ManagementObjectSearcher* class.

3. Declare a *ManagementScope* object, and set the *PathName* and *ConnectionOptions* properties.

4. Create an *ObjectQuery* object, and specify a query to run.

5. Create a *ManagementObjectCollection*, and set it to the return value from the *ManagementObjectSearcher*'s *Get* method.

NOTE **Using** *ConnectionOptions*

There are some security concerns when using this object because anything that can read system resources has the potential to be misused. One area that needs special care is the *ConnectionOptions* class. Because it contains a user name and a password, great care should be taken to keep this information secure. Unfortunately, at this time the *ConnectionOptions* class does not use a *SecureString* object to hold the password.

In each of the examples that will be presented, the process will be logically similar to the steps just listed. In most cases, the only substantive difference will be the object that is queried.

The *System.Management* namespace has many members, but a few in particular account for most of its functionality. Those members are listed in Table 10-8.

Table 10-8   Management Objects in the *System.Management* Namespace

Name	Description
ManagementQuery	Base class used for WMI queries.
EventQuery	Query object used to query WMI objects. *EventQuery* objects are used in conjunction with event watchers.
ObjectQuery	Query object for querying both instances and classes.
ManagementObjectSearcher	Class used to query a collection of *Management-Objects* based on a WMI query.

Enumerating Logical Drives

To enumerate the logical drives by using *System.Management* objects, the main thing that needs to be done is specify a target. In the following example, the *Win32_LogicalDisk* object is going to be queried. The *Size* and *Name* attributes will be returned via a *ManagementObjectCollection*.

```
' VB
Dim DemoOptions As New ConnectionOptions
DemoOptions.Username = "domainname\\username"
DemoOptions.Password = "password"

Dim DemoScope As ManagementScope = New ManagementScope( _
  "\\machinename\root\cimv2", DemoOptions)
Dim DemoQuery As New ObjectQuery( _
  "SELECT Size, Name FROM Win32_LogicalDisk where DriveType=3")
Dim DemoSearcher As New ManagementObjectSearcher(DemoScope, DemoQuery)
Dim AllObjects As ManagementObjectCollection = DemoSearcher.Get

For Each DemoObject As ManagementObject In AllObjects
  Console.WriteLine("Resource Name: " & DemoObject("Name").ToString())
  Console.WriteLine("Resource Size: " & DemoObject("Size").ToString())
Next
```

```csharp
// C#
ConnectionOptions DemoOptions = new ConnectionOptions();
DemoOptions.Username = "domainname\\username";
DemoOptions.Password = "password";

ManagementScope DemoScope = new ManagementScope("\\\\machinename\\root\\cimv2",
  DemoOptions);
ObjectQuery DemoQuery = new
  ObjectQuery("SELECT Size, Name FROM Win32_LogicalDisk where DriveType=3");

ManagementObjectSearcher DemoSearcher =
  new ManagementObjectSearcher(DemoScope, DemoQuery);
ManagementObjectCollection AllObjects = DemoSearcher.Get();

foreach (ManagementObject DemoObject in AllObjects)
{
  Console.WriteLine("Resource Name: " + DemoObject["Name"].ToString());
  Console.WriteLine("Resource Size: " + DemoObject["Size"].ToString());
}
```

Enumerating Network Adapters

Using almost identical methodology to that used in the previous example, you can enumerate all the network adapters on a given machine essentially by just changing the query. The main difference between the previous code and the code used to accomplish this is that the *Win32_NetworkConfiguration* object needs to be queried instead of the *Win32_LogicalDisk*. Network adapters and disk drives have different properties, so the implementation will change slightly to allow each of the different properties to be shown:

```vb
' VB
Public Const IP_Enabled As String = "IPEnabled"
Public Const IP_Address As String = "IPAddress"
Public Const IP_Subnet As String = "IPSubnet"
Public Const DNS_Hostname As String = "DNSHostName"
Public Const DNS_Domain As String = "DNSDomain"

Public Sub EnumerateAllNetworkAdapters()
  Dim DemoQuery As ManagementObjectSearcher = _
    New ManagementObjectSearcher("SELECT * FROM Win32_NetworkAdapterConfiguration")
  Dim DemoQueryCollection As ManagementObjectCollection = DemoQuery.Get()

  For Each DemoManager As ManagementObject In DemoQueryCollection
    Console.WriteLine("Description : " & CType(DemoManager("Description"), String))
    Console.WriteLine("MacAddress : " & CType(DemoManager("MacAddress"), String))

    If (CType(DemoManager(IP_Enabled), Boolean) = True) Then
        Dim IPAddresses() As String = CType(DemoManager(IP_Address), String())
        Dim IPSubnets() As String = CType(DemoManager(IP_Subnet), String())
```

```
      Console.WriteLine(DNS_Hostname & " : " & DemoManager(DNS_Hostname).ToString)
      Console.WriteLine(DNS_Domain & " : " & DemoManager(DNS_Domain).ToString)

      For Each IPAddress As String In IPAddresses
        Console.WriteLine(IP_Address & " : " & IPAddress)
      Next

      For Each IPSubnet As String In IPSubnets
        Console.WriteLine(IP_Subnet & " : " & IPSubnet)
      Next
    End If
  Next
End Sub


// C#
public const String IP_Enabled = "IPEnabled";
public const String IP_Address = "IPAddress";
public const String IP_Subnet = "IPSubnet";
public const String DNS_HostName = "DNSHostName";
public const String DNS_Domain = "DNSDomain";

public static void EnumerateAllNetworkAdapters()
{
  ManagementObjectSearcher DemoQuery =
    new ManagementObjectSearcher("SELECT * FROM Win32_NetworkAdapterConfiguration");
  ManagementObjectCollection DemoQueryCollection = DemoQuery.Get();

  foreach (ManagementObject DemoManager in DemoQueryCollection)
  {
    Console.WriteLine("Description : " + DemoManager["Description"]);
    Console.WriteLine("MacAddress : " + DemoManager["MacAddress"]);

    if (Convert.ToBoolean(DemoManager[IP_Enabled]) == true)
    {
      String[] IPAddresses = DemoManager[IP_Address] as String[];
      String[] IPSubnets = DemoManager[IP_Subnet] as String[];

      Console.WriteLine(DNS_HostName + " : " + DemoManager[DNS_HostName]);
      Console.WriteLine(DNS_Domain + " : " + DemoManager[DNS_Domain]);

      foreach (String IPAddress in IPAddresses)
      {
        Console.WriteLine(IP_Address + " : " + IPAddress);
      }

      foreach (String IPSubnet in IPSubnets)
      {
        Console.WriteLine(IP_Subnet + " : " + IPSubnet);
      }
    }
  }
}
```

Retrieve Information about Services that Are Paused

Retrieving information about Windows Services is just as straightforward as retrieving information about other resources. Just do the following:

1. Create a new *ManagementObjectSearcher* object.

2. Specify a query for it.

3. Call the *Get* method of the *ManagementObjectSearcher* (in the *System.Management* namespace). Here is an example:

```vb
' VB
Private Sub ListPausedServices()
  Dim DemoSearcher As New ManagementObjectSearcher( _
    "SELECT * FROM Win32_Service WHERE Started = FALSE")

  Dim AllObjects As ManagementObjectCollection = DemoSearcher.Get

  For Each PausedService As ManagementObject In AllObjects
    Console.WriteLine("Service = " & CType(PausedService("Caption"), String))
  Next
End Sub
```

```csharp
// C#
private static void ListPausedServices()
{
  ManagementObjectSearcher DemoSearcher = new ManagementObjectSearcher(
    "SELECT * FROM Win32_Service WHERE Started = FALSE");
  ManagementObjectCollection AllObjects = DemoSearcher.Get();

  foreach (ManagementObject PausedService in AllObjects)
  {
    Console.WriteLine("Service = " + PausedService["Caption"]);
  }
}
```

Subscribe to Management Events Using the *ManagementEventWatcher* Class

The *ManagementEventWatcher* class allows for subscription information about events that occur within the WMI context. To use it, perform the following steps:

1. Create a new *ManagementEventWatcher* object.

2. Associate an *EventQuery* object with it.

3. Call the *WaitForNextEvent* method.

4. Stop the notifications.

Here is an example:

```vb
' VB
Public Sub QueryServices()
  Dim DemoQuery As New EventQuery
  DemoQuery.QueryString = _
    "SELECT * FROM __InstanceCreationEvent WITHIN 1 WHERE TargetInstance" & _
    " isa ""Win32_Service"" AND TargetInstance.State = 'Paused'"
  Dim DemoWatcher As New ManagementEventWatcher(DemoQuery)

  DemoWatcher.Options.Timeout = New TimeSpan(0, 0, 20)
  Console.WriteLine("Open an application to trigger WaitForNextEvent")
  Dim e As ManagementBaseObject = DemoWatcher.WaitForNextEvent()
  DemoWatcher.Stop()
End Sub
```

```csharp
// C#
public static void QueryServices()
{
  EventQuery DemoQuery = new EventQuery();
  DemoQuery.QueryString = "SELECT * FROM __InstanceCreationEvent WITHIN 2 " +
    "WHERE TargetInstance isa \"Win32_Service\" AND " +
    "TargetInstance.State = 'Paused'";
  ManagementEventWatcher DemoWatcher =
    new ManagementEventWatcher(DemoQuery);
  DemoWatcher.Options.Timeout = new TimeSpan(0, 0, 10);
  Console.WriteLine("Open an application to trigger WaitForNextEvent");
  ManagementBaseObject Event = DemoWatcher.WaitForNextEvent();
  DemoWatcher.Stop();
}
```

Lab: Write a Management Event to a Log

In this lab, you create an application that writes a management event to a log. If you encounter a problem completing an exercise, the completed projects are available on the companion CD in the Code folder.

1. Open Visual Studio 2005.

2. Select File, New, Project, Visual C#/ Visual Basic .NET, Windows, and then Console Application.

3. Type **ManagementEventDemo** in the Name text box, and click OK.

4. Select the Program.cs file in Visual C# or Module1.vb in Visual Basic.

5. Add the following code to the top of the Program.cs file or Module1.vb file:

```vb
'VB
Imports System.Diagnostics
Imports System.Management
```

```csharp
//C#
using System.Diagnostics;
using System.Management;
```

Note that you will also need to add an assembly reference to System.Management.

6. In Module1.vb or Program.cs, create a new method named WriteToEventLog and insert the following code:

```vb
' VB
Public Sub WriteToEventLog()
  Dim DemoQuery As New WqlEventQuery("__InstanceCreationEvent", _
    New TimeSpan(0, 0, 1), "TargetInstance isa ""Win32_Process""")
  Dim DemoWatcher As New ManagementEventWatcher()

  DemoWatcher.Query = DemoQuery

  DemoWatcher.Options.Timeout = New TimeSpan(0, 0, 30)

  Console.WriteLine("Open an application to trigger an event.")

  Dim e As ManagementBaseObject = DemoWatcher.WaitForNextEvent()
  Dim DemoLog As New EventLog("")
  DemoLog.Source = "Chap10Demo"
  Dim EventName As String = _
    CType(e("TargetInstance"), ManagementBaseObject)("Name").ToString
  Console.WriteLine(EventName)
  DemoLog.WriteEntry(EventName, EventLogEntryType.Information)
  DemoWatcher.Stop()
End Sub
```

```csharp
//C#
public static void WriteToEventLog()
{
    WqlEventQuery DemoQuery =
        new WqlEventQuery("__InstanceCreationEvent",
        new TimeSpan(0, 0, 1),
        "TargetInstance isa \"Win32_Process\"");

    ManagementEventWatcher DemoWatcher =
        new ManagementEventWatcher();
    DemoWatcher.Query = DemoQuery;
    DemoWatcher.Options.Timeout = new TimeSpan(0, 0, 30);

    Console.WriteLine(
        "Open an application to trigger an event.");

    ManagementBaseObject e = DemoWatcher.WaitForNextEvent();

    EventLog DemoLog = new EventLog("");
    DemoLog.Source = "Chap10Demo";
    String EventName = ((ManagementBaseObject)e["TargetInstance"])
["Name"].ToString();
    Console.WriteLine(EventName);
```

```
DemoLog.WriteEntry(EventName, EventLogEntryType.Information);

DemoWatcher.Stop();

}
```

7. Call the WriteToEventLog from Main:

```
'VB
Sub Main()
  WriteToEventLog()
  Console.ReadLine()
End Sub

//C#
static void Main(string[] args)
{
  WriteToEventLog();
  Console.ReadLine();
}
```

8. Compile the application and run it. You will be prompted to open an application (for instance, notepad.exe). You should see the name of the application written out to the console window and written to an event log whose source is "Chapter10Demo".

Lesson Summary

- WMI is a component of the Windows operating system that provides monitoring functionality that spans virtually every machine resource.

- The *EventQuery* class is used within the .NET Framework to represent a WMI query.

- The *Win32_Service* object can be used to query information about Windows services.

- The *ManagementQuery* base class is used as a foundation for all management query objects.

- The *ManagementObjectSearcher* is used to query system resources through WMI.

Lesson Review

You can use the following questions to test your knowledge of the information in Lesson 4, "Detecting Management Events." The questions are also available on the companion CD if you prefer to review them in electronic form.

NOTE   Answers

Answers to these questions and explanations of why each answer choice is right or wrong are located in the "Answers" section at the end of the book.

1. Which of the following items *cannot* be queried via WMI?

    A. Network adapters.

    B. Logical drives on a machine

    C. A list of OleDb-compliant databases on the network

    D. A list of Windows Services on a machine and their respective states

Chapter Review

To further practice and reinforce the skills you learned in this chapter, you can perform the following tasks:

- Review the chapter summary.
- Review the list of key terms introduced in this chapter.
- Complete the case scenarios. These scenarios set up real-world situations involving the topics of this chapter and ask you to create a solution.
- Complete the suggested practices.
- Take a practice test.

Chapter Summary

- The Windows event logging mechanism is an excellent way to record information about an application that has already been deployed. Informational messages, warning messages, security messages, and custom messages can all be stored in the Windows event logs.
- The *Debug* and *Trace* classes are provided to allow for specific application information to be tracked during development and after deployment.
- Listener objects provide a location for *Debug* and *Trace* output to be directed to.
- Visual Studio 2005 provides many new attributes that will allow you to take finely grained control over the debugger. Examples of these new attributes include *DebuggerVisualizerAttribute* and *DebuggerProxyType*.
- Visualizers are a powerful new feature of Visual Studio 2005 that allow developers to see virtually every aspect of an object at debug time.
- Windows Management Instrumentation (WMI) and the *System.Management* namespace provide a framework for querying information about virtually every aspect of a computer's resources.

Key Terms

Do you know what these key terms mean? You can check your answers by looking up the terms in the glossary at the end of the book.

- attribute

- *Debug*
- *Debugger*
- event log
- *ManagementQuery*
- performance counter
- process
- *StackTrace*
- Windows Management Instrumentation

Case Scenario

In the following case scenario, you will apply what you've learned in this chapter. You can find answers to these questions in the "Answers" section at the end of this book.

Case Scenario: Choosing Where to Direct Output

You are working as an application developer in the Application Development department at A Datum Corporation. An application you helped develop has been deployed for about a month, and users have started complaining that performance is sluggish. The Database Administrator (DBA) of your company has been warning the Application Development department that the forecasted load for the new deployments would be too much for the current SQL Server database. Although there are noted hardware deficiencies, the DBA is sure that the many connection timeouts that are occuring are caused by connection leaks. The Network Administrator also had concerns that the Web servers were not going to be able to address the additional load.

The Corporate Vice President recently requested from the Application Development department a definitive list of everything that would be necessary to fix the problem "once and for all." He said that he's willing to purchase whatever resources are necessary, but any additional equipment that needs purchased that is not included in the memo will be purchased with your department's bonus pool money. He also indicated that he wants all the problems fixed, so any bugs that might be causing performance issues in addition to the database and Web server deficiencies had better be included in the memo. Your boss comes by your office and instructs you to write up the list. What do you do to solve this problem?

Suggested Practices

To help you successfully master the objectives covered in this chapter, complete the following tasks.

Embedding configuration, diagnostic, management, and installation features into a .NET Framework application

For this task, you should complete at least Practices 1 and 2. If you want a better understanding of how the *System.Diagnostics* and *System.Management* namespaces work, complete Practices 3 and 4 as well.

- **Practice 1**   Create a new event log that will be used specifically by an application you create. Write values to it, retrieve values written to it, and clear all the values from it.

- **Practice 2**   Use a plaintext string value and convert it to a *SecureString* object. Use this *SecureString* to start a process such as Notepad or Excel.

- **Practice 3**   Start a process without specifying parameters for it. Then do the same, but this time specify parameters for it.

- **Practice 4**   Using the code provided in Lesson 4, run a few queries to learn about your system resources. Use similar methodology to query about objects that weren't specifically mentioned in the lesson.

Take a Practice Test

The practice tests on this book's companion CD offer many options. For example, you can test yourself on just one exam objective or you can test yourself on all the 70-536 certification exam content. You can set up the test so that it closely simulates the experience of taking a certification exam, or you can set it up in study mode so that you can look at the correct answers and explanations after you answer each question.

MORE INFO   Practice tests

For details about all the practice test options available, see the "How to Use the Practice Tests" section in this book's Introduction.

Chapter 11
Application Security

Everyone has heard that you shouldn't log on to your computer as an Administrator. The reason isn't because you don't trust yourself not to delete your hard drive; it's because you don't trust the applications you run. When you run an unmanaged application in Microsoft Windows Server 2003, Microsoft Windows XP, and earlier versions of Windows, that code gets all the privileges your user account has. If you accidentally run a virus or a Trojan horse, the application can do anything your user account has permissions to do. So you are forced to log on with minimal privileges to restrict application permissions.

Code access security (CAS), a concept that the .NET Framework introduced to Windows, enables you to control the permissions that individual applications have. If a friend sends you a new .NET Framework text editor, you can restrict it to opening a window and prompting you to open and save files—and nothing else. The text edited wouldn't be able to send e-mails, upload files to a Web site, or create files, even if you are logged on as an Administrator.

CAS enables users to restrict on a very granular level what managed code can do. As a developer, you must understand how to create applications that work even when some permissions are restricted. You can also use CAS to improve your application's security by restricting which callers can use your code and forcibly limiting your application to a restricted permission set.

Exam objectives in this chapter:
- Implement code access security to improve the security of a.NET Framework application. (Refer *System.Security* namespace)
    - *SecurityManager* class
    - *CodeAccessPermission* class
    - Modify the Code Access Security Policy at the computer, user, and enterprise level by using the Code Access Security Policy tool (Caspol.exe).
    - *PermissionSet* class and *NamedPermissionSet* class
    - Standard Security interfaces

- Control permissions for resources by using the *System.Security.Permission* classes. (Refer *System.Security.Permission* namespace)

  ❑ *SecurityPermission* class

  ❑ *PrincipalPermission* class

  ❑ *FileIOPermission* class

  ❑ *StrongNameIdentityPermission* class

  ❑ *UIPermission* class

  ❑ *UrlIdentityPermission* class

  ❑ *PublisherIdentityPermission* class

  ❑ *GacIdentityPermission* class

  ❑ *FileDialogPermission* class

  ❑ *DataProtectionPermission* class

  ❑ *EnvironmentPermission* class

  ❑ *IUnrestrictedPermission* interface

  ❑ *RegistryPermission* class

  ❑ *IsolatedStorageFilePermission* class

  ❑ *KeyContainerPermission* class

  ❑ *ReflectionPermission* class

  ❑ *StorePermission* class

  ❑ *SiteIdentityPermission* class

  ❑ *ZoneIdentityPermission* class

- Control code privileges by using *System.Security.Policy* classes. (Refer *System.Security.Policy* namespace)

  ❑ *ApplicationSecurityInfo* class and *ApplicationSecurityManager* class

  ❑ *ApplicationTrust* class and *ApplicationTrustCollection* class

  ❑ *Evidence* class and *PermissionRequestEvidence* class

  ❑ *CodeGroup* class, *FileCodeGroup* class, *FirstMatchCodeGroup* class, *NetCodeGroup* class, and *UnionCodeGroup* class

  ❑ *Condition* classes

❑ *PolicyLevel* class and *PolicyStatement* class

❑ *IApplicationTrustManager* interface, *IMembershipCondition* interface, and *IIdentityPermissionFactory* interface

Lessons in this chapter:

Before You Begin

To complete the lessons in this chapter, you should be familiar with Microsoft Visual Basic or C# and be comfortable with the following tasks:

- Create a console application in Microsoft Visual Studio using Visual Basic or C#.

- Add references to system class libraries to a project.

- Write to files and streams.

Lesson 1: Understanding Code Access Security

If you have worked with previous versions of the .NET Framework, you might already be familiar with code access security (CAS) concepts. If you have been a Microsoft Windows developer but haven't previously used the .NET Framework, using CAS requires you to understand completely novel security concepts. This lesson describes the concept behind CAS and each of the components that the .NET Framework uses to implement CAS.

After this lesson, you will be able to:

- Describe the purpose of CAS.
- List the four most important elements of CAS and the significance of each.
- Describe how security policy defines an assembly's permission set.
- Explain how CAS works with operating system security.
- Use the .NET Framework Configuration tool to configure CAS.
- Use Caspol to configure CAS.

Estimated lesson time: 60 minutes

What Is Code Access Security?

Code access security (CAS) is a security system that allows administrators and developers to control application authorization similar to the way they have always been able to authorize users. With CAS, you can allow one application to read and write to the registry, while restricting access for a different application. You can control authorization for most of the same resources you've always been able to restrict using the operating system's role-based security (RBS), including the following:

- The file system
- The registry
- Printers
- The event logs

You can also restrict resources that you can't control using RBS. For example, you can control whether a particular application can send Web requests to the Internet or whether an application can make DNS requests. These are the types of requests that malicious applications are likely to make to abuse a user's privacy, so it makes sense that CAS allows you to restrict those permissions.

Unfortunately, CAS can be applied only to managed applications that use the .NET Framework runtime. Unmanaged applications run without any CAS restrictions and are limited only by the operating system's RBS. If CAS is used to restrict the permissions of an assembly, the assembly is considered *partially trusted*. Partially trusted assemblies must undergo CAS permission checks each time they access a protected resource. Some assemblies are exempt from CAS checks and are considered *fully trusted*. Fully trusted assemblies, like unmanaged code, can access any system resource that the user has permissions to access.

Elements of Code Access Security

Every security system needs a way to identify users and determine what a user can and can't do, and CAS is no exception. However, because CAS identifies and assigns permissions to applications rather than to people, it can't use the user names, passwords, and access control lists (ACLs) that you're accustomed to.

Instead, CAS identifies assemblies using *evidence*. Each piece of evidence is a way that an assembly can be identified, such as the location where the assembly is stored, a hash of the assembly's code, or the assembly's signature. An assembly's evidence determines which code group it belongs to. Code groups, in turn, grant an assembly a permission set. The sections that follow describe each of these components in more detail.

What Is Evidence?

Evidence is the information that the runtime gathers about an assembly to determine which code groups the assembly belongs to. Common forms of evidence include the folder or Web site from which the assembly is running and digital signatures.

NOTE Evidence: a misnomer

Identification might be a better term than *evidence*. Evidence sounds like a set of clues you use to track down someone who didn't want to be identified. In CAS, evidence is used just like a person's passport, password, and PIN—information that proves identity and describes an individual as deserving a certain level of trust.

Table 11-1 shows the common types of evidence that a host can present to the runtime. Each row corresponds to a member class of the *System.Security.Policy* namespace.

Table 11-1   Evidence Types

Evidence	Description
Application directory	The directory in which the assembly resides.
Hash	The cryptographic hash of the assembly, which uniquely identifies a specific version of an assembly. Any modifications to the assembly make the hash invalid.
Publisher	The assembly's publisher's digital signature, which uniquely identifies the software developer. Using Publisher evidence requires the assembly to be signed.
Site	The site from which the assembly was downloaded, such as *www.microsoft.com*.
Strong Name	The cryptographic strong name of the assembly, which uniquely identifies the assembly's namespace. The assembly must be signed to use Strong Name evidence.
URL	The URL from which the assembly was downloaded, such as *www.microsoft.com/assembly.exe*.
Zone	The zone in which the assembly is running, such as the Internet zone or the LocalIntranet zone.

There are two types of evidence: host evidence and assembly evidence. *Host evidence* describes the assembly's origin, such as the application directory, URL, or site. Host evidence can also describe the assembly's identity, such as the hash, publisher, or strong name. *Assembly evidence* is custom user- or developer-provided evidence.

What Is a Permission?

A *permission* is a CAS access control entry. For example, the File Dialog permission determines whether an assembly can prompt the user with the Open dialog box, the Save dialog box, both, or neither. Figure 11-1 shows the File Dialog permission being configured.

By default, 19 permissions are available for configuration in the .NET Framework Configuration tool. Each corresponds to two members of the *System.Security.Permissions* namespace: one for imperative use and one for declarative use. Table 11-2 describes each of these permissions. Additionally, you can add custom permissions.

Figure 11-1 Permissions specify whether an assembly can and can't do specific actions

Table 11-2   Default Permissions

Permission	Description
Directory Services	Grants an assembly access to the Active Directory. You can specify paths, and whether Browse or Write access is available.
DNS	Enables or restricts an assembly's access to submit DNS requests.
Environment Variables	Grants assemblies access to environment variables, such as *Path*, *Username*, and *Number_Of_Processors*. You can grant an assembly access to all environment variables, or specify those that the assembly should be able to access. To view all environment variables, open a command prompt and run the command Set.
Event Log	Provides an assembly access to event logs. You can grant unlimited access or limit access to browsing or auditing.
File Dialog	Controls whether an assembly can prompt the user with the Open dialog box, the Save dialog box, or both.

Table 11-2 Default Permissions

Permission	Description
File IO	Restricts access to files and folders. You can grant an assembly unrestricted access, or you can specify a list of paths and whether each path should grant Read, Write, Append, or Path Discovery access.
Isolated Storage File	Grants assemblies access to isolated storage. You can configure the level of isolation and the size of the disk quota.
Message Queue	Allows an assembly to access message queues, which can be restricted by path and access type.
Performance Counter	Controls whether an assembly can read or write performance counters.
Printing	Limits an assembly's capability to print.
Reflection	Controls whether an assembly can discover member and type information in other assemblies.
Registry	Restricts access to registry keys. You can grant an assembly unrestricted access; or you can specify a list of keys and whether each key should grant Read, Write, or Delete access.
Security	Provides granular control over the assembly's access to various CAS features. All assemblies must at least have the Enable Assembly Execution setting to run. This permission also controls whether assemblies can call unmanaged code, assert permissions, and control threads, among other settings.
Service Controller	Specifies which services, if any, an assembly can browse or control.
Socket Access	Used to control whether an assembly can initiate TCP/IP connections. You can control the destination, port number, and protocol.
SQL Client	Controls whether an assembly can access SQL Server, and whether blank passwords are allowed.

Table 11-2   Default Permissions

Permission	Description
User Interface	Determines whether an assembly can create new windows or access the clipboard.
Web Access	Determines whether the assembly can access Web sites and which Web sites can be accessed.
X509 Store	Grants assemblies access to the X509 certificate store and controls whether they can add, remove, and open certificate stores.

What Is a Permission Set?

A *permission set* is a CAS ACL. For example, the Internet default permission set contains the following permissions:

- File Dialog
- Isolated Storage File
- Security
- User Interface
- Printing

The LocalIntranet zone contains more permissions, based on the theory that code running on your local network deserves more trust than code running from the Internet:

- Environment Variables
- File Dialog
- Isolated Storage File
- Reflection
- Security
- User Interface
- DNS
- Printing

The .NET Framework includes seven default permission sets, as described in Table 11-3.

Table 11-3   Default Permission Sets

Permission Set	Description
FullTrust	Exempts an assembly from CAS permission checks.
SkipVerification	Enables an assembly to bypass permission checks, which can improve performance, but sacrifices security.
Execution	Enables an assembly to run and grants no other permissions.
Nothing	Grants no permissions to an assembly. The assembly is not even allowed to run.
LocalIntranet	Grants a generous set of permissions to assemblies, including the capability to print and access the event log. Notably, it does not allow the assembly to access the file system except through the Open and Save dialog boxes.
Internet	Grants a restricted set of permissions to an assembly. Generally, you can run an assembly with this permission set with very little risk. Even malicious assemblies should not be able to cause any serious damage when run with this permission set.
Everything	Grants assemblies all permissions. This is different from FullTrust, which skips all CAS security checks. Assemblies with the Everything permission set will still be subject to CAS checks.

What Are Code Groups?

Code groups are authorization devices that associate assemblies with permission sets. Code groups provide a similar service to CAS as user groups provide to RBS. For example, if an administrator wants to grant a set of users access to a folder, the administrator creates a user group, adds the users to the group, and then assigns file permissions to the group. Code groups work similarly, except that you don't have to manually add individual assemblies to a group. Instead, group membership is determined by the evidence that you specify as the code group's membership condition.

For example, any code running from the Internet should be a member of the Internet_Zone code group. As you can see from Figure 11-2, the Internet_Zone code group's default membership condition is that the host presents Zone evidence, and that piece of Zone evidence identifies the assembly as being in the Internet zone.

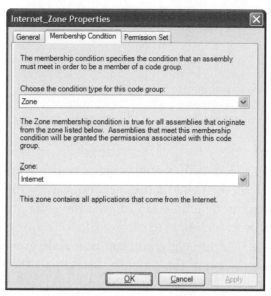

Figure 11-2   The Internet_Zone code group membership is restricted by using Zone evidence

Whereas user groups control authorization based on distributed ACLs associated with each resource, code groups use centralized permission sets. For example, Figure 11-3 shows that the Internet_Zone code group assigns the Internet permission set. For convenience, the dialog box lists the permission set's individual permissions. However, you cannot specify individual permissions for a code group. A code group must be associated with a permission set.

Figure 11-3   The Internet_Zone code group assigns the Internet permission set

---

BEST PRACTICES   Working with files

Applications running in the Internet and LocalIntranet zones do not receive the *FileIOPermission*, and as such, cannot directly access files. They do, however, have *FileDialogPermission*. Therefore, assemblies in the Internet zone can open files by prompting the user to select the file using an *OpenFileDialog* object. Assemblies in the LocalIntranet zone can also save files by using the *Save-FileDialog* object. To access files without *FileIOPermission*, call the *ShowDialog* method of either *OpenFileDialog* or *SaveFileDialog*. If the user selects a file, you can use the file handle returned by the *OpenFile* method to access the file.

It might seem limiting that you can specify only a single type of evidence and a single permission set for a code group. However, just as a user account can be a member of multiple user groups, an assembly can be a member of multiple code groups. The assembly will receive all the permissions assigned to each of the code groups (known as the union of the permission sets). Additionally, you can nest code groups within each other, and assign permissions only if the assembly meets all the evidence requirements of both the parent and child code groups. Nesting code groups allows you to assign permissions based on an assembly having more than one type of evidence. Figure 11-4 shows the Microsoft_Strong_Name code group nested within the My_Computer_Zone code group, which in turn is nested within the All_Code group.

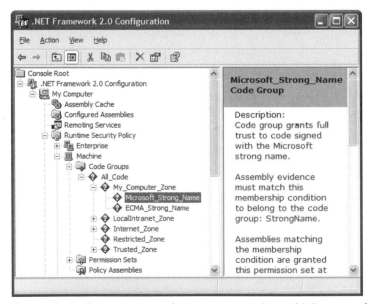

Figure 11-4   You can nest code groups to require multiple types of evidence

Table 11-4 lists the default machine code groups residing directly within the All_Code code group. Additionally, some of these code groups contain nested code groups.

Table 11-4   Default Code Groups

Code Group	Evidence	Permission Set
My_Computer_Zone	Zone: My Computer	FullTrust
LocalIntranet_Zone	Zone: Local Intranet	LocalIntranet
Internet_Zone	Zone: Internet	Internet
Restricted_Zone	Zone: Untrusted sites	Nothing
Trusted_Zone	Zone: Trusted sites	Internet

What Is Security Policy?

A *security policy* is a logical grouping of code groups and permission sets. Additionally, a security policy can contain custom assemblies that define other types of policies. Security policies provide administrators with the flexibility to configure CAS settings at multiple levels. By default, there are four configurable policy levels: Enterprise, Machine, User, and Application Domain. Application Domains were described in Chapter 8, "Application Domains and Services."

The Enterprise level is the highest security policy level, describing security policy for an entire enterprise. Enterprise security policy can be configured by using the Active Directory directory service. Machine policy, the second security policy level, applies to all code run on a particular computer. User policy is the third level, and it defines permissions on a per-user basis. The runtime evaluates the Enterprise, Machine, and User levels separately, and it grants an assembly the minimum set of permissions granted by any of the levels (known as the intersection of the permission sets). By default, the Enterprise and User security policies grant all code full trust, which causes the Machine security policy to alone restrict CAS permissions.

> ### Usefulness of Multiple Layers of Security Policy
>
> To understand how security policies are used, consider an application developer who wants to play with an assembly she downloaded from the Internet. The developer has downloaded the assembly to her local computer, so it will run within the My Computer Zone. The developer's computer is a member of an Active Directory domain, and a domain administrator has created a code group in the Enterprise security policy that grants assemblies on the local computer

the Everything permission set. This is more restrictive than the FullTrust permission set that the Machine security policy grants assemblies in the My Computer zone, so the Everything permission set takes precedence.

The developer isn't sure that the assembly is safe to run, however, so she wants to apply the Internet permission set to prevent the assembly from writing to the disk or communicating across the network. She doesn't log on to her computer as an Administrator, but she can still launch the .NET Framework Configuration tool and modify the User security policy. (Standard users aren't allowed to modify the Machine security policy.) By modifying the User security policy, she can restrict assemblies in the My Computer zone to the Internet permission set. Assemblies that she runs will be restricted without affecting other users of the same computer.

The assembly is a member of three code groups: one in the Enterprise security policy, one in the Machine security policy, and one in the User security policy. The runtime determines the assembly's permissions by comparing each code group's permission sets and using the most restrictive set of permissions shared by all three permission sets (the intersection). Because the FullTrust and Everything permission sets contain all the Internet permission set's permissions (plus a few more permissions), the most restrictive set of permissions is exactly that defined by the Internet permission set.

How CAS Works with Operating System Security

CAS is completely independent of operating system security. In fact, you must use entirely different tools to administer CAS. Although you can control a user's or group's file permissions using Microsoft Windows Explorer, you have to use the .NET Framework Configuration tool to grant or restrict an assembly's file permissions.

CAS works on top of existing operating system security. When determining whether an assembly can take a particular action, both CAS and the operating system security are evaluated. The most restrictive set of permissions is applied. For example, if CAS grants an assembly access to write to the C:\Windows\ folder but the user running the assembly does not have that permission, the assembly *cannot* write to the folder. Figure 11-5 shows how CAS relates to operating system security.

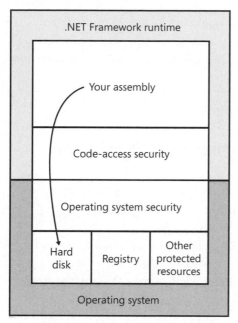

Figure 11-5 CAS complements, but does not replace, role-based security

Exam Tip No assembly can have more permissions than the user running the assembly, regardless of how the assembly uses CAS.

How to Use the .NET Framework Configuration Tool to Configure CAS

The .NET Framework Configuration tool provides a graphical interface for managing .NET Framework security policy and applications that use remoting services. You can perform many different CAS-related tasks, including the following:

- Evaluating an assembly to determine which code groups it is a member of
- Evaluating an assembly to determine which permissions it will be assigned
- Adding new permission sets
- Adding new code groups
- Increasing an assembly's trust
- Adjusting zone security
- Resetting policy levels

MORE INFO .NET Framework Configuration tool

This chapter covers using the .NET Framework Configuration tool only to manage CAS policy. For more information about the .NET Framework Configuration tool, refer to Chapter 9, "Installing and Configuring Applications."

The following sections provide procedures for performing these tasks.

How to Determine Which Code Groups Grant Permissions to an Assembly

When troubleshooting CAS permissions, you might need to determine which code groups grant permissions to your assembly. To do this, launch the .NET Framework Configuration tool and perform the following steps:

1. Click Runtime Security Policy.

2. Click Evaluate Assembly. The Evaluate An Assembly Wizard appears.

3. On the What Would You Like To Evaluate page, click Browse. Select your assembly and then click Open.

4. Click the View Code Groups That Grant Permissions To The Assembly option. Click Next.

5. Expand each policy level to determine which code groups grant permissions to your assembly. Figure 11-6 shows an assembly that receives permissions from the My_Computer_Zone code group.

Figure 11-6 Use the Evaluate An Assembly Wizard to determine which code groups apply permissions to your assembly

6. Click Finish.

How to Determine Total CAS Permissions Granted to an Assembly

When troubleshooting CAS permissions, you might need to determine which permissions the runtime will grant to your assembly. To do this, launch the .NET Framework Configuration tool and perform the following steps:

1. Click Runtime Security Policy.

2. Click Evaluate Assembly. The Evaluate An Assembly Wizard appears.

3. On the What Would You Like To Evaluate page, click Browse. Select your assembly and then click Open.

4. Click the View Permissions Granted To The Assembly option. Click Next.

5. The wizard displays each permission assigned to your assembly. To view the detailed permission settings, select any permission and then click the View Permission button.

6. Click Finish.

How to Add a Permission Set

To create a new permission set, launch the .NET Framework Configuration tool and perform the following steps:

1. Expand Runtime Security Policy.

2. Expand Enterprise, Machine, or User, depending on the policy level in which you want to define the permission set.

3. Click Permission Sets. In the right pane, click Create New Permission Set.

4. On the Identify The New Permission Set page, specify a name and description. Click Next.

5. On the Assign Individual Permissions To Permission Set page, perform the following steps:

    A. Click the permission you want to add to the permission set, and click Add.

    B. For each permission, specify the permission settings that are unique to that permission and click OK.

    C. Repeat this process for each individual permission required by your permission set.

6. Click Finish.

How to Add a Code Group

To add a code group, launch the .NET Framework Configuration tool and perform the following steps:

1. Expand Runtime Security Policy.

2. Expand Enterprise, Machine, or User, depending on the policy level in which you want to define the code group.

3. Expand Code Groups, expand All_Code, and examine the existing child code groups. If the code group you want to create defines a subset of permissions for an existing code group, click that code group. Otherwise, click All_Code.

4. Click Add A Child Code Group.

5. On the Identify The New Code Group page, type a name and a description, and then click Next.

6. On the Choose A Condition Type page, specify the condition type for the code group by choosing the evidence the runtime will use to identify the code. Click Next.

7. On the Assign A Permission Set To The Code Group page, click the Use Existing Permission Set option if one of the current permission sets exactly meets your needs. Otherwise, click Create A New Permission Set. Click Next.

8. If you selected Create A New Permission Set, perform the following steps:

   A. On the Identify The New Permission Set page, specify a name and description. Click Next.

   B. On the Assign Individual Permissions To Permission Set page, click the permissions you want in the permission set and click Add. For each permission, specify the permission settings that are unique to that permission and click OK. Click Next.

9. On the Completing The Wizard page, click Finish.

How to Increase an Assembly's Trust

If you have restricted the default CAS permissions on your computer, you might need to grant additional trust to specific assemblies to grant them the permissions they need to run correctly. To do this, launch the .NET Framework Configuration tool and perform the following steps:

1. Click Runtime Security Policy.

2. Click Increase Assembly Trust. The Trust An Assembly Wizard appears.

3. On the What Would You Like To Modify page, click Make Changes To This Computer to adjust the Machine policy level, or click Make Changes For The Current

User Only to affect the User policy level. Click Next. You must be an administrator to adjust the Machine policy level.

4. On the What Assembly Do You Want To Trust page, click Browse. Select the assembly you want to trust and then click Open. You can trust only assemblies that have a strong name. Click Next.

5. On the Choose The Minimum Level Of Trust For The Assembly page, select the minimum trust level for the assembly. Click Next.

6. On the Completing The Wizard page, review your selections and then click Finish.

How to Adjust Zone Security

By default, the .NET Framework includes five zones, each with a unique set of CAS permissions. You should make use of these default zones whenever possible, but you might need to change the permission set that a zone uses. To do this, launch the .NET Framework Configuration tool and perform the following steps:

1. Expand Runtime Security Policy, expand Machine, expand Code Groups, and then expand All_Code.

2. Click the zone you want to adjust. In the right pane, click Edit Code Group Properties.

3. Click the Permission Set tab (shown in Figure 11-7) and then click an item in the Permission Set list to specify the desired permission set. Click OK.

Figure 11-7 Adjust the permissions assigned to a zone by adjusting the associated code group's properties

As a developer, one of the first things you should do is adjust the permission set assigned to the My_Computer_Zone code group. By default, it's set to Full Trust, which means any CAS statements in your applications will be completely ignored. Change this to the Everything permission set, which grants similar permissions but respects CAS statements in assemblies. Alternatively, you can further restrict access to local assemblies by choosing another permission set.

How to Reset Policy Levels

You might need to restore the default policy levels after making modifications. To do this, launch the .NET Framework Configuration tool and perform the following steps:

1. Click Runtime Security Policy. In the right pane, click Reset All Policy Levels.

2. Click Yes and then click OK.

The .NET Framework Configuration tool restores the original policy level settings, including removing all custom code groups and permission sets that you created.

How to Use the Code Access Security Policy Tool

You can use the Code Access Security Policy tool (Caspol.exe) to examine and modify Machine-, User-, and Enterprise-level code access security policies. Although the .NET Framework Configuration tool is the most convenient tool to use for manual configuration, Caspol provides similar functionality at the command line.

MORE INFO   Caspol

Caspol features a dizzying set of parameters, and this book will cover only a handful of the most common ones. For complete instructions, at the command prompt, run this command:

Caspol -?.

Caspol Parameters

Caspol uses an extremely complicated set of options. Table 11-5 lists the most commonly used options. The −addgroup and −chggroup options take additional parameters in the form of membership conditions and flags. Membership conditions, described in Table 11-6, are the evidence that the .NET Framework uses to determine which code group to assign an assembly. Flags define the name, description, and other options and are listed in Table 11-7.

Table 11-5   **Commonly Used Caspol Options**

Option	Description
-addfulltrust *assembly_file*	Adds an assembly that implements a custom security object (such as a custom permission or a custom membership condition) to the full trust assembly list for a specific policy level. The *assembly_file* argument specifies the assembly to add. This file must be signed with a strong name.
-addgroup *parent_name* *membership_condition* *permission_set_name* [*flags*]	Adds a new code group. The *parent_name* argument specifies the name of the code group that will be the parent of the code group being added. The *membership_condition* argument specifies the membership condition for the new code group (described in Table 11-6). The *permission_set_name* argument is the name of the permission set that will be associated with the new code group. You can also set one or more flags for the new group (described in Table 11-7).
-all	Indicates that all options following this one apply to the Enterprise, Machine, and the current User policy.
-chggroup *name* {*membership_condition* | *permission_set_name* | *flags*}	Changes a code group's membership condition, permission set, or the settings of the exclusive, levelfinal, name, or description flags. The *name* argument specifies the name of the code group to change. The *permission_set_name* argument specifies the name of the permission set to associate with the code group. See Tables 11-6 and 11-7 for information about the *membership_condition* and *flags* arguments.
-enterprise	Indicates that all options following this one apply to the Enterprise level policy. Users who are not enterprise administrators do not have sufficient rights to modify the Enterprise policy, although they can view it.

Table 11-5   Commonly Used Caspol Options

Option	Description
-execution {on | off}	Turns on or off the mechanism that checks for the permission to run before code starts to run.
-help	Displays command syntax and options for Caspol.
-list	Lists the code group hierarchy and the permission sets for the specified Machine, User, or Enterprise policy level or all policy levels.
-listdescription	Lists all code group descriptions for the specified policy level.
-listfulltrust	Lists the contents of the full trust assembly list for the specified policy level.
-listgroups	Displays the code groups of the specified policy level or all policy levels. Caspol displays the code group's label first, followed by the name if it is not null.
-listpset	Displays the permission sets for the specified policy level or all policy levels.
-machine	Indicates that all options following this one apply to the Machine level policy. Users who are not administrators do not have sufficient rights to modify the Machine policy, although they can view it. For administrators, -machine is the default.
-quiet	Temporarily disables the prompt that is normally displayed for an option that causes policy changes.
-recover	Recovers policy from a backup file. Whenever a policy change is made, Caspol stores the old policy in a backup file.
-remgroup *name*	Removes the specified code group. If the specified code group has child code groups, Caspol also removes all the child code groups.

Table 11-5   Commonly Used Caspol Options

Option	Description
-rempset *permission_set_name*	Removes the specified permission set from policy. The *permission_set_name* argument indicates which permission set to remove. Caspol removes the permission set only if it is not associated with any code group. The built-in permission sets cannot be removed.
-reset	Returns policy to its default state.
-resolvegroup *assembly_file*	Shows the code groups to which a specific assembly (*assembly_file*) belongs.
-resolveperm *assembly_file*	Displays all permissions that security policy would grant the assembly (*assembly_file*) if the assembly were allowed to run.
-security {on | off}	Turns code access security on or off. When code access security is disabled, all code access demands succeed.
-user	Indicates that all options following this one apply to the User level policy for the user on whose behalf Caspol is running. For nonadministrative users, -user is the default.
-?	Displays command syntax and options for Caspol.exe.

Table 11-6   Caspol Membership Conditions

This Membership Condition	Specifies
-all	All code.
-appdir	The application directory. If you specify -appdir as the membership condition, the URL evidence of code is compared with the application directory evidence of that code. If both evidence values are the same, this membership condition is satisfied.

Table 11-6   Caspol Membership Conditions

This Membership Condition	Specifies
-hash *hash_algorithm* {-hex *hash_value* | -file *assembly_file* }	Code that has the given assembly hash. To use a hash as a code group membership condition, you must specify either the hash value or the assembly file.
-pub { -cert *cert_file_name* | -file *signed_file_name* | -hex *hex_string* }	Code that has the given software publisher, as denoted by a certificate file, a signature on a file, or the hexadecimal representation of an X509 certificate.
-site *website*	Code that has the given site of origin. For example: -site *www.microsoft.com*.
-strong -file *file_name* {name | -noname} {version | -noversion}	Code that has a specific strong name, as designated by the filename, the assembly name as a string, and the assembly version in the format *major.minor.build.revision*. For example: -strong -file myAssembly.exe myAssembly 1.2.3.4
-url *URL*	Code that originates from the given URL. The URL must include a protocol, such as *http://* or *ftp://*. Additionally, a wildcard character (*) can be used to specify multiple assemblies from a particular URL. To specify a file share on a network, use the syntax "-url *servename**sharename**". The trailing * is required to properly identify the share.
-zone *zonename*	Code with the given zone of origin. The *zonename* argument can be one of the following values: MyComputer, Intranet, Trusted, Internet, or Untrusted.

Table 11-7   Caspol Flags

Flag	Description
-description "*description*"	If used with the −addgroup option, specifies the description for a code group to add. If used with the −chggroup option, specifies the description for a code group to edit. You must add double quotes around the description, even if it does not include spaces.
-exclusive {on | off}	When set to on, indicates that only the permission set associated with the code group you are adding or modifying is considered when some code fits the membership condition of the code group. When this option is set to off, Caspol considers the permission sets of all matching code groups in the policy level.
-levelfinal {on | off}	When set to on, indicates that no policy level below the level in which the added or modified code group occurs is considered. This option is typically used at the Machine policy level. For example, if you set this flag for a code group at the Machine level, and some code matches this code group's membership condition, Caspol does not calculate or apply the user level policy for this code.
-name "*name*"	If used with the −addgroup option, specifies the scripting name for a code group to add. If used with the -chggroup option, specifies the scripting name for a code group to edit. The name argument must be enclosed in double quotation marks, even though it cannot include spaces.

How to Perform Common Tasks with Caspol

The following list provides usage examples for common tasks that you might want to perform with Caspol.

- **To grant an assembly full trust** `Caspol -addfulltrust` *assemblyname.exe*

For example, to grant the C:\Program Files\Mine\Mine.exe assembly full trust, you would run the following command:

```
Caspol -addfulltrust "C:\Program Files\Mine\Mine.exe"
```

- **To add a code group to the Machine policy** `Caspol -machine -addgroup Parent_` `Code_Group  Membership_Conditions  Permission_Set -name "Group_Name"`

For example, to add a code group named My_Code_Group to the Machine policy level's All_Code group, using a URL of *devserver\devshare*\, which grants LocalIntranet permissions, you would run the following command with administrative privileges:

```
Caspol -machine -addgroup All_Code -url \\devserver\devshare\* LocalIntranet
-name "My_Code_Group"
```

- **To add a code group to the User policy** `Caspol -user -addgroup Parent_Code_` `Group Membership_Condition Permission_Set -name "Group_Name"`

Similarly, to add a code group named User_Code_Group to the User policy level's All_Code group, using a site of *www.contoso.com*, which grants FullTrust permissions, you would run the following command:

```
Caspol -user -addgroup All_Code -site www.contoso.com FullTrust -name
"User_Code_Group"
```

NOTE Refreshing the .NET Framework Configuration tool

You must close and reopen the .NET Framework Configuration tool to see changes caused by Caspol. But then again, if you have the .NET Framework Configuration tool open, why are you using Caspol?

- **To adjust zone security for a Machine policy** `Caspol -chggroup Code_Group` `Permission_Set`

For example, to change the Machine My_Computer_Zone security policy to use the Intranet permission set, run the following command with administrative privileges:

```
Caspol -chggroup My_Computer_Zone LocalIntranet
```

- **To reset policy levels for the Machine policy level** `Caspol -recover`

Lab: Configuring Code Access Security

In this lab, you configure CAS using both the graphical .NET Framework Configuration tool and the command-line Caspol tool. Complete Exercises 1 through 3. The last step of Exercise 3 will restore your original settings to ensure future practices work correctly.

▶ **Exercise 1: Compile and Test the Permissions of a Sample Assembly**

In this exercise, you compile and test the permissions of a sample assembly in a restricted My_Computer zone.

1. Log on to your computer as an Administrator.

NOTE   **Logging on as an Administrator**

For other practices in this chapter, and most tasks on your computer, you should be logged on as a standard user. This practice is an exception because it uses the default C$ share, which only administrators have access to by default. You can log on as a standard user if you create a new share that can be accessed by standard users.

---

2. Use Windows Explorer to copy the Chapter11\ListPermissions folder from the companion CD to your My Documents\Visual Studio 2005\Projects\ folder. You can choose either the C# or Visual Basic version.

3. In Windows Explorer, select the My Documents\Visual Studio 2005\Projects\ folder and then double-click ListPermissions.csproj or ListPermissions.vbproj. Visual Studio .NET 2005 opens the ListPermissions project.

4. Click the Build menu and then click Build Solution. Visual Studio .NET 2005 compiles the application.

5. Copy the ListPermissions.exe file to the root of your C drive.

6. Open a command prompt and run the command C:\ListPermissions.exe. List-Permissions runs and displays several common permissions, and whether the assembly currently has that permission. Notice that you have all the listed permissions. Press Enter. Answer the following question:

   ❑ Why does the assembly have all the permissions?

   The assembly is currently running in the My_Computer_Zone because you launched it from the C drive. By default, that zone uses the FullTrust permission set.

7. Run the command \\127.0.0.1\c$\ListPermissions.exe. Notice that you are now missing several permissions; in particular, *IsolatedStorageFilePermission* is missing. Press Enter. Answer the following question:

   ❑ Why is the assembly now missing permissions, and what code group determined the permissions?

   The assembly is now being run from a shared folder, so it is running from the Internet zone. Because the IP address being used is the special loopback address, it is part of the Internet_Same_Site_Access code group.

▶ Exercise 2: Create a Code Group and Permission Set with the .NET Framework
Configuration Tool

In this exercise, you use the .NET Framework Configuration tool to create a code
group that uses a new permission set.

1. Launch the .NET Framework 2.0 Configuration tool. Expand Runtime Security
   Policy, Machine, Code Groups, and then All_Code.

2. Click All_Code and then click Add A Child Code Group in the right pane.

3. In the Name box, type **Local_Shared_Folder**. In the Description box, type **Code
   Run From A Network Drive Mapped To The Local Shared C: Drive**. Click Next.

4. On the Choose A Condition Type page, select URL. In the URL box (as shown in
   Figure 11-8), type **file://127.0.0.1/c$/*** and then click Next.

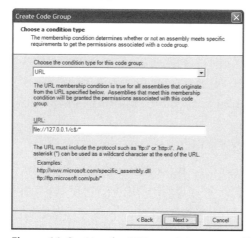

Figure 11-8   Use the URL condition to specify code groups for assemblies running from
shared folders

5. On the Assign A Permission Set To The Code Group page, click the Create A New
   Permission Set option. Click Next.

6. On the Identify The New Permission Set page, type **GenerousPermissions** in the
   Name box. In the Description box, type **Permissions For The ListPermissions
   Assembly**. Click Next.

7. On the Assign Individual Permissions To Permission Set page, double-click Isolated Storage File. In the Permission Settings dialog box, select Grant Assemblies
   Unrestricted Access To File-Based Storage. Click OK and then click Next.

8. On the Completing The Wizard page, click Finish.

9. Open a command prompt, and run the command \\127.0.0.1\c$\ListPermissions.exe. Notice that ListPermission now has the *IsolatedStorageFilePermission*. Press Enter. Answer the following question:

   ❑ Why does the assembly now have *IsolatedStorageFilePermission*?

   The assembly is currently running in both the Local_Shared_Folder code group and the Internet_Same_Site_Access code group. The permissions in the *GenerousPermissions* permission set have been added to the previously existing permissions.

▶ **Exercise 3: Modify a Code Group with the Caspol Tool and Restore Default Settings**

In this exercise, you modify the newly created code group with the Caspol tool, test the change, and then restore the default settings.

1. Open the Visual Studio 2005 Command Prompt, and run the following command to change the Local_Shared_Folder code group permission set to Everything:

   ```
   Caspol -chggroup Local_Shared_Folder Everything
   ```

2. When prompted, press Y and then press Enter.

3. Run \\127.0.0.1\c$\Listpermissions. Notice that the assembly now has all permissions, indicating that the Local_Shared_Folder code group now has the Everything permission set.

4. Restore the default CAS settings by running the command `Caspol -recover`.

Lesson Summary

- CAS is a security system that authorizes managed assemblies to access system resources.

- CAS is implemented by using the following four components:
  - ❑ Evidence, which identifies an assembly
  - ❑ Permissions, which describe which resources an assembly can access
  - ❑ Permission sets, which collect multiple permissions
  - ❑ Code groups, which assign permissions to an assembly based on evidence

- A security policy is a logical grouping of code groups and permission sets. You can use multiple levels of security policy to simplify CAS administration. Assemblies receive the most restrictive set of permissions assigned by each of the policy levels.

- CAS permissions can never override a user's operating system permissions. An assembly's effective permissions are the intersection of the permissions granted to the assembly by CAS and to the user by the operating system.

- The .NET Framework Configuration tool is a graphical tool to configure any aspect of CAS. To use the tool, launch the Microsoft .NET Framework Configuration from the Administrative Tools group.

- The Code Access Security Policy tool, Caspol, is a command-line tool with a large number of options for controlling almost every aspect of CAS behavior. To use Caspol, call it from the directory the .NET Framework is installed into.

Lesson Review

You can use the following questions to test your knowledge of general CAS information. The questions are also available on the companion CD if you prefer to review them in electronic form.

NOTE Answers

Answers to these questions and explanations of why each answer choice is right or wrong are located in the "Answers" section at the end of the book.

---

1. Which of the following evidence types require an assembly to be signed? (Choose all that apply.)

    A. Zone

    B. Strong Name

    C. Hash

    D. Publisher

2. Which permission must an assembly have to connect to a Web server?

    A. *SocketPermission*

    B. *WebPermission*

    C. *DnsPermission*

    D. *ServiceControllerPermission*

3. Which of the following code groups offers the most restrictive permission set?

    A. My_Computer_Zone

    B. LocalIntranet_Zone

    C. Internet_Zone

    D. Restricted_Zone

4. Your user account has Read access to a file named text.txt. You run an assembly in the My_Computer_Zone code group, which grants it the FullTrust permission set. Which of the following actions can the assembly perform on the file?

    A. Read

    B. Write

    C. Change permissions

    D. Delete

Lesson 2: Using Declarative Security to Protect Assemblies

In Lesson 1 you learned that CAS can restrict permissions granted to an application. So you must plan to have your application run in a partially trusted security context. In some situations, CAS security is so restrictive that your application won't have the permissions required for even the most basic functionality, and the runtime should detect this problem and prevent your assembly from running. In other situations, your application will have more permissions than necessary, which violates the principle of least privilege and makes your application unnecessarily vulnerable to abuse.

You can use declarative CAS demands to ensure your assembly has all necessary permissions but none that it does not require. As an additional benefit, administrators deploying your application can examine the assembly's declarative CAS demands to identify the minimum permissions they need to grant to take advantage of all your application's functionality.

After this lesson, you will be able to:

- Describe why you should use CAS assembly declarations.
- List the classes built into the .NET Framework for CAS permissions.
- List the three types of CAS assembly declarations.
- Create CAS assembly declarations.
- Explain the guidelines for effectively implementing CAS assembly declarations.

Estimated lesson time: 45 minutes

Reasons to Use CAS Assembly Declarations

There are three main reasons to use CAS assembly declarations:

- **To ensure that the runtime will never run your application without granting access to required resources** If you have not built exception handling into your application to respond to situations in which your assembly lacks the necessary CAS permissions, use *SecurityAction.RequestMinimum* to declare all CAS permissions required by your application. If a user attempts to run your application and CAS security policy does not grant a required permission, the runtime throws an exception. Users might not be able to identify the problem based on the exception information displayed by the runtime, but an administrator should understand the problem. Either way, using *SecurityAction.RequestMinimum* is better than having unexpected exceptions while your application is running.

■ **To create a small sandbox for your application to ensure that an attacker does not manipulate your application to cause it to access unintended resources**   The principle of least privilege reduces the chances of an attacker abusing your assembly by causing it to take unintended actions, such as revealing the contents of private files, destroying data, or propagating malicious viruses and worms. By using assembly CAS declarations to restrict your assembly's CAS permissions to the bare minimum, you eliminate the risk of an attacker manipulating your application into accessing resources that it would not normally access. This reduces the risk of common attacks, such as canonicalization attacks in which the attacker tricks an application into processing an invalid file by providing a malformed path.

■ **To verify that your application can run with limited CAS permissions and therefore run in partially trusted zones**   There is currently no way to easily identify the permissions required by an application. However, if you develop and test your application using *SecurityAction.RequestOptional* CAS declarations, the runtime grants your assembly only those permissions you specify. If you add code that requires additional permissions, the runtime throws *System.Security.Policy.PolicyException*, indicating the required permission. You can then add another *SecurityAction.RequestOptional* CAS declaration, ensuring that you maintain an accurate list of required permissions.

Classes for CAS Permissions

CAS can restrict access to many types of resources—from files and folders, to printers, to network access. For each type of resource that can be protected, the .NET Framework provides a class. Table 11-8 lists each class used for assembly CAS declarations and the rights that the class represents.

NOTE   **Using attributes**

The .NET Framework also provides attribute classes for each of the classes listed in Table 11-8. The attribute classes have *Attribute* appended to the name. You don't need to worry about this when writing code, however, because the .NET Framework automatically uses the attribute classes when you reference these classes declaratively.

NOTE   **.NET 2.0**

Of the classes used for assembly CAS declarations listed in Table 11-8, the following are new to the .NET Framework 2.0: *DataProtectionPermission*, *GacIdentityPermission*, *KeyContainerPermission*, and *StorePermission*.

Table 11-8   Classes Used for Assembly CAS Declarations

Class	Right Represented
AspNetHostingPermission	Access resources in ASP.NET-hosted environments.
DataProtectionPermission	Access encrypted data and memory. This class is new in the .NET Framework version 2.0.
DirectoryServicesPermission	Access to the System.DirectoryServices classes.
DnsPermission	Access to Domain Name System (DNS).
EnvironmentPermission	Read or write environment variables.
EventLogPermission	Read or write access to event log services.
FileDialogPermission	Access files that have been selected by the user in an Open dialog box.
FileIOPermission	Read, append, or write files or directories.
GacIdentityPermission	Defines the identity permission for files originating in the global assembly cache. This class is new in the .NET Framework version 2.0.
IsolatedStorageFilePermission	Access isolated storage, which is storage that is associated with a specific user and with some aspect of the code's identity, such as its Web site, publisher, or signature.
IUnrestrictedPermission	An interface that allows a permission to expose an unrestricted state.
KeyContainerPermission	Access to public key encryption containers. This class is new in the .NET Framework version 2.0.
MessageQueuePermission	Access message queues through the managed Microsoft Message Queuing (MSMQ) interfaces.
OdbcPermission	Access an ODBC data source.
OleDbPermission	Access databases using OLE DB.
OraclePermission	Access an Oracle database.

Table 11-8   Classes Used for Assembly CAS Declarations

Class	Right Represented
PerformanceCounterPermission	Access performance counters.
PrincipalPermission	Control access based on username and group memberships. This class is discussed in Chapter 12, "User and Data Security."
PrintingPermission	Access printers.
ReflectionPermission	Discover information about a type at run time.
RegistryPermission	Read, write, create, or delete registry keys and values.
SecurityPermission	Execute, assert permissions, call into unmanaged code, skip verification, and other rights.
ServiceControllerPermission	Access running or stopped services.
SiteIdentityPermission	Defines the identity permission for the Web site from which the code originates.
SocketPermission	Make or accept connections on a transport address.
SqlClientPermission	Access SQL databases.
StorePermission	Access stores containing X.509 certificates. This class is new in the .NET Framework version 2.0.
StrongNameIdentityPermission	Defines the identity permission for strong names.
UIPermission	Access user interface functionality. Required to debug an assembly.
UrlIdentityPermission	Defines the identity permission for the URL from which the code originates.
WebPermission	Make or accept connections on a Web address.
ZoneIdentityPermission	Defines the identity permission for the zone from which the code originates.

Each class has unique members that you can use to further control permissions. For example, you can set the *OleDbPermissionAttribute.AllowBlankPassword* property to control whether your assembly will be allowed to use a blank password. Similarly, the *DirectoryServicesPermissionAttribute.Path* property can be defined to limit your assembly's access to a specific branch of the Active Directory. (Because of the large number of classes, this book does not describe the use of each class and property.)

Because the permission attribute classes are inherited from the *CodeAccessSecurityAttribute* class, they share some common properties and methods. However, you usually need to be familiar with only two standard properties:

- **Action**   Specifies the security action to take. Set this using the *SecurityAction* enumeration.

- **Unrestricted**   A *Boolean* value that specifies that the permission enables access to all the class's permissions. Setting this value to true is equivalent to selecting the Grant Assemblies Unrestricted Access To The File System option when specifying permission settings with the .NET Framework Configuration tool.

Types of Assembly Permission Declarations

All permission attribute classes define the *Action* property, which specifies how the runtime will interpret the permission. When creating assembly CAS declarations, you must always set the *Action* property to one of three members of the *SecurityAction* enumeration. The following list describes each of these choices:

- *SecurityAction.RequestMinimum*   Requires a permission for your assembly to run. If your assembly lacks the specified CAS permission, the runtime throws a *System.Security.Policy.PolicyException*.

- *SecurityAction.RequestOptional*   Refuses all permissions not listed in a *SecurityAction.RequestOptional* or *SecurityAction.RequestMinimum* declaration. Defining permissions with this action ensures that your application will have no more permissions than those you have declared. If your assembly lacks the requested CAS permissions, the runtime does *not* throw an exception, unlike its behavior with *SecurityAction.RequestMinimum*. Therefore, use both *SecurityAction.RequestMinimum* and *SecurityAction.RequestOptional* together when your application cannot adapt to a missing permission.

- *SecurityAction.RequestRefuse*   Reduces the permissions assigned to your application. Use this type of declaration to ensure that your application does not have access to critical resources that could potentially be abused. Unlike *SecurityAction.RequestMinimum*, this declaration never causes the runtime to throw an exception at load time.

NOTE Confusing names

If these security action names are confusing, the problem is not you. Why is a declaration called *RequestMinimum* if it's actually a requirement? The name *RequestMinimum* sounds like your code is politely asking for permissions. Given the way *RequestMinimum* behaves, it should be called *RequireMinimum* because the runtime doesn't respond nicely to a request for permissions that it can't provide—it throws an exception and refuses to run your assembly. Also, the runtime will never grant your code permissions that the code wouldn't have had anyway. *RequestOptional* should actually be called *RefuseAllExcept* because the primary purpose is to explicitly list only those CAS permissions your application should have.

How to Create Assembly Declarations

The following code sample shows an assembly that requires CAS read access to the C:\boot.ini file. If security policy does not grant that permission to the assembly, the runtime throws an exception before running the assembly.

```
' VB
Imports System.Security.Permissions

<Assembly: FileIOPermissionAttribute(SecurityAction.RequestMinimum, _
    Read := "C:\boot.ini")>
Module Module1
    Sub Main()
        Console.WriteLine("Hello, World!")
    End Sub
End Module

// C#
using System.Security.Permissions;

[assembly:FileIOPermissionAttribute(SecurityAction.RequestMinimum,
    Read=@"C:\boot.ini")]
namespace DeclarativeExample
{
    class Program
    {
        static void Main(string[] args)
        {
            Console.WriteLine("Hello, World!");
        }
    }
}
```

NOTE What you say you need and what you really need

The sample assembly doesn't actually access the C:\boot.ini file. CAS declarations are completely arbitrary. It's up to you to make sure they're consistent with your application's requirements.

The preceding examples used *SecurityAction.RequestMinimum* to cause the .NET Framework runtime to throw an exception if the assembly did not have CAS permissions to read the C:\boot.ini file. This ensures that the assembly will not run unless the runtime provides the required permission, therefore preventing the application from experiencing problems while running. However, throwing the exception does not improve the security of the assembly because it does nothing to restrict the assembly's permissions.

Exam Tip   For the exam, remember that CAS is significant only for partially trusted assemblies. The runtime completely ignores CAS declarations for fully trusted assemblies.

To improve the assembly's security, specify the *SecurityAction.RequestOptional* or *SecurityAction.RequestRefuse* enumerations for the permission's *Action* property. Optionally, you can combine multiple declarations in a single assembly. For example, if you want the runtime to throw an exception if you don't have access to the HKEY_ LOCAL_MACHINE\Software registry key, and you don't want any other CAS permissions (except, of course, the Enable Assembly Execution security permission), you would use the following declarations:

```vb
' VB
<Assembly: RegistryPermission(SecurityAction.RequestMinimum, _
    Read:="HKEY_LOCAL_MACHINE\Software")>
<Assembly: UIPermission(SecurityAction.RequestOptional, _
    Unrestricted:=True)>
<Assembly: RegistryPermission(SecurityAction.RequestOptional, _
    Read:="HKEY_LOCAL_MACHINE\Software")>
```

```csharp
// C#
[assembly:RegistryPermission(SecurityAction.RequestMinimum,
    Read=@"HKEY_LOCAL_MACHINE\Software")]
[assembly: UIPermission(SecurityAction.RequestMinimum, Unrestricted = true)]
[assembly: RegistryPermission(SecurityAction.RequestOptional,
    Read=@"HKEY_LOCAL_MACHINE\Software")]
```

If you use any *SecurityAction.RequestOptional* declarations and you want to debug your assembly, you must also declare the *UIPermission* attribute and set the *Unrestricted* parameter to *True*, as shown in the second line of the previous example. You can specify either *SecurityAction.RequestOptional* or *SecurityAction.RequestMinimal* for the *UIPermission* attribute. Otherwise, your assembly will not have permission to interact with the debugger. You will be able to run the assembly without a debugger, however.

You can combine *RequestMinimum*, *RequestOptional*, and *RequestRefuse*, but combining *RequestOptional* and *RequestRefuse* might accomplish nothing. After all, *Request-Optional* refuses all permissions except those explicitly listed. The only case in which you would combine *RequestOptional* and *RequestRefuse* is to refuse a subset of the specified *RequestOptional* permissions.

For example, the following declarations would cause the runtime to throw an exception if the assembly did not have CAS printing permissions. The runtime would deny all CAS permissions except printing, opening Windows, and file system access to the C drive. Access to the C:\Windows directory would also be denied.

```vb
' VB
<Assembly: PrintingPermission(SecurityAction.RequestMinimum)>
<Assembly: UIPermission(SecurityAction.RequestOptional, _
    Unrestricted:=True)>
<Assembly: FileIOPermissionAttribute(SecurityAction.RequestOptional, _
    Read:="C:\")>
<Assembly: FileIOPermissionAttribute(SecurityAction.RequestRefuse, _
    Read:="C:\Windows\")>
```

```csharp
// C#
[assembly: PrintingPermission(SecurityAction.RequestMinimum)]
[assembly: UIPermission(SecurityAction.RequestMinimum,
    Unrestricted = true)]
[assembly: FileIOPermissionAttribute(SecurityAction.RequestOptional,
    Read = @"C:\")]
[assembly: FileIOPermissionAttribute(SecurityAction.RequestRefuse,
    Read = @"C:\Windows\")]
```

If you use any *SecurityAction.RequestOptional* declarations, you must also declare the *UIPermission* attribute and set the *Unrestricted* parameter to True to be able to run the assembly with a debugger, as shown in the second line of the previous example. Otherwise, your assembly will not have permission to communicate with the debugger.

BEST PRACTICES   Use *SecurityAction.RequestOptional* assembly declarations

There are whole books about writing secure code, and you should always follow secure coding best practices. We're just human, though. Sometimes, you might simply forget to validate an input or to use strong typing. Other times, you might be rushing to finish a project and just get careless.

Using *SecurityAction.RequestOptional* assembly declarations is the one security best practice that you should always follow. These declarations take very little time to write because it's just a couple lines of code, they're easy to debug because the runtime will throw an easily identifiable exception, and they offer protection for every line of code in your assembly. As an assembly grows in size, this projection decreases some, so you should use method declarations, as discussed in Lesson 3.

Guidelines for Using Assembly Declarations

Follow these guidelines to choose which CAS assembly declarations to use:

- Use *SecurityAction.RequestMinimum* assembly declarations to require every permission needed by your assembly that your assembly does not imperatively check for.

- Use *SecurityAction.RequestOptional* assembly declarations to list every permission your assembly uses. Declare the most granular permissions possible, including specific files or registry keys that will be accessed.

- Use *SecurityAction.RequestRefuse* assembly declarations to further refine permissions listed with *SecurityAction.RequestOptional* assembly declarations.

Lab: Using Assembly Permission Requests

In this lab, you work with CAS declarations to ensure that your assembly has sufficient privileges and to reduce security risks when your assembly runs.

▶ **Exercise: Declare Security Requirements**

In this exercise, you modify an existing assembly to add CAS declarations.

1. Copy either the C# or Visual Basic version of the Chapter11\Lesson2-Exercise1 folder from the companion CD to your hard disk, and open the project.

2. Examine the code to determine what permissions are required. Add the *System.Security.Permissions* namespace to the assembly to allow you to declare the CAS permissions required.

3. Add CAS declarations to declare the minimum permissions required so that the runtime throws an exception if the assembly lacks the necessary permissions. The following code would work:

```
' VB
<Assembly: UIPermission(SecurityAction.RequestMinimum, Unrestricted:=True)>
<Assembly: FileIOPermission(SecurityAction.RequestMinimum, _
    ViewAndModify:="C:\Hello.txt")>

// C#
[assembly: UIPermission(SecurityAction.RequestMinimum,
    Unrestricted = true)]
[assembly: FileIOPermission(SecurityAction.RequestMinimum,
    ViewAndModify = @"C:\Hello.txt")]
```

NOTE   .NET 2.0

The *FileIOPermission* attribute *All* has been replaced by *ViewAndModify*.

4. Run the assembly, and verify that it works correctly.

5. Modify the CAS declarations to refuse permissions other than those required so that the assembly cannot be abused by an attacker and made to do something other than it was intended to do. The following code would work:

```vb
' VB
<Assembly: UIPermission(SecurityAction.RequestOptional, _
    Unrestricted:=True)>
<Assembly: FileIOPermission(SecurityAction.RequestOptional, _
    ViewAndModify:="C:\Hello.txt")>
```

```csharp
// C#
[assembly: UIPermission(SecurityAction.RequestOptional,
    Unrestricted = true)]
[assembly: FileIOPermission(SecurityAction.RequestOptional,
    ViewAndModify = @"C:\Hello.txt")]
```

6. Run the assembly, and verify that it works correctly.

Note that you can use *SecurityAction.RequestOptional* to verify that you are declaring all the permissions required by your assembly, even if you ultimately plan to declare CAS permission requirements using *SecurityAction.RequestMinimum*. For example, in step 3 of this exercise, if you had declared the *FileIOPermission* attribute using *Read* instead of *ViewAndModify*, the runtime would not have thrown an exception even though the assembly writes to the file. However, when you change the declaration to *Security-Action.RequestOptional*, the runtime does throw an exception, verifying that you did not declare all required permissions.

Lesson Summary

- Use CAS assembly declarations because they enable administrators to view the permissions required by your application, prevent your application from running without sufficient permissions, restrict the permissions granted to your application, and enable you to isolate your application to verify compatibility with partially trusted zones.

- The .NET Framework provides more than a dozen classes for CAS permissions, describing resources such as the file system, the registry, and printers.

- There are three types of CAS assembly declarations: *RequestMinimum*, *Request-Optional*, and *RequestRefuse*.

- To create assembly declarations, add assembly attributes by using permission classes.

■ Use *RequestMinimum* declarations when your application doesn't handle missing permissions appropriately, use *RequestOptional* to list every permission required by your application, and use *RequestRefuse* to further restrict your *RequestOptional* permissions.

Lesson Review

You can use the following questions to test your knowledge of declarative assembly security. The questions are also available on the companion CD if you prefer to review them in electronic form.

NOTE   Answers

Answers to these questions and explanations of why each answer choice is right or wrong are located in the "Answers" section at the end of the book.

---

1. An administrator runs the following console application with the Everything permission set. What will the output from the application be?

    ```vb
    ' VB
    <Assembly: UIPermission(SecurityAction.RequestOptional, _
        Unrestricted:=True)>
    <Assembly: FileIOPermissionAttribute(SecurityAction.RequestOptional, _
        Read:="C:\")>
    <Assembly: FileIOPermissionAttribute(SecurityAction.RequestRefuse, _
        Read:="C:\Windows\")>
    Module Module1
        Sub Main()
            Console.WriteLine("Reading one line of the boot.ini file:")
            Dim sr As StreamReader = New StreamReader("C:\boot.ini")
            Console.WriteLine("First line of boot.ini: " + sr.ReadLine)
        End Sub
    End Module
    ```

    ```csharp
    // C#
    [assembly: UIPermission(SecurityAction.RequestOptional,
        Unrestricted = true)]
    [assembly: FileIOPermissionAttribute(SecurityAction.RequestOptional,
        Read = @"C:\")]
    [assembly: FileIOPermissionAttribute(SecurityAction.RequestRefuse,
        Read = @"C:\Windows\")]
    namespace console_cs2
    {
        class Program
        {
            static void Main(string[] args)
            {
                Console.WriteLine("Reading one line of the boot.ini file:");
    ```

```csharp
        StreamReader sr = new StreamReader(@"C:\boot.ini");
        Console.WriteLine("First line of boot.ini: " + sr.ReadLine());
        }
    }
}
```

A.

```
Unhandled Exception: System.Security.SecurityException: Request for the
permission of type 'System.Security.Permissions.
FileIOPermission, mscorlib, Version=2.0.0.0, Culture=neutral,
PublicKeyToken=b77a5c561934e089' failed.
```

B.

```
Reading one line of the boot.ini file:
Unhandled Exception: System.Security.SecurityException: Request for the
permission of type 'System.Security.Permissions.
FileIOPermission, mscorlib, Version=2.0.0.0, Culture=neutral,
PublicKeyToken=b77a5c561934e089' failed.
```

C.

```
Reading one line of the boot.ini file:
First line of boot.ini: [boot loader]
```

D. An unhandled *SecurityException* occurs before the application begins execution.

2. An administrator runs the console application with the Everything permission set. What will the output from the application be?

```vb
' VB
<Assembly: UIPermission(SecurityAction.RequestOptional, _
    Unrestricted:=True)>
<Assembly: FileIOPermissionAttribute(SecurityAction.RequestOptional, _
    Read:="C:\Temp")>
<Assembly: FileIOPermissionAttribute(SecurityAction.RequestRefuse, _
    Read:="C:\Windows\")>
Module Module1
    Sub Main()
        Console.WriteLine("Reading one line of the boot.ini file:")
        Dim sr As StreamReader = New StreamReader("C:\boot.ini")
        Console.WriteLine("First line of boot.ini: " + sr.ReadLine)
    End Sub
End Module
```

```csharp
// C#
[assembly: UIPermission(SecurityAction.RequestOptional,
    Unrestricted = true)]
[assembly: FileIOPermissionAttribute(SecurityAction.RequestOptional,
    Read = @"C:\Temp")]
[assembly: FileIOPermissionAttribute(SecurityAction.RequestRefuse,
    Read = @"C:\Windows\")]
namespace console_cs2
```

```
{
    class Program
    {
        static void Main(string[] args)
        {
            Console.WriteLine("Reading one line of the boot.ini file:");
            StreamReader sr = new StreamReader(@"C:\boot.ini");
            Console.WriteLine("First line of boot.ini: " + sr.ReadLine());
        }
    }
}
```

A.

```
Unhandled Exception: System.Security.SecurityException: Request for the
permission of type 'System.Security.Permissions.
FileIOPermission, mscorlib, Version=2.0.0.0, Culture=neutral,
PublicKeyToken=b77a5c561934e089' failed.
```

B.

```
Reading one line of the boot.ini file:
Unhandled Exception: System.Security.SecurityException: Request for the
permission of type 'System.Security.Permissions.
FileIOPermission, mscorlib, Version=2.0.0.0, Culture=neutral,
PublicKeyToken=b77a5c561934e089' failed.
```

C.

```
Reading one line of the boot.ini file:
First line of boot.ini: [boot loader]
```

D. An unhandled SecurityException occurs before the application begins execution.

3. An administrator runs the following console application with the Everything permission set. What will the output from the application be?

```
' VB
<Assembly: UIPermission(SecurityAction.RequestMinimum, Unrestricted:=True)>
<Assembly: FileIOPermissionAttribute(SecurityAction.RequestMinimum, _
    Read:="C:\Temp")>
<Assembly: FileIOPermissionAttribute(SecurityAction.RequestRefuse, _
    Read:="C:\Windows\")>
Module Module1
    Sub Main()
        Console.WriteLine("Reading one line of the boot.ini file:")
        Dim sr As StreamReader = New StreamReader("C:\boot.ini")
        Console.WriteLine("First line of boot.ini: " + sr.ReadLine)
    End Sub
End Module

// C#
[assembly: UIPermission(SecurityAction.RequestMinimum,
    Unrestricted = true)]
```

```
[assembly: FileIOPermissionAttribute(SecurityAction.RequestMinimum,
    Read = @"C:\Temp")]
[assembly: FileIOPermissionAttribute(SecurityAction.RequestRefuse,
    Read = @"C:\Windows\")]
namespace console_cs2
{
    class Program
    {
        static void Main(string[] args)
        {
            Console.WriteLine("Reading one line of the boot.ini file:");
            StreamReader sr = new StreamReader(@"C:\boot.ini");
            Console.WriteLine("First line of boot.ini: " + sr.ReadLine());
        }
    }
}
```

A.

```
Unhandled Exception: System.Security.SecurityException: Request for the
permission of type 'System.Security.Permissions.
FileIOPermission, mscorlib, Version=2.0.0.0, Culture=neutral,
PublicKeyToken=b77a5c561934e089' failed.
```

B.

```
Reading one line of the boot.ini file:
Unhandled Exception: System.Security.SecurityException: Request for the
permission of type 'System.Security.Permissions.
FileIOPermission, mscorlib, Version=2.0.0.0, Culture=neutral,
PublicKeyToken=b77a5c561934e089' failed.
```

C.

```
Reading one line of the boot.ini file:
First line of boot.ini: [boot loader]
```

D. An unhandled *SecurityException* occurs before the application begins execution.

4. Which of the following permissions is required for all console applications running with a debugger?

   A. *SocketPermission*

   B. *WebPermission*

   C. *UIPermission*

   D. *FileIOPermission*

Lesson 3: Using Declarative and Imperative Security to Protect Methods

CAS can be used either declaratively, in which case the compiler performs security checks prior to running code, or imperatively, in which case the code itself performs security checks and controls what happens if the check fails. In Lesson 2, you learned how to use CAS declarations to protect an entire assembly. You can also use CAS to declaratively protect individual methods within an assembly or use CAS to imperatively protect sections of code within a method. In this lesson you'll learn how and why to use both imperative and declarative CAS demands to protect code within an assembly.

After this lesson, you will be able to:

- List the types of method permission requests.
- Describe how method permission requests should be used to maximize application security.
- Use CAS to require specific permissions for individual methods.
- Restrict permissions for a method to reduce the risk of the method being misused by an attacker.
- Use the *Assert* method to relax permissions and improve performance.
- Use permission sets to demand, restrict, or assert multiple permissions simultaneously.

Estimated lesson time: 45 minutes

Types of Method Permission Requests

Although there are only three types of CAS assembly declarations (*RequestOptional*, *RequestMinimum*, and *RequestRefuse*), you have six options available for imperative and declarative permissions within a method. The following list describes each option:

- **Assert**   Instructs the runtime to ignore the fact that callers might not have the specified permission. Assemblies must have the Assert Any Permission That Has Been Granted security permission setting.

- **Demand**   Instructs the runtime to throw an exception if the caller and all callers higher in the stack lack the specified permission.

- **Deny**   Causes the runtime to reduce the method's access by removing the specified permission.

- **InheritanceDemand**   Instructs the runtime to throw an exception if the assembly inheriting from the class lacks the specified permission.

- **LinkDemand**   Causes the runtime to throw an exception if the immediate caller, but not callers higher in the stack, lack the specified permission.

- **PermitOnly**   Instructs the runtime to reduce the method's access by removing all permissions except for the specified permission.

To understand each of these methods, consider a group of four guests who want to enter an exclusive party. The host (your method) has hired a bouncer (the .NET Framework runtime) to make sure that only guests (calling assemblies) with an invitation (a CAS permission) are allowed to enter the party (call your method).

If the host calls *InvitedGuests.LinkDemand*, the bouncer will check the invitation of the first guest and then allow everyone else into the party. This is quick, but it might let people sneak into the party. If the host calls *InvitedGuests.Demand*, the bouncer will check the invitation of every guest individually. This process takes more time, but it ensures that nobody can sneak in.

To speed up the process of checking invitations, the first invited guests might use *InvitedGuests.Assert* to assure the bouncer that all the guests in the group were invited—assuming that the bouncer trusted the first guest enough. This procedure would also allow the first guest to bring guests who lacked invitations, which might be a good thing if the host wanted to have a lot of people at the party but didn't want to hand out too many invitations (that might fall into the wrong hands). However, it might be a bad thing if a thief discovered that he could sneak into the party.

If the host wanted to ensure that people danced at the party (and never did anything else), the host would use *Dancing.PermitOnly* to instruct the bouncer to make sure that guests stayed on the dance floor. If the host wanted people to do anything *but* dance, the host would use *Dancing.Deny* to prevent anyone from dancing.

Guidelines for Using Method Permission Requests

As a developer, you have many choices for implementing CAS in your applications. Choosing how to implement CAS for a particular situation can be complicated, however. Follow these guidelines to choose which CAS methods to use:

- Use *SecurityAction.PermitOnly* declarations to limit the permissions available to each method. List every permission the method requires.

- Use *SecurityAction.Deny* declarations to further refine the permissions available to each method.

■ Use *CodeAccessPermission.PermitOnly* to imperatively reduce permissions when a section of a method requires fewer permissions than the rest of the method. This is particularly important when calling objects created by third parties. Use *CodeAccessPermission.RevertPermitOnly* to restore the permission.

■ Use *CodeAccessPermission.Assert* when you want to allow partially trusted code to call a method that requires permissions the caller might lack. Review your code carefully for potential security vulnerabilities; *Assert* can be abused by an attacker to gain elevated privileges. After you perform the functions requiring elevated privileges, use *CodeAccessPermission.RevertAssert* to restore the original permissions.

■ Use *CodeAccessPermission.Demand* only when your assembly implements customized functionality that does not rely on functionality built into the .NET Framework, such as calls to unmanaged code.

NOTE Security risks of declarative demands

There's a school of thought that says declarative security demands are less secure than imperative security demands because declarative demands can reveal to attackers too much about the code's design and potential vulnerabilities. It's true that declarative security demands are a bit easier for an attacker to analyze, but a sophisticated attacker could also examine imperative demands by using a tool that analyzes your assembly's Intermediate Language (IL) code. It's a bit harder for the attacker to analyze IL than to analyze the declarative security demands, but it wouldn't make much of a difference to an attacker who was sophisticated enough to make use of security demand information. Also, declarative demands are faster than imperative demands.

Techniques for Demanding Permissions

Two of the *SecurityAction* enumerations and two of the *CodeAccessPermission* methods cause the runtime to throw an exception if the specified CAS permission is missing: *Demand* and *LinkDemand*. The difference between the two enumerations and methods is that *Demand* causes the permission check to verify the access of all callers, whereas *LinkDemand* verifies only the immediate caller.

To understand the difference, compare the *Demand* process demonstrated in Figure 11-9 with the *LinkDemand* process demonstrated in Figure 11-10. As you can see, *Demand* will detect whether any caller lacks the demanded permission or permission set, and will throw an exception. This is more secure than using *LinkDemand*, which checks only the immediate caller. However, as with almost every security mechanism, there is a trade-off. *Demand* requires the runtime to do more checks, which requires more processing time and slows performance. Using *LinkDemand* improves performance but increases the risk of an attacker successfully bypassing the check.

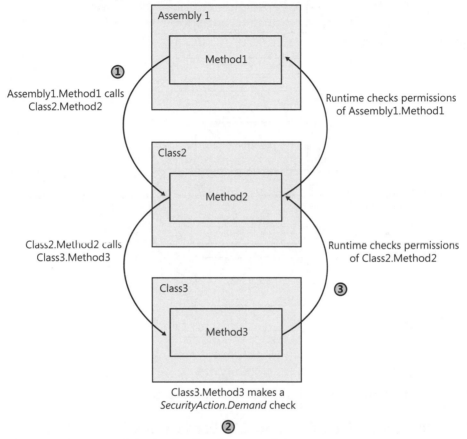

Figure 11-9 *Demand* checks all callers for a permission

IMPORTANT *Demand* and *LinkDemand* check the caller

Demand and *LinkDemand* do *not* check the current method's permissions—they check the caller. However, if your assembly calls a private method that uses *Demand* or *LinkDemand*, the runtime will check your assembly's permission because in this case your assembly is the caller.

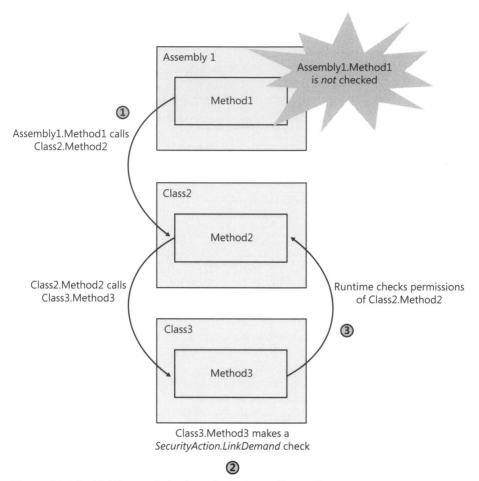

Figure 11-10   *LinkDemand* checks only the immediate caller

How to Declaratively Demand CAS Permissions

Creating CAS method declarations is very similar to creating CAS assembly declarations. However, you must create the declarations as attributes to the method instead of to the assembly and you must use different *SecurityAction* enumerations. To create a declarative request, use one of the classes discussed in Lesson 2 of this chapter with the *SecurityAction.Demand* or *SecurityAction.LinkDemand* enumerations. The following sample shows two methods that use *FileIOPermissionAttribute* (in *System.Security .Permissions*) and *WebPermissionAttribute* (in *System.Net*) classes to declaratively verify that callers of particular methods have access to specific files and the *www .microsoft.com* Web site.

```
' VB
<FileIOPermissionAttribute(SecurityAction.Demand, _
    Write:="C:\Program Files\")> _
Public Sub createProgramFolder()
    ' Method logic
End Sub

<WebPermission(SecurityAction.Demand, _
    ConnectPattern:="http://www\.microsoft\.com/.*")> _
Public Sub requestWebPage()
    ' Method logic
End Sub

// C#
[FileIOPermission(SecurityAction.Demand, Write = @"C:\Program Files\")]
public static void createProgramFolder()
{
    // Method logic
}

[WebPermission(SecurityAction.Demand,
    ConnectPattern = @"http://www\.microsoft\.com/.*")]
public static void requestWebPage()
{
    // Method logic
}
```

If you write classes from which other developers will derive, you can restrict which assemblies can inherit from your classes using the *SecurityAction.InheritanceDemand* enumeration. For example, only assemblies signed with the C:\Certificates\MyCertificate.cer certificate could inherit from the following class:

```
' VB
<PublisherIdentityPermission(SecurityAction.InheritanceDemand, _
    CertFile:="C:\Certificates\MyCertificate.cer")> _
Public Class ProtectedInheritance
    ' Class logic
End Class

// C#
[PublisherIdentityPermission(SecurityAction.InheritanceDemand,
    CertFile = @"C:\Certificates\MyCertificate.cer")]
public class ProtectedInheritance
{
    // Class logic
}
```

You can use the same declarative syntax to protect individual class members from being overridden by a derived class. This approach is necessary only when you want to provide levels of protection for individual members that are higher than those for the base class.

How to Imperatively Demand CAS Permissions

For each of the *SecurityAction* enumerations used to specify CAS declarations, there is a *CodeAccessPermission* method with the same name and function used for imperative permissions. You will use the *SecurityAction* enumerations for declarative security and the *CodeAccessPermission* methods for imperative security. The following sample performs the same checks as the sample code that used declarative CAS demands, but it performs the check imperatively:

```vb
' VB
Public Class CASImperativeClass
    Public Shared Sub createProgramFolder()
        Try
            Dim filePermissions As FileIOPermission = _
                New FileIOPermission(FileIOPermissionAccess.Write, _
                    "C:\Program Files\")
            filePermissions.Demand()
            ' Method logic
        Catch
            ' Error handling logic
        End Try
    End Sub

    Public Shared Sub requestWebPage()
        Try
            Dim connectPattern As Regex = _
                New Regex("http://www\.microsoft\.com/.*")
            Dim webPermissions As WebPermission = _
                New WebPermission(NetworkAccess.Connect, connectPattern)
            webPermissions.Demand()
            ' Method logic
        Catch
            ' Error handling logic
        End Try
    End Sub
End Class

// C#
public static void createProgramFolder()
{
    try
    {
        FileIOPermission filePermissions =
            new FileIOPermission(FileIOPermissionAccess.Write,
                @"C:\Program Files\");
        filePermissions.Demand();
        // Method logic
    }
    catch
    {
        // Error-handling logic
```

```
    }
}

public static void requestWebPage()
{
    try
    {
        Regex connectPattern = new Regex(@"http://www\.microsoft\.com/.*");
        WebPermission webPermissions =
            new WebPermission(NetworkAccess.Connect, connectPattern);
        webPermissions.Demand();
        // Method logic
    }
    catch
    {
        // Error-handling logic
    }
}
```

Remember, the advantage of using imperative demands is that you can catch the security exception within your method and deal with it gracefully. If you just want to throw an exception back to the caller, use a declarative demand.

How to Analyze Granted Permissions

If you need to determine whether your assembly has a particular CAS permission, don't use *Demand*. *Demand* is designed to check an assembly's *caller* for permission, not the assembly itself. Instead, use the *System.Security.SecurityManager.IsGranted* method, as demonstrated by the following code sample:

```
' VB
Dim filePermissions As FileIOPermission = New _
    FileIOPermission(FileIOPermissionAccess.Read, "C:\Windows\")
If SecurityManager.IsGranted(filePermissions) = True Then
    ' Assembly can read the C:\Windows directory
Else
    ' Assembly cannot read the C:\Windows directory
End If

// C#
FileIOPermission filePermissions = new
    FileIOPermission(FileIOPermissionAccess.Read, @"C:\Windows\");
if ( SecurityManager.IsGranted(filePermissions) == true )
    // Assembly can read the C:\Windows directory
else
    // Assembly cannot read the C:\Windows directory
```

The ListPermissions sample application from the Lesson 1 Lab uses this method; examine the source code on the companion CD for a working example.

BEST PRACTICES   Avoid redundant demands

Most classes in the .NET Framework use demands to ensure that callers have the permissions required to use them, so also calling *Demand* is redundant. For example, if you're reading a line from a text file using a *StreamWriter* object, the object itself will demand *FileIOPermission*. Generally, use demands to protect custom resources that require custom permissions.

Techniques for Limiting Permissions

Always use CAS assembly declarations to restrict the CAS permissions granted to your assembly so that your assembly has only the bare minimum required for all functionality. You can control permissions on a more granular level by restricting permissions for individual methods using method declarations or by restricting permissions within methods using imperative statements.

Two of the *SecurityAction* enumerations and permission methods cause the runtime to reduce CAS permissions: *Deny* and *PermitOnly*. The difference between the two enumerations is that *Deny* removes a single permission or permission set, whereas *PermitOnly* removes all permissions except the requested permission or permission set. Recall from Lesson 2 that *Deny* performs a similar function to *RequestRefuse*, whereas *PermitOnly* is similar to *RequestOptional*.

Exam Tip   For the exam, remember to use *RequestRefuse* and *RequestOptional* for assembly declarations, and use *Deny* and *PermitOnly* for methods.

How to Declaratively Limit Method Permissions

The following two declarations demonstrate how to prevent a method from accessing the C:\Windows\ directory and how to limit outgoing Web requests to only *www.microsoft.com*:

```vb
' VB
<FileIOPermissionAttribute(SecurityAction.Deny, _
    ViewAndModify := "C:\Windows\")> _
    <WebPermission(SecurityAction.PermitOnly, _
    ConnectPattern:="http://www\.microsoft\.com/.*")> _
```

```csharp
// C#
[FileIOPermission(SecurityAction.Deny, ViewAndModify = @"C:\Windows\")]
[WebPermission(SecurityAction.PermitOnly,
    ConnectPattern = @"http://www\.microsoft\.com/.*")]
```

> **NOTE** Limitations of declarative security
>
> Declarative security criteria must be static. If you need to dynamically generate file paths, Web addresses, or any other aspects of the security criteria, you must enforce the security limitations imperatively.

How to Imperatively Limit Permissions

The following sample forces the same limitations as the sample code that used declarative CAS demands, but it limits the permissions imperatively:

```vb
' VB
' Deny access to the Windows directory
Dim filePermissions As FileIOPermission = New _
    FileIOPermission(FileIOPermissionAccess.AllAccess, "C:\Windows\")
filePermissions.Deny()
' Method logic

' Permit only Web access, and limit it to www.microsoft.com
Dim connectPattern As Regex = New Regex("http://www\.microsoft\.com/.*")
Dim webPermissions As WebPermission = _
    New WebPermission(NetworkAccess.Connect, connectPattern)
webPermissions.PermitOnly()
' Method logic
```

```csharp
// C#
// Deny access to the Windows directory
FileIOPermission filePermissions =
    new FileIOPermission(FileIOPermissionAccess.AllAccess, @"C:\Windows\");
filePermissions.Deny();
// Method logic

// Permit only Web access, and limit it to www.microsoft.com
Regex connectPattern = new Regex(@"http://www\.microsoft\.com/.*");
WebPermission webPermissions = new WebPermission(NetworkAccess.Connect,
    connectPattern);
webPermissions.PermitOnly();
// Method logic
```

If part of your code needs to use a permission that you previously blocked with *Deny* or *PermitOnly*, use the *System.Security.CodeAccessPermission.RevertDeny* or *System.Security .CodeAccessPermission.RevertPermitOnly* static methods to reenable the permission.

Best Practice for Handling Errors

Use *PermitOnly* to limit permissions during error-handling routines. Attackers often initiate an error condition in an application and then abuse that error condition to perform tasks that would not be possible under normal circumstances. Using *PermitOnly* to limit CAS permissions to the bare minimum required to log the event and report an error to the user significantly reduces the risk that your error-handling routine can be abused. If your application will continue running after the error, be sure to revert to your original permissions—otherwise, normal application functionality will not be available.

For example, the following code catches an exception, restricts CAS permissions to those required to add events, and then reverts to the previous permission set:

```
' VB
Try
    ' Assembly logic
Catch
    Dim errorPerms As EventLogPermission = _
        New EventLogPermission (PermissionState.Unrestricted)
    errorPerms.PermitOnly
    ' Log event
    CodeAccessPermission.RevertPermitOnly
End Try

// C#
try
{
    // Assembly logic
}
catch
{
    EventLogPermission errorPerms = new
        EventLogPermission(PermissionState.Unrestricted);
    errorPerms.PermitOnly();
    // Log event
    CodeAccessPermission.RevertPermitOnly();
}
```

Restricting permissions to those required for a specific block of code is an excellent example of following the principle of least privilege. Although it's particularly important during error-catching routines, you can use this technique to limit the permissions of any block of code.

How to Relax Permissions and Potentially Improve Performance

Using CAS demands improves the security of an assembly but can decrease performance. In particular, calling a permission's *Demand* method is costly because it forces the runtime to systematically check the permission of every caller. *LinkDemand*, discussed earlier, is one way to improve upon the performance of the *Demand* method, but it sacrifices some level of security. Another technique is the *Assert* method, which causes the runtime to bypass any security checks.

IMPORTANT   **Compared with assert in C++**

CodeAccessPermission.Assert is nothing like the *assert* function in C or C++.

Permission objects include the *Assert* method to enable a method to vouch for all callers. Figure 11-11 shows how a call to *Assert* stops the runtime from checking the CAS permissions of assemblies higher in the stack. This has two effects: improving performance by reducing the number of permission checks and allowing underprivileged code to call methods with higher CAS permission requirements.

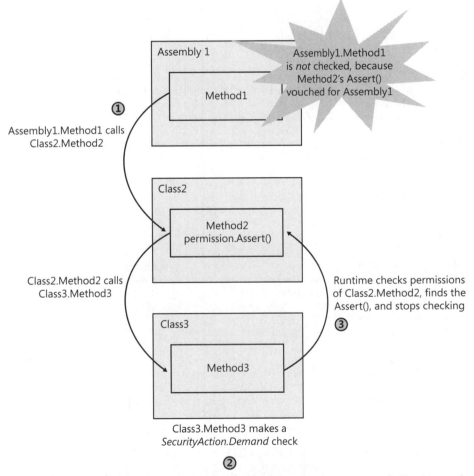

Figure 11-11   Assert blocks demand checks, increasing performance and allowing underprivileged code to call methods with CAS permission requirements

For example, if you create a *RegistryPermission* object and call the *Assert* method, your assembly must be granted *RegistryPermission*, but any code calling your assembly does not require the permission. If you call another method that uses *Demand* to require *RegistryPermission*, *Demand* will succeed whether or not your caller has been granted *RegistryPermission*.

You can use *Assert* either declaratively or imperatively, and the syntax is identical to other types of CAS declarations. The following example asserts permissions declaratively:

```
' VB
<FileIOPermissionAttribute(SecurityAction.Assert, _
    ViewAndModify := "C:\Program Files\")> _
    <WebPermission(SecurityAction.Assert, _
    ConnectPattern:="http://www\.microsoft\.com/.*")> _
```

```
// C#
[FileIOPermission(SecurityAction.Assert, ViewAndModify = @"C:\Windows\")]
[WebPermission(SecurityAction.Assert,
    ConnectPattern = @"http://www\.microsoft\.com/.*")]
```

Although the following example asserts permissions imperatively:

```
' VB
' Block all CAS permission checks for file access to the Windows directory
Dim filePermissions As FileIOPermission = _
    New FileIOPermission(FileIOPermissionAccess.AllAccess, "C:\Windows\")
filePermissions.Assert()
' Method logic

' Block all CAS permission checks for Web access to www.microsoft.com
Dim connectPattern As Regex = New Regex("http://www\.microsoft\.com/.*")
Dim webPermissions As WebPermission = _
    New WebPermission(NetworkAccess.Connect, connectPattern)
webPermissions.Assert()
' Method logic
```

```
// C#
// Block all CAS permission checks for file access to the Windows directory
FileIOPermission filePermissions =
    new FileIOPermission(FileIOPermissionAccess.AllAccess, @"C:\Windows\");
filePermissions.Assert();
// Method logic

// Block all CAS permission checks for Web access to www.microsoft.com
Regex connectPattern = new Regex(@"http://www\.microsoft\.com/.*");
WebPermission webPermissions = new WebPermission(NetworkAccess.Connect, connectPattern);
webPermissions.Assert();
// Method logic
```

To successfully use *Assert*, the assembly must have the *SecurityPermissionFlag.Assertion* privilege as well as the privilege being asserted. In the .NET Framework Configuration tool, *SecurityPermissionFlag.Assertion* is represented by the Assert Any Permission That Has Been Granted item in the Security permission properties dialog box. The Full-Trust, LocalIntranet, and Everything permission sets have this permission.

Using *Assert* allows an assembly to vouch for the security of lesser-privileged assemblies. This is an excellent way to grant additional functionality to assemblies that would normally lack CAS permissions. For example, you can use an *Assert* to allow an assembly in the Internet zone to save a file to the user's disk. Simply create an assembly with the *AllowPartiallyTrustedCallersAttribute*. Then create a public method that writes the file, create a *FileIOPermission* object, and call the *Assert* method before writing the file. The assembly in the Internet zone can save a file to a user's disk without requiring the administrators to grant file permissions to the Internet zone.

To decrease the opportunity for an attacker to abuse asserted permissions, use the *CodeAccessPermission.RevertAssert* static method. As the name suggests, calling this method erases the assertion and returns CAS permission checking to the normal state. Use a *try/finally* block to ensure that you call *RevertAssert* after every *Assert*, even if a failure occurs. The following method demonstrates this and is also an excellent example of how to fail to a more secure permission set:

```vb
' VB
Dim filePermissions As FileIOPermission = _
    New FileIOPermission (FileIOPermissionAccess.Write, _
    "C:\Inetpub\NewFile.txt")
filePermissions.Assert
Try
    Dim newFile As StreamWriter = New StreamWriter _
        ("C:\Inetpub\NewFile.txt")
    newFile.WriteLine("Lesser privileged applications can save a file.")
    newFile.Close
Finally
    CodeAccessPermission.RevertAssert
End Try
```

```csharp
// C#
FileIOPermission filePermissions =
    new FileIOPermission(FileIOPermissionAccess.Write, @"C:\Inetpub\");
filePermissions.Assert();
try
{
    StreamWriter newFile = new StreamWriter(@"C:\Inetpub\NewFile.txt");
    newFile.WriteLine("Lesser privileged applications can save a file.");
    newFile.Close();
}
```

```
finally
{
    CodeAccessPermission.RevertAssert();
}
```

Assert does have a few limitations. You can use *Assert* only once in a method. If you have to assert multiple permissions, you need to create a custom permission set (described later in this lesson). Second, *Assert* doesn't override the operating system's role-based security, regardless of the assembly's CAS permissions. If a user lacks permission to write to the D drive and runs an assembly with full trust that asserts that file permission, the *Assert* will succeed, but the assembly still can't write to the D drive. The assembly is still limited by the user's access restrictions.

How to Call Trusted Code from Partially Trusted Code

To prevent partially trusted code from bypassing security checks, partially trusted code can't call strong-named assemblies by default. You can control this on an assembly-by-assembly basis, however, by adding the *AllowPartiallyTrustedCallersAttribute* assembly-level custom attribute:

```
[assembly:AllowPartiallyTrustedCallers]
```

If your assembly doesn't have a strong name, partially trusted code can access your public methods even when you don't add that attribute.

How to Use Permission Sets

Permission sets are a collection of permissions that can be used imperatively in the same ways you use individual permissions. Use the *System.Security.Permissions .PermissionSet* class to create a permission set and then use the *AddPermission* method to specify the permissions that define the permission set. Then you can call any standard permission methods, including *Assert*, *Demand*, *Deny*, and *PermitOnly*.

For example, the following code creates a permission set consisting of read access to the C:\Windows folder, write access to the C:\Inetpub\ folder, and read access to the HKEY_LOCAL_MACHINE\Software registry key. Then it demands access to all those resources to cause the runtime to throw an exception if any of the specified permissions are not available.

```
' VB
Dim myPerms As PermissionSet = New PermissionSet(PermissionState.None)
myPerms.AddPermission(New FileIOPermission _
    (FileIOPermissionAccess.Read, "C:\Windows"))
myPerms.AddPermission(New FileIOPermission _
    (FileIOPermissionAccess.Write, "C:\Inetpub"))
```

```
myPerms.AddPermission(New _
    RegistryPermission (RegistryPermissionAccess.Write, _
    "HKEY_LOCAL_MACHINE"))
myPerms.Demand

// C#
PermissionSet myPerms = new PermissionSet(PermissionState.None);
myPerms.AddPermission(new FileIOPermission(
    FileIOPermissionAccess.Read, @"C:\Windows"));
myPerms.AddPermission(new FileIOPermission(
    FileIOPermissionAccess.Write, @"C:\Inetpub"));
myPerms.AddPermission(new
    RegistryPermission(RegistryPermissionAccess.Write,
    @"HKEY_LOCAL_MACHINE\Software"));
myPerms.Demand();
```

You can call *Assert* only once in a method, so if you need to assert multiple permissions, you *must* use a permission set.

Lab: Protecting Methods with Code Access Security Demands

In this lab, you work with *Deny* and *Assert* methods to validate your understanding of both declarative and imperative CAS permissions. Complete Exercises 1 through 4. You will reset all policy levels and the end of Exercise 4.

▶ **Exercise 1: Experiment with the Default Permission Set**

In this exercise, you experiment with declarative and imperative CAS demands and determine how each reacts when CAS is not restricted. To complete this exercise, you must have a folder named C:\Documents and Settings\Administrator\. If this folder is not present, create it prior to performing this exercise.

1. Copy either the C# or Visual Basic version of the Chapter11\CASDemands folder from the companion CD to your hard disk, and open the project. Build the project and copy the resulting executable file to a folder on your computer that standard users (users who are not a member of the Administrators group) can access.

2. Log on to your computer as a standard user account and run the CASDemands.exe file.

3. In the Code Access Security Demands application, click the Create File With No Demand button and then answer the following questions:

   A. In which zone is the assembly running?

   The assembly is using the My_Computer_Zone because it is being run from the computer's local file system.

B. What permission set did the .NET Framework runtime grant the assembly?

By default, the My_Computer_Zone grants assemblies the FullTrust permission set.

C. What type of exception was thrown, and why was that particular type of exception thrown?

The .NET Framework threw a *System.UnauthorizedAccessException* because the user, StandardUser, did not have access to create new files within the C:\Documents and Settings\Administrator\ folder.

4. In the Code Access Security Demands application, click the Create File With Declarative Demand button and then answer the following questions.

A. What type of exception was thrown, and why was that particular type of exception thrown?

The .NET Framework threw a *System.UnauthorizedAccessException* because the user, StandardUser, did not have access to create new files within the C:\Documents and Settings\Administrator\ folder.

B. Notice that the error message reads Failed When Attempting To Create File, not Failed Before Attempting To Create File. Use Visual Studio .NET to examine the *declarativeDemandButton_Click* method. This method calls the *declarativeCreateFile* method, which requires write access to a file that the user lacks permission to create. Why was the exception thrown within the *createFile* method, and not thrown when the declarative security demand was processed before the *declarativeCreateFile* method was run?

Declarative code access security demands will cause an exception to be thrown when the *code* itself lacks the required permission. In this case, the *user* lacks the required permission, but the code does have CAS permissions to create the file. Therefore, the declarative security demand is successful, but the more restricted role-based security requirement enforced by the operating system causes the .NET Framework runtime to throw an exception when the application attempts to create the file itself in the *createFile* method.

5. In the Code Access Security Demands application, click the Create File With Imperative Demand button and then answer the following question:

□ What type of exception was thrown, and why was that particular type of exception thrown?

The .NET Framework threw a *System.UnauthorizedAccessException*, just as it did for the other buttons, because CAS is not being taken into account because the assembly is running with the FullTrust permission set.

6. Close the Code Access Security Demands application.

▶ **Exercise 2: Restrict Permissions to the My_Computer_Zone**

In this exercise, you restrict permissions to the My_Computer_Zone.

1. Log on to your computer as an administrator.

2. Launch the Microsoft .NET Framework 2.0 Configuration. In the .NET Framework Configuration tool, expand Runtime Security Policy, expand Machine, expand Code Groups, and then expand All_Code. Right-click My_Computer_Zone, and then click Properties.

3. Click the Permission Set tab and then set Permission Set to Internet. Then click OK.

4. Log on to your computer as a standard user account.

5. Run the CASDemands.exe file. As shown in Figure 11-12, the assembly no longer has unrestricted permissions, and the .NET Framework displays a security warning. Close the bubble.

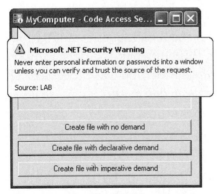

Figure 11-12   The .NET Framework provides a security warning because the application is running in a partially trusted context

6. In the Code Access Security Demands application, click the Create File With No Demand button and then answer the following questions.

   A. In which zone is the assembly running?

      The assembly is using the My_Computer_Zone because it is being run from the computer's local file system.

    B. What permission set did the .NET Framework runtime grant the assembly?

        Because you used the Administrator account to modify the default configuration, the My_Computer_Zone will grant the Internet permission set to the assembly.

    C. What type of exception was thrown, and why was that particular type of exception thrown?

        The .NET Framework threw a *System.Security.SecurityException* because the application, running in the Internet zone, did not have CAS permissions to use the file system.

7. In the Code Access Security Demands application, click the Create File With Declarative Demand button and then answer the following questions:

    A. What type of exception was thrown, and why was that particular type of exception thrown?

        The .NET Framework threw a *System.Security.SecurityException* for the same reasons it threw the exception when you clicked the Create File With No Demand button.

    B. In which method was the exception caught?

        The Failed Before Attempting To Create File error message indicates that the exception was caught in the *declarativeDemandButton_Click* method because the exception was thrown when the declarative demand associated with the *declarativeCreateFile* method was processed. The .NET Framework runtime never ran the *createFile* method because it was prevented by the security demand.

8. In the Code Access Security Demands application, click the Create File With Imperative Demand button and then answer the following question:

    ❑ A. What type of exception was thrown, and what method caught the exception?

        As with the declarative security demand, the *System.Security.SecurityException* was caught before it reached the *createFile* method. In this case, the exception was caught in the *imperativeDemandButton_Click* method.

9. Finally, use the .NET Framework Configuration tool with administrative privileges to reset all policy levels, as described in Lesson 1 of this chapter.

▶ **Exercise 3: Grant Access to Partially Trusted Code**

In this exercise, you modify a class to enable code without *FileIOPermission* to write to the disk.

1. Log on to your computer as an administrator. Use Windows Explorer to copy the Chapter11\TrustedClass and Chapter11\PartiallyTrustedAssembly folders from the companion CD to your computer in either Visual Basic or C#.

2. Open the TrustedClass.sln file, and build the solution. While you have the solution open, examine the *Distrust* class. Note that it has one member: *WriteToFile*, which uses a *StreamWriter* class, which automatically demands *FileIOPermission*.

3. Copy the TrustedClass.dll file to C:\TrustedClass\TrustedClass.dll.

4. At a command prompt, run the following command to share the folder:

   ```
   net share trusted="C:\TrustedClass"
   ```

5. Open the PartiallyTrustedAssembly.sln file.

6. Click Project and then click Add Reference. In the Add Reference dialog box, click the Browse tab. In the File Name box, type **\\127.0.0.1\Trusted\TrustedClass.dll**. Click OK.

7. Build the solution and then copy both the PartiallyTrustedAssembly.exe file and the TrustedClass.dll file to C:\PartiallyTrustedAssembly\.

8. At a command prompt, run the following command to share the folder:

   ```
   net share untrusted="C:\PartiallyTrustedAssembly"
   ```

9. At a command prompt, issue the following command:

   ```
   \\127.0.0.1\untrusted\PartiallyTrustedAssembly
   ```

   Answer the following questions:

   A. PartiallyTrustedAssembly attempts to write to a file. Did it succeed?

   No, it failed and reported a *SecurityException* because a request for *FileIO-Permission* failed.

   B. Examine the source code and explain the behavior.

   PartiallyTrustedAssembly calls the *TrustedClass.Distrust.WriteToFile* method. This method uses the .NET Framework's *StreamWriter* object, which contains a demand for *FileIOPermission*. After the *StreamWriter* object issues the demand, the runtime checks each caller for the CAS permission. Because PartiallyTrustedAssembly lacks the permission, the runtime throws a *SecurityException*.

10. Add a method to *TrustedClass.Distrust* named *WriteToFile*Wrapper that uses *Assert* to block the *FileIOPermission* demand, rebuild the assembly, and copy it to C:\TrustedClass.

11. In the PartiallyTrustedAssembly solution, remove and re-add the TrustedClass reference. Then modify the PartiallyTrustedAssembly source code to call *Write-ToFileWrapper* instead of *WriteToFile*. Answer the following questions:

    ❑ What code did you write to create the assembly?

    The exact code will vary, but it should resemble the following:

    ```vb
    ' VB
    Public Shared Sub WriteToFileWrapper(ByVal fileName As String, _
        ByVal contents As String)
        ' Assert permission to allow caller to bypass security check
        Dim newFilePermission As FileIOPermission = _
            New FileIOPermission(FileIOPermissionAccess.Write, fileName)
        newFilePermission.Assert()
        Try
            WriteToFile(fileName, contents)
        Finally
            ' Clean up the assertion
            CodeAccessPermission.RevertAssert()
        End Try
    End Sub
    ```

    ```csharp
    // C#
    public static void WriteToFileWrapper(string fileName, string contents)
    {
        // Assert permission to allow caller to bypass security check
        FileIOPermission newFilePermission =
            new FileIOPermission(FileIOPermissionAccess.Write, fileName);
        newFilePermission.Assert();
        try
        {
            WriteToFile(fileName, contents);
        }
        finally
        {
            // Clean up the assertion
            CodeAccessPermission.RevertAssert();
        }
    }
    ```

12. Rebuild the solution and then copy both the PartiallyTrustedAssembly.exe file and the TrustedClass.dll file to C:\PartiallyTrustedAssembly\.

13. At the command prompt, issue the following command:

    ```
    \\127.0.0.1\Untrusted\PartiallyTrustedAssembly
    ```

Answer the following question:

❑ PartiallyTrustedAssembly attempts to write to a file. Did it succeed? Why or why not?

No, it failed and reported a *SecurityException* because a request for *Security-Permission* failed. The new method attempts to use an *Assert*, which is a security permission it lacks because of the permission set assigned to *TrustedClass*.

14. Now, you must increase the *TrustedClass* assembly's trust to enable it to use an *Assert*. However, before you can increase an assembly's trust, it must be signed. Therefore, in the TrustedClass solution, modify the project properties to sign the assembly. For detailed instructions, read "How to: Sign a Visual Basic or Visual C# Assembly" at *http://msdn2.microsoft.com/en-us/library/ms180781.aspx*. Then rebuild the assembly, and copy it to C:\TrustedClass\.

15. Launch the .NET Framework 2.0 Configuration tool. Click Runtime Security Policy, and then click Increase Assembly Trust in the right pane.

16. On the What Would You Like To Modify page, click Make Changes To This Computer and then click Next.

17. On the Which Assembly Do You Want To Trust page, type **\\127.0.0.1\trusted\trustedclass.dll** and then click Next.

18. On the Trust This Assembly Or All Assemblies From This Publisher page, click This One Assembly. Click Next.

19. On the Choose The Minimum Level Of Trust For The Assembly page, move the slider to Full Trust. Click Next and then click Finish.

20. In the PartiallyTrustedAssembly solution, remove and readd the TrustedClass reference. Rebuild the solution and then copy both the PartiallyTrustedAssembly .exe file and the TrustedClass.dll file to C:\PartiallyTrustedAssembly\.

21. At the command prompt, issue the following command:

```
\\127.0.0.1\Untrusted\PartiallyTrustedAssembly
```

Answer the following question:

❑ A. PartiallyTrustedAssembly attempts to write to a file. Did it succeed? Why or why not?

Yes, it succeeded because the *WriteToFileWrapper* method includes an *Assert* that blocks the *StreamWriter*'s inherent *Demand* from checking the permissions of PartiallyTrustedAssembly. Additionally, *TrustedClass* has sufficient trust to use the *Assert*.

22. Remove the shares you created by running the following commands at an Administrator command prompt:

```
net share trusted /delete
net share untrusted /delete
```

23. Finally, use the .NET Framework Configuration Tool with administrative privileges to reset all policy levels, as described in Lesson 1 of this chapter.

Lesson Summary

- You can use six different methods to control permissions in an assembly: *Assert*, *Demand*, *Deny*, *InheritanceDemand*, *LinkDemand*, and *PermitOnly*.

- You should use *PermitOnly* and *Deny* within an assembly to reduce the likelihood of the assembly being misused by an attacker. Use *Demand* and *LinkDemand* only when accessing custom resources or unmanaged code.

- You can use *Demand* and *LinkDemand* to protect methods either declaratively or imperatively. You can use *InheritanceDemand* declaratively to restrict which assemblies can derive new classes from your own.

- You can use *PermitOnly* and *Deny* both declaratively and imperatively to restrict the permissions assigned to a method.

- To bypass CAS demands and enable underprivileged assemblies to call privileged methods, use *Assert*.

- Permission sets have the same capabilities as individual permissions, but apply a single action to multiple permissions simultaneously. To create a permission set, use the *System.Security.Permissions.PermissionSet* class and then use the *AddPermission* method to specify the permissions that define the permission set. Then you can call any standard permission methods, including *Assert*, *Demand*, *Deny*, and *PermitOnly*.

Lesson Review

You can use the following questions to test your knowledge of declarative and imperative method security. The questions are also available on the companion CD if you prefer to review them in electronic form.

NOTE   Answers

Answers to these questions and explanations of why each answer choice is right or wrong are located in the "Answers" section at the end of the book.

---

1. Which of the following would you use within a method to throw an exception if the assembly lacked a specific privilege?

   A. *SecurityAction.Demand*

   B. *SecurityAction.Deny*

   C. *SecurityAction.Assert*

   D. *SecurityAction.RequestMinimum*

2. Which of the following would you use to throw an exception before method execution begins if a caller lacked a specific privilege?

   A. *SecurityAction.Demand*

   B. *SecurityAction.Deny*

   C. *SecurityAction.Assert*

   D. *SecurityAction.RequestMinimum*

3. You have created a *FileIOPermission* object named *fp*. Which method would you use to determine whether the current assembly had a specific permission without throwing an exception?

   A. *fp.Deny*

   B. *fp.IsGranted*

   C. *SecurityManager.Deny(fp)*

   D. *SecurityManager.IsGranted(fp)*

4. Given the best answer, which of the following lines of code would reverse the security restriction? (Choose all that apply.)

```
' VB
Dim e As EventLogPermission = _
    New EventLogPermission (PermissionState.Unrestricted)
e.PermitOnly

// C#
EventLogPermission e =
    new EventLogPermission(PermissionState.Unrestricted);
e.PermitOnly();
```

   A. *e.RevertPermitOnly*

   B. *CodeAccessPermission.RevertPermitOnly*

   C. *e.RevertAll*

   D. *CodeAccessPermission.RevertAll*

   E. *e.RevertDeny*

   F. *CodeAccessPermission.RevertDeny*

Chapter Review

To further practice and reinforce the skills you learned in this chapter, you can perform the following tasks:

- Review the chapter summary.
- Review the list of key terms introduced in this chapter.
- Complete the case scenarios. These scenarios set up real-world situations involving the topics of this chapter and ask you to create a solution.
- Complete the suggested practices.
- Take a practice test.

Chapter Summary

- CAS controls managed code's access similarly to the way that operating system security restricts a user's access to system resources. You can configure CAS by using either the .NET Framework Configuration tool or the Caspol command-line tool.
- Assembly permission requests enable administrators to view the permission requirements of an assembly. They can also dramatically reduce the likelihood of an assembly being abused by ensuring that the assembly cannot access any system resources that it does not require.
- You can control CAS permissions within an assembly either imperatively or declaratively, allowing more granular control than can be accomplished with assembly declarations. This further increases the application's security.

Key Terms

Do you know what these key terms mean? You can check your answers by looking up the terms in the glossary at the end of the book.

- assembly evidence
- code access security (CAS)
- code group
- evidence
- fully trusted

- host evidence
- partially trusted code
- permission
- permission set
- security policy

Case Scenarios

In the following case scenarios, you will apply what you've learned about how to implement and apply code access security. You can find answers to these questions in the "Answers" section at the end of this book.

Case Scenario 1: Explaining Code Access Security

You are a developer at Blue Yonder Airlines. The CEO of your company read an article that quoted a security analyst who stated that the CAS in the .NET Framework could be used to prevent viruses from spreading. You run into him in the hallway and he says, "Hey, I just read this article in the paper. What's this about the .NET Framework? It's got some kind of new security that can stop programs from doing bad things, eh? Maybe you can install it on my computer so that I don't have to worry about viruses spreading or about other dangerous software sending my private files off to the Internet somewhere." He then asks you a series of questions.

Questions

Answer the following questions for your CEO:

1. Can .NET Framework CAS prevent viruses from spreading? Why or why not?

2. Will installing the .NET Framework on my computer improve the security? If not, what will it accomplish?

3. Could a .NET Framework-based virus running in the Internet zone with the default CAS permissions effectively replicate itself across our network? Why or why not?

4. Could a malicious .NET Framework–based assembly running in the Intranet zone with the default CAS permissions delete files on your hard drive? Why or why not?

Case Scenario 2: Customizing Code Access Security

You are an application developer for Contoso, Inc. You and your coworkers have been creating applications for internal use using the .NET Framework since version 1.0. However, you have never made use of CAS. Now, managers are requesting that partners outside your organization install your client application. However, they are concerned that your application might have security vulnerabilities that could expose partners to security risks, potentially tarnishing Contoso's reputation. CAS might be able to limit your risk.

In a meeting, your manager tells you, "The people in charge of customer and partner relations are begging us to let outsiders install your app. I'm concerned about security, especially because some clients will be installing the app on public kiosk computers that people are constantly trying to hack into. I'd like some assurance that if someone installs our app, an attacker can't abuse it to gain elevated privileges, or write a virus to the disk of the local computer, etcetera."

Questions

Answer the following questions for your manager:

1. How can you let partners and customers install your application while virtually eliminating the possibility that the application could be misused to read or write to the file system?

2. What class would you use to restrict your application's access to the file system?

3. How will end users be affected by implementing CAS security?

Suggested Practices

To help you successfully master the "Improving the security of .NET Framework applications by using the .NET Framework 2.0 security features" exam objective, complete the following tasks.

Implement Code Access Security to Improve the Security of a .NET Framework Application

For this task, you should complete at least Practice 1. If you want a solid understanding of how to analyze permissions, complete Practices 2 and 3 as well.

- **Practice 1**   Use the Caspol tool to add a code group to the Machine policy level. Then use the .NET Framework 2.0 Configuration tool to remove the code group.

- **Practice 2** Create an assembly that retrieves Web pages and saves them to a file on the local hard disk. Imperatively verify that the user has sufficient privileges by using *SecurityManager.IsGranted* to check the most granular permissions possible. Display an error message if the user lacks the necessary permissions.

- **Practice 3** Create an assembly that retrieves Web pages and saves them to a file on the local hard disk. Verify that the user has sufficient privileges by creating an instance of *PermissionSet* with the most granular permissions possible and calling *PermissionSet.Demand*.

Control Permissions for Resources by Using the *System.Security.Permission* Classes

For this task, you should complete all three practices to gain experience using *Permission* classes with a real-world application.

- **Practice 1** Open the last assembly that you created as part of your job, and add the most granular assembly permission requests possible. Be very specific—if your assembly needs access to only a single file, limit your file system access to that file. If you use Web services, restrict the *WebPermission* object to allow your assembly access only to the server and path that the Web service uses. If your assembly does not explicitly check for the permissions, configure the assembly permission requests so that the runtime will throw an exception if the permissions are not present before the runtime runs the assembly.

- **Practice 2** Using the same assembly as in Practice 1, add permission declarations to each method.

- **Practice 3** Again using the same assembly, add imperative security where required.

Control Code Privileges by Using *System.Security.Policy* Classes

For this task, you should complete at least Practice 1. If you want a deeper understanding of how to analyze evidence, complete Practice 2 as well.

- **Practice 1** Create a new code group that requires an assembly to be signed with your publisher certificate. Then verify that the .NET Framework correctly analyzes the evidence and places the assembly in the correct code group.

- **Practice 2** Write a console application that displays the current assembly's evidence.

Take a Practice Test

The practice tests on this book's companion CD offer many options. For example, you can test yourself on just one exam objective, or you can test yourself on all the 70-536 certification exam content. You can set up the test so that it closely simulates the experience of taking a certification exam, or you can set it up in study mode so that you can look at the correct answers and explanations after you answer each question.

MORE INFO   Practice tests

For details about all the practice test options available, see the "How to Use the Practice Tests" section in this book's Introduction.

Chapter 12
User and Data Security

Businesses must be able to control who can access confidential data. For example, an expense-tracking application should show users their own expenses, but only managers should be able to view other people's expenses. Unauthorized users should not be able to view any of the data—even if they manage to bypass your application's built-in protection.

Protecting data requires coordinating several different technologies. *Role-based security (RBS)* allows you to control what users can access based on their user name and group memberships. With the .NET Framework, you can make RBS decisions based on the local user database, an Active Directory domain, or a custom user database. You can also use the .NET Framework to configure *access control lists* (ACLs). ACLs are the operating system's method for tracking who should have access to what, and determining which actions require adding an event to the event log. Finally, to protect data if an attacker bypasses operating system security, the .NET Framework provides cryptography tools for encrypting, validating, and signing data.

Exam objectives in this chapter:
- Access and modify identity information by using the *System.Security.Principal* classes. (Refer *System.Security.Principal* namespace.)
  - ❏ *GenericIdentity* class and *GenericPrincipal* class
  - ❏ *WindowsIdentity* class and *WindowsPrincipal* class
  - ❏ *NTAccount* class and *SecurityIdentifier* class
  - ❏ *IIdentity* interface and *IPrincipal* interface
  - ❏ *WindowsImpersonationContext* class
  - ❏ *IdentityReference* class and *IdentityReferenceCollection* class
- Implement a custom authentication scheme by using the *System.Security.Authentication* classes. (Refer *System.Security.Authentication* namespace.)

  Implement access control by using the *System.Security.AccessControl* classes.
  - ❏ *DirectorySecurity* class, *FileSecurity* class, *FileSystemSecurity* class, and *RegistrySecurity* class

- ❑ *AccessRule* class

- ❑ *AuthorizationRule* class and *AuthorizationRuleCollection* class

- ❑ *CommonAce* class, *CommonAcl* class, *CompoundAce* class, *GeneralAce* class, and *GeneralAcl* class

- ❑ *AuditRule* class

- ❑ *MutexSecurity* class, *ObjectSecurity* class, and *SemaphoreSecurity* class

- Encrypt, decrypt, and hash data by using the *System.Security.Cryptography* classes. (Refer *System.Security.Cryptography* namespace)

  - ❑ *DES* class and *DESCryptoServiceProvider* class

  - ❑ *HashAlgorithm* class

  - ❑ *DSA* Class and *DSACryptoServiceProvider* Class

  - ❑ *SHA1* class and *SHA1CryptoServiceProvider* class

  - ❑ *TripleDES* and *TripleDESCryptoServiceProvider* class

  - ❑ *MD5* class and *MD5CryptoServiceProvider* class

  - ❑ *RSA* class and *RSACryptoServiceProvider* class

  - ❑ *RandomNumberGenerator* class

  - ❑ *CryptoStream* class

  - ❑ *CryptoConfig* class

  - ❑ *RC2* class and *RC2CryptoServiceProvider* class

  - ❑ *AsymetricAlgorithm* class

  - ❑ *ProtectedData* class and *ProtectedMemory* class

  - ❑ *RijndaelManaged* class and *RijndaelManagedTransform* class

  - ❑ *CspParameters* class

  - ❑ *CryptoAPITransform* class

  - ❑ Hash-based Message Authentication Code (HMAC)

Lessons in this chapter:

Before You Begin

To complete the lessons in this chapter, you should be familiar with Microsoft Visual Basic or C# and be comfortable with the following tasks:

- Create a console application in Microsoft Visual Studio using Visual Basic or C#
- Write to files and streams
- Manage user accounts with the graphical tools built into Microsoft Windows
- Manage file permissions with the graphical tools built into Windows

Lesson 1: Authenticating and Authorizing Users

In this lesson, you will learn the meaning of the term authentication and how it differs from authorization. You will then learn how to implement and analyze both authentication (checking a user's identity) and authorization (verifying a user's right to access resources). You can use the techniques described in this lesson to protect portions of your code from unauthorized use, so that only specific users or members of specific groups can run an assembly, method, or code segment.

If your organization uses Active Directory or local user databases, you can integrate your application's authorization controls into your existing directory service using the *WindowsIdentity* and *WindowsPrincipal* classes. You can also build your own authentication system or integrate into a non-Microsoft directory service. For straightforward user databases, you can use the *GenericIdentity* and *GenericPrincipal* classes. If you need complete control over users and roles, you can implement the *IIdentity* and *IPrincipal* interfaces.

After this lesson, you will be able to:

- Explain how authorization relates to authentication.
- Use the *WindowsIdentity* class to examine a user's name and authentication type to make decisions within your application.
- Explain the purpose of the *WindowsPrincipal* class.
- Describe the purpose of the *PrincipalPermission* class.
- Use declarative RBS demands to restrict access to methods.
- Use imperative RBS demands to create applications that restrict access to portions of your application's logic.
- Create custom identity classes by using the *IIdentity* interface, the *IPrincipal* interface, the *GenericIdentity* class, and the *GenericPrincipal* class.
- Describe the different circumstances in which the runtime uses *AuthenticationException* and *InvalidCredentialException*.

Estimated lesson time: 90 minutes

Authentication and Authorization Overview

Authentication is the process of identifying a user and is the most visible and fundamental concept in security. From personal identification numbers (PINs) to driver's licenses to user names and passwords, authentication is a part of everyone's daily life.

Without authentication, restricting access to resources based on a person's identity would be impossible.

Authorization is the process of verifying that a user is allowed to access a requested resource. Authorization generally happens only after authentication. After all, how can you determine whether someone is allowed to do something if you don't yet know who they are? Figure 12-1 shows how authentication and authorization together provide a user's identity and validate the user's permissions.

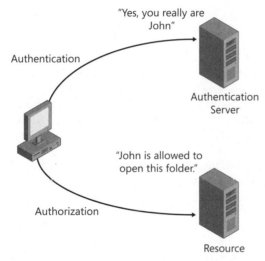

Figure 12-1   To access a resource, a user must be authenticated and then authorized

Whether you're withdrawing money from a bank, entering a restricted building, or boarding an airplane, gaining access to a restricted resource requires both authentication and authorization. The two processes are closely related and often confused. To understand the difference between authentication and authorization, consider an example in the physical world that most people are familiar with: boarding an airplane. Before you can board a plane, you must present both your identification and your ticket. Your identification, typically a driver's license or a passport, enables the airport staff to determine who you are. Validating your identity is the *authentication* part of the boarding process. The airport staff also checks your ticket to make sure that the flight you are boarding is the correct one. Verifying that you are allowed to board the plane is the *authorization* process.

On networks, authentication is often performed by providing a user name and password. The user name identifies you, and the password offers the computer system some assurance that you really are who you claim to be. After you are authenticated, the computer agrees that you are who you claim to be. However, it doesn't yet know whether you are allowed to access the resource you are requesting. For example, help desk support staff should have the right to reset a user's password, but members of the accounting department should be able to change only their own passwords. To authorize the user, the computer system typically checks an ACL, which lists users and groups of users who are permitted to access a resource.

WindowsIdentity Class

The *System.Security.Principal.WindowsIdentity* class represents a Windows user account. This class provides access to the current user's name, authentication type, and account token. It does not allow you to authenticate a user; Windows has already taken care of the authentication. *WindowsIdentity* simply stores the results of the authentication, including the user's name and authentication token.

Generally, when you create an instance of the *WindowsIdentity* class, you call one of three methods to create the object:

- **GetAnonymous** Returns a *WindowsIdentity* object that represents an anonymous, unauthenticated Windows user. You can use this method to impersonate an anonymous user to ensure that your code operates without credentials.

- **GetCurrent** Returns a *WindowsIdentity* object that represents the current Windows user. You can use this method to examine the current user's user name and group memberships.

- **Impersonate** Returns a *WindowsImpersonationContext* object that represents a specified user on the system. You can use this method to impersonate a particular user account when your application has access to the user's credentials.

For example, the following code (which requires the *System.Security.Principal* namespace) creates a *WindowsIdentity* object named *currentIdentity* that represents the current user:

```
' VB
Dim currentIdentity As WindowsIdentity =  WindowsIdentity.GetCurrent()

// C#
WindowsIdentity currentIdentity = WindowsIdentity.GetCurrent();
```

After the variable is assigned, you can access several useful properties that provide information about the user:

- **AuthenticationType** A string representing the authentication method. This is usually "NTLM".

- *IsAnonymous*   A Boolean value set to true if the user is anonymous.

- *IsAuthenticated*   A Boolean value set to true if the user is authenticated.

- *IsGuest*   A Boolean value set to true if the user is a guest.

- *IsSystem*   A Boolean value set to true if the user is part of the system.

- *Name*   A string representing the authentication domain and user name of the user, separated by a backslash in the format, "DOMAIN\Username". If the user's account is in the local user database, the domain is the machine name. Otherwise, domain represents the name of the Active Directory domain.

- *Token*   An integer representing the user's authentication token, assigned by the computer that authenticated the user.

Use the *WindowsIdentity* class to examine the current user's name and authentication type to determine whether the user is authorized to run privileged portions of your code. Examining objects of this class is useful if, for example, a section of your code displays information that should be available only to authenticated users.

The following simple console application (which requires the *System.Security.Principal* namespace) demonstrates the use of the *WindowsIdentity* class by displaying information about the current user:

```vb
' VB
' Grab the current user
Dim currentIdentity As WindowsIdentity = WindowsIdentity.GetCurrent()

' Display the name, token, and authentication type
' for the current user
Console.WriteLine("Name: " + currentIdentity.Name)
Console.WriteLine("Token: " + currentIdentity.Token.ToString())
Console.WriteLine("Authentication Type: " _
    + currentIdentity.AuthenticationType)

' Display information based on Boolean properties of the current user
If currentIdentity.IsAnonymous = True Then
    Console.WriteLine("Is an anonymous user")
End If
If currentIdentity.IsAuthenticated = True Then
    Console.WriteLine("Is an authenticated user")
End If
If currentIdentity.IsSystem = True Then
    Console.WriteLine("Is part of the system")
End If
If currentIdentity.IsGuest = True Then
    Console.WriteLine("Is a guest")
End If
```

```csharp
// C#
// Grab the current user
WindowsIdentity currentIdentity = WindowsIdentity.GetCurrent();

// Display the name, token, and authentication type
// for the current user
Console.WriteLine("Name: " + currentIdentity.Name);
Console.WriteLine("Token: " + currentIdentity.Token.ToString());
Console.WriteLine("Authentication Type: "
    + currentIdentity.AuthenticationType);

// Display information based on Boolean properties of
// the current user
if (currentIdentity.IsAnonymous)
    Console.WriteLine("Is an anonymous user");
if (currentIdentity.IsAuthenticated)
    Console.WriteLine("Is an authenticated user");
if (currentIdentity.IsGuest)
    Console.WriteLine("Is a guest");
if (currentIdentity.IsSystem)
    Console.WriteLine("Is part of the system");
```

WindowsPrincipal Class

The *System.Security.Principal.WindowsPrincipal* class provides access to a user's group memberships. This class must be created by using an instance of the *WindowsIdentity* class. For example, the following code creates a *WindowsIdentity* object named *currentIdentity* that represents the current user, and then it creates a *WindowsPrincipal* object named *currentPrincipal* that represents the current user by creating the object using an existing *WindowsIdentity* object:

```vb
' VB
Dim currentIdentity As WindowsIdentity = WindowsIdentity.GetCurrent()
Dim currentPrincipal As WindowsPrincipal = _
    New WindowsPrincipal(currentIdentity)
```

```csharp
// C#
WindowsIdentity currentIdentity = WindowsIdentity.GetCurrent();
WindowsPrincipal currentPrincipal = new WindowsPrincipal(currentIdentity);
```

As an alternative to creating a *WindowsIdentity* object using the *WindowsIdentity.GetCurrent* method, you can extract the current *WindowsPrincipal* object by querying the current thread directly. To do this, first set the current *principal policy* to use Windows security, and then create a new *WindowsPrincipal* object by casting *System.Threading.Thread.CurrentPrincipal* as a *WindowsPrincipal* object. The following code (which requires both the *System.Security.Principal* and *System.Threading* namespaces) demonstrates this:

```vb
' VB
' Specify that WindowsPrincipal should be used
AppDomain.CurrentDomain.SetPrincipalPolicy(PrincipalPolicy.WindowsPrincipal)
```

```
' Cast the current principal as a WindowsPrincipal object
Dim currentPrincipal As WindowsPrincipal = _
    CType(Thread.CurrentPrincipal, WindowsPrincipal)

// C#
// Specify that WindowsPrincipal should be used
AppDomain.CurrentDomain.SetPrincipalPolicy(PrincipalPolicy.WindowsPrincipal);

// Cast the current principal as a WindowsPrincipal object
WindowsPrincipal currentPrincipal = (WindowsPrincipal)Thread.CurrentPrincipal;
```

You can use the *WindowsPrincipal* class to determine which groups a user is a member of. To query for built-in groups, pass to the *WindowsPrincipal.IsInRole* method a member of the *System.Security.Principal.WindowsBuiltInRole* class. Each member of the *WindowsBuiltInRole* class represents a built-in group that exists either within the computer's local user database, or within an Active Directory domain. For example, the following portion of a console application checks three separate members of the *WindowsBuiltInRole* class and displays whether the current local user is a member:

```
' VB
' Create a WindowsIdentity object representing the current user
Dim currentIdentity As WindowsIdentity =  WindowsIdentity.GetCurrent()

' Create a WindowsPrincipal object representing the current user
Dim currentPrincipal As WindowsPrincipal = _
    New WindowsPrincipal(currentIdentity)

Console.WriteLine("The current user is a member of the following roles: ")

' Check for three common group memberships
If currentPrincipal.IsInRole(WindowsBuiltInRole.Administrator) Then
    Console.WriteLine(WindowsBuiltInRole.Administrator.ToString())
End If
If currentPrincipal.IsInRole(WindowsBuiltInRole.PowerUser) Then
    Console.WriteLine(WindowsBuiltInRole.PowerUser.ToString())
End If
If currentPrincipal.IsInRole(WindowsBuiltInRole.User) Then
    Console.WriteLine(WindowsBuiltInRole.User.ToString())
End If

// C#
// Create a WindowsIdentity object representing the current user
WindowsIdentity currentIdentity = WindowsIdentity.GetCurrent();

// Create a WindowsPrincipal object representing the current user
WindowsPrincipal currentPrincipal = new WindowsPrincipal(currentIdentity);

Console.WriteLine("The current user is a member of the following roles: ");

// Check for three common group memberships
if (currentPrincipal.IsInRole(WindowsBuiltInRole.Administrator))
    Console.WriteLine(WindowsBuiltInRole.Administrator.ToString());
```

```
if (currentPrincipal.IsInRole(WindowsBuiltInRole.PowerUser))
    Console.WriteLine(WindowsBuiltInRole.PowerUser.ToString());
if (currentPrincipal.IsInRole(WindowsBuiltInRole.User))
    Console.WriteLine(WindowsBuiltInRole.User.ToString());
```

The presence of built-in groups varies depending on the operating system and whether the computer is a domain controller, so always be prepared to catch an exception when checking user roles.

To query for custom groups or groups in a domain rather than for the local user database, pass a string value to the overloaded *IsInRole* method in the format "*DOMAIN\ Group Name*". For example, if you have code that should execute only if the user is a member of the CONTOSO\Accountants group, you could use the following *if* statement:

```
' VB
If currentPrincipal.IsInRole("CONTOSO\Accounting") Then
    Console.WriteLine("User is in Accounting")
End If
```

```
// C#
if (currentPrincipal.IsInRole(@"CONTOSO\Accounting"))
    Console.WriteLine("User is in Accounting");
```

In most circumstances, however, you will not know the computer name or domain name ahead of time to insert it into the string you pass the *IsInRole* method. Instead, construct it using the *System.Environment.MachineName* string property or the *System.Environment.UserDomainName* string property. *System.Environment.MachineName* can be used to specify group names only on the local computer. Use *System.Environment.UserDomainName* to specify group names that exist on the local computer or in the Active Directory domain, depending on how the user logged on.

PrincipalPermission Class

The *System.Security.Permissions.PrincipalPermission* class and the related *PrincipalPermissionAttribute* class enable you to check the active principal for both declarative and imperative security actions. They (collectively referred to as *PrincipalPermission*) are typically used to declaratively demand that users running your code have been authenticated or belong to a specified role. By passing identity information (user name and/or role) to the constructor, *PrincipalPermission* can be used to demand that the identity of the active principal match this information.

You can set any combination of three properties for *PrincipalPermission*:

- **Authenticated** A Boolean value. If set to true, the permission requires the user to be authenticated.

- *Name* A string that must match the identity's user name.
- *Role* A string that must match one of the principal's roles.

Exam Tip   Memorize these three properties. Remember, *PrincipalPermission* doesn't expose any other properties—not a user's full name, phone number, password, or any other attribute.

PrincipalPermission has several methods; however, only the *PrincipalPermission* *.Demand* method is used with the RBS techniques described in this chapter. The *Demand* method verifies that the active principal meets the requirements specified in the *Authenticated*, *Name*, and *Role* properties. If the principal does not match any properties that are not null, the principal throws an exception.

How to Use Declarative Role-Based Security Demands to Restrict Access to Methods

Declarative RBS demands instruct the runtime to perform an RBS check before running a method. This is the most secure way to use RBS to restrict access to code because security is enforced by the runtime before it runs your code. There are two primary disadvantages to declarative RBS demands:

- They can be used only to restrict access to entire methods.
- They might result in the runtime throwing an exception. If the method was called by a Windows event, Windows catches the exception, and your application might stop running.

To use declarative RBS demands, you must have three elements in your code:

- The *System.AppDomain.CurrentDomain.SetPrincipalPolicy* method to specify the principal security policy
- A *Try/Catch* block to catch underprivileged access attempts and to report the error appropriately
- A *PrincipalPermission* attribute to declare the method's access requirements

First, specify the principal policy for the thread from within your application using the *System.AppDomain.CurrentDomain.SetPrincipalPolicy* method, as described earlier in this lesson. Next, create a *Try/Catch* block to catch the *System.Security.SecurityException* exceptions that the runtime will throw when it attempts to run the method but lacks the permission demanded. It's important to catch this type of exception and provide a useful error message to the user because without the error message, the user could quickly become frustrated and might spend a significant amount of time attempting to troubleshoot the access problem. Additionally, log failed access attempts so that administrators can analyze the events to detect potential compromises.

For example, the following code calls a method named *AdministratorsOnlyMethod* (not shown) that is protected with a declarative RBS demand and displays a message box if the user lacks the necessary permission:

```
' VB
Try
    AdministratorsOnlyMethod()
Catch ex As System.Security.SecurityException
    MessageBox.Show("Your account lacks permission to that function.")
End Try
```

```
// C#
try
    { AdministratorsOnlyMethod(); }
catch (System.Security.SecurityException ex)
    { MessageBox.Show("Your account lacks permission to that function."); }
```

Finally, add declarative permission statements using the *PrincipalPermission* class before each method you need to restrict access to. You must define two things for *PrincipalPermission*:

- The action *PrincipalPermission* will take using the *System.Security.Permissions. SecurityAction* enumeration. Typically, you use *SecurityAction.Demand* for declarative RBS.

- One or more *PrincipalPermission* properties. Use *Authenticated* to restrict access to authenticated users, *Role* to restrict access by group memberships, and *User* to restrict access to a specific user name.

For example, the following code (which requires the System.Security.Permissions namespace) causes the runtime to throw a *System.Security.SecurityException* exception when the user is not a member of the local Administrators group:

```
' VB
<PrincipalPermission(SecurityAction.Demand, Role:="BUILTIN\Administrators")> _
Private Sub AdministratorsOnlyMethod ()
    ' Code that can only be run by Administrators
End Sub
```

```
// C#
[PrincipalPermission(SecurityAction.Demand, Role = @"BUILTIN\Administrators")]
static void AdministratorsOnlyMethod()
{ // Code that can only be run by Administrators }
```

You can also use multiple declarative demands to enable users who meet any of the demands to execute the code. The following code enables any of the following to run the method:

- Members of the local Administrators group

- A user named CONTOSO\User1 who is also a member of the CONTOSO\Managers group

- Any user who is authenticated

```vb
' VB
<PrincipalPermission(SecurityAction.Demand, _
    Name:="CONTOSO\Administrator")> _
<PrincipalPermission(SecurityAction.Demand, _
    Name:="CONTOSO\User1", Role:="CONTOSO\Managers")> _
<PrincipalPermission(SecurityAction.Demand, Authenticated:=True)> _
Private Sub AdministratorsOnlyMethod ()
    ' Code that can only be run by CONTOSO\Administrator
End Sub
```

```csharp
// C#
[PrincipalPermission(SecurityAction.Demand,
    Name = @"CONTOSO\Administrator")]
[PrincipalPermission(SecurityAction.Demand,
    Name = @"CONTOSO\User1", Role = @"CONTOSO\Managers")]
[PrincipalPermission(SecurityAction.Demand, Authenticated = true)]
static void AdministratorsOnlyMethod()
{ // Code that can only be run by CONTOSO\Administrator }
```

How to Use Imperative Role-Based Security Demands to Create Applications that Restrict Access to Portions of Their Logic

Imperative RBS demands are declared within your code and can be used to restrict access to portions of code on a more granular basis than declarative RBS demands. In other words, imperative RBS demands allow you to restrict portions of a method, whereas declarative RBS demands require you to restrict entire methods. To use imperative RBS demands, you must have four elements in your code:

- The *System.AppDomain.CurrentDomain.SetPrincipalPolicy* method to specify the principal security policy

- A *Try/Catch* block to catch underprivileged access attempts and report the error appropriately

- A *PrincipalPermission* object, with properties set according to the restrictions you want to impose

- A call to the *PrincipalPermission.Demand* method to declare the method's access requirements

The first two elements are exactly the same as those required by declarative RBS demands and should be implemented in exactly the same way. The use of the *Principal-Permission* class is different, however. First, you must create a new *PrincipalPermission* object. *PrincipalPermission* has three overloaded constructors:

- **PrincipalPermission(PermissionState)**   Enables you to specify the *PrincipalPermisson* object's properties by using a *System.Security.Permissions.PermissionState* object.

- **PrincipalPermission(Name, Role)**   Specifies values for the new object's *Name* and *Role* properties. If you want to specify only a user name or a role, simply specify null for the other value.

- **PrincipalPermission(Name, Role, Authenticated)**   Specifies values for the new object's *Name*, *Role*, and *Authenticated* properties. Specify null for any properties that you do not want to use to restrict access.

The following two lines of code throw an exception when the user is not a member of the local Administrators group. Note that the first argument to the *PrincipalPermission* constructor is null, which indicates that no particular user name is required. The last argument, set to true, requires that the user be authenticated (which is redundant and could effectively be left out because no unauthenticated user would be a member of the Administrators group).

```
' VB
Dim p As PrincipalPermission= New PrincipalPermission (Nothing, _
    "BUILTIN\Administrators", True)
p.Demand
```

```
// C#
PrincipalPermission p = new PrincipalPermission(null,
    @"BUILTIN\Administrators", true);
p.Demand();
```

To tie the imperative use of the *PrincipalPermission* object into a larger application, consider the following console application. This application displays "Access allowed." if the current user is a member of the local VS Developers group. Otherwise, it catches the exception thrown by the *PrincipalPermission.Demand* method and displays "Access denied".

```
' VB
' Define the security policy in use as Windows security
System.AppDomain.CurrentDomain.SetPrincipalPolicy(PrincipalPolicy.WindowsPrincipal)
```

```
' Concatenate the group name as "MachineName\VS Developers"
Dim r As String = System.Environment.MachineName + "\VS Developers"

' Catch any security denied exceptions so that they can be logged
Try
    ' Create and demand the PrincipalPermission object
    Dim p As PrincipalPermission = New PrincipalPermission(Nothing, r, True)
    p.Demand()
    Console.WriteLine("Access allowed.")
    ' TODO: Main application
Catch ex As System.Security.SecurityException
    Console.WriteLine("Access denied: " + ex.Message)
    ' TODO: Log error
End Try
```

```
// C#
// Define the security policy in use as Windows security
System.AppDomain.CurrentDomain.SetPrincipalPolicy(PrincipalPolicy.WindowsPrincipal);

// Concatenate the group name as "MachineName\VS Developers"
string r = System.Environment.MachineName + @"\VS Developers";

// Catch any security denied exceptions so that they can be logged
try
{
    // Create and demand the PrincipalPermission object
    PrincipalPermission p = new PrincipalPermission(null, r, true);
    p.Demand();

    Console.WriteLine("Access allowed.");
    // TODO: Main application
}
catch(System.Security.SecurityException ex)
{
    Console.WriteLine("Access denied: " + ex.Message);
    // TODO: Log error
}
```

How to Implement Custom Users and Roles

If you need to authenticate users against a custom database, you can use the *System .Security.Principal.IIdentity* and *System.Security.Principal.IPrincipal* interfaces. You can extend these interfaces by implementing your own classes with additional properties and functionalities. For example, you could create your own *IIdentity*-based class that includes custom user attributes such as name and address, or you could create your own *IPrincipal*-based class that implements hierarchical roles.

How to Create a Custom Identity Class

The *IIdentity* interface is a template for creating identity classes. The *WindowsIdentity* class is an implementation of *IIdentity*, and the bulk of *WindowsIdentity*'s properties and methods are inherited directly from *IIdentity*. Similarly, *FormsIdentity* and *PassportIdentity* implement *IIdentity* for working with Web authentication, and the *GenericIdentity* class provides a very flexible implementation of *IIdentity*.

If none of the existing implementations of *IIdentity* suits your needs, you can extend *IIdentity*'s functionality by creating your own class based on it. By doing this, you can add any properties you see fit. After creating the class, you can use the new class in the same ways you used *WindowsIdentity*.

To implement *IIdentity*, you must implement the following properties:

- **AuthenticationType**   A string used to store a description of the user's authentication mechanism. Applications can use this property to determine whether the authentication mechanism can be trusted. For example, one application might determine that Passport authentication meets the security requirements but Basic authentication does not. If you create a custom authentication mechanism, specify a unique *AuthenticationType*.

- **IsAuthenticated**   A Boolean value that should be set to true if the user has been authenticated. If you create your own custom authentication mechanism, set this value when the user is authenticated.

- **Name**   A string that stores the user's user name. This property must exist, even when your authentication mechanism does not use a user name. It must uniquely identify the user; only one account should have any given name.

Additionally, you will need to implement a constructor that defines each of the object's properties.

The following class implements *IIdentity* and adds properties for the user's first and last name, address, city, state, and postal code. This class provides two constructors: one that takes no parameters and initializes all properties as null, and a second one that initializes every property.

```
' VB
Public Class CustomIdentity
    Implements IIdentity
    Private _isAuthenticated As Boolean
    Private _name As String
    Private _authenticationType As String
    Private _firstName As String
```

```vb
Private _lastName As String
Private _address As String
Private _city As String
Private _state As String
Private _zip As String

Public Sub New()
    Me._name = String.Empty
    Me._isAuthenticated = False
    Me._authenticationType = "None"
    Me._firstName = String.Empty
    Me._lastName = String.Empty
    Me._address = String.Empty
    Me._city = String.Empty
    Me._state = String.Empty
    Me._zip = String.Empty
End Sub

Public Sub New(ByVal isLogin As Boolean, _
    ByVal newAuthenticationType As String, _
    ByVal newFirstName As String, ByVal newLastName As String, _
    ByVal newAddress As String, _
    ByVal newCity As String, ByVal newState As String, _
    ByVal newZip As String)

    Me._name = newFirstName + newLastName
    Me._isAuthenticated = isLogin
    Me._authenticationType = newAuthenticationType
    Me._firstName = newFirstName
    Me._lastName = newLastName
    Me._address = newAddress
    Me._city = newCity
    Me._state = newState
    Me._zip = newZip
End Sub

Public ReadOnly Property IsAuthenticated() As Boolean _
    Implements IIdentity.IsAuthenticated

    Get
        Return Me._isAuthenticated
    End Get
End Property

Public ReadOnly Property Name() As String Implements IIdentity.Name
    Get
        Return Me._name
    End Get
End Property

Public ReadOnly Property AuthenticationType() As String _
    Implements IIdentity.AuthenticationType
```

```
            Get
                Return Me._authenticationType
            End Get
        End Property

        Public ReadOnly Property FirstName() As String
            Get
                Return Me._firstName
            End Get
        End Property

        Public ReadOnly Property LastName() As String
            Get
                Return Me._lastName
            End Get
        End Property

        Public ReadOnly Property Address() As String
            Get
                Return Me._address
            End Get
        End Property

        Public ReadOnly Property City() As String
            Get
                Return Me._city
            End Get
        End Property

        Public ReadOnly Property State() As String
            Get
                Return Me._state
            End Get
        End Property

        Public ReadOnly Property Zip() As String
            Get
                Return Me._zip
            End Get
        End Property
    End Class

// C#
class CustomIdentity : IIdentity
{
    // Implement private variables for standard properties
    private bool isAuthenticated;
    private string name, authenticationType;

    // Implement private variables for custom properties
    private string firstName, lastName, address, city, state, zip;
```

```csharp
// Allow the creation of an empty object
public CustomIdentity()
{
    this.name = String.Empty;
    this.isAuthenticated = false;
    this.authenticationType = "None";

    this.firstName = String.Empty;
    this.lastName = String.Empty;
    this.address = String.Empty;
    this.city = String.Empty;
    this.state = String.Empty;
    this.zip = String.Empty;
}

// Allow caller to create the object and specify all properties
public CustomIdentity(bool isLogin, string newAuthenticationType,
    string newFirstName,
    string newLastName, string newAddress, string newCity,
    string newState, string newZip)
{
    // Create a unique username by concatenating first and last name
    this.name = newFirstName + newLastName;
    this.isAuthenticated = isLogin;
    this.authenticationType = newAuthenticationType;

    this.firstName = newFirstName;
    this.lastName = newLastName;
    this.address = newAddress;
    this.city = newCity;
    this.state = newState;
    this.zip = newZip;
}

// Implement public read-only interfaces for standard properties
public bool IsAuthenticated
{ get { return this.isAuthenticated; } }

public string Name
{ get { return this.name; } }

public string AuthenticationType
{ get { return this.authenticationType; } }

// Implement public, read-only interfaces for custom properties
public string FirstName
{ get { return this.firstName; } }

public string LastName
{ get { return this.lastName; } }

public string Address
{ get { return this.address; } }
```

```
public string City
{ get { return this.city; } }

public string State
{ get { return this.state; } }

public string Zip
{ get { return this.zip; } }
}
```

BEST PRACTICES **When not to implement** *IIdentity*

This code shows how to implement a custom identity based on *IIdentity*. However, if you want to add properties to a Windows logon while still using the Windows token or other Windows security properties, base your custom identity on the *WindowsIdentity* class instead. The same applies for *IPrincipal* and *WindowsPrincipal*.

How to Create a Custom Principal Class

Just as *WindowsIdentity* is based on *IIdentity*, the *WindowsPrincipal* and *GenericPrincipal* classes are based on the *IPrincipal* interface. Objects based on the *IPrincipal* interface represent the security context of a user, including that user's identity and any roles or groups to which they belong.

To implement *IPrincipal*, you must implement at least one constructor, one property, and one method. The constructor must accept an *IIdentity* object and an array of strings containing the identity's roles, although you can add overloaded constructors. The property that you must implement is *IPrincipal.Identity*, which should return the principal's identity object (which must be defined when the object is constructed). The method is the Boolean *IPrincipal.IsInRole*, which takes a single string and the role being queried, and returns true when the principal's identity is a member of that role. Otherwise, it returns false.

You can add some interesting functionality by overriding *IPrincipal*:

- Add a *Roles* property that returns an array of strings containing the roles the user is a member of.

- Add *IsInAllRoles* and *IsInAnyRole* methods that determine whether the user is a member of multiple roles.

- Add *IsHigherThanRole* and *IsLowerThanRole* methods to enable hierarchical group memberships. For example, a principal who is a member of the Presidents role would evaluate *IPrincipal.IsHigherThanRole("Vice-Presidents")* as true.

To create a custom principal class, implement it based on *IPrincipal*; and at a minimum override the constructor, the *Identity* property, and the *IsInRole* method. For example, the following class implements the *IPrincipal* interface without extending the functionality:

```vb
' VB
Public Class CustomPrincipal
    Implements IPrincipal

    ' Implement private variables for standard properties
    Private _identity As IIdentity
    Private _roles As String()

    ' Allow caller to create the object and specify all properties
    Public Sub New(ByVal identity As IIdentity, ByVal roles As String())
        _identity = identity
        roles.CopyTo(_roles, 0)
        Array.Sort(_roles)
    End Sub

    ' Implement public read-only interfaces for standard properties
    Public Function IsInRole(ByVal role As String) As Boolean _
        Implements IPrincipal.IsInRole

        If Array.BinarySearch(_roles, role) >= 0 Then
            Return True
        Else
            Return False
        End If
    End Function

    Public ReadOnly Property Identity() As IIdentity _
        Implements IPrincipal.Identity

        Get
            Return _identity
        End Get
    End Property
End Class


// C#
class CustomPrincipal : IPrincipal
{
    private IIdentity _identity;
    private string[] _roles;

    // Allow caller to create the object and specify all properties
    public CustomPrincipal(IIdentity identity, string[] roles)
    {
        _identity = identity;
```

```
        roles = new string[roles.Length];
        roles.CopyTo(_roles, 0);
        Array.Sort(_roles);
    }

    public IIdentity Identity
    { get { return _identity; } }

    public bool IsInRole(string role)
    { return Array.BinarySearch(_roles, role) >= 0 ? true : false; }
}
```

How to Create Simple Custom User Privilege Models

If you don't want to use any of the classes based on *IIdentity* and *IPrincipal* that are built into the runtime, and you need only the basic functionality provided by the *IIdentity* and *IPrincipal* interfaces, use *System.Security.Principal.GenericIdentity* and *System.Security.Principal.GenericPrincipal*. These classes, provided by the runtime, implement only the properties and methods required by the interfaces. They each provide constructors that your application must use to specify each class's properties.

GenericIdentity has two overloaded constructors. To create a new *GenericIdentity* object, you can use just a user name, or you can use both a user name and an authentication type. You can't later change these values; you must specify them when the object is created. The following code sample demonstrates both usages:

```
' VB
Dim myUser1 As GenericIdentity = New GenericIdentity("AHankin")
Dim myUser2 As GenericIdentity = New GenericIdentity("TAdams", "SmartCard")

// C#
GenericIdentity myUser1 = new GenericIdentity("AHankin");
GenericIdentity myUser2 = new GenericIdentity("TAdams", "SmartCard");
```

GenericPrincipal has only a single constructor that requires both a *GenericIdentity* object and an array of strings containing the identity's roles. The following code sample extends the previous code sample to demonstrate how to create a *GenericPrincipal* object, where *myUser1* is a *GenericIdentity* object that was previously created:

```
' VB
Dim myUser1Roles() As String = _
    New String() {"IT", "Users", "Administrators"}
Dim myPrincipal1 As GenericPrincipal = _
    New GenericPrincipal(myUser1, myUser1Roles)

// C#
String[] myUser1Roles = new String[]{"IT", "Users", "Administrators"};
GenericPrincipal myPrincipal1 =
    new GenericPrincipal(myUser1, myUser1Roles);
```

After creating the principal object in the previous code sample, *myPrincipal1.IsIn-Role("Users")* method would return true.

How to Use RBS Demands with Custom Identities and Principals

Whether you define custom *IIdentity* and *IPrincipal* interfaces or use *GenericIdentity* and *GenericPrincipal*, you can take advantage of the same declarative and imperative RBS techniques used for *WindowsIdentity* and *WindowsPrincipal*. To do this, perform the following steps in your application:

1. Create an *IIdentity* or *GenericIdentity* object representing the current user.

2. Create an *IPrincipal* or *GenericPrincipal* object based on your *IIdentity* object.

3. Set the *Thread.CurrentPrincipal* property to your *IPrincipal* object.

4. Add any declarative or imperative RBS demands required.

The following console application (which requires the *System.Security.Permissions*, *System.Security.Principal*, and *System.Threading* namespaces) performs all these steps to demonstrate how to use declarative RBS demands with the *GenericIdentity* and *GenericPrincipal* classes. In this example, only members of the IT role can run the *Test-Security* method. Two identities and principals are created. The object *myUser1*, with the user name AHankin, is a member of the IT role and should be able to run the method. The object *myUser2*, with the user name TAdams, is not a member of that role.

```vb
' VB
Sub Main()
    Dim myUser1 As GenericIdentity = New GenericIdentity("AHankin")
    Dim myUser1Roles As String() = New String() {"IT", "Users", _
        "Administrators"}
    Dim myPrincipal1 As GenericPrincipal = _
        New GenericPrincipal(myUser1, myUser1Roles)

    Dim myUser2 As GenericIdentity = New GenericIdentity("TAdams")
    Dim myUser2Roles As String() = New String() {"Users"}
    Dim myPrincipal2 As GenericPrincipal = _
        New GenericPrincipal(myUser2, myUser2Roles)

    Try
        Thread.CurrentPrincipal = myPrincipal1
        TestSecurity()

        Thread.CurrentPrincipal = myPrincipal2
        TestSecurity()
    Catch ex As Exception
        Console.WriteLine(ex.GetType.ToString + " caused by " + _
            Thread.CurrentPrincipal.Identity.Name)
    End Try
End Sub
```

```
<PrincipalPermissionAttribute(SecurityAction.Demand, Role:="IT")> _
Private Sub TestSecurity()
    Console.WriteLine(Thread.CurrentPrincipal.Identity.Name + " is in IT.")
End Sub

// C#
static void Main(string[] args)
{
    GenericIdentity myUser1 = new GenericIdentity("AHankin");
    String[] myUser1Roles = new String[]{"IT", "Users", "Administrators"};
    GenericPrincipal myPrincipal1 =
        new GenericPrincipal(myUser1, myUser1Roles);

    GenericIdentity myUser2 = new GenericIdentity("TAdams");
    String[] myUser2Roles = new String[]{"Users"};
    GenericPrincipal myPrincipal2 =
        new GenericPrincipal(myUser2, myUser2Roles);

    try
    {
        Thread.CurrentPrincipal = myPrincipal1;
        TestSecurity();

        Thread.CurrentPrincipal = myPrincipal2;
        TestSecurity();
    }
    catch(Exception ex)
    { Console.WriteLine(ex.GetType().ToString() + " caused by " +
            Thread.CurrentPrincipal.Identity.Name); }
}

[PrincipalPermission(SecurityAction.Demand, Role = "IT")]
private static void TestSecurity()
{ Console.WriteLine(Thread.CurrentPrincipal.Identity.Name + " is in IT."); }
```

This application produces the following output, which verifies that the declarative RBS demand does protect the *TestSecurity* method from users who are not in the IT role:

```
AHankin is in IT.
System.Security.SecurityException caused by TAdams
```

Handling Authentication Exceptions in Streams

When authenticating to remote computers using the *System.Net.Security.Negotiate-Stream* or *System.Net.Security.SslStream* classes, the .NET Framework will throw an exception if either the client or server cannot be properly authenticated. Therefore, you should always be prepared to catch one of the following exceptions when using *NegotiateStream* or *SslStream*:

- **System.Security.Authentication.AuthenticationException**   An exception of this type indicates that you should prompt the user for different credentials and retry authentication.

- *System.Security.Authentication.InvalidCredentialException*   An exception of this type indicates that the underlying stream is not in a valid state, and you cannot retry authentication.

Lab: Adding Role-Based Security to an Application

In this lab, you add security to an application so that features are limited based on the user's name and group membership. If you encounter a problem completing an exercise, the completed projects are available on the companion CD in the Code folder.

▶ **Exercise: Protect an Application with Role-Based Security**

In this exercise, you update a Windows Forms calculator application to include RBS. You should use the most secure techniques possible and meet the following requirements:

- Only members of the Users group can run the method linked to the Add button.

- Only members of the Administrators group can run the *multiply* method.

- Only the CPhilp user can run the method linked to the Divide button.

- You must hide buttons users do not have access to.

1. Use Windows Explorer to copy either the C# or Visual Basic version of the Chapter12\Lesson1-Exercise1 folder from the companion CD to your My Documents\Visual Studio Projects\ folder. Then open the solution.

2. Add the *System.Security.Permissions* and *System.Security.Principal* namespaces to your code.

3. To enable you to check Windows group memberships, set the principal policy to Windows Policy. You should do this in a method that will run when the form opens, such as the form constructor. The following code would work:

```
' VB
Public Sub New()
    MyBase.New()
    InitializeComponent()

    ' Set the security policy context to Windows security
    System.AppDomain.CurrentDomain.SetPrincipalPolicy( _
        PrincipalPolicy.WindowsPrincipal)
End Sub

// C#
public Form1()
{
    InitializeComponent();
```

```
    // Set the security policy context to Windows security
    System.AppDomain.CurrentDomain.SetPrincipalPolicy(
        PrincipalPolicy.WindowsPrincipal);
}
```

4. Address the first requirement, "Only members of the Users group can run the method linked to the Add button." The following code would work for the *addButton_Click* method:

```vb
' VB
Try
    ' Demand that user is member of the built-in Users group
    ' Because this method is called by a Windows event, protect it
    ' with a imperative RBS demand
    Dim userPermission As PrincipalPermission = _
        New PrincipalPermission(Nothing, "BUILTIN\Users")
    userPermission.Demand()

    ' Perform calculations
    Dim answer As Integer = (Integer.Parse(integer1.Text) + _
        Integer.Parse(integer2.Text))
    answerLabel.Text = answer.ToString()
Catch ex As System.Security.SecurityException
    ' Display message box explaining access denial
    MessageBox.Show("You have been denied access: " + ex.Message)
    ' TODO: Log error
End Try
```

```csharp
// C#
try
{
    // Demand that user is member of the built-in Users group
    // Because this method is called by a Windows event, protect it with
    // a imperative RBS demand
    PrincipalPermission userPermission =
        new PrincipalPermission(null, @"BUILTIN\Users");
    userPermission.Demand();

    // Perform the calculation
    int answer = (int.Parse(integer1.Text) + int.Parse(integer2.Text));
    answerLabel.Text = answer.ToString();
}
catch (System.Security.SecurityException ex)
{
    // Display message box explaining access denial
    MessageBox.Show("You have been denied access: " + ex.Message);
    // TODO: Log error
}
```

5. Address the second requirement, "Only members of the Administrators group can run the *multiply* method." Because the multiply method is not directly called

by a Windows event, you can use declarative security. The following code declaration would protect the *multiply* method:

```vb
' VB
<PrincipalPermission(SecurityAction.Demand, _
    Role:="BUILTIN\Administrators")> _
```

```csharp
// C#
[PrincipalPermission(SecurityAction.Demand,
    Role = @"BUILTIN\Administrators")]
```

6. Address the third requirement, "Only the CPhilp user can run the method linked to the Divide button." The following code would work for the *divideButton_Click* method:

```vb
' VB
' Concatenate the computer and username
Dim allowUser As String = System.Environment.MachineName + "\cphilp"
Try
    ' Demand that user has the username "cphilp" on the local
    ' computer. Because this method is called by a Windows event,
    ' protect it with a imperative RBS demand
    Dim p As PrincipalPermission = _
        New PrincipalPermission(allowUser, Nothing)
    p.Demand()

    ' Perform super-secret mathematical calculations
    Dim answer As Decimal = (Decimal.Parse(integer1.Text) _
        / Decimal.Parse(integer2.Text))
    answerLabel.Text = Decimal.Round(answer, 2).ToString()
Catch ex As System.Security.SecurityException
    ' Display message box explaining access denial
    MessageBox.Show("You have been denied access: " + ex.Message)
    ' TODO: Log error
End Try
```

```csharp
// C#
// Concatenate the computer and username
string allowUser = System.Environment.MachineName + @"\cphilp";
try
{
    // Demand that user has the username "cphilp" on the local
    // computer. Because this method is called by a Windows event,
    // protect it with a imperative RBS demand
    PrincipalPermission p = new PrincipalPermission(allowUser, null);
    p.Demand();

    // Perform super-secret mathematical calculations
    Decimal answer = (Decimal.Parse(integer1.Text)
        / Decimal.Parse(integer2.Text));
    answerLabel.Text = Decimal.Round(answer, 2).ToString();
}
```

```
catch (System.Security.SecurityException ex)
{
    // Display message box explaining access denial
    MessageBox.Show("You have been denied access: " + ex.Message);
    // TODO: Log error
}
```

7. Address the fourth requirement, "You must hide buttons users do not have access to." You should do this in a method that will run when the form opens, such as the form constructor. The following code would work:

```
' VB
Public Sub New()
    MyBase.New()
    InitializeComponent()

    ' Create a WindowsIdentity object representing the current user
    Dim currentIdentity As WindowsIdentity = WindowsIdentity.GetCurrent()

    ' Create a WindowsPrincipal object representing the current user
    Dim currentPrincipal As WindowsPrincipal = _
        New WindowsPrincipal(currentIdentity)

    ' Set the security policy context to Windows security
    System.AppDomain.CurrentDomain.SetPrincipalPolicy( _
        PrincipalPolicy.WindowsPrincipal)

    ' Hide the subtract and multiply buttons if the user
    ' is not an Administrator
    If Not currentPrincipal.IsInRole(WindowsBuiltInRole.Administrator) Then
        subtractButton.Visible = False
        multiplyButton.Visible = False
    End If

    ' Hide the Add button if the user is not in the Users group
    If Not currentPrincipal.IsInRole(WindowsBuiltInRole.User) Then
        addButton.Visible = False
    End If

    ' Hide the Divide button if the user is not named CPhilp
    If Not (currentIdentity.Name.ToLower() = _
        System.Environment.MachineName.ToLower() + "\cphilp") Then
        divideButton.Visible = False
    End If
End Sub

// C#
public Form1()
{
    InitializeComponent();

    // Create a WindowsIdentity object representing the current user
    WindowsIdentity currentIdentity = WindowsIdentity.GetCurrent();
```

```
// Create a WindowsPrincipal object representing the current user
WindowsPrincipal currentPrincipal =
    new WindowsPrincipal(currentIdentity);

// Set the security policy context to Windows security
System.AppDomain.CurrentDomain.SetPrincipalPolicy(
    PrincipalPolicy.WindowsPrincipal);

// Hide the subtract and multiply buttons if the user
// is not an Administrator
if (!currentPrincipal.IsInRole(WindowsBuiltInRole.Administrator))
{
    subtractButton.Visible = false;
    multiplyButton.Visible = false;
}

// Hide the Add button if the user is not in the Users group
if (!currentPrincipal.IsInRole(WindowsBuiltInRole.User))
    addButton.Visible = false;

// Hide the Divide button if the user is not named CPhilp
if (!(currentIdentity.Name.ToLower() ==
    System.Environment.MachineName.ToLower() + @"\cphilp"))
    divideButton.Visible = false;
}
```

8. Build and run your project. Test it when running with different user accounts, including a user account named *Cphilp*, a user account that is a member of the Administrators group, and a user account that is only a member of the Users group.

Lesson Summary

- *Authentication,* such as checking your photo identification, verifies your identity by requiring you to provide unique credentials that are not easily impersonated. *Authorization,* such as checking your plane ticket, verifies that you have permission to perform the action you are attempting. Authentication, determining who you are, must happen before authorization, which determines whether you are allowed to access a resource.

- The *WindowsIdentity* class provides .NET Framework applications access to a Windows user's account properties. You can examine the current user's user name and authentication type by creating a new *WindowsIdentity* object by using the *WindowsIdentity.GetCurrent* method.

- The *WindowsPrincipal* class enables assemblies to query the Windows security database to determine whether a user is a member of a particular group. To examine the current user's group memberships, create a *WindowsPrincipal* object by using the current user's identity and then call the *WindowsPrincipal.IsInRole* method.

- You use the *PrincipalPermission* class to specify user name, role, and authentication requirements.

- Declarative RBS demands restrict access to an entire method by throwing an exception if the current principal does not meet the specified access requirements. Use declarative RBS demands by setting the principal policy, creating a *try/catch* block to handle users with insufficient privileges, and declaring a *PrincipalPermission* attribute to declare the method's access requirements.

- Use imperative RBS demands by setting the principal policy, creating a *try/catch* block to handle users with insufficient privileges, creating a *PrincipalPermission* object to declare the method's access requirements, and then calling the *PrincipalPermission.Demand* method. Use the *WindowsPrincipal.IsInRole* method to make decisions based on group memberships. Declarative RBS demands are perfect for situations in which your application calls a method directly, and access to the entire method must be restricted. Use imperative RBS demands when you need to protect only a portion of a method or when you are protecting a method that can be called by a Windows event.

- To create a custom identity and principal classes, extend the *IIdentity* and *IPrincipal* interfaces by overriding the existing properties and adding your custom methods and properties. To create simple custom user models, use the *GenericIdentity* and *GenericPrincipal* classes instead of the *IIdentity* and *IPrincipal* interfaces. To create declarative and imperative RBS demands with a custom identities and principals, set the *Thread.CurrentPrincipal* property to your custom principal.

- If you are establishing an *SslStream* connection, you should catch different types of exceptions. If you catch an *AuthenticationException*, you should prompt the user for different credentials. If you catch an *InvalidCredentialException*, some aspect of the stream is corrupted, and you cannot retry authentication.

Lesson Review

You can use the following questions to test your knowledge of the information in Lesson 1, Authenticating and Authorizing Users." The questions are also available on the companion CD if you prefer to review them in electronic form.

NOTE Answers

Answers to these questions and explanations of why each answer choice is right or wrong are located in the "Answers" section at the end of the book.

---

1. You must restrict access to a method based on a user's group memberships in the local user database. You want to use the most secure method possible. Which technique will you use?

   A. *WindowsPrincipal.IsInRole*

   B. *WindowsIdentity.IsInRole*

   C. Imperative RBS demands

   D. Declarative RBS demands

2. You must restrict access to a method that is called by a Windows event based on a user's group memberships in the local user database. If the user lacks sufficient access, you want to log an event and display a message to the user. You want to use the most secure method possible. Which technique will you use?

   A. *WindowsPrincipal.IsInRole*

   B. *WindowsIdentity.IsInRole*

   C. Imperative RBS demands

   D. Declarative RBS demands

3. You are writing a method for a console application that lists options available to a user based on his group memberships. Which technique should you use?

   A. *WindowsPrincipal.IsInRole*

   B. *WindowsIdentity.IsInRole*

   C. Imperative RBS demands

   D. Declarative RBS demands

4. You are creating a front-end interface to a back-end database that stores user names and groups within the database itself. The user database is very simple, storing only user names and group memberships. You want to be able to use imperative and declarative RBS demands within your application based on the custom user database. Which of the following classes meets your requirements and would be most efficient to implement? (Choose all that apply.)

   A. *GenericIdentity*

   B. *GenericPrincipal*

   C. *IIdentity*

   D. *IPrincipal*

Lesson 2: Using Access Control Lists

In Lesson 1, you learned how to use permission demands to restrict access to portions of your code to specific users. Operating systems use ACLs to provide similar functionality. ACLs are the most common technique for restricting access to files, folders, printers, services, registry values, and just about every other operating system resource. As a developer, you must understand ACLs for two important reasons:

- You can configure them to restrict access to sensitive files, folders, and other objects used by your application.

- You can configure them to allow users to access files and other objects that they are not typically allowed to access but that the application needs to access.

In this lesson you will learn the fundamentals of ACLs and how to analyze and configure them from within your application.

After this lesson, you will be able to:
- Explain the purpose of a discretionary ACL, and describe how Windows calculates effective permissions.
- Explain the purpose of a security ACL.
- View and configure ACLs using the *System.Security.AccessControl* namespace.

Estimated lesson time: 30 minutes

What Is a Discretionary Access Control List?

A *discretionary access control list (DACL)* is an authorization restriction mechanism that identifies the users and groups that are allowed or denied access to an object. Windows XP and Windows Server 2003, like all recent members of the Microsoft Windows family, keep track of the privileges users have for accessing resources by using a DACL. If a DACL does not explicitly identify a user or any groups that a user is a member of, the user is denied access to that object. By default, a DACL is controlled by the owner of an object or the person who created the object, and it contains access control entries (ACEs) that determine user access to the object. An ACE is an entry in an object's DACL that grants permissions to a user or group.

Explicit and Inherited Permissions

When you assign a DACL directly to an object, you create an explicit permission. Assigning explicit permissions to every individual folder, file, registry value, and

Active Directory object would be a ponderous task. In fact, managing the massive number of ACLs that would be required would have a significant negative impact on the performance of Windows.

To make managing permissions more efficient, Windows includes the concept of inheritance. When Windows is initially installed, most objects have only inherited permissions. *Inherited permissions* propagate to an object from its parent object. For example, the file system uses inherited permissions. Therefore, each new folder you create in the root C:\ folder inherits the exact permissions assigned to the C:\ folder. Similarly, each subkey you create in the HKEY_LOCAL_MACHINE\Software\ key inherits the exact permissions assigned to the parent key.

Because of inheritance, you typically do not need to explicitly specify permissions when creating a file, folder, registry key, or other object. The new object will inherit its parent's permissions. Systems administrators often put a great deal of time and energy into choosing permissions and configuring inheritance, and in most circumstances, you should trust the system administrator's judgment. However, it is important to use care to create objects in the proper place. For example, you should create temporary files in the temporary folder and save user files in user directories.

How Windows Calculates Effective Permissions

Calculating a user's effective permissions requires Windows to do more than simply look up that user's name in the ACL. ACEs can assign rights directly to the user, or they can assign rights to a group. Additionally, users can be members of multiple groups, and groups can be nested within each other. Therefore, a single user can have several different ACEs in a single ACL. To understand what a user's effective permissions will be, you must understand how permissions are calculated when multiple ACEs apply to the user.

Permissions that are granted to a user or the groups to which the user belongs are cumulative. If Mary is a member of both the Accounting group and the Managers group, and the ACL for a file grants Mary's user account Read privileges, the Accounting group Modify privileges, and the Managers group Full Control privileges, Mary will have Full Control privileges. There's a catch, though. ACEs that deny access always override ACEs that grant access. Therefore, if the Accounting group is explicitly denied access to the file, Mary cannot open the file. Even though Mary is a member of the Managers group, and the Managers group has Full Control privileges, the Deny ACE means that all members of the Managers group are denied access to the file.

If no ACEs in an ACL apply to a user, that user is denied access to the object. In other words, not explicitly having privileges to an object is exactly the same as being explicitly denied access.

ACEs in the .NET Framework

Different resources have unique permissions that are used to define an ACE. Although both files and the registry have Full Control and Delete permissions, the Read & Execute permission is unique to files and folders, and the Query Values permission is unique to the registry. Therefore, each resource has its own set of classes in the .NET Framework. Fortunately, permissions for different resources function similarly, and all classes inherit from common base classes.

In the .NET Framework, you use the *FileSystemRights* enumeration to specify file and folder permissions. This enumeration has 24 members that correspond to the standard and special permissions you can view and edit using the Windows Explorer tool. Table 12-1 lists the members that correspond to the standard file and folder permissions.

Table 12-1   Standard File and Folder Permissions

FileSystemRights Member	Standard Permission	Description
FullControl	Full Control	Users can perform any action on the file or folder, including creating and deleting it, and modifying its permissions.
Modify	Modify	Users can read, edit, and delete files and folders.
ReadAndExecute	Read & Execute	Users can view files and run applications.
ListDirectory	List Folder Contents	Users can browse a folder.
Read	Read	Users can view a file or the contents of a folder. If an executable file has Read permission but not Read & Execute permission, the user cannot start the executable.

Table 12-1 Standard File and Folder Permissions

FileSystemRights Member	Standard Permission	Description
Write	Write	Users can create files in a directory, but they cannot necessarily read them. This permission is useful for creating a folder in which multiple users can copy files but not access each other's files or even see what other files exist.
Other members	Special Permissions	Special permissions are more granular permissions that make up the standard permissions you will work with most often.

What Is a Security Access Control List?

A *security access control list* (SACL) is a usage event logging mechanism that determines how file or folder access is audited. Unlike a DACL, an SACL cannot restrict access to a file or folder. However, an SACL can cause an event to be recorded in the security event log when a user accesses a file or folder. This auditing can be used to troubleshoot access problems or identify intrusions.

To a security professional, an SACL is a critical tool for intrusion detection. A systems administrator is more likely to use SACLs to identify permissions that need to be granted to a user to allow an application to run correctly. A developer uses SACLs to track resources that her application is denied access to so that she can customize the application to allow it to run without problems under a less privileged account.

NOTE The difference between SACLs and DACLs

It's important to understand the difference between SACLs and DACLs for the exam. The difference between the two is also a common question in technical interviews. Fortunately, it's simple: DACLs restrict access, whereas SACLs audit access. Realistically, though, you're not going to spend much time thinking about SACLs when you write an application. You might, however, dedicate many hours to troubleshooting problems relating to DACLs. For that reason, this book uses the term ACL to refer to DACLs.

By default, Windows does not log auditing events, even if you add an SACL. First, you must enable the Audit Object Access security policy on a computer by following these steps:

1. Open the Local Security Policy console from within Administrative Tools.

2. Expand Local Policies and click Audit Policy.

3. In the right pane, double-click Audit Object Access. Select Failure to enable failure auditing, and select Success to enable success auditing.

In an Active Directory domain, domain administrators can enable object auditing for all member computers using Group Policy settings.

How to View and Configure ACLs from Within an Assembly

The *System.Security.AccessControl* namespace contains a variety of classes for viewing and configuring ACLs for different types of objects. The sections that follow give an overview of this namespace and describe how to analyze and change ACLs.

Overview of the *System.Security.AccessControl* Namespace

You can use the classes in the *System.Security.AccessControl* namespace to programmatically access DACLs, SACLs, and ACEs for files, folders, registry keys, cryptographic keys, Event Wait handles, mutexes, and semaphores.

NOTE   .NET 2.0

The entire *System.Security.AccessControl* namespace is new in .NET 2.0. Previously, developers were forced to make calls to unmanaged code to analyze or modify ACLs.

For each resource type, the *System.Security.AccessControl* namespace provides three ACL classes:

- *<Type>Security*   The most commonly used class, these classes provide methods for retrieving a collection of DACLs (*GetAccessRules*) or SACLs (*GetAuditRules*) and adding and removing ACLs (*AddAccessRule*, *RemoveAccessRule*, *AddAuditRule*, and *RemoveAuditRule*). These classes all inherit from *NativeObjectSecurity*.

- *<Type>AccessRule*   Represents a set of access rights allowed or denied for a user or group. These classes all inherit from *AccessRule*, which in turn inherits from *AuthorizationRule*.

- **<Type>AuditRule**   Represents a set of access rights to be audited for a user or group. These classes all inherit from *AuditRule*, which in turn inherits from *AuthorizationRule*.

Additionally, you can retrieve an instance of the *AuthorizationRuleCollection* class by calling *<Type>Security.GetAccessRules*. This class contains a collection of *<Type>AccessRule* or *<Type>AuditRule* instances that you can iterate through to analyze an object's ACLs.

How to Analyze ACLs

To analyze ACLs, follow these steps:

1. Create an instance of a class that inherits from *NativeObjectSecurity*, such as *DirectorySecurity*, *FileSecurity*, *RegistrySecurity*, or *MutexSecurity*. Several classes in the *Microsoft.Win32* namespace include a *GetAccessControl* method for creating these objects.

2. Call the *GetAccessRules* method to retrieve an instance of *AuthorizationRuleCollection*.

3. Iterate through items in the *AuthorizationRuleCollection* instance to retrieve and analyze individual ACLs.

The following code sample (which requires both the *System.Security.AccessControl* and *System.Security.Principal* namespaces) demonstrates how to display access rules (DACLs) for a folder; however, the same technique could be used to analyze a file, registry value, or other object:

```vb
' VB
' You could also call Directory.GetAccessControl for the following line
Dim ds As DirectorySecurity = New DirectorySecurity("C:\Program Files", _
    AccessControlSections.Access)
Dim arc As AuthorizationRuleCollection = ds.GetAccessRules(True, _
    True, GetType(NTAccount))
For Each ar As FileSystemAccessRule In arc
    Console.WriteLine(ar.IdentityReference.ToString + ": " + _
        ar.AccessControlType.ToString + " " + ar.FileSystemRights.ToString)
Next
```

```csharp
// C#
// You could also call Directory.GetAccessControl for the following line
DirectorySecurity ds = new DirectorySecurity(@"C:\Program Files",
    AccessControlSections.Access);
AuthorizationRuleCollection arc = ds.GetAccessRules(true, true,
    typeof(NTAccount));
foreach (FileSystemAccessRule ar in arc)
    Console.WriteLine(ar.IdentityReference + ": " + ar.AccessControlType +
        " " + ar.FileSystemRights);
```

You can follow the same general procedure for other object types, though the specific classes you use to retrieve the object vary. For example, the following code sample (which requires the *System.Security.AccessControl*, *System.Security.Principal*, and *Microsoft.Win32* namespaces) displays access rules for the HKEY_LOCAL_MACHINE registry key:

```
' VB
Dim rs As RegistrySecurity = Registry.LocalMachine.GetAccessControl
Dim arc As AuthorizationRuleCollection = rs.GetAccessRules(True, _
    True, GetType(NTAccount))
For Each ar As RegistryAccessRule In arc
    Console.WriteLine(ar.IdentityReference.ToString + ": " _
        + ar.AccessControlType.ToString + " " + ar.RegistryRights.ToString)
Next
```

```
// C#
RegistrySecurity rs = Registry.LocalMachine.GetAccessControl();
AuthorizationRuleCollection arc = rs.GetAccessRules(true,
    true, typeof(NTAccount));
foreach (RegistryAccessRule ar in arc)
    Console.WriteLine(ar.IdentityReference + ": "
        + ar.AccessControlType + " " + ar.RegistryRights);
```

To analyze SACLs, follow the same steps, but call *GetAuditRules* instead of *GetAccessRules*, and substitute audit classes where necessary.

How to Configure ACLs

To configure ACLs, follow these steps:

1. Call the *GetAccessControl* method to get an instance of a class that inherits from *NativeObjectSecurity*, such as *DirectorySecurity*, *FileSecurity*, *RegistrySecurity*, or *MutexSecurity*.

2. Add or remove ACL entries from the object. Typically, you will provide a user or group name, an enumeration describing the rights (such as *FileSystemRights* or *RegistryRights*), and an *AccessControlType* enumeration specifying whether to allow or deny the rights.

3. Call the *SetAccessControl* method to apply the changes.

The following code sample (which requires both the *System.Security.AccessControl* and *System.IO* namespaces) demonstrates how to add an access rule to a folder by granting the Guest user Read access to the "C:\test" folder. The same general technique could be used to add an ACL to a file, registry value, or other object:

```
' VB
Dim dir As String = "C:\test"
```

```
Dim ds As DirectorySecurity = Directory.GetAccessControl(dir)
ds.AddAccessRule(New FileSystemAccessRule("Guest", _
    FileSystemRights.Read, AccessControlType.Allow))
Directory.SetAccessControl(dir, ds)

// C#
string dir = @"C:\test";
DirectorySecurity ds = Directory.GetAccessControl(dir);
ds.AddAccessRule(new FileSystemAccessRule("Guest",
    FileSystemRights.Read, AccessControlType.Allow));
Directory.SetAccessControl(dir, ds);
```

To remove an access rule, simply replace *AddAccessRule* with *RemoveAccessRule*.

Lab: Working with DACLs and Inheritance

In this lab, you will work with file and folder DACLs, and you will learn how to rescue folders created with permissions that make them inaccessible. If you encounter a problem completing an exercise, the completed projects are available on the companion CD in the Code folder.

▶ **Exercise: Create a Folder with Explicit Permissions**

In this exercise, you will write an application that creates a folder named C:\Guest and grants the Guest user Read access to the folder. Then you will create a file within that folder and display the permissions assigned to both the folder and the file to verify that your application functioned correctly.

1. Create a new console application in either Visual Basic or C#.

2. Add the *System.Security.AccessControl*, *System.Security.Policy*, *System.Security.Principal*, and *System.IO* namespaces to your project.

3. In the *Main* method, write code to create a *DirectorySecurity* object that grants the Guest user Read access to the folder. Create the folder by specifying the *DirectorySecurity* object. Do not create the folder before creating the *DirectorySecurity* object. For example, the following code would work:

```
' VB
Dim ds As DirectorySecurity = New DirectorySecurity
ds.AddAccessRule(New FileSystemAccessRule("Guest", _
    FileSystemRights.Read, AccessControlType.Allow))
Directory.CreateDirectory("C:\Guest", ds)

// C#
DirectorySecurity ds = new DirectorySecurity();
ds.AddAccessRule(new FileSystemAccessRule("Guest",
    FileSystemRights.Read, AccessControlType.Allow));
Directory.CreateDirectory(@"C:\Guest", ds);
```

4. Now, create a file within the folder named "Data.dat", as the following code demonstrates:

```
' VB
File.Create("C:\Guest\Data.Dat")
```

```
// C#
File.Create(@"C:\Guest\Data.Dat");
```

5. Build and run your application. The runtime should throw an exception when you attempt to create the file because you did not grant yourself permissions to modify the folder. The folder did not inherit the parent's permissions because you explicitly provided access controls when creating the folder. If you had first created the folder without specifying access permissions and then modified the permissions, the parent's permissions would have been inherited.

6. Use Windows Explorer to view the permissions assigned to the C:\Guest folder. If your application worked properly, the Guest account should have Read permissions, and no other account should have access.

MORE INFO   File Permissions in Windows XP

For detailed instructions on how to view and edit file permissions in Windows XP, read Microsoft Knowledge Base article #308418 at *http://support.microsoft.com/kb/308418*.

---

7. Before you can delete the C:\Guest folder, you must take ownership of it. While logged on as a member of the Administrators group, open the C:\Guest properties dialog box. On the Security tab of the Guest Properties dialog box, click the Advanced button. Then click the Owner tab, select the Replace Owner On Subcontainers And Objects check box, and click OK. Click Yes, and then click OK again.

8. Now, use Windows Explorer to delete the C:\Guest folder.

Lesson Summary

- DACLs are used to restrict access to files, folders, and other operating system objects. By default, child objects (such as a subfolder) inherit ACLs from their parent object (such as a root folder).

- SACLs determine the conditions under which object access is audited.

- You can use the members of the *System.Security.AccessControl* namespace to view and configure ACLs for a variety of objects, including files, folders, registry keys, cryptographic keys, Event Wait handles, semaphores, and mutexes. Each object type has three classes: an object derived from *NativeObjectSecurity*, an object derived from *AccessRule*, and an object derived from *AuditRule*.

Lesson Review

You can use the following questions to test your knowledge of the information in Lesson 2, "Using Access Control Lists." The questions are also available on the companion CD if you prefer to review them in electronic form.

NOTE Answers

Answers to these questions and explanations of why each answer choice is right or wrong are located in the "Answers" section at the end of the book.

---

1. Which of the following resources can you control access to using the .NET Framework? (Choose all that apply.)

   A. Files

   B. Registry keys

   C. Printers

   D. Network shares

2. Given the following code sample, which line correctly finalizes the ACL changes?

```vb
' VB
Dim dir As String = "C:\MyApp"
Dim ds As DirectorySecurity = Directory.GetAccessControl(dir)
ds.AddAccessRule(New FileSystemAccessRule("Administrator", _
    FileSystemRights.FullControl, AccessControlType.Allow))
Directory.SetAccessControl(dir, ds)
```

```csharp
// C#
string dir = @"C:\myApp";
DirectorySecurity ds = Directory.GetAccessControl(dir);
ds.AddAccessRule(new FileSystemAccessRule("Guest",
    FileSystemRights.FullControl, AccessControlType.Allow));
Directory.SetAccessControl(dir, ds);
```

   A.

```vb
' VB
Directory.SetAccessControl(dir, ds)
```

```csharp
// C#
Directory.SetAccessControl(dir, ds);
```

B.

```
' VB
Directory.CreateDirectory(dir, ds)

// C#
Directory.CreateDirectory(dir, ds);
```

C.

```
' VB
Directory.SetAccessControl(ds)

// C#
Directory.SetAccessControl(ds);
```

D.

```
' VB
Directory.CreateDirectory(ds)

// C#
Directory.CreateDirectory(ds);
```

3. Which of the following classes describes an SACL for a registry key?

   A. *RegistryAccessRule*

   B. *RegistryAuditRule*

   C. *AccessRule*

   D. *AuditRule*

4. Which of the following is returned by the *DirectorySecurity.GetAccessRules* method?

   A. A generic *Collection* object containing *AccessRule* objects

   B. A generic *Collection* object containing *FileSystemAccessRule* objects

   C. An instance of *AuthorizationRuleCollection* containing *FileSystemAccessRule* objects

   D. An instance of *AuthorizationRuleCollection* containing *AuthorizationRule* objects

Lesson 3: Encrypting and Decrypting Data

Data is most vulnerable when it is stored persistently or transferred across a network. Although you can use permission demands to control access to your application and ACLs to protect data, an attacker with access to the hard disk or network infrastructure can bypass software security and either extract private information from the data or modify the data. However, you are not defenseless. You can use cryptography to protect the privacy and integrity of the data that your application stores or transfers. The .NET Framework provides classes for several different types of cryptography, including symmetric and asymmetric encryption, hashing, and digital signatures. In this lesson you will learn when and how to use each type of cryptography.

After this lesson, you will be able to:

- Encrypt and decrypt data using secret-key encryption (also known as symmetric encryption).
- Encrypt and decrypt data using public-key encryption (also known as asymmetric encryption).
- Use hashing to validate the integrity of data
- Sign files with digital signatures to verify that the file is authentic and has not been modified.

Estimated lesson time: 90 minutes

Encrypting and Decrypting Data with Symmetric Keys

Many people are introduced to encryption at an early age. Children protect even the most mundane communications from imaginary spies with a secret decoder ring—a toy with two rings that translates encrypted characters to unencrypted characters. The rings on a decoder ring rotate, and a message can be decrypted only when the two rings are lined up correctly. To exchange an encrypted message, the children must first agree on how the rings will line up. After they have exchanged this secret piece of information, they can freely pass encrypted messages without worrying that someone will be able to decrypt them. Even if an imaginary spy had a decoder ring, the spy would need to know how to position the rings to decrypt the message.

Because both the sender and the recipient of the message must know the same secret to encrypt and decrypt a message, secret decoder rings are an example of symmetric key encryption. Symmetric key encryption is a game for children, but it is also the foundation for most encrypted communications today. As children know, encryption is a fun topic. You should enjoy building it into your application, and you'll greatly reduce the chance of private data being compromised.

What Is Symmetric Key Encryption?

Symmetric key encryption, also known as secret-key encryption, is a cryptography technique that uses a single secret key to both encrypt and decrypt data. *Symmetric encryption* algorithms (also called ciphers) process plain text with the secret *encryption key* to create encrypted data called *cipher text*. The cipher text cannot easily be decrypted into the plain text without possession of the secret key. Figure 12-2 shows symmetric key encryption and decryption.

Encryption

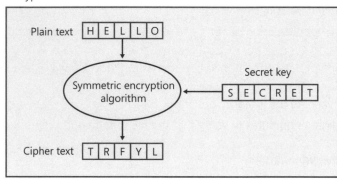

Decryption

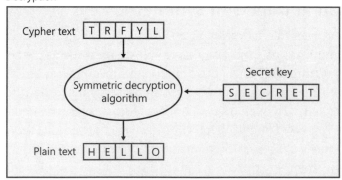

Figure 12-2 Symmetric encryption uses the same key for encryption and decryption

Symmetric algorithms are extremely fast and are well suited for encrypting large quantities of data. Even though symmetric encryption is very secure, an attacker can identify the plain text, given the cipher text and enough time. To identify the plain text, the attacker needs to use only a brute force attack to sequentially generate symmetric keys until the attacker has tried every single possibility. Typically, the time required to try all keys is hundreds of years, if not longer, because the attacker would need to try at least 2^{56} key possibilities. More secure symmetric algorithms use longer keys that would take exponentially longer to crack.

The disadvantage of secret-key encryption is that it presumes that two parties have already agreed on a key. Agreeing on a symmetric key is a challenge because the key itself cannot be encrypted. If you've decided to use encryption, it must be because you don't trust your system to prevent an attacker from gaining access to your data. Therefore, users must find a secure way to exchange secret keys. After the secret keys are exchanged, encrypted data can be freely exchanged between the parties. However, keys should be changed on a regular basis for the same reasons that passwords should be changed regularly. Each time the key must be changed, users must resort to the secure communication mechanism.

Figure 12-3 shows how users must transfer both the encrypted message and the key using different communication mechanisms to enable the recipient to decrypt the message, while preventing an attacker who can capture your communications across only a single network from decrypting the message. Keys are often transferred by voice across the phone network, sent physically through the mail system, or carried to the recipient. After the *shared secret* has been established, the two peers can use it to encrypt and decrypt any number of messages.

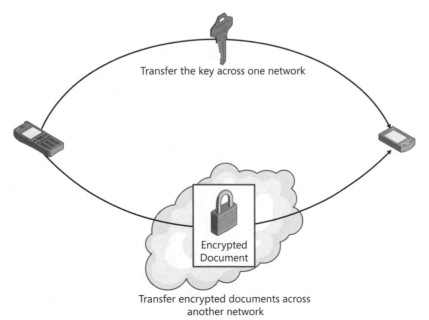

Figure 12-3   Symmetric key encryption requires separately exchanging both the key and the encrypted document

The need to establish a shared secret key rules out relying solely on symmetric encryption for encrypting spontaneous network communications. For example, symmetric key encryption is not initially used between a Web client and Web server because users on the Internet aren't typically willing to wait several days while the Web site physically mails them a secret key. Instead, Web sessions are initially established by using asymmetric keys.

Symmetric Algorithm Classes in the .NET Framework

Most of the .NET Framework's cryptography functionality is built into the *System.Security.Cryptography* namespace, including the four implementations of symmetric encryption algorithms. Table 12-2 shows symmetric encryption algorithm classes.

Table 12-2   Symmetric Cryptography Classes

Class	Key Length	Description
RijndaelManaged	128 through 256 bits, in 32-bit increments	The .NET Framework implementation of the Rijndael symmetric encryption algorithm. As a government encryption standard, this algorithm is also known as *Advanced Encryption Standard*, or *AES*. *RijndaelManaged* is the only .NET Framework symmetric encryption class that is fully managed. All other encryption classes call unmanaged code. Because of this, *RijndaelManaged* is the preferred choice when your application will be running in a partially trusted environment.
RC2	Variable	An encryption standard designed to replace *DES* that uses variable key sizes.
DES	56 bits	The *Data Encryption Standard (DES)* is a symmetric encryption algorithm that uses relatively short key lengths that are vulnerable to cracking attacks. As a result, it should be avoided. However, it remains commonly used because it is compatible with a wide range of legacy platforms.

Table 12-2   Symmetric Cryptography Classes

Class	Key Length	Description
TripleDES	156 bits, of which only 112 bits are effectively used for encryption	The .NET Framework implementation of the *Triple DES (3DES)* symmetric encryption algorithm, it essentially applies the DES algorithm three times.

All symmetric algorithm classes are derived from the *System.Security.Cryptography.SymmetricAlgorithm* base class and share the following properties:

- **BlockSize** Gets or sets the block size of the cryptographic operation in bits. The block size is the number of bits that the algorithm processes at a single time and can usually be ignored when creating applications that use encryption.

- **FeedbackSize** Gets or sets the feedback size of the cryptographic operation in bits. The feedback size determines one aspect of the algorithm's encryption technique; however, as a developer, you can safely ignore this property.

- **IV** Gets or sets the initialization vector for the symmetric algorithm. Like the *Key* property, both the encryptor and decryptor must specify the same value. To avoid the overhead of transferring the IV securely between the encryptor and decryptor, you might choose to statically define the IV in your application, or to derive this from the *Key* property.

NOTE   Understanding initialization vectors (IVs)

An *initialization vector (IV)* is data that symmetric encryption algorithms use to further obscure the first block of data being encrypted, which makes unauthorized decrypting more difficult. You don't need to understand what IVs do to use encryption, as long as you know that you must synchronize the IV values for both the encryptor and decryptor.

- **Key** Gets or sets the secret key for the symmetric algorithm. Keys are automatically generated if you have not specifically defined them. After encryption, you must store this value and transfer it to the decryptor. During decryption, you must specify the same key used during encryption.

- **KeySize** Gets or sets the size of the secret key used by the symmetric algorithm in bits. When you create a symmetric algorithm object, the runtime will choose the largest key size supported by the platform. As a result, you can usually ignore this property. However, if the message's recipient does not support the same key sizes as the sender, you must set this property to the highest value supported by both the encryptor and the decryptor.

- **LegalBlockSizes** A *KeySizes* array that gets the block sizes that are supported by the symmetric algorithm. Each array member contains *MinSize* and *MaxSize* properties, which define the valid key ranges in bits; and a *SkipSize* property that specifies in bits the interval between valid key sizes.

- **LegalKeySizes** A *KeySizes* array that gets the key sizes that are supported by the symmetric algorithm. Each array member contains *MinSize* and *MaxSize* properties that define the valid key ranges in bits, and a *SkipSize* property that specifies the interval between valid key sizes in bits.

- **Mode** A property set to one of the *CipherMode* enumeration values that determines one aspect of the encryption algorithm's behavior. This property is usually set to Cipher Block Chaining (CBC), the default. You should usually leave this set to CBC. If you do change this value, you must change it at both the encryptor and decryptor.

- **Padding** A *PaddingMode* enumeration value, this property determines how the encryption algorithm fills out any difference between the algorithm's block size and the length of the plain text. You should generally not change this property.

Additionally, the symmetric algorithm classes each share the following methods (standard object methods have been omitted):

- **CreateDecryptor** To decrypt messages, you must create a symmetric algorithm object and call this method to create an *ICryptoTransform* object that a *Crypto-Stream* object can use to decrypt the stream.

- **CreateEncryptor** Creates a symmetric encryptor object used by *CryptoStream* objects to encrypt a stream.

- **GenerateIV** Generates a random IV to be used for the algorithm. Generally, there is no need to call this method because IVs are automatically randomly generated unless you specifically define them. You will call this method only if you have defined IV and later need to use a different random IV.

- **GenerateKey** Generates a random key to be used for the algorithm. Like *GenerateIV*, you need to call this method only if you have already defined the *Key* property and later need to use a random key.

- **ValidKeySize** Determines whether the specified key size is valid for the current algorithm and returns a Boolean value. Use this method when you are working with an unknown symmetric algorithm class to verify that your key is valid for the given algorithm.

BEST PRACTICES Choosing a symmetric key algorithm

Use the Rijndael algorithm whenever both the encryptor and decryptor are running on Windows XP or later operating systems; otherwise, use Triple DES. Out of all symmetric-key algorithms supported by the .NET Framework, the U.S. government–approved Rijndael algorithm is considered the most secure. This algorithm supports 128-, 192-, and 256-bit keys. Another reason to choose Rijndael is that it is the only implementation that is natively supported by the .NET Framework. The other algorithms must make calls to unmanaged code.

How to Establish a Symmetric Key

Before you can encrypt and decrypt messages by using symmetric encryption, both the encryptor and decryptor must have the same key. You can't use just any piece of data as a key, however. Symmetric encryption algorithms must use keys of a specific length, so you cannot simply set the *Key* property to a user-provided password. To generate a random key, simply create and use a symmetric algorithm object. If you specify a value for the *Key* property and later want to use a random key, call the *GenerateKey* method.

You can also generate a valid key based on a user-provided password if you can rely on users to transfer the password between the encryptor and decryptor. You cannot directly use passwords as encryption keys, but you can use the *System.Security .Cryptography.Rfc2898DeriveBytes* class to turn a password into a key. This is particularly useful when a shared secret has already been established between an encryptor and a decryptor. For example, if you create a custom authentication mechanism and your application is privy to the user's user name and password, you could concatenate the user's own user name and password to derive the same key at both the encryptor and decryptor.

NOTE .NET 2.0

Rfc2898DeriveBytes is new to the .NET Framework. It functions almost exactly like *PasswordDeriveBytes*, but is preferred because it is standards-based. *PasswordDeriveBytes* also gives you the ability to specify the hashing algorithm, should you need that level of control.

Rfc2898DeriveBytes requires three values in addition to the user's password: a salt value, an IV, and the number of iterations used to generate the key. Ideally, all these values are randomly generated. Changing any of these values produces a different key, requiring you to use the same values at both the encryptor and decryptor. Therefore, when random values are used, the values must be exchanged in the same way the password is exchanged. For this reason, it is usually not possible to securely exchange these values in addition to the password. Instead, you can specify static values that both the encryptor and decryptor applications have stored within their source code, but it is more secure to generate the values based on other shared secret information, such as the password.

Creating symmetric keys based on a password requires several different values to be synchronized between the encryptor and decryptor:

- The password
- The salt value
- The number of iterations used to generate the key (or you can accept the default)

The simplest way to specify these values is to pass them to the *Rfc2898DeriveBytes* constructor. After initialization, you can retrieve a key by calling the *Rfc2898DeriveBytes .GetBytes* method. *GetBytes* accepts the number of bytes to return as an integer. When deriving a key, determine the length based on the number of bits required by the algorithm object's *KeySize* and *BlockSize* properties. Note that both *KeySize* and *BlockSize* are defined as a number of bits, whereas the *Rfc2898DeriveBytes.GetBytes* method requires a number of bytes. You must divide the number of bits required for the key by 8 to determine the number of bytes required.

Besides the key, the encryption algorithm must also have the same IV specified at both the encryptor and decryptor. For optimal security, when only a password is shared between the encryptor and decryptor, you should also generate the IV based on the password. Whereas the length of the key being generated must be based on the *KeySize* property, the length of the IV must be based on the encryption algorithm's *BlockSize* property.

The following sample code generates a key and IV for the *myAlg SymmetricAlgorithm* object using a static password, which should be provided by the user in practice:

```
' VB
' In practice, the user would provide the password
Dim password As String = "P@S5w0r]>"

' Create an algorithm object
Dim myAlg As RijndaelManaged = New RijndaelManaged()

' Derive the key and use it to define the algorithm
Dim salt As Byte() = System.Text.Encoding.ASCII.GetBytes("This is my salt")
Dim key As Rfc2898DeriveBytes = New Rfc2898DeriveBytes(password, salt)
myAlg.Key = key.GetBytes(myAlg.KeySize / 8)
myAlg.IV = key.GetBytes(myAlg.BlockSize / 8)
```

```csharp
// C#
// In practice, the user would provide the password
string password = "P@S5wOr]>";

// Create an algorithm object
RijndaelManaged myAlg = new RijndaelManaged();

// Derive the key and use it to define the algorithm
byte[] salt = Encoding.ASCII.GetBytes("This is my salt");
Rfc2898DeriveBytes key = new Rfc2898DeriveBytes(password, salt);
myAlg.Key = key.GetBytes(myAlg.KeySize / 8);
myAlg.IV = key.GetBytes(myAlg.BlockSize / 8);
```

How to Encrypt and Decrypt Messages Using Symmetric Keys

After both the encryptor and decryptor have the same key, they can begin exchanging encrypted messages. The .NET Framework makes this process easy. In fact, using encryption is similar to reading and writing to standard files and streams, and it requires only a few additional lines of code. To encrypt or decrypt messages in your application, perform the following tasks:

1. Create a *Stream* object to interface with the memory or file that you will be reading from or writing to.

2. Create a *SymmetricAlgorithm* object.

3. Specify the algorithm's key, the IV, or both.

4. Call *SymmetricAlgorithm.CreateEncryptor()* or *SymmetricAlgorithm.CreateDecryptor()* to create a *ICryptoTransform* object.

5. Create a *CryptoStream* object using the *Stream* object and the *ICryptoTransform* object.

6. Read from or write to the *CryptoStream* object just like any other *Stream* object.

The following console application demonstrates these steps by reading an unencrypted file (the C:\Boot.ini file), encrypting it with the Rijndael algorithm, and saving the encrypted results as a new file. The application requires the *System.IO* and *System.Security.Cryptography* namespaces.

```vb
' VB
Dim inFileName As String = "C:\Boot.ini"
Dim outFileName As String = "C:\Boot.ini.enc"

' Step 1: Create the Stream objects
Dim inFile As FileStream = New FileStream(inFileName, FileMode.Open, FileAccess.Read)
Dim outFile As FileStream = New FileStream(outFileName, FileMode.OpenOrCreate, FileAccess.Write)
```

```vbnet
' Step 2: Create the SymmetricAlgorithm object
Dim myAlg As SymmetricAlgorithm = New RijndaelManaged

' Step 3: Specify a key (optional)
myAlg.GenerateKey()

' Read the unencrypted file into fileData
Dim fileData(inFile.Length - 1) As Byte
inFile.Read(fileData, 0, CType(inFile.Length, Integer))

' Step 4: Create the ICryptoTransform object
Dim encryptor As ICryptoTransform = myAlg.CreateEncryptor

' Step 5: Create the CryptoStream object
Dim encryptStream As CryptoStream = New CryptoStream(outFile, encryptor, _
CryptoStreamMode.Write)

' Step 6: Write the contents to the CryptoStream
encryptStream.Write(fileData, 0, fileData.Length)

' Close the file handles
encryptStream.Close()
inFile.Close()
outFile.Close()

// C#
string inFileName = @"C:\Boot.ini";
string outFileName = @"C:\Boot.ini.enc";

// Step 1: Create the Stream objects
FileStream inFile = new FileStream(inFileName, FileMode.Open, FileAccess.Read);
FileStream outFile = new FileStream(outFileName, FileMode.OpenOrCreate, FileAccess.Write);

// Step 2: Create the SymmetricAlgorithm object
SymmetricAlgorithm myAlg = new RijndaelManaged();

// Step 3: Specify a key (optional)
myAlg.GenerateKey();

// Read the unencrypted file into fileData
byte[] fileData = new byte[inFile.Length];
inFile.Read(fileData, 0, (int)inFile.Length);

// Step 4: Create the ICryptoTransform object
ICryptoTransform encryptor = myAlg.CreateEncryptor();

// Step 5: Create the CryptoStream object
CryptoStream encryptStream = new CryptoStream(outFile, encryptor, CryptoStreamMode.Write);

// Step 6: Write the contents to the CryptoStream
encryptStream.Write(fileData, 0, fileData.Length);
```

```
// Close the file handles
encryptStream.Close();
inFile.Close();
outFile.Close();
```

Because the key is randomly generated, running the application repeatedly generates different results each time. Because the key is not stored, the file can never be decrypted. The key is simply an array of bytes and can be stored by using the *BinaryWriter* object or by transferring the key across a network.

The code for decrypting a file is almost identical to the code for encrypting a file, except that it must read the encryption key that was used to encrypt the data rather than randomly generate it, and it must call decryption methods instead of encryption methods. To reverse the process to decrypt a file, simply make the following changes to an application:

- Change the code for step 3 to read the key and IV that was used to encrypt the data.

- Change the code for step 4 to use the *CreateDecryptor* method instead of *Create-Encryptor*.

- Change the code for step 5 to use the *CryptoStreamMode.Read* enumeration instead of *CryptoStreamMode.Write*.

- Change the code for step 6 to read from the *CryptoStream* object.

Encrypting and Decrypting Data with Asymmetric Keys

Asymmetric encryption, also known as public-key encryption, overcomes symmetric encryption's most significant disability: requiring both the encryptor and decryptor to know a shared secret. Asymmetric encryption relies on key pairs. In a key pair, there is one public key and one private key. The public key can be freely shared because it cannot be easily abused, even by an attacker. Messages encrypted with the public key can be decrypted only with the private key, allowing anyone to send encrypted messages that can be decrypted only by a single individual.

The asymmetric encryption process begins with a public key being exchanged. Generally, both the client and server exchange public keys. However, if only one side of the communication needs to be encrypted, only the peer receiving encrypted communications must provide a public key. After the public keys are exchanged, communications are encrypted using the recipient's public key. Such communications can be decrypted only by the recipient because only the recipient holds the private key that matches the public key. Figure 12-1 shows a simple asymmetric encryption arrangement in which only one side of the communications provides a public key.

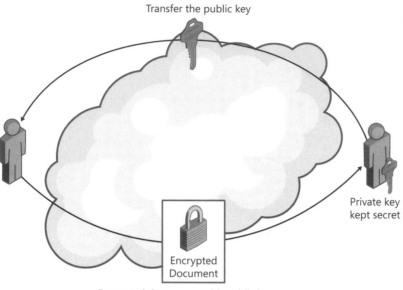

Figure 12-4   Asymmetric cryptography uses separate keys for encryption and decryption

Asymmetric algorithms are not as fast as symmetric algorithms, but are much more difficult to break. Asymmetric algorithms are not well suited to encrypting large amounts of data because of the performance overhead. One common use of asymmetric algorithms is to encrypt and transfer a symmetric key and IV. The symmetric encryption algorithm is then used for all messages being sent back and forth. This is the technique used by HTTPS and Secure Sockets Layer (SSL) to encrypt Web communications—asymmetric encryption is used only during session establishment. This common combination of asymmetric and symmetric encryption is shown in Figure 12-5.

The other significant challenge of asymmetric encryption is key management. To manage keys, organizations typically implement a public key infrastructure (PKI), such as Certificate Services included with Windows Server 2003. A PKI is an infrastructure for distributing, managing, and revoking certificates in an organization. As a developer, you will generally not be responsible for configuring a PKI.

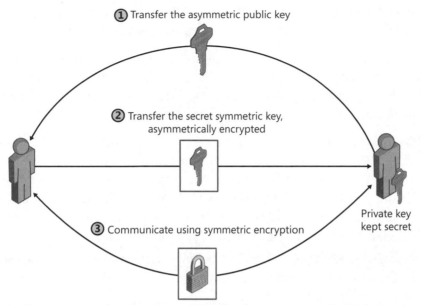

Figure 12-5 Combine asymmetric and symmetric algorithms to optimize security and performance

Asymmetric Algorithm Classes in the .NET Framework

The .NET Framework provides two classes for working with asymmetric encryption, and they are both based on the *System.Security.Cryptography.AsymmetricAlgorithm* class. This base class has the following properties, several of which are identical to the *SymmetricAlgorithm* counterparts:

- **KeyExchangeAlgorithm** Gets the name of the key exchange algorithm. Generally, you do not need to directly access this property.

- **KeySize** Gets or sets the size of the secret key used by the symmetric algorithm in bits. Asymmetric keys are much larger than symmetric keys. For example, although a typical symmetric key is 182 bits, the .NET Framework implementation of the RSA algorithm supports key lengths from 384 through 16384 bits.

- **LegalKeySizes** A *KeySizes* array that gets the key sizes that are supported by the symmetric algorithm. Each array member contains *MinSize* and *MaxSize* properties that define the valid key ranges in bits, and a *SkipSize* property that specifies the interval between valid key sizes in bits.

- *SignatureAlgorithm*   Gets the URL of an XML document describing the signature algorithm. Generally, you do not need to directly access this property.

Unlike the *SymmetricAlgorithm* base class, the *AsymmetricAlgorithm* base class has no useful methods. Instead, the encryption functionality is built into the objects that implement the *AsymmetricAlgorithm* class. The .NET Framework provides two implementations of this class:

- *RSACryptoServiceProvider*   Used for all asymmetric encryption and decryption. *RSACryptoServiceProvider* is the .NET Framework implementation of the RSA algorithm. RSA is named for the last initial of its three creators—Ronald Rivest, Adi Shamir, and Leonard Adleman—who developed the algorithm in 1977. The *RSACryptoServiceProvider* class is a managed wrapper around the unmanaged RSA implementation provided by the Cryptography API.

- *DSACryptoServiceProvider*   Used for digitally signing messages, it is also a managed wrapper around unmanaged code.

In addition to the properties provided by *AsymmetricAlgorithm*, *RSACryptoServiceProvider* provides the following properties:

- *PersistKeyInCsp*   Gets or sets a value indicating whether the key should be persisted in the CSP. Set this to true when you want to reuse the key without exporting it.

- *UseMachineKeyStore*   Gets or sets a value indicating whether the key should be persisted in the computer's key store instead of the user profile store.

The default constructors always populate the algorithm parameters with the strongest defaults available to the run-time environment, giving you the strongest algorithm possible without changing any settings. The *RSACryptoServiceProvider* class also includes methods for encrypting and decrypting, as well as for importing and exporting keys. The following list describes each of these methods:

- *Decrypt*   Decrypts data with the RSA algorithm.
- *Encrypt*   Encrypts data with the RSA algorithm.
- *ExportParameters*   Exports an *RSAParameters* structure, which defines the algorithm's key pair. Pass true to this method to export both the private and public key, or pass false to export only the public key.
- *FromXmlString*   Imports a key pair from an XML string.

- ***ImportParameters***   Imports to a public key or key pair the specified *RSAParameters* object.

- ***SignData***   Computes the hash value of the specified data and stores the signature in a byte array.

- ***SignHash***   Computes the signature for the specified hash value by encrypting it with the private key and storing the signature in a byte array.

- ***VerifyData***   Verifies the specified signature data by comparing it with the signature computed for the specified data.

- ***VerifyHash***   Verifies the specified signature data by comparing it with the signature computed for the specified hash value.

How to Export and Import Asymmetric Keys and Key Pairs

RSA keys are much more complex than symmetric encryption keys. In fact, RSA keys are called parameters and are represented by an *RSAParameters* structure. Table 12-3 lists the significant members of this structure and their purpose. The structure includes several parameters that are not listed, but you will not need to directly access these: *DP*, *DQ*, *InverseQ*, *P*, and *Q*.

Table 12-3   ***RSAParameters* Structure Members**

Parameter	Description
D	The private key.
Exponent	Also known as *e*, this is the short part of the public key.
Modulus	Also known as *n*, this is the long part of the public key.

You will almost always need to export your public key because without the public key, nobody can send encrypted messages to you. To export your public key to an instance of the *RSAParamaters* structure, use the *RSACryptoServiceProvider.ExportParameters* method, and pass it a Boolean *false* parameter. The *false* parameter causes the method to export only the public key. If it were set to true, *ExportParameters* would export both the public and private key.

IMPORTANT   **Exporting the private key**

Export your private key only if you need to reuse it later. If you do store it, your application must protect the privacy of the private key.

The following code sample demonstrates how to create a new instance of an RSA algorithm and export its automatically generated public key to an *RSAParameters* object named *publicKey*:

```
' VB
' Create an instance of the RSA algorithm object
Dim myRSA As RSACryptoServiceProvider = New RSACryptoServiceProvider

' Create a new RSAParameters object with only the public key
Dim publicKey As RSAParameters = myRSA.ExportParameters(False)

// C#
// Create an instance of the RSA algorithm object
RSACryptoServiceProvider myRSA = new RSACryptoServiceProvider();

// Create a new RSAParameters object with only the public key
RSAParameters publicKey = myRSA.ExportParameters(false);
```

After you create an *RSAParameters* object, you can freely access any of the byte array parameters described in Table 12-3. If you need to store or transmit the export key or keys, you should use the *RSACryptoServiceProvider.ToXmlString* method instead. Like *ExportParameters*, this method takes a Boolean value that indicates whether the private key should be exported. However, *ToXmlString* stores the data in an XML format that can be easily stored, transferred, and imported with the *FromXmlString* method. The following example shows an abbreviated version of an exported RSA key pair created by calling *RSACryptoServiceProvider.ToXmlString(true)*:

```
<RSAKeyValue>
    <Modulus>vilaR5C3XtmH5…IGZNTs=</Modulus>
    <Exponent>AQAB</Exponent>
    <P>699j5bpTO4JlVkjz…66sYYxLG6VQ==</P>
    <Q>zmNovTJlGllamlJ1Vk…EMtEJqhZqzhTw==</Q>
    <DP>OWBf5p7qB6JzB7xek…tkQGoiMBK+Q==</DP>
    <DQ>NLbZUrGjduA/99K…scf2pOzQTvKw==</DQ>
    <InverseQ>BYZ3vVwb/N+…HjPcGz7Yg==</InverseQ>
    <D>Jz81qMuPbP4MdEaF/…hYZ5WmrzeRRE=</D>
</RSAKeyValue>
```

How to Store Key Pairs for Later Reuse

You can also export keys to the CSP by using *CryptoAPI* key storage. To store your private keys persistently, add the following elements to your code:

1. Create a *CspParameters* object.
2. Specify the *CspParameters.KeyContainerName* property.

3. Create a *RSACryptoServiceProvider* object using the overloaded constructor that accepts a *CspParameters* object.

4. Set the *RSACryptoServiceProvider.PersistKeyInCsp* property to true.

The .NET Framework handles creating and retrieving keys automatically. The first time you specify a *CspParameters* object and set the *PersistKeyInCsp* property to true, the .NET Framework will create the key container and store your key. If you run the same application again, the .NET Framework will detect that a key container with that name already exists and will retrieve the stored private key. For example, if you run this console application repeatedly, it will display the same private key every time:

```vb
' VB
' Create a CspParameters object
Dim persistantCsp As CspParameters = New CspParameters
persistantCsp.KeyContainerName = "AsymmetricExample"

' Create an instance of the RSA algorithm object
Dim myRSA As RSACryptoServiceProvider = _
    New RSACryptoServiceProvider (persistantCsp)

' Specify that the private key should be stored in the CSP
myRSA.PersistKeyInCsp = True

' Create a new RSAParameters object with the private key
Dim privateKey As RSAParameters = myRSA.ExportParameters(True)

' Display the private key
For Each thisByte As Byte In privateKey.D
    Console.Write(thisByte.ToString("X2") + " ")
Next
```

```csharp
// C#
// Create a CspParameters object
CspParameters persistantCsp = new CspParameters();
persistantCsp.KeyContainerName = "AsymmetricExample";

// Create an instance of the RSA algorithm object
RSACryptoServiceProvider myRSA = new RSACryptoServiceProvider(persistantCsp);

// Specify that the private key should be stored in the CSP
myRSA.PersistKeyInCsp = true;

// Create a new RSAParameters object with the private key
RSAParameters privateKey = myRSA.ExportParameters(true);

// Display the private key
foreach (byte thisByte in privateKey.D)
    Console.Write(thisByte.ToString("X2") + " ");
```

However, if you change the *KeyContainerName* value and rerun the application, the application will display a new private key because the .NET Framework will not find an existing key container.

How to Encrypt and Decrypt Messages Using Asymmetric Encryption

To encrypt and decrypt messages using asymmetric encryption, call the *RSACryptoServiceProvider.Encrypt* and *RSACryptoServiceProvider.Decrypt* methods. Both take two parameters:

- **byte[] rgb**   An array of bytes containing the message to be encrypted or decrypted.

- **bool fOAEP**   A Boolean value. When set to true, encryption and encryption will use OAEP data padding, which is supported only on Windows XP and later operating systems. When set to false, PKCS#1 v1.5 data padding will be used. Both the encryption and decryption methods *must* use the same data padding.

The most challenging aspect of encryption is converting data into the byte array format. To convert strings to byte arrays, use the *System.Text.Encoding.Unicode.GetBytes* and *System.Text.Encoding.Unicode.GetString* methods. For example, the following console application encrypts a string using PKCS#1 v1.5 data padding, and then immediately decrypts and displays the string:

```
' VB
Dim messageString As String = "Hello, World!"
Dim myRsa As RSACryptoServiceProvider = New RSACryptoServiceProvider

Dim messageBytes As Byte() = Encoding.Unicode.GetBytes(messageString)
Dim encryptedMessage As Byte() = myRsa.Encrypt(messageBytes, False)

Dim decryptedBytes As Byte() = myRsa.Decrypt(encryptedMessage, False)
Console.WriteLine(Encoding.Unicode.GetString(decryptedBytes))

// C#
string messageString = "Hello, World!";
RSACryptoServiceProvider myRsa = new RSACryptoServiceProvider();

byte[] messageBytes = Encoding.Unicode.GetBytes(messageString);
byte[] encryptedMessage = myRsa.Encrypt(messageBytes, false);

byte[] decryptedBytes = myRsa.Decrypt(encryptedMessage, false);
Console.WriteLine(Encoding.Unicode.GetString(decryptedBytes));
```

Whichever encoding method you use to convert the data into a byte array, be sure you use a matching decoding method after decrypting the data.

Validating Data Integrity with Hashes

Another important use of cryptography is protecting data integrity by using hashes. A *hash* is a checksum that is unique to a specific file or piece of data. You can use a hash value to verify that a file has not been modified after the hash was generated.

Unlike encryption, you cannot derive the original data from the hash, even if the original data is very small. In other words, creating a hash is a one-way operation. Hashes are often used to enable passwords to be verified without storing the password itself. After the hash of the password has been stored, the application can verify the password by calculating the hash of the provided password and comparing it with the stored hash. The two hash values will match if the user has provided the same password; however, an attacker cannot determine the original password, even if the attacker gains access to the password's hash value.

Hash Algorithms in the .NET Framework

The .NET Framework includes six nonkeyed hash algorithms and two keyed hash algorithms. Table 12-4 lists each of the nonkeyed hash algorithms included with the .NET Framework. Each is member of the *System.Security.Cryptography* class, and is derived from *System.Security.Cryptography.HashAlgorithm*.

Table 12-4   Nonkeyed Hashing Algorithms

Abstract Class	Implementation Class	Description
MD5	MD5CryptoService-Provider	The Message Digest algorithm. The hash size for the MD5 algorithm is 128 bits.
RIPEMD160	RIPEMD160Managed	The MD160 hash algorithm. The has size for the MD160 hash algorithm is 160 bits.
SHA1	SHA1CryptoService-Provider	The Secure Hash Algorithm 1. The hash size for the SHA1 algorithm is 160 bits.
SHA256	SHA256Managed	The Secure Hash Algorithm 256. The hash is 256 bits.
SHA384	SHA384Managed	The Secure Hash Algorithm 384. The hash is 384 bits.
SHA512	SHA512Managed	The Secure Hash Algorithm 512. The hash is 512 bits.

NOTE .NET 2.0

RIPEMD160 is new in .NET 2.0 and is intended as a replacement for MD5.

You have to take care to prevent attackers from modifying a hash value. If an attacker can modify a hash, he or she can effectively defeat the purpose of the hash. *Keyed hash algorithms* are algorithms that protect against modification of the hash by encrypting it by using a secret key that both the sender and receiver must have. Table 12-5 lists both of the keyed hash algorithms included with the .NET Framework, both derived from *System.Security.Cryptography.KeyedHashAlgorithm.*

Table 12-5 Keyed Hashing Algorithms

Class	Description
HMACSHA1	Hash-based Message Authentication Code using *SHA1.* Used to determine whether a message sent over an insecure channel has been tampered with, provided that the sender and receiver share a secret key. HMACSHA1 accepts keys of any size, and produces a hash sequence of length 20 bytes.
MACTripleDES	Message Authentication Code using *TripleDES.* Like HMACSHA1, *MACTripleDES* is used to determine whether a message sent over an insecure channel has been tampered with, provided that the sender and receiver share a secret key. *MACTripleDES* uses a key of length 8, 16, or 24 bytes, and produces a hash sequence of length 8 bytes.

Real World: Hash Algorithms Aren't Always Unique

Tony Northrup

Many years ago, I was a developer creating a database that indexed thousands of files for one of the first major Internet download services. A single file was often submitted using multiple file names, so avoiding duplicate files required more than simply checking to see whether the file name already existed. Initially, I sorted through the files to verify that each was unique by examining the size and contents of the files. However, this was an extremely slow process.

I decided to create an index of files by using an MD5 hash of each file. Then my application could check whether a file already existed simply by looking up the

MD5 hash. I was surprised when my application found a duplicate file. After checking into it further, I discovered that it had found two unique files that produced the same hash! This was supposed to be mathematically impossible; however, because the size of the MD5 was a reasonably small 128 bits and the size of the files was much larger, the possibility existed that multiple files would produce the same hash. In my case, I had stumbled across such an unlikely occurrence. Using a longer hash, such as SHA512, further reduces the likelihood of such an occurrence.

How to Compute a Nonkeyed Hash

To compute a nonkeyed hash, perform the following steps in your code:

1. Create the hash algorithm object.

2. Store the data to be hashed in a byte array.

3. Call the *HashAlgorithm.ComputeHash* method.

4. Retrieve the *HashAlgorithm.Hash* byte array, which contains the hash value.

The following console application demonstrates how to create a hash by calculating the hash of the file specified in *args[0]*, and displaying the hash using Base64 text encoding:

```
' VB
Sub Main(ByVal args As String())
    ' Step 1: Create the hash algorithm object
    Dim myHash As MD5 = New MD5CryptoServiceProvider

    ' Step 2: Store the data to be hashed in a byte array
    Dim file As FileStream = New FileStream (args(0), _
        FileMode.Open, FileAccess.Read)
    Dim reader As BinaryReader = New BinaryReader (file)

    ' Step 3: Call the HashAlgorithm.ComputeHash method
    myHash.ComputeHash(reader.ReadBytes(CType(file.Length, Integer)))

    ' Step 4: Retrieve the HashAlgorithm.Hash byte array
    Console.WriteLine(Convert.ToBase64String(myHash.Hash))
End Sub

// C#
// Step 1: Create the hash algorithm object
MD5 myHash = new MD5CryptoServiceProvider();
```

```
// Step 2: Store the data to be hashed in a byte array
FileStream file = new FileStream(args[0], FileMode.Open, FileAccess.Read);
BinaryReader reader = new BinaryReader(file);

// Step 3: Call the HashAlgorithm.ComputeHash method
myHash.ComputeHash(reader.ReadBytes((int)file.Length));

// Step 4: Retrieve the HashAlgorithm.Hash byte array
Console.WriteLine(Convert.ToBase64String(myHash.Hash));
```

Repeatedly running that console application to calculate the hash of a single file will always produce the same hash result until the file is modified. After the file is modified, the hash result also changes. Consider the following console output, which creates a new text file, computes the hash repeatedly, and then modifies the file. After the file is modified, the hash also changes:

```
C:\>echo Hello, World! > HashThis.txt

C:\>HashExample HashThis.txt
h7GTmgvuZdNOSGROA6qdBA==

C:\>HashExample HashThis.txt
h7GTmgvuZdNOSGROA6qdBA==

C:\>echo Hello, again. >> HashThis.txt

C:\>HashExample HashThis.txt
F1QQWOeK/Yc2EwNR2BxCuw==
```

Because all nonkeyed hash algorithms are derived from a single class, you can change the hash algorithm used simply by changing the algorithm declaration. The more bits used in the hash, the longer the hash that will be displayed. To later verify that the data has not been modified, simply recalculate the hash using the same algorithm and compare the two values.

How to Compute a Keyed Hash

To compute a keyed hash, perform the following steps in your code:

1. Create a secret key that is shared among all parties who will compute or verify the hash.

2. Create the hash algorithm object using the secret key. If you do not provide a secret key, one will be automatically generated for you.

3. Store the data to be hashed in a byte array.

4. Call the *KeyedHashAlgorithm.ComputeHash* method.

5. Retrieve the *KeyedHashAlgorithm.Hash* byte array, which contains the hash value.

The following console application demonstrates how to create a HMACSHA1 hash by calculating the hash of the file specified in *args[1]* by using a password specified in *args[0]* to generate a secret key:

```vb
' VB
Sub Main(ByVal args As String())
    ' Step 1: Create a secret key
    Dim saltValueBytes As Byte() = System.Text.Encoding.ASCII.GetBytes("This is my salt")
    Dim key As Rfc2898DeriveBytes = _
        New Rfc2898DeriveBytes(args(0), saltValueBytes)
    Dim secretKey As Byte() = key.GetBytes(16)

    ' Step 2: Create the hash algorithm object
    Dim myHash As HMACSHA1 = New HMACSHA1(secretKey)

    ' Step 3: Store the data to be hashed in a byte array
    Dim file As FileStream = _
        New FileStream(args(1), FileMode.Open, FileAccess.Read)
    Dim reader As BinaryReader = New BinaryReader(file)

    ' Step 4: Call the HashAlgorithm.ComputeHash method
    myHash.ComputeHash(reader.ReadBytes(CType(file.Length, Integer)))

    ' Step 5: Retrieve the HashAlgorithm.Hash byte array
    Console.WriteLine(System.Convert.ToBase64String(myHash.Hash))
End Sub

// C#
byte[] saltValueBytes  = Encoding.ASCII.GetBytes("This is my salt");
Rfc2898DeriveBytes passwordKey =
    new Rfc2898DeriveBytes(args[0], saltValueBytes);
byte[] secretKey = passwordKey.GetBytes(16);

// Step 2: Create the hash algorithm object
HMACSHA1 myHash = new HMACSHA1(secretKey);

// Step 3: Store the data to be hashed in a byte array
FileStream file = new FileStream(args[1], FileMode.Open, FileAccess.Read);
BinaryReader reader = new BinaryReader(file);

// Step 4: Call the HashAlgorithm.ComputeHash method
myHash.ComputeHash(reader.ReadBytes((int)file.Length));

// Step 5: Retrieve the HashAlgorithm.Hash byte array
Console.WriteLine(Convert.ToBase64String(myHash.Hash));
```

If either the file contents or the password changes, the computed hash will also change. This ensures that both the sender and recipient used the same password to generate the hash, which prevents an attacker from modifying the hash. Consider the following console output, which creates a new text file, computes the hash repeatedly, and then modifies the file. After either the file or the password (and key) is modified, the hash also changes:

```
C:\>echo Hello, World! > HashThis.txt

C:\>KeyedHashExample SomePassword HashThis.txt
t04kYA9Z2ki+JbzUqe7lIE6EjN4=

C:\>KeyedHashExample SomePassword HashThis.txt
t04kYA9Z2ki+JbzUqe7lIE6EjN4=

C:\>KeyedHashExample NotSomePassword HashThis.txt
TFNPh9TspBobOvixy1yJOfX/+vo=

C:\>echo Hello, again. >> HashThis.txt

C:\>KeyedHashExample SomePassword HashThis.txt
yW6K6G7diJEV3bV2nNttgtcCMOo=
```

Either HMACSHA1 or MACTripleDES can be used for the previous example. However, whereas HMACSHA1 accepts a secret key of any length, MACTripleDES accepts only secret keys of 8, 16, or 24 bytes.

Signing Files

A *digital signature* is a value that can be appended to electronic data to prove that it was created by someone who possesses a specific private key. Public-key algorithms can also be used to form digital signatures. Digital signatures authenticate the identity of a sender (if you trust the sender's public key) and help protect the integrity of data. A signature can be verified by anyone because the sender's public key can be publicly accessible and is typically included in the digital signature format.

IMPORTANT **The difference between digital signatures and encryption**

Digital signatures do not protect the secrecy of the data being signed. To protect the secrecy of the file, you must encrypt it.

Digital Signature Classes in the .NET Framework

The .NET Framework provides two classes for generating and verifying digital signatures: *DSACryptoServiceProvider* and *RSACryptoServiceProvider*. These classes use different algorithms but provide similar functionality. Each implements the following four methods for use with digital signatures:

- **SignHash**   Generates a digital signature based on the hash of a file.
- **SignData**   Generates a digital signature by first generating the hash for a file, and then generating a signature based on the hash.
- **VerifyHash**   Verifies a digital signature based on the hash of a file.
- **VerifyData**   Verifies a digital signature given the entire file's contents.

Digital signatures provide separate methods for signing and verifying data, whereas hashes do not provide separate methods for verification. The reason that hash algorithms do not need a separate method for signing and verifying is that the recipient can easily re-create the hash and then compare the hash she generated with the hash the sender provided. However, digital signatures use asymmetric encryption. Therefore, the recipient cannot regenerate the signature without the sender's private key, although the signature can be verified by using the sender's public key. The *VerifyData* and *VerifyHash* methods use the public sender's public key; the *SignData* and *SignHash* methods use the sender's private key.

How to Generate and Verify a Digital Signature for a File

To generate a digital signature for a file, perform the following steps in your code:

1. Create the digital signature algorithm object.
2. Store the data to be signed in a byte array.
3. Call the *SignData* method and store the signature.
4. Export the public key.

To verify the digital signature, perform the following steps:

1. Create the digital signature algorithm object.
2. Import the signature and public key.
3. Store the data to be verified in a byte array.
4. Call the *VerifyData* method.

The following code sample is the *Main* method of a console application that accepts a file name as a command-line argument and displays a Base64-encoded digital signature for the file based on a dynamically generated key pair. The public key and digital signature are stored in variables. Then the application verifies the signature with the public key by creating new objects.

```vb
' VB
Sub Main(ByVal args As String())
    ' Signing Step 1: Create the digital signature algorithm object
    Dim signer As DSACryptoServiceProvider = New DSACryptoServiceProvider

    ' Signing Step 2: Store the data to be signed in a byte array.
    Dim file As FileStream = _
        New FileStream(args(0), FileMode.Open, FileAccess.Read)
    Dim reader As BinaryReader = New BinaryReader(file)
    Dim data As Byte() = reader.ReadBytes(CType(file.Length, Integer))

    ' Signing Step 3: Call the SignData method and store the signature
    Dim signature As Byte() = signer.SignData(data)

    ' Signing Step 4: Export the public key
    Dim publicKey As String = signer.ToXmlString(False)
    Console.WriteLine("Signature: " + Convert.ToBase64String(signature))
    reader.Close()
    file.Close()

    ' Verifying Step 1: Create the digital signature algorithm object
    Dim verifier As DSACryptoServiceProvider = New DSACryptoServiceProvider

    ' Verifying Step 2: Import the signature and public key.
    verifier.FromXmlString(publicKey)

    ' Verifying Step 3: Store the data to be verified in a byte array
    Dim file2 As FileStream = _
        New FileStream(args(0), FileMode.Open, FileAccess.Read)
    Dim reader2 As BinaryReader = New BinaryReader(file2)
    Dim data2 As Byte() = reader2.ReadBytes(CType(file2.Length, Integer))

    ' Verifying Step 4: Call the VerifyData method
    If verifier.VerifyData(data2, signature) Then
        Console.WriteLine("Signature verified")
    Else
        Console.WriteLine("Signature NOT verified")
    End If
    reader2.Close()
    file2.Close()
End Sub
```

```csharp
// C#
// Signing Step 1: Create the digital signature algorithm object
DSACryptoServiceProvider signer = new DSACryptoServiceProvider();

// Signing Step 2: Store the data to be signed in a byte array.
FileStream file = new FileStream(args[0], FileMode.Open, FileAccess.Read);
BinaryReader reader = new BinaryReader(file);
byte[] data = reader.ReadBytes((int)file.Length);

// Signing Step 3: Call the SignData method and store the signature
byte[] signature = signer.SignData(data);
```

```
// Signing Step 4: Export the public key
string publicKey = signer.ToXmlString(false);

Console.WriteLine("Signature: " + Convert.ToBase64String(signature));
reader.Close();
file.Close();

// Verifying Step 1: Create the digital signature algorithm object
DSACryptoServiceProvider verifier = new DSACryptoServiceProvider();

// Verifying Step 2: Import the signature and public key.
verifier.FromXmlString(publicKey);

// Verifying Step 3: Store the data to be verified in a byte array
FileStream file2 = new FileStream(args[0], FileMode.Open, FileAccess.Read);
BinaryReader reader2 = new BinaryReader(file2);
byte[] data2 = reader2.ReadBytes((int)file2.Length);

// Verifying Step 4: Call the VerifyData method
if (verifier.VerifyData(data2, signature))
    Console.WriteLine("Signature verified");
else
    Console.WriteLine("Signature NOT verified");
reader2.Close();
file2.Close();
```

The previous example uses the *DSACryptoServiceProvider* class, but you can also use *RSACryptoServiceProvider* for digital signatures. *RSACryptoServiceProvider* usage is similar, but requires providing a hash algorithm object for both the *SignData* and *Verify-Data* methods. The following code sample shows only the lines that would need to change from the previous example to use *RSACryptoServiceProvider* with the *SHA1CryptoServiceProvider* hash algorithm:

```
' VB
' Signing Step 1: Create the digital signature algorithm object
Dim signer As RSACryptoServiceProvider = New RSACryptoServiceProvider

' Signing Step 3: Call the SignData method and store the signature
Dim signature As Byte() = _
    signer.SignData(data, New SHA1CryptoServiceProvider)

' Verifying Step 1: Create the digital signature algorithm object
Dim verifier As RSACryptoServiceProvider = New RSACryptoServiceProvider

' Verifying Step 4: Call the VerifyData method
If verifier.VerifyData(data2, New SHA1CryptoServiceProvider, signature) Then

// C#
// Signing Step 1: Create the digital signature algorithm object
RSACryptoServiceProvider signer = new RSACryptoServiceProvider();
```

```
// Signing Step 3: Call the SignData method and store the signature
byte[] signature = signer.SignData(data, new SHA1CryptoServiceProvider());

// Verifying Step 1: Create the digital signature algorithm object
RSACryptoServiceProvider verifier = new RSACryptoServiceProvider();

// Verifying Step 4: Call the VerifyData method
if (verifier.VerifyData(data2, new SHA1CryptoServiceProvider(), signature))
```

Although this simplified example creates and verifies a signature within a single application, you will typically transfer the public key and digital signature across a network. The most convenient way to transfer digital signatures is to create a binary file that contains the public key, the digital signature, and the file data itself. However, you can also transmit them as separate files or separate network communications.

Lab: Encrypting and Decrypting Files

In this lab, you will write console applications that encrypt and decrypt files using a password. The console applications should take three parameters: the file name of the unencrypted file to read, the file name of the encrypted file to write, and the password. If you encounter a problem completing an exercise, the completed projects are available on the companion CD in the Code folder.

▶ **Exercise 1: Write a Console Application to Encrypt Files**

In this exercise, you create a console application that encrypts files using a password.

1. Create a new console application in either Visual Basic or C#.

2. Add the *System.Security.Cryptography* and *System.IO* namespaces to your project.

3. Add code to read the command-line parameters into strings. If you are using Visual Basic, you will have to change the *Main* parameter declaration to accept an array of strings—for example, *"Sub Main(ByVal args As String())"*. The following code would work, though you should add error handling that displays usage information if the user does not provide the correct parameters:

```
' VB
Dim inFileName As String = args(0)
Dim outFileName As String = args(1)
Dim password As String = args(2)

// C#
string inFileName = args[0];
string outFileName = args[1];
string password = args[2];
```

4. Write code to create the encryption object and specify the key and IV based on the provided password. The following code would work:

```vb
' VB
' Create the password key
Dim saltValueBytes As Byte() = _
    System.Text.Encoding.ASCII.GetBytes("This is my salt")
Dim passwordKey As Rfc2898DeriveBytes = _
    New Rfc2898DeriveBytes(password, saltValueBytes)

' Create the algorithm and specify the key and IV
Dim alg As RijndaelManaged = New RijndaelManaged
alg.Key = passwordKey.GetBytes(alg.KeySize / 8)
alg.IV = passwordKey.GetBytes(alg.BlockSize / 8)
```

```csharp
// C#
// Create the password key
byte[] saltValueBytes  = Encoding.ASCII.GetBytes("This is my salt");
Rfc2898DeriveBytes passwordKey =
    new Rfc2898DeriveBytes(password, saltValueBytes);

// Create the algorithm and specify the key and IV
RijndaelManaged alg = new RijndaelManaged();
alg.Key = passwordKey.GetBytes(alg.KeySize/8);
alg.IV = passwordKey.GetBytes(alg.BlockSize/8);
```

5. Read the unencrypted file into a byte array, as the following code demonstrates:

```vb
' VB
' Read the unencrypted file into fileData
Dim inFile As FileStream = New FileStream(inFileName, _
    FileMode.Open, FileAccess.Read)
Dim fileData(inFile.Length) As Byte
inFile.Read(fileData, 0, CType(inFile.Length, Integer))
```

```csharp
// C#
// Read the unencrypted file into fileData
FileStream inFile = new FileStream(inFileName,
    FileMode.Open, FileAccess.Read);
byte[] fileData = new byte[inFile.Length];
inFile.Read(fileData, 0, (int)inFile.Length);
```

6. Create the *ICryptoTransform* object based on your cryptography algorithm. Then create a *FileStream* object to write the encrypted file. Create a *CryptoStream* object based on the *ICryptoTransform* object and the *FileStream* object, and then write the contents of the unencrypted file to the *CryptoStream*.

```vb
' VB
' Create the ICryptoTransform and CryptoStream object
Dim encryptor As ICryptoTransform = alg.CreateEncryptor
Dim outFile As FileStream = New FileStream(outFileName, FileMode.OpenOrCreate,
FileAccess.Write)
```

```
Dim encryptStream As CryptoStream = _
    New CryptoStream(outFile, encryptor, CryptoStreamMode.Write)

' Write the contents to the CryptoStream
encryptStream.Write(fileData, 0, fileData.Length)

// C#
// Create the ICryptoTransform and CryptoStream object
ICryptoTransform encryptor = alg.CreateEncryptor();
FileStream outFile =
    new FileStream(outFileName, FileMode.OpenOrCreate, FileAccess.Write);
CryptoStream encryptStream = new CryptoStream(outFile, encryptor,
CryptoStreamMode.Write);

// Write the contents to the CryptoStream
encryptStream.Write(fileData, 0, fileData.Length);
```

7. Finally, close the files.

```
' VB
' Close the file handles
encryptStream.Close()
inFile.Close()
outFile.Close()

// C#
// Close the file handles
encryptStream.Close();
inFile.Close();
outFile.Close();
```

Now, open a command prompt and use your application to encrypt a text file and an image file. Verify that the size of the encrypted files is approximately the same as the size of the unencrypted files. (It might be slightly larger due to padding added during encryption.) Attempt to open the encrypted files, and verify that they are unreadable.

Exercise 2: Write a Console Application to Decrypt Files

In this exercise, you create a console application that decrypts files using a password.

1. Create a new console application in either Visual Basic or C#.

2. Add the *System.Security.Cryptography* and *System.IO* namespaces to your project.

3. Similar to the application you wrote for Exercise 1, create a console application that creates an encryption algorithm object based on a password, reads an encrypted file, and writes a decrypted file. For example, the following code would work:

```
' VB
Sub Main(ByVal args As String())
    ' Read the command-line parameters
```

```vb
    Dim inFileName As String = args(0)
    Dim outFileName As String = args(1)
    Dim password As String = args(2)

    ' Create the password key
    Dim saltValueBytes As Byte() = System.Text.Encoding.ASCII.GetBytes("This is my salt")
    Dim passwordKey As Rfc2898DeriveBytes = New Rfc2898DeriveBytes(password, _
saltValueBytes)

    ' Create the algorithm and specify the key and IV
    Dim alg As RijndaelManaged = New RijndaelManaged
    alg.Key = passwordKey.GetBytes(alg.KeySize / 8)
    alg.IV = passwordKey.GetBytes(alg.BlockSize / 8)

    ' Read the encrypted file into fileData
    Dim decryptor As ICryptoTransform = alg.CreateDecryptor
    Dim inFile As FileStream = _
        New FileStream(inFileName, FileMode.Open, FileAccess.Read)
    Dim decryptStream As CryptoStream = _
        New CryptoStream(inFile, decryptor, CryptoStreamMode.Read)
    Dim fileData(inFile.Length) As Byte
    decryptStream.Read(fileData, 0, CType(inFile.Length, Integer))

    ' Write the contents of the unencrypted file
    Dim outFile As FileStream = _
        New FileStream(outFileName, FileMode.OpenOrCreate, _
        FileAccess.Write)
    outFile.Write(fileData, 0, fileData.Length)

    ' Close the file handles
    decryptStream.Close()
    inFile.Close()
    outFile.Close()
End Sub

// C#
// Read the command-line parameters
string inFileName = args[0];
string outFileName = args[1];
string password = args[2];

// Create the password key
byte[] saltValueBytes = Encoding.ASCII.GetBytes("This is my salt");
Rfc2898DeriveBytes passwordKey = new Rfc2898DeriveBytes(password, saltValueBytes);

// Create the algorithm and specify the key and IV
RijndaelManaged alg = new RijndaelManaged();
alg.Key = passwordKey.GetBytes(alg.KeySize / 8);
alg.IV = passwordKey.GetBytes(alg.BlockSize / 8);

// Read the encrypted file into fileData
ICryptoTransform decryptor = alg.CreateDecryptor();
```

```
FileStream inFile =
    new FileStream(inFileName, FileMode.Open, FileAccess.Read);
CryptoStream decryptStream =
    new CryptoStream(inFile, decryptor, CryptoStreamMode.Read);
byte[] fileData = new byte[inFile.Length];
decryptStream.Read(fileData, 0, (int)inFile.Length);

// Write the contents of the unencrypted file
FileStream outFile = new FileStream(outFileName, FileMode.OpenOrCreate, FileAccess.Write);
outFile.Write(fileData, 0, fileData.Length);

// Close the file handles
decryptStream.Close();
inFile.Close();
outFile.Close();
```

4. Add code to read the command-line parameters into strings. If you are using Visual Basic, you have to change the *Main* parameter declaration to accept an array of strings. The following code would work, though you should add error-handling that displays usage information if the user does not provide the correct parameters:

```
' VB
Dim inFileName As String = args(0)
Dim outFileName As String = args(1)
Dim password As String = args(2)

// C#
string inFileName = args[0];
string outFileName = args[1];
string password = args[2];
```

Now, open a command prompt and use your application to decrypt the text file and image files that you encrypted earlier. Attempt to open the decrypted files, and verify that they are readable. Attempt to decrypt the files with the incorrect password and note that the application throws a *System.Security.Cryptography.CryptographicException*. You should catch this exception and display a friendly error message to the user indicating that they probably mistyped the password.

Lesson Summary

- Symmetric key encryption is a cryptographic technique for protecting the privacy of data in situations where both the encryptor and decryptor have access to the same secret key. There are four symmetric algorithm classes in the .NET Framework: *RijndaelManaged*, *DES*, *TripleDES*, and *RC2*. The primary disadvantage of symmetric key encryption is that you have to transfer the key between the sender and receiver, and the key can be very complex. Alternatively, you can generate a key based on a user password by using the *Rfc2898DeriveBytes* class.

■ Asymmetric key encryption is a cryptographic technique for encrypting data using key pairs, in which one key performs the encryption, and the other key must be used to perform decryption. There are two asymmetric algorithm classes in the .NET Framework: *RSACryptoServiceProvider* and *DSACryptoService-Provider* (used only for creating digital signatures).

■ Hashes process a file and produce a unique key that can be used to validate the integrity of the file. If the file is modified in any way, the hash will also be changed. Therefore, hashing is useful when you want to ensure that a file has not been changed.

■ Digital signatures enable you to use a public key to verify that a file is signed with a private key. In environments with a public key infrastructure, you can use digital signatures to verify that a specific user created a file.

Lesson Review

You can use the following questions to test your knowledge of the information in Lesson 3, "Encrypting and Decrypting Data." The questions are also available on the companion CD if you prefer to review them in electronic form.

NOTE Answers

Answers to these questions and explanations of why each answer choice is right or wrong are located in the "Answers" section at the end of the book.

---

1. Which of the following classes requires both the encryptor and decryptor to have the same key? (Choose all that apply.)

   A. *RSACryptoServiceProvider*

   B. *RijndaelManaged*

   C. *TripleDES*

   D. *DSACryptoServiceProvider*

   E. *DES*

   F. *RC2*

2. Which of the following must be synchronized between the encryptor and decryptor when using symmetric encryption? (Choose all that apply.)

   A. *SymmetricAlgorithm.Key*

   B. *SymmetricAlgorithm.Salt*

     C. *SymmetricAlgorithm.IV*

     D. *SymmetricAlgorithm.Mode*

3. Under which circumstances should you export the private key from an asymmetric encryption algorithm?

     A. When transferring data across a network for a single session

     B. When a remote computer will be sending you a private file that you must be able to decrypt

     C. When you are encrypting a file that needs to be read later

     D. When you are sending a remote computer a private file that the remote computer must be able to decrypt

4. Which of the following are keyed hashing algorithms? (Choose all that apply.)

     A. *RIPEMD160*

     B. *HMACSHA1*

     C. *SHA512*

     D. *MACTripleDES*

     E. *MD5*

Chapter Review

To further practice and reinforce the skills you learned in this chapter, you can perform the following tasks:

- Review the chapter summary.
- Review the list of key terms introduced in this chapter.
- Complete the case scenarios. These scenarios set up real-world situations involving the topics of this chapter and ask you to create a solution.
- Complete the suggested practices.
- Take a practice test.

Chapter Summary

Use role-based security (RBS) to control which users can access which aspects of your application. You can base RBS on the local Windows user database, an Active Directory domain, or a custom user database.

- Discretionary access control lists (DACLs) define which users can access which objects, whereas security access control lists (SACLs) define what logging is performed when users attempt to access a file. You can use classes in the *System.Security.AccessControl* namespace to view and manipulate both types of ACLs.
- The cryptography classes in the *System.Security.Cryptography* namespace enable you to encrypt and decrypt data (using either symmetric or asymmetric algorithms), validate data (using hashing), and sign data (using digital signatures).

Key Terms

Do you know what these key terms mean? You can check your answers by looking up the terms in the glossary at the end of the book.

- access control list (ACL)
- Advanced Encryption Standard (AES)
- asymmetric encryption
- authentication
- authorization

- cipher text
- Data Encryption Standard (DES)
- declarative RBS demands
- digital signature
- discretionary access control list (DACL)
- encryption key
- hash
- imperative RBS demands
- inherited permission
- initialization vector (IV)
- keyed hash algorithms
- MD5
- principal policy
- RC2
- Rijndael
- role-based security (RBS)
- security access control list (SACL)
- SHA1
- shared secret
- symmetric encryption
- Triple DES

Case Scenarios

In the following case scenarios, you will apply what you've learned about user and application security. You can find answers to these questions in the "Answers" section at the end of this book.

Case Scenario 1: Creating Custom Authentication Methods

You are a developer in the IT department of Litware, Inc., a company that manages electronic distribution for software companies. Your manager asks you to develop a

Windows Forms application for the Accounting department. The application needs to work with the existing database to enable the Accounting team to keep track of accounts payable, and, for authorized users, to issue payments. You interview key personnel and review technical requirements before coming up with your solution.

Interviews

Following is a list of company personnel interviewed and their statements:

- **IT Manager** "The accounting team wanted to upgrade their commercial accounting package, but it costs like a zillion dollars and I said we could write our own program to add the new functionality they needed for, like, half that cost. They just need to enter payments when a bill comes in and then click a button to make the payment. Oh, they're concerned about security because apparently they don't trust some of their people. I'm not sure how they want to control things, but I will tell you that the user accounts and groups they use to access the application are stored in the database, not in our Active Directory."

- **Accountant** "Our needs, actually, are pretty simple. We have three different types of employees: temps, accountants, and managers. The temps do data entry and create new accounts payable entries. The accountants pay bills, but only if these bills are less than $1,500. Any bill $1,500 or higher must be paid by a manager."

- **Database Administrator** "This accounting database is a nightmare, but we're stuck with it. There's one big table, called Users, that has a row for each user containing the user name and password *in clear-text*. Yeah, I told you it was bad, but at least you won't have to fool with encryption. There's another table named Groups that contains a row for every group membership. So, for example, John the temp has a row in the Users table containing his user name and password, and a row in the Groups table that indicates he is a member of the Temps group. Lori the IT manager happens to be in both the Accountants and Managers groups, so she has one row in the Users table and two rows in the Groups table. Make sense?"

Technical Requirements

Create a Windows Forms application that implements a customized authentication mechanism that queries the accounting database. Assume that you will have two methods: *AddBill* and *PayBill*. Use each user's group memberships to determine whether the user can run a particular method.

Questions

Your manager shows up and asks you the following questions:

1. Which classes or interfaces will you use to implement the custom authentication mechanism?

2. How will you restrict access to the *AddBill* method?

3. How will you restrict access to the *PayBill* method?

Case Scenario 2: Protecting Data by Using Cryptography

You are a developer for Blue Yonder Airlines. Blue Yonder Airlines is a national airline that has been growing rapidly in the past two years and has more than quadrupled the number of flights in that time period. Blue Yonder Airlines has only a handful of developers, however. Your manager recently sent you to security training, and now plans to use your skills to provide recommendations for different security problems throughout the organization.

Questions

Answer the following questions for your manager:

1. We keep the master records of all flights and passengers in a centralized database. An application that our team created then transfers that data to remote offices. What's the best way to encrypt this data?

2. Our application stores user names and passwords in a database. How should we protect those passwords?

3. Occasionally, we distribute bonuses to employees and customers in the form of frequent flier miles and upgrades. These bonuses are always distributed from the central office. We want the application running at the remote offices to be able to verify that the bonus originated from the central office. How can we do this?

Suggested Practices

To help you successfully master the "Improving the security of .NET Framework applications by using the .NET Framework 2.0 security features" exam objective, complete the following tasks.

Implement a Custom Authentication Scheme by Using the *System.Security.Authentication* Classes

To master this objective, you should complete Practices 1 and 2.

- **Practice 1** Create a client/server application that establishes an *SslStream* connection between the two hosts.

- **Practice 2** Add authentication error handling to the application created in Practice 1 by catching multiple types of exceptions based on classes in the *System.Security.Authentication* namespace.

Access and Modify Identity Information by Using the *System.Security.Principal* Classes

For this task, you should complete at least Practices 1 and 2. If you want a better understanding of how you can implement custom authentication, complete Practice 3. If you have written an application that uses other authentication techniques, complete Practice 4 as well.

- **Practice 1** List every time you have been authenticated in the past week.

- **Practice 2** Write an application that implements a custom authentication scheme by implementing the *GenericIdentity* and *GenericPrincipal* classes.

- **Practice 3** Write an application that implements a custom authentication scheme by implementing the *IIdentity* and *IPrincipal* interfaces.

- **Practice 4** If you have written an application that authenticates users to a database, update the application to make use of the *System.Security.Authentication* classes.

Implement Access Control by Using the *System.Security.AccessControl* Classes

For this task, you should complete all three practices to gain a good understanding of how to view and control ACLs.

- **Practice 1** Write an application that analyzes every folder on your hard drive and displays folders for which the Everyone group has access.

- **Practice 2** Write a console application named CopyACLs that functions exactly like the Copy command-line tool, but copies both files and ACLs.

- **Practice 3**   Write an application that enables auditing for successfully adding values to the *Run* and *RunOnce* registry keys located in HKEY_LOCAL_ MACHINE\Software\Microsoft\Windows\CurrentVersion\ and HKEY_ CURRENT_USER\Software\Microsoft\Windows\CurrentVersion\.

Encrypt, Decrypt, and Hash Data by Using the *System.Security.Cryptography* Classes

For this task, you should at least complete Practices 1 and 2 to understand how to use digital signatures and hashing in the real world. Complete Practice 3 to gain a better understanding of how to use asymmetric encryption.

- **Practice 1**   Write an application to sign files and then verify the digital signature.
- **Practice 2**   Write an application that stores hashes of every .dll and .exe file on your computer, and that later analyzes the files for changes and shows you which files have been modified.
- **Practice 3**   Write a client/server application that encrypts files on the client using a public key provided by the server, transfers them across a network, and then decrypts them on the server using the private key.

Take a Practice Test

The practice tests on this book's companion CD offer many options. For example, you can test yourself on just one exam objective, or you can test yourself on all the 70-536 certification exam content. You can set up the test so that it closely simulates the experience of taking a certification exam, or you can set it up in study mode so that you can look at the correct answers and explanations after you answer each question.

MORE INFO   **Practice tests**

For details about all the practice test options available, see the "How to Use the Practice Tests" section in this book's Introduction.

Chapter 13
Interoperation

Interoperation is a generic name used to refer to the process of interacting with unmanaged code from within managed code. Although the .NET Framework 2.0 provides a vast amount of functionality, two issues make Interoperation necessary:

- Many companies have a large amount of legacy code, code that was expensive to develop and has already been tested.

- Not every Microsoft Windows API has been wrapped for the .NET Framework 2.0, so some tasks are possible only if you use Interoperation.

For example, an application might need to take control of Microsoft Office Excel and perform a processing routine. Because the Excel library isn't written in .NET, you need to access it through Component Object Model (COM). COM and .NET are two very different execution environments, so the only way to share libraries between them is to use Interoperation, which is also known as *Interop*.

Exam objectives in this chapter:
- Expose COM components to the .NET Framework and the .NET Framework components to COM. (Refer *System.Runtime.InteropServices* namespace)
  - Import a type library as an assembly.
  - Create COM types in managed code.
  - Compile an Interop project.
  - Deploy an Interop application.
  - Qualify the .NET Framework types for Interoperation.
  - Apply Interop attributes, such as the *ComVisibleAttribute* class.
  - Package an assembly for COM.
  - Deploy an application for COM access.
- Call unmanaged DLL functions in a .NET Framework application, and control the marshaling of data in a .NET Framework application. (Refer *System.Runtime.InteropServices* namespace)
  - Platform Invoke

❑ Create a class to hold DLL functions.

❑ Create prototypes in managed code.

❑ Call a DLL function.

❑ Call a DLL function in special cases, such as passing structures and implementing callback functions.

❑ Create a new Exception class and map it to an HRESULT

❑ Default marshaling behavior

❑ Marshal data with Platform Invoke

❑ Marshal data with COM Interop

❑ *MarshalAsAttribute* class and *Marshal* class

Real World

William Ryan

A company I used to work for made a decision to adopt .NET soon after the Framework was released. However, we had more than 200,000 lines of legacy code. If we had had to rewrite and retest this code prior to launching any new application developed in .NET, we would have never made the switch. Using an "all or nothing" approach with migrating to .NET is simply too expensive and time consuming for many companies with investments in legacy code. By taking advantage of Interoperation, we were able to migrate our existing applications little by little, in a manner that was virtually transparent to clients. Were it not for Interoperation, the aforementioned company (and most others) would have never made the migration.

Lessons in this chapter:

Before You Begin

To complete the lessons in this chapter, you should be familiar with Visual Basic or C# and be comfortable with the following tasks:

- Create a console application in Visual Studio using Visual Basic or C#.
- Add references to system class libraries to a project.
- Create text files.

Lesson 1: Using COM Objects

Prior to the advent of the .NET Framework, COM was the primary framework for Windows developers to interact with the Windows operating system. Whether you're using COM components or pure .NET components, one thing is similar—external libraries need to be imported in order to be consumed. After you have a reference in place, you can declare and instantiate new objects just like anything else. Like many other aspects of .NET development, you can import types either by using the command line or by letting Microsoft Visual Studio 2005 do it for you.

After this lesson, you will be able to:

- Understand the tools Visual Studio 2005 provides for manipulating COM components.
- Consume a COM component in a .NET application.
- Deal with COM component exceptions.

Estimated lesson time: 20 minutes

Importing Type Libraries

The .NET Framework provides ample support for COM Interoperability, and the ability to import type libraries is included. The mechanism that serves as a proxy so that the .NET runtime can communicate with a COM component is known as a Runtime Callable Wrapper (RCW). The RCW handles the majority of the work between .NET and COM for you, including marshaling data types, handling events, and handling interfaces.

Unlike pure .NET components, COM components must be registered before they can be used. After they are registered, these components need to be imported by using Visual Studio 2005 or the Type Library Importer tool (TlbImp.exe). If you have a particular COM dynamic-link library (DLL) that you would like to use for the examples in this chapter, feel free to do so; otherwise, assume the following structure of a *Person* object contained in Person.dll:

```
' VB 6.0
Private mFirstName As String
Private mLastName As String

Property Get Firstname() As String
    mFirstName = Firstname
End Property
Property Let Firstname(Value As String)
    mFirstName = Value
End Property
```

```
Property Get Lastname() As String
    mLastName = Firstname
End Property
Property Let Lastname(Value As String)
    mLastName = Value
End Property
```

Perform the following steps to execute the Regsvr32 command to ensure that Person.dll (or whatever COM DLL you are using) is registered:

1. Open a new Command window or the Run dialog box (which you can access by choosing Start and then Run).

2. Execute Regsvr32 Person.dll.

Now that the DLL has been registered, you have two ways to import it:

- Visual Studio 2005

- TlbImp.exe

Strictly speaking, you can also use some of the services available in the *System.Runtime.InteropServices* namespace, but doing so is cumbersome and error prone. For the sake of this lesson, we'll focus on the two approaches just listed.

Using Visual Studio 2005 to Import a Type

With one minor exception, importing a COM library is virtually indistinguishable from importing any other type. The exception is that most of the DLLs you reference will be located on the COM tab of the Add Reference dialog box, as illustrated in Figure 13-1.

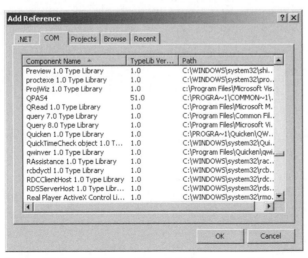

Figure 13-1   COM tab of the Add Reference dialog box

All registered COM components will be visible here, so simply do the following to finalize the process:

1. Create a new blank solution named COMDemos.

2. Create a new Visual Basic 2005 or C# 2005 project, and name it TypeDemo.

3. Right-click the TypeDemo project in Solution Explorer, and click Add Reference. In the Add Reference dialog box, click the COM tab.

4. Find the component you want to register, and click OK.

After you have followed the steps just shown, the component should be imported and referenced. If the component has been registered correctly, it will be visible on the COM tab.

Using TlbImp.exe to Import a Type

Using the Type Library Importer utility (TlbImp.exe) is a little more intricate but still quite straightforward. To import a library using the TlbImp.exe, do the following:

1. Open the Visual Studio 2005 command prompt.

2. Navigate to the location of the DLL you want to import.

3. Type **tlbimp** *<dllname>***.dll**

    This will import the DLL and create a .NET assembly with its original name. For example, Person.dll will be imported as Person.dll, MyObject will be imported as MyObject.dll, and so forth.

4. If you want a name to be used other than the original DLL name, type **tlbimp** *<dllname>***.dll /out:***<DesiredName>***.dll**.

Now add a reference to the assembly name you chose just as you would for any other .NET assembly. The important thing to remember is that TlbImp.exe is creating a new assembly for you from the COM library. So now you have a brand new .NET assembly, and it will be visible only under the .NET tab of the Add Reference dialog box.

Although it would be almost fair to say that either of the preceding approaches is all that you need to know about the subject, that wouldn't be entirely true. One area in particular might give you a lot of headaches, mainly because of the inherent differences between Visual Basic 2005 and C#. C# doesn't support optional parameters whereas Visual Basic 2005 does. So what's the problem? COM components don't support parameter overloading, so for each value in a parameter list, you've got to pass in something, even if it does nothing. Moreover, COM parameters are always passed by reference, which means that you can't pass in a null value.

In Visual Basic 2005, this isn't really an issue because many of these parameters are optional and you can just leave them out (or include them) as you see fit. C# doesn't support this, though, so you have to create object variables (remember, they can't be null) and then pass them in. This approach is problematic for the following reasons:

■ It leads to unnecessary and confusing code.

■ In many instances, it leads to code that's virtually unreadable. (Imagine a 15-item parameter list, for instance.)

To address this problem, a new feature of the *Type* class has been provided: *Type.Missing*. Examine the following code samples:

```
' VB
Imports Microsoft.Office.Core
Imports Microsoft.Office.Interop.Excel ' Must have Office installed for this demo
Dim NewExcelApp As New Microsoft.Office.Interop.Excel.Application
'This works fine
NewExcelApp.Worksheets.Add()
```

```
// C#
using Microsoft.Office.Core;
using Microsoft.Office.Interop.Excel; // Must have Office installed for this demo
Application NewExcelApp = new Application();
// This will not compile.
NewExcelApp.Worksheets.Add();
```

Instead of creating "dummy" object variables, the *Type.Missing* field can be used. That field can be passed in with the C# code and the application will work as expected. In a pure sense, this approach is unnecessary in Visual Basic 2005 because of optional parameter support; however, many consider the use of optional parameters problematic and avoid them. (Optional parameters are included in this book for consistency.)

BEST PRACTICES   Avoiding optional parameters

There are many reasons to avoid Visual Basic's optional parameter feature, although this is an area that's frequently disputed. The primary reason to avoid them, in my opinion, is that they aren't supported in all .NET languages. Developers who didn't know Visual Basic and were trying to translate the code would have a difficult time—they'd wonder why something worked in one context and not the other. Similarly, many argue that optional parameters are remnants of the previous non-.NET Visual Basic and, as such, should be avoided.

Here is an example of using the *Type.Missing* field:

```
' VB
Module Module1
    Private OptionalParamHandler As Object = Type.Missing
    Sub Main()
        Dim NewExcelApp As New Microsoft.Office.Interop.Excel.Application
        NewExcelApp.Worksheets.Add(OptionalParamHandler, _
            OptionalParamHandler, OptionalParamHandler, _
            OptionalParamHandler)
    End Sub
End Module

// C#
class Program
    {
        private static Object OptionalParamHandler = Type.Missing;

        static void Main(string[] args)
        {
            Application NewExcelApp = new Application();
            NewExcelApp.Worksheets.Add(OptionalParamHandler,
                OptionalParamHandler, OptionalParamHandler,
                OptionalParamHandler);
        }
    }
```

This approach accomplishes two things: it allows the code to work in C#, and it makes the code more intelligible. (No one will have to guess why you created objects that never get used for any apparent reason.)

Tools Used by COM Interop

Both the .NET Framework 2.0 and Visual Studio 2005 provide multiple tools that are used by COM Interop. The .NET tools and their uses are explained in Table 13-1.

Table 13-1   Tools for Managing COM Interop from .NET

Name	Description	Application Name
Type Library Importer	Imports a new .NET assembly based on the COM component	TlbImp.exe
Type Library Exporter	Creates a COM type library that can be consumed by a COM application	TlbExp.exe

Table 13-1 Tools for Managing COM Interop from .NET

Name	Description	Application Name
Registry Editor	All COM components must have an entry in the Windows registry. Although not exclusive to COM Interop, the Registry Editor allows you to search for and manage existing registry entries.	Regedit.exe
Intermediate Language Disassembler	Although not exclusive to COM Interop, this tool enables you to view a visual representation of the Intermediate Language (IL).	Ildasm.exe
Assembly Registration Tool	Enables you to add .NET assemblies to and remove .NET assemblies from the system registration database.	Regasm.exe

NOTE Portability

Platforms other than Windows that the .NET Framework has been ported to (such as Linux and Macintosh) do not have a Registry. These tools are available only with Windows.

Using COM Objects in Code

After the steps in the "Importing Type Libraries" section have been performed, using an object contained in a given library is virtually identical to using one created purely in .NET. In the following example, the Adobe Acrobat Reader 7.0 Browser Document COM component will be used to open and read a .pdf file. If you don't have Adobe Acrobat Reader 7.0 installed, it's available for free at *http://www.adobe.com/products/ acrobat/readstep2_allversions.html*. For the sake of simplicity, add the Adobe PDF Reader component to your toolbox and drag the component onto a Windows form. (Detailed instructions for how to do this are provided in the "Lab" section at the end of this lesson.)

```vb
' VB
AxAcroPDF1.LoadFile("SamplePDFDocument.pdf")
AxAcroPDF1.Print()
```

```csharp
// C#
axAcroPDF1.LoadFile(@"SamplePDFDocument.pdf");
axAcroPDF1.Print();
```

This might seem surprisingly easy. It certainly did to me when I first encountered it. And after a type is imported, that's all there is to it. At first glance, it might not seem obvious why that is. However, think about what happens when a DLL is imported. A new .NET assembly is created from it. From your code's perspective, there's no notion of where the code originated, so it makes perfect sense that the behavior would seem identical.

Handling Exceptions in COM Interop

Dealing with exceptions is one area that has changed drastically (albeit transparently in many instances) with regard to consuming COM objects in .NET 2.0. In prior versions of the Framework, *System.Exception* sat at the top of the *Exception* object hierarchy chain. This meant that that trapping a *System.Exception* object would catch anything wrong in an application. Well, not exactly. Although this is a widely held belief, it's a misconception. What *System.Exception* would handle is any Common Language Specification (CLS)-compliant exception. Because your COM errors won't be CLS compliant, they won't be caught. Because so many developers mistakenly understood the behavior of trapping *System.Exception*, quite a bit of unstable code and code with serious potential security implications was developed.

In version 2.0 of the .NET Framework, the *RuntimeWrappedException* class was introduced into the *System.Runtime.CompilerServices* namespace. Table 13-2 lists the properties of the *RuntimeWrappedException,* from the MSDN documentation.

Table 13-2 *RuntimeWrappedException* Properties

Name	Description
Data	Gets a collection of key/value pairs that provide additional, user-defined information about the exception
HelpLink	Gets or sets a link to the help file associated with this exception
InnerException	Gets the *Exception* instance that caused the current exception
Message	Gets a message that describes the current exception
Source	Gets or sets the name of the application or object that caused the error
StackTrace	Gets a string representation of the frames on the call stack at the time the current exception was thrown

Table 13-2 *RuntimeWrappedException* **Properties**

Name	Description
TargetSite	Gets the method that throws the current exception
WrappedException	Gets the object that was wrapped by the *RuntimeWrapped-Exception* object

With the exception (no pun intended) of *WrappedException*, each of these properties is inherited from the *System.Exception* class. So the main distinction is the *Wrapped-Exception* property, which is of type *Object*. Why does all this matter? Under the .NET Framework 2.0, when a non-CLS-compliant exception is thrown, the common language runtime (CLR) creates an instance of this class and then sets the *Wrapped-Exception* property to the object that was thrown. This behavior is handled by default and is transparent to the developer, but it's important to be aware of. The following code illustrates this behavior.

```vb
' VB
Private Sub IllustrateExceptions()
    Try
        ' Something that throws an exception
    Catch ex As Exception
        ' In the previous versions this will catch only CLS-Compliant
        ' In the current version both CLS and Non CLS-Compliant will
        ' be caught by this block.
    End Try ' There is no equivalent for Catch without an exception
            ' because it's considered unreachable.
End Sub
```

```csharp
// C#
private static void IllustrateExceptions()
{
    try
    {
        // Something that throws an exception
    }
    catch (Exception ex)
    {
        // In the previous versions this will catch only CLS-Compliant
        // In the current version both CLS and Non CLS-Compliant will
        // be caught by this block.
    }
    catch
    {
        // All exceptions, CLS-Compliant and Non CLS-Compliant are caught
    }
}
```

To turn off this behavior, you can use the *RuntimeCompatibility* attribute, as illustrated here:

```
' VB
Imports System.Runtime.CompilerServices
<Assembly: RuntimeCompatibility(WrapNonExceptionThrows:=False)>

// C#
using System.Runtime.CompilerServices;
[assembly: RuntimeCompatibility(WrapNonExceptionThrows=false)]
```

MORE INFO   **Exception management**

Exception management in COM Interop applications is discussed further in the "Exception Handling in Managed Code" section of Lesson 3.

Limitations of COM Interop

Since the advent of .NET, there have been some shortcomings with using COM Interop, and they are largely related to inherent differences (improvements, in my opinion) that .NET has compared to previous development methodologies. Following is a list of these shortcomings:

- **Static/shared members**   COM objects are fundamentally different from .NET types. One of the differences is lack of support for static/shared members.

- **Parameterized constructors**   COM types don't allow parameters to be passed into a constructor. This limits the control you have over initialization and the use of overloaded constructors.

- **Inheritance**   One of the biggest issues is the limitations COM objects place on the inheritance chain. Members that shadow members in a base class aren't recognizable, and therefore, aren't callable or usable in any real sense.

- **Portability**   Operating systems other than Windows don't have a registry. Reliance on the Windows registry limits the number of environments a .NET application can be ported to.

Lab: Use a COM Application from .NET

In this lab, you create an application that consumes an Adobe PDF Reader COM component (or any other component that you prefer). If you encounter a problem completing an exercise, the completed projects are available on the companion CD in the Code folder.

1. Open Visual Studio 2005, and create a new C# or Visual Basic 2005 Winforms application.

2. Name the project TypeDemo.

3. From the main menu, select Tools, Choose Toolbox Items. A dialog box appears that has two or more tabs. On the COM Components tab, select the Adobe PDF Reader component and click OK.

4. Open Form1 in Design view and drag a new Adobe PDF Reader component onto the form. By default, this component will be named AxAcroPDF1 (VB) or axAcroPDF1 (C#).

5. Double-click Form1.cs or Form1.vb to automatically register the *Load* event for the form and go to the code window. Add the following code to the *Form_Load* event, adding the path to the SamplePDFDocument.pdf document, which is located in the \Code\Chapter13 folder on the companion CD.

```
' VB
AxAcroPDF1.LoadFile("SamplePDFDocument.pdf")
AxAcroPDF1.Print()

// C#
axAcroPDF1.LoadFile(@"SamplePDFDocument.pdf");
axAcroPDF1.Print();
```

6. Build the project, and resolve any errors. If everything works correctly, a window similar to the one shown in Figure 13-2 will appear and you can print the PDF document.

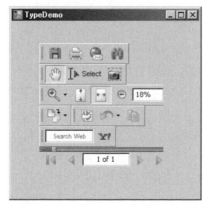

Figure 13-2   The TypeDemo window

Lesson Summary

- COM components can easily be consumed in a .NET application, although the reasons for doing so need to be carefully considered.

- You can use the COM tab of the Add Reference dialog box to add a reference to registered COM components.

- The TlbImp.exe tool is a command-line mechanism to import a COM component.

- The *out* switch of the TlbImp.exe tool can be used to change the name of the assembly that will be imported from its original name to a preferred one.

- The default behavior when catching *System.Exception* objects now catches both CLS-compliant and non-CLS-compliant exceptions.

- The *RuntimeCompatibilty* attribute can be used to change whether non-CLS-compliant exceptions will be trapped by default.

Lesson Review

You can use the following questions to test your knowledge of the information in Lesson 1, "Using COM Objects." The questions are also available on the companion CD if you prefer to review them in electronic form.

NOTE Answers

Answers to these questions and explanations of why each answer choice is right or wrong are located in the "Answers" section at the end of the book.

---

1. Which methods allow COM components to be used in .NET applications? (Choose all that apply.)

   A. Add a reference to the component through Microsoft Visual Studio 2005.

   B. Use the Type Library Import tool (TlbImport.exe).

   C. Use the Regsvr32 tool.

   D. Ensure that the application is registered, using the RegSvr tool if necessary. Then either add a reference to it from the COM tab of the Add Reference dialog box or use TblImp.exe.

2. How should non-CLS-compliant exceptions be trapped when running under the .NET Framework 2.0? (Choose all that apply.)

   A. Trap an instance of the *ApplicationException*.

    B. Trap an instance of *System.Exception*, and set the *RuntimeCompatibilty* attribute to false.

    C. Simply trap an instance of a *System.Exception* object.

    D. Trap an instance of *System.Exception*, and set the *RuntimeCompatibilty* attribute to true.

3. Which items are generally considered shortcomings associated with using COM Interop? (Choose all that apply.)

    A. Lack of support for Shared members (in Visual Basic) and Static members (in C#)

    B. Inability to use parameterized constructors

    C. Limited portability between different operating systems

    D. Limited ability to use inheritance hierarchies

4. Which tools can be used to manipulate COM Interop? (Choose all that apply.)

    A. Intermediate Language Disassembler (Ildasm.exe).

    B. The .NET Framework 2.0 Configuration Tool.

    C. Type Library Importer (TlbImp.exe).

    D. The Windows Registry Editor.

Lesson 2: Exposing .NET Components to COM

So far, we've focused on getting at COM data from within a .NET context. Now we're going to examine the mirror opposite, exposing .NET components to COM.

After this lesson, you will be able to:

■ Build a .NET component that can be consumed by COM

■ Hide public data from COM components

■ Deploy COM-enabled assemblies

Estimated lesson time: 20 minutes

Building .NET Components for Use by COM

Just as COM components can be consumed by .NET applications, the reverse is true. When .NET components are consumed by COM, a proxy known as a COM Callable Wrapper (CCW) handles marshaling items between .NET and COM.

NOTE   COM Callable Wrapper behavior

No matter how many COM clients consume a given managed object, the .NET runtime will create only one CCW.

There's one additional step that needs to be performed for components that will be consumed by COM versus ones that won't. To accomplish this task from start to finish, perform the following steps:

1. Create a .NET class library just like you normally would.

2. Open the Project Properties dialog box by right-clicking the project and selecting Properties.

3. Click the Build tab, which is located on the right side of the dialog box.

4. Select the Register For COM Interop option in the Output section of the tab, as shown in Figure 13-3.

5. Build the application.

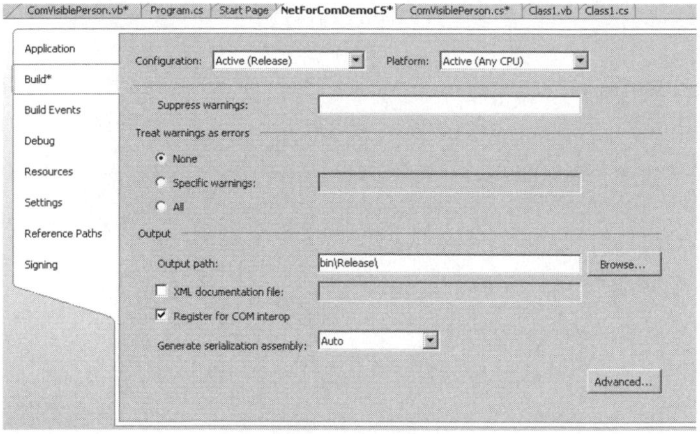

Figure 13-3 Project properties manager

After the project is built, the necessary type library information will be created by Visual Studio 2005, which will also register each of the objects as COM objects for you. The following listing is an example of code you might use in your project to create a .NET component that can be used by COM.

```vb
' VB
Public Class ComVisiblePerson
    Private _firstName As String
    Private _lastName As String

    Public Property FirstName() As String
        Get
            Return Me._firstName
        End Get
        Set(ByVal value As String)
            Me._firstName = value
        End Set
    End Property

    Public Property LastName() As String
        Get
            Return Me._lastName
        End Get
        Set(ByVal value As String)
            Me._lastName = value
        End Set
    End Property
End Class
```

```
// C#
namespace NetForComDemoCS
{
    class ComVisiblePerson
    {

        private String firstName;
        private String lastName;

        public String FirstName
        {
            get { return firstName; }
            set { firstName = value; }
        }

        public String LastName
        {
            get { return lastName; }
            set { lastName = value; }
        }
    }
}
```

If you compile the application with the code just shown and there are no errors, the assembly will be visible to COM.

Hiding Public .NET Classes from COM

The first thing you need to be aware of when considering visibility is whether you want everything to be visible or invisible (making everything invisible makes little sense) and the level of granularity of this visibility.

To set COM Visibility to either On or Off by default, simply set the *ComVisible Assembly* attribute to true or false, respectively.

```
' VB
<Assembly: ComVisible(False)> ' Visibility disabled by default
```

```
// C#
[assembly: ComVisible(false)]
```

Next, for each class and each member that you want to have visible or invisible, simply use the *ComVisible* attribute individually for each of them:

```
' VB
Imports System.Runtime.CompilerServices
Imports System.Runtime.InteropServices

<ComVisible(False)> _
Public Class ComVisiblePerson
  Private _firstName As String
```

```vb
    Private _lastName As String
    Private _salary As Int32

    <ComVisible(True)> _
    Public Property FirstName() As String
      Get
         Return Me._firstName
      End Get
      Set(ByVal value As String)
        Me._firstName = value
      End Set
    End Property

      <ComVisible(True)> _
    Public Property LastName() As String
      Get
        Return Me._lastName
      End Get
      Set(ByVal value As String)
        Me._lastName = value
      End Set
    End Property

    <ComVisible(False)> _
    Public Property Salary() As Int32
      Get
        Return Me._salary
      End Get
      Set(ByVal value As Int32)
        Me._salary = value
      End Set
    End Property
End Class

// C#
using System.Runtime.CompilerServices;
using System.Runtime.InteropServices;

namespace NetForComDemoCS
{
    [ComVisible(false)]
    class ComVisiblePerson
    {

        private String firstName;
        private String lastName;
        private Int32 salary;

        [ComVisible(true)]
        public String FirstName
        {
            get { return firstName; }
            set { firstName = value; }
```

```
        }

        [ComVisible(true)]
        public String LastName
        {
            get { return lastName; }
            set { lastName = value; }
        }

        [ComVisible(false)]
        public Int32 Salary
        {
            get { return salary; }
            set { salary = value; }
        }
    }
}
```

Deploying COM-Enabled Assemblies

Although an assembly can be created visible to COM, the MSDN documentation provides the following guidelines to ensure that things work as planned:

- All classes must use a default constructor with no parameters.

- Any type that is to be exposed must be public.

- Any member that is to be exposed must be public.

- Abstract classes will not be able to be consumed.

After these criteria are met, the assembly is essentially ready to be exported. There are two mechanisms for doing this. As with many other tasks, you can use either Visual Studio 2005 or a command-line utility (TlbExp.exe). First, you need to compile the type through Visual Studio's build mechanism or through the command-line compiler. Here is an example:

```
' VB
vbc /t:library ComVisiblePerson.vb

// C#
csc /t:library ComVisiblePerson.cs
```

Next you need to use the Type Library Exporter Utility. This should be done from the Visual Studio 2005 command prompt:

```
tlbexp ComVisiblePerson.dll /out:ComVisiblePersonlib.tlb
```

Next you need to create a resource script (ComVisiblePerson.res) with the following statement:

```
IDR_TYPELIB1 typelib "ComVisiblePersonlib.tlb"
```

To generate the resource file, you compile the script by using the Resource Compiler, as shown here:

```
rc ComVisiblePersonLib.res
```

Then you recompile the assembly with the type library embedded as a Win32 resource file, as shown here:

```
' VB
vbc /t:library ComVisiblePerson.vb /win32res:ComVisiblePersonLib.res
```

```
// C#
csc /t:library ComVisiblePerson.cs /win32res:ComVisiblePersonLib.res
```

Lab: Build a COM-Enabled Assembly

In this lab, you create a simple .NET assembly and class that can be consumed by a COM component. If you encounter a problem completing an exercise, the completed projects are available on the companion CD in the Code folder.

NOTE Additional code on CD

The files for this lab on the companion CD contain additional code not shown here.

---

1. Open Visual Studio 2005, and create a new C# or Visual Basic 2005 Class Library project.

2. Create a class called *ComVisiblePerson*, or rename the existing Class1 class.

3. Replace the code in the *ComVisiblePerson* class with the following code:

```
' VB
Imports System.Runtime.CompilerServices
Imports System.Runtime.InteropServices
<ComVisible(False)> _
Public Class ComVisiblePerson
  Private _firstName As String
  Private _lastName As String
  Private _salary As Int32

  <ComVisible(True)> _
  Public Property FirstName() As String
    Get
      Return Me._firstName
    End Get
```

```vbnet
      Set(ByVal value As String)
        Me._firstName = value
      End Set
    End Property

    <ComVisible(True)> _
    Public Property LastName() As String
      Get
        Return Me._lastName
      End Get
      Set(ByVal value As String)
        Me._lastName = value
      End Set
    End Property

    <ComVisible(False)> _
    Public Property Salary() As Int32
      Get
        Return Me._salary
      End Get
      Set(ByVal value As Int32)
        Me._salary = value
      End Set
    End Property
End Class
```

```csharp
// C#
using System;
using System.Runtime.CompilerServices;
using System.Runtime.InteropServices;

namespace NetForComDemo
{
  [ComVisible(false)]
  class ComVisiblePerson
  {
    private String firstName;
    private String lastName;
    private Int32 salary;

    [ComVisible(true)]
    public String FirstName
    {
      get
      {
        return firstName;
      }
      set
      {
        firstName = value;
      }
    }
```

```
[ComVisible(true)]
public String LastName
{
  get
  {
    return lastName;
  }
  set
  {
    lastName = value;
  }
}

[ComVisible(false)]
public Int32 Salary
{
  get
  {
    return salary;
  }
  set
  {
    salary = value;
  }
}
  }
}
```

4. Right-click the project, and select the Properties option.

5. Click the Compile (VB) or Build (C#) page, and select the Register For COM Interop option.

6. On the Debug tab of the project Properties dialog box, select the Release Configuration option.

7. Build the project, and resolve any errors.

The output DLL is now able to be consumed by a COM-based application.

Lesson Summary

- The Register For COM Interop option under the build configuration automates the process of exposing .NET assemblies to COM components.

- The primary mechanism for exposing .NET assemblies to COM components is the *ComVisible* attribute.

- The *ComVisible* attribute can be set to apply to an entire assembly, an entire class, or individual members.

■ The more granular the application of the *ComVisible* attribute, the more it takes precedence. A class, for example, can be marked with *ComVisible* set to false and with a given member set to true. The member that is set to true will be visible to COM components.

Lesson Review

You can use the following questions to test your knowledge of the information in Lesson 2, "Exposing .NET Components to COM." The questions are also available on the companion CD if you prefer to review them in electronic form.

NOTE Answers

Answers to these questions and explanations of why each answer choice is right or wrong are located in the "Answers" section at the end of the book.

---

1. What is necessary to make a .NET assembly visible to a COM component? (Choose all that apply.)

   A. Set the Register For COM option under the build configuration.

   B. Set the *ComVisible* attribute to true for each class you want exposed.

   C. Set the *ComVisible* attribute to false for any class members you want hidden.

   D. Set the *ComVisible* attribute to true for any class members that you want visible.

2. Which tool can be used to create a COM consumable type?

   A. TlbImp.exe

   B. TlbExp.exe

   C. Regedit.exe

   D. csc.exe

3. Which of the following choices is true with respect to making types available to COM components?

   A. A default constructor with no parameters should be used.

   B. Class definitions can be marked public or private.

   C. Members can be marked public or private.

   D. Both concrete and abstract classes can be used.

Lesson 3: Using Unmanaged Code

As mentioned previously, the .NET Framework provides an abundance of functionality, but there are areas that have not yet been wrapped for .NET. This is the case with legacy code obviously, but it is also the case with Windows API functionality. With each new version of the Framework, the number of Windows APIs that aren't wrapped gets smaller, but gaps still exist. In this lesson, you will learn how to bridge those gaps.

After this lesson, you will be able to:

■ Use Platform Invoke (P/Invoke) to access unmanaged code.

■ Encapsulate DLL functions.

■ Convert data types between managed and unmanaged code.

Estimated lesson time: 20 minutes

Calling Platform Invoke

Platform Invoke, or P/Invoke as it's commonly called, is critical in many instances where, for example, you need to call an unmanaged Windows API. If the .NET Framework doesn't have an existing wrapper and you don't have legacy code to do something, P/Invoke is often the only viable solution.

NOTE Use cases for Windows API calls

With respect to the Windows API, the following list provides typical use case scenarios:

■ Functionality specific to the Windows operating system, context switching, and file I/O.

■ Advanced manipulation of windows, menus, dialog boxes, and icons. For example, if you want to customize a *MessageBox* outside of what the .NET Framework provides, the only way to do it is through the Windows API.

■ Advanced drawing functionality.

You manage P/Invoke through the *System.Runtime.InteropServices* namespace, just as you would manage other unmanaged code. To use P/Invoke, you do the following:

1. Create a new static/shared external method with the name of the function you want to call.

2. Decorate it with the *DllImport* attribute specifying the library that it should call.

3. Call the method from your code.

In the following example, we're going to use the *GetWindowText* Windows API. To do this, we need to ensure that we are accurately referencing the active window running on the operating system, which might not be our application.

```vb
' VB
Imports System.Text
Imports System.Runtime.InteropServices

Public Class WindowExample
  Private Const BufferSize As Int32 = 256

  <DllImport("user32.dll")> _
  Private Shared Function GetForegroundWindow() As IntPtr
  End Function

  <DllImport("user32.dll")> _
  Private Shared Function GetWindowText(ByVal hWnd As IntPtr, _
    ByVal textValue As StringBuilder, ByVal counter As Int32) As Int32

  End Function

  Public Shared Sub GetScreenDemo()
    Dim DemoBuilder As New StringBuilder(BufferSize)
    Dim DemoHandle As IntPtr = GetForegroundWindow()

    If GetWindowText(DemoHandle, DemoBuilder, BufferSize) > 0 Then
      Console.WriteLine(DemoBuilder.ToString())
    End If
  End Sub
End Class
```

```csharp
// C#
using System.Runtime.InteropServices;
class WindowExample
{
  private const Int32 BufferSize = 256;

  [DllImport("user32.dll")]
  private static extern IntPtr GetForegroundWindow();

  [DllImport("user32.dll")]
  private static extern Int32 GetWindowText(IntPtr hWnd,
    StringBuilder textValue, Int32 counter);

  public static void GetScreenDemo()
  {
    StringBuilder DemoBuilder = new StringBuilder(BufferSize);
    IntPtr DemoHandle = GetForegroundWindow();

    if (GetWindowText(DemoHandle, DemoBuilder, BufferSize) > 0)
    {
      Console.WriteLine(DemoBuilder.ToString());
    }
```

```
    }
}
```

BEST PRACTICES   *StringBuilder* objects are preferable to *String* objects in P/Invoke calls

When using Platform Invoke, use a *StringBuilder* object instead of a *String*. A *StringBuilder* is a reference type with no atypical behavior and is needed because of the way P/Invoke internals work.

Encapsulating DLL Functions

Because P/Invoke calls can be less than elegant, at least in terms of what most .NET developers are accustomed to doing, it's often beneficial to create a class that exposes them and wraps this functionality. After all, much of the .NET Framework is composed of precisely this methodology. This approach has the following benefits:

- Consumers of your class will not know this code from any other "normal" code they are used to dealing with.

- It relieves developers of having to remember the API call names and their respective parameters. You can create it once and then use it like any other .NET method.

- It will be less error prone. Even slight typing differences can cause P/Invoke calls to break. Even if you are a perfect typist and never forget anything, it's doubtful that everyone you work with will have the same capability. And if they don't, they will invariable type something incorrectly, miss a parameter, or forget the name of something.

Assume that we are using the *WindowsExample* class shown in the previous section. Wrapping it so that it can be used like a "normal" .NET class is already taken care of. Instead of repetitiously writing the code in the *GetScreenDemo* method each time you need that functionality, you can simply do the following:

```
' VB
WindowExample.GetScreenDemo()
```

```
// C#
WindowExample.GetScreenDemo();
```

Converting Data Types

Chances are that if you've created even a rudimentary .NET application you've converted data from one type to another. Perhaps the most common conversion is the *ToString()* method. Every time you call *ToString()*, you are taking a given object and converting it to its *String* representation. In fully managed applications, you can specify conversion functionality by using the *TypeConverter* class. When using unmanaged code, however, you typically need to take a different approach.

The first mechanism for converting data types is the *MarshalAs* attribute. *MarshalAs* can be applied to a property or a parameter. Either way, it works essentially the same. You simply create your property, decorate it with the *MarshalAs* attribute, and then specify the type it should be converted from, as shown here:

```vb
' VB
Imports System.Runtime.CompilerServices
Imports System.Runtime.InteropServices

Public Class MarshalAsDemo

    <MarshalAs(UnmanagedType.LPStr)> _
    Public FirstName As String
    Public LastName As String
    <MarshalAs(UnmanagedType.Bool)> _
    Public IsCurrentlyWorking As Boolean

End Class
```

```csharp
// C#
using System.Runtime.CompilerServices;
using System.Runtime.InteropServices;

namespace NetForComDemoCS
{
    class MarshalAsDemo
    {
        [MarshalAs(UnmanagedType.LPStr)]
        public String FirstName;
        public String LastName;
        [MarshalAs(UnmanagedType.Bool)]
        public Boolean IsCurrentlyWorking;
    }
}
```

One convenient feature of using this attribute is that it has full Microsoft IntelliSense support, so you can find the equivalent data type much more easily.

Just as this attribute can be applied to a method or property, it can be applied to a parameter as well. The following code shows the same sample with the *LastName* property converted to a function that takes a *String* type named *firstName*:

```vb
' VB
Imports System.Runtime.CompilerServices
Imports System.Runtime.InteropServices
```

```
Public Class MarshalAsDemo
  <MarshalAs(UnmanagedType.LPStr)> _
  Public FirstName As String

  Public Function LastName( _
    <MarshalAs(UnmanagedType.LPStr)> ByVal firstName As String) As String
  End Function

  <MarshalAs(UnmanagedType.Bool)> _
  Public IsCurrentlyWorking As Boolean
End Class

// C#
using System.Runtime.CompilerServices;
using System.Runtime.InteropServices;


namespace NetForComDemoCS
{
    class MarshalAsDemo
    {
        [MarshalAs(UnmanagedType.LPStr)]
        public String FirstName;
        public String LastName(
        [MarshalAs(UnmanagedType.LPStr)] String firstName) { }
        [MarshalAs(UnmanagedType.Bool)]
        public Boolean IsCurrentlyWorking;
    }
}
```

Marshaling Structures

Structures are commonly used in many Windows APIs and methods that you will use through P/Invoke. So to understand how the unmanaged structures are marshaled, it's worth a brief discussion of how managed types are handled as well.

Performance is a major objective of the CLR and, as a general rule, it's safe to assume that the CLR will optimize performance wherever it can. Types provide the best illustration. When the *Type* class is created, its developer can lay out the class's members however she sees fit. Typically, you'll see members arranged in an aesthetically pleasing and logical manner. "Aesthetically pleasing" and "logical," however, are subjective assessments. What's logical and intuitive to one developer might be quite different to another. Microsoft has published standards for library developers, and most companies have a set of rules that developers are encouraged to conform to. However, compliance to such standards largely remains the responsibility of the developer.

MORE INFO Suggestions for code library developers

Tools such as Microsoft FX Cop (which can be found at *http://www.gotdotnet.com/team/fxcop/*) can help ensure compliance to standards.

Microsoft has a set of recommended rules for library developers, and they are available at *http://www.gotdotnet.com/team/libraries/*.

By default, when a type is created, the CLR will decide how best to arrange the class's members. To manually direct the CLR about how to handle (or not handle) the layout of a type, the *System.Runtime.InteropServices.StructLayoutAttribute* attribute is provided. Table 13-3 lists the definition of the *StructLayoutAttribute* from the MSDN documentation.

Table 13-3 *StructLayoutAttribute* Definition

Name	Scope/Definition	Description
StructLayoutAttribute Constructor		
StructLayoutAttribute	Public/Constructor	Overloaded. Initializes a new instance of the *StructLayout Attribute* class.
StructLayoutAttribute Public Fields		
CharSet	Public/Field	Indicates how string data fields within the class should be marshaled as *LPWSTR* or *LPSTR*. (The default is *LPSTR*.)
Pack	Public/Field	Controls the alignment of data fields of a class or structure in memory.
Size	Public/Field	Indicates the absolute size of the class or structure.

Table 13-3 *StructLayoutAttribute* Definition

Name	Scope/Definition	Description
StructLayoutAttribute Public Properties		
TypeId	Public/Property	When implemented in a derived class, gets a unique identifier for this attribute. (Inherited from the *Attribute* class.)
Value	Public/Property	Gets the *LayoutKind* value that specifies how the class or structure is arranged.
StructLayoutAttribute Public Methods		
Equals	Public/Method	Overloaded. (Inherited from the *Attribute* class.)
GetCustomAttribute	Public/Method	Overloaded. Retrieves a custom attribute of a specified type applied to an assembly, module, type member, or method parameter. (Inherited from the *Attribute* class.)
GetCustomAttributes	Public/Method	Overloaded. Retrieves an array of the custom attributes applied to an assembly, module, type member, or method parameter. (Inherited from the *Attribute* class.)
GetHashCode	Public/Method	Returns the hash code for this instance. (Inherited from the *Attribute* class.)

Table 13-3   *StructLayoutAttribute* Definition

Name	Scope/Definition	Description
GetType	Public/Method	Gets the type of the current instance. (Inherited from the *Object* class.)
IsDefaultAttribute	Public/Method	When overridden in a derived class, indicates whether the value of this instance is the default value for the derived class. (Inherited from the *Attribute* class.)
IsDefined	Public/Method	Overloaded. Determines whether any custom attributes of a specified type are applied to an assembly, module, type member, or method parameter. (Inherited from the *Attribute* class.)
Match	Public/Method	When overridden in a derived class, returns a value that indicates whether this instance equals a specified object. (Inherited from the *Attribute* class.)
ReferenceEquals	Public/Method	Determines whether the specified object instances are the same instance. (Inherited from *Object* class.)
ToString	Public/Method	Returns a string that represents the current object. (Inherited from the *Object* class.)

Arguably the most important aspect of using the *StructLayoutAttribute* attribute is the constructor, which takes one of the following three values:

- *LayoutKind.Auto*   Causes the developer to relinquish all control over the layout to the CLR
- *LayoutKind.Sequential*   Causes the CLR to preserve the layout specified by the developer

- **LayoutKind.Explicit**   Causes the CLR to use the layout explicitly specified by the developer by using memory offsets

---

NOTE   Make sure the correct layout is used for structures

By default, the CLR will use *LayoutKind.Auto* for *Reference* types and use *LayoutKind.Sequential* for value types. Because this section of the book is about structures, *LayoutKind.Sequential* is used by default.

For the sake of illustration, we are going to use the *OSVersionInfo* structure, which is used to provide information about the *OperatingSystemVersion*.

LayoutKind.Sequential

The first method to use is the *LayoutKind.Sequential* option. This method indicates that structure values will appear exactly as they should in the called library:

```vb
' VB
Imports System.Runtime.CompilerServices
Imports System.Runtime.InteropServices
<StructLayout(LayoutKind.Sequential)> _
Public Class OSVersionInfo

    Public dwOSVersionInfoSize As Int32
    Public dwMajorVersion As Int32
    Public dwMinorVersion As Int32
    Public dwBuildNumber As Int32
    Public dwPlatformId As Int32
    <MarshalAs(UnmanagedType.ByValTStr, SizeConst:=128)> _
    Public szCSDVersion As String
End Class
```

```csharp
// C#
using System.Runtime.CompilerServices;
using System.Runtime.InteropServices;
namespace NetForComDemoCS
{
    [StructLayout(LayoutKind.Sequential)]
    class OSVersionInfo
    {
        public Int32 dwOSVersionInfoSize;
        public Int32 dwMajorVersion;
        public Int32 dwMinorVersion;
        public Int32 dwBuildNumber;
        public Int32 dwPlatformId;
        [MarshalAs(UnmanagedType.ByValTStr, SizeConst=128)]
        public String szCSDVersion;
    }
}
```

LayoutKind.Explicit

The other option is to use the Explicit mode. With this method, two things must be done:

- The *LayoutKind* enumeration needs to be set to Explicit.
- The offset in bytes must be specified for each field.

Other than these differences, using either approach is virtually indistinguishable from using *Sequential* layouts.

```
' VB
Imports System.Runtime.CompilerServices
Imports System.Runtime.InteropServices

<StructLayout(LayoutKind.Explicit)> _
Public Class OSVersionInfo

    <FieldOffset(0)> Public dwOSVersionInfoSize As Int32
    <FieldOffset(4)> Public dwMajorVersion As Int32
    <FieldOffset(8)> Public dwMinorVersion As Int32
    <FieldOffset(12)> Public dwBuildNumber As Int32
    <FieldOffset(16)> Public dwPlatformId As Int32
    <MarshalAs(UnmanagedType.ByValTStr, SizeConst:=128)> _
    <FieldOffset(20)> Public szCSDVersion As String
End Class

// C#
using System.Runtime.CompilerServices;
using System.Runtime.InteropServices;
namespace NetForComDemoCS
{
    [StructLayout(LayoutKind.Explicit)]
    class OSVersionInfo
    {
        [FieldOffset(0)]
        public Int32 dwOSVersionInfoSize;
        [FieldOffset(4)]
        public Int32 dwMajorVersion;
        [FieldOffset(8)]
        public Int32 dwMinorVersion;
        [FieldOffset(12)]
        public Int32 dwBuildNumber;
        [FieldOffset(16)]
        public Int32 dwPlatformId;
        [MarshalAs(UnmanagedType.ByValTStr, SizeConst = 128)]
        [FieldOffset(20)]
        public String szCSDVersion;
    }
}
```

Using a Callback with Unmanaged Code

Callback functions are an extremely important tool in any developer's library. Callbacks are used throughout the .NET Framework and Framework Class Library extensively, and most nontrivial applications will employ them in some fashion or another. Just as callbacks are important in a totally managed environment, they are also important in an unmanaged environment.

Traditionally, callbacks were implemented with pointers. This approach afforded a tremendous amount of power to the programmer, but it also had some inherent shortcomings, such as lack of type safety. To address this issue, the .NET Framework provides *Delegate* objects, which can be used to manage callbacks in a "type-safe" fashion.

MORE INFO Definition of *type safe*

Although the term *type safe* has different meanings in different environments, in general it refers to verification of a given type so that mismatches cannot present themselves. An in-depth discussion is available at Wikipedia (*http://en.wikipedia.org/wiki/Type_safety*).

To use *Delegate* objects correctly, perform the following steps:

1. Create a *Delegate* object with the same signature as the callback.

2. Substitute the *Delegate* for the callback, and make the call. The following listing is an example of using an unmanaged callback:

```vb
' VB
Imports System.Text
Imports System.Runtime.InteropServices
Imports System.Runtime.CompilerServices

Public Class UnmanagedCallbackDemo
  Public Delegate Function DemoCallback(ByVal hWnd As IntPtr, _
    ByVal lParam As Int32) As Boolean

  Private Const UserReference As String = "user32.dll"
  Private Const BufferSize As Int32 = 100

  <DllImport(UserReference)> _
  Public Shared Function EnumWindows(ByVal callback As DemoCallback, _
    ByVal param As Int32) As Int32
  End Function

  <DllImport(UserReference)> _
  Public Shared Function GetWindowText(ByVal hWnd As IntPtr, _
    ByVal lpString As StringBuilder, ByVal nMaxCount As Int32) As Int32
  End Function
```

```
      Public Shared Function DisplayWindowInfo(ByVal hWnd As IntPtr, _
        ByVal lParam As Int32) As Boolean

        Dim DemoBuilder As New StringBuilder(BufferSize)

        If GetWindowText(hWnd, DemoBuilder, BufferSize) <> 0 Then
          Console.WriteLine("Demo Output: " + DemoBuilder.ToString())
        End If

        Return True
    End Function

      Public Shared Sub RunDemo()
        EnumWindows(AddressOf DisplayWindowInfo, 0)
        Console.WriteLine("Beginning process...")
        Console.ReadLine()
      End Sub
    End Class

    // C#
    using System.Text;
    using System.Runtime.CompilerServices;
    using System.Runtime.InteropServices;

    namespace NetForComDemoCS
    {

        public class UnmanagedCallbackDemo
          {
              public delegate Boolean DemoCallback(IntPtr hWnd, Int32 lParam);

              private const String UserReference = "user32.dll";
              private const Int32 BufferSize = 100;

              [DllImport(UserReference)]
              public static extern Int32 EnumWindows(DemoCallback callback, Int32 param);
              [DllImport(UserReference)]
              public static extern Int32 GetWindowText(IntPtr hWnd,
                StringBuilder lpString, Int32 nMaxCount);

              public static Boolean DisplayWindowInfo(IntPtr hWnd, Int32 lParam)
              {
                StringBuilder DemoBuilder = new StringBuilder(BufferSize);

                if (GetWindowText(hWnd, DemoBuilder, BufferSize) != 0)
                {
                    Console.WriteLine("Demo Output: " + DemoBuilder.ToString());
                }
                return true;
              }

              public static void RunDemo()
              {
                EnumWindows(DisplayWindowInfo, 0);
                Console.WriteLine("Beginning process...");
```

```
        Console.ReadLine();
      }
    }
  }
```

When the application is run, the output should approximate that shown in Figure 13-4.

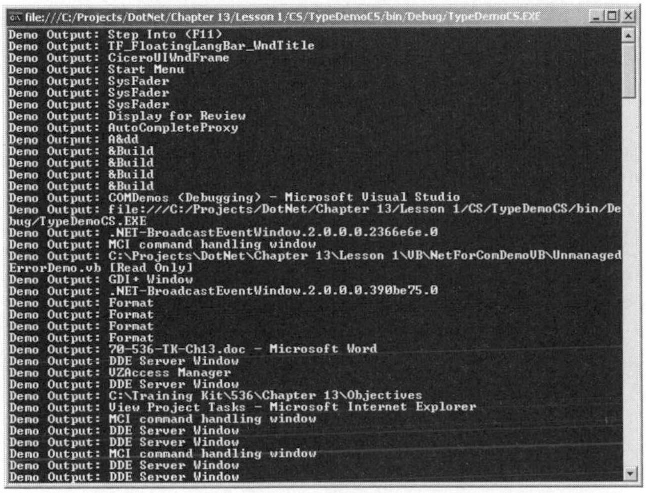

Figure 13-4   Output from unmanaged callback

Exception Handling in Managed Code

Exceptions in unmanaged code are markedly different from those thrown in managed code. In the earlier COM days, you could use the *GetLastError* function to get the last error that was raised. This approach won't work in a managed application because the return value of *GetLastError* might not be the correct one. Why? Because the *GetLast-Error* method can be set by either a .NET Framework object or the common language runtime (CLR).

Because you can't use the *GetLastError* method, you need to do something else. After all, the only thing more problematic than no exception handling is bad exception handling. Here is an example of error handling in managed code:

```vb
' VB
Imports System.Runtime.CompilerServices
Imports System.Runtime.InteropServices

Public Class UnmanagedErrorDemo
  Private Const KernelReference As String = "kernel32.dll"
  Private Const UserReference As String = "user32.dll"
  Private Const MessageSize As Int32 = 255

  <DllImport(KernelReference)> _
```

```vb
    Private Shared Function FormatMessage(ByVal dwFlags As Int32, _
        ByVal lpSource As Int32, ByVal dwMessageId As Int32, _
        ByVal dwLanguageId As Int32, ByRef lpBuffer As String, _
        ByVal nSize As Int32, ByVal Arguments As Int32) As Int32
    End Function

    <DllImport(UserReference, SetLastError:=True)> _
    Private Shared Function MessageBox(ByVal hWnd As Int32, _
        ByVal pText As String, ByVal pCaption As String, _
        ByVal uType As Int32) As Int32
    End Function

    Public Shared Sub ThrowMessageBoxException()
      Dim ProblemCauser As IntPtr = CType(-100, IntPtr)

      MessageBox(CType(ProblemCauser, Int32), "This won't work", _
        "Caption - This won't work", 0)

      Dim ErrorCode As Int32 = Marshal.GetLastWin32Error()

      Console.WriteLine("Error Code: " & ErrorCode.ToString())
      Console.WriteLine("Real Error: " & GetLastErrorMessage(ErrorCode))
    End Sub

    Public Shared Function GetLastErrorMessage( _
      ByVal errorValue As Int32) As String

      ' This order doesn't matter but should be kept
      ' for logical consistency
      Dim FORMAT_MESSAGE_ALLOCATE_BUFFER As Int32 = &H100
      Dim FORMAT_MESSAGE_IGNORE_INSERTS As Int32 = &H200
      Dim FORMAT_MESSAGE_FROM_SYSTEM As Int32 = &H1000
      Dim lpMsgBuf As String = String.Empty
      Dim dwFlags As Int32 = FORMAT_MESSAGE_ALLOCATE_BUFFER Or _
        FORMAT_MESSAGE_FROM_SYSTEM Or FORMAT_MESSAGE_IGNORE_INSERTS
      Dim ReturnValue As Int32 = FormatMessage(dwFlags, 0, errorValue, _
        0, lpMsgBuf, MessageSize, 0)

      If ReturnValue = 0 Then
          Return Nothing
      Else
          Return lpMsgBuf
      End If
    End Function
End Class

// C#
using System.Runtime.CompilerServices;
using System.Runtime.InteropServices;

namespace NetForComDemoCS
{
  public class UnmanagedErrorDemo
  {
```

```
private const String KernelReference = "kernel32.dll";
private const String UserReference = "user32.dll";
private const Int32 MessageSize = 255;

[DllImport(KernelReference)]
private static extern Int32 FormatMessage(Int32 dwFlags,
  Int32 lpSource, Int32 intdwMessageId, Int32 dwLanguageId,
  ref String lpBuffer, Int32 nSize, Int32 Arguments);

[DllImport(UserReference, SetLastError = true)]
private static extern Int32 MessageBox(IntPtr hWnd,
  String pText, String pCaption, Int32 uType);

public static void ThrowMessageBoxException()
{
  IntPtr ProblemCauser = (IntPtr) (-100);

  MessageBox(ProblemCauser, "This won't work",
    "Caption - This won't work", 0);

  Int32 ErrorCode = Marshal.GetLastWin32Error();

  Console.WriteLine("Error Code: " + ErrorCode.ToString());
  Console.WriteLine("Real Error: " +
    GetLastErrorMessage(ErrorCode));
}

public static String GetLastErrorMessage(Int32 errorValue)
{
  // This order doesn't matter but should be kept
  // for logical consistency
  Int32 FORMAT_MESSAGE_ALLOCATE_BUFFER = 0x00000100;
  Int32 FORMAT_MESSAGE_IGNORE_INSERTS = 0x00000200;
  Int32 FORMAT_MESSAGE_FROM_SYSTEM = 0x00001000;

  String lpMsgBuf = String.Empty;

  Int32 dwFlags = FORMAT_MESSAGE_ALLOCATE_BUFFER |
    FORMAT_MESSAGE_FROM_SYSTEM | FORMAT_MESSAGE_IGNORE_INSERTS;
  Int32 ReturnValue = FormatMessage(dwFlags, 0, errorValue,
    0, ref lpMsgBuf, MessageSize, 0);

  if (ReturnValue == 0)
  {
    return null;
  }
  else
  {
    return lpMsgBuf;
  }
}
}
}
```

If this code is run correctly, you'll get a return value indicating that there was a bad pointer instead of just a numeric value.

Limitations of Unmanaged Code

Since the advent of .NET, there have been some shortcomings with using unmanaged code. They are largely related to inherent differences between .NET and previous development methodologies. Following is a list of those shortcomings:

- **Performance**   I mention this with hesitation because a common misconception is that the performance Interop code is much less than its .NET equivalent. This might be the case, but performance varies from one instance to another. Code that isn't managed by a runtime will typically have the ability to perform faster than equivalent code that is managed. However, this benefit might not necessarily be realized. This is because of the overhead associated with marshaling information between the unmanaged code and the .NET 2.0 runtime. It's important to remember that unmanaged code can easily introduce issues such as memory leaks.

- **Type safety**   Unmanaged code is sometimes not type safe. This deficiency can have multiple implications, including decreased readability and security issues. One of the most widely touted benefits of Visual Basic 2005 over previous versions is enhanced type strength, so this point should not be trivialized. Moreover, there's no guarantee that type library definitions are accurate, so depending on the metadata, there could be some definitions that are inaccurate or missing.

- **Code security**   The .NET Framework security model didn't exist previously. There's no way that code written prior to this model can take advantage of it. Features such as declarative security are not available in unmanaged code, which can mean your new .NET code will be forced to accommodate this inconsistency.

- **Versioning**   As is the case with security, versioning (which incidentally was a huge issue in prior development environments) didn't exist in the form it does now. Therefore, side-by-side execution might not be available when using unmanaged code.

Lab: Call Windows DLL Functions

In this lab, you create a simple method to call a Windows DLL. If you encounter a problem completing an exercise, the completed projects are available on the companion CD in the Code folder.

▶ **Exercise 1: Calling a Windows API**

In this exercise, you'll call a *MessageBox* Windows API.

1. Open Visual Studio 2005, and create a new C# or Visual Basic 2005 console application.

2. Open Program.cs or Module1.vb, depending on your language of preference.

3. Import the *System.Runtime.InteropServices* namespace, and add the following code:

```
' VB
Public Const UserReference As String = "user32.dll"

<DllImport(UserReference, SetLastError:=True)> _
Private Function MessageBox(ByVal hWnd As Int32, _
    ByVal pText As String, ByVal pCaption As String, _
    ByVal uType As Int32) As Int32
End Function

//C#
public const String UserReference = "user32.dll";

[DllImport(UserReference, SetLastError = true)]
private static extern Int32 MessageBox(IntPtr hWnd, String pText,
    String pCaption, Int32 uType);
```

4. Build the project, and resolve any errors.

Lesson Summary

- The .NET Framework provides a mechanism to call Windows API calls and unmanaged code through Platform Invoke.

- To use P/Invoke, you use the *DllImport* attribute and the name of the DLL you are referencing.

- You must use the private and static/shared attributes for P/Invoke calls.

- To allow default positioning in a structure that's to be marshaled, you can use the *Layout.Sequential* attribute.

- To specify a value for the positioning in a structure, you can use the *Layout .Explicit* attribute.

- Error messages from unmanaged code behave differently from managed exceptions. To trap them correctly, the Windows API can be used.

Lesson Review

You can use the following questions to test your knowledge of the information in Lesson 3, "Using Unmanaged Code." The questions are also available on the companion CD if you prefer to review them in electronic form.

NOTE Answers

Answers to these questions and explanations of why each answer choice is right or wrong are located in the "Answers" section at the end of the book.

---

1. Which of the following choices is true regarding Platform Invoke?

    A. The *DllImport* attribute should be used.

    B. A Runtime Callable Wrapper can be used instead of P/Invoke, which will wrap all the needed functionality of the library.

    C. If a parameter has no meaningful value, it's best to leave it out of the call.

    D. *String* objects are preferred to *StringBuilder* objects because *String*s are reference types.

2. You need to use a structure for a given P/Invoke call. What should you do? (Choose all that apply.)

    A. Define the structure in your .NET code first.

    B. Use the *SizeOf* method of the *System.Runtime.Marshal* class if the size of the structure is needed.

    C. Use the *StructLayout* attribute if positioning within the structure is important.

    D. Create a new structure, and use the Type Library Exporter to create a type library. Reference this from your assembly, and it will serve as the necessary proxy for your Structure.

3. What purpose does the *MarshalAs* attribute serve? (Choose all that apply.)

    A. Allows mapping between pre-existing types and current .NET types where mismatches exist.

    B. It is necessary for correct data marshaling for all P/Invoke calls.

    C. It allows missing types to simply be ignored by the runtime when calls are made.

    D. It can be used to explicitly indicate what types are being moved around

Chapter Review

To further practice and reinforce the skills you learned in this chapter, you can perform the following tasks:

- Review the chapter summary.
- Review the list of key terms introduced in this chapter.
- Complete the case scenarios. These scenarios set up real-world situations involving the topics of this chapter and ask you to create a solution.
- Complete the suggested practices.
- Take a practice test.

Chapter Summary

- Because of its dependence on the Windows registry, COM Interop limits the platforms an application can run on.
- The TlbImp.exe tool is a command-line mechanism you can use to import a COM component.
- The default behavior when catching *System.Exception* objects now catches both CLS-compliant and non-CLS-compliant exceptions.
- The *ComVisible* attribute can be set to apply to an entire assembly, an entire class, or individual members.
- To use P/Invoke, you use the *DllImport* attribute and the name of the DLL you are referencing.
- You must use the private and static/shared attributes for P/Invoke calls.

Key Terms

Do you know what these key terms mean? You can check your answers by looking up the terms in the glossary at the end of the book.

- CLS-compliant exception
- COM (Component Object Model)
- COM Callable Wrapper (CCW)
- Interop

- managed code
- marshaling
- memory leak
- Platform Invoke
- Runtime Callable Wrapper (RCW)
- Type Library Exporter
- Type Library Importer
- type safety

Case Scenario: Incorporating Legacy Code into a .NET Project

In the following case scenario, you will apply what you've learned about how to use the *System.Runtime.InteropServices* namespace. You can find answers to these questions in the "Answers" section at the end of this book.

A common problem when a project is moved to the .NET Framework is rewriting large amounts of legacy code. In this scenario, a company is trying to port an application to the .NET Framework, but it has a huge existing code base of fully developed and fully tested code.

Interviews

Following is a list of company personnel interviewed and their statements:

- **IT Department Head**   "Since we've started using .NET, our developers have been more productive than ever. Based on this productivity increase, we've adjusted our priorities so that a full system rewrite will be done for our two flagship products, WinformsProduct and WebProduct. Since both products share the same business and data access layers currently, the same should be the case with the new products. We have a tremendous investment in our COM libraries and while we want full rewrites of each, we need to get out what we can as quickly as we can. Hence, we're going to rewrite our business and data access libraries one at a time. We still have some new feature requests that will be included in our existing applications but this shouldn't be a problem since we heard that COM components will be able to consume our .new .NET libraries."

- **Lead Business Analyst** "Like most companies, we have to deal with battling the status quo. Our existing product lines both work very well and the users really like them. We know that the .NET products will afford much shorter development cycles and will give use the ability to do many things that were effectively out of the question because of complexity, but there's one area that we can't compromise on: If a feature exists in either application now, it needs to be in the new application. A friend of mine in another company was telling me that when they migrated to Java, they lost some features because Java wasn't as powerful as C++. This simply can't happen and if we get in a situation where we hear ".NET doesn't support it," regarding features that we currently have, it will be a deal breaker.

We have a lot of current features that users really love, and I've heard they aren't natively supported by .NET. For instance, we have a really involved Help system intertwined with Windows *MessageBox* objects, and these absolutely have to ship with the new products. Other features, like our Automatic Screen Captures, which are transparently e-mailed to tech support have been true life savers. This allows support personnel to see exactly what the user was doing when the failure occurred without depending on the user to know how to retrieve a screen capture and e-mail it to us. Every one of these features must be in the new product."

- **CIO** "We've invested almost $1,000,000 in our current libraries, and although I'm OK with moving to .NET, I don't believe in trend surfing. Our existing components are completed and tested and work very well, and I must insist that we take advantage of our existing investment as much as possible. I understand that all new development entails some problems, but until we're convinced that the new libraries are ready for prime time, let's use our existing investment as much as possible."

Questions

Answer the following questions for your manager:

1. What should approach we use with respect to unmanaged Windows APIs?
2. What criteria should we use to determine the order that libraries should be rewritten in?
3. How will we test our new components?
4. Are Windows API calls and calls to unmanaged resources really necessary?

Suggested Practices

To help you successfully master the objectives covered in this chapter, complete the following tasks.

Practice Managing Interoperation Code

For this task, you should complete at least Practices 1 and 2. You can do Practices 3 for a more in-depth understanding of Interoperation.

- **Practice 1**   Create a reference to the Excel Object library and manipulate it from .NET. For instance, create a new workbook, create a new worksheet, delete an existing worksheet and rename a given worksheet.

- **Practice 2**   Use the Windows API to retrieve the text from whatever window is currently active on the user's computer.

- **Practice 3**   Use the Type Library Exporter to make a .NET component consumable from COM.

Take a Practice Test

The practice tests on this book's companion CD offer many options. For example, you can test yourself on just one exam objective, or you can test yourself on all the 70-536 certification exam content. You can set up the test so that it closely simulates the experience of taking a certification exam, or you can set it up in study mode so that you can look at the correct answers and explanations after you answer each question.

MORE INFO   Practice tests

For details about all the practice test options available, see the "How to Use the Practice Tests" section in this book's Introduction.

Chapter 14
Reflection

One of the major benefits of the .NET Framework—and the common language runtime (CLR) in particular—is the richness of the type information available at runtime. The reflection system enables you to navigate and interrogate this type information. This capability allows for very dynamic systems to be created and makes creating plug-in architectures straightforward.

Exam objectives in this chapter:
- Implement reflection functionality in a .NET Framework application (refer *System.Reflection* namespace), and create metadata, Microsoft intermediate language (MSIL), and a PE file by using the *System.Reflection.Emit* namespace.
    - ❑ *Assembly* class
    - ❑ Assembly attributes
    - ❑ Info classes
    - ❑ *Binder* class and *BindingFlags*
    - ❑ *MethodBase* class and *MethodBody* class
    - ❑ *Builder* classes

Real World

Shawn Wildermuth

Reflection is a crucial tool in the toolboxes of most large application developers these days. In an application I created several years ago, I used reflection to detect whether some of the objects running in a system were using certain custom attributes that we had written. We used attributes to know how to serialize objects to and from the database by specifying whether an object was an atomic piece of data or whether each item in the object needed its own column. This approach allowed us to save data based on the developers' needs without requiring them to change the database on every object they wrote.

Lessons in this chapter:

Before You Begin

To complete the lessons in this chapter, you should be familiar with Microsoft Visual Basic or C# and be comfortable with the following tasks:

- Create a console application in Microsoft Visual Studio using Visual Basic or C#.
- Add references to system class libraries to a project.
- Create text files.

Lesson 1: Understanding Reflection

The reflection system in .NET is used to interrogate types in the type system as well as to create code on the fly. At its root, reflection presents code as an object model. From assemblies and modules all the way down to the individual statements that are part of a line of code, reflection allows you to both interrogate and generate code in .NET.

After this lesson, you will be able to:

- Use the *Assembly* class.
- Understand the relationship between assemblies and modules.
- Dynamically load an assembly.
- List the modules in an assembly.

Estimated lesson time: 15 minutes

Understanding Assemblies and Modules

Code in the CLR is packaged in an assembly. This metadata is the data that the CLR uses to load and execute code, and it includes type information for all the classes, structures, delegates, and interfaces in the assembly. The type information includes every method, property, event, delegate, and enumeration of each type. Additionally, there is even metadata about the actual code, including the size of the code and any local variables.

Even though it is often thought of as a file, an assembly is actually a logical container for different parts of the data the CLR needs to execute code. These parts include the following:

- Assembly metadata
- Type metadata
- Code (Intermediate Language code)
- Resources

Assembly metadata includes data that defined the assembly, such as the name, version, strong name, and culture information. The assembly metadata is also called the *manifest*. Type metadata is all the information that describes what a type looks like, including the namespace and type names (that is, class names), the individual members of a type (such as methods, properties, and constructors), and their parameters if any. The code is the actual Intermediate Language (IL) code that is compiled to machine code as the assembly is executed. Finally, resources are objects (such as strings, images, or files) that are used from the code.

Most of the time, all these parts of an assembly are compiled into a single file, as shown in Figure 14-1.

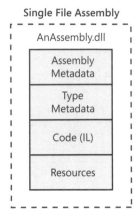

Figure 14-1   Single file assembly

There is no requirement that an assembly be contained in a single file. In fact, in some instances you might want to separate your assembly into multiple files. (For example, when they are deployed in a click-once application, the parts of the assembly will be pulled down only as they are used.) The assembly metadata needs to be in the main assembly file. You can keep some type metadata, code, and resources in the main assembly file as well, but you can refer to other files for additional type metadata and code and have some resources outside the main assembly file. This multifile approach is shown in Figure 14-2.

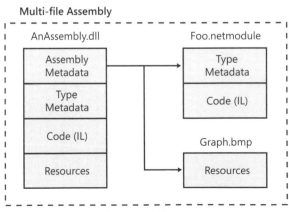

Figure 14-2   Multifile assembly

Modules, on the other hand, are containers for types within an individual assembly. A module can be a container within a single assembly, or more likely it is part of a multifile assembly. In general, you will use multiple modules per assembly only in very special cases where you need to do things like mix source languages within a single assembly or provide support for modular downloading of modules. Visual Studio does not support multiple modules per assembly, so piecing together multimodule assemblies is a task that must be done either at the command line or from other tools (for example, MSBuild).

Examining an Assembly

Before we can start to examine an assembly, we need to get an instance of the *Assembly* class. The *Assembly* class supports a number of static methods to create instances of the class. Table 14-1 shows these static methods.

Table 14-1 *Assembly* **Class Static Methods**

Name	Description
GetAssembly	Returns an *Assembly* that contains a specified type
GetCallingAssembly	Returns the *Assembly* that contains the code that called the current method
GetEntryAssembly	Returns the *Assembly* that contains the code that started up the current process
GetExecutingAssembly	Returns the *Assembly* that contains the currently executing code
Load	Loads an *Assembly* into the current *AppDomain*
LoadFile	Loads an *Assembly* by specifying the path
LoadFrom	Loads an *Assembly* into the current *AppDomain* located at a specific path
ReflectionOnlyLoad	Loads an *Assembly*, but allows only interrogation of the assembly, not execution
ReflectionOnlyLoadFrom	Loads an *Assembly* located at a specific path, but allows only interrogation of the assembly, not execution

The static methods shown in Table 14-1 all return instances of a particular *Assembly*. Using *GetAssembly* or any of the *Load* methods allows you to load an *Assembly* that is not currently loaded.

More interesting are the *GetCallingAssembly*, *GetEntryAssembly*, and *GetExecuting-Assembly* calls. These methods allow you to retrieve an instance of the *Assembly* class for assemblies that are part of the current call stack. *GetEntryAssembly* returns an instance of the assembly that contains the start-up method (usually the executable assembly for a desktop application).

You can retrieve the assembly for the currently running code by calling *GetExecuting-Assembly*. In contrast, the *GetCallingAssembly* retrieves an instance of the *Assembly* class for the method one level up in the call stack. In other words, it retrieves the assembly that contains the method that called the currently executing code. See the following example.

```
' VB
Dim theAssembly As Assembly = Assembly.GetExecutingAssembly
```

```
// C#
Assembly theAssembly = Assembly.GetExecutingAssembly();
```

Once you have an instance of the *Assembly* class, you can interrogate the properties of the assembly itself. The *Assembly* class's instance properties and methods are detailed in Table 14-2 and Table 14-3, respectively.

Table 14-2   *Assembly* Class Properties

Name	Description
EntryPoint	Gets the method that represents the first code to be executed in an assembly
FullName	Gets the fully qualified name of the assembly
GlobalAssemblyCache	Gets a value that indicates whether the assembly was loaded from the global assembly cache
Location	Gets the path to the assembly
ReflectionOnly	Gets a value that indicates whether the assembly was loaded just for reflection

Table 14-3 *Assembly* Class Methods

Name	Description
CreateInstance	Creates an instance of a specified type that exists in the assembly
GetCustomAttributes	Returns an array of attributes for the assembly
GetExportedTypes	Returns a collection of types that are publicly visible outside the assembly
GetFile	Returns a *FileStream* object for a file contained in the resources of the assembly
GetFiles	Returns an array of *FileStream* objects that represents all the files contained in the resources of the assembly
GetLoadedModules	Returns an array of the currently loaded modules in the assembly
GetModule	Returns a specified module from the assembly
GetModules	Returns all the modules from the assembly
GetName	Returns an *AssemblyName* object that represents the fully qualified name of the assembly
GetSatelliteAssembly	Returns a satellite assembly for a specific culture if one exists
GetTypes	Returns an array of all the types defined in all modules of the assembly
IsDefined	Returns a value that indicates whether a specific attribute is defined in the assembly

Once you have an instance of the *Assembly* class, you can get information about the assembly itself:

```
' VB
Dim a As Assembly = Assembly.GetExecutingAssembly()

Console.WriteLine("Full Name: {0}", a.FullName)
Console.WriteLine("Location: {0}", a.Location)
Console.WriteLine("Only Reflection?: {0}", a.ReflectionOnly)
```

```csharp
// C#
Assembly a = Assembly.GetExecutingAssembly();

Console.WriteLine("Full Name: {0}", a.FullName);
Console.WriteLine("Location: {0}", a.Location);
Console.WriteLine("Only Reflection?: {0}", a.ReflectionOnly);
```

The *Assembly* class also supports loading assemblies just to interrogate the information in the assembly. The idea here is that when loading an assembly, there is a bit of work involved with reading an assembly to be executed in an *AppDomain*. At times, you need to load up an assembly to read through its type information, but you do not expect to execute code or create types. To make this process more efficient, the *Assembly* class now supports the *ReflectionOnlyLoad* and *ReflectionOnlyLoadFrom* methods. These methods return instances of the *Assembly* class just like the other static methods, but they do not support certain calls (for example, *CreateInstance*). For example, to load an assembly for reflection you can do the following:

```vb
' VB
Dim fullName As String = "System.Transactions, Version=2.0.0.0, " + _
    "Culture=neutral, PublicKeyToken=b77a5c561934e089"

Dim theAssembly As Assembly = Assembly.ReflectionOnlyLoad(fullName)

Console.Write("Location: {0}", theAssembly.Location)
 ' Throws an exception because we loaded it for reflection only
Dim o As Object = _
    theAssembly.CreateInstance("System.Transactions.TransactionScope")
```

```csharp
// C#
string fullName = "System.Transactions, Version=2.0.0.0, " +
    "Culture=neutral, PublicKeyToken=b77a5c561934e089";

Assembly theAssembly = Assembly.ReflectionOnlyLoad(fullName);

Console.Write("Location: {0}", theAssembly.Location);

// Throws an exception because we loaded it for reflection only
object o =
    theAssembly.CreateInstance("System.Transactions.TransactionScope");
```

Each assembly contains one or more modules that represent containers for type information. You can ask the *Assembly* class to return the modules in an assembly by calling the *GetModules* method, as shown in the following example:

```vb
' VB
Dim a As Assembly = Assembly.GetExecutingAssembly()

Dim mods() As [Module] = a.GetModules()
```

```vb
For Each m As [Module] In mods
    Console.WriteLine("Module Name: {0}", m.Name)
Next

// C#
Assembly a = Assembly.GetExecutingAssembly();

Module[] mods = a.GetModules();
foreach (Module m in mods)
{
    Console.WriteLine("Module Name: {0}", m.Name);
}
```

The *Module* class's properties and methods are shown in Table 14-4 and Table 14-5, respectively.

Table 14-4   *Module* Properties

Name	Description
Assembly	Gets the assembly that this module resides in
FullyQualifiedName	Gets the full name to this module, including the path to the module if any
Name	Gets the name of the module (without the path to the module)

Table 14-5   *Module* Methods

Name	Description
FindTypes	Searches the module for types matching certain criteria
GetCustomAttributes	Gets the attributes associated with this module
GetField	Returns a specific field in the module
GetFields	Returns all the fields in the module
GetMethod	Returns a specific method in the module
GetMethods	Returns all the methods in the module
GetTypes	Returns all the types in the module
IsResource	Used to determine if certain objects are resources in the module

The *Module* class can be used to retrieve or search for types contained within a specified module. For assemblies originally written in languages that support the notion of modules (for example, Visual Basic), it also supports *GetField*, *GetFields*, *GetMethod*, and *GetMethods* methods. In those types of modules, fields and methods can be attached directly to a module. In Lesson 3, you'll learn more about how to use reflection on fields and methods.

Lab: Use the .NET Tools to Examine an Assembly

In this lab, you will create a console application that creates two instances of the *Assembly* class and shows some of its properties. If you encounter a problem completing an exercise, the completed projects are available on the companion CD in the Code folder.

1. Create a new console application, and call it AssemblyDemo.

2. Add a *using* statement (or the *Imports* statement for Visual Basic) to the *System.Reflection* namespace to the main code file.

3. Create a new static method called *ShowAssemblyInfo* that takes an instance of the *Assembly* class as a parameter.

4. Inside the new *ShowAssemblyInfo* method, write out the *FullName*, *GlobalAssemblyCache*, *Location*, and *ImageRuntimeVersion* properties to the console.

5. Next iterate through each of the *Modules* in the *Assembly*, and show each module's name in the console.

6. In the main method of the project, load the System.dll assembly from the framework directory under the Windows directory using the *Assembly.LoadFile* method.

7. Call the *ShowAssemblyInfo* method with the new assembly instance.

8. Create a new instance of the *Assembly* class by getting the currently executing assembly.

9. Call the *ShowAssemblyInfo* method again with the *Assembly* instance from the executing assembly. Your code might look something like this:

```
' VB
Imports System.Reflection

Class Program

    Public Shared Sub Main(ByVal args() As String)

        Dim path As String = _
            "C:\WINDOWS\Microsoft.NET\Framework\v2.0.50727\System.dll"
```

```vb
    ' Load a specific Assembly
    Dim a As Assembly = Assembly.LoadFile(path)
    ShowAssemblyInfo(a)

    ' Get our Assembly
    Dim ourAssembly As Assembly = Assembly.GetExecutingAssembly
    ShowAssemblyInfo(ourAssembly)

    Console.Read()

End Sub

Shared Sub ShowAssemblyInfo(ByVal a As Assembly)

    Console.WriteLine(a.FullName)
    Console.WriteLine("From GAC? {0}", a.GlobalAssemblyCache)
    Console.WriteLine("Path:     {0}", a.Location)
    Console.WriteLine("Version:  {0}", a.ImageRuntimeVersion)

    ' Show Modules
        For Each m As [Module] In a.GetModules
            Console.WriteLine("  Mod: {0}", m.Name)
    Next

    Console.WriteLine()

    End Sub
End Class

// C#
using System.Reflection;

class Program
{
    static void Main(string[] args)
    {
        string path =
            @"C:\WINDOWS\Microsoft.NET\Framework\v2.0.50727\System.dll";

        // Load a specific Assembly
        Assembly a = Assembly.LoadFile(path);
        ShowAssemblyInfo(a);

        // Get our Assembly
        Assembly ourAssembly = Assembly.GetExecutingAssembly();
        ShowAssemblyInfo(ourAssembly);

        Console.Read();
    }

    static void ShowAssemblyInfo(Assembly a)
    {
        Console.WriteLine(a.FullName);
```

```
            Console.WriteLine("From GAC? {0}", a.GlobalAssemblyCache);
            Console.WriteLine("Path:     {0}", a.Location);
            Console.WriteLine("Version:  {0}", a.ImageRuntimeVersion);

            // Show Modules
            foreach (Module m in a.GetModules())
            {
                Console.WriteLine("  Mod: {0}", m.Name);
            }

            Console.WriteLine();
        }
    }
```

10. Build the project, and resolve any errors. Verify that the console application successfully shows both the assemblies and their modules.

Lesson Summary

- Assemblies are containers for modules, and modules are containers for types.

- To access assemblies that are related to the currently running code, load ad-hoc assemblies, and list the modules in an assembly, use the *Assembly* class.

Lesson Review

You can use the following questions to test your knowledge of the information in Lesson 1, "Understanding Reflection." The questions are also available on the companion CD if you prefer to review them in electronic form.

NOTE   Answers

Answers to these questions and explanations of why each answer choice is right or wrong are located in the "Answers" section at the end of the book.

---

1. What static method of the *Assembly* class is guaranteed to return an instance that represents the assembly that contains the startup object (or entry point) of the application?

   A. *Assembly.GetCallingAssembly*

   B. *Assembly.GetExecutingAssembly*

   C. *Assembly.GetEntryAssembly*

   D. *Assembly.Load*

2. Which statements are true when referring to an assembly and module? (Choose all that apply.)

    A. An assembly can contain one or many other assemblies.

    B. An assembly can contain one or many modules.

    C. An assembly can directly contain types.

    D. A module can directly contain types.

Lesson 2: Assembly Attributes

Now that you have seen the *Assembly* class, you might notice that there are many pieces of information about an assembly that are not readily available to this class. These additional pieces of information are captured as part of the assembly as attributes on the assembly. These additional pieces of information include copyright and company information as well as run-time information such as culture and key file information.

After this lesson, you will be able to:

- Use common assembly attributes.
- Query an assembly for attributes.

Estimated lesson time: 20 minutes

Common Attributes

Assembly attributes can adorn assemblies to provide additional information about the assembly. There are a number of built-in assembly attributes that you will find useful in everyday development.

Typically you add assembly attributes to the AssemblyInfo file (AssemblyInfo.cs for C# and AssemblyInfo.vb for Visual Basic). You add them to this file by specifying that they are an assembly attribute using the assembly prefix (*assembly:* in C# and *Assembly:* in Visual Basic) on the assembly in the AssemblyInfo. The following lines of code demonstrate how to do this:

```
' VB
<Assembly: AssemblyCompany("Proseware, Inc.")>
```

```
// C#
[assembly: AssemblyCompany("Proseware, Inc.")]
```

The attribute name is the same as the attribute class, but with the omission of the *Attribute*. For example, the *AssemblyCompanyAttribute* class represents the *Assembly-Company* attribute shown in the preceding code.

The following sections detail the most common of these attributes and explain how and why they are used.

AssemblyAlgorithmIdAttribute Class

The *AssemblyAlgorithmId* attribute is used to specify which hash algorithm to use when reading file hashes in the assembly manifest, as shown in this example:

```
' VB
<Assembly: AssemblyAlgorithmId(AssemblyHashAlgorithm.MD5)>
```

```
// C#
[assembly: AssemblyAlgorithmId(AssemblyHashAlgorithm.MD5)]
```

AssemblyCompanyAttribute Class

The *AssemblyCompany* attribute is used to specify the company that produced the assembly. It is used by the compiler to put the company name in the .DLL header as well, as shown here:

```
' VB
<Assembly: AssemblyCompany("Proseware, Inc.")>
```

```
// C#
[assembly: AssemblyCompany("Proseware, Inc.")]
```

AssemblyConfigurationAttribute Class

The *AssemblyConfiguration* attribute is used to specify which configuration is used for the assembly, such as "DEBUG" or "RELEASE". Tools such as Visual Studio usually specify this attribute for you based on your configuration, but you can override the attribute if necessary, as shown in this example:

```
' VB
<Assembly: AssemblyConfiguration("DEBUG")>
```

```
// C#
[assembly: AssemblyConfiguration("DEBUG")]
```

AssemblyCopyrightAttribute Class

The *AssemblyCopyright* attribute is used to specify the copyright information for the assembly, as shown in the following example:

```
' VB
<Assembly: AssemblyCopyright("Copyright © Proseware, Inc. 2006")>
```

```
// C#
[assembly: AssemblyCopyright("Copyright © Proseware, Inc. 2006")]
```

AssemblyCultureAttribute Class

The *AssemblyCulture* attribute is used to specify the culture of an assembly. Normally assemblies are culture neutral, but in the case of satellite assemblies you use this attribute to specify the culture for the assembly. The following code provides an example:

```
' VB
<Assembly: AssemblyCulture("de")> ' German
```

```
// C#
[assembly: AssemblyCulture("de")] // German
```

AssemblyDefaultAliasAttribute Class

The *AssemblyDefaultAlias* attribute is used to simplify the name of an assembly. This attribute is used when the name of the assembly is long or convoluted. For example, if the name of the assembly is "*Proseware.Framework.Foundation.DataLayer*", you might simplify it by specifying its default alias as "*DataLayer*". The following lines of code provide an example:

```
' VB
<Assembly: AssemblyDefaultAlias("DataLayer")>
```

```
// C#
[assembly: AssemblyDefaultAlias("DataLayer")]
```

AssemblyDelaySignAttribute Class

The *AssemblyDelaySign* attribute is used to specify that the assembly will be signed (or strongly named) after compilation but will be marked as a strongly named assembly. If this attribute is specified, you must supply the *AssemblyKeyFile* attribute to specify a temporary key, as shown in the following example:

```
' VB
<Assembly: AssemblyDelaySign(True)>
```

```
// C#
[assembly: AssemblyDelaySign(true)]
```

AssemblyDescriptionAttribute Class

The *AssemblyDescription* attribute is used to annotate the assembly with a description for human consumption, as shown in the following example:

```
' VB
<Assembly: AssemblyDescription("This the Data Access Layer")>
```

```
// C#
[assembly: AssemblyDescription("This the Data Access Layer")]
```

AssemblyFileVersionAttribute Class

The *AssemblyFileVersion* attribute is used to specify the file version of this assembly. The file version is accessible in the Property dialog box of the file system. If it is not supplied, the *AssemblyVersion* attribute's value is used instead.

AssemblyFlagsAttribute Class

The *AssemblyFlags* attribute is used to specify one or more of the *AssemblyNameFlags* values to the assembly. The *AssemblyNameFlags* enumeration is detailed in Table 14-6.

Table 14-6 *AssemblyNameFlags* **Enumeration**

Name	Description
EnableJITcompile-Optimizer	Enables the just-in-time (JIT) compiler optimization
EnableJITcompile-Tracking	Enables the just-in-time (JIT) compiler tracking
None	No flags are in effect
PublicKey	Enables creation of the public key of the assembly to be based on the actual public key specified instead of on the public key token
Retargetable	Allows for the assembly to be retargeted to an assembly from a different publisher

You can use the *AssemblyFlags* attribute by specifying one or more of the *AssemblyNameFlags* enumerations, as shown in the following example:

```
' VB
<assembly: _
    AssemblyFlags(AssemblyNameFlags.EnableJITcompileOptimizer Or _
                AssemblyNameFlags.EnableJITcompileTracking)>
```

```
// C#
[assembly: AssemblyFlags(AssemblyNameFlags.EnableJITcompileOptimizer |
                AssemblyNameFlags.EnableJITcompileTracking)]
```

AssemblyInformationalVersionAttribute Class

The *AssemblyInformationalVersion* attribute is used to specify a version that is used just for information purposes. The runtime never uses this version for runtime versioning or side-by-side versioning of the assembly. The following lines of code show how to use this attribute:

```
' VB
<Assembly: AssemblyInformationalVersion("1.0.0.1")>
```

```
// C#
[assembly: AssemblyInformationalVersion("1.0.0.1")]
```

AssemblyKeyFileAttribute Class

The *AssemblyKeyFile* attribute is used to specify the path to a key file to use to sign (or strongly name) this assembly. The sn.exe tool that ships with the .NET Framework SDK can be used to create a key file. To use this attribute, specify the full path to a key file, like so:

```
' VB
<Assembly: AssemblyKeyFile("../key.snk")>
```

```
// C#
[assembly: AssemblyKeyFile("../key.snk")]
```

AssemblyTitleAttribute Class

The *AssemblyTitle* attribute is used to specify a title for this assembly in the manifest, as shown in the following example:

```
' VB
<Assembly: AssemblyTitle("Proseware.Framework.DataLayer")>
```

```
// C#
[assembly: AssemblyTitle("Proseware.Framework.DataLayer")]
```

AssemblyTrademarkAttribute Class

The *AssemblyTrademark* attribute is used to specify any trademark information about this assembly, as shown in the following example:

```
' VB
<Assembly: AssemblyTrademark("Proseware®")>
```

```
// C#
[assembly: AssemblyTrademark("Proseware®")]
```

AssemblyVersionAttribute Class

The *AssemblyVersion* attribute is used to specify the version of the assembly. The assembly version is made up of four elements separated by period:

```
<major version>.<minor version>.<build number>.<revision>
```

For example,

```
1.2.3.4
```

The *AssemblyVersion* attribute allows you to replace the build number and the revision with an asterisk. Using the asterisk tells the compiler to update the build number and revision with an autogenerated value. The autogenerated build number is an autoincrementing number that updates once per day. The autogenerated revision number is a randomly generated number. If you specify a revision number, you cannot use an asterisk for the build number. You can specify the *AssemblyVersion* using the attribute, like so:

```
' VB
<Assembly: AssemblyVersion("1.2.*.*")>
```

```
// C#
[assembly: AssemblyVersion("1.2.*.*")]
```

Getting Assembly Attributes

Setting attributes on an assembly is only part of the job. You also need to be able to get the attributes for an assembly. The main way you can get the attributes is by calling the *GetCustomAttributes* method on the *Assembly* class. This method is part of the *ICustomAttributeProvider* interface. The *ICustomAttributeProvider* interface is used to find what types provide custom attributes. Because of this, the *GetCustomAttributes* allows for a Boolean value to indicate whether to get inherited attributes. As you will see in Lesson 3, this is a very useful idea. But because *GetCustomAttributes* is on the *Assembly* class, the .NET Framework completely ignores the Boolean value. (There is no inheritance tree for assemblies.)

You can call the *GetCustomAttributes* method to get all the attributes on the assembly, like so:

```
' VB
Dim a As Assembly = Assembly.GetExecutingAssembly()

Dim attrs() As Object = a.GetCustomAttributes(false)
For Each attr As Attribute In attrs
    Console.WriteLine("Attribute: {0}", attr.GetType.Name)
Next
```

```
// C#
Assembly a = Assembly.GetExecutingAssembly();

object[] attrs = a.GetCustomAttributes(false);
foreach (Attribute attr in attrs)
{
    Console.WriteLine("Attribute: {0}", attr.GetType().Name);
}
```

In cases where you need to get a specific attribute, you can call the *GetCustomAttributes* method and specify the type of the attribute you are looking for. Here is an example of getting the *AssemblyDescription* attribute:

```
' VB
Dim a As Assembly = Assembly.GetExecutingAssembly()

Dim attrType As Type = GetType(AssemblyDescriptionAttribute)
Dim versionAttrs() As Object = a.GetCustomAttributes(attrType, false)
If (versionAttrs.Length > 0) Then
    Dim desc As AssemblyDescriptionAttribute = _
        CType(versionAttrs(0), AssemblyDescriptionAttribute)
    Console.WriteLine("Found Description!")
    Console.WriteLine("Desc: {0}", desc.Description)
End If

// C#
Assembly a = Assembly.GetExecutingAssembly();

Type attrType = typeof(AssemblyDescriptionAttribute);
object[] versionAttrs = a.GetCustomAttributes(attrType, false);
if (versionAttrs.Length > 0)
{
    AssemblyDescriptionAttribute desc =
        (AssemblyDescriptionAttribute)versionAttrs[0];
    Console.WriteLine("Found Description!");
    Console.WriteLine("Desc: {0}", desc.Description);
}
```

Lab: Set Assembly Attributes and Display Them at Runtime

In this lab, you will set the attributes on an assembly and then display them in the console. If you encounter a problem completing an exercise, the completed projects are available on the companion CD in the Code folder.

1. Create a new console application, and call it AssemblyAttrDemo.

2. Open the assemblyinfo file (AssemblyInfo.cs for C# and AssemblyInfo.vb for Visual Basic). In C#, you will find it in the Properties folder. In Visual Basic, click the Show All Files button and look for it under the My Project folder.

3. Set the *AssemblyDescription* attribute to "This is a demo of the AssemblyDescription attribute".

4. Open the main code file in the new project, and add a *using* statement (or *Imports* in Visual Basic) to the *System.Reflection* namespace.

5. In the startup method of the project, create an instance of the *Assembly* class and instantiate it with the assembly from the currently executing code.

6. Create a new local variable to hold an instance of the *Type* class, and assign it the type of the *AssemblyDescriptionAttribute* class.

7. Call the *Assembly* instance's *GetCustomAttributes* method, specifying the *Type* instance you built in step 6 and *false* for inheritance. Then store the result in a new local variable that holds an array of objects.

8. If the length of the array of objects is greater than zero, create a new variable to store an *AssemblyDescriptionAttribute* object and cast the first item of the *Object* array to the new variable.

9. Write out to the console the description that the *AssemblyDescriptionAttribute* variable holds. Your code might look something like this:

```
' VB
Imports System.Reflection

Class Program

    Public Shared Sub Main(ByVal args() As String)

        Dim a As Assembly = Assembly.GetExecutingAssembly

        Dim attrType As Type = GetType(AssemblyDescriptionAttribute)

        Dim attrs() As Object = a.GetCustomAttributes(attrType, False)

        If (attrs.Length > 0) Then

          Dim desc As AssemblyDescriptionAttribute = _
              CType(attrs(0), AssemblyDescriptionAttribute)
          Console.WriteLine("Description is: {0}", desc.Description)

        End If

    End Sub
End Class


// C#
using System.Reflection;
```

```
class Program
{
    static void Main(string[] args)
    {
        Assembly a = Assembly.GetExecutingAssembly();

        Type attrType = typeof(AssemblyDescriptionAttribute);

        object[] attrs = a.GetCustomAttributes(attrType, false);

        if (attrs.Length > 0)
        {
            AssemblyDescriptionAttribute desc =
                (AssemblyDescriptionAttribute)attrs[0];
            Console.WriteLine("Description is: {0}", desc.Description);
        }

    }
}
```

10. Build the project, and resolve any errors. Verify that the console application successfully shows the description in the console window.

Lesson Summary

- To specify assembly metadata, use common assembly attributes.

- To query an assembly for individual attributes, use the *GetCustomAttributes* method.

Lesson Review

You can use the following questions to test your knowledge of the information in Lesson 2, "Assembly Attributes." The questions are also available on the companion CD if you prefer to review them in electronic form.

NOTE Answers

Answers to these questions and explanations of why each answer choice is right or wrong are located in the "Answers" section at the end of the book.

---

1. What does using the *AssemblyCultureAttribute* with a specific culture indicate about an assembly?

   A. The assembly's entry point is meant to be used only on machines that support a specific locale.

   B. The assembly is a satellite assembly.

   C. It does not indicate anything; it is merely informative.

   D. It allows the resources in the assembly to be translated into the specified locale.

2. What does specifying an asterisk as the revision number part of the version in the *AssemblyVersionAttribute* (for example, "1.0.0.*") indicate to the compiler?

   A. Specifying an asterisk here does not indicate anything; asterisks are valid parts of a version number.

   B. Specifying an asterisk here indicates that this assembly will work with any other assemblies with versions that start with *"1.0.0"*.

   C. Specifying an asterisk indicates that the asterisk should be replaced with an autoincrementing number by the compiler.

   D. Specifying an asterisk here indicates that the asterisk should be replaced with a random number by the compiler.

Lesson 3: Reflecting Types

Up to now, we have been delving into the specifics of containers of code, specifically assemblies and modules. In this lesson, we dive into the heart of the matter and start looking at reflecting through the members of a type.

After this lesson, you will be able to:

■ Access type information without iterating through an assembly.

■ Query types for attributes.

■ Enumerate type members.

■ Enumerate types in an assembly.

■ Use the *BindingFlags* enumeration to have more control over what members to retrieve from a *Type*.

Estimated lesson time: 25 minutes

Getting Types

Before you can start looking at type information, you have to understand how to get *Type* objects. You can get *Type* objects in a number of ways:

■ From the *Assembly* class

■ From the *Module* class

■ From instances of *Object*

■ Using the *typeof* keyword in C# or *GetType* in Visual Basic

When working with an *Assembly* instance, you can ask it for all the *Types* in all the modules of the assembly by calling the *GetTypes* method:

```
' VB
Dim a As Assembly = Assembly.GetExecutingAssembly()

' Get all the types in the Assembly
Dim assemblytypes() As Type = a.GetTypes()

// C#
Assembly a = Assembly.GetExecutingAssembly();

// Get all the types in the Assembly
Type[] assemblytypes = a.GetTypes();
```

When working with a *Module* object, you can also ask for all the *Types* associated with it by calling the *Module* class's *GetTypes* method:

```
' VB
Dim mods() As [Module] =  a.GetModules()
Dim m As [Module] =  mods(0)

' Get all the Types from a particular Module
Dim moduleTypes() As Type = m.GetTypes()

// C#
Module[] mods = a.GetModules();
Module m = mods[0];

// Get all the Types from a particular Module
Type[] moduleTypes = m.GetTypes();
```

You can also get the type of the instance of an object by calling its *GetType* method:

```
' VB
Dim o As New Object()

' Get the Type of an instance
Dim objType As Type = o.GetType()

// C#
object o = new object();

// Get the Type of an instance
Type objType = o.GetType();
```

Finally, you can create a *Type* object using the C# *typeof* keyword or Visual Basic *GetType* keyword:

```
' VB
Dim specificType As Type = GetType(Int32)

// C#
Type specificType = typeof(Int32);
```

Now that you can get a *Type* object, let's see what it can do. The *Type* class represents a single type, allowing you to look at the methods, properties, events, interfaces, and inheritance tree of a particular type in the system. Before we delve into parts of a *Type* that can be reflected, let's look at the *Type* class itself. The most important properties and methods of the *Type* class are detailed in Table 14-7 and Table 14-8, respectively.

Table 14-7   *Type* **Class Properties**

Name	Description
Assembly	Gets the *Assembly* that this type is associated with
AssemblyQualifiedName	Gets a fully qualified name of the type, including the name of the assembly
Attributes	Gets the attributes on this *Type*
BaseType	Gets the *Type* from which this *Type* directly inherits
FullName	Gets a fully qualified name for the *Type*, without the assembly information
HasElementType	Get a value that indicates whether this *Type* encompasses another *Type* (usually indicates that the *Type* is an *Array* of another *Type*)
IsAbstract	Gets a value that indicates whether this *Type* refers to an abstract class
IsByRef	Gets a value that indicates whether this *Type* is passed by reference
IsClass	Gets a value that indicates whether this *Type* refers to a class
IsEnum	Gets a value that indicates whether this *Type* refers to an enumeration
IsGenericType	Gets a value that indicates whether this *Type* contains generic parameters
IsInterface	Gets a value that indicates whether this *Type* refers to an interface
IsMarshalByRef	Gets a value that indicates whether this *Type* is marshaled by reference
IsNotPublic	Gets a value that indicates whether this *Type* is not public
IsPrimitive	Gets a value that indicates whether this *Type* is a primitive type (for example, *Boolean*, *Byte*, *SByte*, *Int16*, *UInt16*, *Int32*, *UInt32*, *Int64*, *UInt64*, *Char*, *Double*, or *Single*)

Table 14-7   *Type* Class Properties

Name	Description
IsPublic	Gets a value that indicates whether this *Type* is public
IsSealed	Gets a value that indicates whether this *Type* is sealed or not inheritable
IsValueType	Gets a value that indicates whether this *Type* is a value type
IsVisible	Gets a value that indicates whether this *Type* can be accessed outside of its assembly
Module	Gets the *Module* that this *Type* resides in
Namespace	Gets the namespace for this *Type*

Table 14-8   *Type* Class Methods

Name	Description
GetConstructor	Retrieves a specific *ConstructorInfo* object that is associated with this *Type*
GetConstructors	Retrieves all the *ConstructorInfo* objects that are associated with this *Type*
GetElementType	Retrieves the *Type* that this *Type* encompasses (usually only valid if this *Type* is an array)
GetEvent	Retrieves a specific *EventInfo* object that is associated with this *Type*
GetEvents	Retrieves all the *EventInfo* objects that are associated with this *Type*
GetField	Retrieves a specific *FieldInfo* object that is associated with this *Type*
GetFields	Retrieves all the *FieldInfo* objects that are associated with this *Type*
GetInterface	Retrieves a specific *Type* object that is associated with this *Type*

Table 14-8   *Type* Class Methods

Name	Description
GetInterfaces	Retrieves all the *Type* objects that are associated with this *Type*
GetMember	Retrieves a specific *MemberInfo* object that is associated with this *Type*
GetMembers	Retrieves all the *MemberInfo* objects that are associated with this *Type*
GetMethod	Retrieves a specific *MethodInfo* object that is associated with this *Type*
GetMethods	Retrieves all the *MethodInfo* objects that are associated with this *Type*
GetNestedType	Retrieves a specific *Type* object that is nested within this *Type*
GetNestedTypes	Retrieves all the *Type* objects that are nested within this *Type*
GetProperty	Retrieves a specific *PropertyInfo* object that is associated with this *Type*
GetProperties	Retrieves all the *PropertyInfo* objects that are associated with this *Type*
IsInstanceOfType	Tests an object to see whether it is an instance of this *Type*
IsSubclassOf	Tests to see whether this *Type* ultimately derives from a specific *Type*

Once you get an instance of *Type*, you can use it to get information about the type, like so:

```
' VB
Dim t as Type = GetType(String)

Console.WriteLine("Type: {0}", t.Name)
Console.WriteLine("  Namespace    : {0}", t.Namespace)
Console.WriteLine("  FullName     : {0}", t.FullName)
```

```
Console.WriteLine(" Is ValueType?: {0}", t.IsValueType)
Console.WriteLine(" Is Sealed?   : {0}", t.IsSealed)
Console.WriteLine(" Is Abstract? : {0}", t.IsAbstract)
Console.WriteLine(" Is Public?   : {0}", t.IsPublic)
Console.WriteLine(" Is Class?    : {0}", t.IsClass)

// C#
Type t = typeof(String);

Console.WriteLine("Type: {0}", t.Name);
Console.WriteLine(" Namespace    : {0}", t.Namespace);
Console.WriteLine(" FullName     : {0}", t.FullName);
Console.WriteLine(" Is ValueType?: {0}", t.IsValueType);
Console.WriteLine(" Is Sealed?   : {0}", t.IsSealed);
Console.WriteLine(" Is Abstract? : {0}", t.IsAbstract);
Console.WriteLine(" Is Public?   : {0}", t.IsPublic);
Console.WriteLine(" Is Class?    : {0}", t.IsClass);
```

In addition, you can check for attributes of a class in a similar fashion to the way you check for attributes of an assembly:

```
' VB
For Each attr As Attribute In t.GetCustomAttributes(false)
    Console.WriteLine("    {0}", attr.GetType.Name)
Next

// C#
foreach (Attribute attr in t.GetCustomAttributes(false))
{
    Console.WriteLine("    {0}", attr.GetType().Name);
}
```

The big difference between attributes of types and attributes of assemblies is that the *inherit* Boolean parameter that was ignored in the *Assembly* class is not ignored here. Because you can add attributes to any class in a class hierarchy, the *inherit* parameter tells the reflection system whether to get attributes that are on this specific type or attributes of all types in the inheritance hierarchy.

What Type Is that Object?

Ultimately, every object derives from the *Object* class that is at the top of the hierarchy. The *Object* class supports a method called *GetType*. This method returns a *Type* object that refers to the actual *Type* of an object. For example, say you create an *Animal* class:

```
' VB
Public Class Animal

End Class
```

```
// C#
public class Animal
{
}
```

Now you create two classes that derive from this new class:

```
' VB
Public Class Dog
    Inherits Animal

End Class
Public Class Cat
    Inherits Animal

End Class
```

```
// C#
public class Dog : Animal
{
}

public class Cat : Animal
{
}
```

You can then create three instances, one of each of these classes. However, store them all as *Animals* and then show the *Type*'s name in the console window:

```
' VB
Dim anAnimal As Animal = New Animal
Dim dogAnimal As Animal = New Dog
Dim catAnimal As Animal = New Cat

Console.WriteLine("Typename for anAnimal is {0}", _
    anAnimal.GetType.Name)
Console.WriteLine("Typename for dogAnimal is {0}", _
    dogAnimal.GetType.Name)
Console.WriteLine("Typename for catAnimal is {0}", _
    catAnimal.GetType.Name)

// C#
Animal anAnimal = new Animal();
Animal dogAnimal = new Dog();
Animal catAnimal = new Cat();

Console.WriteLine("Typename for anAnimal is {0}",
    anAnimal.GetType().Name);
Console.WriteLine("Typename for dogAnimal is {0}",
    dogAnimal.GetType().Name);
Console.WriteLine("Typename for catAnimal is {0}",
    catAnimal.GetType().Name);
```

When you output the type names for the three instances, you get the name of the type that was created, not the local variable:

```
Typename for anAnimal is Animal
Typename for dogAnimal is Dog
Typename for catAnimal is Cat
```

Why is this? An object is always of a single type. The fact that it can be cast to one of its base types or to one of the interfaces it implements does not change that the object is still of one and only one type.

Enumerating Class Members

Within the *Type* class, there are methods for getting different parts of a *Type*, including methods, properties, fields, and events. Each of these parts of a *Type* is represented by a class within the reflection system that ends with the name *Info*. Therefore, the class that represents a field is called *FieldInfo*, the class that represents an event is called *EventInfo*, and so on. All these info classes derive from a common abstract class called *MemberInfo*. In fact, the *Type* class also derives from the *MemberInfo* class. The *Member-Info* class contains common functionality. Most of the interesting data about each of the members of a type is contained in the derived classes.

As you saw earlier in the explanation of the *Type* class, a number of methods on the *Type* class allow you to get each of the parts of the type. These match the info classes as well. For example, the *GetEvent* and *GetEvents* methods return an *EventInfo* object (or objects), and the *GetField* and *GetFields* methods return a *FieldInfo* object (or objects). So iterating through each of these parts of the *Type* is very straightforward. For example, to enumerate all the properties of a class, you could write code like so:

```vb
' VB
For Each prop As PropertyInfo In t.GetProperties()
    Console.WriteLine("    {0}", prop.Name)
Next
```

```csharp
// C#
foreach (PropertyInfo prop in t.GetProperties())
{
    Console.WriteLine("    {0}", prop.Name);
}
```

In addition to parts of a type, a *Type* class supports returning types that are nested within a type. These can be nested classes, interfaces, enumerations, and so on. You can get at these by calling the *GetNestedType* or *GetNestedTypes* method. These methods return *Type* objects instead of a specialized info class. Because the *Type* class derives from the *MemberInfo* class, the *Type* class is really an info class anyway. You can get at nested types like so:

```vb
' VB
For Each nestedType As Type In t.GetNestedTypes()
    Console.WriteLine("    {0}", nestedType.Name)
Next
```

```csharp
// C#
foreach (Type nestedType in t.GetNestedTypes())
{
    Console.WriteLine("    {0}", nestedType.Name);
}
```

In addition, you can iterate through all the parts of a *Type* by using the *GetMembers* call. This method, which is shown in the following example, returns an array of *MemberInfo* objects:

```vb
' VB
For Each member As MemberInfo In t.GetMembers()
    Console.WriteLine("    {0}: {1}", member.MemberType, member.Name)
Next
```

```csharp
// C#
foreach (MemberInfo member in t.GetMembers())
{
    Console.WriteLine("    {0}: {1}", member.MemberType, member.Name);
}
```

Each of these info classes has a specialized use for working with part of the *Type* object. Table 14-9 shows each of these *MemberInfo* derived classes and what objects they represent.

Table 14-9 *MemberInfo* **Derived Classes**

Name	Description
ConstructorInfo	Represents a constructor.
EventInfo	Represents an event.
FieldInfo	Represents a field.
LocalVariableInfo	Represents a local variable inside a method's body.
MethodBase	Represents any member that can contain code. This includes methods and constructors. This is the actual base class for *ConstructorInfo* and *MethodInfo*.

Table 14-9 *MemberInfo* Derived Classes

Name	Description
MethodInfo	Represents a method.
PropertyInfo	Represents a property. Properties are accompanied by methods for the get and/or set operations that are specified for a property.
Type	Represents a single type in the system. It can be a nested type within another type or a stand-alone type.

You can see the type of member each of these *MemberInfo* objects is by checking the *MemberType* property on the *MemberInfo* class. This property contains an enumeration value that can represent all the different types of members that a *MemberInfo* object can represent. You can also cast the *MemberInfo* objects into their derived form, like so:

```
' VB
If (member.MemberType = MemberTypes.Property) Then
    Dim prop As PropertyInfo = CType(member,PropertyInfo)
    Console.WriteLine("        Property Type: {0}", prop.PropertyType.Name)
End If

// C#
if (member.MemberType == MemberTypes.Property)
{
    PropertyInfo prop = (PropertyInfo)member;
    Console.WriteLine("        Property Type: {0}", prop.PropertyType.Name);
}
```

Enumerating through members of a type allowed you to find only publicly available members. It also returned all publicly available members whether they were static members or instance members. Finally, it only supported returning all the members that the class has, including those that it inherited. To allow more control over the retrieval of type members, the reflection system supports an enumeration where you can decide what members to return. This feature is called the *BindingFlags* enumeration.

Understanding the *MethodBody*

Iterating through the type information as you have done will allow you to look at the structure of a type, but it won't necessarily allow you to look at the code the type contains. This is where the *MethodBody* object comes in to play. The *MethodBody* is a special sort of container that contains local variables and the actual Intermediate Language (IL) instructions that are compiled into machine code at runtime. You get the *MethodBody* by using the *GetMethodBody* call on a *MethodBase* instance (*ConstructorInfo* or *MethodInfo* class):

```
' VB
Dim body As MethodBody = meth.GetMethodBody()
```

```
// C#
MethodBody body = meth.GetMethodBody();
```

Once you have an instance of the *MethodBody* class, you can get the local variables and the stack size, like so:

```
' VB
Console.WriteLine("  MaxStack: {0}", body.MaxStackSize)
For Each local As LocalVariableInfo In body.LocalVariables
    Console.WriteLine("Local Var ({0}): {1}", _
        local.LocalType, local.LocalIndex)
Next
```

```
// C#
Console.WriteLine("  MaxStack: {0}", body.MaxStackSize);
foreach (LocalVariableInfo local in body.LocalVariables)
{
    Console.WriteLine("Local Var ({0}): {1}",
        local.LocalType, local.LocalIndex);
}
```

The local variables return as an array of *LocalVariableInfo* objects that contain information about the type of each variable. The name of the variable is not available because the metadata about a type doesn't keep the name of the variable, only its order.

Finally, by using the *GetILAsByteArray* method, you can get at an array of bytes that is the actual IL code that the CLR uses to compile and run as machine code. The IL is returned as an array of bytes, as shown in the following example:

```
' VB
For Each b As Byte In body.GetILAsByteArray()
    Console.Write("{0:x2} ", b)
Next
```

```
// C#
foreach (Byte b in body.GetILAsByteArray())
{
    Console.Write("{0:x2} ", b);
}
```

MORE INFO   Intermediate Language

The structure of what IL is and what IL is composed of is an advanced subject that is not covered in this book. Please refer to the MSDN Web site for good sources of information about IL.

Using the *BindingFlags*

The *BindingFlags* enumeration is used to control how members of a type are retrieved using the *GetMembers* method (as well as the specific methods for each member type). The *BindingFlags* enumeration is a flagged enumeration, which means that more than one value can be used. Table 14-10 details each member of the *BindingFlags* enumeration that is used when enumerating members and explains what each value means.

Table 14-10 *BindingFlags* **Enumeration**

Name	Description
DeclaredOnly	Members directly declared on the specific type are included. Inherited members are ignored.
Default	No binding flag is used.
FlattenHierarchy	Declared and inherited members should be returned, but also returns protected members.
IgnoreCase	A case-insensitive matching of the member name should be used.
Instance	Members that are part of an instance of type will be included.
NonPublic	Members that are not public (protected, internal—or friend in Visual Basic—and private) are included.
Public	Members that are public are included.
Static	Members that are defined as static are included.

To use the *BindingFlags*, you combine multiple flags to determine what members you are trying to access. For example, to get all members (public and nonpublic) of a type but limited to only instance members, you would do the following:

```
' VB
Dim t As Type = GetType(String)

' Specify public and non-public, but only instance members
Dim flags As BindingFlags = _
    BindingFlags.Public Or BindingFlags.NonPublic Or BindingFlags.Instance
```

```
' Use the flags to get the members
Dim members() As MemberInfo = t.GetMembers(flags)

For Each member as MemberInfo In members
    Console.WriteLine("Member: {0}", member.Name)
Next

// C#
Type t = typeof(String);

// Specify public and non-public, but only instance members
BindingFlags flags =
    BindingFlags.Public | BindingFlags.NonPublic | BindingFlags.Instance;

// Use the flags to get the members
MemberInfo[] members = t.GetMembers(flags);

foreach (MemberInfo member in members)
{
    Console.WriteLine("Member: {0}", member.Name);
}
```

Lab: Load an Assembly, and Dump Its Type Information

In this lab, you create a console application to load an assembly and show all the type information. If you encounter a problem completing an exercise, the completed projects are available on the companion CD in the Code folder.

1. Create a new console application, and call it AssemblyDemo.

2. Add a *using* statement (or *Imports* in Visual Basic) to the *System.Reflection* namespace to the main code file.

3. In the main method body, create a local string that contains the path to a well-known assembly. The *System.ServiceProcess* assembly in the .NET Framework is a small assembly and works well with this project.

4. Create a local *BindingFlags* variable, and store the flags to get only directly declared, public instance members.

5. Create a new instance of the *Assembly* class by loading the assembly that the local string points to from step 3.

6. Write out the *Assembly*'s full name to the console.

7. Next, get all the types from the *Assembly* object you created in step 5.

8. Iterate through all the types that were returned.

9. Inside the iteration loop, write out the name of the type to the console.

10. Continue inside the iteration loop, and get all the members from each type using the *BindingFlags* variable from step 4.

11. Iterate through each member that was returned, and show the *MemberType* and the name of the member in the console window. Your code might look something like this:

```vb
' VB
Imports System.Reflection
Class Program

    Public Overloads Shared Sub Main()

        Dim path As String = _
            "C:\WINDOWS\Microsoft.NET\Framework\v2.0.50727\" + _
            "System.ServiceProcess.dll"

        ' Using BindingFlags to only get declared public instance members
        Dim flags As BindingFlags = _
            BindingFlags.DeclaredOnly Or _
            BindingFlags.Public Or _
            BindingFlags.Instance

        ' Load the Assembly from the path
        Dim theAssembly As Assembly = Assembly.LoadFrom(path)
        Console.WriteLine(theAssembly.FullName)

        Dim types() As Type = theAssembly.GetTypes
        For Each t As Type In types
            Console.WriteLine(" Type: {0}", t.Name)

            Dim members() As MemberInfo = t.GetMembers(flags)
            For Each member As MemberInfo In members
                Console.WriteLine("    {0}: {1}", member.MemberType, _
                    member.Name)
            Next

        Next

        Console.Read()
    End Sub
End Class

// C#
using System.Reflection;

class Program
{
    static void Main(string[] args)
    {
        string path = @"C:\WINDOWS\Microsoft.NET\Framework\v2.0.50727\" +
            "System.ServiceProcess.dll";
```

```
// Using BindingFlags to only get declared and instance members
BindingFlags flags =
    BindingFlags.DeclaredOnly |
    BindingFlags.Public |
    BindingFlags.Instance;

// Load the Assembly from the path
Assembly theAssembly = Assembly.LoadFrom(path);

Console.WriteLine(theAssembly.FullName);

Type[] types = theAssembly.GetTypes();

foreach (Type t in types)
{
    Console.WriteLine("  Type: {0}", t.Name);

    MemberInfo[] members = t.GetMembers(flags);

    foreach (MemberInfo member in members)
    {
        Console.WriteLine("    {0}: {1}", member.MemberType,
            member.Name);
    }
}

Console.Read();
        }
    }
}
```

12. Build the project, and resolve any errors. Verify that the console application successfully shows all the types in a specified assembly.

Lesson Summary

■ To access type information directly from any object, call the *GetType* method of the *Object* class.

■ To enumerate type members, including methods, properties, fields, events, and enumerations, use the *MemberInfo* and *MemberInfoCollection* classes.

■ To enumerate all the types in a particular assembly, call the *GetTypes* method of the *Assembly* class.

■ To have more control over what members to retrieve from a *Type,* use the *Binding-Flags* enumeration.

Lesson Review

You can use the following questions to test your knowledge of the information in Lesson 3, "Reflecting Types." The questions are also available on the companion CD if you prefer to review them in electronic form.

NOTE Answers

Answers to these questions and explanations of why each answer choice is right or wrong are located in the "Answers" section at the end of the book.

---

1. What classes derive from the *MemberInfo* class? (Choose all that apply.)

   A. *FieldInfo* class

   B. *MethodInfo* class

   C. *Assembly* class

   D. *Type* class

2. What values of the *BindingFlags* enumeration do you need to specify when searching for public instance members directly on a type (not inherited members)? (Choose all that apply.)

   A. *BindingFlags.Public*

   B. *BindingFlags.Static*

   C. *BindingFlags.DeclaredOnly*

   D. *BindingFlags.Instance*

Lesson 4: Writing Dynamic Code

Up to now, you have been looking at type information in an assembly and reporting it to users. At times, you will want to be able to run code in those assemblies. And there are times when you do not have access to code during compile time. Being able to dynamically load an assembly and run code in that assembly without early access to the code is the goal of dynamic code.

After this lesson, you will be able to:

- Use the *ConstructorInfo* class to create a new instance of a type.
- Use the info classes to execute arbitrary code.
- Call static methods and properties.

Estimated lesson time: 15 minutes

Using Dynamic Code

The reflection system allows you to create objects dynamically, even from assemblies you have not referenced ahead of time. Although this is more difficult than writing type-safe compiler-checked code, at times it is necessary.

When you create an object with standard code, how do you do it? You use the constructor. For example, consider the following simple code that creates a *Hashtable*, adds an element, and returns the count:

IMPORTANT   Special consideration about this example

This example uses the *Hashtable,* which most applications already contain references to because the mscorlib assembly is required by nearly every .NET application. The usual case for creating dynamic code is when you need to load code that you have not referenced while developing and compiling your application.

```
' VB
Dim tbl As New Hashtable()
tbl.Add("Hi", "Hello")
Console.WriteLine("Hash count: {0}", tbl.Count)

// C#
Hashtable tbl = new Hashtable();
tbl.Add("Hi", "Hello");
Console.WriteLine("Hash count: {0}", tbl.Count);
```

Creating Objects

You can create this same code dynamically by using the type information you can gather with reflection. The first step is getting the type information, as you did in Lesson 3:

```vb
' VB
Dim path As String = "C:\WINDOWS\Microsoft.NET\Framework\v2.0.50727\" + _
    "mscorlib.dll"

' Get the assembly
Dim theAssembly As Assembly = Assembly.LoadFile(path)

' Get the Hashtable type
Dim hashType As Type = theAssembly.GetType("System.Collections.Hashtable")
```

```csharp
// C#
string path = @"C:\WINDOWS\Microsoft.NET\Framework\v2.0.50727\" +
    "mscorlib.dll";

// Get the assembly
Assembly theAssembly = Assembly.LoadFile(path);

// Get the Hashtable type
Type hashType = theAssembly.GetType("System.Collections.Hashtable");
```

Once you have the type, you can ask it for a *ConstructorInfo* object to use to construct your new type:

```vb
' VB
Dim argumentTypes() As Type = Type.EmptyTypes ' Empty Constructor
Dim ctor As ConstructorInfo = hashType.GetConstructor(argumentTypes)
```

```csharp
// C#
Type[] argumentTypes = Type.EmptyTypes; // Empty Constructor
ConstructorInfo ctor = hashType.GetConstructor(argumentTypes);
```

The method represented in a *ConstructorInfo* object is a specialized *MethodBase* object that looks and acts like a typical method but always returns an instance of a specific type. In this example, you are asking the *Type* class to return an empty constructor. (You are supplying an empty *Array* of *Types* to specify the empty constructor.) You could also ask for a constructor with specific arguments by supplying an array of the constructor argument types, like so:

```vb
' VB
Dim argumentTypes() As Type = _
    New Type() {GetType(System.Int32)} ' One argument of type Int32
Dim ctor As ConstructorInfo = hashType.GetConstructor(argumentTypes)
```

```csharp
// C#
Type[] argumentTypes =
    new Type[] { typeof(int) }; // One argument of type int
ConstructorInfo ctor = hashType.GetConstructor(argumentTypes);
```

Once you have the *ConstructorInfo* object, creating an object is as simple as invoking the constructor. Here is how to invoke the empty constructor:

```
' VB
Dim newHash as Object = ctor.Invoke(New Object() {})
```

```
// C#
object newHash = ctor.Invoke(new object[] {});
```

Invoking Members

Once you have an instance of an object, you simply use reflection to get the info class you need to call, and then you invoke the info class to execute the code. For example, call the *Add* method on your new *Hashtable* instance:

```
' VB
Dim meth As MethodInfo = hashType.GetMethod("Add")
meth.Invoke(newHash, New Object() {"Hi", "Hello"})
```

```
// C#
MethodInfo meth = hashType.GetMethod("Add");
meth.Invoke(newHash, new object[] { "Hi", "Hello" });
```

The *Invoke* call on the *MethodInfo* class requires that you supply it with the object to invoke the member on and an array of parameters that match one of the overloads of the method. In this case, you are calling *Invoke* on your dynamically created *Hashtable* and you are supplying the two arguments that allow you to add a key and value to the *Hashtable*. You can now use the *PropertyInfo* class to get the count of the items in your *Hashtable* to verify that the *Add* worked as you expected it to:

```
' VB
Dim prop As PropertyInfo = hashType.GetProperty("Count")
Dim count As Integer = CType(prop.GetValue(newHash, Nothing),Integer)
```

```
// C#
PropertyInfo prop = hashType.GetProperty("Count");
int count = (int) prop.GetValue(newHash, null);
```

The *PropertyInfo* class supports getting or setting an individual property. In this case, you are calling the *GetValue* method of the *PropertyInfo* class to get the value of the "*Count*" property. When calling the *GetValue* method, it works much like the *Invoke* call shown previously. It requires that you specify an object on which to call the "*Get*" method and that you specify any parameters. Parameters are supplied only for indexer properties.

MORE INFO **Other info classes**

This same pattern for calling code on a particular object follows for the different info classes (*FieldInfo, EventInfo,* and so on). Please see the MSDN documentation for examples of how to invoke each of these types of info classes.

Invoking Static Members

Not all dynamic code requires that you have an instance of a class. When you need to dynamically call static methods, you can skip creation of an object. For example, you can get the *Type* object of the *System.Console* class and grab the *MethodInfo* for *Write-Line* (a static method):

```vb
' VB
Dim consoleType As Type = GetType(Console)
Dim writeLineMethod As System.Reflection.MethodInfo = _
    consoleType.GetMethod("WriteLine", New Type() {GetType(String)})
```

```csharp
// C#
Type consoleType = typeof(Console);
MethodInfo writeLineMethod =
    consoleType.GetMethod("WriteLine", new Type[] { typeof(string) });
```

In this example, you are getting the *MethodInfo* for the overload of the *WriteLine* method that takes a single *String* and writes it out to the console. It is not really different than what you saw earlier in this lesson, except that this is a static method, so you can call it like so:

```vb
' VB
writeLineMethod.Invoke(Nothing, New Object() {count.ToString})
```

```csharp
// C#
writeLineMethod.Invoke(null, new object[] { count.ToString() });
```

Because this is a static method, you specify a null in the parameter that would ordinarily take the instance of the class on which to run the method. You specify the parameters the same as we did in the earlier instanced example.

The *Binder* Class

When using dynamic code, you can construct your own *Binder* class that is responsible for determining how to do type conversions and where to locate dynamic code. An instance of the *Binder* class is an optional argument to the methods of the *Type* class that return members of a type. If an instance of a custom class derived from *Binder* is not specified, the system uses its default binder. A custom *Binder* class is useful if you expect to have to do type conversions or other parameter matching to find the correct method, property, or events when trying to find the implementation of an info class.

MORE INFO   *Binder* class

See the MSDN documentation and its thorough example of how a *Binder* class is created.

Lab: Invoke Members through Reflection

In this lab, you will create a simple console application that loads the *HttpUtility* class from the *System.Web* assembly and use it to encode some text in HTML. If you encounter a problem completing an exercise, the completed projects are available on the companion CD in the Code folder.

1. Create a console application, and call it DynamicCodeDemo.

2. In the main code file, add a *using* statement (or *Imports* for Visual Basic) to the *System.Reflection* namespace.

3. In the main method of the code file, create a new string that is a file path to the *System.Web* assembly in the Framework directory.

4. Create a new *Assembly* object, and load the *System.Web* assembly using the string from step 3.

5. Create a new instance of the *Type* class to get the *System.Web.HttpUtility* class inside the *Assembly* object created in step 4.

6. Get *MethodInfo* objects for the *HtmlEncode* and *HtmlDecode* methods by calling *GetMethod* on the new *Type* object.

7. Create a new string that has elements that would need to be encoded (for example, '<', '>', or '&'). Write the string out to the console.

8. Using the *HttpEncode*'s *MethodInfo* object, encode your string to create a new encoded string. Write this string out to the console.

9. Using the *HttpDecode*'s *MethodInfo* object, decode your string to create a new decoded string. Write this string out to the console. The resulting code might look similar to this:

```
' VB
Imports System.Reflection

Class Program
```

```
    Public Overloads Shared Sub Main()

        Dim path As String = "C:\WINDOWS\Microsoft.NET\Framework\" + _
            "v2.0.50727\System.Web.dll"

        ' Get the Assembly from the file
        Dim webAssembly As Assembly = Assembly.LoadFile(path)

        ' Get the Type object to the HttpUtility class
        Dim utilType As Type = _
            webAssembly.GetType("System.Web.HttpUtility")

        ' Get the static HtmlEncode and HtmlDecode methods
        Dim encode As MethodInfo = utilType.GetMethod("HtmlEncode", _
            New Type() {GetType(System.String)})
        Dim decode As MethodInfo = utilType.GetMethod("HtmlDecode", _
            New Type() {GetType(System.String)})

        ' Create a string to be encoded
        Dim originalString As String = _
            "This is Sally & Jack's Anniversary <sic>"
        Console.WriteLine(originalString)

        ' encode it and show the encoded value
        Dim encoded As String = _
            CType(encode.Invoke(Nothing, New Object() {originalString}), _
                String)
        Console.WriteLine(encoded)

        ' decode it to make sure it comes back right
        Dim decoded As String = _
            CType(decode.Invoke(Nothing, New Object() {encoded}), String)
        Console.WriteLine(decoded)

    End Sub

End Class

// C#
using System.Reflection;

class Program
{
    static void Main(string[] args)
    {
        string path = @"C:\WINDOWS\Microsoft.NET\Framework\" +
            @"v2.0.50727\System.Web.dll";

        // Get the Assembly from the file
        Assembly webAssembly = Assembly.LoadFile(path);

        // Get the Type object to the HttpUtility class
        Type utilType = webAssembly.GetType("System.Web.HttpUtility");
```

```
// Get the static HtmlEncode and HtmlDecode methods
MethodInfo encode = utilType.GetMethod("HtmlEncode",
    new Type[] { typeof(string) });
MethodInfo decode = utilType.GetMethod("HtmlDecode",
    new Type[] { typeof(string) });

// Create a string to be encoded
string originalString =
    "This is Sally & Jack's Anniversary <sic>";
Console.WriteLine(originalString);

// encode it and show the encoded value
string encoded =
    (string) encode.Invoke(null, new object[] { originalString });
Console.WriteLine(encoded);

// decode it to make sure it comes back right
string decoded =
    (string) decode.Invoke(null, new object[] { encoded });
Console.WriteLine(decoded);
        }
    }
```

10. Build the project, and resolve any errors. Verify that the console application successfully encodes and decodes the string.

Lesson Summary

- To create a new instance of a type, use the *Type* class and the *ConstructorInfo* class.

- To execute arbitrary code for a specific instance of a type, use the *MemberInfo* classes.

- To execute static code that is associated with a specific type, use the *MemberInfo* classes.

Lesson Review

You can use the following questions to test your knowledge of the information in Lesson 4, "Writing Dynamic Code." The questions are also available on the companion CD if you prefer to review them in electronic form.

NOTE   Answers

Answers to these questions and explanations of why each answer choice is right or wrong are located in the "Answers" section at the end of the book.

---

1. What method of the *MethodBase* class allows for synchronous execution of a method with two parameters and returns a Boolean value?

   A.

   ```
   ' VB
   method.Invoke(returnValue, param1, param2)
   // C#
   method.Invoke(ref returnValue, param1, param2);
   ```

   B.

   ```
   ' VB
   Dim result As Boolean = CType(method.Invoke(param1, param2),Boolean)
   // C#
   bool result = (bool)method.Invoke(param1, param2);
   ```

   C.

   ```
   ' VB
   Dim result As Boolean = _
     CType(method.Invoke(theInstance, param1, param2),Boolean)
   // C#
   bool result = (bool)method.Invoke(theInstance, param1, param2);
   ```

   D.

   ```
   ' VB
   Dim result As Boolean = CType(method.Invoke(theInstance, _
                           new Object() { param1, param2 }),Boolean)
   // C#
   bool result = (bool)method.Invoke(theInstance,
                           new object[] {param1, param2});
   ```

2. Can the *MethodBody* class be used to invoke part of the body of a method?

   A. Yes.

   B. No.

Lesson 5: Creating Code at Runtime

Reflection is not limited to detecting information about assemblies and types. You can also define this information at runtime and even create your own assemblies (either for in-memory consumption or serialized to disk for reuse).

After this lesson, you will be able to:

- Create a dynamic assembly.
- Create a dynamic module within a new assembly.
- Use the builder classes to build new types.
- Serialize a newly created assembly to disk.

Estimated lesson time: 10 minutes

Building Your Own Code

The reflection system includes a sub-namespace called *Emit* (*System.Reflection.Emit*) that contains a set of builder classes that are used to build assemblies, types, methods, and so on. To build code at runtime, you have to encapsulate it like any other code. (Create an assembly, then a module within the assembly, and finally types within the module.) Each of these builder classes derives from its info class counterpart. For example, *AssemblyBuilder* derives from *Assembly*, *MethodBuilder* derives from *Method-Info*, and *TypeBuilder* derives from *Type*. Table 14-11 lists all the builder classes and their role in creating code at runtime.

Table 14-11   *Builder* Classes

Name	Description
AssemblyBuilder	Used to build assemblies at runtime
ConstructorBuilder	Used to build constructors at runtime
EnumBuilder	Used to build enumerations at runtime
EventBuilder	Used to build events at runtime
FieldBuilder	Used to build fields at runtime
LocalBuilder	Used to build local variables for methods and constructors
MethodBuilder	Used to build methods at runtime

Table 14-11 *Builder* Classes

Name	Description
ModuleBuilder	Used to build modules at runtime
ParameterBuilder	Used to build method parameters at runtime
PropertyBuilder	Used to build properties at runtime
TypeBuilder	Used to build types at runtime

Creating an Assembly and Module

Before you can define any types, you need to create an assembly and module. To do this, you need to ask an *AppDomain* to create a dynamic assembly. The *AppDomain* class has a *DefineDynamicAssembly* method that takes an *AssemblyName* parameter and an *AssemblyBuilderAccess* parameter. The *AssemblyName* object contains each part of the full assembly name. The only required part of the assembly name you need in this case is the simple name. You can construct an *AssemblyName* object like so:

```
' VB
Dim tempName As New AssemblyName()
tempName.Name = "MyTempAssembly"
```

```
// C#
AssemblyName tempName = new AssemblyName();
tempName.Name = "MyTempAssembly";
```

The *AssemblyBuilderAccess* specifies what you can do with the new dynamic assembly. You can specify *ReflectionOnly*, *Run*, *Save*, or *RunAndSave*, depending on what you intend to do with the new assembly. With these two pieces of information, you can now create your dynamic assembly by calling your current *AppDomain*'s *DefineDynamicAssembly* method:

```
' VB
Dim assemBldr As AssemblyBuilder = _
    AppDomain.CurrentDomain.DefineDynamicAssembly(tempName, _
    AssemblyBuilderAccess.RunAndSave)
```

```
// C#
AssemblyBuilder assemBldr =
    AppDomain.CurrentDomain.DefineDynamicAssembly(tempName,
    AssemblyBuilderAccess.RunAndSave);
```

Now that you have an *AssemblyBuilder* object, you can create a *ModuleBuilder* so that you can start creating type information. This is done by simply specifying a name and the filename of the assembly when calling the *AssemblyBuilder.DefineDynamicModule* method:

```vb
' VB
Dim modBldr As ModuleBuilder = assemBldr.DefineDynamicModule("MainMod", _
    "MyTempAssembly.dll")
```

```csharp
// C#
ModuleBuilder modBldr = assemBldr.DefineDynamicModule("MainMod",       "MyTempAssembly.dll");
```

If you want a single file assembly and are serializing the assembly to disk, the filename specified here should be the same as the one you use in the *Save* method that will be shown later in the lesson. With the *ModuleBuilder* in hand, you can now create a dynamic type.

Defining a Type

Creating a dynamic type starts with calling the *ModuleBuilder*'s *DefineType* method. This method takes a type name and *TypeAttributes* enumeration value. The *Type-Attributes* specifies options for the type. In this case, use it to specify that the type will be publicly available and that it is a class (instead of being a struct, interface, and so on):

```vb
' VB
Dim typeBldr As TypeBuilder = modBldr.DefineType("MyNewType", _
    TypeAttributes.Public Or TypeAttributes.Class)
```

```csharp
// C#
TypeBuilder typeBldr = modBldr.DefineType("MyNewType",
    TypeAttributes.Public | TypeAttributes.Class);
```

You can also specify the base class and interfaces that it supports by using overrides of the *DefineType* method, which takes a third parameter as the base class and a fourth parameter that contains an array of types that define the interfaces implemented on the type:

```vb
' VB
Dim typeBldr2 As TypeBuilder = modBldr.DefineType("MyNewType", _
    (TypeAttributes.Public Or TypeAttributes.Class), _
    GetType(Hashtable), _
    New Type() {GetType(IDisposable)})
```
```csharp
// C#
TypeBuilder typeBldr2 = modBldr.DefineType("MyNewType",
    TypeAttributes.Public | TypeAttributes.Class,
    typeof(Hashtable),
    new Type[] { typeof(IDisposable) });
```

Creating Members

The *TypeBuilder* object that the *DefineType* method returns is central to creating dynamic code. The *TypeBuilder* allows you to define any elements of the type. Table 14-12 shows the various methods of the *TypeBuilder* that help you define the members of a type.

Table 14-12 *TypeBuilder* **Definition Methods**

Name	Description
DefineConstructor	Used to define constructors
DefineDefaultConstructor	Used to define a parameterless constructor
DefineEvent	Used to define events
DefineField	Used to define fields
DefineGenericParameters	Used to define generic parameters for generic types
DefineMethod	Used to define methods
DefineMethodOverride	Used to define overloads for methods
DefineNestedType	Used to define new types that are nested in another type
DefinePInvokeMethod	Used to define calls to external code using the *PInvoke* functionality
DefineProperty	Used to define properties

The first thing you need to do on a new type is create a constructor. In this case, you want a default (or parameterless constructor), so you use the *DefineDefaultConstructor* method, like so:

```
' VB
Dim ctorBldr As ConstructorBuilder =
    typeBldr.DefineDefaultConstructor(MethodAttributes.Public)
```

```
// C#
ConstructorBuilder ctorBldr =
    typeBldr.DefineDefaultConstructor(MethodAttributes.Public);
```

The *DefineDefaultConstructor* method takes a *MethodAttributes* enumeration value that dictates the kind of constructor. In this case, you are marking your default constructor as publicly available.

The real magic happens here when you can actually write your own code. You can now take your builder object and create an *ILGenerator* object. The *ILGenerator* class is used to generate local variables and IL code. For example, your constructor is going to do nothing but return, so you can write the code like so:

```
' VB
Dim codeGen As ILGenerator = ctorBldr.GetILGenerator()
codeGen.Emit(OpCodes.Ret)
```

```
// C#
ILGenerator codeGen = ctorBldr.GetILGenerator();
codeGen.Emit(OpCodes.Ret);
```

The *ILGenerator.Emit* call inserts a new line of IL code into the constructor (or any method) that the *ILGenerator* was created from. The *OpCodes* class exposes each of the different IL OpCodes as a separate static member. The *OpCodes.Ret* specifies the IL code for return.

MORE INFO   **Microsoft Intermediate Language**

Before you can really define code inside constructors or methods, you need to understand how IL works. Because this is an advanced topic that is not covered in the exam, it is not covered in this book. Microsoft's implementation of IL is called MSIL. Please see MSDN Online for more information on MSIL (*http://msdn2.microsoft.com/en-US/library/8ffc3x75(VS.80).aspx*).

Creating a constructor is only the beginning of what you can do. You can also create other members of the type. Next let's create a method. Specifying a method requires you to decide on both a return type and the parameter types. The following code provides an example:

```
' VB
Dim methBldr As MethodBuilder = typeBldr.DefineMethod("Add", _
    MethodAttributes.Public, _
    Nothing, _
    New Type() {GetType(System.String)})

// C#
MethodBuilder methBldr = typeBldr.DefineMethod("Add",
    MethodAttributes.Public,
    null,
    new Type[] { typeof(string) });
```

Again, like the other methods, this definition method has its own attributes enumeration to define the method. The third and fourth parameters of the *DefineMethod* method are the return and parameter types.

You can define a static method (or a shared one in Visual Basic) by simply adding *MethodAttributes.Static* to the attributes, like so:

```
' VB
Dim methBldr As MethodBuilder = typeBldr.DefineMethod("Add", _
    MethodAttributes.Public Or MethodAttributes.Static, _
    Nothing, _
    New Type() {GetType(System.String)})

// C#
MethodBuilder methBldr = typeBldr.DefineMethod("Add",
```

```
MethodAttributes.Public | MethodAttributes.Static,
null,
new Type[] { typeof(string) });
```

Next define a new private field called _count that holds the actual count of your new type:

```
' VB
Dim fieldBldr As FieldBuilder = typeBldr.DefineField("_count", _
    GetType(System.Int32), _
    FieldAttributes.Private)
```

```
// C#
FieldBuilder fieldBldr = typeBldr.DefineField("_count",
    typeof(int),
    FieldAttributes.Private);
```

Following the pattern of the other builder class, the *FieldBuilder* also has a *FieldAttributes* enumeration to specify attributes of the field. In this case, you're specifying the field as private.

Finally, you can add a property to the type to expose your new field. You define the property using the *DefineProperty* method.

```
' VB
Dim propBldr As PropertyBuilder = typeBldr.DefineProperty("Count", _
    PropertyAttributes.None, _
    GetType(System.Int32), _
    Type.EmptyTypes)
```

```
// C#
PropertyBuilder propBldr = typeBldr.DefineProperty("Count",
    PropertyAttributes.None,
    typeof(int),
    Type.EmptyTypes);
```

Although defining the property is much like defining a method, the *PropertyAttributes* enumeration does not allow defining as many aspects of the properties as you might expect. For example, you do not specify the visibility of the property in the *PropertyBuilder*. Instead, you need to also define methods that perform the get or set operations on a property. The following code provides an example:

```
' VB
Dim getAttributes As MethodAttributes = MethodAttributes.Public _
    Or MethodAttributes.SpecialName Or _
    MethodAttributes.HideBySig

Dim propGetBldr As MethodBuilder = typeBldr.DefineMethod("get_Count", _
    getAttributes, _
    GetType(System.Int32), _
    Type.EmptyTypes)
```

```
// C#
MethodAttributes getAttributes = MethodAttributes.Public |
    MethodAttributes.SpecialName |
    MethodAttributes.HideBySig;
MethodBuilder propGetBldr = typeBldr.DefineMethod("get_Count",
    getAttributes,
    typeof(int),
    Type.EmptyTypes);
```

You create this new method using the *MethodAttributes* of *SpecialName* and *HideBySig*. These attributes specify that this method is special and it will likely not be part of the public interface. When you name the method, it must be called with *get_XXXX* for the property get operation or *set_XXXX* for the set operation. (You would replace *XXXX* with the name of the property.) In this case, this is *get_Count*. Once you have the get method, you can then associate it with your property by calling the *SetGetMethod* (or *SetSetMethod* for a set operation method):

```
' VB
propBldr.SetGetMethod(propGetBldr)
```

```
// C#
propBldr.SetGetMethod(propGetBldr);
```

Persisting to Disk

You can use your dynamic type and execute code at any point (assuming you specified that the *Assembly* was allowed to run). But in this case, let's now save this assembly to the disk. Once it has been written, any process can attempt to load it and it is exactly like any other assembly in the system. To save the assembly, simply call the *Save* method, like so:

```
' VB
assemBldr.Save("MyTempAssembly.dll")
```

```
// C#
assemBldr.Save("MyTempAssembly.dll");
```

Lab: Create a Dynamic Assembly

In this lab, you will create a console application that will emit a new assembly. If you encounter a problem completing an exercise, the completed projects are available on the companion CD in the Code folder.

1. Create a new console application called DemoDynamic.
2. In the main code file, add *using* statements (or *Imports* statements for Visual Basic) for *System.Reflection* and *System.Reflection.Emit* namespaces.

3. In the main code body, create a new *AssemblyName* object and assign a name and a new version.

4. Create a new *AppDomain* variable, and store the current *AppDomain* in it.

5. Create a new *AssemblyBuilder* object by calling the *AppDomain*'s *DefineDynamic-Assembly* method, specifying the *AssemblyName* from step 3 and that this assembly will be used only for reflection.

6. Define a new *ModuleBuilder* object from the *AssemblyBuilder* created in step 5.

7. Next, define a new *TypeBuilder* using the *ModuleBuilder* object from step 6.

8. Finally, use the *TypeBuilder* to create a *Type* object of the newly created type and iterate through all the members of the new type to see what methods, properties, events, and fields are on the newly created type. Your code might look something like this:

```vb
' VB
Imports System.Reflection
Imports System.Reflection.Emit

Class Program

    Public Shared Sub Main(ByVal args() As String)

        ' Create an Assembly Name
        Dim theName As AssemblyName = New AssemblyName
        theName.Name = "DemoAssembly"
        theName.Version = New Version("1.0.0.0")

        ' Get the AppDomain to put our assembly in
        Dim domain As AppDomain = AppDomain.CurrentDomain

        ' Create the Assembly
        Dim assemBldr As AssemblyBuilder = _
            domain.DefineDynamicAssembly(theName, _
            AssemblyBuilderAccess.ReflectionOnly)

        ' Define a module to hold our type
        Dim modBldr As ModuleBuilder = _
            assemBldr.DefineDynamicModule("CodeModule", "DemoAssembly.dll")

    ' Create a new type
        Dim animalBldr As TypeBuilder = modBldr.DefineType("Animal", _
            TypeAttributes.Public)

        ' Display the new Type
        Dim animal As Type = animalBldr.CreateType
        Console.WriteLine(animal.FullName)
        For Each m As MemberInfo In animal.GetMembers
            Console.WriteLine("  Member ({0}): {1}", m.MemberType, m.Name)
        Next
```

```
            Console.Read()
        End Sub
    End Class

    // C#
    using System.Reflection;
    using System.Reflection.Emit;

    class Program
    {
        static void Main(string[] args)
        {
            // Create an Assembly Name
            AssemblyName theName = new AssemblyName();
            theName.Name = "DemoAssembly";
            theName.Version = new Version("1.0.0.0");

            // Get the AppDomain to put our assembly in
            AppDomain domain = AppDomain.CurrentDomain;

            // Create the Assembly
            AssemblyBuilder assemBldr =
                domain.DefineDynamicAssembly(theName,
                AssemblyBuilderAccess.ReflectionOnly);

            // Define a module to hold our type
            ModuleBuilder modBldr =
                assemBldr.DefineDynamicModule("CodeModule",
                "DemoAssembly.dll");

            // Create a new type
            TypeBuilder animalBldr = modBldr.DefineType("Animal",
                TypeAttributes.Public);

            // Display the new Type
            Type animal = animalBldr.CreateType();
            Console.WriteLine(animal.FullName);
            foreach (MemberInfo m in animal.GetMembers())
            {
                Console.WriteLine("  Member ({0}): {1}", m.MemberType, m.Name);
            }

            Console.Read();
        }
    }
```

9. Build the project, and resolve any errors. Verify that the console application successfully creates an assembly, module, and type and shows the members from the class derived from *Object*.

Lesson Summary

- To create an assembly dynamically at runtime, use the *DefineDynamicAssembly* method of the *AppDomain* class.

- To create a module within a dynamic assembly, call the *DefineDynamicModule* by using the *AssemblyBuilder* class.

- To build types at runtime, use the *ModuleBuilder* class's *DefineType* method.

- To create members of a type, use the *TypeBuilder* class's definition methods, such as *DefineConstructor*, *DefineMethod*, *DefineProperty*, and *DefineField*.

- To save a dynamic assembly to disk, call the *AssemblyBuilder* class's *Save* method.

Lesson Review

You can use the following questions to test your knowledge of the information in Lesson 5, "Creating Code at Runtime." The questions are also available on the companion CD if you prefer to review them in electronic form.

NOTE   Answers

Answers to these questions and explanations of why each answer choice is right or wrong are located in the "Answers" section at the end of the book.

---

1. What class allows the creation of a dynamic assembly (an instance of the *AssemblyBuilder* class)?

    A. *AssemblyBuilder* (because it has a public constructor or static method)

    B. *ModuleBuilder*

    C. *AppDomain*

    D. *Application*

2. What values of the *AssemblyBuilderAccess* enumeration allow you to execute the assembly? (Choose all that apply.)

    A. *AssemblyBuilderAccess.Run*

    B. *AssemblyBuilderAccess.ReflectionOnly*

    C. *AssemblyBuilderAccess.RunAndSave*

    D. *AssemblyBuilderAccess.Save*

Chapter Review

To further practice and reinforce the skills you learned in this chapter, you can perform the following tasks:

- Review the chapter summary.
- Review the list of key terms introduced in this chapter.
- Complete the case scenarios. These scenarios set up real-world situations involving the topics of this chapter and ask you to create a solution.
- Complete the suggested practices.
- Take a practice test.

Chapter Summary

- The *Reflection* namespace includes classes for interrogating the metadata about assemblies, modules, and types in the CLR.
- A number of assembly-specific attributes can be used to specify information about an assembly, such as the copyright, the version, and trademark information.
- A number of classes that are used to hold metadata information derive from the *MemberInfo* class. These include *Type*, *MethodInfo*, and *FieldInfo*.
- The *BindingFlags* enumeration is used to define different options for finding and executing members of various types.
- The *MemberInfo* classes can be used to execute code at runtime, even if you do not have the project referenced during compilation.
- The builder classes can be used to build assemblies, modules, and types at runtime, and they can even allow you to persist new assemblies to disk.

Key Terms

Do you know what these key terms mean? You can check your answers by looking up the terms in the glossary at the end of the book.

- module
- multifile assemblies
- satellite assemblies

Case Scenario: Create a Plugin Architecture

In the following case scenario, you will apply what you've learned about the topics of this chapter. You can find answers to the questions presented in this section in the "Answers" section at the end of this book.

You work for a small ISV. Your main application allows customers to draw network diagrams. Your company is trying to get other companies to provide new functionality to your software that your customers can purchase. Your manager wants you to recommend how to allow this type of change to your application.

Interviews

Following is a list of company personnel interviewed and their statements:

- **Development Manager**   "We want them to be able to drop their code in our application and have it just work. We cannot expect that the .NET SDK will be on each client's machine, so we can't recompile our application based on other companies' components."

Questions

Answer the following questions for your manager:

1. How do you intend to make this happen?
2. How can you show any trademark or company information of your partners in the application?

Suggested Practices

To help you successfully master the objectives covered in this chapter, complete the following tasks.

Write an Assembly Explorer Application

For this task, you should complete at least Practices 1 and 2. You can do Practice 3 for a more in-depth understanding of reflection.

Practice 1

- Create a Windows Forms application that will load a specific assembly and show all the reflected data as a hierarchy.

- Allow the users to list all the attributes for any parts of the hierarchy by testing for *ICustomAttributeProvider* and calling *GetCustomAttributes*.

Practice 2

- Add functionality to allow the user to create instances of any type.
- Allow users to set properties and run methods on the created instances.
- Allow users to run static methods on the types.

Practice 3

- Allow users to copy types into new dynamic assemblies and save the new assemblies.

Take a Practice Test

The practice tests on this book's companion CD offer many options. For example, you can test yourself on just one exam objective, or you can test yourself on all the 70-536 certification exam content. You can set up the test so that it closely simulates the experience of taking a certification exam, or you can set it up in study mode so that you can look at the correct answers and explanations after you answer each question.

MORE INFO   **Practice tests**

For details about all the practice test options available, see the "How to Use the Practice Tests" section in this book's Introduction.

Chapter 15
Mail

E-mail is an extremely popular communication mechanism. Unlike the telephone and most other ways of communicating, e-mail is easy for applications to use. For a developer, e-mail is an effective way to allow an application to send files or reports to users and to notify users of problems or events.

The .NET Framework version 2.0 adds the *System.Net.Mail* namespace, which provides classes that enable you to easily create and transmit e-mail messages. Messages can include plain text, HTML, and file attachments. At a high level, sending e-mail has two steps: creating the mail message, and then sending the message to an SMTP (Simple Mail Transfer Protocol) server. Lesson 1 covers how to create a message, and Lesson 2 covers how to send the message.

NOTE   .NET 2.0

The *System.Net.Mail* namespace is new in .NET Framework version 2.0.

Exam objectives in this chapter:
- Send electronic mail to a Simple Mail Transfer Protocol (SMTP) server for delivery from a .NET Framework application. (Refer *System.Net.Mail* namespace)
  - ❏ *MailMessage* class
  - ❏ *MailAddress* class and *MailAddressCollection* class
  - ❏ *SmtpClient* class, *SmtpPermission* class, and *SmtpPermissionAttribute* class
  - ❏ *Attachment* class, *AttachmentBase* class, and *AttachmentCollection* class
  - ❏ *SmtpException* class, *SmtpFailedRecipientException* class, and *SmtpFailedRecipientsException* class
  - ❏ *SendCompletedEventHandler* delegate
  - ❏ *LinkedResource* class and *LinkedResourceCollection* class
  - ❏ *AlternateView* class and *AlternateViewCollection* class

Lessons in this chapter:

Before You Begin

To complete the lessons in this chapter, you should be familiar with Microsoft Visual Basic or C# and be comfortable with the following tasks:

- Create a console application in Microsoft Visual Studio using Visual Basic or C#.
- Add references to system class libraries to a project.

Lesson 1: Creating a Mail Message

Creating an e-mail message can be simple or complex. At its simplest, an e-mail message has a sender, recipient, subject, and body. These simple messages can be created with a single line of code using the .NET Framework. At their most complex, e-mail messages can have custom encoding types, multiple views for plain text and HTML, attachments, and images embedded within HTML.

After this lesson, you will be able to:

- Describe the process of creating and sending an e-mail.
- Create a *MailMessage* object.
- Attach one or more files to an e-mail message.
- Create HTML e-mails with or without pictures.
- Catch and respond to different exceptions that might be thrown while creating a message.

Estimated lesson time: 30 minutes

The Process of Creating and Sending an E-mail Message

To create and send an e-mail message, follow these steps:

1. Create a *MailMessage* object. *MailMessage* and other mail-related classes are in the *System.Net.Mail* namespace.

2. If you did not specify the recipients in the *MailMessage* constructor, add them to the *MailMessage* object.

3. If you need to provide multiple views (such as plain text and HTML), create *AlternateView* objects and add them to the *MailMessage* object.

4. If necessary, create one or more *Attachment* objects and add them to the *MailMessage* object.

5. Create an *SmtpClient* object, and specify the SMTP server.

6. If the SMTP server requires clients to authenticate, add credentials to the *SmtpClient* object.

7. Pass your *MailMessage* object to the *SmtpClient.Send* method. Alternatively, you can use *SmtpClient.SendAsync* to send the message asynchronously.

Steps 5 through 7 are described in detail in Lesson 2.

How to Create a *MailMessage* Object

The *MailMessage* object has four different constructors that allow you to create a blank *MailMessage*; specify both the sender and recipient; or specify the sender, recipient, subject, and message body. If you are creating a simple message with a single recipient, you can do the bulk of the work in the *MailMessage* constructor:

```vb
' VB
Dim m As MailMessage = New MailMessage _
    ("jane@contoso.com", _
     "ben@contoso.com", _
     "Quarterly data report.", _
     "See the attached spreadsheet.")
```

```csharp
// C#
MailMessage m = new MailMessage
    ("jane@contoso.com",
     "ben@contoso.com",
     "Quarterly data report.",
     "See the attached spreadsheet.");
```

NOTE Sending quick messages

You can also use an overload of the *SmtpClient.Send* method to send an e-mail without creating a *MailMessage* object. *SmtpClient* is described in Lesson 2.

You can specify the sender and the recipient as either a string or *MailAddress* object. The *MailAddress* object allows you to specify an e-mail address, a display name, and an encoding type, as the following code sample demonstrates:

```vb
' VB
Dim m As MailMessage = New MailMessage _
    (New MailAddress("lance@contoso.com", "Lance Tucker"), _
     New MailAddress("ben@contoso.com", "Ben Miller"))
```

```csharp
// C#
MailMessage m = new MailMessage
    (new MailAddress("lance@contoso.com", "Lance Tucker"),
     new MailAddress("ben@contoso.com", "Ben Miller"));
```

NOTE Encoding types

Specifying the encoding type for e-mail addresses is rarely necessary.

If you need to specify multiple recipients, use the blank *MailMessage* constructor. Then add *MailAddress* objects to the *MailMessage.To* property (which is of the

MailAddressCollection type), and specify *MailMessage.From*, *MailMessage.Subject*, and *MailMessage.Body*:

```vb
' VB
Dim m As MailMessage = New MailMessage()
m.From = New MailAddress("lance@contoso.com", "Lance Tucker")
m.To.Add(New MailAddress("james@contoso.com", "James van Eaton"))
m.To.Add(New MailAddress("ben@contoso.com", "Ben Miller"))
m.To.Add(New MailAddress("burke@contoso.com", "Burke Fewel"))
m.Subject = "Quarterly data report."
m.Body = "See the attached spreadsheet."
```

```csharp
// C#
MailMessage m = new MailMessage();
m.From = new MailAddress("lance@contoso.com", "Lance Tucker");
m.To.Add(new MailAddress("james@contoso.com", "James van Eaton"));
m.To.Add(new MailAddress("ben@contoso.com", "Ben Miller"));
m.To.Add(new MailAddress("burke@contoso.com", "Burke Fewel"));
m.Subject = "Quarterly data report.";
m.Body = "See the attached spreadsheet.";
```

Additionally, you can add recipients to the *MailMessage.Cc* and *MailMessage.Bcc* properties in exactly the same way as you would add recipients to *MailMessage.From*. Recipients specified with *MailMessage.Cc* will receive the message, and their names will show up on the CC line of the e-mail, which is visible to all recipients. Recipients specified with *MailMessage.Bcc* will receive the message, but their names will not be visible to other recipients. BCC stands for "blind carbon copy," a term that originated when people made duplicates of typed paper memos using carbon paper.

NOTE **The risk of BCC**

Instead of using BCC, you should send a separate copy of your message to each recipient that you want to receive a blind copy. The problem with BCC is that spam filters frequently block messages that do not have the recipient's e-mail address in the From header. Therefore, if you use BCC, the message will very likely be filtered.

MailMessage has the following less frequently used properties:

- **DeliveryNotificationOptions** Instructs the SMTP server to send a message to the address specified in *MailMessage.From* if a message is delayed, fails, or is successfully delivered or relayed to another server. The enumeration is of type *DeliveryNotificationOptions*, and the values are *OnSuccess*, *OnFailure*, *Delay*, *None*, and *Never*.

- **ReplyTo** The e-mail address that replies will be sent to. Because the .NET Framework does not act as an e-mail client, and therefore your application will not

typically be receiving e-mail, in most cases you should simply set *MailMessage*
.From to the address that should receive replies instead of using *ReplyTo*.

■ *Priority*   The priority of the message. This does not in any way affect how the
.NET Framework or the mail server handles the message. However, the priority
might be visible in the recipient's e-mail client. The priority is also useful for filtering automatically generated e-mail based on the priority of the event that initiated the e-mail. This enumeration is of type *MailPriority* and can have values of
Normal, *High*, and *Low*.

How to Attach Files

To attach a file, add it to the *MailMessage.Attachments AttachmentCollection* by calling
the *MailMessage.Attachments.Add* method. The simplest way to add a file is to specify
the file name:

```
' VB
Dim m As MailMessage = New MailMessage()
m.Attachments.Add(New Attachment("C:\boot.ini"))
```

```
// C#
MailMessage m = new MailMessage();
m.Attachments.Add(new Attachment(@"C:\boot.ini"));
```

You can also specify a MIME (Multipurpose Internet Mail Extensions) content type
using the *System.Net.Mime.MediaTypeNames* enumeration. There are special MIME
types for text and images, but you will typically specify *MediaTypeNames.Applica-
tion.Octet*. The following code sample (which requires *System.IO* and *System.Net.Mime*
in addition to *System.Net.Mail*) demonstrates how to use a *Stream* as a file attachment
and how to specify the MIME type:

```
' VB
Dim m As MailMessage = New MailMessage()
Dim sr As Stream = New FileStream("C:\Boot.ini", FileMode.Open, FileAccess.Read)
m.Attachments.Add(New Attachment(sr, "myfile.txt", MediaTypeNames.Application.Octet))
```

```
// C#
MailMessage m = new MailMessage();
Stream sr = new FileStream(@"C:\Boot.ini", FileMode.Open, FileAccess.Read);
m.Attachments.Add(new Attachment(sr, "myfile.txt", MediaTypeNames.Application.Octet));
```

As the previous example demonstrates, you should specify a filename when creating
an attachment from a *Stream* object. Otherwise, the attachment will be labeled with a
generic name such as "application_octect-stream.dat". Because the file extension
would be incorrect, users would not be able to easily open the attachment in the correct application.

How to Create HTML E-mails

To create an HTML e-mail message, supply HTML-tagged content for *MailMessage* *.Body* and set the *MailMessage.IsBodyHtml* attribute to True, as the following code sample demonstrates:

```
' VB
Dim m As MailMessage = New MailMessage
m.From = New MailAddress("lance@contoso.com", "Lance Tucker")
m.To.Add(New MailAddress("burke@contoso.com", "Burke Fewel"))
m.Subject = "Testing HTML"

' Specify an HTML message body
m.Body = "<html><body><h1>My Message</h1><br>This is an HTML message.</body></html>"
m.IsBodyHtml = True

' Send the message
Dim client As SmtpClient = New SmtpClient("smtp.contoso.com")
client.Send(m)

// C#
MailMessage m = new MailMessage();
m.From = new MailAddress("lance@contoso.com", "Lance Tucker");
m.To.Add(new MailAddress("burke@contoso.com", "Burke Fewel"));
m.Subject = "Testing HTML";

// Specify an HTML message body
m.Body = "<html><body><h1>My Message</h1><br>This is an HTML message.</body></html>";
m.IsBodyHtml = true;

// Send the message
SmtpClient client = new SmtpClient("smtp.contoso.com");
client.Send(m);
```

MailMessage.Subject is always plain text. You can define *MailMessage.Body* just like any HTML Web page. However, most e-mail clients will ignore the <head> section, will ignore any client-side scripts, and will not automatically download images from Web sites.

To embed images into an HTML message so that they appear when the user clicks the message (without requiring the user to explicitly choose to download images), use the *AlternateView* and *LinkedResource* classes. First, create an HTML message using *AlternateView*, and then add images using *LinkedResource*, as the following sample code demonstrates:

```
' VB
' Create the HTML message body
' Reference embedded images using the content ID
Dim htmlBody As String = "<html><body><h1>Picture</h1><br>" + _
    "<img src=""cid:Pic1""></body></html>"
```

```
Dim avHtml As AlternateView = AlternateView.CreateAlternateViewFromString _
    (htmlBody, Nothing, MediaTypeNames.Text.Html)

' Create a LinkedResource object for each embedded image
Dim pic1 As LinkedResource = New LinkedResource("pic.jpg", MediaTypeNames.Image.Jpeg)
pic1.ContentId = "Pic1"
avHtml.LinkedResources.Add(pic1)

' Create an alternate view for unsupported clients
Dim textBody As String = "You must use an e-mail client that supports HTML messages"
Dim avText As AlternateView = AlternateView.CreateAlternateViewFromString _
    (textBody, Nothing, MediaTypeNames.Text.Plain)

' Add the alternate views instead of using MailMessage.Body
Dim m As MailMessage = New MailMessage
m.AlternateViews.Add(avHtml)
m.AlternateViews.Add(avText)

' Address and send the message
m.From = New MailAddress("lance@contoso.com", "Lance Tucker")
m.To.Add(New MailAddress("james@contoso.com", "James van Eaton"))
m.Subject = "A picture using alternate views"
Dim client As SmtpClient = New SmtpClient("smtp.contoso.com")
client.Send(m)

// C#
// Create the HTML message body
// Reference embedded images using the content ID
string htmlBody = "<html><body><h1>Picture</h1><br><img src=\"cid:Pic1\"></body></html>";
AlternateView avHtml = AlternateView.CreateAlternateViewFromString
    (htmlBody, null, MediaTypeNames.Text.Html);

// Create a LinkedResource object for each embedded image
LinkedResource pic1 = new LinkedResource("pic.jpg", MediaTypeNames.Image.Jpeg);
pic1.ContentId = "Pic1";
avHtml.LinkedResources.Add(pic1);

// Create an alternate view for unsupported clients
string textBody = "You must use an e-mail client that supports HTML messages";
AlternateView avText = AlternateView.CreateAlternateViewFromString
    (textBody, null, MediaTypeNames.Text.Plain);

// Add the alternate views instead of using MailMessage.Body
MailMessage m = new MailMessage();
m.AlternateViews.Add(avHtml);
m.AlternateViews.Add(avText);

// Address and send the message
m.From = new MailAddress("lance@contoso.com", "Lance Tucker");
m.To.Add(new MailAddress("james@contoso.com", "James van Eaton"));
m.Subject = "A picture using alternate views";
SmtpClient client = new SmtpClient("smtp.contoso.com");
client.Send(m);
```

This code produces the HTML message shown in Figure 15-1 (assuming pic.jpg was a picture of a cute puppy stored in the same folder as the assembly).

Figure 15-1 Using *AlternateView* and *LinkedResource* to embed images in emails

To reference images attached as linked resources from your HTML message body, use "cid:*contentID*" in the <img> tag. Then specify the same name for the *LinkedResource.ContentID* property. In the previous example, the body of the HTML message contained the tag <img src=\"cid:Pic1\">, and *LinkedResource.ContentID* was set to "Pic1". Each *LinkedResource* should have a unique *ContentID*.

Lab: Create a *MailMessage* Object

In this lab, you create a *MailMessage* object based on user input into a Microsoft Windows Forms application that is provided for you. If you encounter a problem completing an exercise, the completed projects are available on the companion CD in the Code folder.

1. Use Windows Explorer to copy either the C# or Visual Basic version of the Chapter15\Lesson1-Exercise1 folder from the companion CD to your My Documents\Visual Studio Projects\ folder. Then open the solution.

2. Add the *System.Net.Mail* namespace to your code.

3. The runtime calls the *sendButton_Click* method when you click the Send button in the form. You now need to add logic to create a *MailMessage* object using user input, as the following code demonstrates:

```
' VB
' Create a MailMessage object
Dim mm As MailMessage = New MailMessage
```

```
// C#
// Create a MailMessage object
MailMessage mm = new MailMessage();
```

4. Now, specify the sender and recipient. Note that it's okay if the user hasn't typed display names for the To and From addresses, because the *MailAddress* constructor can accept a Null value for the second string. This code demonstrates how to do this:

```
' VB
' Define the sender and recipient
mm.From = New MailAddress(fromEmailAddress.Text, fromDisplayName.Text)
mm.To.Add(New MailAddress(toEmailAddress.Text, toDisplayName.Text))
```

```
// C#
// Define the sender and recipient
mm.From = new MailAddress(fromEmailAddress.Text, fromDisplayName.Text);
mm.To.Add(new MailAddress(toEmailAddress.Text, toDisplayName.Text));
```

5. Next, define the subject and body, as the following code demonstrates:

```
' VB
' Define the subject and body
mm.Subject = subjectTextBox.Text
mm.Body = bodyTextBox.Text
mm.IsBodyHtml = htmlRadioButton.Checked
```

```
// C#
// Define the subject and body
mm.Subject = subjectTextBox.Text;
mm.Body = bodyTextBox.Text;
mm.IsBodyHtml = htmlRadioButton.Checked;
```

6. Build and run your project in Debug mode. Without typing anything, click the Send button. Notice that the runtime throws an *ArgumentException*. Create a Try/Catch block around your code to catch an *ArgumentException* and display a message to the user, as the following code demonstrates:

```
' VB
Try
    ' Method logic omitted
Catch ex As ArgumentException
```

```
      MessageBox.Show("You must type from and to e-mail addresses", _
          "Invalid input", MessageBoxButtons.OK, MessageBoxIcon.Error)
End Try

// C#
try
{
    // Method logic omitted
}
catch (ArgumentException)
{
    MessageBox.Show("You must type from and to e-mail addresses",
        "Invalid input", MessageBoxButtons.OK, MessageBoxIcon.Error);
}
```

NOTE **Why not manually validate input?**

In Chapter 3, "Searching, Modifying, and Encoding Text," you learned how to use regular expressions to validate user input. There are even specific examples in Chapter 3 for validating e-mail addresses. Although you could use regular expressions to validate input in this example, it would be redundant. The *MailMessage* object includes logic for validating input, as the next step demonstrates. In some circumstances, security might be important enough to justify having two levels of validation. In this example, the additional complexity and increased chance of introducing a bug are not justified.

---

7. Build and run your project in Debug mode again. This time, type "hello" into the To and From e-mail address boxes, and then click the Send button. Notice that the runtime throws a *FormatException* if the user provides an e-mail address in an invalid format. Add a *Catch* block to catch a *FormatException* and display a message to the user, as the following code demonstrates:

```
' VB
Catch ex As FormatException
    MessageBox.Show("You must provide valid from and to e-mail addresses", _
        "Invalid input", MessageBoxButtons.OK, MessageBoxIcon.Error)

// C#
catch (FormatException)
{
    MessageBox.Show("You must provide valid from and to e-mail addresses",
        "Invalid input", MessageBoxButtons.OK, MessageBoxIcon.Error);
}
```

8. Build and run your project. Populate the form's text boxes with valid data, and click Send. Nothing will happen yet because you haven't written code to send the message. You will complete this application in Lesson 2.

Lesson Summary

- To send an e-mail message, create a *MailMessage* object, specify the sender, subject, and body; and add recipients, alternate views, and file attachments. Then create an instance of the *SmtpClient* class, and call *SmtpClient.Send* or *SmtpClient.SendAsync* (covered in Lesson 2).

- The *MailMessage* object includes constructors that allow you to create simple messages with a single line of code. More complex messages and messages with multiple recipients will require adding more code.

- To attach a file, create an instance of the *Attachment* class and add it to the *MailMessage.Attachments* collection.

- Creating an HTML message without images is as simple as specifying HTML in the body and setting *MailMessage.IsBodyHtml* to True. If you need to include images in the message, create an *AlternateView* object and a *LinkedResource* object for each image.

Lesson Review

You can use the following questions to test your knowledge of the information in Lesson 1, "Creating a Mail Message." The questions are also available on the companion CD if you prefer to review them in electronic form.

NOTE Answers

Answers to these questions and explanations of why each answer choice is right or wrong are located in the "Answers" section at the end of the book.

---

1. From which of the following sources can you attach a file to an e-mail message? (Choose all that apply.)

   A. Local file system

   B. *Stream*

   C. Web site

   D. An incoming e-mail message

2. Which of the following are required to send an HTML e-mail message? (Choose all that apply.)

   A. Set *MailMessage.Body* to an HTML message.

   B. Set *MailMessage.Head* to an HTML header.

    C. Set *MailMessage.IsBodyHtml* to True.

    D. Set *MailMessage.Subject* to an HTML message.

3. Which of the following HTML tags correctly references the following linked resource as an image?

```
' VB
' Create a LinkedResource object for each embedded image
Dim lr As LinkedResource = New LinkedResource("myPic.jpg", MediaTypeNames.Image.Jpeg)
lr.ContentId = "myPic"

// C#
// Create a LinkedResource object for each embedded image
LinkedResource lr = new LinkedResource("myPic.jpg", MediaTypeNames.Image.Jpeg);
lr.ContentId = "myPic";
```

    A. `<img src="cid:myPic">`

    B. `<img src="cid:myPic.jpg">`

    C. `<img src="myPic">`

    D. `<img src="myPic.jpg">`

4. You want to send an HTML message that is also viewable in clients that do not support HTML. Which class should you use?

    A. *LinkedResource*

    B. *Attachment*

    C. *AlternateView*

    D. *SmtpClient*

Lesson 2: Sending Mail

Often, sending an e-mail message is simple and requires only two lines of code. However, as with any network communication, it can become much more complex. If the server is unresponsive, you need to allow users to decide whether to wait for or cancel the message transfer. Some servers require valid user credentials, so you might need to provide a username and password. When possible, you should enable the Secure Sockets Layer (SSL) to encrypt the message in transit and reduce your security risks.

After this lesson, you will be able to:

- Configure an SMTP server, and send an e-mail message.
- Provide a username and password when required to authenticate to an SMTP server.
- Enable SSL to encrypt SMTP communications.
- Send a message asynchronously to allow your application to respond to the user or perform other tasks while an e-mail is being sent.
- Catch and respond to different exceptions that might be thrown while sending a message.

Estimated lesson time: 30 minutes

How to Send a Message

Once you create a message, you need to send it through an SMTP (Simple Message Transfer Protocol) server, which in turn will forward it to the recipient. In the .NET Framework, the *SmtpClient* class represents the SMTP server. Most of the time, sending a message is as simple as this sample code (where "smtp.contoso.com" is the name of the local SMTP server):

```
' VB
Dim m As MailMessage = New MailMessage _
    ("jane@contoso.com", _
     "ben@contoso.com", _
     "Quarterly data report.", _
     "See the attached spreadsheet.")
Dim client As SmtpClient = New SmtpClient("smtp.contoso.com")
client.Send(m)

// C#
MailMessage m = new MailMessage
    ("jane@northrup.org",
     "ben@northrup.org",
     "Quarterly data report.",
```

```
    "See the attached spreadsheet.");
SmtpClient client = new SmtpClient("smtp.contoso.com");
client.Send(m);
```

To send a message, call *SmtpClient.Send*.

NOTE   The *SmtpClient.PickupDirectoryLocation* property

The *SmtpClient.PickupDirectoryLocation* property is intended for Web applications. To send messages through an IIS-based SMTP server, specify the host name of the IIS server just like you would any other SMTP server. To specify the local computer, use "localhost" or "127.0.0.1".

> **Real World**
>
> *Tony Northrup*
>
> Years ago, I used to recommend that everyone install IIS, enable the SMTP service on the computer that would be running their application, and send messages through the local SMTP server. This process is much more efficient than using a remote SMTP server because the local IIS SMTP server will directly contact each recipient's SMTP servers to send the message. Additionally, you don't have to deal with network connections.
>
> However, this approach became unreliable as organizations battled against spam. Organizations now block incoming messages from large blocks of IP addresses. Even if you are not a spammer, messages sent from a local SMTP server might be rejected if your IP address appears on one of these lists. To make it more complicated, you might be able to send messages to most domains but be rejected by others.
>
> Ultimately, the job of managing SMTP servers is now too complex to have every user running their own mail server. As a result, I now recommend people use their ISP's or their organization's mail server for outgoing messages.

How to Handle Mail Exceptions

Many things can go wrong when sending e-mail. For example, the mail server might not be available, the server might reject your user credentials, or the server might determine that one of your recipients is invalid. In each of these circumstances, the runtime will throw an exception, and your application must be prepared to catch the exception.

When you send a message, you should always be prepared to catch an *SmtpException*. Messages are frequently rejected because the SMTP server cannot be found, the server identified the message as spam, or the server requires a username and password.

You should also catch *SmtpFailedRecipientException*, which the runtime will throw if the SMTP server rejects a recipient e-mail address. SMTP servers reject only local recipients. In other words, if you are sending a message to tony@contoso.com and are using Contoso's SMTP server, the server is likely to reject the message if tony@contoso.com is not a valid address (causing the runtime to throw a *SmtpFailed-RecipientException*). However, if you are sending a message to the same invalid address using Fabrikam's SMTP server, the SMTP server will not be able to identify that the e-mail address is invalid. Therefore, the runtime will not throw an exception.

Table 15-1 summarizes these and other exceptions that the runtime might throw.

Table 15-1   Exceptions that Can Occur when Sending Mail

Situation	Exception	Synchronous or Asynchronous
You did not define the server hostname.	*InvalidOperationException*	Both
The server hostname could not be found.	*SmtpException* with an inner *WebException*	Both
You are sending a message to a recipient at your local mail server, but the recipient does not have a mailbox.	*SmtpFailedRecipient-Exception*	Synchronous
You are not a valid user, or other message transmission problems.	*SmtpException*	Both

When using *SmtpClient.SendAsync*, invalid recipients and several other events do not result in an exception. Instead, the runtime will call the *SmtpClient.SendCompleted* event. If *AsyncCompletedEventArgs.Error* is not Null, an error occurred.

How to Configure Credentials

To reduce spam, all SMTP servers should reject messages from unauthorized users when the message recipients are not hosted by the SMTP server. SMTP servers provided by ISPs typically determine whether a user is authorized based on the user's IP address; if you are part of the ISP's network, you are allowed to use the SMTP server.

Other SMTP servers (and some ISP SMTP servers) require users to provide a valid username and password. To use the default network credentials, set *SmtpClient .UseDefaultCredentials* to True. Alternatively, you can set *SmtpClient.Credentials* to *CredentialCache.DefaultNetworkCredentials* (in the *System.Net* namespace), as the following code demonstrates:

```
' VB
Dim client As SmtpClient = New SmtpClient("smtp.contoso.com")
client.Credentials = CredentialCache.DefaultNetworkCredentials

// C#
SmtpClient client = new SmtpClient("smtp.contoso.com");
client.Credentials = CredentialCache.DefaultNetworkCredentials;
```

To specify the username and password, create an instance of the *System.Net.NetworkCredential* class and use it to define *SmtpClient.Credentials*. The following example shows hard-coded credentials; however, you should always prompt the user for credentials:

```
' VB
Dim client As SmtpClient = New SmtpClient("smtp.contoso.com")
client.Credentials = New NetworkCredential("user", "password")

// C#
SmtpClient client = new SmtpClient("smtp.contoso.com");
client.Credentials = new NetworkCredential("user", "password");
```

How to Configure SSL

Another important security-related property is *SmtpClient.EnableSsl*. When you set this value to True, the runtime will encrypt the SMTP communications using SSL. Not all SMTP servers support SSL, but you should always enable this property if support is available.

NOTE .NET 2.0

SmtpClient.EnableSsl is new in .NET 2.0.

How to Send a Message Asynchronously

Sending an e-mail message often takes less than a second. Other times, however, the SMTP server might be slow or completely unresponsive, causing your application to wait for the value specified by *SmtpClient.Timeout*. While your application waits for the SMTP server (up to 100 seconds by default), your application will be unresponsive and the cursor will change to an hourglass. Users don't have much patience for unresponsive applications, and there is a good chance they will terminate your application.

Fortunately, you can send e-mails asynchronously to enable your application to respond to the user while you wait for the message to be sent. You can even give the user the opportunity to cancel the e-mail transmission. To send a message asynchronously, perform these tasks:

1. Create a method to respond to the *SmtpClient.SendCompleted* event. This method needs to determine whether the transmission was successful, unsuccessful, or cancelled.

2. Add your event handler to *SmtpClient.SendCompleted*.

3. Call *SmtpClient.SendAsync*.

4. Optionally, provide the user the opportunity to cancel the e-mail by calling the *SmtpClient.SendAsyncCancel* method.

For example, the following method responds to an *SmtpClient.SendCompleted* event (it requires the *System.ComponentModel* namespace):

```vb
' VB
Sub sc_SendCompleted(ByVal sender As Object, ByVal e As AsyncCompletedEventArgs)
    If e.Cancelled Then
        Console.WriteLine("Message cancelled")
    Else
        If Not (e.Error Is Nothing) Then
            Console.WriteLine("Error: " + e.Error.ToString)
        Else
            Console.WriteLine("Message sent")
        End If
    End If
End Sub
```

```csharp
// C#
void sc_SendCompleted(object sender, AsyncCompletedEventArgs e)
{
    if (e.Cancelled)
        Console.WriteLine("Message cancelled");
    else if (e.Error != null)
        Console.WriteLine("Error: " + e.Error.ToString());
    else
        Console.WriteLine("Message sent");
}
```

And the following code creates the *SmtpClient* object, adds the event handler, calls the asynchronous send, and then immediately cancels the send. Naturally, in real code, you would wait for the user to initiate a cancellation. This code assumes a *MailMessage* object named *mm* already exists.

```
' VB
SmtpClient sc = new SmtpClient("server_name");

' Add the event handler
AddHandler sc.SendCompleted, AddressOf sc_SendCompleted

' Send the message asynchronously
sc.SendAsync(mm, Nothing)

' Cancel the send
sc.SendAsyncCancel()


// C#
sc = new SmtpClient("server_name");

// Add the event handler
sc.SendCompleted += new SendCompletedEventHandler(sc_SendCompleted);

// Send the message asynchronously
sc.SendAsync(mm, null);

// Cancel the send
sc.SendAsyncCancel();
```

SmtpClient.SendAsync accepts two parameters: the *MailMessage* object to be sent and a generic *Object*. You can specify Null or any other object for the second parameter; it is strictly for your own use. The .NET Framework simply passes it to the event handler. If you were sending multiple messages asynchronously, you could use the second parameter to keep track of which message generated the event.

Lab: Send an E-mail Message

In this lab, you complete the application you created in Lesson 1 by sending the e-mail message. If you encounter a problem completing an exercise, the completed projects are available on the companion CD in the Code folder.

▶ **Exercise 1: Create an *SmtpClient* Object to Send a *MailMessage* Object**

In this exercise, you extend an existing application to create an *SmtpClient* object and send an e-mail message.

1. Use Windows Explorer to copy either the C# or Visual Basic version of the Chapter 15\Lesson2-Exercise1 folder from the companion CD to your My Documents\ Visual Studio Projects\ folder. Then open the solution. Alternatively, you can continue working with the application you created in Lesson 1, Exercise 1, adding new code right after the mail message definitions.

2. Add the *System.Net* namespace to your code. (You will need the *System.Net.Network-Credential* class.)

3. Write code to create an instance of *SmtpClient*, enable SSL if required, and configure credentials if required. The following code demonstrates this:

```
' VB
' Configure the mail server
Dim sc As SmtpClient = New SmtpClient(serverTextBox.Text)
sc.EnableSsl = sslCheckBox.Checked
If Not String.IsNullOrEmpty(usernameTextBox.Text) Then
    sc.Credentials = New NetworkCredential(usernameTextBox.Text, passwordTextBox.Text)
End If

// C#
// Configure the mail server
SmtpClient sc = new SmtpClient(serverTextBox.Text);
sc.EnableSsl = sslCheckBox.Checked;
if (!String.IsNullOrEmpty(usernameTextBox.Text))
    sc.Credentials = new NetworkCredential(usernameTextBox.Text, passwordTextBox.Text);
```

4. Write code to send the e-mail message, and notify the user that the message was sent successfully, as the following code demonstrates:

```
' VB
' Send the message and notify the user of success
sc.Send(mm)
MessageBox.Show("Message sent successfully. ", _
    "Success", MessageBoxButtons.OK, MessageBoxIcon.Information)

// C#
// Send the message and notify the user of success
sc.Send(mm);
MessageBox.Show("Message sent successfully.",
    "Success", MessageBoxButtons.OK, MessageBoxIcon.Information);
```

5. Build and run your project in Debug mode. Type e-mail addresses in the From and To boxes, and then click the Send button without typing the server name. Notice that the runtime throws an *InvalidOperationException*. Create a *Catch* block to catch an *InvalidOperationException*, and display a message to the user, as the following code demonstrates:

```
' VB
Catch ex As InvalidOperationException
```

```
    MessageBox.Show("Please provide a server name.", "No SMTP server provided", _
        MessageBoxButtons.OK, MessageBoxIcon.Error)

// C#
catch (InvalidOperationException)
{
    MessageBox.Show("Please provide a server name.",
        "No SMTP server provided", MessageBoxButtons.OK, MessageBoxIcon.Error);
}
```

6. Re-run your project. This time, provide an invalid server name, and then click Send. Notice that the runtime throws an *SmtpException*. Using the debugger, examine the exception. The *SmtpException* object doesn't provide a useful description of the problem. However, the inner exception object is a *WebException* instance, which describes the problem accurately as an invalid DNS name. Write code to catch *SmtpException* and display the message from the base exception type, as the following sample demonstrates:

```
' VB
Catch ex As SmtpException
    ' Invalid hostnames result in a WebException InnerException that provides
    ' a more descriptive error, so get the base exception
    Dim inner As Exception = ex.GetBaseException
    MessageBox.Show("Could not send message: " + inner.Message, _
        "Problem sending message", MessageBoxButtons.OK, MessageBoxIcon.Error)

// C#
catch (SmtpException ex)
{
    // Invalid hostnames result in a WebException InnerException that provides
    // a more descriptive error, so get the base exception
    Exception inner = ex.GetBaseException();
    MessageBox.Show("Could not send message: " + inner.Message,
        "Problem sending message", MessageBoxButtons.OK, MessageBoxIcon.Error);
}
```

7. Re-run your project. This time, type your SMTP server's hostname. In the To box, provide an invalid e-mail address in your local domain. Then click Send. The runtime should throw an *SmtpFailedRecipientException* (though SMTP server behavior can vary). Write code to catch *SmtpFailedRecipientException* and display a message to the user:

```
' VB
Catch ex As SmtpFailedRecipientException
    MessageBox.Show("The mail server says that there is no mailbox for " + _
        toEmailAddress.Text + ".", "Invalid recipient", _
        MessageBoxButtons.OK, MessageBoxIcon.Error)
```

```
// C#
catch (SmtpFailedRecipientException)
{
    MessageBox.Show("The mail server says that there is no mailbox for " +
        toEmailAddress.Text + ".", "Invalid recipient",
        MessageBoxButtons.OK, MessageBoxIcon.Error);
}
```

8. Finally, re-run your project and send yourself an e-mail message to verify that your application works properly.

▶ **Exercise 2: Send an E-mail Asynchronously**

In this exercise, you modify the application you created earlier to allow the user to cancel the message before the transaction is completed. To do this, you change the *SmtpClient.Send* method to *SmtpClient.SendAsync*, change the Send button to Cancel while a message is being sent, and respond to a user clicking the Cancel button.

1. Use Windows Explorer to copy either the C# or Visual Basic version of the Chapter 15\ Lesson2-Exercise 2 folder from the companion CD to your My Documents\Visual Studio Projects\ folder. Then open the solution. Alternatively, you can continue working with the application you created in the previous exercise.

2. First, comment out the existing *SmtpClient.Send* line.

3. You need to respond after the message is sent, so add an event handler to the *SmtpClient.SendCompleted* event. Then call *SmtpClient.SendAsync*, and pass the *MailMessage* object. Remove the code that displays a message box indicating that the message was transmitted successfully, because the runtime will immediately continue processing and will not wait for the message to be successfully transmitted. The following code demonstrates this:

```
' VB
' Send the message and notify the user of success
' sc.Send(mm)
AddHandler sc.SendCompleted, AddressOf sc_SendCompleted
sc.SendAsync(mm, Nothing)
```

```
// C#
// Send the message and notify the user of success
//              sc.Send(mm);
sc.SendCompleted += new SendCompletedEventHandler(sc_SendCompleted);
sc.SendAsync(mm, null);
```

4. To allow access to the *SmtpClient* variable from more than one method, move the variable declaration to the class level. You still need to define the variable by setting the value equal to *serverTextBox.Text* in the *sendButton_Click* method, however.

5. After you start sending the message, you need to give the user an opportunity to cancel the transmission. You could add a second button labeled Cancel, or you could change the Send button to Cancel. Either way, if the user clicks Cancel, you need to call *SmtpClient.SendAsyncCancel*. The following code demonstrates how to do this by adding an *If* statement to the *sendButton_Click* method that determines whether the user has clicked the button while in a Send or Cancel state:

```vb
' VB
If sendButton.Text = "Send" Then
    ' ... code omitted for simplicity ...

    ' Send the message and notify the user of success
    ' sc.Send(mm)
    AddHandler sc.SendCompleted, AddressOf sc_SendCompleted
    sc.SendAsync(mm, Nothing)
    sendButton.Text = "Cancel"
Else
    sc.SendAsyncCancel()
End If
```

```csharp
// C#
if (sendButton.Text == "Send")
{
    // ... code omitted for simplicity ...

    // Send the message and notify the user of success
    //              sc.Send(mm);
    sc.SendCompleted += new SendCompletedEventHandler(sc_SendCompleted);
    sc.SendAsync(mm, null);
    sendButton.Text = "Cancel";
}
else
{
    sc.SendAsyncCancel();
}
```

6. Next, write a method to respond to the *SmtpClient.SendCompleted* event. Based on the variable name *sc*, Visual Studio generated a method named *sc_SendCompleted*. Within the method, you need to perform the following tasks:

   ❑ If the *SendAsync* was cancelled, display a message confirming the cancellation.

   ❑ If there was an error, display the error message to the user.

   ❑ If the transmission was successful, inform the user.

The following code demonstrates this. If you are using Visual Basic, you will need to add the *System.ComponentModel* namespace:

```vb
' VB
Sub sc_SendCompleted(ByVal sender As Object, ByVal e As AsyncCompletedEventArgs)
    If e.Cancelled Then
        MessageBox.Show("Message cancelled.", "Cancelled", _
            MessageBoxButtons.OK, MessageBoxIcon.Error)
    Else
        If Not (e.Error Is Nothing) Then
            MessageBox.Show("Error: " + e.Error.ToString, "Error", _
                MessageBoxButtons.OK, MessageBoxIcon.Error)
        Else
            MessageBox.Show("Message sent successfully.", "Success", _
                MessageBoxButtons.OK, MessageBoxIcon.Information)
        End If
    End If
    sendButton.Text = "Send"
End Sub
```

```csharp
// C#
void sc_SendCompleted(object sender, AsyncCompletedEventArgs e)
{
    if (e.Cancelled)
        MessageBox.Show("Message cancelled.",
            "Cancelled", MessageBoxButtons.OK, MessageBoxIcon.Error);
    else if(e.Error != null)
        MessageBox.Show("Error: " + e.Error.ToString(),
            "Error", MessageBoxButtons.OK, MessageBoxIcon.Error);
        else
        MessageBox.Show("Message sent successfully.",
            "Success", MessageBoxButtons.OK, MessageBoxIcon.Information);
    sendButton.Text = "Send";
}
```

7. Now, build and run your code. Verify that you can successfully transmit a message.

8. Next, send a message, but immediately click Cancel. If your SMTP server is extremely responsive, the Cancel button might disappear very quickly. Verify that your application correctly handles the cancellation and informs the user.

9. Finally, verify that your application correctly responds to incorrect server names, invalid users, and invalid credentials. Note whether an invalid server name is handled by the *SmtpClient.SendCompleted* event or the *sendButton_Click* exception handling.

Lesson Summary

- To send a message, create an instance of *SmtpClient*. Configure the SMTP server host name, and then call *SmtpClient.Send*.

- If you call *SmtpClient.Send* without defining the server hostname, the runtime will throw an *InvalidOperationException*. If the hostname is defined but the server cannot be found, the runtime will throw an *SmtpException* with an inner *WebException*. If the SMTP server reports that the recipient is invalid, the runtime will throw an *SmtpFailedRecipientException*. All other problems sending e-mail result in an *SmtpException*.

- To use the default network credentials, set *SmtpClient.UseDefaultCredentials* to True. To specify the username and password, create an instance of the *System. Net.NetworkCredential* class, and use it to define *SmtpClient.Credentials*.

- To enable SSL encryption for the SMTP connection, set *SmtpClient.EnableSsl* to True. Not all SMTP servers support SSL.

- To send a message asynchronously, first create a method to respond to the *SmtpClient .SendCompleted* event. Then add your event handler to *SmtpClient.SendCompleted*, and call *SmtpClient.SendAsync*. You can call *SmtpClient.SendAsyncCancel* to cancel an asynchronous message transmission before it has completed.

Lesson Review

You can use the following questions to test your knowledge of the information in Lesson 2, "Sending Mail." The questions are also available on the companion CD if you prefer to review them in electronic form.

NOTE Answers

Answers to these questions and explanations of why each answer choice is right or wrong are located in the "Answers" section at the end of the book.

---

1. Which method would you call to send an e-mail message and wait for the transmission to complete before proceeding?

   A. *MailMessage.Send*

   B. *SmtpClient.Send*

   C. *SmtpClient.SendAsync*

   D. *MailMessage.SendAsync*

2. You need to send e-mail messages from your assembly. The computer that will run your assembly also hosts an SMTP server. Which of the following are valid values for *SmtpClient.Host*? (Choose all that apply.)

   A. self

   B. 10.1.1.1

    C. localhost

    D. 127.0.0.1

3. What type of exception will the runtime throw if the SMTP server rejects a recipient e-mail address?

    A. *SmtpFailedRecipientException*

    B. *SmtpFailedRecipientsException*

    C. *SmtpException*

    D. *SmtpClientException*

4. You want to send an e-mail message to an SMTP server while encrypting the network communications. Which property do you need to modify from its default settings?

    A. *SmtpClient.Credentials*

    B. *SmtpClient.DeliveryMethod*

    C. *SmtpClient.Port*

    D. *SmtpClient.EnableSsl*

Chapter Review

To further practice and reinforce the skills you learned in this chapter, you can perform the following tasks:

- Review the chapter summary.
- Review the list of key terms introduced in this chapter.
- Complete the case scenarios. These scenarios set up real-world situations involving the topics of this chapter and ask you to create a solution.
- Complete the suggested practices.
- Take a practice test.

Chapter Summary

- To create an e-mail message, use the *System.Net.MailMessage* class. This class supports simple text e-mails, HTML e-mails, e-mails with multiple views and different encoding standards, and attachments.
- To send an e-mail message, use the *System.Net.SmtpClient* class. This class supports SMTP servers that accept anonymous connections, servers that require authentication, and servers that support SSL encryption. Additionally, you can send messages asynchronously to allow users to cancel a message before the transmission has completed.

Key Terms

Do you know what these key terms mean? You can check your answers by looking up the terms in the glossary at the end of the book.

- Multipurpose Internet Mail Extensions (MIME)
- Secure Sockets Layer (SSL)
- Simple Message Transfer Protocol (SMTP)

Case Scenario: Add E-mail Capabilities to an Existing Application

In the following case scenario, you will apply what you've learned about how to send e-mails. You can find answers to these questions in the "Answers" section at the end of this book.

You are an application developer for Contoso, Inc. For the last two years, you have been developing and maintaining an internal customer relationship management system. Recently, the Contoso Sales group has asked for a way to send confirmation e-mails to customers before making changes to their account information. Your manager asks you to interview key people and then come to her office to answer her questions about your design choices.

Interviews

Following is a list of company personnel interviewed and their statements:

- **Sales Manager** "It's critical to customer satisfaction that our client database is accurate. We've had several situations where someone mistyped an address or a phone number, and this resulted in missed deliveries, unsatisfied customers, and lost sales. What we'd like is to automatically send a confirmation e-mail to customers when we make a change to their contact information. If the change is incorrect, the customer should be able to reject the change. I suppose they could either reply to the e-mail, click a link, or call us, based on how hard it is for you to develop the solution. The rejections shouldn't be that common."

- **Chief Security Officer** "I understand the desire to confirm changes to contact information; however, we need to manage our risk. Sending confidential information through e-mail is never good. You can, and should, encrypt the connection to the SMTP server, but you lose any control over the security of the data after you hand it off. Messages often bounce through several different servers, and most connections are not encrypted. Being that this is just contact information, I'm okay with sending the messages, but please do use security when possible."

Questions

Answer the following questions for your manager.

1. What .NET Framework classes will you use to send the e-mails?
2. How could you process e-mail responses from customers?
3. How can you protect the data in the e-mail messages?

Suggested Practices

To help you successfully master the "Implementing interoperability, reflection, and mailing functionality in a .NET Framework application" exam objective, complete the following tasks.

Send Electronic Mail to a Simple Mail Transfer Protocol (SMTP) Server for Delivery from a .NET Framework Application

For this task, you should complete at least Practices 1 and 2. If you want a better understanding of how to work with file attachments, complete Practices 3 through 5. For a detailed understanding of the importance of using SSL, complete Practice 6 as well.

- **Practice 1**   Use the application you created in the labs in this chapter, and attempt to send messages through different SMTP servers. Note how different servers respond. To look up the SMTP server for any domain, open a command prompt and run the command *nslookup -type=mx domain* (for example, *nslookup -type=mx contoso.com*).

- **Practice 2**   Expand the application you created in the labs in this chapter to enable the user to attach files.

- **Practice 3**   Attempt to send increasingly larger file attachments until the SMTP server rejects your message. Test several different SMTP servers. Note the maximum file size.

- **Practice 4**   Using a text file as an attachment, change the file extension to .txt, .jpg, .bat, .cmd, .dll, and .exe. Note which file extensions different mail servers allow, and which of the attachments can be viewed using e-mail clients such as Microsoft Outlook.

- **Practice 5**   In Chapter 6, "Graphics," you created an application that generates a chart. Add a button to the application that sends the chart as an e-mail attachment.

- **Practice 6**   Using a protocol analyzer (also known as a *sniffer*) such as Microsoft Network Monitor, capture the network communications created when sending a message using standard SMTP, standard SMTP with user credentials, and SMTP protected by SSL. Use the protocol analyzer to view the raw packets and determine whether an attacker with access to the network could view your message and user credentials.

Take a Practice Test

The practice tests on this book's companion CD offer many options. For example, you can test yourself on just one exam objective, or you can test yourself on all the 70-536 certification exam content. You can set up the test so that it closely simulates the experience of taking a certification exam, or you can set it up in study mode so that you can look at the correct answers and explanations after you answer each question.

MORE INFO   Practice tests

For details about all the practice test options available, see the "How to Use the Practice Tests" section in this book's Introduction.

Chapter 16
Globalization

The .NET Framework 2.0 has an incredibly feature rich set of tools that can be used to create applications that will run in dispersed geographical regions. An application can be written that will function equally well in Japan as it will in Great Britain, with virtually no changes needed to the code. To accomplish such tasks, the *System.Globalization* namespace is provided.

Exam objectives in this chapter:
- Format data based on culture information. (Refer *System.Globalization* namespace)
    - Access culture and region information in a .NET Framework application.
    - Format date and time values based on the culture.
    - Format number values based on the culture.
    - Perform culture-sensitive string comparison.
    - Build a custom culture class based on existing culture and region classes.

Lessons in this chapter:

Before You Begin

To complete the lessons in this chapter, you should be familiar with Microsoft Visual Basic or C# and be comfortable with the following tasks:

- Create a console application in Microsoft Visual Studio using Visual Basic or C#.
- Add references to system class libraries to a project.

Lesson 1: Using Culture Information

The geographical scope of applications is steadily increasing. The costs of not knowing who will be using the applications are increasing as well. Dealing with issues as an afterthought is always more costly than designing for them, and building applications for different locales is no different in this respect. The .NET Framework provides the *System.Globalization* namespace to help developers address such concerns.

After this lesson, you will be able to:

■ Detect a user's culture.

■ Respond to the current culture.

■ Set the current culture.

Estimated lesson time: 20 minutes

CultureInfo Class

One of the core tools for manipulating and retrieving information about the cultural context an application is running in is the *CultureInfo* class. This class provides culture-specific information such as the format of numbers and dates, and casing conventions. More broadly, it represents the name of a culture, the culture's writing system, the culture's calendar, the culture's language and sublanguages if applicable, and the country and region of the culture, and it provides methods to manipulate all these aspects. The basic uses of the *CultureInfo* class are shown in the following list:

■ Control how string comparisons are performed.

■ Control how number comparisons and formats are performed.

■ Control how date comparisons and formats are performed.

■ Control how resources are retrieved and used.

IMPORTANT All cultures are represented by the Neutral Culture—Specific Culture format

The cultures "zh-CHS" (Simplified Chinese) and "zh-CHT" (Traditional Chinese) are neutral cultures, and therefore, are the two exceptions to the standard format for expressing specific cultures, which uses a neutral culture followed by a hyphen followed by a specific culture.

As a rule, a culture will be grouped into one of three categories: an *invariant* culture, a *neutral* culture, or a *specific* culture. The distinctions between these categories are detailed in the following list:

- **Invariant Culture** This culture category is culture-insensitive. The category is to be used as essentially a default culture when consistency is desired. One situation where this category might be desirable to use is creating a trial application with a hard-coded expiration date. Using an invariant will allow you to check for a specific date, regardless of the culture's format, which will greatly simplify the task of comparing these dates. The invariant culture is not based on the English language per se, but it is associated with it and bears more similarities to it than to any other identifiable culture. Although it might be tempting to use the invariant culture for every possible comparison and just ignore specific cultural comparisons, doing so is a great mistake. Without intending to do so, you can overuse an invariant culture and end up with language that is syntactically incorrect or inappropriate.

- **Neutral Culture** English (en), French (fr), and Spanish (sp) are all neutral cultures. A neutral culture is associated with a language but has no relationship to countries or regions. For instance, the English spoken in England is different from that spoken in the United States. The same holds true for Spanish spoken in Mexico versus that spoken in Spain. As mentioned earlier, the neutral culture will be designated by the first two characters in the *CultureInfo* class. If only two letters are specified, they will be the *Neutral* class. Although neutral cultures, like the invariant culture, might be tempting to use, they should be avoided as well, if possible, for the same reasons that invariants should be avoided. The language spoken in different countries that are covered by a neutral culture will almost certainly be different in at least a few respects. In reality, the differences will be many. Therefore, overuse of neutral cultures can result in incorrect or inappropriate language.

- **Specific Culture** This is the most precise of the three categories and is represented by a neutral culture, a hyphen, and then a specific culture abbreviation. For instance, in the designations "fr-FR" and "en-US", *fr* and *en* represent the neutral culture (French and English, respectively), and *FR* and *US* represent the specific culture (France and the United States, respectively). Specific cultures should be used if at all possible.

To detect a user's current culture information, use the *CurrentCulture* property of the executing thread's *CurrentThread* property, as shown in the following code sample:

```
' VB
Dim usersCulture As CultureInfo = Thread.CurrentThread.CurrentCulture

Console.WriteLine("The current culture of this application is : " _
    & usersCulture.Name)
Console.WriteLine("The Display Name of this application is : " _
    & usersCulture.DisplayName)
Console.WriteLine("The Native Name of this application is : " _
    & usersCulture.NativeName)
Console.WriteLine("The ISO Abbreviation of this application is : " _
    & usersCulture.TwoLetterISOLanguageName)

// C#
CultureInfo usersCulture = Thread.CurrentThread.CurrentCulture;

Console.WriteLine("The current culture of this application is : "
    + usersCulture.Name);
Console.WriteLine("The Display Name of this application is : "
    + usersCulture.DisplayName);
Console.WriteLine("The Native Name of this application is : "
    + usersCulture.NativeName);
Console.WriteLine("The ISO Abbreviation of this application is : "
    + usersCulture.TwoLetterISOLanguageName);
```

If you compile and run the application, you should see results similar to those shown in Figure 16-1. (Results will vary based on machine configuration.)

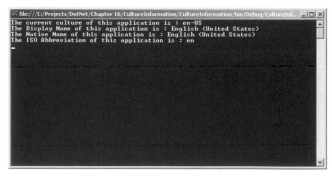

Figure 16-1   Output of *CurrentCulture* information

One aspect that is critical here is how strings are handled. If you hard code many values, as opposed to using formatters, cultural differences will not be visible. Examine the following examples:

```
' VB
salaryTextBox.Text = "$100,000.00"

// C#
salaryTextBox.Text = "$100,000.00";
```

If you changed the *CurrentCulture* to say, Japanese, and re-ran it, you might expect to see the Yen symbol (which after all is Japan's currency). However, you wouldn't. What you would see is "$100,000.00". This might seem contrary to what was discussed earlier—changing to *CurrentCulture* is supposed to change the formatting after all. And that's exactly what it does, it changes formatting. However, if you use hard-coded values instead of formatting them, there's no way for the runtime to know that something should be changed.

Using formatting would change this scenario so that changes to *CurrentCulture* would propagate to changes in everything else related—for instance, *salaryTextBox*:

```
' VB
salaryTextBox.Text = Format(100000, "Currency")
```

```
// C#
salaryTextBox.Text = (100000).ToString("C");
```

Another important feature is the *CurrentUICulture* property of the *CultureInfo* class. Although this property is often the same as the *CurrentCulture* property of the *CultureInfo* class, they can and very well might be different. Hence, one culture can be used for calculations and internal manipulation and another can be used for display purposes. The *CurrentUICulture* of the application can be accessed via the *CurrentUICulture* property of the *CurrentThread* class.

```
' VB
Dim usersCulture As CultureInfo = Thread.CurrentThread.CurrentUICulture

Console.WriteLine("The current UI culture of this application is : " _
    & usersCulture.Name)
```

```
// C#
CultureInfo usersCulture = Thread.CurrentThread.CurrentUICulture;

Console.WriteLine("The current UI culture of this application is : "
    + usersCulture.Name);
```

NOTE *CurrentUICulture* **must be set at the application's startup**

The *CurrentCulture* can be manipulated at any time during execution. However, this is not the case with the *CurrentUICulture*. To be used correctly, the *CurrentUICulture* must be set at the onset of the application (ideally in the *Main* method) or in a form's constructor. Failure to do so can result in unexpected behavior.

Setting the current culture is similar to retrieving it. *CurrentCulture* is a property of the *CurrentThread* property of the *Thread* class; therefore, all that's needed to change or set this property is to specify a different value for it, as shown in the following code:

```
' VB
Dim usersCulture As CultureInfo = Thread.CurrentThread.CurrentCulture

Console.WriteLine("The current culture of this application is : " _
    & usersCulture.Name)
' Change this to Spanish/Venezuela
Thread.CurrentThread.CurrentCulture = New CultureInfo("es-VE")
Console.WriteLine("The current culture of this application is : " _
    & Thread.CurrentThread.CurrentCulture.Name)

// C#
CultureInfo usersCulture = Thread.CurrentThread.CurrentCulture;

Console.WriteLine("The current culture of this application is : "
    + usersCulture.Name);
// Change this to Spanish/Venezuela
Thread.CurrentThread.CurrentCulture = new CultureInfo("es-VE");
Console.WriteLine("The current culture of this application is : "
    + Thread.CurrentThread.CurrentCulture);
```

NOTE Unexpected behavior with the *ClearCacheData* method

The *ClearCacheData* method of the *CultureInfo* class has some odd behavior. It's implemented as an instance method, and there's no static equivalent. However, the method applies to a class that's shared between all instances of *CultureInfo*. As you might be thinking, "shared between all instances of a class" sounds remarkably like the behavior of a *Static* or *Shared* property. In fact, this is how the method behaves. It has no effect whatsoever on individual instances and, as such, causes one to wonder whether the method was meant to be implemented as a *Static* or *Shared* property in the first place.

If the preceding code is run, the resulting output will show that the *CurrentCulture* will first be en-US and then is changed to es-VE. The output from this code should resemble that shown in Figure 16-2.

Figure 16-2   Change of current culture from US English to Venezuelan Spanish

The *CultureInfo* class also provides a mechanism for detecting a user's culture information—namely, the *GetCultures* method. The *GetCultures* method takes a single parameter of type *CultureTypes*.

CultureTypes Enumeration

CultureTypes is an enumeration marked with the *FlagsAttribute* attribute, which allows users to specify multiple values.

Table 16-1   The *CultureTypes* Enumeration

Name	Description
AllCultures	As the name implies, refers to all available cultures
FrameworkCultures	Both neutral and specific cultures that are included with the .NET Framework (new .NET Framework 2.0 feature)
InstalledWin32Cultures	Includes all cultures that are installed on the Windows operating system
NeutralCultures	Includes cultures that are associated with a language but are not specific to a country/region
ReplacementCultures	Includes custom cultures created by the user that replace cultures shipped with the .NET Framework (new .NET Framework 2.0 feature)
SpecificCultures	Includes cultures that are specific to a country/region
UserCustomCulture	Includes custom cultures created by the user (new .NET Framework 2.0 feature)
WindowsOnlyCultures	Includes cultures installed in the Windows system but not in the .NET Framework. The *WindowsOnlyCultures* value is mutually exclusive with the *FrameworkCultures* value. (New .NET Framework 2.0 feature)

Using the information in Table 16-1, the *GetCultures* method of the *CultureInfo* class can be called passing in one or more of each value. The following example illustrates how to use the *GetCultures* method, specifying the *SpecificCultures* value of the *CultureType* enumeration:

```vb
' VB
For Each usersCulture As CultureInfo In _
  CultureInfo.GetCultures(CultureTypes.SpecificCultures)

  Console.WriteLine("Culture: " & usersCulture.Name)
Next
```

```
// C#
foreach (CultureInfo usersCulture in
  CultureInfo.GetCultures(CultureTypes.SpecificCultures))
{
  Console.WriteLine("Culture: " + usersCulture.Name);
}
```

RegionInfo Class

Although the *CultureInfo* class provides fairly detailed information about a given culture, more granular information is sometimes needed. The *RegionInfo* is one mechanism to provide more detailed information. In short, the *RegionInfo* class provides specific information about a particular country or region.

The *CultureInfo* has two types of property that will allow it to work in conjunction with the *RegionInfo* class: nominal identifiers (such as the *Name* property) and numeric identifiers (such as *LCID*). Either approach will have the same ultimate result:

```
' VB
Dim usersCulture As CultureInfo = Thread.CurrentThread.CurrentCulture
Dim demoRegion As RegionInfo = New RegionInfo(usersCulture.LCID)
```

Or:

```
' VB
Dim usersCulture As CultureInfo = Thread.CurrentThread.CurrentCulture
Dim demoRegion As RegionInfo = New RegionInfo(usersCulture.Name)
```

```
// C#
CultureInfo usersCulture = Thread.CurrentThread.CurrentCulture;
RegionInfo demoRegion = new RegionInfo(usersCulture.LCID);
```

Or:

```
// C#
CultureInfo usersCulture = Thread.CurrentThread.CurrentCulture;
RegionInfo demoRegion = new RegionInfo(usersCulture.Name);
```

Afterward, any of the desired properties can be accessed directly just like any other class:

```
' VB
Dim usersCulture As CultureInfo = Thread.CurrentThread.CurrentCulture
Dim demoRegion As RegionInfo = New RegionInfo(usersCulture.LCID)

Console.WriteLine("English Name: " & demoRegion.EnglishName)
Console.WriteLine("Display Name: " & demoRegion.DisplayName)
Console.WriteLine("Currency Symbol: " & demoRegion.CurrencySymbol)
```

```
// C#
CultureInfo usersCulture = Thread.CurrentThread.CurrentCulture;
RegionInfo demoRegion = new RegionInfo(usersCulture.LCID);
```

```
Console.WriteLine("English Name: " + demoRegion.EnglishName);
Console.WriteLine("Display Name: " + demoRegion.DisplayName);
Console.WriteLine("Currency Symbol: " + demoRegion.CurrencySymbol);
```

If you compile and run the application, you should see results similar to those shown in Figure 16-3. (Results will vary based on machine configuration.)

Figure 16-3   Output of *RegionInfo* information

DateTimeFormatInfo and *NumberFormatInfo* Classes

When dealing with applications that cross cultural boundaries, uninitiated developers might make a few incorrect assumptions, including the following ones:

- They assume that dates and date formats will be the same across boundaries.

- They assume that numbers and number formats will be the same across boundaries.

- They assume that currency values will be the same across boundaries.

If you were to compare United States English and, say, Japanese, you probably would not be surprised that the word for the first workday of the week, for instance, is different in each language. It's expected that most words will be different from language to language. For some reason, though, people all too often assume that the opposite will be true with dates, currency, or numbers. The United States uses the dollar as its primary currency, whereas Japan uses the yen, and it shouldn't be a big surprise that the two currencies are formatted and represented differently.

A similar situation occurs with respect to dates. Employing the example we've been using so far, Venezuela's date format differs markedly from that of the United States. Venezuela uses the Day/Month/Year format, whereas the US uses Month/Day/Year.

The *DateTimeFormatInfo* class and the *NumberFormatInfo* class provide mechanisms for manipulating how these differences are handled. The *CultureInfo* class has properties that provide information about a specific culture.

The *DateTimeFormatInfo* class provides a comprehensive set of methods and properties to handle and respond to the dates of different cultures. Examine the following code:

```
' VB
Dim usersCulture As CultureInfo = New CultureInfo("es-VE")
Dim days() As String = usersCulture.DateTimeFormat.DayNames

For Each day As String In days
  Console.WriteLine("Day Name for Venezuelan Spanish : " & day)
Next
```

```
// C#
CultureInfo usersCulture = new CultureInfo("es-VE");
String[] days = usersCulture.DateTimeFormat.DayNames;

foreach (String day in days)
{
  Console.WriteLine("Day Name for Venezuelan Spanish : " + day);
}
```

The corresponding output should resemble that shown in Figure 16-4.

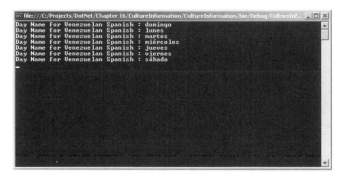

Figure 16-4   Each day of the week in Venezuelan Spanish

If this same code was run with United States English as the *CurrentCulture*, the output would be Sunday, Monday, Tuesday, Wednesday, Thursday, Friday, and Saturday, respectively. The same differences exist with respect to months, as shown in the following code:

```
' VB
Dim usersCulture As CultureInfo = New CultureInfo("es-VE")
Dim months() As String = usersCulture.DateTimeFormat.MonthNames
For Each month As String In months
Console.WriteLine("Month Name for Venezuelan Spanish : " & month)
Next
```

```
// C#
CultureInfo usersCulture = new CultureInfo("es-VE");
String[] months = usersCulture.DateTimeFormat.MonthNames;

foreach (String month in months)
{
  Console.WriteLine("Month Name for Venezuelan Spanish : " + month);
}
```

Again, when this code is run, the name of each month in Venezuelan Spanish will be shown. There are many other properties corresponding to just about every conceivable facet of date manipulation.

One of the reasons this is so important is because of evaluation and comparisons. If one culture has a date format in mm/dd/yyyy format and the other stores the values in dd/mm/yyyy format, what would happen if you tried to compare them? Chances are that you'd end up with erroneous comparisons. However, by specifying that the dates are from different cultures, comparisons will work correctly.

The same problem exists when dealing with numbers and currency, and essentially the same solution is in place—using the *NumberFormatInfo* class instead of the *DateFormatInfo* class. This can be easily illustrated by using the same code we used previously, but with a slight modification:

```
' VB
Dim usersCulture As CultureInfo = New CultureInfo("es-VE")

Console.WriteLine("Venezuelan Currency Symbol: " _
  & usersCulture.NumberFormat.CurrencySymbol)
Console.WriteLine("Number Decimal Symbol: " _
  & usersCulture.NumberFormat.NumberDecimalSeparator)

// C#
CultureInfo usersCulture = new CultureInfo("es-VE");

Console.WriteLine("Venezuelan Currency Symbol: "
  + usersCulture.NumberFormat.CurrencySymbol);
Console.WriteLine("Number Decimal Symbol: "
  + usersCulture.NumberFormat.NumberDecimalSeparator);
```

As shown by the output from this code, the Venezuelan currency abbreviation is "Bs" and a comma is used as the decimal separator when writing numbers.

Using the *CompareInfo* Class and *CompareOptions* Enumeration for Culturally Aware Comparisons

One important reason to use the *CultureInfo* class is to allow for culturally aware string comparisons. To do this, the *CultureInfo* class has a *CompareInfo* property, which is an instance of the *CompareInfo* class. You can create a new instance of the *CompareInfo* class or, more practically, you can set it to the *CompareInfo* property of the *CurrentCulture*. The following code shows the results from outputting the current *CompareInfo* associated with the *CurrentCulture* on your machine:

```vb
' VB
Dim demoInfo As CompareInfo = _
   Thread.CurrentThread.CurrentCulture.CompareInfo
Console.WriteLine(demoInfo.Name)
Console.WriteLine(demoInfo.LCID)
```

```csharp
// C#
CompareInfo demoInfo =
   Thread.CurrentThread.CurrentCulture.CompareInfo;
Console.WriteLine(demoInfo.Name);
Console.WriteLine(demoInfo.LCID);
```

Comparisons are typically based on one specific culture. (For instance, if an application was written in the United States, all comparisons would probably be based on en-US.) Because of this, it's generally best to create a *CompareInfo* object based on the current culture. If necessary, however, you can also create a new *CultureInfo* object based on any culture you'd like, as shown in the following code:

```vb
' VB
Dim demoInfo As CompareInfo = New CultureInfo("en-US").CompareInfo
Console.WriteLine(demoInfo.Name)
Console.WriteLine(demoInfo.LCID)
```

```csharp
// C#
CompareInfo demoInfo = new CultureInfo("en-US").CompareInfo;
Console.WriteLine(demoInfo.Name);
Console.WriteLine(demoInfo.LCID);
```

The most basic approach to using the *CompareInfo* class is to call the *Compare* method, passing in the values to be compared. The following code illustrates comparing two words for equivalency using the *Compare* method of the *CompareInfo* class:

```vb
' VB
Dim firstString As String = "Coté"
Dim secondString As String = "coté"
Dim demoInfo As CompareInfo = New CultureInfo("fr-FR").CompareInfo

demoInfo.Compare(firstString, secondString)
```

```csharp
// C#
String firstString = "Coté";
String secondString = "coté";
CompareInfo demoInfo = new CultureInfo("fr-FR").CompareInfo;

demoInfo.Compare(firstString, secondString);
```

If you run this code, the two strings will not be considered equal. Even though the cultural information will evaluate to true, the casing is different. To handle items like this, you can use members of the *CompareOptions* enumeration to control how comparisons are performed. According to the MSDN documentation, the members are defined as shown in Table 16-2.

Table 16-2   The *CompareOptions* Enumeration Members

Name	Description
IgnoreCase	Indicates that the string comparison must ignore case.
IgnoreKanaType	Indicates that the string comparison must ignore the Kana type. Kana type refers to Japanese hiragana and katakana characters, which represent phonetic sounds in the Japanese language. Hiragana is used for native Japanese expressions and words, and katakana is used for words borrowed from other languages, such as "computer" and "Internet." A phonetic sound can be expressed in both hiragana and katakana. If this value is selected, the hiragana character for one sound is considered equal to the katakana character for the same sound.
IgnoreNonSpace	Indicates that the string comparison must ignore nonspacing combining characters, such as diacritics. The Unicode Standard defines combining characters as characters that are combined with base characters to produce a new character. Nonspacing combining characters do not occupy a spacing position by themselves when rendered. For more information on nonspacing combining characters, see The Unicode Standard at *http://www.unicode.org*.
IgnoreSymbols	Indicates that the string comparison must ignore symbols, such as white-space characters, punctuation, currency symbols, the percent sign, mathematical symbols, the ampersand, and so on.
IgnoreWidth	Indicates that the string comparison must ignore the character width. For example, Japanese katakana characters can be written as full-width or half-width and, if this value is selected, the katakana characters written as full-width are considered equal to the same characters written in half-width.

Table 16-2 The *CompareOptions* Enumeration Members

Name	Description
None	Indicates the default option settings for string comparisons.
Ordinal	Indicates that the string comparison must be done using the Unicode values of each character, which is a fast comparison but is culture-insensitive. A string starting with "U+xxxx" comes before a string starting with "U+yyyy" if xxxx is less than yyyy. This flag cannot be combined with other flags and must be used alone.
OrdinalIgnoreCase	Indicates that the string comparison must ignore case, and then perform an ordinal comparison. This is equivalent to converting the string to uppercase using the invariant culture and then performing an ordinal comparison on the result.
StringSort	Indicates that the string comparison must use the string sort algorithm, where the hyphen and the apostrophe, as well as other nonalphanumeric symbols, come before alphanumeric characters.

So if the same code used in the previous example is used with one modification, it will work as expected. (The modification is that a *CompareOptions* enumeration is specified with the *IgnoreCase* option specified.) The following code illustrates this change:

```
' VB
Dim firstString As String - "Coté"
Dim secondString As String = "coté"
Dim demoInfo As CompareInfo = New CultureInfo("fr-FR").CompareInfo

demoInfo.Compare(firstString, secondString, CompareOptions.IgnoreCase)

// C#
String firstString = "Coté";
String secondString = "coté";
CompareInfo demoInfo = new CultureInfo("fr-FR").CompareInfo;

demoInfo.Compare(firstString, secondString, CompareOptions.IgnoreCase);
```

Lab: Write Code that Adjusts to Culture

In this lab, you'll write code that recognizes changes in culture. If you encounter a problem completing an exercise, the completed projects are available on the companion CD in the Code folder.

1. Open Visual Studio 2005.

2. Create a new console application in Microsoft C# 2005 or in Microsoft Visual Basic 2005. Visual Basic 2005 creates a module for you, along with an empty *Main* procedure. Visual C# creates a Program.cs class for you with an empty *Main* procedure.

3. Make sure that the *System, System.Threading*, and *System.Globalization* namespaces are imported in the Module1.vb or Program.cs file.

4. Within the *Main* procedure, add the following code:

```vb
' VB
Console.WriteLine("Please select a Culture format [i.e. en-US, es-ES]")
Dim original As String = Console.ReadLine()

Dim usersCulture As CultureInfo = New CultureInfo(original)
Dim days As String() = usersCulture.DateTimeFormat.DayNames

For Each day As String In days
  Console.WriteLine("Day Name for " & usersCulture.DisplayName & _
    " " & day)
Next

Console.WriteLine("Please select a NEW Culture format [i.e. en-US, es-ES]")
Dim modified As String = Console.ReadLine()

Dim modifiedUsersCulture As CultureInfo = New CultureInfo(modified)
Dim modifiedDays As String() = modifiedUsersCulture.DateTimeFormat.DayNames

For Each day As String In ModifiedDays
  Console.WriteLine("Day Name for " & modifiedUsersCulture.DisplayName & _
    " " & day)
Next

Console.ReadLine()
```

```csharp
// C#
Console.WriteLine("Please select a Culture format [i.e. en-US, es-ES]");
String original = Console.ReadLine();

CultureInfo usersCulture = new CultureInfo(original);
String[] days = usersCulture.DateTimeFormat.DayNames;

foreach (String day in days)
{
  Console.WriteLine("Day Name for "
    + usersCulture.DisplayName + " " + day);
}

Console.WriteLine("Please select a NEW Culture format [i.e. en-US, es-ES]");
String modified = Console.ReadLine();

CultureInfo modifiedUsersCulture = new CultureInfo(modified);
String[] modifiedDays = modifiedUsersCulture.DateTimeFormat.DayNames;

foreach (String day in modifiedDays)
```

```
    {
        Console.WriteLine("Day Name for "
            + modifiedUsersCulture.DisplayName + " " + day);
    }

    Console.ReadLine();
```

5. Build the program and fix any errors, and then run the application.

6. At the first prompt, enter a specific culture. If you don't know one, use *es-ES*.

7. At the second prompt, enter a different culture. If you don't know one, use *en-US*.

8. Compare the output. If you used the values recommended in this example, you should spot a profound difference in how the application responded.

Lesson Summary

- Cultures are represented by the *CultureInfo* class.

- The current culture of an application can be retrieved by examining the *Current-Culture* property of the *CultureInfo* class. The current culture of the application can be changed by simply setting the *CurrentCulture* property to another culture.

- To effectively implement globalization, data must be formatted instead of being hard coded. (The first method shown in the following code samples should be avoided, while the second method should be used.)

```
' VB
Dim dollarValue As String = "$20.00"

// C#
String dollarValue = "$20.00";

' VB
Dim dollarValue As String = Format(20.0, "Currency")

// C#
String dollarValue = (20).ToString("C");
```

- The *CultureInfo* class is the primary vehicle used to manipulate cultural information.

- The *CurrentCulture* property of the *CurrentThread* class is used to both retrieve and set culture information for the current application.

- The *CurrentUICulture* property of the *CurrentThread* class is used to retrieve and set culture information about visual aspects of the application. Unlike the *CurrentCulture* property, this property should be set only when the application starts or in an object's constructor.

- The *NumberFormatInfo* class provides a mechanism for displaying how numbers are represented and displayed.

- The *DateFormatInfo* class provides a mechanism for displaying how dates are represented and displayed.

Lesson Review

You can use the following questions to test your knowledge of the information in Lesson 1, "Using Culture Information." The questions are also available on the companion CD if you prefer to review them in electronic form.

NOTE Answers

Answers to these questions and explanations of why each answer choice is right or wrong are located in the "Answers" section at the end of the book.

---

1. Which method illustrates how to retrieve information for the current culture of the application? (Choose all that apply.)

   A. Create a new instance of the *CultureInfo* class, and instantiate it with no values specified in the constructor.

   B. Use the *CurrentCulture* property of the *CurrentThread* property of the *Thread* instance.

   C. Create a new instance of the *CultureInfo* class, and use an invariant culture.

   D. Create an instance of the *CultureInfo* class using a specific culture, and check the *CurrentCulture* property.

2. Which of the following statements describes the neutral and specific culture "en-US"?

   A. The specific culture is *en*, and *US* is the neutral culture.

   B. The specific culture is US, and en is the neutral culture.

   C. The combination of both represents a neutral culture.

   D. The neutral culture is *en-US*, and no specific culture is specified.

3. What method should be used to perform case-insensitive, culturally aware *String* comparisons?

   A. Specify a culture for each string. Create a *CompareInfo* class, and call its *Compare* method, passing in both strings.

   B. Specify a culture for each string. Create a *CompareInfo* class, and call its *Compare* method, passing in both strings and specifying *CompareOptions.IgnoreCase*.

   C. Use the *String.CompareTo* method, and just specify the other string.

   D. Use the *ToUpper* or *ToLower* method of each string, and simply ensure that they are both the same case.

Lesson 2: Creating a Custom Culture

At times, the existing cultures provided by the .NET Framework will not be sufficient for your needs. The Framework provides a mechanism for overcoming this problem. The *CultureAndRegionInfoBuilder* class enables you to create and use a customized culture. Furthermore, it enables you to install this culture on a given machine now or on other machines in the future.

NOTE .NET 2.0

The *CultureAndRegionInfoBuilder* class is new in .NET 2.0.

NOTE Installing a custom culture

To install a culture that you create, a few things must be considered. According to MSDN, "a custom culture can be registered on a computer only by a user who has administrative rights on that computer. Consequently, typical applications cannot create a custom culture. Instead, use the *CultureAndRegionInfoBuilder* class to build a tool that an administrator can use to create and register a custom culture. After the custom culture is registered on a computer, use the *CultureInfo* class to create an instance of the custom culture just as you would a predefined culture."

Using the *CultureAndRegionInfoBuilder* you can create a culture totally from scratch, base a new culture on an existing one, or use an existing one entirely. The code shown next illustrates how to use an existing culture.

NOTE A reference to sysglobl.dll must be included to use a
CultureAndRegionInfoBuilder object

In the previous lessons, simply having a reference and including *System.Globalization* as a *using* or *Imports* statement was all that was needed. However, this approach will not work here. If you try to instantiate an instance of the *CultureAndRegionInfoBuilder* class, you will get a "type not defined" error. You need to add a specific reference to the sysglobl.dll, which is usually located in %SystemRoot%\Microsoft.NET\Framework\[VERSION]\sysglobl.dll.

```vb
' VB
Dim demoBuilder As New CultureAndRegionInfoBuilder("en-US", _
  CultureAndRegionModifiers.Neutral)
```

```csharp
// C#
CultureAndRegionInfoBuilder demoBuilder =
   new CultureAndRegionInfoBuilder("en-US",
   CultureAndRegionModifiers.Neutral);
```

All you need to do is instantiate a new instance of the *CultureAndRegionInfoBuilder* class, use an existing culture, and specify a *CultureAndRegionModifiers* value, which will be discussed shortly. You can also use existing *RegionInfo* objects, *CultureInfo* objects, or both to populate a *CultureAndRegionInfoBuilder* object. This is illustrated in the following code:

```vb
' VB
Dim usCulture As New CultureInfo("en-US")
Dim usRegion As New RegionInfo("en-US")
Dim demoBuilder As New CultureAndRegionInfoBuilder("en-US", _
  CultureAndRegionModifiers.Neutral)

demoBuilder.LoadDataFromCultureInfo(usCulture)
demoBuilder.LoadDataFromRegionInfo(usRegion)
```

```csharp
// C#
CultureInfo usCulture = new CultureInfo("en-US");
RegionInfo usRegion = new RegionInfo("US");
CultureAndRegionInfoBuilder demoBuilder =
  new CultureAndRegionInfoBuilder("en-US",
  CultureAndRegionModifiers.Neutral);

demoBuilder.LoadDataFromCultureInfo(usCulture);
demoBuilder.LoadDataFromRegionInfo(usRegion);
```

If you want to create a customized culture of your own, the process is not much different than the one just shown. The first thing you need to do is figure out what you want to call the culture and determine whether it will be based on an existing one. So let's say we wanted to create a new culture based on United States English specific to Microsoft Corporation. The following code illustrates how to do this:

```vb
' VB
Dim usCulture As New CultureInfo("en-US")
Dim usRegion As New RegionInfo("en-US")
Dim demoBuilder As _
  New CultureAndRegionInfoBuilder("en-MS", _
  CultureAndRegionModifiers.None)

demoBuilder.LoadDataFromCultureInfo(usCulture)
demoBuilder.LoadDataFromRegionInfo(usRegion)
```

```csharp
// C#
CultureInfo usCulture = new CultureInfo("en-US");
RegionInfo usRegion = new RegionInfo("US");
CultureAndRegionInfoBuilder demoBuilder =
  new CultureAndRegionInfoBuilder("en-MS",
  CultureAndRegionModifiers.None);

demoBuilder.LoadDataFromCultureInfo(usCulture);
demoBuilder.LoadDataFromRegionInfo(usRegion);
```

All that's being done here, in its simplest form, is creating a new culture (en-MS) and basing it on the *en* and *US* definitions. Afterwards, we can set any properties that we want to, such as *CurrencyName*, *CultureName*, *NumberFormat*, or any other available properties.

To use the *CultureAndRegionInfoBuilder* class, the constructor takes an argument from the *CultureAndRegionModifiers* enumeration. This is a very straightforward enumeration with only three values. According to the MSDN documentation, they are each defined as shown in Table 16-3.

Table 16-3   *CultureAndRegionModifiers* Enumeration

Name	Description
Neutral	A neutral custom culture
None	A specific, supplemental custom culture
Replacement	A custom culture that replaces an existing .NET Framework culture or Windows Locale

If you wanted to use an existing culture but no region, you would specify the *Neutral* option. If you were going to specify supplemental information for the object, you would specify *None* (so that the amount of information inherited would be minimal). If you were going to do a replacement, you would specify *Replacement*, which would mandate that you set all the properties yourself.

Lab: Create Your Own Culture

In this lab, you'll create a culture of your own. If you encounter a problem completing an exercise, the completed projects are available on the companion CD in the Code folder.

1. Open Visual Studio 2005.

2. Create a new console application in Microsoft C# 2005 or in Microsoft Visual Basic 2005. Visual Basic 2005 creates a module for you, along with an empty *Main* procedure. Visual C# creates a Program.cs class for you with an empty *Main* procedure.

3. Make sure that the *System* and *System.Globalization* namespaces are imported in the Module1.vb or Program.cs file.

4. Add a reference to sysglobl.dll, as described earlier in this chapter.

5. Within the *Main* procedure, add the following code:

```
' VB
Dim usCulture As New CultureInfo("en-US")
Dim usRegion As New RegionInfo("en-US")
Dim demoBuilder As New CultureAndRegionInfoBuilder("x-en-US-sample", _
  CultureAndRegionModifiers.None)
```

```
demoBuilder.LoadDataFromCultureInfo(usCulture)
demoBuilder.LoadDataFromRegionInfo(usRegion)

// C#
CultureInfo usCulture = new CultureInfo("en-US");
RegionInfo usRegion = new RegionInfo("US");
CultureAndRegionInfoBuilder demoBuilder =
  new CultureAndRegionInfoBuilder("x-en-US-sample",
  CultureAndRegionModifiers.None);

demoBuilder.LoadDataFromCultureInfo(usCulture);
demoBuilder.LoadDataFromRegionInfo(usRegion);
```

6. Add a *NumberFormatInfo* object, and set the properties as illustrated in the following code:

```
' VB
Dim numberInfo As New NumberFormatInfo()
    numberInfo.CurrencySymbol = "@"
    numberInfo.CurrencyDecimalDigits = 4
    demoBuilder.NumberFormat = numberInfo

// C#
NumberFormatInfo numberInfo = new NumberFormatInfo();
numberInfo.CurrencySymbol = "@";
numberInfo.CurrencyDecimalDigits = 4;
demoBuilder.NumberFormat = numberInfo;
```

7. Add a *DateTimeFormatInfo* object, and set the properties as illustrated in the following code:

```
' VB
Dim dateInfo As DateTimeFormatInfo = New DateTimeFormatInfo()
dateInfo.DateSeparator = "."
dateInfo.DayNames = New String() {"FirstDay", "SecondDay", _
    "ThirdDay", "FourthDay", "FifthDay", "SixthDay", "SeventhDay"}

// C#
DateTimeFormatInfo dateInfo = new DateTimeFormatInfo();
dateInfo.DateSeparator = ".";
dateInfo.DayNames = new String[] { "FirstDay", "SecondDay",
    "ThirdDay", "FourthDay", "FifthDay", "SixthDay", "SeventhDay" };
```

8. Build the program, fix any errors, and then run the application.

9. Use the *CultureInfo* class to interrogate the properties of your new culture.

Lesson Summary

- Custom cultures can be created with the *CultureAndInfoRegionBuilder* class.

- The culture of a *CultureAndRegionInfoBuilder* class can be inherited from a parent setting.

- The region of a *CultureAndRegionInfoBuilder* class can also be inherited from a parent setting.

- The number formatting of custom classes can be manipulated through the *NumberFormat* property of the *CultureAndRegionInfoBuilder* class.

Lesson Review

You can use the following questions to test your knowledge of the information in Lesson 2, "Creating a Custom Culture." The questions are also available on the companion CD if you prefer to review them in electronic form.

NOTE   Answers

Answers to these questions and explanations of why each answer choice is right or wrong are located in the "Answers" section at the end of the book.

1. What reason best describes why an application would use the *CultureAndRegionInfoBuilder* class?

    A. The current culture works properly, but items such as the currency symbol might change because of political, economic, or other reasons.

    B. The current culture works properly, but items such as the date formatting might change because of political or other reasons.

    C. There is a need for a specific culture that does not currently exist.

    D. You don't like the way a culture is represented and want to completely change it.

2. If you were creating a culture of your own using the *CultureAndRegionInfoBuilder* class, which value would you set for the *CultureAndRegionModifiers* parameter?

    A. None

    B. Neutral

    C. Replacement

Chapter Review

To further practice and reinforce the skills you learned in this chapter, you can do any of the following tasks:

- Review the chapter summary.
- Review the list of key terms introduced in this chapter.
- Complete the case scenarios. These scenarios set up real-world situations involving the topics of this chapter and ask you to create a solution.
- Complete the suggested practices.
- Take a practice test.

Chapter Summary

- The .NET Framework provides the *System.Globalization* namespace to give applications the ability to run seamlessly in multiple locales.
- The *NumberFormatInfo* class provides a mechanism to retrieve and manipulate number and currency formatting.
- The *DateTimeFormatInfo* class provides a mechanism to retrieve and manipulate date and time formatting.
- To effectively implement globalization, data must be formatted instead of being hard coded. (The first method shown in the following code samples should be avoided, while the second method should be used.)

```
' VB
Dim dollarValue As String = "$20.00"
```

```
// C#
String dollarValue = "$20.00";
```

```
' VB
Dim dollarValue As String = Format(20.00, "Currency")
```

```
// C#
String dollarValue = (20).ToString("C");
```

- Custom cultures can be created with the *CultureAndRegionInfoBuilder* class.
- The number formatting of custom classes can be manipulated through the *NumberFormat* property of the *CultureAndRegionInfoBuilder* class.

- The date and time formatting of a custom class can be manipulated through the *GregorianDateTimeFormat* property of the *CultureAndRegionInfoBuilder* class.

Key Terms

Do you know what these key terms mean? You can check your answers by looking up the terms in the glossary at the end of the book.

- current culture
- current UI culture
- globalization
- localization

Case Scenario

In the following case scenario, you will apply what you've learned about how to create custom cultures. You can find answers to these questions in the "Answers" section at the end of this book.

Case Scenario: Installing and Configuring a New Application

You are a software developer at A Datum Corporation, and you are working on its new application named A-Datum 2005. This application is a Windows Forms application written in C#, although you are free to use Visual Basic assemblies if you want to. A-Datum 2004, the previous version, was sold exclusively in the United States, the same country it was developed in. Because of that, the previous version did not have any issues related to cultural differences. However, the company has now signed multiple contracts with partners all over the world, and it needs to support formatting for many locales where French and Spanish are spoken. Soon the scope might expand to include many other cultures as well, so you need to take this into account.

Interviews

Following is a list of company personnel interviewed and their statements:

- **IT Manager** "The biggest problem we're running into is currency and date differences. We have a ton of hard-coded dates and currency thresholds, and those are blowing up every time the program runs outside of the United States."

■ **Programming Manager**   "We've often developed our software by the seat of our pants and have taken short cuts because we needed to get the product out the door. This has worked for us in the past, but now that we're going global, it won't work any more. We can finally take the time to do things right, and taking into account the date and currency differences is absolutely critical to getting this right. Even if the product ships, I won't consider it "complete" until it works correctly in every locale that's using it."

Questions

Answer the following questions for your manager:

1. What can be done to get around the hard-coded value problem?

2. What can be done to perform culture-insensitive date and currency comparisons?

3. How can the user interface be built so that cultural differences are taken into account?

Suggested Practices

To help you successfully master the objectives covered in this chapter, complete the following tasks.

Using Culture Information

■ **Practice 1**   Create a simple application that makes extensive use of currencies and dates. At first, ignore any culture settings. Now pick three cultures that you aren't familiar with (if you're familiar with all of them, just randomly pick three), and one by one, change the current culture to each of those three. Examine the dates and the currencies, and see the effects of your changes.

■ **Practice 2**   Create a Winforms application that uses en-US as the default culture. Create the resource files and culture settings so that a dialog box is presented that allows the user to choose a culture. Have your application respond to a user's change of culture.

Create a Custom Culture

■ **Practice 1**   Think of one area you have lived or visited outside of where you currently live. Create a specific culture to represent that area. Choose any symbol you like to represent the currency, and choose a date format you've never seen before. Make sure you use resource files, and treat this just as you would any other culture, ensuring that your application can respond to this new culture appropriately.

Take a Practice Test

The practice tests on this book's companion CD offer many options. For example, you can test yourself on just one exam objective, or you can test yourself on all the 70-536 certification exam content. You can set up the test so that it closely simulates the experience of taking a certification exam, or you can set it up in study mode so that you can look at the correct answers and explanations after you answer each question.

MORE INFO Practice tests

For details about all the practice test options available, see the "How to Use the Practice Tests" section in this book's Introduction.

Answers

Chapter 1: Lesson Review Answers

Lesson 1

1. **Correct Answers: A, C, and D**

    A. **Correct:** *Decimal* is a value type.

    B. **Incorrect:** *String* is a reference type.

    C. **Correct:** *System.Drawing.Point* is a value type.

    D. **Correct:** *Integer* is a value type.

2. **Correct Answer: B**

    A. **Incorrect:** First, value types must be initialized before being passed to a procedure unless they are specifically declared as *nullable*. Second, passing a *null* value would not affect the behavior of a value type.

    B. **Correct:** Procedures work with a copy of variables when you pass a value type by value. Therefore, any modifications that were made to the copy would not affect the original value.

    C. **Incorrect:** The variable might have been redeclared, but it would not affect the value of the variable.

    D. **Incorrect:** If the variable had been passed by reference, the original value would have been modified.

3. **Correct Answer: B**

    A. **Incorrect:** The Visual Basic sample uses angle brackets rather than parentheses. The C# sample uses parentheses rather than angle brackets.

    B. **Correct:** This is the proper way to declare and assign a nullable integer. In C#, you could also use the following: int? i = null;

    C. **Incorrect:** You must use the *Nullable* generic to declare an integer as nullable. By default, integers are not nullable.

    D. **Incorrect:** This is not the correct syntax for using the *Nullable* generic.

4. **Correct Answer: D**

   A. **Incorrect:** You could pass a class by reference; however, it could be modified when passed to a procedure.

   B. **Incorrect:** You could pass a structure by reference; however, it could be modified when passed to a procedure.

   C. **Incorrect:** You could pass a class by value; however passing structures by value tends to be more efficient.

   D. **Correct:** Structures passed by value are typically the most efficient.

Lesson 2

1. **Correct Answers: B and C**

   A. **Incorrect:** Types declared as *Nullable* can only be value types.

   B. **Correct:** Strings are reference types.

   C. **Correct:** Exceptions are reference types.

   D. **Incorrect:** Value types derive from *System.Object*, so not all derived types are reference types.

2. **Correct Answer: C**

   A. **Incorrect:** You should order *Catch* clauses from most specific to most general.

   B. **Incorrect:** The first type that matches is caught and subsequent *Catch* clauses are skipped.

   C. **Correct:** The first type that matches is caught, and subsequent *Catch* clauses are skipped. Therefore, you should order *Catch* clauses from most specific to most general to enable you to catch errors that you have specific error-handling for, while still catching other exceptions with the more general *Catch* clauses.

   D. **Incorrect:** The first type that matches is caught and subsequent *Catch* clauses are skipped.

3. **Correct Answer: A**

   A. **Correct:** Using the *String* type to construct a dynamic string can result in a lot of temporary strings in memory because the *String* type is immutable. Therefore, using the *StringBuilder* class is preferable.

   B. **Incorrect:** Strings are limited to 32,767 bytes, not 256 bytes.

C. **Incorrect:** You can search and replace with a standard *String* class.

D. **Incorrect:** Strings are never value types; they are reference types.

4. **Correct Answer: B**

A. **Incorrect:** While this statement is true, the real advantage of using a *Finally* block is that code is executed even if the runtime does not throw an exception. Code in a *Catch* block is executed only if an exception occurs.

B. **Correct:** Use *Finally* blocks for code that should run whether or not an exception occurs.

C. **Incorrect:** The compiler will not throw an error if you do not include a *Finally* block. *Finally* blocks are optional.

D. **Incorrect:** You can dispose of resources in a *Catch* block. However, the code will run only if an exception occurs. Typically, you need to dispose of resources whether or not an exception occurs.

Lesson 3

1. **Correct Answers: B and C**

A. **Incorrect:** Interfaces define a contract between types; inheritance derives a type from a base type.

B. **Correct:** Interfaces define a contract between types, ensuring that a class implements specific members.

C. **Correct:** Inheritance derives a type from a base type, automatically implementing all members of the base class, while allowing the derived class to extend or override the existing functionality.

D. **Incorrect:** Interfaces define a contract between types; inheritance derives a type from a base type.

2. **Correct Answers: A and C**

A. **Correct:** *Nullable* is a generic type.

B. **Incorrect:** *Boolean* is a nongeneric value type.

C. **Correct:** *EventHandler* is a generic type.

D. **Incorrect:** *System.Drawing.Point* is a structure and is not generic.

3. **Correct Answer: D**

   A. **Incorrect:** The *Object* class does not have a *Dispose* member method. Additionally, you would need to use a constraint to mandate types implementing the *IDisposable* interface to call the *Dispose* method.

   B. **Incorrect:** Implementing an interface does not enable generic types to use interface methods.

   C. **Incorrect:** Deriving the generic class from an interface does not enable generic types to use interface methods.

   D. **Correct:** If you use constraints to require types to implement a specific interface, you can call any methods used in the interface.

4. **Correct Answer: A**

   A. **Correct:** Delegates define the signature (arguments and return type) for the entry point.

   B. **Incorrect:** Event procedures can be *Shared/static* or instance members.

   C. **Incorrect:** If you mistyped the event procedure name, you would receive a different compiler error.

   D. **Incorrect:** Events work equally well, regardless of the language used.

Lesson 4

1. **Correct Answer: A**

   A. **Correct:** The primary reason to avoid boxing is because it adds overhead.

   B. **Incorrect:** Boxing requires no special privileges.

   C. **Incorrect:** Boxing does not make code less readable.

2. **Correct Answers: A and B**

   A. **Correct:** Value types are boxed when an abstract method inherited from *System.Object* is called. Overriding the method avoids boxing.

   B. **Correct:** By default, the *ToString* method simply returns the type name, which is typically not useful for a consuming application.

   C. **Incorrect:** The compiler does not require structures to override the *ToString* method.

   D. **Incorrect:** *ToString* never causes a run-time error; it simply returns the type name unless overridden.

3. **Correct Answer: B**

   A. **Incorrect:** You can't omit a member of an interface and still conform to that interface.

   B. **Correct:** *InvalidCastException* is the recommended exception to throw.

   C. **Incorrect:** While you could throw a custom exception, using standard exception types makes it easier for developers writing code to consume your type to catch specific exceptions.

   D. **Incorrect:** You must return a value for each conversion member.

4. **Correct Answers: A and C**

   A. **Correct:** You can convert from *Int16* to *Int32* because that is considered a widening conversion. Because *Int32* can store any value of *Int16*, implicit conversion is allowed.

   B. **Incorrect:** You cannot convert from *Int32* to *Int16* because that is considered a narrowing conversion. Because *Int16* cannot store any value of *Int32*, implicit conversion is not allowed.

   C. **Correct:** You can convert from *Int16* to *Double* because that is considered a widening conversion. Because *Double* can store any value of *Int16*, implicit conversion is allowed.

   D. **Incorrect:** You cannot convert from *Double* to *Int16* because that is considered a narrowing conversion. Because *Int16* cannot store any value of *Double*, implicit conversion is not allowed.

Chapter 1: Case Scenario Answers

Case Scenario: Designing an Application

1. Both subscribers and doctors will have a lot of information in common, including names, phone numbers, and addresses. However, they will each have unique information, also. For example, you need to track the subscription plan and payment information for subscribers. For doctors, you need to track contract details, medical certifications, and specialties. Therefore, you should create separate classes for subscribers and doctors, but derive them from a single class that contains all members shared by both classes. To do this, you could create a base class named *Person*, and derive both the *Subscriber* and *Doctor* classes from *Person*.

2. You can use an array to store a group of subscribers.

3. Yes, you can use generics to create a method that can accept both subscribers and doctors. To access the information in the base class that both classes share, you would need to make the base class a constraint for the generic method.

4. The security error would generate an exception. Therefore, to respond to the exception, you should wrap the code in a *Try/Catch* block. Within the *Catch* block, you should inform the user that he should contact his manager.

Chapter 2: Lesson Review Answers

Lesson 1

1. **Correct Answers: A, B, and D**

   A. **Correct:** Not specifying the *FileAccess* on *File.Open* defaults to read/write access.

   B. **Correct:** Explicitly using the *FileAccess.Write* value allows you to write to the file.

   C. **Incorrect:** Explicitly using the *FileAccess.Read* prohibits writing to the file.

   D. **Correct:** Creating a new *FileInfo* object and opening it with FileMode.Create defaults to read/write access to the file.

2. **Correct Answers: A, B, C, and D**

   A. **Correct:** The *FileSystemWatcher* can report on new files.

   B. **Correct:** The *FileSystemWatcher* can report on new directories.

   C. **Correct:** The *FileSystemWatcher* can report on file changes.

   D. **Correct:** The *FileSystemWatcher* can report on renamed files.

   E. **Incorrect**: All of these changes can be detected.

3. **Correct Answer: A**

   A. **Correct:** The *Path* class deals only with the string of a path. It makes no changes to the file system.

   B. **Incorrect:** The *Path* class deals only with the string of a path. It makes no changes to the file system.

Lesson 2

1. **Correct Answers: A, C, and D**

   A. **Correct:** This method reads from the file and moves the position forward.

   B. **Incorrect:** *Lock* has no affect on the position.

   C. **Correct:** This method writes to the file and moves the position forward.

   D. **Correct:** This method moves the position to another place in the file.

2. **Correct Answers: A, B, and C**

   A. **Correct:** Closing the *StreamWriter* causes the data to be flushed, but doing so will also close the underlying stream.

   B. **Correct:** The *Flush* method causes the data to be flushed.

   C. **Correct:** Setting *AutoFlush* forces every call to the *StreamWriter* to flush the data to the stream.

   D. **Incorrect:** Closing the stream does not cause the data to be flushed, and subsequent use of the *StreamWriter* (including *StreamWriter.Close*) will cause an exception.

3. **Correct Answers: A and C**

   A. **Correct:** Creating a new instance of the *FileStream* class with *FileMode.OpenOrCreate* will open an existing file or create a new one if necessary.

   B. **Incorrect:** *File.Create* will overwrite an existing file if one exists.

   C. **Correct:** Calling *File.Open* with *FileMode.OpenOrCreate* will open an existing file or create a new one if necessary.

   D. **Incorrect:** Calling *File.Open* with *FileMode.Open* will open an existing file only. It will not create a new one if necessary.

Lesson 3

1. **Correct Answer: B**

   A. **Incorrect:** The *BaseStream* property is read-only, and there is no *CompressionMode* property.

   B. **Correct:** You specify the stream and the mode in the constructor.

   C. **Incorrect:** The *Write* method does not specify a stream.

   D. **Incorrect:** The *DeflateStream* class does not have a *BaseStream* event.

2. **Correct Answers: C and D**

  A. **Incorrect:** Any file can be compressed, but there is a 4-GB limit to the compression size.

  B. **Incorrect:** Any data can be compressed, but it is limited to 4 GB.

  C. **Correct:** True.

  D. **Correct:** True.

Lesson 4

1. **Correct Answers: A, B, and C**

  A. **Correct:** The *GetStore* method allows you to get advanced types of stores.

  B. **Correct:** The *GetMachineStoreForAssembly* method allows you to get a machine-level store for the calling assembly.

  C. **Correct:** The *GetUserStoreForAssembly* method allows you to get a user-specific store for the calling assembly.

  D. **Incorrect:** The constructor is not publicly available.

2. **Correct Answer: A**

  A. **Correct:** The *IsolatedStorageFileStream* derives from *FileStream*; therefore, it can be used just like any other object *FileStream* creates.

  B. **Incorrect:** The *IsolatedStorageFileStream* class derives from the *FileStream* class, so you can use any files *IsolatedStorageFileStream* creates just like a file that *FileStream* creates.

Chapter 2: Case Scenario Answers

Case Scenario 1: Saving User Settings

1. The company should use isolated storage to store the information for the users. By using an assembly/user-level scope for an isolated storage store, you can affirm that multiple users on the same machine will not have access to each other's data, as well as allow the application to run with very few security permissions.

2. To limit the size of the disk space, you would probably suggest using *GZipStream* (or *DeflateStream*) to minimize the size of the settings file.

Case Scenario 2: Monitoring Old Servers

1. You should create a simple service that could be run continuously.

2. You should suggest using a *FileSystemWatcher* and registering to view new files, changes, and deletions. When a file has changed, you could use the *FileInfo* object to get the access control list to find out who created the file and e-mail that information to the IT department.

3. By using the *FileSystemWatcher* class, you can alleviate the Development Manager's performance concerns because the file system will alert you to changes instead of storing information about every file and using a brute-force comparison.

Chapter 3: Lesson Review Answers

Lesson 1

1. **Correct Answer: C**

    A. **Incorrect:** This code sample would work correctly; however, it performs a case-sensitive replacement. Therefore, it would not correctly replace "HTTP://".

    B. **Incorrect:** This code sample has the parameters reversed and would replace "https://" with "http://".

    C. **Correct:** This code sample correctly replaces "http://" with "https://" regardless of case.

    D. **Incorrect:** This code sample has the parameters reversed and would replace "https://" with "http://".

2. **Correct Answer: A**

    A. **Correct:** This code sample correctly specifies the *RegexOptions.Multiline* option and does not use angle brackets to name regular expression groups.

    B. **Incorrect:** You must specify the *RegexOptions.Multiline* option to process multiline input.

    C. **Incorrect:** When naming a group, you should not include the angle brackets.

    D. **Incorrect:** When naming a group, you should not include the angle brackets. Additionally, you must specify the *RegexOptions.Multiline* option to process multiline input.

3.   **Correct Answer: B**

   A. **Incorrect:** This regular expression would match "zoot", but it does not match "zot".

   B. **Correct:** This regular expression matches both strings.

   C. **Incorrect:** This regular expression does not match either string because it begins with the "$" symbol, which matches the end of the string.

   D. **Incorrect:** This regular expression does match "zot", but it does not match "zoot".

4.   **Correct Answers: A, C, and E**

   A. **Correct:** This string does match the regular expression.

   B. **Incorrect:** This string does not match the regular expression because the fourth character does not match.

   C. **Correct:** This string does match the regular expression.

   D. **Incorrect:** This string does not match the regular expression because the second and third characters must be "mo".

   E. **Correct:** This string does match the regular expression.

Lesson 2

1.   **Correct Answer: A**

   A. **Correct:** UTF-32 has the largest byte size and will yield the largest file size.

   B. **Incorrect:** UTF-16 has a smaller byte size than UTF-32

   C. **Incorrect:** UTF-8 has a smaller byte size than UTF-32

   D. **Incorrect:** ASCII has a smaller byte size than UTF-32

2.   **Correct Answers: A, B, and C**

   A. **Correct:** UTF-32 provides large enough bytes to support Chinese Unicode characters.

   B. **Correct:** UTF-16 provides large enough bytes to support Chinese Unicode characters.

   C. **Correct:** UTF-8 provides large enough bytes to support Chinese Unicode characters.

   D. **Incorrect:** ASCII supports only English-language characters.

3. **Correct Answers: C and D**

   A. **Incorrect:** ASCII uses 8-bit bytes, whereas UTF-32 uses larger bytes.

   B. **Incorrect:** ASCII uses 8-bit bytes, whereas UTF-16 uses larger bytes.

   C. **Correct:** UTF-8 uses 8-bit bytes for characters in the ASCII range and is backward-compatible with ASCII.

   D. **Correct:** UTF-7 will correctly decode ASCII files.

4. **Correct Answer: D**

   A. **Incorrect:** iso-2022-kr does provide support for Korean characters. However, Unicode also provides support for the Korean language, as well as other languages in the same file, and it provides the widest-ranging compatibility.

   B. **Incorrect:** x-EBCDIC-KoreanExtended does provide support for Korean characters. However, Unicode also provides support for the Korean language, as well as other languages in the same file, and it provides the widest-ranging compatibility.

   C. **Incorrect:** x-mac-korean does provide support for Korean characters. However, Unicode also provides support for the Korean language, as well as other languages in the same file, and it provides the widest-ranging compatibility.

   D. **Correct:** Though you could use one of several different Korean code pages, Unicode provides support for the Korean language and is the best choice for creating new documents.

Chapter 3: Case Scenario Answers

Case Scenario 1: Validating Input

1. You can use separate ASP.NET *RegularExpressionValidator* controls to restrict the input for each of the three boxes. For the company name validator, set the *ValidationExpression* property to "[a-zA-Z'`-Ã,Â´\s]{1,40}". For the contact name validator, you can use the regular expression, "[a-zA-Z'`-Ã,Â´\s]{1,30}". Finally, for the phone number validator, you can use ASP.NET's built-in regular expression, "((\(\d{3}\) ?)|(\d{3}-))?\d{3}-\d{4}".

2. You can write code to further constrain, reject, and sanitize the input. In particular, if the database developer provides further restrictions such as not allowing

apostrophes or percent symbols, you can remove those symbols from the input by using the *String.Replace* method.

Case Scenario 2: Processing Data from a Legacy Computer

1. Yes, you can extract data from text reports using regular expressions. You could use the *Regex.Match* method and the *Match.Groups* collection to extract the important data.

2. Yes, you can read ASCII files. You do not need to specify a certain type of encoding to read ASCII files because the standard settings for file streams will process ASCII correctly.

Chapter 4: Lesson Review Answers

Lesson 1

1. **Correct Answers: B and C**

   A. **Incorrect:** *Remove* will return without exception, regardless of whether the item exists in the collection.

   B. **Correct:** *Contains* can be used to test to whether the item exists in the collection.

   C. **Correct:** *IndexOf* will return -1 if the item does not exist in the collection.

   D. **Incorrect:** Returning the count of the collection will not reveal whether an item is in the collection.

2. **Correct Answers: A, C, and D**

   A. **Correct:** *Comparer* will compare two objects and return an integer that represents whether the left-hand object is less than, equal to, or greater than the right-hand object.

   B. **Incorrect:** The class compares two objects relatively, not for identity of references.

   C. **Correct:** It is used in the *ArrayList.Sort* method to do the default sorting.

   D. **Correct:** It is the default implementation of the *IComparer* implementation.

Lesson 2

1. **Correct Answers: A and C**

Lesson 2

1. **Correct Answers: A and C**

   A. **Correct:** It does retrieve the item from the front of the collection.

   B. **Incorrect:** It does not add an item to the collection.

   C. **Correct:** As it retrieves an item, it also removes it from the collection.

   D. **Incorrect:** It does not clear the collection.

2. **Correct Answer: C**

   A. **Incorrect:** The stack is a last-in, first-out collection.

   B. **Incorrect:** The stack is a last-in, first-out collection.

   C. **Correct:** It is a last-in, first-out collection.

   D. **Incorrect:** The stack is a last-in, first-out collection.

Lesson 3

1. **Correct Answers: B and D**

   A. **Incorrect:** *GetType* is not called to determine uniqueness.

   B. **Correct:** The hash value from the object is used to see whether the hash has been used in the collection.

   C. **Incorrect:** The string representation of the object does not determine whether the key is unique. The *Hashtable* class only uses the hash value to determine uniqueness.

   D. **Correct:** If two hash values are identical, *Equals* can be called to determine whether two objects are in fact equal before assigning the value to a key.

2. **Correct Answer: A**

   A. **Correct:** You pass an object that supports the interface to override the way that uniqueness is compared.

   B. **Incorrect:** You cannot assign an *IEqualityComparer* once the *Hashtable* has been created.

   C. **Incorrect:** You can use *IEqualityComparer* with a *Hashtable*.

   D. **Incorrect:** The *Hashtable* supports a constructor that accepts an *IEquality-Comparer*, but it does not implement the interface itself.

Lesson 4

1. **Correct Answers: C and D**

   A. **Incorrect:** Only case-insensitive *Hashtable* and *SortedList* objects can be made from the *CollectionUtil* class.

   B. **Incorrect:** Only case-insensitive *Hashtable* objects can be made from the *CollectionUtil* class, not culture-invariant ones.

   C. **Correct:** Case-insensitive *Hashtable* objects can be created with the *CollectionUtil* class.

   D. **Correct:** Case-insensitive *SortedList* objects can be created with the *CollectionUtil* class.

2. **Correct Answer: A**

   A. **Correct:** Only strings can be stored as a *Value* in *StringDictionary*.

   B. **Incorrect:** Only strings can be stored as a *Value* in *StringDictionary*.

   C. **Incorrect:** Only strings can be stored as a *Value* in *StringDictionary*.

   D. **Incorrect:** Only strings can be stored as a *Value* in *StringDictionary*.

Lesson 5

1. **Correct Answer: B**

   A. **Incorrect:** The enumerator is type-safe to return a *KeyValuePair*.

   B. **Correct:** The enumerator is type-safe to return a *KeyValuePair*.

   C. **Incorrect:** The enumerator is type-safe to return a *KeyValuePair*.

   D. **Incorrect:** The enumerator is type-safe to return a *KeyValuePair*.

2. **Correct Answers: A, B, C, and D**

   A. **Correct:** You can add at the beginning of the *LinkedList*.

   B. **Correct:** You can add before a specific node in the *LinkedList*.

   C. **Correct:** You can add after a specific node in the *LinkedList*.

   D. **Correct:** You can add at the end of the *LinkedList*.

   E. **Incorrect:** You cannot insert by index.

Chapter 4: Case Scenario Answers

Case Scenario 1: Use an *ArrayList* to Store Status Codes

1. Use an *ArrayList* to keep the codes because there aren't likely to be very many, and doing so will allow the company to add new ones without much trouble.

2. Use the *ArrayList*'s *Sort* function to sort the codes per user.

Case Scenario 2: Select the Correct Collection

1. Use a *HybridDictionary*, as it will provide both the lookup via sales person code you need as well as good performance with both small and large lists.

2. By storing the agent names in an in-memory collection, the list won't need to be continually loading into memory, so the performance should not change to a noticeable extent.

Case Scenario 3: Rewrite to Use a Type-Safe Collection

1. Use a generic *List* collection, and make it type safe to bank activity objects. This collection will accept only the right types of objects, and if the wrong type is used it will cause a compile error. Compilation errors will be evident to the developer so that he or she can fix the issue before it ever gets to the tellers.

2. The speed of the collection will be on par with or better than the current one. All the type-checking code that you would expect to slow down the object will be done at compile-time, so the code will be cleaner and probably faster.

Chapter 5: Lesson Review Answers

Lesson 1

1. **Correct Answers: A and D**

   A. **Correct:** You must call the *BinaryFormatter.Serialize* method to serialize an object.

   B. **Incorrect:** You do not necessarily need file permissions to serialize an object. You can also serialize an object to a network stream.

   C. **Incorrect:** Internet Information Services is not required for serialization; however, serialized objects are often transferred to Web services.

D. **Correct:** The *BinaryFormatter.Serialize* method requires a stream object to act as the destination for the serialization.

2. **Correct Answer: B**

A. **Incorrect:** *ISerializable* is an interface that you can implement to perform custom serialization. It is not an attribute.

B. **Correct:** Classes must have the *Serializable* attribute to be serialized.

C. **Incorrect:** *SoapInclude* is used when generating schemas for SOAP serialization. It is not required to enable serialization.

D. **Incorrect:** *OnDeserialization* is an *ISerializable* method that you can implement to control serialization behavior. It is not an attribute.

3. **Correct Answer: A**

A. **Correct:** The *NonSerialized* attribute prevents a member from being serialized.

B. **Incorrect:** *Serializable* is an attribute that specifies a class should be serialized. It does not apply to members.

C. **Incorrect:** *SerializationException* is an exception class called when a serialization error occurs. It is not an attribute.

D. **Incorrect:** The *SoapIgnore* attribute prevents a member from being serialized only by *SoapFormatter*. It does not apply to *BinaryFormatter*.

4. **Correct Answer: C**

A. **Incorrect:** *IFormatter* provides functionality for formatting serialized objects.

B. **Incorrect:** *ISerializable* allows an object to control its own serialization and deserialization.

C. **Correct:** Implement the *IDeserializationCallback* interface and the *IDeserializationCallback.OnDeserialization* method to run code after an object is serialized.

D. **Incorrect:** *IObjectReferences* indicates that the current interface implementer is a reference to another object.

Lesson 2

1. **Correct Answers: A and C**

   A. **Correct:** Classes serialized with XML serialization must be public.

   B. **Incorrect:** You cannot use XML serialization on private classes.

   C. **Correct:** For XML serialization to work, the class must have a parameter-less constructor.

   D. **Incorrect:** XML serialization does not require the *SerializationInfo* parameter.

2. **Correct Answer: D**

   A. **Incorrect:** *XmlAnyAttribute* causes an array to be filled with *XmlAttribute* objects that represent all XML attributes unknown to the schema. It is used during deserialization, and it is not used during serialization.

   B. **Incorrect:** Use the *XMLType* attribute to specify the name and namespace of the XML type.

   C. **Incorrect:** *XMLElement* causes the field or property to be serialized as an XML element.

   D. **Correct:** By default, members are serialized as elements. Add the *XMLAttribute* attribute to serialize a member as an attribute.

3. **Correct Answer: A**

   A. **Correct:** You can use the Xsd.exe tool to create classes based on an XML schema.

   B. **Incorrect:** Xdcmake.exe is the Microsoft XML Document Contents Merge Tool. It cannot be used to create a class that conforms to an XML schema.

   C. **Incorrect:** XPadsi90.exe is used to register a SQL Server in an Active Directory. It cannot be used to create a class that conforms to an XML schema.

   D. **Incorrect:** Xcacls.exe is used to configure access control lists (ACLs) on files. It cannot be used to create a class that conforms to an XML schema.

4. **Correct Answer: B**

   A. **Incorrect:** Use the *XMLType* attribute to specify the name and namespace of the XML type.

   B. **Correct:** Use the *XMLIgnore* attribute to prevent a member from being serialized during XML serialization.

C. **Incorrect:** *XMLElement* causes the field or property to be serialized as an XML element.

D. **Incorrect:** *XMLAttribute* causes the field or property to be serialized as an XML attribute.

Lesson 3

1. **Correct Answers: A and C**

A. **Correct:** The deserialization constructor must accept two objects of types *SerializationInfo* and *StreamingContext*.

B. **Incorrect:** Although the *Formatter* class is used during serialization, it is not passed to the deserialization constructor.

C. **Correct:** The deserialization constructor must accept two objects of types *SerializationInfo* and *StreamingContext*.

D. **Incorrect:** Although the *ObjectManager* class is used during serialization, it is not passed to the deserialization constructor.

2. **Correct Answer: B**

A. **Incorrect:** *OnSerializing* occurs before serialization, not before deserialization.

B. **Correct:** *OnDeserializing* occurs immediately before deserialization.

C. **Incorrect:** *OnSerialized* occurs after serialization, not immediately before deserialization.

D. **Incorrect:** *OnDeserialized* occurs after deserialization, not before deserialization.

3. **Correct Answer: C**

A. **Incorrect:** *OnSerializing* occurs before serialization, not after serialization.

B. **Incorrect:** *OnDeserializing* occurs before deserialization, not immediately after serializing.

C. **Correct:** *OnSerialized* occurs immediately after serialization.

D. **Incorrect:** *OnDeserialized* occurs after deserialization, not immediately after serialization.

4. **Correct Answers: A and C**

    A. **Correct:** Methods that are called in response to a serialization event must accept a *StreamingContext* object as a parameter.

    B. **Incorrect:** Methods that are called in response to a serialization event must accept a *StreamingContext* object as a parameter and are not required to accept a *SerializationInfo* parameter.

    C. **Correct:** Methods that are called in response to a serialization event must return void.

    D. **Incorrect:** Methods that are called in response to a serialization event must return void, and cannot return a *StreamingContext* object.

Chapter 5: Case Scenario Answers

Case Scenario 1: Choosing a Serialization Technique

1. You should use *BinaryFormatter* serialization. In this case, you will be communicating only with other .NET Framework–based applications. Additionally, the network manager asked you to conserve bandwidth.

2. In all likelihood, you will need to add only the *Serializable* attribute to enable serialization.

3. It depends on how you establish the network connection, but the serialization itself should require only two or three lines of code.

Case Scenario 2: Serializing Between Versions

1. Yes, *BinaryFormatter* can deserialize objects serialized with .NET 1.0.

2. Yes, you can deserialize the *Preferences* class, even if the serialized class is missing members. However, you will need to add the *OptionalField* attribute to any new members to prevent the runtime from throwing a serialization exception. Then you will need to initialize the new members with default values after deserialization by either implementing *IDeserializationCallback* or creating a method for the *OnDeserialized* event.

3. There's nothing to prevent the same class from being serialized by either *Binary-Formatter* or *XmlSerializer*. Your application should first check for the preferences of a serialized XML file. If the file does not exist, it would then attempt to deserialize the binary file.

Chapter 6: Lesson Review Answers

Lesson 1

1. **Correct Answer: E**

   A. **Incorrect:** *Graphics.DrawLines* draws multiple, connected lines. This method can be used to draw a square, but it cannot be used to draw a filled square.

   B. **Incorrect:** *Graphics.DrawRectangle* would be the most efficient way to draw an empty square. However, it cannot be used to draw a filled square.

   C. **Incorrect:** *Graphics.DrawPolygon* could be used to draw an empty square. However, it cannot be used to draw a filled square.

   D. **Incorrect:** *Graphics.DrawEllipse* is used to draw oval shapes and cannot be used to draw a filled square.

   E. **Correct:** *Graphics.FillRectangle* is used to draw filled squares or rectangles.

   F. **Incorrect:** *Graphics.FillPolygon* could be used to draw a filled square. However, it is not as efficient as using *FillRectangle*.

   G. **Incorrect:** *Graphics.FillEllipse* is used to draw oval shapes and cannot be used to draw a square.

2. **Correct Answer: C**

   A. **Incorrect:** *Graphics.DrawLines* draws multiple, connected lines. This method can be used to draw an empty triangle, but it is not the most efficient way.

   B. **Incorrect:** *Graphics.DrawRectangle* draws empty squares or rectangles. However, it cannot be used to draw a triangle.

   C. **Correct:** *Graphics.DrawPolygon* is the most efficient way to draw an empty triangle.

   D. **Incorrect:** *Graphics.DrawEllipse* is used to draw oval shapes and cannot be used to draw an empty triangle.

   E. **Incorrect:** *Graphics.FillRectangle* is used to draw filled squares or rectangles and cannot be used to draw an empty triangle.

   F. **Incorrect:** *Graphics.FillPolygon* could be used to draw a filled triangle. However, it cannot be used to draw an empty triangle.

   G. **Incorrect:** *Graphics.FillEllipse* is used to draw oval shapes and cannot be used to draw an empty triangle.

3. **Correct Answers: A and B**

   A. **Correct:** To draw a circle, call the *Graphics.DrawEllipse* method using an instance of the *Graphics* class.

   B. **Correct:** To call the *Graphics.DrawEllipse* method, you must provide an instance of the *Pen* class.

   C. **Incorrect:** *System.Drawing.Brush* is used to draw filled shapes, not empty shapes.

   D. **Incorrect:** You can create a *Graphics* object from *System.Drawing.Bitmap*; however, there are many better ways to create a *Graphics* class.

4. **Correct Answer: B**

   A. **Incorrect:** *HatchBrush* defines a rectangular brush with a hatch style, foreground color, and background color.

   B. **Correct:** *LinearGradientBrush* can be used to fill objects with a color that gradually fades to a second color.

   C. **Incorrect:** *PathGradientBrush* can be used to fill objects with a color that gradually fades to a second color; however, *LinearGradientBrush* is more efficient.

   D. **Incorrect:** *SolidBrush* fills objects with only a single color.

   E. **Incorrect:** *TextureBrush* is used to fill objects with an image.

5. **Correct Answer: D**

   A. **Incorrect:** The arrow points to the right.

   B. **Incorrect:** The arrow points to the right.

   C. **Incorrect:** The arrow points to the right.

   D. **Correct:** The arrow points to the right.

Lesson 2

1. **Correct Answers: A and B**

   A. **Correct:** You can load a picture from a file using the *Image* constructor, and then call *Graphics.DrawImage* to display the picture in the form.

   B. **Correct:** The *Bitmap* class inherits from the *Image* class and can be used in most places where the *Image* class is used.

   C. **Incorrect:** You cannot use the *MetaFile* class to load a JPEG image.

D. **Incorrect:** The *PictureBox* class is used to display pictures in a form, but it does not include a method to load a picture from a file.

2. **Correct Answer: C**

A. **Incorrect:** You cannot directly create a *Graphics* object from a picture saved to the disk.

B. **Incorrect:** The *Bitmap* class does not have methods for drawing graphics.

C. **Correct:** You must first create a *Bitmap* object, and then create a *Graphics* object from the *Bitmap* before saving it.

D. **Incorrect:** There is no *Bitmap.CreateGraphics* method. Instead, you must call *Graphics.FromImage* to create a *Graphics* object.

3. **Correct Answer: C**

A. **Incorrect:** You can use the BMP format to store photographs; however, the JPEG format uses much less space.

B. **Incorrect:** The GIF format is not ideal for storing photographs.

C. **Correct:** The JPEG format offers excellent quality and compression for photographs with almost universal application support.

D. **Incorrect:** The PNG format is very efficient; however, it is not as universally compatible as GIF and JPEG.

4. **Correct Answer: B**

A. **Incorrect:** You can use the BMP format to store charts; however, the GIF format uses much less space.

B. **Correct:** The GIF format is ideal for storing charts.

C. **Incorrect:** You can use the JPEG format to store charts; however, the results may not be as clear as the GIF format.

D. **Incorrect:** The PNG format is very efficient; however, it is not as universally compatible as GIF and JPEG.

Lesson 3

1. **Correct Answer: B**

A. **Incorrect:** The *string* class does not have a *Draw* method.

B. **Correct:** You add text by calling *Graphics.DrawString*, which requires a *Graphics* object, a *Font* object, and a *Brush* object.

    C. **Incorrect:** *Graphics.DrawString* requires a *Brush* object, not a *Pen* object.

    D. **Incorrect:** The *Bitmap* class does not have a *DrawString* method.

2. **Correct Answer: A**

    A. **Correct:** Create an instance of the *StringFormat* class, and pass it to *Graphics.DrawString* to control the alignment of a string.

    B. **Incorrect:** *StringAlignment* can be used when specifying the formatting of a string; however, it is an enumeration and you cannot create an instance of it.

    C. **Incorrect:** *FormatFlags* can be used when specifying the formatting of a string; however, it is a property of *StringFormat* and you cannot create an instance of it.

    D. **Incorrect:** *LineAlignment* can be used when specifying the formatting of a string; however, it is a property of *StringFormat* and you cannot create an instance of it.

3. **Correct Answer: C**

    A. **Incorrect:** This statement would cause the line to be drawn at the top of the bounding rectangle.

    B. **Incorrect:** This statement would cause the line to be drawn at the bottom of the bounding rectangle.

    C. **Correct:** This statement would cause the line to be drawn at the left of the bounding rectangle.

    D. **Incorrect:** This statement would cause the line to be drawn at the right of the bounding rectangle.

Chapter 6: Case Scenario Answers

Case Scenario 1: Choosing Graphics Techniques

1. You can specify the size of an image as part of the *Bitmap* constructor, and the .NET Framework will automatically resize the image. Note, however, that to ensure the image is scaled proportionally (and not squeezed vertically or horizontally), you should open the image, check the size, and calculate a new size for the image that uses the same proportions.

2. First open the image file in a *Bitmap* object. Then create a *Graphics* object from the *Bitmap* object, and call *Graphics.DrawImage* to draw the corporate logo. The logo background will need to be transparent.

3. Determine a percentage of the horizontal and vertical area that the logo will consume as a maximum, calculate the maximum number of pixels as a percentage of the size of the splash screen, and then resize the logo.

4. This will not require using graphics at all—simply specify a different size for labels and text boxes by editing the properties of the controls.

Case Scenario 2: Creating Simple Charts

1. You should use a *PictureBox* control.

2. *Graphics.DrawLines*

3. *Graphics.DrawRectangles*

4. You can call the *PictureBox.Image.Save* method.

Chapter 7: Lesson Review Answers

Lesson 1

1. **Correct Answer: B**

   A. **Incorrect:** The *ThreadStart* delegate does not allow a parameter to be passed.

   B. **Correct:** The *ParameterizedThreadStart* delegate expects a single parameter.

   C. **Incorrect:** The *SynchronizationContact* class has nothing to do with starting a thread.

   D. **Incorrect:** The *ExecutionContext* class is not required when starting a thread with a single parameter.

2. **Correct Answer: C**

   A. **Incorrect:** *Thread.Suspend* is no longer supported and would only pause a thread, not stop it.

   B. **Incorrect:** *Thread.Resume* is no longer supported and does not stop a thread.

C. **Correct:** The *Thread.Abort* method tells the thread to stop by firing a *ThreadAbortException*.

D. **Incorrect:** *Thread.Join* waits until the thread is complete. It does not stop a thread.

Lesson 2

1.   **Correct Answer: D**

A. **Incorrect:** There is not a limit to the number of readers a *ReaderWriterLock* allows.

B. **Incorrect:** There is not a limit to the number of readers a *ReaderWriterLock* allows.

C. **Incorrect:** There is not a limit to the number of readers a *ReaderWriterLock* allows.

D. **Correct:** Yes, there is no limit to the number of readers.

2.   **Correct Answers: B and C**

A. **Incorrect:** The *Monitor* class cannot be shared across *AppDomain* and process boundaries.

B. **Correct:** *Mutex*es can be named, so they can be shared across *AppDomain* and process boundaries.

C. **Correct:** *Semaphore*s can be named, so they can be shared across *AppDomain* and process boundaries.

D. **Incorrect:** The *lock* (C#) and *SyncLock* (Visual Basic) keywords use a *Monitor* to perform locking, and the *Monitor* cannot be shared across *AppDomain* and process boundaries.

Lesson 3

1.   **Correct Answers: B and D**

A. **Incorrect:** *RegisterWaitForSingleObject* is used to wait for *WaitHandles* to be signaled.

B. **Correct:** *QueueUserWorkItem* is used to have a pool thread run code.

C. **Incorrect:** *UnsafeRegisterWaitForSingleObject* is used to wait for *WaitHandles* to be signaled.

D. **Correct:** *UnsafeQueueUserWorkItem* is used to have a pool thread run code.

2. **Correct Answer: B**

A. **Incorrect:** Disposing the *Timer* will stop the timer, and you will not be able to restart it.

B. **Correct:** Using *Timer.Change* and *Timeout.Infinite* is correct.

C. **Incorrect:** Allowing the *Timer* object to go out of scope will not stop the *Timer* from firing until garbage is collected, which could be anywhere from immediately to a long time down the road.

D. **Incorrect**: Setting the timeout to zero will cause the timer to continue to fire as often as possible, the exact opposite of the requested result.

Chapter 7: Case Scenario Answers

Case Scenario 1: Improving Server Processing

1. The current application is single threaded, so only the main thread is running any code.

2. Make the application multithreaded to use equally well both the CPU that is currently being used and all available CPUs.

3. Use the *ThreadPool*, which scales up the number of available threads based on the number of CPUs on a machine.

Case Scenario 2: Multiple Applications

1. Use a named *Mutex* to make sure only one application can get to the interface at a time.

2. The *Mutex* is an operating-system-level object (a kernel object), so there is a performance impact, but in this case the performance should be plenty fast.

Chapter 8: Lesson Review Answers

Lesson 1

1. **Correct Answers: B and D**

A. **Incorrect:** There are other ways to launch separate processes.

B. **Correct:** You can call *AppDomain.Unload* to close the application domain and free up resources.

C. **Incorrect:** Creating a separate application domain does not improve performance.

D. **Correct:** Application domains provide a layer of separation. Additionally, you can limit the application domain's privileges, reducing the risk of a security vulnerability being exploited in an assembly.

2. **Correct Answers: B and C**

A. **Incorrect:** *AppDomain.CreateDomain* creates a new application domain, but it does not run an assembly.

B. **Correct:** You can use *AppDomain.ExecuteAssembly* to run an assembly given the path to the executable file.

C. **Correct:** You can use *AppDomain.ExecuteAssemblyByName* to run an assembly given the name of the assembly and a reference to the assembly.

D. **Incorrect:** *AppDomain.ApplicationIdentity* is a property and cannot be used to run an assembly.

3. **Correct Answer: D**

A. **Incorrect:** *AppDomain.DomainUnload* is an event that is called when an application domain is unloaded.

B. **Incorrect:** Setting an application domain to *null* does not cause it to be unloaded.

C. **Incorrect:** Instances of the *AppDomain* class do not contain an *Unload* method.

D. **Correct:** To unload an *AppDomain* object, pass it to the static *AppDomain.Unload* method.

Lesson 2

1. **Correct Answer: C**

A. **Incorrect:** Evidence cannot be used to affect a process's priority.

B. **Incorrect:** While evidence can identify the author of an assembly, the runtime uses this information only if security settings have been specifically configured for a given author.

C. **Correct:** The primary purpose of providing evidence for an application domain is to modify the privileges that the runtime assigns to the application domain.

D. **Incorrect:** Evidence is not related to auditing.

2. **Correct Answers: A and D**

   A. **Correct:** You can pass evidence to the *AppDomain.CreateDomain* method to apply the evidence to any assemblies run within that application domain.

   B. **Incorrect:** You can read, but not set, *AppDomain.Evidence*. To specify evidence for an *AppDomain*, you must pass the *Evidence* as part of the constructor.

   C. **Incorrect:** *AppDomain.ExecuteAssembly* does not accept a zone as a parameter. You must add the zone to an *Evidence* object to pass it to the *ExecuteAssembly* method.

   D. **Correct:** You can pass evidence to the *AppDomain.ExecuteAssembly* method to associate the evidence with the specified assembly.

3. **Correct Answer: D**

   A. **Incorrect:** *DynamicDirectory* is read-only. Additionally, it specifies the location where dynamically generated files will be located. It does not specify the base directory for an application.

   B. **Incorrect:** *BaseDirectory* is read-only.

   C. **Incorrect:** The *DynamicBase* property specifies the location where dynamically generated files will be located. It does not specify the base directory for an application.

   D. **Correct:** Use an instance of the *AppDomainSetup* class to configure an application domain, and set the *AppDomainSetup.ApplicationBase* property to set the name of the directory containing the application.

4. **Correct Answer: A**

   A. **Correct:** This Boolean property indicates whether the current application domain is allowed to download assemblies.

   B. **Incorrect:** The *DisallowCodeDownload* property is located within *AppDomain.CurrentDomain.SetupInformation*.

   C. **Incorrect:** The *DisallowPublisherPolicy* property gets or sets a value indicating whether the publisher policy section of the configuration file is applied to an application domain. You need to examine *DisallowCodeDownload* instead.

D. **Incorrect:** First, the *DisallowPublisherPolicy* property is located within *App-Domain.CurrentDomain.SetupInformation*. Second, you need to examine *DisallowCodeDownload* instead.

Lesson 3

1. **Correct Answer: A**

    A. **Correct:** *LocalService* causes your service to run in the context of an account that acts as a nonprivileged user on the local computer, and it presents anonymous credentials to any remote server. Using *LocalService* is the best way to minimize security risks because it limits the damage a service can do if successfully exploited.

    B. **Incorrect:** *NetworkService* can present authentication credentials to remote computers, which could be a security risk, though minimal.

    C. **Incorrect:** *LocalSystem* has almost unlimited privileges on the local computer, which enables a successful exploit of the service to perform almost any action on the computer.

    D. **Incorrect:** *User* causes the system to prompt for a valid user name and password when the service is installed. While this user account could have restricted privileges, the risk is likely to be greater than using *LocalService*.

2. **Correct Answer: C**

    A. **Incorrect:** *LocalService* causes your service to run in the context of an account that acts as a nonprivileged user on the local computer. Using *LocalService* is the best way to minimize security risks, but it can cause security problems when performing common tasks such as writing to the file system.

    B. **Incorrect:** *NetworkService* should be used when the service needs to authenticate to remote computers. It is not recommended for services that need access only to the local computer.

    C. **Correct:** *LocalSystem* has almost unlimited privileges on the local computer, which enables a service to take almost any action. You should use *LocalSystem* only when security is not a concern.

    D. **Incorrect:** *User* causes the system to prompt for a valid user name and password when the service is installed. While this user account could have sufficient privileges, *LocalSystem* guarantees that you will have unlimited privileges on the local computer.

3. **Correct Answers: B and D**

   A. **Incorrect:** While you could launch an assembly automatically by adding it to the Startup group, you cannot launch a service this way.

   B. **Correct:** You can use the InstallUtil command-line tool to install a service manually.

   C. **Incorrect:** While you could launch an assembly automatically by adding it to Scheduled Tasks, you cannot launch a service this way.

   D. **Correct:** The most user-friendly way to install a service is to use Visual Studio to create an installer for your service.

4. **Correct Answer: B**

   A. **Incorrect:** My Computer does not contain a tool to configure user accounts for services.

   B. **Correct:** Computer Management contains the Services snap-in, which you can use to configure user accounts for services.

   C. **Incorrect:** While you can use the Net command-line tool to start, stop, pause, and continue service, you cannot use Net to configure user accounts for services.

   D. **Incorrect:** The Microsoft .NET Framework 0 Configuration tool does not contain a tool to configure user accounts for services.

Chapter 8: Case Scenario Answers

Case Scenario 1: Creating a Testing Tool

1. You should create an application that prompts the user to select a zone and an assembly. Based on their selections, you should launch the assembly in an application domain with evidence that would cause it to be assigned to the code group corresponding to the selected zone.

2. Although several techniques would work, the simplest way to do this is to assign Internet zone evidence to the assembly, as the following code demonstrates:

```vb
' VB
Dim hostEvidence As Object() = {New Zone (SecurityZone.Internet)}
Dim internetEvidence As Evidence = New Evidence (hostEvidence, Nothing)

Dim myDomain As AppDomain = AppDomain.CreateDomain("QADomain")
myDomain.ExecuteAssembly("C:\path\CASDemands.exe", internetEvidence)
```

```
// C#
object [] hostEvidence = {new Zone(SecurityZone.Internet)};
Evidence internetEvidence = new Evidence(hostEvidence, null);

AppDomain myDomain = AppDomain.CreateDomain("QADomain");
myDomain.ExecuteAssembly(@"C:\path\CASDemands.exe", internetEvidence);
```

When the CASDemand application runs, the runtime should warn you that the application is running in a partially trusted context. If you do not receive this warning, you have not successfully restricted the assembly's permissions.

Case Scenario 2: Monitoring a File

1. You should create a Windows Service.

2. You will need to create a setup project for the service. The setup project will generate an MSI file that IT can distribute by using Systems Management Server (SMS).

3. You should set the startup type to Automatic.

4. You should specify the User account type, and ask the IT department to create a user account that has only privileges to read the configuration file and add events. *LocalService* would not have sufficient privileges, and *LocalSystem* would have excessive privileges.

Chapter 9: Lesson Review Answers

Lesson 1

1. **Correct Answer: D**

   A. **Incorrect:** Although the overall approach is correct, "Hello World" is the value that's being retrieved, not the key. Using the configuration file shown, this line of code would return a null object because there is no *Key* value of "Hello World".

   B. **Incorrect:** Although *AppSettings* will technically work, it's obsolete and cannot be guaranteed to be supported in future releases. Using this approach will result in a compiler warning and, depending on the build settings, might not even compile.

   C. **Incorrect:** The overall approach is correct here; however, there is only one value in the configuration file. The index references here is 5. There aren't 5 objects in the collection, so using this line of code will result in a null reference exception.

    D. **Correct:** The *AppSettings* property of the *ConfigurationManager* object will return a *NameValueCollection*. This collection can be referenced by *Key*. There is a *Key* for *"Foo"*, and using this approach will return the value "Hello World".

2. **Correct Answer: D**

    A. **Incorrect:** There is no section named *SqlConnectionStrings*, so this code will result in a failure.

    B. **Incorrect:** Using the *<clear/>* tag is the only safe way to approach this scenario. As such, if any other connection strings are already stored or if the file has already been read, there won't be a problem with duplicate keys.

    C. **Incorrect:** There is no *SqlConnectionString* property in the *ConfigurationManager* object.

    D. **Correct:** As mentioned, there is no *SqlConnectionStrings* property of the *ConfigurationManager* object. For this code to work, *connectionStrings* would need to be used instead.

3. **Correct Answer: D**

    A. **Incorrect:** The *IConfigurationSectionHandler* is a viable interface for implementing custom configuration section management. However, *ApplicationSettingsBase* is the most appropriate choice.

    B. **Incorrect:** The *ConfigurationValidatorBase* is used to validate values in a configuration file. It's not used for implementation.

    C. **Incorrect:** The *IConfigurationSystem* interface is intended for use internally by the .NET Framework and should not be used directly.

    D. **Correct:** The *ApplicationSettingsBase* object is a valid way to handle custom configuration and, in many ways, is a preferred object to use.

Lesson 2

1. **Correct Answer: D**

    A. **Incorrect:** *InstallContext* is a property and not a class from which objects can be derived.

    B. **Incorrect:** The *InstallerCollection* is a collection of *Installer* objects and, as such, would not make a viable candidate for a base class from which to create an installer.

C. **Incorrect:** The *ManagedInstallerClass* class is used to support the .NET Framework internally and is not meant to be used by developers.

D. **Correct:** The *Installer* class is the base class from which all *Installer* objects should be derived.

2. **Correct Answer: A**

A. **Correct:** The *Rollback* method is the method of the *Installer* class that is made to handle undoing the installation in the case of failure.

B. **Incorrect:** There is no *Undo* method of the *Installer* class.

C. **Incorrect:** There is no *Clear* method of the *Installer* class. All that's needed to roll back an installation is the *Rollback* method.

D. **Incorrect:** The *Uninstall* method is used to remove existing installed applications, not ones that have failed midway through installation.

Lesson 3

1. **Correct Answers: C and D**

A. **Incorrect:** Processes can be viewed with the *Process* class but not with the .NET Framework 2.0 Configuration tool.

B. **Incorrect:** Services cannot be viewed with the .NET Framework 2.0 Configuration tool.

C. **Correct:** Any application that has been configured can be managed under the Applications node.

D. **Correct:** Assemblies in the global assembly cache (GAC) can be managed under the Assembly Cache node.

2. **Correct Answer: A**

A. **Correct:** Permission sets are one of the items that can be added and managed with the configuration tool

B. **Incorrect:** Code Groups can be managed with the tool, but there is no code set.

C. **Incorrect:** There is no such thing as an assembly set.

D. **Incorrect:** There is no such thing as an application set.

Lesson 4

1. Correct Answers: A, B, C, and D

   A. **Correct:** *OpenExeConfiguration* is a valid method to open a configuration file.

   B. **Correct:** *OpenMachineConfiguration* is a valid method to open the machine configuration file.

   C. **Correct:** *OpenMappedExeConfiguration* is a valid method to open a configuration file as long as a mapping is specified.

   D. **Correct:** *OpenMappedMachineConfiguration* is a valid method to open a machine configuration file as long as a mapping is specified.

2. Correct Answer: A

   A. **Correct:** *Create* is the only method in the *IConfigurationSectionHandler* interface that needs to be implemented.

   B. **Incorrect:** *ReadSection* is not a valid method of the *IConfigurationSectionHandler* interface.

   C. **Incorrect:** *GetConfig* is not applicable in this setting.

   D. **Incorrect:** *GetAppSettings* is not applicable in this setting.

Chapter 9: Case Scenario Answers

Case Scenario: Installing and Configuring a New Application

1. A human-readable format is going to be the only viable way to do this. Users want to be able to change settings, and a human-readable format such as XML is probably the best way to facilitate this.

2. A desktop shortcut menu would be nice to include in the solution, and the application needs to be added to the Start menu. Any files that the application writes should have an associated file type as well.

Chapter 10: Lesson Review Answers

Lesson 1

1. **Correct Answer: B**

   A. **Incorrect:** Because the code might be used by partial trust objects that have a malicious purpose, care needs to be taken and *EventLog* objects should be used with caution.

   B. **Correct:** *EventLog* objects are secure to use as long as they are not used by partial trust assemblies. If partial trust assemblies are avoided, there should be no security issues.

   C. **Incorrect:** It is secure to use *EventLog* objects as long as they are used with the proper security boundaries in place.

   D. **Incorrect:** There is no practical way to implement this solution. Therefore, this answer choice is incorrect.

2. **Correct Answer: A, B, and C**

   A. **Correct:** There are disk space limitations, so overuse of *EventLog* objects can cause problems.

   B. **Correct:** Use of *EventLog* objects in partial trust scenarios poses multiple security risks.

   C. **Correct:** *EventLog* objects use many system resources, so unrestrained use of them can put unnecessary strains on the system.

   D. **Incorrect:** They are secure if used correctly; however, they do require special permissions and do have partial trust implications.

3. **Correct Answer: C**

   A. **Incorrect** Calling *Clear* will handle all entries, so it does not need to be called individually.

   B. **Incorrect:** The *Clear* method alone accomplishes the task.

   C. **Correct:** This is the only available method that accomplishes the task.

   D. **Incorrect:** There is no *ClearAll* method. The *Clear* method accomplishes the task.

4.   **Correct Answer: C**

A.   **Incorrect:** There is no *ClearLog* method of the *EventLog* class.

B.   **Incorrect:** There is no *RemoveLog* method of the *EventLog* class.

C.   **Correct:** The *Delete* method is the only available choice to delete an *Event-Log* object.

D.   **Incorrect:** There is no *RemoveLog* method of the *EventLog* class.

5.   **Correct Answers: A, B, C, and D**

A.   **Correct:** Error entries are valid.

B.   **Correct:** Warning entries are valid

C.   **Correct:** Information entries are valid.

D.   **Correct:** SuccessAudit entries are valid.

6.   **Correct Answers: A, B, and C**

A.   **Correct:** By default, the Application log is provided.

B.   **Correct:** By default, the Security log is provided.

C.   **Correct:** By default, the System log is provided.

D.   **Incorrect:** Although a specific event log named Audit could be created, there is no such log provided by default.

Lesson 2

1.   **Correct Answer: A**

A.   **Correct:** The primary function of the *CorrelationManager* is to keep the identities unique.

B.   **Incorrect:** Although a *TraceSwitch* can be used to modify trace information, using it in this context would not accomplish the required task and would only serve to convolute the logic.

C.   **Incorrect:** Specifying a different *TracelLevel* for each process will change the output of the traces, but it will do nothing to keep them logically separated.

D.   **Incorrect:** Although the *CorrelationManager* is used to accomplish the desired results, there is no *Correlation* object that can be managed with it.

2. **Correct Answer: B**

   A. **Incorrect:** The *DebuggerDisplayAttribute* will not specify a visualizer.

   B. **Correct:** The *DebuggerVisualizerAttribute* is the only attribute that can specify a visualizer.

   C. **Incorrect:** The *DebuggerStepThroughAttribute* is used to step over code and has no bearing on what visualizer is used.

   D. **Incorrect:** The *DebuggableAttribute* will not attach a visualizer.

Lesson 3

1. **Correct Answer: C**

   A. **Incorrect:** Although this method will start an instance of Internet Explorer, it will not navigate to any specific page.

   B. **Incorrect:** This will treat all of the input as one value and result in an error.

   C. **Correct:** This method specifies the application name as the first parameter and the correct URL as the only command-line argument.

   D. **Incorrect:** *Process.Run* is not a method of the *Process* class.

2. **Correct Answer: D**

   A. **Incorrect:** *Debug.Assert* takes an expression to evaluate, not a *String*.

   B. **Incorrect:** This method will cause the assertion to fail but will not output the *StackTrace*. Instead, it will output the entire exception. Furthermore, it will not direct the output to the console window.

   C. **Incorrect:** This call will output the *StackTrace* to the console window, but it will output the entire exception as well.

   D. **Correct:** This method specifically outputs the *StackTrace* and nothing else, and it writes the output only to the console window.

3. **Correct Answer: D**

   A. **Incorrect:** For security reasons, a *String* object should not be used for passwords.

   B. **Incorrect:** A *Char* array, although different from a *String*, fails to provide an optimal level of security..

   C. **Incorrect:** Using one value of a *String* array has the same effect as using an individual string.

    D. **Correct:** A *System.Security.SecureString* is the correct type for the *ProcessStartInfo* object's *Password* property. It affords the highest level of security of the methods listed.

Lesson 4

  1. **Correct Answer: C**

    A. **Incorrect:** Network Adapters can be discovered using WMI.

    B. **Incorrect:** Logical drives can be discovered and interrogated using WMI.

    C. **Correct:** Although some database information can be retrieved using WMI, a list of all OleDb-compliant databases cannot be determined using the WMI query syntax

    D. **Incorrect:** A list of Windows Services running on a machine, and their respective states, can be queried via WMI.

Chapter 10: Case Scenario Answers

Case Scenario: Choosing Where to Direct Outupt

To find out exactly what is needed, you will need to employ a strategy that encompasses the following tasks:

  1. Rework the Data Access Layer components to include the use of performance counters. Use the .NET Data Provider for SQL Server. Track all the metrics related to *Connection* objects because there's a suspicion of a leak. Specifically, carefully watch the number of pooled connections and the number of reclaimed connections monitors.

  2. On each of the Web components, add counters corresponding to ASP.NET. The Web server is a suspected cause of the performance issues, but it's not suspected to be as significant a cause as the database, so a small sample of counters should suffice.

  3. Monitor the network utilization of your application by including the .NET CLR Networking performance counter.

  4. On the client code, put similar measurement strategies in place. Keep track of memory utilization, network traffic, and file input/output.

5. Use the Windows event log to log any conditions where the application causes processor utilization to go above a given threshold.

6. Include assertions throughout your code to ensure that all your assumptions are correct.

7. Enable tracing, and insert copious code to track all instances of exceptions and items that caused them.

Chapter 11: Lesson Review Answers

Lesson 1

1. **Correct Answers: B and D**

   A. **Incorrect:** Zone evidence is based on the location from which the assembly runs. It does not require a strong name.

   B. **Correct:** To provide the Strong Name evidence type, an assembly must be signed.

   C. **Incorrect:** Hash evidence is based on a unique signature generated using the assembly's binary. It does not require a strong name.

   D. **Correct:** To provide the Publisher evidence type, an assembly must be signed.

2. **Correct Answer: B**

   A. **Incorrect:** *SocketPermission* is related to networking; however, it is required for initiating raw TCP/IP connections rather than HTTP Web connections.

   B. **Correct:** You must have WebPermission to initiate HTTP requests to a Web server.

   C. **Incorrect:** You need DnsPermission to look up DNS addresses, which is often part of sending a Web request. However, it is not a requirement.

   D. **Incorrect:** *ServiceControllerPermission* controls the ability to start, stop, and pause services.

3. **Correct Answer: D**

   A. **Incorrect:** My_Computer_Zone uses the FullTrust permission set and offers the highest level of privileges.

   B. **Incorrect:** LocalIntranet_Zone uses the LocalIntranet permission set, which provides a moderately high level of privileges.

C. **Incorrect:** Internet_Zone uses the Internet permission set, which provides a very restrictive level of privileges. However, it is not as restrictive as Restricted_Zone.

D. **Correct:** Restricted_Zone uses the Nothing permission set, which grants no privileges.

4. **Correct Answer: A**

A. **Correct:** You can read the file because both your user account and the assembly's CAS allow reading the file.

B. **Incorrect:** Although the assembly's CAS allows writing to the file, your user permissions restrict you to read access.

C. **Incorrect:** Although the assembly's CAS allows changing the permissions of the file, your user permissions restrict you to read access.

D. **Incorrect:** Although the assembly's CAS allows you to delete the file, your user permissions restrict you to read access.

Lesson 2

1. **Correct Answer: C**

A. **Incorrect:** The Everything permission set is sufficient for the application to run.

B. **Incorrect:** The Everything permission set is sufficient for the application to run.

C. **Correct:** The declarative permissions will not stop the assembly from reading the first line of the C:\boot.ini file.

D. **Incorrect:** A security exception prior to execution would occur only if the administrator were running the assembly with a debugger and the request for UIPermission was removed.

2. **Correct Answer: B**

A. **Incorrect:** The permissions are sufficient for the first line to be displayed, but the runtime throws an exception when the assembly attempts to access a file in the root of the C:\ drive.

B. **Correct:** The runtime throws an exception when the assembly attempts to access a file in the root of the C:\ drive because the *SecurityAction.Request-*

Optional FileIOPermissionAttribute declaration refuses access to everything except for the C:\Temp folder.

 C. **Incorrect:** The SecurityAction.RequestOptional declarative permission refuses permission to the root of the C:\ drive.

 D. **Incorrect:** A security exception prior to execution would occur only if the administrator were running the assembly with a debugger and the request for UIPermission was removed.

3. **Correct Answer: C**

 A. **Incorrect:** There are no *SecurityAction.RequestOptional* requests. Therefore, the only permissions denied to the assembly are those listed with *Security-Action.RequestRefuse*.

 B. **Incorrect:** There are no *SecurityAction.RequestOptional* requests. Therefore, the only permissions denied to the assembly are those listed with *Security-Action.RequestRefuse*.

 C. **Correct:** The assembly has permission to read a file in the root of the C:\ drive because it has the Everything permission set, and the permission is not explicitly refused.

 D. **Incorrect:** A security exception prior to execution would occur only if the administrator were running the assembly with a debugger and the request for UIPermission was removed.

4. **Correct Answer: C**

 A. **Incorrect:** *SocketPermission* controls access to networking. This is not required for console applications.

 B. **Incorrect:** *WebPermission* controls access to HTTP requests. This is not required for console applications.

 C. **Correct:** *UIPermission* is required for console applications running with a debugger to enable the application to communicate with the debugger.

 D. **Incorrect:** *FileIOPermission* controls access to the file system. This is not required for console applications.

Lesson 3

1. **Correct Answer: A**

   A. **Correct:** *SecurityAction.Demand* instructs the runtime to throw an exception if the caller and all callers higher in the stack lack the specified permission.

   B. **Incorrect:** *SecurityAction.Deny* causes the runtime to reduce the method's access by removing the specified permission.

   C. **Incorrect:** *SecurityAction.Assert* instructs the runtime to ignore the fact that callers might not have the specified permission. Assemblies must have the Assert Any Permission That Has Been Granted security permission setting.

   D. **Incorrect:** *SecurityAction.RequestMinimum* is used for declaratively checking permissions.

2. **Correct Answer: D**

   A. **Incorrect:** *SecurityAction.Demand* instructs the runtime to throw an exception if the caller and all callers higher in the stack lack the specified permission. However, *SecurityAction.Demand* must be used imperatively, and the question describes a need for declarative security.

   B. **Incorrect:** *SecurityAction.Deny* causes the runtime to reduce the method's access by removing the specified permission.

   C. **Incorrect:** *SecurityAction.Assert* instructs the runtime to ignore the fact that callers might not have the specified permission.

   D. **Correct:** *SecurityAction.RequestMinimum* is used for declaratively checking permissions. If the caller lacks the privilege, the runtime will throw an exception.

3. **Correct Answer: D**

   A. **Incorrect:** Calling *IPermission.Deny* throws an exception if the permission is missing.

   B. **Incorrect:** The *IsGranted* method is a member of the *SecurityManager* class, not *IPermission*.

   C. **Incorrect:** The *Deny* method is a member of the *IPermission* interface, not the *SecurityManager* class.

   D. **Correct:** Use the *Boolean SecurityManager.IsGranted* method to determine whether the assembly has a specific permission.

4. **Correct Answers: B and D**

   A. **Incorrect:** There is no *EventLogPermission.RevertPermitOnly* method.

   B. **Correct:** Call *CodeAccessPermission.RevertPermitOnly* to remove a previous *EventLogPermission.PermitOnly* call.

   C. **Incorrect:** The *RevertAll* method is a member of the *CodeAccessPermission* class, not *EventLogPermission*.

   D. **Correct:** Call *CodeAccessPermission.RevertAll* to remove a previous *EventLogPermission.PermitOnly* or *EventLogPermission.Deny* call.

   E. **Incorrect:** The *RevertDeny* method is a member of the *CodeAccessPermission* class, not *EventLogPermission*.

   F. **Incorrect:** You should call *CodeAccessPermission.RevertDeny* to remove a previous *EventLogPermission.Deny* call. However, it cannot remove an *EventLogPermission.PermitOnly* call.

Chapter 11: Case Scenario Answers

Case Scenario 1: Explaining Code Access Security

1. No. As long as operating systems enable unmanaged code to run, viruses can bypass CAS simply by not leveraging the .NET Framework. Unmanaged code is exempt from CAS permission checks.

2. No. It will, however, let him run applications that use the .NET Framework.

3. No, a virus based on the .NET Framework would be restricted by the Internet permission set, which restricts assemblies from communicating across the network except to contact the site from which the assembly originated.

4. No. The Intranet zone does not allow assemblies to directly access the file system. The most the assembly could do is prompt you to open or save files.

Case Scenario 2: Customizing Code Access Security

1. You can build CAS functionality into your application to limit the permissions available and specifically restrict access to the file system. Use assembly declarations to limit the permissions your assembly receives to the bare minimum. Protect methods using method declarations. Finally, you can use imperative CAS security to control permissions within a method. If a method does need to write to the file system, you can ensure that the window of opportunity is as small as possible.

2. You would use *FileIOPermission*.

3. They shouldn't be negatively affected at all.

Chapter 12: Lesson Review Answers

Lesson 1

1. **Correct Answer: D**

   A. **Incorrect:** You could use *WindowsPrincipal.IsInRole* to imperatively check for a group membership; however, declarative RBS demands offer greater security by performing the security check before running a method.

   B. **Incorrect:** The *IsInRole* method is a member of *WindowsPrincipal*, not *WindowsIdentity*.

   C. **Incorrect:** You could use imperative RBS demands to check for a group membership; however, declarative RBS demands offer greater security by performing the security check before running a method.

   D. **Correct:** Declarative RBS demands restrict access to an entire method while offering the highest level of resistance to security vulnerabilities.

2. **Correct Answer: C**

   A. **Incorrect:** You could use *WindowsPrincipal.IsInRole* to imperatively check for a group membership; however, imperative RBS demands are more secure because they throw an exception that prevents further processing.

   B. **Incorrect:** The *IsInRole* method is a member of *WindowsPrincipal*, not *WindowsIdentity*.

   C. **Correct:** Imperative RBS demands restrict access to code by throwing an exception. You can easily catch this exception and display an error message to the user.

   D. **Incorrect:** Although declarative RBS demands are more secure than imperative RBS demands, declarative RBS demands are defined as an attribute to a method, and it is difficult to catch security exceptions thrown by a declarative RBS demand when the method is called by a Windows event.

3. **Correct Answer: A**

    A. **Correct:** *WindowsPrincipal.IsInRole* is perfect when you simply need to branch your code based on user memberships, and the code is not performing security-sensitive tasks.

    B. **Incorrect:** The *IsInRole* method is a member of *WindowsPrincipal*, not *WindowsIdentity*.

    C. **Incorrect:** Imperative RBS demands restrict access to code by throwing an exception. Exceptions interrupt processing; therefore, you should use an imperative RBS demand only when you need to completely prevent a user from running code.

    D. **Incorrect:** Declarative RBS demands completely prevent a user from running a method. In this scenario, the method should simply make a decision based on the group membership, and *WindowsPrincipal.IsInRole* allows that without blocking access to the entire method.

4. **Correct Answers: A and B**

    A. **Correct:** *GenericIdentity* represents individual users, supports imperative and declarative RBS demands, and meets the simple requirements.

    B. **Correct:** *GenericPrincipal* represents user groups, supports imperative and declarative RBS demands, and meets the simple requirements.

    C. **Incorrect:** You could implement *IIdentity* to represent users; however, *GenericIdentity* meets your requirements and would be more efficient to implement.

    D. **Incorrect:** You could implement *IPrincipal* to represent users; however, *GenericPrincipal* meets your requirements and would be more efficient to implement.

Lesson 2

1. **Correct Answers: A and B**

    A. **Correct:** You can control access to files using the *FileSecurity* class.

    B. **Correct:** You can control access to registry keys using the *RegistrySecurity* class.

    C. **Incorrect:** The .NET Framework does not provide libraries for configuring printer permissions.

    D. **Incorrect:** The .NET Framework does not provide libraries for configuring share permissions.

2. **Correct Answer: A**

   A. **Correct:** To apply ACL changes to a folder, call *Directory.SetAccessControl*. This method requires two parameters: the directory and the *DirectorySecurity* object containing the ACLs.

   B. **Incorrect:** Although you can create a new directory by specifying a *DirectorySecurity* object, in this example, the directory must already exist for the code to work properly.

   C. **Incorrect:** You must provide both a path and a *DirectorySecurity* object to *Directory.SetAccessControl*.

   D. **Incorrect:** Although you can create a new directory by specifying a *DirectorySecurity* object, in this example, the directory must already exist for the code to work properly. Additionally, you cannot create a directory by specifying only a *DirectorySecurity* object.

3. **Correct Answer: B**

   A. **Incorrect:** *RegistryAccessRule* describes a DACL for a registry key.

   B. **Correct:** *RegistryAuditRule* describes an SACL for a registry key.

   C. **Incorrect:** *AccessRule* is the base class for all DACLs.

   D. **Incorrect:** *AuditRule* is the base class for all SACLs. However, it is not specific to registry keys. *RegistryAuditRule* inherits from *AuditRule* and specifically describes registry key SACLs.

4. **Correct Answer: C**

   A. **Incorrect:** *DirectorySecurity.GetAccessRules* returns an instance of *AuthorizationRuleCollection* containing *FileSystemAccessRule* objects.

   B. **Incorrect:** *DirectorySecurity.GetAccessRules* returns an instance of *AuthorizationRuleCollection* containing *FileSystemAccessRule* objects.

   C. **Correct:** *DirectorySecurity.GetAccessRules* returns an instance of *AuthorizationRuleCollection* containing *FileSystemAccessRule* objects.

   D. **Incorrect:** Although you could iterate through an instance of *AuthorizationRuleCollection* using *AuthorizationRule* objects, you would not have access to important elements of file system ACLs. Instead, you should use *FileSystemAccessRule*, which derives from *AuthorizationRule*.

Lesson 3

1. **Correct Answers: B, C, E, and F**

   A. **Incorrect:** The *RSACryptoServiceProvider* class provides asymmetric encryption, which requires the encryptor and decryptor to have related but different keys.

   B. **Correct:** The *RijndaelManaged* class provides symmetric encryption, which requires the encryptor and decryptor to have the same keys.

   C. **Correct:** The *TripleDES* class provides symmetric encryption, which requires the encryptor and decryptor to have the same keys.

   D. **Incorrect:** The *DSACryptoServiceProvider* class provides asymmetric digital signing, which requires the encryptor and decryptor to have related but different keys.

   E. **Correct:** The *DES* class provides symmetric encryption, which requires the encryptor and decryptor to have the same keys.

   F. **Correct:** The *RC2* class provides symmetric encryption, which requires the encryptor and decryptor to have the same keys.

2. **Correct Answers: A, C, and D**

   A. **Correct:** *SymmetricAlgorithm.Key* must be the same on both the encryptor and decryptor.

   B. **Incorrect:** Symmetric encryption algorithms do not use a salt. Salts are used when creating keys from passwords using the *Rfc2898DeriveBytes* class.

   C. **Correct:** *SymmetricAlgorithm.IV* must be the same on both the encryptor and decryptor.

   D. **Correct:** *SymmetricAlgorithm.Mode* must be the same on both the encryptor and decryptor.

3. **Correct Answer: C**

   A. **Incorrect:** When transferring data across a network, you need to export only the public key. Because you can create new keys for future network sessions, there is no need to save the private key.

   B. **Incorrect:** If you are decrypting a file encrypted by a remote computer, you should provide the remote computer your public key. You do not need to export your private key.

C. **Correct:** If you need to decrypt a file at a later time, you must export the private key.

D. **Incorrect:** If you are sending a file to a remote computer, you should encrypt it with the remote computer's private key. You do not need to generate or export encryption keys at all.

4. **Correct Answers: B and D**

A. **Incorrect:** *RIPEMD160* is a nonkeyed hashing algorithm.

B. **Correct:** *HMACSHA1* is a keyed hashing algorithm.

C. **Incorrect:** *SHA512* is a nonkeyed hashing algorithm.

D. **Correct:** *MACTripleDES* is a keyed hashing algorithm.

E. **Incorrect:** *MD5* is a nonkeyed hashing algorithm.

Chapter 12: Case Scenario Answers

Case Scenario 1: Creating Custom Authentication Methods

1. Use *GenericIdentity* and *GenericPrincipal* because the simple relationship between users and groups used by the accounting application does not require you to create custom classes based on *IIdentity* and *IPrincipal*.

2. Use declarative RBS demands to restrict access to *AddBill*. As long as a user is authenticated and is a member of one of the Temps, Accountants, or Managers group, the user can use that method.

3. Use declarative RBS demands to restrict access to authenticated members of the Accountants or Managers group. Within the method, use the *GenericPrincipal.IsInRole* method to verify that the user is a member of the Managers role if the value of the bill being paid is $1,500 or higher.

Case Scenario 2: Protecting Data by Using Cryptography

1. Both symmetric and asymmetric encryption can meet the requirements, but symmetric encryption is the best choice because it minimizes administrative overhead. You can use symmetric key encryption because the data will be transferred between relatively stable computers in remote offices, and because configuring each with a secret key would be easy. Alternatively, you can use asymmetric encryption, configure a key pair at the centralized database, and distribute the public key to each of the remote offices. The application could then use asym-

metric encryption to establish session keys to enable symmetric key encryption during the data transfers.

2. At the very least, you should store hashes of the password. A keyed hashing algorithm would be more secure than a nonkeyed algorithm. Your primary deterrence must be preventing attackers from gaining access to the password database, however.

3. You should use digital signatures. Store a key pair at the central office, and distribute the public key to each of the remote offices. Sign all bonus communications with the private key, and then verify the signature at the remote offices.

Chapter 13: Lesson Review Answers

Lesson 1

1. **Correct Answers: A, B, and D**

   A. **Correct:** Adding a reference through Visual Studio 2005 will automate all the actions that are necessary to import a COM Library.

   B. **Correct:** TlbImport.exe allows you to import the type, although it's a command-line utility and generally considered less convenient than adding a reference.

   C. **Incorrect:** Regsrv registers a COM component, and used alone it does nothing for a .NET application.

   D. **Correct:** By using the Regsvr tool, you can first verify that a COM component has been properly registered. Afterward, either of the two methods will successfully import it.

2. **Correct Answers: C and D**

   A. **Incorrect:** Trapping an *ApplicationException* object will trap only CLS-compliant applications specific to that application.

   B. **Incorrect:** Setting the *RuntimeCompatibilty* attribute to false will turn off the default behavior, which will cause *System.Exceptions* to be caught only if they are CLS compliant.

   C. **Correct:** Trapping *System.Exception* will trap both CLS-compliant and non-CLS-compliant exceptions.

D. **Correct:** This would be unnecessary because this feature is enabled by default, but it would allow *System.Exception* to catch both CLS-compliant and non-CLS-compliant exceptions.

3. **Correct Answers: A, B, C and D**

A. **Correct:** All members of COM objects have to be implemented as instance members as opposed to static or shared members. In the .NET Framework, there is extensive use of shared/static members, so there stands to be a great behavior difference between objects created in each environment.

B. **Correct:** COM does not provide support for parameterized constructors whereas the .NET Framework does.

C. **Correct:** COM objects must be registered in the Windows registry. This is not available in other operating systems.

D. **Correct:** COM flattens the inheritance chain and as such, places significant restrictions on what can be done with inheritance.

4. **Correct Answers: A, C, and D**

A. **Correct:** This will allow you to view the Intermediate Language instructions issued after a COM component has been imported.

B. **Incorrect:** While this tool is very powerful, it provides no facility to manage COM Interop.

C. **Correct:** This tool will allow you to import COM components and change the name they'll be imported as.

D. **Correct:** Since all COM components must be registered properly (which entails Windows registry entries), this tool enables you to view what has been entered into the Windows registry.

Lesson 2

1. **Correct Answers: A, B, C, and D**

A. **Correct:** This option alone will make the assembly consumable by COM.

B. **Correct:** This option can be set to either true or false, but setting it to true would make the class visible to COM provided all other members didn't override it.

C. **Correct:** Members that should not be exposed to COM should have the *ComVisible* attribute set to false.

D. Correct: Members that should be exposed to COM should have the *ComVisible* attribute set to true or left blank (if the class or assembly was marked as Visible). Setting it to true will not cause any problems if it has already been set to true at an upper level.

2. **Correct Answer: B**

   A. **Incorrect:** The TlbImp.exe tool will import a type, not export it.

   B. **Correct:** TlbExp.exe is the only tool that can export a type.

   C. **Incorrect:** Regedit.exe cannot export a type; however, it can interrogate registry entries associated with a type.

   D. **Incorrect:** The csc.exe tool can compile an application, but alone it cannot make anything visible to COM.

3. **Correct Answer: A**

   A. **Correct:** COM will recognize only constructors without any parameters specified.

   B. **Incorrect:** If a class is defined as private, it will not be visible to a COM component.

   C. **Incorrect:** If a member is marked as private, it will not be visible to a COM component.

   D. **Incorrect:** Abstract classes will not be recognized by a COM component.

Lesson 3

1. **Correct Answer: A**

   A. **Correct:** The *DllImport* attribute must be used in conjunction with the name of the dynamic-link library (DLL) being called.

   B. **Incorrect:** A Runtime Callable Wrapper can be used to facilitate addressing external libraries, but it has no direct purpose in this context.

   C. **Incorrect:** Parameter signatures must match those in the DLL as closely as possible. Although the call might still work without it, it's extremely unlikely and will probably cause undesired behavior.

   D. **Incorrect:** *String* objects are reference types, but so are *StringBuilder* objects. Unlike *String* objects, *StringBuilder* objects behave as a pure reference type and are the best choice.

2. **Correct Answers: A, B, and C**

    A. **Correct:** To use a structure, you will first need to define it. Although the types might vary, the *MarshalAs* method can be used to overcode this.

    B. **Correct:** The *SizeOf* method is the only mechanism to determine the size of the structure.

    C. **Correct:** The *StructLayout* attribute lets you specify the positioning and layout of your structure if it should be different from what the library expects.

    D. **Incorrect:** Although TlbExport will create the necessary type library, it will not do any of the necessary tasks related to passing the structure.

3. **Correct Answers: A and D**

    A. **Correct:** Type mapping is the primary purpose of this attribute.

    B. **Incorrect:** It is certainly necessary in some P/Invoke calls, but not every call has a type mismatch that needs to be addressed.

    C. **Incorrect:** Type mismatches cannot be ignored. (And even if they could, they shouldn't be.)

    D. **Correct:** Although this is unnecessary, it will not cause any problems and will explicitly define relationships, which might help other developers understand the code's purpose.

Chapter 13: Case Scenario Answers

Case Scenario: Incorporating Legacy Code into a .NET Project

1. A substantial amount of research needs to be performed first. Each function that is mission critical needs to be examined and documented. For each such function, analysis needs to be performed to determine whether there's an existing .NET object or tool that can perform the function. If so, it should be used. If not, the task should be listed and wrapped in a library.

2. With respect to specific conversions, the driving consideration should be whether there's an existing managed library and, where there's not one, we need to determine to what extent there are managed classes that can comprise a library.

3. New features in the .NET Framework 0 allow developers to trap both managed and unmanaged exceptions. The trapping of *System.Exception* objects has new

behaviors in the Framework, but overall there's not any notable difference in how new components should be tested.

4. The necessity of particular calls depends entirely on the goal of a given piece of code, but in many instances the answer is, "Yes, the calls are necessary." There are areas of the Windows API, for instance, that do not have wrappers in the .NET Framework yet. If you want to provide certain functionality, using unmanaged code might be unavoidable.

Chapter 14: Lesson Review Answers

Lesson 1

1. **Correct Answer: C**

   A. **Incorrect:** *GetCallingAssembly* returns the assembly that contains the code that called the current method. This is not necessarily the assembly that contains the startup object (or entry point).

   B. **Incorrect:** *GetExecutingAssembly* returns the assembly that contains the code that is currently being executed. This is not necessarily the assembly that contains the startup object (or entry point).

   C. **Correct:** *GetEntryAssembly* returns the assembly that contains the startup object (or entry point).

   D. **Incorrect:** *Assembly.Load* returns an assembly that is not currently loaded, and therefore it cannot be the assembly that contains the startup object or entry point.

2. **Correct Answers: B and D**

   A. **Incorrect:** Assemblies cannot contain other assemblies.

   B. **Correct:** Assemblies can contain one or more modules.

   C. **Incorrect:** Assemblies cannot directly contain types. Only modules can contain types directly. Assemblies contain types indirectly because they contain modules.

   D. **Correct:** Only modules can directly contain types.

Lesson 2

1. **Correct Answer: B**

   A. **Incorrect:** Specifying the attribute tells the compiler that this is a satellite assembly with specific resources for the specified locale. It cannot be used independent of the main assembly.

   B. **Correct:** It tells the compiler that this is a satellite assembly for a particular locale and cannot be used as a main assembly.

   C. **Incorrect:** Specifying the attribute tells the compiler that this is a satellite assembly with specific resources for the specified locale. It cannot be used independent of the main assembly.

   D. **Incorrect:** Specifying the attribute tells the compiler that this is a satellite assembly with specific resources for the specified locale. It cannot be used independent of the main assembly.

2. **Correct Answer: D**

   A. **Incorrect:** The asterisk is not a valid part of the a version number. Build numbers are autoincrementing, not revision numbers.

   B. **Incorrect:** The asterisk has nothing to do with compatibility with other assemblies. Build numbers are autoincrementing, not revision numbers.

   C. **Incorrect:** It indicates to the compiler to create a random value for the revision number. Build numbers are autoincrementing, not revision numbers.

   D. **Correct:** It indicates to the compiler to create a random value for the revision number.

Lesson 3

1. **Correct Answers: A, B, and D**

   A. **Correct:** The *FieldInfo* class does derive from the *MemberInfo* class.

   B. **Correct:** The *MethodInfo* class does derive from the *MemberInfo* class.

   C. **Incorrect:** The *Assembly* class does *not* derive from the *MemberInfo* class.

   D. **Correct:** The *Type* class does derive from the *MemberInfo* class.

2. **Correct Answers: A, C, and D**

   A. **Correct:** *BindingFlags.Public* indicates you want publicly available members.

B.   Incorrect: *BindingFlags.Static* indicates you want static members; use *BindingFlags.Instance* to get nonstatic members.

C.   Correct: *BindingFlags.DeclaredOnly* indicates you want members of the specific type, not the inherited members.

D.   Correct: *BindingFlags.Instance* indicates you want members of an instance of the class, not static members.

Lesson 4

1.   **Correct Answer: D**

   A.   Incorrect: The return value is returned from the *Invoke* call, you don't have an instance to run the method on, and parameters are passed in as an array of objects.

   B.   Incorrect: You don't have an instance to run the method on, and parameters are passed in as an array of objects.

   C.   Incorrect: Parameters are passed in as an array of objects.

   D.   Correct: The return value is returned from the *Invoke* call, you have an instance to run the method on, and parameters are passed in as an array of objects.

2.   **Correct Answer: B**

   A.   Incorrect: No, the *MethodBody* class can be used to interrogate the Intermediate Language or other properties of the body of a method, but it cannot execute part of the method.

   B.   Correct: The *MethodBody* class can be used to interrogate the Intermediate Language or other properties of the body of a method, but it cannot execute part of the method.

Lesson 5

1.   **Correct Answer: C**

   A.   Incorrect: The *AssemblyBuilder* class has no methods (static or constructors) to create an instance of the *AssemblyBuilder* class.

   B.   Incorrect: The *ModuleBuilder* class has no methods to create an instance of the *AssemblyBuilder* class.

C. **Correct:** The *AppDomain* class has the *DefineDynamicAssembly* method to create an instance of the *AssemblyBuilder* class.

D. **Incorrect:** The *Application* class has no methods to create an instance of the *AssemblyBuilder* class.

2. **Correct Answers: A and C**

A. **Correct:** *AssemblyBuilderAccess.Run* allows execution of the dynamic assembly.

B. **Incorrect:** *AssemblyBuilderAccess.ReflectionOnly* only allows for the interrogating of the type information, not execution of the code.

C. **Correct:** *AssemblyBuilderAccess.RunAndSave* allows execution of the dynamic assembly.

D. **Incorrect:** *AssemblyBuilderAccess.Save* does not allow execution of the code, only serializing the assembly.

Chapter 14: Case Scenario Answers

Case Scenario: Create a Plugin Architecture

1. Assuming your customers use .NET to develop their components, you can load their assemblies at runtime and add their components to your application. The application would not need to change every time someone added a component. It would just require a restart. They can drop their components into a specified directory where you would load them from.

2. You can look at the assembly attributes that hold company and trademark information when you load their components so that you can show that information in your application (perhaps on the splash screen or in the About dialog box).

Chapter 15: Lesson Review Answers

Lesson 1

Correct Answers: A and B

A. **Correct:** You can attach a file from the local file system by specifying the file-name.

B. **Correct:** You can attach a file using a Stream object, providing a great deal of flexibility for the source of the file.

C. **Incorrect:** You cannot directly attach a file from a Web site. You would need to first download and save the file.

D. **Incorrect:** The .NET Framework does not provide support for receiving incoming e-mail messages.

Correct Answers: A and C

A. **Correct:** To send an HTML message, you should set *MailMessage.Body* to HTML.

B. **Incorrect:** There is no *MailMessage.Head* property. Instead, you should include any headers in the body of the message (though e-mail clients will not typically process the header).

C. **Correct:** To send an HTML message, you must set *MailMessage.IsBodyHtml* to True.

D. **Incorrect:** *MailMessage.Subject* should always be text, not HTML.

Correct Answer: A

A. **Correct:** To reference a linked resource as an image, use

```
<img src="cid:ContentID">
```

B. **Incorrect:** You should not provide the image's filename.

C. **Incorrect:** You must preface the content ID with

```
cid:
```

D. **Incorrect:** You should not provide the image's filename.

Correct Answer: C

A. **Incorrect:** Use *LinkedResource* for embedded images.

B. **Incorrect:** Use *Attachment* to attach files to a message.

C. **Correct:** You can provide multiple versions of an e-mail message by using *AlternateView*. The e-mail client can then display the appropriate version.

D. **Incorrect:** Use *SmtpClient* to send e-mail messages.

Lesson 2

1. **Correct Answer: B**

   A. **Incorrect:** The *MailMessage* class does not have a Send method.

   B. **Correct:** To send a message, create an instance of *SmtpClient* and call the *Send* method.

   C. **Incorrect:** There is no SmtpServer class.

   D. **Incorrect:** There is no *MailClient* class.

2. **Correct Answers: C and D**

   A. **Incorrect:** "self" is not a special keyword. The runtime would attempt to resolve the name as a DNS address.

   B. **Incorrect:** 10.1 is a private IP address, but it does not describe the local computer. The runtime would attempt to deliver the message to a computer at that IP address.

   C. **Correct:** "localhost" is a special keyword that always describes the local computer.

   D. **Correct:** 120.0.1 is a special IP address that always describes the local computer.

3. **Correct Answer: A**

   A. **Correct:** The runtime throws *SmtpFailedReceipientException* if the SMTP server rejects an e-mail address.

   B. **Incorrect:** *SmtpFailedReceipientsException* is used internally by the runtime. Your application will never catch an exception of this type.

   C. **Incorrect:** The runtime throws *SmtpException* for problems related to contacting the SMTP server.

   D. **Incorrect:** There is no *SmtpClientException* class.

4. **Correct Answer: D**

   A. **Incorrect:** You do not need to specify credentials to use SSL.

   B. **Incorrect:** You do not need to change the delivery method. The default value of *SmtpDeliveryMethod.Network* is correct.

   C. **Incorrect:** You do not need to change the port. SMTP uses the same port for both encrypted and non-encrypted communications (TCP 25).

   D. **Correct:** The only property you need to set is *EnableSsl*. It should be set to True.

Chapter 15: Case Scenario Answers

Case Scenario: Add E-mail Capabilities to an Existing Application

1. You can use the *System.Net.MailMessage* and *System.Net.SmtpClient* classes to send the e-mails.

2. The .NET Framework doesn't include classes to process incoming e-mail, and it would be very time-consuming to create. Instead, you could set the From address to an e-mail address that someone in Sales manages so that they can manually correct any errors. Alternatively, you could set up an ASP.NET Web site and include a link to that Web site to allow customers to manage their own contact information.

3. You can enable SSL when sending the messages to the SMTP server. However, as the CSO mentioned, this does not protect the messages after the server receives them.

Chapter 16: Lesson Review Answers

Lesson 1

1. **Correct Answers: B and D**

    A. **Incorrect:** This method might work, but it's not reliable. If a culture other than the current one was set before checking this property, it would yield that culture instead of the current one.

    B. **Correct:** *Thread.CurrentThread.CurrentCulture* will retrieve the default setting unless it has been changed.

    C. **Incorrect:** Using an invariant will do just that, return the invariant culture that's specified.

    D. **Correct:** This will return the current culture if none is specified.

2. **Correct Answer: B**

    A. **Incorrect:** *US* is the specific culture, and *en* is the neutral culture.

    B. **Correct:** *US* is the specific culture, and *en* is the neutral culture.

    C. **Incorrect:** The neutral culture is *en*, not the combination of *en* and *US*.

    D. **Incorrect:** *US* is the specific culture, and it has been specified.

3.   **Correct Answer: B**

   A.   **Incorrect:** This method will result in a case-sensitive comparison, which is not what's required.

   B.   **Correct:** The *IgnoreCase* value of the *CompareOptions* enumeration will accomplish a case-insensitive comparison.

   C.   **Incorrect:** The *CompareTo* method will not accomplish this.

   D.   **Incorrect:** Although this approach will ultimately work, it will work only because it changes the case of each *String*. The comparison will still be cases sensitive, but this approach will simply ensure that they are both cased the same way.

Lesson 2

1.   **Correct Answer: C**

   A.   **Incorrect:** The currency format can be changed by simply using the *NumberFormatInfo* class.

   B.   **Incorrect:** The date format can be changed by simply using the *DateTimeFormatInfo* class.

   C.   **Correct:** This is the exact use case for this object.

   D.   **Incorrect:** If you don't like the way an existing culture is represented, you can change specific properties. Changing the entire thing could be a huge source of problems for others who aren't aware that you changed it.

2.   **Correct Answer: C**

   A.   **Incorrect:** None would not be an appropriate value to use if you were creating a culture from scratch.

   B.   **Incorrect:** Neutral would not be appropriate either because of the values that would be already set.

   C.   **Correct:** Replacement is specifically put in place for scenarios where you completely override existing values and create your own culture.

Chapter 16: Case Scenario Answers

Case Scenario: Installing and Configuring a New Application

1. Dates and currency symbols must no longer be hard-coded. Instead, formatters should be used. No assumption should be made about what the date format will be or what the currency will be—that way nothing will be culture-bound.

2. If formatters are used, many things can be done. The main thing is to use an invariant culture as a base for appropriate comparisons. Another is to simply change the *CurrentCulture* of the application.

3. Creating localized resources for each culture the application will be used in is the first step. Next, make sure to set the *CurrentUICulture* for each of these, and make sure you detect the culture and respond accordingly.

Glossary

access control list (ACL)   A term most commonly used to refer to a discretionary access control list (DACL), which is an authorization restriction mechanism that identifies the users and groups that are assigned or denied access permissions on an object.

Advanced Encryption Standard (AES)   A synonym for Rijndael, which is a symmetric encryption algorithm that uses key sizes of 128 through 256 bits.

application domain   A logical container that allows multiple assemblies to run within a single process, while preventing them from directly accessing another assembly's memory.

application setting   A custom setting that the application reads, writes, or both.

assembly evidence   Evidence that an assembly presents that describes the assembly's identity, such as the hash, the publisher, or the strong name.

asymmetric encryption   A cryptography technique that uses separate private and public keys to encrypt and decrypt data. Also known as public-key encryption.

Asynchronous Programming Model   A pattern of working with specific types of .NET classes that use *Begin/End* method pairs to provide asynchronous execution of certain methods.

attribute   A specific class type in the .NET Framework that allows for declarative binding of code.

authentication   The process of identifying a user.

authorization   The process of verifying that a user is allowed to access a requested resource.

BinaryFormatter   Located in the *System.Runtime.Serialization.Formatters.Binary* namespace, this formatter is the most efficient way to serialize objects that will be read only by .NET Framework–based applications.

Bitmap   Located in the *System.Drawing* namespace, this class provides methods for loading and saving images, and editing individual pixels.

boxing   Converting from a value type to a reference type, which often occurs implicitly.

Brush   Located in the *System.Drawing* namespace, classes derived from the *Brush* class are required for drawing text and filling in shapes.

CAS (code access security)   A security system that enables administrators and developers to authorize applications, similar to the way they have always been able to authorize users.

cast   A conversion from one type to another.

CCW (COM Callable Wrapper)   A proxy class that sits between a .NET assembly and a COM component and that allows the COM component to consume the .NET assembly.

cipher text   Encrypted text generated by an encryption algorithm that cannot be converted to plain text without a secret key.

CLS-compliant exception   Any exception object managed by the .NET Framework. All CLS-compliant exceptions derive from the *System.Exception* hierarchy. CLS stands for Common Language Specification.

code access security (CAS)   A security system that enables administrators and developers to authorize applications, similar to the way they have always been able to authorize users.

code group   Authorization device that associates assemblies with permission sets.

code page   A list of selected character codes (with characters represented as code points) in a certain order. Code pages are usually defined to support specific languages or groups of languages that share common writing systems. Windows code pages contain 256 code points and are zero-based.

collection   Any class that allows for gathering items into lists and for iterating through those items.

COM (Component Object Model)   Prior to .NET, COM was the fundamental development framework from Microsoft.

COM Callable Wrapper (CCW)   A proxy class that sits between a .NET assembly and a COM component and that allows the COM component to consume the .NET assembly.

configuration management   The practice of handling and managing how an application is set up and configured.

connection string   A specific value used by an application to connect to a given database. All ODBC- and OleDb-compliant databases (which means databases from all major vendors) use a connection string. For security, these should always be encrypted.

constraint A condition on a type parameter that restricts the type argument you can supply for it. A constraint can require that the type argument implement a particular interface, be or inherit from a particular class, have an accessible parameterless constructor, or be a reference type or a value type. You can combine these constraints, but you can specify at most one class.

contract *See* interface.

current culture The culture that the application is currently configured to run under.

current UI culture The culture used to display many visual interface elements. This might or might not be the same as the current culture.

DACL (discretionary access control list) An authorization restriction mechanism that identifies the users and groups that are assigned or denied access permissions on an object.

Data Encryption Standard (DES) A symmetric encryption algorithm that uses relatively short key lengths that are vulnerable to cracking attacks.

Debug A specific constant defined in an application that allows *Debugger* objects to be attached to code.

Debugger A class that provides access to the default debugger attached to an application.

declarative RBS demands Access restrictions that are declared as an attribute to a method and that instruct the runtime to perform an access check before running the method.

defense-in-depth The security principle of providing multiple levels of protection so that your system is still protected in the event of a vulnerability.

deflate An industry standard for compressing data that is efficient, commonly used, and patent free.

DES (Data Encryption Standard) A symmetric encryption algorithm that uses relatively short key lengths that are vulnerable to cracking attacks.

deserialization The process of converting a previously serialized sequence of bytes into an object.

digital signature A value that can be appended to electronic data to prove that it was created by someone who possesses a specific private key.

discretionary access control list (DACL) An authorization restriction mechanism that identifies the users and groups that are assigned or denied access permissions on an object.

encryption key   A value that can be used to encrypt and decrypt data. When used with symmetric encryption, this is also known as a shared secret.

event log   A mechanism that allows an application to record information about its state and persist it permanently.

evidence   The way an assembly is identified, such as the location where the assembly is stored, a hash of the assembly's code, or the assembly's signature.

exception   Unexpected events that interrupt normal execution of an assembly.

file system   The operating-system-provided mechanism for storing files in folders and drives.

filtering exceptions   The process of ordering *Catch* clauses so that specific exception types are caught before general exception types.

fully trusted   An assembly that is exempt from code access security (CAS) permission checks.

garbage collection   Recovery of memory in the heap through removal of dereferenced items.

generic type   A single programming element that adapts to perform the same functionality for a variety of data types.

globalization   The process of enabling an application to format numbers and dates for a particular culture.

Graphics   Located in the *System.Drawing* namespace, this class provides methods for drawing lines, shapes, and text.

gzip   An industry standard extension to the deflate compression agorithm that allows for a header to carry additional information.

hash   A value that summarizes a larger piece of data and can be used to verify that the data has not been modified since the hash was generated.

heap   Area of memory where reference types are stored.

host evidence   Evidence that an assembly's host presents describing the assembly's origin, such as the application directory, URL, or site.

imperative role-based security (RBS) demands   Access restrictions that are declared within your code and can be used to restrict access to portions of code on a very granular basis.

inherited permission   Permissions that propagate to an object from its parent object.

initialization vector (IV)   Data that symmetric encryption algorithms use to further obscure the first block of data being encrypted, which makes unauthorized decrypting more difficult.

interface   Defines a common set of members that all classes that implement the interface must provide.

Interop   An abbreviation of the word *Interoperation*, which means managed and unmanaged code working together.

isolated storage   A protected place in a user's system to store data without requiring high-level rights to an application and that is scoped by user, assembly, or application.

iteration   The process of moving through a collection of items.

IV (initialization vector)   Data that symmetric encryption algorithms use to further obscure the first block of data being encrypted, which makes unauthorized decrypting more difficult.

keyed hash algorithms   Algorithms that protect against modification of the hash by encrypting it by using a secret key that both the sender and receiver must have.

localization   The process of enabling an application to format numbers and dates based on a specific locale.

LocalService   A service account that runs with very limited privileges.

LocalSystem   A service account that runs with almost unlimited privileges.

managed code   Code that is managed by the .NET Framework runtime.

ManagementQuery   A request for information about a Windows Management Instrumentation object.

marshaling   Moving type data across different execution environments.

MD5   The Message Digest hashing algorithm. The hash size for the MD5 algorithm is 128 bits.

memory leak   The problem of resource leakage related to memory that is not reclaimed.

module   A single container for types inside an assembly. An assembly can contain one or more modules.

multifile assemblies   An assembly that is broken up into several modules that can be loaded as independently as necessary.

Multipurpose Internet Mail Extensions (MIME) A standard that enables binary data to be published and read on the Internet. The header of a file with binary data contains the MIME type of the data. This informs client programs (such as Web browsers and e-mail clients) that they cannot process the data as straight text.

narrowing Converting a value from one type to another when the destination type can't accommodate all possible values from the source type. These conversions must be explicit in C# and in Visual Basic if Option Strict is on.

.NET Framework 2.0 Configuration tool A tool provided by the .NET Framework that allows visual configuration and management of applications and assemblies.

NetworkService A service account that is capable of authenticating to remote computers.

nullable type A value type that can be set to *Nothing/null*.

partially trusted code An assembly that must undergo code access security (CAS) permission checks each time it accesses a protected resource.

Pen Located in the *System.Drawing* namespace, this class is used to specify the color and width of drawings.

performance counter A mechanism to measure performance of code that is executing.

permission A code access security (CAS) access control entry (ACL).

permission set A CAS ACL consisting of multiple permissions.

Platform Invoke A mechanism used to call unmanaged code from managed code.

principal policy The scheme that the .NET Framework uses to determine which default principal will be returned when the current principal is queried by an application.

process An application that is currently running. Processes allow for resource isolation.

RC2 A symmetric encryption standard designed to replace Data Encryption Standard (DES) that uses variable key sizes.

RCW (Runtime Callable Wrapper) A proxy class that sits between a .COM component and a .NET assembly and that allows the .NET assembly to consume the component.

regular expression A set of characters that can be compared to a string to determine whether the string meets specified format requirements so that it can be used to extract portions of the text or to replace text.

Rijndael A symmetric encryption algorithm that uses key sizes of 128 through 256 bits. As a government encryption standard, this algorithm is also known as AES.

role-based security (RBS) Authenticating users and then authorizing them based on the permissions assigned to their user accounts and group memberships.

roll back An action taken in cases where an installation does not complete successfully. To *roll back* means to undo any changes made up until the point of failure so that the machine is returned to the state it was in prior to the installation attempt.

Runtime Callable Wrapper (RCW) A proxy class that sits between a .COM component and a .NET assembly and that allows the .NET assembly to consume the component.

satellite assemblies Assemblies that contain localization resources for different cultures and reside outside the main assembly.

Secure Sockets Layer (SSL) A standard that uses public-key encryption to protect network communications.

security access control list (SACL) A usage event logging mechanism that determines how file or folder access is audited.

security policy A logical grouping of code groups, permission sets, and custom policy assemblies.

serialization The process of serializing and deserializing objects so that they can be stored or transferred and then later re-created.

service A process that runs in the background, without a user interface, in its own user session.

SHA1 The Secure Hash Algorithm 1. The hash size for the SHA1 algorithm is 160 bits.

shared secret A symmetric encryption key.

signature The return type, parameter count, and parameter types of a member.

Simple Message Transfer Protocol (SMTP) The standard clients use to transmit e-mail messages to mail servers and mail servers use to transmit messages between themselves.

SoapFormatter Located in the *System.Runtime.Serialization.Formatters.Soap* namespace, this XML-based formatter is the most reliable way to serialize objects that will be transmitted across a network or read by non–.NET Framework applications. *SoapFormatter* is more likely to successfully traverse firewalls than *BinaryFormatter*.

SSL (Secure Sockets Layer) A standard that uses public-key encryption to protect network communications.

stack   An area of memory where value types are stored.

StackTrace   An ordered collection of one or more *StackFrame* objects.

structure   A user-defined value type made up of other types.

symmetric encryption   A cryptography technique that uses a single secret key to encrypt and decrypt data. Also known as secret-key encryption.

thread   A single synchronous line of execution of code.

Triple DES   A symmetric encryption standard that uses 156-bit keys. Essentially, Triple DES repeats the (Data Encryption Standard) DES algorithm three times.

Type Library Exporter   A tool used to export a .NET type to COM (Component Object Model).

Type Library Importer   A tool used to import a COM type into .NET.

type safety   Verification of a given type so that mismatches cannot occur.

unboxing   Converting back from a reference type to a value type after boxing has occurred.

Unicode   A massive code page with tens of thousands of characters that support most languages and scripts, including Latin, Greek, Cyrillic, Hebrew, Arabic, Chinese, and Japanese (and many other scripts).

uninstall   Getting rid of any remnants of an application so that the machine looks identical to how it would have had the application never been installed.

widening   Converting a value from one type to another when the destination type can accommodate all possible values from the source type. These conversions can be implicit.

Windows kernel objects   Operating-system-provided mechanisms that perform cross-process synchronization. These include mutexes, semaphores, and events.

Windows Management Instrumentation   A technology that provides access to information about objects in a managed environment.

XML (eXtensible Markup Language)   A standardized, text-based document format for storing application-readable information.

Index

Additional Resources for C# Developers

Published and Forthcoming Titles from Microsoft Press

Microsoft® Visual C#® 2005 Express Edition: Build a Program Now!

Patrice Pelland • ISBN 0-7356-2229-9

In this lively, eye-opening, and hands-on book, all you need is a computer and the desire to learn how to program with Visual C# 2005 Express Edition. Featuring a full working edition of the software, this fun and highly visual guide walks you through a complete programming project—a desktop weather-reporting application—from start to finish. You'll get an unintimidating introduction to the Microsoft Visual Studio® development environment and learn how to put the lightweight, easy-to-use tools in Visual C# Express to work right away—creating, compiling, testing, and delivering your first, ready-to-use program. You'll get expert tips, coaching, and visual examples at each step of the way, along with pointers to additional learning resources.

Microsoft Visual C# 2005 *Step by Step*

John Sharp • ISBN 0-7356-2129-2

Visual C#, a feature of Visual Studio 2005, is a modern programming language designed to deliver a productive environment for creating business frameworks and reusable object-oriented components. Now you can teach yourself essential techniques with Visual C#—and start building components and Microsoft Windows®–based applications—one step at a time. With *Step by Step*, you work at your own pace through hands-on, learn-by-doing exercises. Whether you're a beginning programmer or new to this particular language, you'll learn how, when, and why to use specific features of Visual C# 2005. Each chapter puts you to work, building your knowledge of core capabilities and guiding you as you create your first C#-based applications for Windows, data management, and the Web.

Programming Microsoft Visual C# 2005 Framework Reference

Francesco Balena • ISBN 0-7356-2182-9

Complementing *Programming Microsoft Visual C# 2005 Core Reference*, this book covers a wide range of additional topics and information critical to Visual C# developers, including Windows Forms, working with Microsoft ADO.NET 2.0 and Microsoft ASP.NET 2.0, Web services, security, remoting, and much more. Packed with sample code and real-world examples, this book will help developers move from understanding to mastery.

Programming Microsoft Visual C# 2005 *Core Reference*

Donis Marshall • ISBN 0-7356-2181-0

Get the in-depth reference and pragmatic, real-world insights you need to exploit the enhanced language features and core capabilities in Visual C# 2005. Programming expert Donis Marshall deftly builds your proficiency with classes, structs, and other fundamentals, and advances your expertise with more advanced topics such as debugging, threading, and memory management. Combining incisive reference with hands-on coding examples and best practices, this *Core Reference* focuses on mastering the C# skills you need to build innovative solutions for smart clients and the Web.

CLR via C#, Second Edition

Jeffrey Richter • ISBN 0-7356-2163-2

In this new edition of Jeffrey Richter's popular book, you get focused, pragmatic guidance on how to exploit the common language runtime (CLR) functionality in Microsoft .NET Framework 2.0 for applications of all types— from Web Forms, Windows Forms, and Web services to solutions for Microsoft SQL Server™, Microsoft code names "Avalon" and "Indigo," consoles, Microsoft Windows NT® Service, and more. Targeted to advanced developers and software designers, this book takes you under the covers of .NET for an in-depth understanding of its structure, functions, and operational components, demonstrating the most practical ways to apply this knowledge to your own development efforts. You'll master fundamental design tenets for .NET and get hands-on insights for creating high-performance applications more easily and efficiently. The book features extensive code examples in Visual C# 2005.

Programming Microsoft Windows Forms
Charles Petzold • ISBN 0-7356-2153-5

CLR via C++
Jeffrey Richter with Stanley B. Lippman
ISBN 0-7356-2248-5

Programming Microsoft Web Forms
Douglas J. Reilly • ISBN 0-7356-2179-9

Debugging, Tuning, and Testing Microsoft .NET 2.0 Applications
John Robbins • ISBN 0-7356-2202-7

For more information about Microsoft Press® books and other learning products, visit: **www.microsoft.com/books** *and* **www.microsoft.com/learning**

Additional Resources for Web Developers

Published and Forthcoming Titles from Microsoft Press

Microsoft® Visual Web Developer™ 2005 Express Edition: Build a Web Site Now!
Jim Buyens • ISBN 0-7356-2212-4

With this lively, eye-opening, and hands-on book, all you need is a computer and the desire to learn how to create Web pages now using Visual Web Developer Express Edition! Featuring a full working edition of the software, this fun and highly visual guide walks you through a complete Web page project from set-up to launch. You'll get an introduction to the Microsoft Visual Studio® environment and learn how to put the light-weight, easy-to-use tools in Visual Web Developer Express to work right away—building your first, dynamic Web pages with Microsoft ASP.NET 2.0. You'll get expert tips, coaching, and visual examples at each step of the way, along with pointers to additional learning resources.

Microsoft ASP.NET 2.0 Programming
Step by Step
George Shepherd • ISBN 0-7356-2201-9

With dramatic improvements in performance, productivity, and security features, Visual Studio 2005 and ASP.NET 2.0 deliver a simplified, high-performance, and powerful Web development experience. ASP.NET 2.0 features a new set of controls and infrastructure that simplify Web-based data access and include functionality that facilitates code reuse, visual consistency, and aesthetic appeal. Now you can teach yourself the essentials of working with ASP.NET 2.0 in the Visual Studio environment—one step at a time. With *Step by Step*, you work at your own pace through hands-on, learn-by-doing exercises. Whether you're a beginning programmer or new to this version of the technology, you'll understand the core capabilities and fundamental techniques for ASP.NET 2.0. Each chapter puts you to work, showing you how, when, and why to use specific features of the ASP.NET 2.0 rapid application development environment and guiding you as you create actual components and working applications for the Web, including advanced features such as personalization.

Programming Microsoft ASP.NET 2.0
Core Reference
Dino Esposito • ISBN 0-7356-2176-4

Delve into the core topics for ASP.NET 2.0 programming, mastering the essential skills and capabilities needed to build high-performance Web applications successfully. Well-known ASP.NET author Dino Esposito deftly builds your expertise with Web forms, Visual Studio, core controls, master pages, data access, data binding, state management, security services, and other must-know topics—combining definitive reference with practical, hands-on programming instruction. Packed with expert guidance and pragmatic examples, this *Core Reference* delivers the key resources that you need to develop professional-level Web programming skills.

Programming Microsoft ASP.NET 2.0
Applications: *Advanced Topics*
Dino Esposito • ISBN 0-7356-2177-2

Master advanced topics in ASP.NET 2.0 programming—gaining the essential insights and in-depth understanding that you need to build sophisticated, highly functional Web applications successfully. Topics include Web forms, Visual Studio 2005, core controls, master pages, data access, data binding, state management, and security considerations. Developers often discover that the more they use ASP.NET, the more they need to know. With expert guidance from ASP.NET authority Dino Esposito, you get the in-depth, comprehensive information that leads to full mastery of the technology.

Programming Microsoft Windows® Forms
Charles Petzold • ISBN 0-7356-2153-5

Programming Microsoft Web Forms
Douglas J. Reilly • ISBN 0-7356-2179-9

CLR via C++
Jeffrey Richter with Stanley B. Lippman
ISBN 0-7356-2248-5

Debugging, Tuning, and Testing Microsoft .NET 2.0 Applications
John Robbins • ISBN 0-7356-2202-7

CLR via C#, Second Edition
Jeffrey Richter • ISBN 0-7356-2163-2

For more information about Microsoft Press® books and other learning products, visit: **www.microsoft.com/books** *and* **www.microsoft.com/learning**

Additional Resources for Visual Basic Developers

Published and Forthcoming Titles from Microsoft Press

Microsoft® Visual Basic® 2005 Express Edition: Build a Program Now!
Patrice Pelland • ISBN 0-7356-2213-2

Featuring a full working edition of the software, this fun and highly visual guide walks you through a complete programming project—a desktop weather-reporting application—from start to finish. You'll get an introduction to the Microsoft Visual Studio® development environment and learn how to put the lightweight, easy-to-use tools in Visual Basic Express to work right away—creating, compiling, testing, and delivering your first ready-to-use program. You'll get expert tips, coaching, and visual examples each step of the way, along with pointers to additional learning resources.

Microsoft Visual Basic 2005 *Step by Step*
Michael Halvorson • ISBN 0-7356-2131-4

With enhancements across its visual designers, code editor, language, and debugger that help accelerate the development and deployment of robust, elegant applications across the Web, a business group, or an enterprise, Visual Basic 2005 focuses on enabling developers to rapidly build applications. Now you can teach yourself the essentials of working with Visual Studio 2005 and the new features of the Visual Basic language—one step at a time. Each chapter puts you to work, showing you how, when, and why to use specific features of Visual Basic and guiding as you create actual components and working applications for Microsoft Windows®. You'll also explore data management and Web-based development topics.

Programming Microsoft Visual Basic 2005 *Core Reference*
Francesco Balena • ISBN 0-7356-2183-7

Get the expert insights, indispensable reference, and practical instruction needed to exploit the core language features and capabilities in Visual Basic 2005. Well-known Visual Basic programming author Francesco Balena expertly guides you through the fundamentals, including modules, keywords, and inheritance, and builds your mastery of more advanced topics such as delegates, assemblies, and My Namespace. Combining in-depth reference with extensive, hands-on code examples and best-practices advice, this *Core Reference* delivers the key resources that you need to develop professional-level programming skills for smart clients and the Web.

Programming Microsoft Visual Basic 2005 Framework Reference
Francesco Balena • ISBN 0-7356-2175-6

Complementing *Programming Microsoft Visual Basic 2005 Core Reference*, this book covers a wide range of additional topics and information critical to Visual Basic developers, including Windows Forms, working with Microsoft ADO.NET 2.0 and ASP.NET 2.0, Web services, security, remoting, and much more. Packed with sample code and real-world examples, this book will help developers move from understanding to mastery.

Programming Microsoft Windows Forms
Charles Petzold • ISBN 0-7356-2153-5

Programming Microsoft Web Forms
Douglas J. Reilly • ISBN 0-7356-2179-9

Debugging, Tuning, and Testing Microsoft .NET 2.0 Applications
John Robbins • ISBN 0-7356-2202-7

Microsoft ASP.NET 2.0 *Step by Step*
George Shepherd • ISBN 0-7356-2201-9

Microsoft ADO.NET 2.0 *Step by Step*
Rebecca Riordan • ISBN 0-7356-2164-0

Programming Microsoft ASP.NET 2.0 *Core Reference*
Dino Esposito • ISBN 0-7356-2176-4

For more information about Microsoft Press® books and other learning products, visit: **www.microsoft.com/books** *and* **www.microsoft.com/learning**

System Requirements

We recommend that you use a computer that is not your primary workstation to do the practice exercises in this book because you will make changes to the operating system and application configuration.

Hardware Requirements

The following hardware is required to complete the practice exercises:

- Computer with a 600-MHz or faster processor (1-GHz recommended)
- 192 MB of RAM or more (512 MB recommended)
- 2 GB of available hard disk space
- DVD-ROM drive
- 1,024 x 768 or higher resolution display with 256 colors
- Keyboard and Microsoft mouse, or compatible pointing device

Software Requirements

The following software is required to complete the practice exercises:

- One of the following operating systems:
    - Windows 2000 with Service Pack 4
    - Windows XP with Service Pack 2
    - Windows XP Professional x64 Edition (WOW)
    - Windows Server 2003 with Service Pack 1
    - Windows Server 2003, x64 Editions (WOW)
    - Windows Server 2003 R2
    - Windows Server 2003 R2, x64 Editions (WOW)
    - Microsoft Windows Vista

- Visual Studio 2005 (A 90-day evaluation edition of Visual Studio 2005 Professional Edition is included on DVD with this book.)

IMPORTANT Evaluation edition is not the full retail product

The 90-day evaluation edition of Microsoft Visual Studio 2005 Professional Edition provided with this training kit is not the full retail product and is provided only for the purposes of training and evaluation. Microsoft and Microsoft Technical Support do not support this evaluation edition.

Information about any issues relating to the use of this evaluation edition with this training kit is posted to the Support section of the Microsoft Press Web site (*www.microsoft.com/learning/support/books/*). For information about ordering the full version of any Microsoft software, please call Microsoft Sales at (800) 426-9400 or visit *www.microsoft.com*.

What do you think of this book? We want to hear from you!

Do you have a few minutes to participate in a brief online survey? Microsoft is interested in hearing your feedback about this publication so that we can continually improve our books and learning resources for you.

To participate in our survey, please visit:

www.microsoft.com/learning/booksurvey

And enter this book's ISBN, 0-7356-2277-9. As a thank-you to survey participants in the United States and Canada, each month we'll randomly select five respondents to win one of five $100 gift certificates from a leading online merchant.* At the conclusion of the survey, you can enter the drawing by providing your e-mail address, which will be used for prize notification *only*.

Thanks in advance for your input. Your opinion counts!

Sincerely,

Microsoft Learning

Learn More. Go Further.

To see special offers on Microsoft Learning products for developers, IT professionals, and home and office users, visit: *www.microsoft.com/learning/booksurvey*

Save 15%
on your Microsoft® Certification exam fee

Present this discount voucher to any of 5,000 testing centers worldwide for 15% off one Microsoft Certification exam fee. Or, use the discount code on the voucher to register online or via phone with the Microsoft Certified Exam Provider of your choice.

Microsoft | Learning

Good for 15% off one exam fee in the Microsoft Certified Professional Program

Offer expires 12/31/2010

Your voucher discount code

Redeemable at Microsoft Certified Exam Providers worldwide.
For locations, visit: www.microsoft.com/mcp/exams

Promotion Terms and Conditions:

- Offer good for 15% off one exam fee in the Microsoft Certified Professional Program.
- Voucher code can be redeemed online or at Microsoft Certified Exam Providers worldwide.
- Exam purchased using this voucher code must be taken on or before December 31, 2010.
- Inform your Microsoft Certified Exam Provider that you want to use the voucher discount code at the time you register for the exam.

Voucher Terms and Conditions

- Expired vouchers will not be replaced.
- Each voucher code may only be used for one exam and must be presented at time of registration.
- This voucher may not be combined with other vouchers or discounts.
- This voucher is nontransferable and is void if altered or revised in any way.
- It may not be sold or redeemed for cash, credit, or refund.

Microsoft

X11-56768